Inside Linux

Other Books by New Riders Publishing

Cisco Router Configuration & Troubleshooting, 2E
Mark Tripod
0-7357-0999-8

Developing Linux Applications
Eric Harlow
0-7357-0021-4

GIMP Essential Reference
Alex Harford
0-7357-0911-4

GTK+/Gnome Application Development
Havoc Pennington
0-7357-0078-8

KDE Application Development
Uwe Thiem
1-57870-201-1

Linux Essential Reference
Ed Petron
0-7357-0852-5

Linux Firewalls
Robert Ziegler
0-7357-0900-9

Linux System Administration
M Carling, Stephen Degler, and James Dennis
1-56205-934-3

Lotus Notes & Domino Essential Reference
Tim Bankes and Dave Hatter
0-7357-0007-9

MySQL
Paul DuBois
0-7357-0921-1

Network Intrusion Detection: An Analyst's Handbook, 2E
Stephen Northcutt and Judy Novak
0-7357-1008-2

Solaris Essential Reference
John Mulligan
0-7357-0023-0

Understanding Data Communications, Sixth Edition
Gilbert Held
0-7357-0036-2

Inside Linux

201 West 103rd Street,
Indianapolis, Indiana 46290

Michael J. Tobler

Inside Linux

Copyright © 2001 by New Riders Publishing

All rights reserved. No part of this book shall be reproduced, stored in a retrieval system, or transmitted by any means, electronic, mechanical, photocopying, recording, or otherwise, without written permission from the publisher. No patent liability is assumed with respect to the use of the information contained herein. Although every precaution has been taken in the preparation of this book, the publisher and author assume no responsibility for errors or omissions. Neither is any liability assumed for damages resulting from the use of the information contained herein.

International Standard Book Number: 0-7357-0940-8

Library of Congress Catalog Card Number: 99-067436

Printed in the United States of America

First Printing: October

03 02 01 00   7 6 5 4 3 2 1

Interpretation of the printing code: The rightmost double-digit number is the year of the book's printing; the rightmost single-digit number is the number of the book's printing. For example, the printing code 00-1 shows that the first printing of the book occurred in 2000.

Trademarks

All terms mentioned in this book that are known to be trademarks or service marks have been appropriately capitalized. New Riders Publishing cannot attest to the accuracy of this information. Use of a term in this book should not be regarded as affecting the validity of any trademark or service mark.

Warning and Disclaimer

Every effort has been made to make this book as complete and as accurate as possible, but no warranty or fitness is implied. The information provided is on an "as is" basis. The author and the publisher shall have neither liability nor responsibility to any person or entity with respect to any loss or damages arising from the information contained in this book.

Publisher
David Dwyer

Executive Editor
Al Valvano

Acquisitions Editors
Stacey Beheler
Katie Purdum

Marketing Manager
Stephanie Layton

Publicity Manager
Susan Petro

Managing Editor
Sarah Kearns

Development Editor
Chris Zahn

Project Editor
Jennifer Chisholm

Copy Editors
Barbara Hacha
Gayle Johnson

Technical Reviewer
Scott Orr

Indexer
Cheryl Lenser

Proofreaders
Debra Neel
Daryl Kessler

Compositor
Wil Cruz

Manufacturing Coordinator
Chris Moos

Book Designer
Louisa Klucznik

Contents

I Getting Started   1

1 Introduction to Linux   3
The Purpose of This Book   4
What Is Linux?   4
Linux: Its Past and Present   6
The Driving Forces Behind Linux   6
How Is Linux Used?   7
The Future of Linux   8
Linux Distributions   9
Sources of Linux Information and Documentation   10
Summary   13

2 Installing Linux   15
Requirements Checklist   16
Planning Your Installation   26
Distribution-Specific Installations   29
Summary   53

3 Using Linux   55
Linux Startup   55
Linux Shutdown   56
Logging In to Linux   58
Logging Out of Linux   59
Managing User Accounts   59
Moving Around in Linux   64
Using Files and Directories   77
Some Basic Commands   85
Summary   92

4 Installing X Windows   93
XFree86 Defined   94
Installing XFree86   95
Configuring XFree86   101
Summary   130

5 Using X Windows 131
Overview of the Graphical Environment 132
Navigating X 134
Window Managers 135
Exploring the Graphical Environment 138
KDE 138
GNOME 158
Summary 171

II Configuration 173

6 Network Configuration 175
TCP/IP Overview 175
Hardware Requirements 180
Configuring TCP/IP 181
The rc Files 185
Testing the Network 195
Summary 198

7 Hardware Configuration 201
Overview 201
Hard Drives 202
Modems 205
Mouse 205
Peripheral Computer Interface (PCI) 206
Video Cards 207
Serial Ports 210
Sound Cards 216
Summary 221

III Linux Services 223

8 Email Services: SMTP and POP 225
Overview 225
Comprehending Electronic Mail 226
MUA Programs 230
Using MUAs 231
The sendmail Package 243
Summary 254

9 File Transfer Protocol (FTP) 255
FTP Overview 255
FTP Commands 257
Using ftp 265
Configuring an FTP Server 274
Summary 279

10 Domain Name Service (DNS) 281
DNS Overview 282
DNS Configuration 287
Summary 301

11 Network Information Service (NIS) 303
Overview 303
The NIS Model 305
Structuring NIS 307
Configuring NIS 308
Additional NIS Commands and Files 319
Summary 324

12 Network File Service (NFS) 325
Overview 325
NFS Design and Architecture 328
NFS and Linux 332
Using the NFS Client 344
Optimizing NFS on Low-Bandwidth Connections 348
Summary 349

13 Dial-Up Networking Services: SLIP and PPP 351
Serial Line Internet Protocol (SLIP) 351
Point-to-Point Protocol (PPP) 372
Summary 385

14 UNIX-to-UNIX Copy Program 387
UUCP Overview 387
Basic UUCP Configuration 388
A UUCP Session 404
Summary 410

15 Samba: Merging Linux and Windows   413
Overview   413
Obtaining and Installing Samba   416
Configuring Samba   420
Executing Samba   435
Using smbclient   438
Summary   442

16 Apache Web Server   443
Apache Overview   443
Choosing an Apache Package   444
Obtaining and Installing Apache   445
Apache Runtime Configuration   459
Starting and Stopping the Server   461
Apache Log Files   465
Special-Purpose Environment Variables   465
Apache's Handler Use   466
Summary   467

17 Internet News Service   469
Overview   469
Basic Usenet Mechanics   471
Common Usenet Terms   481
NNTP Protocol   484
Configuring the NNTP Server   495
Summary   497

18 Print Services   499
Print Overview   499
Printer Preliminaries   500
Configuring Print Services   505
Summary   523

IV System Administration 525

19 The Tools 527
Overview 527
Configuration, Maintenance, and Management Tools 528
Productivity Tools 565
Summary 567

20 Booting and Shutdown 569
Overview 569
The init Process 572
Using LILO, the Linux Loader 577
Using LOADLIN, another Linux Loader 580
Emergency Boot Floppy Disks 583
Summary 584

21 Security 585
Overview 585
Physical Security 587
Threats to Security Caused By Social Engineering 591
Authentication 592
File Security 599
Network Access 601
Summary 607

22 Managing Accounts 609
Overview 609
Managing Users 611
Managing Groups 620
Summary 622

23 Other Administrative Tasks 625
Overview 625
Root Account 626
Rotating User Passwords 627
System Backup and Restoration 628
Using `cron` and `crontab` Files 636
System Monitoring 637
Summary 646

V Quick Reference 649

24 Utility Programs 651
Overview 651
Online Help 652
Process Commands 657
Summary 665

25 Regular Expressions 667
Overview 667
Pattern Matching 668
Metacharacters 670
Escaping 683
Whole Words 685
Summary 687

VI Appendixes 689

A Other Sources of Information 691
Books 691
Magazines 693
Usenet Newsgroups 694
Mailing Lists 699
Linux Web Sites 701
Linux FTP Sites 707

B Common Questions 709
Overview 709
So What Is Linux? 710
What Distributions of Linux Are Available? 710
What Processors Does Linux Run On? 716
What Are Some of the Requirements of Linux? 717
Where Can I Get Linux? 718
Where Can I Find Software for Linux? 719
Can I Access Data on Drive Types Other Than Linux? 719
Can I Run Software Written for Other Operating Systems? 720

Where Can I Get Linux Information on the Internet? 720
Are Disk and File Utilities Available for Linux? 722
What Do I Do If I Forgot the root Password? 724
How Can I Share Linux/Windows Printers and Filesystems? 725
How Can I Mount a Windows95 Filesystem? 725
Do Viruses Exist on Linux? 725
How Are Linux Passwords Encrypted? 726
How Large Can a File Be Under Linux? 726
Are There Comparisons of Linux to Other Operating Systems? 726
What Is the Legal Status of Linux? 726
Do I Need to Repartition to Use Linux? 727
Can I Get Linux Preinstalled on a New Computer? 727

Index   729

About the Author

Michael J. Tobler is a software consultant based in Houston, Texas. He has more than 17 years experience working on software development projects. Michael specializes in the planning, designing, and development of Web-based multi-tier systems using C++, Java, and CORBA. A dedicated methodologist, Michael is a practitioner of the Rational Unified Process (RUP) and the Extreme Programming (XP) discipline.

Michael is president of the Houston Java Users Group and a contributing author of The Waite Group's *C++ How-To* and Sams' *C++ Unleashed*. He is the technical editor of The Waite Group's *C Primer Plus* and Sams' *Teach Yourself UML in 24 Hours*.

Michael is a devoted Linux user and advocate and has been using Linux for over eight years, designing and developing multi-tier systems to run under Linux (and Unix).

Michael's personal activities include motorcycling and skydiving and hopes to surf Waimea and Maverick's soon. He can be reached via email at mjtobler@consultant.com.

About the Technical Reviewer

Scott Orr has been involved with the networking efforts of the Purdue School of Engineering and Technology at Indiana University-Purdue University at Indianapolis from the very beginning. Starting out as a 20-node Novell network, the program expanded to more than 400 Microsoft- and UNIX-based workstations within several years. Since then, he moved to the Computer Science department where he manages all student and research lab PC and UNIX clusters. In addition, he teaches undergraduate courses and conducts research in the areas of computer security, networking, and UNIX system administration. Scott also has made numerous presentations to local industry on the deployment of Internet security measures and has assisted several large corporations with the configuration and testing of their firewalls.

For:

Valarie Anna Findlay
My true love, without your presence I could not have written this

And ...

My Mom, Sonja
In memory of my Dad, John.
My children: Madison, Ashton, and Drew

-*Michael J. Tobler*

Acknowledgments

The Acknowledgment of a book seems to be the most difficult portion to write. Many people contribute in some form or fashion. Writing a book is a difficult and time-consuming endeavor and not only affects the writer, but everyone around the writer.

I would to thank all educators in my family. To Louis, who always makes me stop to think problems through before giving up. To James, for his considerable feedback and suggestions.

I would like to acknowledge everyone at New Riders (and others within Macmillan Publishing). I want to thank Al Valvano for ensuring that this book made it to the bookshelves. Stacey Beheler, acquisitions editor, who has had to endure countless meetings explaining yet another slipped deadline. To Katie Purdum, acquisitions editor, who introduced me to and raised me in the world of publishing. Cheers to both! Thanks go to Chris Zahn, Ph.D., development editor, who was always patiently (maybe not) awaiting the author reviews and other miscellaneous corrections.
In addition, I want to thank Scott Orr, technical editor, for keeping me on track technically. Lastly, I want to thank Jennifer Chisholm and Wil Cruz.

I know I am missing many people at New Riders—people that have contributed to the success of this book. My hat is off to all the ladies and gents at New Riders.

To all my colleagues and clients, past and present—they too have spent countless moments listening to the Linux dialogue. And especially to those who have supported the Linux movement with me.

I would also like to thank everyone in the Linux community. Without everyone's support, drive, and determination, we would not be where we are today—or in the future.

Tell Us What You Think!

As the reader of this book, *you* are our most important critic and commentator. We value your opinion and want to know what we're doing right, what we could do better, what areas you'd like to see us publish in, and any other words of wisdom you're willing to pass our way.

As the executive editor for the Open Source, Linux team at New Riders Publishing, I welcome your comments. You can fax, email, or write me directly to let me know what you did or didn't like about this book—as well as what we can do to make our books stronger.

Please note that I cannot help you with technical problems related to the topic of this book, and that due to the high volume of mail I receive, I might not be able to reply to every message.

When you write, please be sure to include this book's title, author, and ISBN number (found on the back cover of the book above the bar code), as well as your name and phone or fax number. I will carefully review your comments and share them with the author and editors who worked on the book.

Fax: 317-581-4663
Email: nrfeedback@newriders.com
Mail: Stephanie Wall
Executive Editor
Open Source, Linux
New Riders Publishing
201 West 103rd Street
Indianapolis, IN 46290 USA

I

Getting Started

1 Introduction to Linux

2 Installing Linux

3 Using Linux

4 Installing X Windows

5 Using X Windows

1

Introduction to Linux

WELCOME TO THE WONDERFUL WORLD OF LINUX! There is no need to fear Linux, as users often did in Linux's infancy. During those early days of Linux, it took a dedicated and determined hacker to get Linux installed and running. Today, however, any PC user—from a weekend user to a power user—can install a copy of Linux and reap its rewards within a couple of hours. This book provides you with the knowledge to exploit Linux's power.

> **Hacker Denotations**
>
> The term *hacker*, as previously used, describes a person who wants to know absolutely everything about a system and is committed to that goal. The term hacker is sometimes used synonymously with cracker.
>
> A *cracker* is someone who breaks the security on a computer system. The term was coined around 1985 by hackers in defense of journalistic misuse of the term hacker.

Because Linux is a UNIX clone, PC users who want to gain knowledge of UNIX can do so without paying exorbitant licensing fees. Any Intel 386, 486, or Pentium-class computer can be used as a Linux workstation or server. Releases of Linux also are available for other processors, such as Digital Alpha, Sun SPARC, MIPS, ARM, 680x0, and PPC processors, among many others. Currently, a complete Linux system can be downloaded for free, or a commercial-grade version can be purchased for less than $50.

Linux is not just for hobbyists any more—many businesses are using it to run their day-to-day operations. Hospitals, financial institutions, telecommunications companies, and oil and gas industries are utilizing Linux to help run their businesses. Colleges and universities also use Linux extensively to facilitate their admissions and financial departments. Linux has come to be known as a stable and fully featured platform for hosting mission-critical applications.

Linux is a very cooperative operating system when networked with other non-Linux operating systems. Linux can read and write files that reside on DOS partitions and floppy disks. You can also find kernel support for Windows 9x and Windows NT systems that use the VFAT file system. The newer Linux kernel (2.0.34 and newer) supports FAT32 partitions. Linux also provides read-and-write access to Windows for Workgroups and Windows NT SMB volumes. The UFS file system (System V and others) and IBM's OS/2 volumes can be accessed in read-only mode. This list is not comprehensive—Appendix A, "Other Sources of Information," can lead you to additional sources of information about Linux and its interoperability.

The unique aspect of Linux is that it is free. Linus Torvalds, the creator of Linux, owns the Linux kernel copyright and has placed it under the GNU General Public License. What does this mean to you? It allows you to freely copy, change, and distribute Linux—but you cannot place any restrictions on further distribution, and you must make the source code available.

The Purpose of This Book

Part I of this book, "Getting Started," is designed to guide you through the installation of Linux. Part II, "Configuration," guides you through the configuration of Linux. Although some configuration is taken care of during the installation process, you eventually have to configure other aspects of the system after installation is complete. Part III, "Linux Services," describes the important services that Linux provides, such as email and networking. This section is a mixture of a how-to and a reference. In Part IV, "System Administration," we discuss the essentials of system administration. A quick reference can be found in Part V, "Quick Reference." Part VI, "Appendixes," provides you with additional helpful information.

We do not claim that this book is an exhaustive reference, but that it provides a good foundation of information required to install and use Linux. This book will no doubt find its place both on the system administrator's and the Linux hobbyist's desk.

What Is Linux?

First things first—the generally accepted pronunciation for Linux is "Lynn-ucks" (short i). A second opinion is that Linux should be pronounced "Line-ucks" (long i). An audio file is included on the CD-ROM; this audio file is a recording of Linus Torvalds himself pronouncing Linux (Linus pronounces Linux as "Leen-ucks"). You be the judge.

Linux can be viewed from three angles. First, Linux is a clone of the UNIX operating system. It is primarily designed to run on Intel 386, 486, and Pentium-class computers. Linux is written from the ground up to be a UNIX clone and does not contain any proprietary UNIX code. Second, Linux refers to the core kernel. When you boot Linux, the kernel is the heart of the system; it is the master controller between you and the peripherals, the applications, and the CPU. Third, and most important, Linux is a complete package of software tools and applications.

Because Linux is a UNIX clone, most of the features of UNIX are available to you. Linux is a preemptive, multitasking operating system, which means that you can have more than one program running simultaneously. Linux takes care of switching between the various processes, without the processes' knowledge. This is in contrast to cooperative multitasking operating systems, such as Windows 3.1. With a cooperative multitasking operating system, each application is responsible to yield processor time—if an application never yields, other applications will not receive any processor time.

Linux is also a multiuser operating system. This allows multiple users to be logged on to one machine and to utilize its services. This may not make sense when using a standalone home PC, unless you consider Linux's support for virtual terminals (or consoles). A virtual terminal allows a single PC to have multiple text-mode screen sessions running concurrently—you use a predefined keystroke sequence to switch between the running screen sessions. This allows you to have a text editor running on one virtual screen, for example, and to switch to another virtual screen to view a directory listing.

Linux supports the concept of virtual memory. By using a dedicated portion of a machine's hard drive, called the *swap partition*, Linux swaps pages of memory in and out of the swap space as required. To Linux and any running applications, the machine appears to have more physical memory than what actually exists. This, of course, comes at a cost—the cost of reading and writing to the hard drive.

Linux also supports dynamically shared libraries. What is a shared library? A shared library contains one or more "common" functions that multiple, concurrent programs can execute in a shared fashion. These concurrent programs can all share a single library file and call on any functions contained within it. This reduces the size of the individual applications because they don't have to contain the shared functions.

The Graphical User Interface (GUI) found on a UNIX system is known as X Windows. Linux provides a clone of the X Windows GUI that is called

XFree86. XFree86 provides a graphical, windowed interface to the Linux system. Multiple, overlapping windows with most of the graphical widgets you expect are supported. A *window manager* is responsible for the management of the graphical display, such as the placement and resizing of windows and the overall appearance of the graphical display. Different window managers are available, ranging from simple (*twm*) to powerful and elegant (*KDE*).

Linux: Its Past and Present

No Linux text worth its salt can continue without mentioning Linus Torvalds—the father of Linux. The name Linux is derived partly from Linus and partly from Minix, an early implementation of UNIX for the PC.

Linux began its life as a university project; its author is Linus. Linus, a student at the University of Helsinki (Finland), wrote a tiny task-switcher for the 386 PC. The functionality of this task-switcher consisted merely of two processes that alternately printed As and Bs to a terminal. The first official version of Linux was 0.02 in October 1991, and the first release was delivered in March 1992. Linux was—and still is—developed by many programmers (primarily UNIX programmers) from across the globe. Linux is a freely distributed version of UNIX, governed by the GNU General Public License.

So, where are we today with Linux? Linux is a very viable multitasking, multiuser operating system. Linux is constantly in the news, whether that news is computer related or business related. More and more companies are using Linux as file servers, print servers, Web and application servers, and workstations. Linux is a scalable operating system—it can serve up an office with two PCs or accommodate a Fortune 100 company with thousands of PCs.

The Driving Forces Behind Linux

Many reasons exist for the strong surge of Linux use. One reason is its power and lean profile. Linux is a strong multitasking and multiuser operating system, requiring a minimum of hardware resources.

A second reason is the ever-increasing availability of robust utility and business software. Any seasoned UNIX programmer can easily move to, and develop for, Linux.

Another reason is its extensibility. Because source code for the operating system is freely available, Linux can be modified and tuned to meet the needs of the company.

An important reason for the Linux surge is available support. When you purchase a commercial version of Linux, you are actually paying for support from the vendor. However, it is important to realize that beyond that vendor's support staff, a vast pasture of Linux expertise can be found in the world. Many Linux newsgroups, user-group organizations, chat rooms, Web sites, and extensive amounts of Linux documentation provide support for Linux. An answer to virtually any Linux issue can be unearthed quickly.

How Is Linux Used?

Today, Linux is first and foremost a server operating system. Although many applications are now appearing that allow Linux to be used as a primary workstation or a desktop system, most users of Linux focus on the server capabilities of the operating system. Some of the reasons that Linux makes a very strong server include the following:

- **Performance.** Linux has a high performance-to-cost ratio and runs as well as any other operating system, given the same hardware (it may even run better).
- **Security.** Security issues are resolved quickly and distribution is immediate. Commercially oriented vendors may take weeks or months to fix and distribute patches.
- **Bang for the Buck.** You can get Linux for the cost of a download, or you can purchase a CD-ROM packed with Linux and supporting software for less than $20. If you want "commercial" peace of mind, you can get commercial distributions, such as Red Hat and Caldera OpenLinux, which range in price from $30 to $80. With commercial distributions, you get the operating system, the source code, and a wealth of supporting programs and utilities. In some cases, commercial software is also bundled at no extra charge.

How else is Linux used? The most popular uses of Linux are the following:

- FTP server
- Email server
- Web server
- Distributed software server
- DNS (domain name) server
- Database server
- Samba (Windows) server

> **Database Support for Linux**
> Some well-known database vendors, such as Oracle, Informix, Sybase, and IBM, provide support for Linux.

Linux is a very powerful workstation, used for computer graphics (CAD/CAM), software development, Internet access, and office applications. Linux is also ideal for the home PC market, providing a robust operating system and a balance of software for the cost of a download.

As mentioned previously, office applications are available, rivaling products from other well-known vendors. Products from Sun Microsystems (StarOffice) and Corel (WordPerfect) provide the capability to read and write Microsoft Word 95 and 97 file formats. This enables Linux users to exchange word processing documents with Microsoft Word users. Both StarOffice and ApplixWare provide office suite products that compete with the Microsoft Office suite. I use the StarOffice suite and find it easier and more elegant to use than the Microsoft Office suite. As of this writing, you can get the StarOffice 5.1 Personal Edition for free (available for many platforms).

The Future of Linux

Linux has a very bright future, indeed. Many companies are choosing Linux as the operating system of choice for workstations and servers, and, in many cases, companies are replacing currently installed UNIX and Windows machines with Linux machines. The reasons are clear, as stated in previous sections.

Linux, when combined with the Apache Web server, makes an ideal Web server. You might be interested to learn that Apache is the most widely used Web server to date (Apache is not dependent on Linux; it can run on any UNIX-based system). Linux is also the clear choice for hosting the application server for distributed software systems.

You can now purchase new computer systems preinstalled with Linux from major computer manufacturers. An added bonus is that most of the manufacturers include Linux technical support as part of the package.

Hardware requirements for running Linux are minimal when compared to other operating systems. Many companies are using Intel Pentium 133 and 166 MHz machines to run their Linux-powered Web, email, FTP, and application servers. In addition, some system administrators are digging out retired Intel 386 computers to use as print servers and desktop workstations. Linux, at a minimum, requires only an Intel 386, 4MB of RAM, a hard disk with at least 40MB, a floppy disk drive, and a video adapter and monitor. If you want to run the XFree86 windowing system, your machine should have 16MB of RAM to provide the best performance.

Linux continues to evolve, with kernel releases coming out regularly.

Linux Distributions

Numerous organizations, both commercial and public, distribute their own unique version of Linux. Do not confuse a Linux distribution with a Linux release; these two terms have different meanings. A Linux release refers to a specific version of the Linux kernel and a core set of programs and files. A distribution refers to a packaging of a Linux release with various software utilities and applications.

Many distributions of Linux are available, such as Red Hat, Slackware, TAMU (from Texas A&M University), Debian, Caldera, SuSE, Yggdrasil, and many others. No two distributions are alike; each is packaged differently and each supplies a different installation procedure. Differences also exist between the Linux kernel version bundled with each distribution. In addition, some distributions include experimental Linux kernels, XFree86 servers, and hardware drivers.

Because so many distributions are available, deciding which distribution is right for you or your organization can be difficult. If you are interested only in trying out Linux on your home PC, downloading Linux from an anonymous FTP site is an inexpensive option. Of course, you have to pay the cost of the connection time required to download the distribution. An alternative to downloading Linux is to purchase a CD-ROM distribution, such as Slackware, from your local software store. Some bookstores and mail order houses also carry these CD-ROM distributions. The cost for a CD-ROM package is generally less than $20. Some CD-ROM packages contain multiple distributions. For example, one CD-ROM package consists of six CD-ROMs; four of the CD-ROMs have different distributions of Linux. This allows you to install one distribution and have the benefit of switching to another distribution in the future.

If you decide to purchase a CD-ROM pack, pay particular attention to the version number of the distribution. Some packages have the Linux kernel version printed on the jewel case sleeve. Some commercial distributions of Linux use a version of the kernel that is one or two minor versions behind the current release. This delay is for time spent by development staff to stabilize the kernel, ensuring a reliable kernel. This development effort is reflected in the additional cost for a commercial distribution.

See Appendix A for more information concerning Linux distributions.

Sources of Linux Information and Documentation

As discussed in a previous section, numerous sources of information and documentation are available for Linux. One important source of information is this book, which covers installing and configuring Linux, the major Linux services, and system administration. Beyond this book, a wealth of documentation and support is available to you.

This section provides a brief summary of Linux information and sources of Linux documentation; a more comprehensive list can be found in Appendix A.

Books can provide a great deal of information—do not feel compelled to choose Linux-only books. If you want to be a serious Linux user, it is wise to invest in some general-purpose UNIX books. This is more important if you are a developer and want to write software for Linux. If you are new to Linux and UNIX, you should spend time in the bookstore exploring books that meet your needs.

If you want to keep up with the world of Linux, the *Linux Journal* is a good source of information. This is a monthly magazine dedicated to the world of Linux. Packed into every issue is information for users and developers alike. Another monthly magazine is *Sys Admin*, which is targeted to UNIX system administrators. This magazine now includes a section dedicated solely to Linux. Another good magazine, *Network World* (previously titled *UnixWorld*), is dedicated to networking professionals.

In addition to the printed magazines, there are some very good e-zines. *Linux World* is a good source of information and is found at `http://www.linuxworld.com`. Another Web magazine providing current news on Linux is *Linux Weekly News*; its address is `http://lwn.net`. The *Linux Gazette* states, "the Linux Gazette, a member of the Linux Documentation Project, is an online WWW publication dedicated to two simple ideas: making Linux just a little more fun and sharing ideas and discoveries." You can visit the *Linux Gazette* at `http://www.linuxgazette.com`.

The home of the Linux Documentation Project (LDP), probably the most important Web site for information concerning Linux, is found at `http://metalab.unc.edu/mdw`. This site is your central source for comprehensive Linux documentation. You will find the official Linux Guides, HOWTOs, man pages, and FAQs here.

The Linux Guides provide in-depth coverage of installing and using Linux. Some of the guides that are available are as follows:

- "Installation and Getting Started Guide," by Matt Welsh and others
- "The Linux Kernel," by David A. Rusling

- "The Linux Kernel Hackers' Guide," by Michael K. Johnson
- "The Linux Kernel Module Programming Guide," by Ori Pomerantz
- "The Linux Network Administrators' Guide," by Olaf Kirch
- "The Linux Programmer's Guide," by B. Scott Burkett, Sven Goldt, John D. Harper, Sven van der Meer, and Matt Welsh
- "The Linux System Administrators' Guide," by Lars Wirzenius
- "The Linux Users' Guide," by Larry Greenfield

The Linux HOWTOs, including the mini-HOWTOs, are formatted as "how to" documents on specific Linux subjects. Most, but not all, of the HOWTOs are available in plain text, PostScript, DVI, HTML, and SGML output formats. The following is a partial list of HOWTOs:

- Config HOWTO, by Guido Gonzato
- DOS/Win to Linux HOWTO, by Guido Gonzato
- Ethernet HOWTO, by Paul Gortmaker
- Installation HOWTO, by Eric S. Raymond
- PalmOS HOWTO, by David H. Silber
- XFree86 HOWTO, by Eric S. Raymond

The collection of online help files for Linux, known as the man pages, are accessed using the Linux man command (*man* is short for manual). If you require the most up-to-date version of the man pages, this is the place to get them.

The Frequently Asked Questions (FAQs) provide answers to the most common questions about Linux. The FAQs are categorized by subject matter, such as "Introduction and General Information," "Compatibility with Other Operating Systems," and "Frequently Encountered Error Messages." The following is a partial list of FAQs:

- How much hard disk space does Linux need?
- How much memory does Linux need?
- I don't have FTP access. Where do I get Linux?
- I don't have Usenet access. Where do I get information?
- Can Linux share my disk with DOS? OS/2? 386BSD? Win95?
- How can I get Linux to work with my disk?
- How can I undelete files?
- How do I compile programs?

- I have screwed up my system and can't log in to fix it.
- How do I upgrade/recompile my kernel?
- How many people use Linux?
- I can't get X Windows to work right.

The site also hosts general and introductory Linux information, upcoming events, and Linux links. Also available is information concerning Linux development projects, such as hardware ports, kernel, device drivers, file systems, networking, and distributions. A comprehensive links list covers such topics as hardware, software, and multimedia.

If you have access to Usenet newsgroups, you will find this to be a valuable resource of Linux information. For those of you who are unaware of Usenet, now is the time to discover the strength of newsgroups. Usenet newsgroups are electronic discussion and news forums; each newsgroup forum is dedicated to a specific topic. A program called a *newsreader* is used to access a newsgroup forum. A newsreader allows you to read, post, reply, and search a newsgroup forum that you have selected. Most online services, such as America Online and CompuServe, also provide access to Usenet newsgroups. A short list of Linux newsgroups follows:

- **comp.os.linux.advocacy.** Benefits of Linux compared to other operating systems
- **comp.os.linux.networking.** Networking and communications under Linux
- **comp.os.linux.setup.** Linux installation and system administration
- **comp.os.linux.development.apps.** Writing Linux applications; porting to Linux

If you do not have Usenet access but have Internet access, Deja.com is the site for you. Formerly known as DejaNews, this Web site provides the functionality of a newsreader through a Web interface. A benefit of Deja.com is that most newsgroup forums are archived, enabling you to search for specific subject matter. For example, suppose that you want to find discussions with a subject line containing "sound card," in newsgroup comp.os.linux.setup, within the date range of January 1, 1998 through June 27, 1999. On the day that I specified this search, more than 11,000 matches were returned!

Additional sources of Linux information can be found at various Internet FTP sites. *FTP* is an acronym for File Transfer Protocol. FTP is a TCP/IP protocol dedicated to transferring files from one machine to another across the Internet. After you are logged in to an FTP site and have the proper user rights, you can change directories, list directory contents, and download files. Some FTP sites will also allow you to upload files to their site. The following is a short list of Linux FTP sites:

- **sunsite.unc.edu.** The main Linux archive site
- **tsx-11.mit.edu.** Official sites for Linux's GCC
- **net.tamu.edu.** Home of TAMU Linux distribution

If you do not have FTP capability but have email facilities, you may be able to use the ftpmail utility program. The ftpmail utility allows you to send requests for file(s) using the facilities of electronic mail. The process is straightforward: You simply embed the FTP commands within the body of your email. For example, to retrieve a file named ##### from sunsite.unc.edu, the body text should appear as follows:

```
open sunsite.unc.edu
cd /pub/Linux
binary
get #####
close
quit
```

The email address you use is ftpmail@sunsite.unc.edu. To obtain a list of available ftpmail commands for a particular site—for example, sunsite.unc.edu—type the word **help** as the subject line, leave the body empty, and send the mail to the address ftpmail@sunsite.unc.edu.

Summary

This chapter introduced the Linux system. Linux can be viewed from three angles: It is a UNIX operating system clone, it is the core kernel, and it is the complete package of software tools and applications.

We also discussed the past, present, and future of Linux. The first official release of Linux was in March 1992. Linux has grown to be a powerful, stable, and feature-rich operating system providing many business benefits to organizations of all sizes.

Finally, we covered some Linux distributions and references to Linux information.

Chapter 2, "Installing Linux," covers Linux installation. It details the installation of four different distributions: OpenLinux 2.2, Red Hat 6.0, Slackware 4.0, and SuSE 6.1. In Chapter 3, "Using Linux," we cover the basics of using Linux. These two chapters will guide you through the installation and use of Linux, giving you a productive jump-start with Linux. Enjoy!

2
Installing Linux

IN THIS CHAPTER, WE WILL DISCUSS what it takes to install Linux. Planning is one of the most important steps for installing any operating system, including Linux. Many people want to simply insert CD-ROM #1 into the drive and begin installation. Unfortunately, installing any operating system is not that simple. It is important to go through a checklist and address any issues *before* you begin installation. This is especially important if you want Linux to coexist with one or more operating systems on the same machine.

We will also discuss how to install Linux on a machine that has a preexisting operating system. This is easily achieved with the proper tools and planning. Many people find it beneficial to have multiple operating systems on their machine.

The last four sections of this chapter are dedicated to the installation of specific Linux distributions: Caldera OpenLinux, Red Hat, Slackware, and SuSE. These are by far the most popular distributions of Linux.

Installing Linux can be an effortless or a difficult task. The degree of difficulty is proportional to the amount of preparatory effort you exert. The more you can anticipate before installation, the smoother the process will be.

Now that you have been forewarned, grab some paper and a pencil and let's prepare for installation.

Requirements Checklist

Before we actually install Linux, we need to go through our preflight checklist. This will help prepare us for our journey through the installation process. It is very frustrating to be halfway through the installation procedure only to discover that you do not have the required hardware. Or, to find out the machine is out of hard disk space when the installation is ninety percent complete.

The following is a list of hardware components that must meet minimum requirements to support Linux. Each will be discussed in detail in the sections that follow:

- CPU requirements
- Memory requirements
- Bus architecture requirements
- Video requirements
- Network card requirements
- Modem requirements
- CD-ROM requirements
- Disk drive requirements
- Mouse requirements
- Miscellaneous hardware requirements

As we go through the checklist, mark off each bulleted item that is within the requirements of Linux. Alternatively, a System Planning Worksheet is provided for you in the section that follows. Be sure to make note of any component(s) that may not be Linux compatible. This will be helpful if you must obtain technical support.

System Planning Worksheet

General:
Processor
Type   386   486   Pentium Pro
Speed (optional) _____

Mfg   Intel   AMD   Cyrix
Motherboard   _____
Make   _____
Chip Set   _____

Mouse   _____
Mfg   _____
Type   bus   PS/2   serial-port
If serial   COM1 (ttyS0)   COM2 (ttyS1)

Hard disk drive(s):
Type   IDE/MFM/RLL/ESDI SCSI
Size (list each drive) _____
                  _____
                  _____

SCSI Controller:
Make   _____
Model   _____

Boot: Linux   DOS/Windows   OS/2   Other

Disk _____   Partition _____   Size _____
Boot _____   Mount point _____
Disk _____   Partition _____   Size: _____
Boot _____   Mount point _____
Disk _____   Partition _____   Size _____
Boot _____   Mount point _____
Disk _____   Partition _____   Size _____
Boot _____   Mount point _____

CD-ROM: IDE/ATAPI   SCSI   Proprietary
Mfg _____   Model _____

X Windows _____

Video Card _____
Mfg   _____
Model _____

Chapter 2 Installing Linux

RAM: 1MB   2MB   4MB   8MB   16MB

Monitor   _____
Mfg   _____
Model   _____
Max scan rate   _____

Networking   _____

Modem   _____
Mfg   _____
Model   _____

Serial port: COM1   COM2   COM3   COM4
                    (ttyS0)   (ttyS1)   (ttyS2)   (ttyS3)

Computer hostname   _____
(Example: rainier)

The following answers are needed only if using a network interface card.

NIC Type: ethernet   token ring   FDDI   other

NIC Mfg   _____
Model   _____

Network domain name   _____
(Example: mountains.net)

IP Address   _____
(Example: 192.168.1.2)

Network address   _____
(Example: 192.168.1.0)

Netmask   _____
(Example: 255.255.255.0)

Broadcast address   _____
(Example: 192.168.1.255)

Gateway(s)   _____
(Example: none or 192.168.1.1)

DNS(s)   _____
(Example: 192.168.1.2)

General Requirements for Linux

This first section discusses only the general requirements necessary to install most any Linux distribution. Refer to the distribution-specific sections that follow to determine their supported hardware.

CPU Requirements

Linux can be installed on any IBM-compatible PC with an Intel 386, 486, or Pentium processor. All the various processor types, such as the 80386SX, 80486SX, and 80486DX, are fully supported by Linux. A floating-point math coprocessor is not required because Linux can emulate it via software.

Use an Integrated Math Coprocessor

The 80486SX series and the 80386 family of processors do not have an integrated math coprocessor. If you want ultimate performance from Linux, you should use a processor with an integrated coprocessor or ensure that your machine has a math coprocessor installed.

Linux supports other processors, such as the Sun SPARC, Digital Alpha, MIPS, ARM, 680x0, and PPC processors. This book does not address any machine equipped with a processor other than an Intel PC processor. Two chip manufacturers, Advanced Micro Devices and Cyrix, make processors that mimic Intel's 80386, 80486, and Pentium processors. These processors are fully supported by Linux.

If you are doing development work, an Intel 80486DX (or comparable clone) is the minimum requirement. Compilers and linkers tend to soak up a lot of processor time. If you plan to run a local SQL database, Java, a CORBA ORB, or Smalltalk, you should not consider anything less than an Intel Pentium (or comparable) processor.

One final consideration is multiuser support. For a non-GUI machine that will support up to two users, an Intel 80486DX should be sufficient. Beyond two users, including XFree86 support, an Intel Pentium should be the only consideration.

Minimum (character-based Linux installation):

- IBM-compatible PC with an Intel 80386 or comparable processor from AMD or Cyrix. Floating-point math coprocessor is recommended.

Recommended (Xfree86 GUI Linux installation):

- IBM-compatible PC with an Intel Pentium or comparable processor from AMD or Cyrix.

Memory Requirements

In this day and age of bloated operating systems, it is refreshing to discover that 2MB of Random Access Memory (RAM) is the minimum requirement to run a true multitasking, multiuser operating system. Of course, if you run Linux with 2MB of RAM, you will have to dedicate some hard disk space for a swap partition. Although Linux can run on 2MB of RAM, it is recommended that you have at least 4MB of RAM—the performance gain will be significant. The more RAM your machine has, the better Linux performs. One catch that I have yet to mention: With fewer than 16MB of RAM, Linux will run only in text mode. Even if you do get XFree86 to run with 8MB of RAM, your Linux system will run painfully slow.

XFree86 is to Linux what X Windows is to UNIX. XFree86 is a clone of X Windows, providing a windowing environment to the system. If you plan to run XFree86, be sure you have at least 16MB of virtual memory. Notice that I say *virtual* memory. The total amount of virtual memory is the sum of physical memory plus the size of the swap partition. Suppose, for example, that your machine has 12MB of RAM and you have devoted 4MB of disk space for the swap partition. This gives your Linux system 16MB of virtual memory.

Virtual Memory Rule

Although it is stated that 16MB of virtual memory is sufficient to run Linux and XFree86, the proper ratio of physical RAM to swap partition size must be considered. Linux will run sluggishly with 4MB of RAM and a 12MB swap partition. The general rule is that physical RAM should constitute 50% of total virtual memory. Ideally though, the swap partition size should be twice the amount of physical RAM, if you have the resources available.

If you are a developer and write Java or Smalltalk applications or run a CORBA ORB or SQL database server locally, you should have 32 megabytes of virtual memory as a minimum.

A Linux machine that will support multiple users will require more memory. For a non-GUI machine that will support up to two users, an Intel 80486DX should be sufficient. Beyond two users, including XFree86 support, an Intel Pentium should be the only consideration.

Minimum:

- Character-based installation: 4MB RAM
- Xfree86 GUI installation: 16MB virtual memory

Recommended (the more RAM, the better):

- Character-based installation: 8MB RAM
- Xfree86 GUI installation: 32MB virtual memory

Bus Architecture Requirements

Linux supports most PC motherboard bus architectures, which include Industry Standard Architecture (ISA), Extended Industry Standard Architecture (EISA), VESA Local-bus systems, and Peripheral Component Interconnect (PCI).

Surprisingly enough, Linux now supports the IBM MicroChannel Architecture (MCA). The reason this is surprising is that many PS/2 machines have been decommissioned by organizations that used them. If you have a PS/2 in your closet, you now have a reason to dust it off and turn it on.

Supported:

- ISA, EISA, VESA Local-bus, IBM MCA, and PCI.

Video Requirements

Linux supports a broad range of PC video cards. The list includes the Hercules, IBM monochrome, CGA, EGA, VGA, and SVGA video cards. Many accelerated video cards are also supported by Linux; be sure to check the supported cards for the Linux distribution you are installing.

Accelerated Video Cards
If your computer has an accelerated video card that is not supported by your distribution, you may still be able to install and run Linux. This is because most accelerated video cards can run in VGA and SVGA modes.

If you experience a flickering (snow) effect while running Linux, check to see if your machine has an IBM CGA card. You may need to upgrade the video card because there is no other solution to this problem.

If you intend to run XFree86 under Linux, your video card must use one of the chipsets listed in Table 2.1. Refer to the documentation provided with your video card to determine the chipset used.

All video monitors that are plug-compatible with the previous list of video cards should work under Linux.

Table 2.1 **Chipsets Supported by Linux**

Card Manufacturer	Chipset
ATI	28800-4, 28800-5, 28800-a
Cirrus Logic	CLGD5420, CLGD5422, CLGD5424, CLGD5426, CLGD5428, CLGD6205, CLGD6215, CLGD6225, CLGD6235

continues ▶

Table 2.1 **Continued**

Card Manufacturer	Chipset
Compaq	AVGA
NCR	77C22, 77C22E, 77C22E+
OAK	OTI067, OTI077
Paradise	PVGA1
S3	86C911, 86C924, 86C801, 86C805, 86C805i, 86C928
Trident	TVGA8800CS, TVGA8900B, TVGA8900C, TVGA8900CL, TVGA9000, TVGA9000i, TVGA9100B, TVGA9200CX, TVGA9320, TVGA9400CX, TVGA9420
Tseng	ET3000, ET4000AX, ET4000/W32
Western Digital	WD90C00, WD90C10, WD90C11, WD90C24, WD90C30

This chipset list is ever evolving. To check on the current list of supported chipsets, refer to the XFree86 Web site at http://www.xfree86.org. Other important information concerning the support and use of XFree86 can also be found there.

Network Card Requirements

Linux supports a wide range of network interface cards. Most Ethernet, FDDI, Frame Relay, Token Ring, and ARCnet cards are supported, the most popular being Ethernet cards. Your Linux distribution should contain a list of supported network cards. Table 2.2 contains a partial list of ethernet cards supported by Linux.

Table 2.2 **Partial List of Ethernet Cards Supported by Linux**

Card Manufacturer	Card
3Com	3c501 3c503, 3c505, 3c507, 3c509, 3c509B (ISA), 3c579 (EISA), Etherlink III Vortex Ethercards (3c590, 3c592, 3c595, 3c597), Etherlink XL Boomerang (3c900, 3c905), Fast EtherLink Ethercard
AMD	LANCE (79C960), PCnet-ISA/PCI (AT1500, HP J2405A, NE1500/NE2100)
AT&T	GIS WaveLAN
Allied Telesis	AT1700, LA100PCI-T, AT2400T/BT
Ansel Communications	AC3200 (EISA)

Card Manufacturer	Card
Apricot	Xen-II, 82596
Cabletron	E21xx
Cogent	EM110
Crystal Lan	CS8920, Cs8900
Danpex	EN-9400
DEC	DE425, DE434, DE435, DE450, DE500, DE450, DE500-XA, DEPCA and EtherWORKS, EtherWORKS 3, QSilver's DLink DE-220P, DE-528CT, DE-530+, DFE-500TX, DFE-530TX
Fujitsu	FMV-181, 182, 183, 184
HP PCLAN	27245, 27xxx series, PLUS (27247B and 27252A) 100VG PCLAN (J2577, J2573, 27248B, J2585)
Intel	EtherExpress, EtherExpress Pro
KTI	ET16/P-D2, ET16/P-DC ISA
Macromate	MN-220P (PnP or NE2000 mode)
NCR	WaveLAN NE2000/NE1000
Netgear	FA-310TX
SMC	Ultra, EtherEZ (ISA), 9000 series, PCI EtherPower 10/100, EtherPower II
Western Digital	WD80x3

Modem Requirements

Linux supports a vast array of internal and external serial modems. If you are using a serial mouse and a modem, be sure that both devices are configured to avoid conflicts. Most internal and external serial modems are supported, with the exception of Wintel modems (usually found in laptops). Support may be provided for these modems in the future.

CD-ROM Requirements

The easiest way to install Linux is to use CD-ROM media. Of course, for the installation to succeed, Linux must support the CD-ROM. CD-ROM drives must interface with a drive controller; the most common interfaces are IDE, EIDE, ATAPI, and SCSI. A SCSI interface can have multiple devices daisy-chained on a single controller. The rule with SCSI CD-ROMs is that as long as Linux supports the SCSI controller, the CD-ROM is accessible by Linux.

Many after-market multimedia products, such as PC sound systems, bundle CD-ROM drives in their package. A majority of these products uses a proprietary interface to the CD-ROM and therefore will not work with Linux. One exception is the CD-ROM bundled with Creative Labs' Sound Blaster package. Furthermore, some proprietary interfaces are also supported, such as the Sony CDU-541 and CDU-31a, NEC CDR-74, and Mitsumi. Current day machines with a CD-ROM drive use either an (E)IDE or SCSI interface, which Linux supports.

Linux can read only two CD-ROM file system formats: ISO 9660 and the High Sierra extensions. If Linux can spin up the CD-ROM drive but cannot mount the media, chances are that the CD-ROM format is incompatible.

Disk Drive Requirements

Believe it or not, Linux can actually be run from a floppy disk. In addition, some distributions allow you to run Linux as a live file system existing on a CD-ROM.

The optimal configuration, of course, is to install Linux to a hard disk. You will realize better performance if Linux is run from the hard drive.

Linux supports all MFM, IDE, EIDE controllers, and most RLL and ESDI controllers. As discussed in the previous CD-ROM section, Linux supports a wide range of SCSI controllers: manufacturers such as Adaptec, Future Domain, and Buslogic.

Linux can support more than one hard drive on the same machine. In fact, Linux can be installed across multiple drives. This is, in fact, the way most UNIX systems are configured. Maintenance of the operating system is easier and a slight gain in performance occurs.

The amount of disk space required for an installation is largely dependent on the parts of the operating system you require. A bare-bones system, without X Windows, will consume around 20MB of disk space. For a complete installation, including X Windows and development support, count on 250MB of disk space to be exhausted. Some of the commercial distributions, such as Caldera and Red Hat, can devour more than 400MB of disk space! Be sure to check the literature supplied with the distribution to determine the amount of storage required for your configuration.

One last consideration for disk consumption relates to the swap partition. Most Linux configurations can benefit from a swap partition, even if sufficient physical memory exists. Consider dedicating an amount equal to or double the amount of physical memory to a swap partition. For example, if you have 32MB of physical memory installed, consider creating a swap partition that is 32 to 64MB in size.

> **Swap Partition Upper Limits**
>
> The upper limit for a Linux swap partition is 128MB. Linux does allow up to 16 swap partitions. If your machine has multiple hard disks, the swap partition(s) should be placed on the least-used drive.

As we discussed in the earlier section "Memory Requirements," a swap partition is always recommended, especially if you have a limited amount (less than 16MB) of physical memory.

Mouse Requirements

A mouse is required if you intend to use the Linux X Windows GUI, XFree86. Linux supports serial, bus, and PS/2 mouse interfaces. Pointing devices, such as trackballs and touchpads, should work under Linux because these devices emulate mice.

Mouse use under Linux is not restricted to the XFree86 GUI. Linux supports the use of a mouse when in text mode—you can use the mouse to cut and paste text from one part of the screen to another (or to another virtual console). In addition, several text mode Linux applications use a mouse.

Linux supports serial mice from Mouseman, Logitech, Microsoft, and Mouse Systems. Linux also supports bus interface mice from Microsoft, Logitech, and ATIXL. In addition, Linux supports mice that use the PS/2 mouse interface.

Miscellaneous Hardware Requirements

In this section, we address the assorted hardware that you might have installed on your machine, such as a tape drive and a printer. Other sources of information concerning unique hardware can be found on the Web at http://metalab.unc.edu/mdw/index.html, which is the home of the Linux Documentation Project.

Tape Drives

Linux supports most SCSI tape drives as long as the SCSI controller is supported. Some other tape drives, namely QIC drives, that interface with the floppy controller or parallel port are also supported. Linux also supports other interfaces, such as QIC-02.

Most QIC drives can write data directly as raw bytes or, using a proprietary compression scheme, can compress the data to the tape, effectively storing more data. Unfortunately, you may not be able to utilize the compression option of these drives under Linux.

Printers

Linux supports practically every parallel-port printer. The rule here, as with other hardware devices, is if the printer is supported under MS-DOS, Linux should support it.

Although a serial printer can be used under Linux, it is not recommended. Documentation for serial printer configuration and use is hard to come by. Be prepared for some work if you are determined to use a serial printer.

The standard UNIX line printer software, lp and lpr, are available under Linux. Additionally, Linux bundles software that enables you to print to PostScript printers.

Planning Your Installation

As mentioned previously, a successful installation requires planning and preparation. This enables you to deal with issues before you are in the middle of the installation process. In this section, we address the various methods for installation, co-mingling Linux with other operating systems, and hard-disk partitioning.

Methods of Installation

There are a few methods of installing Linux. For example, you can install Linux from a CD-ROM, floppy disks, a DOS partition, NFS, or FTP. This flexibility is good for special situations; for example, maybe the machine you're installing lacks a CD-ROM drive.

Because most modern machines have a CD-ROM, this book approaches the installation of Linux using a CD-ROM.

Multiple Operating Systems on One Machine

A very appealing aspect of Linux is that it can coexist with other operating systems on your machine. Linux is quite happy to live with MS-DOS, Microsoft Windows, OS/2, or another distribution of Linux. For example, I have IBM-DOS 6.0, Windows 3.11, OS/2 Warp, Windows 98, Windows NT, Slackware Linux 4.0, Red Hat Linux 6.0, SuSE Linux 6.1, and Caldera Open Linux 2.2 all installed on a single machine!

This does not mean that you must have an existing operating system to install or run Linux. If you want to dedicate the entire machine to Linux, so be it.

Be sure that you spend some extra time planning your installation if Linux is to coexist with other operating systems. Because Linux must live in its own partition, you will have to repartition your hard disk to accommodate Linux.

> **Back Up Your System!**
> If you are going to retain any operating systems, be sure to back up your system. Replacing the boot manager is a destructive process because the boot sector is rewritten. If the boot sector is damaged for any reason, you may not be able to recover the original boot sector.

Linux provides a boot loader, called LILO (LInux LOader), which is used to boot Linux and other operating systems. After powering up your machine, you are presented with a choice of systems. Simply select one and LILO boots the corresponding operating system.

If you are serious about multiboot functionality, I recommend that you invest in a commercial boot manager, such as System Commander from V Communications or BootMagic from PowerQuest. These products are necessary if you're a multiplatform developer, a technical support engineer, or if you simply want to investigate various operating systems. As an added bonus, some of these products also bundle partitioning software with them.

In the next section, we discuss hard-disk partitioning. Also, we continue the discussion of booting multiple operating systems; be sure to continue through the next section to get a complete understanding of booting.

Hard Disk Partitioning

Before you can install Linux, you will have to prepare the hard drive. We prepare a hard drive by partitioning it. Partitioning a hard disk is not specific to Linux—all hard disks must eventually be partitioned and formatted to meet the requirements of any operating system. If you purchased your computer with an operating system preinstalled, you never had to think about partitioning and formatting the hard disk. Also, many after-market hard disks are partitioned and preformatted.

Partitioning is a good way to organize a hard drive. (Drive partitioning is common practice in organizations that use UNIX). An optimal system will have one partition dedicated to the operating system, another partition for the software, and a third partition for the data. Systems that use the FAT file system can benefit by partitioning the hard disk and creating logical drives. By reducing the size of a logical drive, you are effectively increasing the storage capacity (because the cluster size decreases as the size of the drive decreases).

Hard disks are divided into partitions. Each hard disk can have up to four *primary* partitions (the partition table is just large enough to describe four). Only one primary partition can be active (or "visible") at a time. In other words, a program in the active partition cannot access any files in another (inactive) partition on the same drive. A special section of each hard drive contains a partition table. This table provides information about each partition, such as size, location, type, and status.

Another type of partition is known as an *extended* partition. An extended partition can contain many logical partitions (or drives); a primary partition cannot. All extended partitions, and drives within them, are visible from the active (primary) partition. In addition, a program running in a logical partition can see all other logical partitions and the primary partition.

The active partition on the first drive is assigned the first hard drive designation, which would be c under DOS and Windows. (See Figure 2.1 for a visual representation.) If a second hard drive exists, the visible primary partition on that drive will get the next letter designation. Next, if an extended partition exists on the first drive, all logical drives within that partition are named. Finally, the extended partition on the second drive is visited, and all logical drives contained are named. Again, take a look at Figure 2.1 to see this graphically.

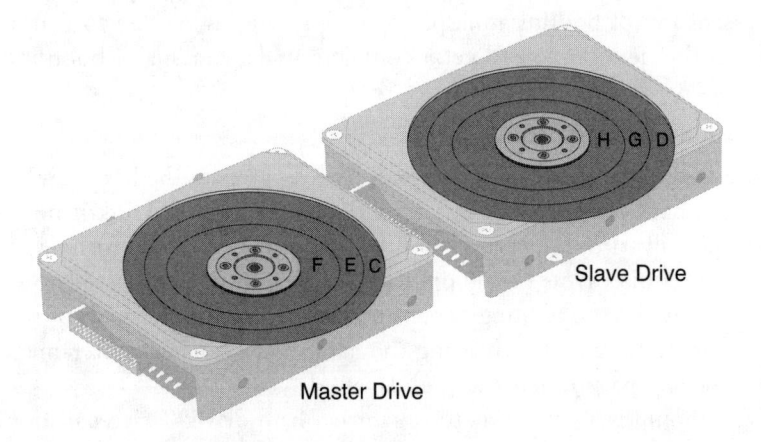

Figure 2.1 Layout of primary and logical partitions in DOS.

Linux and UNIX do not use drive letters to designate partitions. Directory names are used to refer to partitions. If this is your first exposure to Linux or UNIX, this might take time to sink in.

Booting a system is the act of loading an operating system from a hard drive. Booting is a well-defined process. After you power up the computer, the BIOS looks for the partition table on the first drive. Next, a search is made for the first primary partition that is marked as active. The boot loader is then executed to boot the operating system.

Some operating systems, such as DOS, must be in the first primary partition of the first drive to boot. That partition must also be marked as active. Linux, and other operating systems, do not have this restriction and can be booted from a logical drive (partition) in an extended partition. Everything we have talked about so far is very important to understand, especially if Linux is to coexist with one or more operating systems.

If you are using Linux as the sole operating system for your machine, partitioning the hard drive is a simple task. The simplest configuration is to create two partitions: one as a primary and the other as a logical. The primary will contain the operating system and all files. The logical partition will be the swap partition and will house the swap file. However, any seasoned Linux (or UNIX) user will tell you that this is not the optimal configuration. At a minimum, I recommend that you create one partition for / (root), one partition for /home, one partition for /usr, and one partition for swap.

If you are serious about partitioning, and you anticipate rearranging partitions in the future, I recommend that you invest in a commercial partitioning product, such as Partition Magic from PowerQuest or Partition Commander from V Communications. These products enable you to partition your hard drive with ease and confidence. As an added bonus, some of these products also bundle a boot manager with them.

Distribution-Specific Installations

In this section, we truly begin our journey with Linux. The journey begins with installation. As mentioned at the beginning of this chapter, installing Linux can be an effortless or a difficult event. The degree of difficulty depends on the amount of preplanning effort you exerted. If you followed all the preplanning, installation will be an effortless event.

This section deals with the installation of four different distributions. Why were these distributions selected? First, they are the most popular distributions. Virtually every computer store carries these distributions. Some stores carry all four packages, along with others. Second, more and more organizations (and hobbyists) are using Linux for their day-to-day operations. The third reason is ease of installation. Each of these distributions includes a comprehensive and flexible installation program. If it's easy to install, people will purchase it.

The following list identifies the distributions we will be installing and their version numbers:

- Caldera OpenLinux 2.2
- Red Hat Linux 6.0
- Slackware Linux 4.0
- SuSE Linux 6.1

The first distribution we will install is Caldera's OpenLinux 2.2. The second section will address the installation of Red Hat Linux v6.0. The third section tackles installing Slackware Linux v4.0, and in the final section, we will install SuSE Linux 6.1.

Caldera OpenLinux Installation

Caldera was founded in 1994 and is one of the oldest Linux vendors. Caldera Systems has been a leader in promoting Linux as an alternative to other operating systems.

The newest release of OpenLinux (2.2) provides a Windows-based installation. You can start your OpenLinux installation process from within Windows 95/98/NT. In addition, Caldera has packaged PartitionMagic for drive partitioning and BootMagic for booting multiple operating systems on a single machine. These products are discussed in previous sections of this chapter.

Quoted from the OpenLinux documentation:

"The easiest way to install OpenLinux 2.2 is to start by installing the Windows components of OpenLinux. By installing these tools, you can:

- Learn about OpenLinux in a familiar environment.
- Prepare any additional items you need for installation (for example, some users may need to create an Installation diskette).
- Prepare a separate partition of your hard disk on which to install OpenLinux using a graphical tool called PartitionMagic, from PowerQuest.
- Start the actual installation directly from your Windows Start menu."

We will not detail the Windows-based installation in this section. Rather, we will utilize the boot disk and CD-ROM provided. There is, however, an advantage to using the Windows installation. The hard disk partitioning software included enables you to easily prepare your hard drive (only) for OpenLinux or to partition the disk to allow the coexistence of multiple operating systems.

An assumption is made that your hard drive has an extra partition or some spare space to install OpenLinux. If not, you will need to prepare your hard drive before proceeding here.

When your machine is partitioned and ready for OpenLinux, move on to the following section.

CD-ROM Installation

To begin, insert the boot floppy disk and the OpenLinux CD-ROM, and reboot your computer. When installation begins, a graphical window is displayed showing the Linux kernel boot process and status of hardware probing. When probing has completed, a Caldera OpenLinux logo appears, and then disappears.

Next, the Language Selection window is displayed, enabling you to select the language to use for installation. Use the tab and the up and down arrow keys to choose the appropriate option (the mouse may not work yet) and select Next.

The Set Up Mouse window is displayed next, enabling you to specify your mouse. The program attempts to detect the mouse. Choose the appropriate option and select Next.

Next, the Installation Target window is shown, enabling you to define where on your hard disk OpenLinux should be installed. You can choose from Entire Hard Disk, Prepared Partitions, and Custom (Expert only). We're assuming that Linux partitions have already been prepared, so Prepared Partitions should be selected. To continue, select Next.

The next window, Select Root Partition, is displayed, prompting you to identify the (target) partition to use for OpenLinux. Choose the partition and select Next.

Next, the Partition Information window is revealed. This window shows the root and swap partitions. When you select Format Chosen Partitions, the install program formats the selected partitions. Select Next to continue.

The next screen, Select Installation, enables you to select the packages to install. Your choices are as follows:

- **Minimal Installation.** Consumes about 160MB. Consists of a complete Linux operating system, but without many of the preferred utilities and applications.

- **All Recommended Packages.** Consumes about 500MB. Consists of a complete Linux system with standard graphical tools and applications. About everything you could want.
- **Recommended Packages Plus Commercial Products.** Consumes about 800MB. Similar to the All Recommended Packages installation; it also installs WordPerfect for Linux (word processor) and other commercial software.
- **All Packages.** Consumes about 1.4GB! Installs all binary packages and software development tools from the CD-ROM.

Choose the installation that best fits your needs and select Next. (You can add or remove software packages after the installation is completed.)

The following set of screens is used to configure the X Windows (graphical) system. The first screen is Select Keyboard Type, which allows you to select your keyboard configuration. Choose your keyboard type and select Next.

The Select Video Card window is shown. You will identify the video card that your machine uses. You can select the Probe button to get more accurate card information. If you select Probe, a dialog window is shown—simply select the Probe button in the dialog box to continue. Then select OK in the dialog box. The Select Video Card window is fully revealed again. Select Next to continue.

The Select Monitor window is shown next. If your monitor is not available in the vendor list, choose Typical. To continue, select Next.

The Select Video Mode screen is shown, allowing you to choose a default video mode. Choose a mode and color depth and select Test This Mode to confirm that the mode is usable. When you are satisfied, select Next to continue.

In the Set Root Password screen, you will need to specify a password for the root account. After the password is accepted (you have to type it twice), select Next.

The Set Login Name(s) window enables you to create regular user accounts. Simply provide the information required and choose Add User. Continue this process to add additional regular users. When finished, select Next to continue. You should create at least one regular user account, as the root account should only be used for administrative purposes.

The Set Up Networking screen allows you to define networking information you might require. There are three options: No Ethernet, Ethernet Configured Using DHCP, and Ethernet Configured Statically. Choose the appropriate options and select Next. If you choose Ethernet Configured Statically, you will need to supply the IP Address, Name Server,

Netmask, Backup #1 (name server), Gateway Address, and NIS Domain. Enter the values appropriately for your system.

In the Choose Time Zone screen, you will need to specify your time zone. Select Next to continue.

The screen that appears reveals a Tetris (game) clone. You can play this game while the installation continues in the background. After the packages are installed and configured, the Finish button becomes available. To complete the installation, choose Finish.

The system boots the new OpenLinux system and the initialization screen is displayed. Be sure to remove the CD-ROM and the installation disk before rebooting.

After the kernel has started, the hardware is examined, the system switches into graphics mode, and then the graphical login window is displayed. You are ready to log in to your new Open Linux system!

After login, you can begin working with Open Linux. You should now jump to Chapter 3, "Using Linux," which provides a good foundation of knowledge to maneuver within Linux.

Red Hat Linux Installation

Red Hat introduced its distribution back in 1994. The Red Hat distribution introduced the concept of a package. A *package* is a software product that is tested, configured, and bundled up ready to install and execute. *Product* can refer to shareware or commercial software.

The staff at Red Hat put much effort into making Linux reliable and robust. Red Hat was Linux Journal's 1998 Readers' Choice winner and was awarded PC Magazine's Technical Innovation Award in 1998. Red Hat Linux was also selected as Operating System Product of the Year for three years running. It is easy to see why it has received these awards.

Installing and maintaining Red Hat Linux is a snap. Most installations take anywhere from 15 to 30 minutes. After installation, the Red Hat Package Manager (RPM) enables you to install and uninstall software packages with ease. The administrative tools provided with Red Hat help automate the configuration process. Finally, complete source code is provided for the freely distributable portion of the distribution.

Preparation

As I've said in earlier sections, you should always be prepared before beginning an installation. In addition to information provided here, you can refer to Red Hat's Web site at http://www.redhat.com.

The installation program can detect most hardware automatically on newer computers. Nevertheless, you should gather this information and be prepared. The following is a quick checklist of the items for which you need to have information during installation:

- **Hard drives.** Be sure you have the number, size, and type of drives in your system. If your machine has more than one drive, be sure you know which is the master, which is the slave, and on which interface they reside. You should know if you have IDE or SCSI drives, and see if they are accessed in LBA mode. Prepare yourself with the documentation for your hard drive(s) and computer.
- **SCSI adapter.** If you have one, record the make and model of the adapter.
- **CD-ROM.** As with hard drives, you should know whether the interface is IDE or SCSI. If possible, you should get the make and model of the CD-ROM drive.
- **Memory.** The amount of RAM installed.
- **Network card.** If applicable, record the make and model of the network interface card.
- **Video card and monitor.** If you plan to run the X Windows System, have your documentation ready for your video card and monitor. Technical specifications for both the video card and monitor can be critical. Be prepared.
- **Mouse.** Be prepared to specify the type of mouse, such as serial, PS/2, or bus.

If your system is going to be a member of a network, you should have the following information available:

- **IP address.** If statically configured or if using DHCP
- **Netmask.** If required
- **Gateway IP address.** If required
- **Name server IP addresses.** If required
- **Domain name.** Your organization's domain name
- **Hostname.** Your computer's name

You should consult your system administrator for this information. If you are using another operating system, such as Windows, you may be able to acquire much of the information in this section from its configuration.

An assumption is made that your hard drive has an extra partition or some spare space to install Red Hat. If not, you will need to prepare your hard drive before proceeding.

The *FIPS* program can be used to split a single partition into two. See the later section "Disk Partitioning" (in the section on installing Slackware UNIX) for more detail.

When your machine is partitioned and ready for Red Hat, go to the following section.

CD-ROM Installation

Red Hat's installation program is screen based, similar to a graphical interface. The interface is very intuitive and should be easy to follow. Some of the interface elements you will interact with are windows, text boxes, check boxes, scrollbars, and buttons. Follow along as we begin.

Insert the boot disk into the disk drive and reboot your machine. After a moment, the boot prompt appears. A number of boot options are presented. If you need help with any of these options, you can press the appropriate function key shown at the bottom of the screen. For most installations, just press Enter. After boot up, a welcome message is displayed; press Enter to continue.

Alternatively, if you have a newer computer that allows booting from a CD-ROM, you can insert the CD-ROM and reboot your machine. Be sure that your BIOS settings are set to boot from CD-ROM.

In the Choose a Language window, use the up and down arrow keys to highlight the appropriate choice and select OK.

The Keyboard Type window is displayed, enabling you to select a keyboard type. Highlight the appropriate type and press Enter.

The installation program checks your computer for PCMCIA support. If a PCMCIA card is detected, the program asks if you want PCMCIA support. Answer appropriately and select OK.

Next, the installation method is requested. (This section assumes CD-ROM installation.) Choose CD-ROM and select OK. Next, the program prompts you to insert the Red Hat CD-ROM. Select OK when you have done so. The program attempts to identify the CD-ROM drive. If the CD-ROM is found, the installation continues. You may be asked the type of CD-ROM if it is not found. You should choose from either an IDE or a SCSI drive type.

The Installation Path window is displayed. Select either Install.

The Installation Class window pops up. You should choose one of the following classes: Workstation, Server, or Custom.

The program checks the computer for any SCSI controllers. You may be asked if you have any SCSI adapters. If you select Yes, a list of SCSI drivers is displayed. Choose the appropriate SCSI adapter from the list.

The Disk Setup window is displayed next. The installation program needs to know where Red Hat should be installed. You will define the mount points of the partitions where Red Hat Linux will be installed. You should select Disk Druid (it is easier to use).

The Current Disk Partitions window is displayed (Disk Druid). Highlight the partition for the mount point and select Edit. The Edit New Partition window is displayed. Supply the partition's mount point. If the mount point should be root, type /, and then select OK. The Current Disk Partitions window is shown again. Select OK to continue.

The Active Swap Space window is shown, allowing you to activate the swap partition. Using the Spacebar, select the partitions you want to initialize. Also, if you want to check bad blocks, select the appropriate box. Choose OK to continue.

Next, the Partitions to Format window pops up. Any new partitions or existing partitions that you want to wipe should be formatted. Highlight the partition(s) to format and press the Spacebar. Select OK to continue.

The Components to Install window is shown, allowing you to select the software packages you want installed on the system. Select each component you desire and press the Spacebar. The Everything choice installs everything and requires about 1GB of space. If you want to select individual packages for each component, check the Select Individual Packages check box with the spacebar. This will take extra time, but will allow you to fine-tune the packages you install.

After you have selected the packages to install, the installation program displays a dialog box telling you that the /tmp/install.log file will contain the list of packages installed. Select OK to continue.

The installation program formats any partitions you selected. Afterward, the program starts installing the packages you selected. The Install Status window is displayed. It shows the package being installed, the size of the package, and a description of the package. Two progress bars are shown: one for the current package and one for the overall installation.

Next, the Configure Mouse window is shown, enabling you to specify the type of mouse you use. If you have a two-button mouse, you might want to select Emulate Three Buttons. Choose the appropriate mouse and select OK. If you chose a serial mouse, the Mouse Port window is displayed. Choose the appropriate port and select OK.

The Network Configuration window pops up, enabling you to specify whether you want networking support. Select Yes or No, as appropriate. If you choose networking support, you will be presented with a number of network configuration windows. The Boot Protocol window requires you to choose between Static IP Address, BOOTP, or DHCP. Next, the Configure TCP/IP window is shown, requesting IP Address, Netmask, Default Gateway, and Primary Name Server. The Configure Network window may be shown, requiring entries for Domain Name, Host Name, Secondary Name Server, and Tertiary Name Server.

The Configure Timezones window is then displayed. Choose the appropriate time zone and select OK.

The Services window is shown, enabling you to choose the services you would like automatically started at every boot. Choose the services you want started and select OK.

The following window asks if you want to configure a printer. If so, select Yes. The Select Printer Connection window is displayed next. Choose either Local, Remote lpd, SMB/Windows 95/NT, or NetWare and select OK. The Standard Printer Options window is displayed, requiring the name of the queue and the spool directory. You should accept the defaults supplied.

The Root Password window is displayed next, requiring you to enter a password for the root account. You must enter the password twice, and then select OK.

The Authentication Configuration window pops up. Choose the options appropriate for your requirements and select OK to continue.

The Bootdisk window is shown, asking if you want to create a bootdisk. It is always wise to do so.

The LILO Installation window is shown next. You should choose First Sector of Boot Partition and select OK. You should select Skip if you will be starting from the bootdisk. Installing LILO to the correct location on the hard drive is critical to the success of booting other operating systems. Installing LILO to the boot partition could overwrite other operating system boot loaders or multiboot software. Refer to the HOWTO titled "Multiboot using LILO mini-HOWTO" (http://metalab.unc.edu/mdw/index.html). This HOWTO addresses multibooting Windows 95, Windows NT, and Linux.

If you elected to install the X Windows System, you now have the opportunity to configure X. Various prompts will guide you through the configuration.

The last window displayed is the Done window, congratulating you on a job well done. When you select the OK button, the system will reboot. Be sure to remove all media from their respective drives.

After the system boots, you can log in and begin working with Red Hat Linux. You should jump to Chapter 3, which provides a good foundation of knowledge to maneuver within Linux.

Slackware Linux Installation

The newer releases of Slackware, from version 4.0 and later, are very stable and have a straightforward installation program. The release we are installing is 4.0.

To be exact, this distribution is the Linux Slackware 4.0 four CD-ROM set from Walnut Creek. Disc 1 contains the installation files and Linux source code. Disc 2 contains a ready-to-boot Linux system with source code for the kernel and X, and GNU archives. This disk contains a live Linux file system, allowing you to use it instead of installing the system to your hard disk. This is good if all you want to do is "demo" Linux. Discs 3 and 4 contain the Linux Archives from `Sunsite.unc.edu`.

Hardware Requirements

You can refer to the Linux Hardware HOWTO to see a listing of hardware that Linux supports. You can also refer to the Linux INFO-SHEET.

The basic list follows:

- You will need at least 8MB of RAM. Less than this and it's a trip to the computer store for more RAM. You can attempt some of the suggestions in `LOWMEM.TXT`, but you are much better off getting more physical RAM.
- For disk space, you will need 500MB (or more) to install Slackware. For a complete installation, you'll probably want to devote a 500MB or larger partition completely to Slackware. You could try and get away with a 20MB install, but you won't be a happy camper. Most installs range from 200MB to 400MB.
- As far as drives and controllers go, Slackware supports most MFM, RLL, and ATAPI/IDE drives and controllers. If you're installing from the CD-ROM (which we assume), be sure your CD-ROM drive is supported.
- You can have any one of CGA, EGA, Hercules, or (Super) VGA video adapters and monitors. As a rule, if your video system works with MS-DOS, it should work with Linux. But if you want to execute X Windows, you will have to refer to the XFree86 hardware list.

Linux can coexist with MS-DOS and Windows 96/98/NT (among others). Also, Linux can read/write MS-DOS files. Linux lives in its own partition, so it is not dependent on other operating systems. Linux is self-sustaining and does not require another operating system on the computer.

Required Disk Space

No document details the disk space consumption for Slackware. The Slackware installation is partitioned into disk sets; this is because in the early days, the distribution had to fit onto floppy disks.

The following is an overview of the disk sets and their space requirements:

- **A.** The base Slackware system. Contains everything to get Slackware up and running. Editors and the installation utilities are available. Consumes about 25MB. This is a minimal system; nothing else is required.
- **AP.** Applications. Contains more editors, file utilities, man pages (plus groff), director browsers, more command shells, and other utilities. Consumes about 20MB.
- **D.** Development. Consists of compilers, linkers, interpreters. Language support includes C, C++, Common LISP, FORTRAN-77, Objective-C, Pascal, and Perl, among others. If you are going to recompile the kernel, you will need to install this set. Consumes about 50MB.
- **E.** GNU Emacs. An incredibly powerful and feature-rich editor. Among other things, you can edit and compile programs and read email. Consumes about 35MB.
- **F.** Frequently Asked Questions (FAQs). Provides answers to commonly asked questions about Linux (includes the Linux HOWTOs). Consumes about 12MB.
- **K.** Linux kernel source. Contains the source code for the Linux 2.0.35 kernel. If you want to recompile the kernel, you need this set and the D set. Consumes about 27MB.
- **N.** Networking. Contains TCP/IP, UUCP, SLIP/PPP, pine and sendmail, trn and nn, Apache Web server (Netscape is in XAP set), and LYNX Web browser. Consumes about 25MB.
- **T.** TeX. TeX is a typesetting language for formatting and printing high-quality output to many printers. Consumes about 42MB.
- **TCL.** The Tcl, Tk, and TclX scripting languages. Consumes about 10MB.
- **X.** The X Window System (XFree86 3.3.3.1). The graphical user interface (GUI) environment for Slackware. Consumes about 70MB.

- **XAP.** X Windows System Applications. GUI programs to run under X. Examples are TkDesk and xfilemanager. Various window managers: fvwm95, fvwm, and twm. Web browsers, such as Netscape and Arena; image editors; GNU GIMP; and much, much more. Consumes about 70MB.
- **XD.** Tools for recompiling X servers. Not required to develop X applications, but to rebuild the X servers. Most people won't need this set. Consumes about 15MB.
- **XV.** xview3.2p1-X11R6. Provides support for Open Look (window manager); also for building XView applications. Consumes about 15MB.
- **Y.** Contains a collection of games. Consumes about 10MB.

The A set must be installed, if nothing else. A decent Linux system will consist of A, AP, D, and N. If you want X Windows—and who doesn't?—add X, XAP, and XV sets. For a robust Linux system, put everything on.

Methods of Installation

We assume installation from CD-ROM. If your machine has a bootable CD-ROM drive, you can simply boot Disc 1. Check your CMOS settings for information. If you cannot boot a CD-ROM, you'll have to create a boot and root floppy. The boot floppy holds the Linux kernel (albeit a small one) and the root floppy holds a Linux system plus installation software. If you plan to boot Linux from a floppy disk, you'll need another floppy on hand.

Other methods of installation include NFS, floppy disk, and MS-DOS partition. These methods are outside the scope of this book. Refer to the Slackware documentation for details on these methods.

In the next section, we list the available boot and root images, and then we describe how to create those floppies.

Creating the Boot and Root Floppies

First, round up two high-density (formatted) MS-DOS floppies. The boot and root images are written to the floppy disks using the `RAWRITE.EXE` program (on the CD-ROM).

Alternatively, you can use the `VIEW.EXE` program (CD-ROM) to create the floppies. The VIEW program is a much easier method of installing the boot and root images. Not only can you use VIEW to navigate the CD-ROM and write the images, you can view descriptions for the entries you are browsing. The VIEW program is found in the root directory of Disc 1.

Using RAWRITE Under Windows

Using RAWRITE or VIEW to write the images under Windows95/98/NT may not work. Switch to DOS real mode before attempting to write the disks.

Using VIEW

Launch the VIEW program, found in the root directory on Disc 1 of the Slackware distribution. A welcome screen is displayed. Use the down arrow key to highlight the bootdsks.144 or bootdsks.12 directory and press Enter. The directory list is shown. You can choose from two directories: ide-bat and scsi.bat. If you are not sure which one you should choose, read the WHICH.ONE file. Select one of the directories. Next, highlight the boot image that is appropriate for your system. Label one floppy as "boot" and insert it into the floppy drive. Now press the Enter key. Press Enter to begin writing. A status screen is displayed, showing the current progress of the image write. When it is finished, remove the floppy. Press Esc twice to return to the root directory.

Use the down arrow key to highlight the rootdsks directory, and press Enter. The directory list for rootdsks is shown. Next, highlight the root image that is appropriate for installation. This is most likely color.bat. Label the second floppy "root" and insert it into the floppy drive. Now press the Enter key. Press a key to begin writing. A status screen is displayed, showing the current progress of the image write. When it is finished, remove the floppy.

Put the two floppies aside and press the Esc key until the VIEW program terminates.

Using RAWRITE

RAWRITE copies a file to a floppy disk directly, track by track. Label a floppy disk "boot" and insert it into the floppy drive.

Make the CD-ROM drive current and change to the bootsdks.144 or bootdsks.12 directory. Next, write the appropriate boot image to the floppy using RAWRITE, as the following dialog demonstrates (take note of the DIR command; this is required because of a flaw in RAWRITE):

```
C:\> d:    (CDROM drive letter)
D:\> CD \BOOTDSKS.144
D:\> DIR A:
E:\BOOTDSKS.144> RAWRITE BARE.I A:
```

Press Enter to begin writing. A status screen is displayed, showing the current progress of the image write. When it is finished, remove the floppy. In the previous example, BARE.I is written to the boot disk. You will need to use the appropriate boot image for your system.

Next, we need to pick and write a root disk. Change to the `rootdsks` directory. In almost all cases, you will choose the `COLOR.GZ` image. Check the `README.TXT` file for a list of available choices. If you have not removed the boot floppy, do so now and place the floppy labeled root in the drive. Use RAWRITE to write the appropriate image to the floppy. The following is a sample dialog:

```
D:\> CD \rootdsks
D:\> DIR A:
E:\ROOTDSKS> RAWRITE COLOR.GZ A:
```

Press Enter to begin writing. A status screen is displayed, showing the current progress of the image write. When it is finished, remove the floppy.

Disk Partitioning

No beating around the bush here. If you have an operating system installed and you want to retain it, repartitioning software is the way to go. Read the previous sections titled "Multiple Operating Systems on One Machine" and "Hard Disk Partitioning" for more information.

If you do not want to invest in repartitioning software, you can use a program called FIPS to split a DOS partition into two. It is located in the `install\fips##` directory (the # character may be replaced with a number). All the documentation for FIPS is located there, also.

One other thing to consider is that you will have to defragment your hard disk *before* using FIPS; otherwise, you may end up lopping off the tail end of files.

Consider this section a sort of boot camp for repartitioning. We will not spend much time describing what is happening or the philosophy behind the action. We are here to readjust the number and size of the disk's partitions to accommodate Linux. Refer to the `FIPS.DOC` and `SPECIAL.DOC` files found in the `install\fips##` directory. In addition, you can refer to articles on the CD such as "Partition mini-HOWTO," by Kristian Koehntopp, "Installation HOWTO," by Eric S. Raymond, and "Installation and Getting Started Guide," by Matt Welsh for more information.

We will be using FIPS for this repartitioning exercise. Before we start, be sure you have defragged the target hard drive.

Get a blank floppy and format it with the `/s` switch, as shown in the following:

```
C:\> format a: /s
```

This will install the DOS system files to the floppy. Next, copy FIPS.EXE to the floppy. Now, reboot the system, leaving the floppy in the drive.

As soon as the A: prompt appears, execute FIPS. FIPS will ask which drive you want to repartition. Select the drive to shrink.

Confirm your drive choice and tell FIPS to copy the boot and root sectors.

FIPS asks if all free space on the partition is to be used to create a second partition. Select No. This allows you to alter the partition size.

Rearrange the table until the partition size is to your liking. Confirm the changes and write out the table.

When FIPS is finished, remove the floppy and reboot the machine. That is it for now. In the section that follows, we will boot the system into Linux and begin installation.

Performing the Installation

Ready, set, …

Slide the Slackware *boot* disk into the drive and reset your machine. A Welcome screen is displayed, and you have the opportunity to supply any kernel flags required for unique hardware configurations. Check the BOOTING.TXT file on the CD-ROM if your hardware is not detected.

If you are ready, press the Enter key to load the kernel. The following message will unfurl on the screen:

```
LILO loading ramdisk........
```

As the kernel boots, a generous amount of diagnostic messages are output to the screen. Shortly thereafter, you will see the following:

```
VFS: Insert root floppy disk to be loaded into ramdisk and press ENTER
```

Remove the boot disk from the floppy drive and insert the root disk. Press the Enter key, after which a login prompt appears.

Log in to the system as root, as in the following dialog:

```
slackware login:
slackware login: root
```

In a moment, the shell prompt will appear. Execute the fdisk utility, as shown in the following dialog:

```
#
# fdisk
```

Follow along as we set up a couple of partitions for Linux. One partition is for the root file system and the second is for swap.

44   Chapter 2 Installing Linux

The `fdisk` prompt appears and awaits input. Issue the `p` (partition) command to display the current partition table. The first partition is a DOS partition consisting of 61693 blocks.

```
Command (m for help):   p
Disk /dev/hda: 16 heads, 38 sectors, 683 cylinders
Units = cylinders of 608 * 512 bytes

    Device Boot   Begin   Start     End   Blocks    Id  System
  /dev/hda1    *      1       1     203   61693      6  DOS 16-bit >=32M
Command (m for help):
```

The prompt is offered again; issue the **n** (new) command. This allows us to create a new partition.

```
Command (m for help):  n
Command action
   e   extended
   p   primary partition (1-4)
```

Now we have to specify whether the partition should be an extended or a primary partition. If you currently have only the DOS partition, select `p` for primary.

```
Partition number (1-4): 2
First cylinder (204-1700):   204
Last cylinder or +size or +sizeM or +sizeK (204-683): +500M
```

We are prompted for the partition number; type **2**. Enter a starting cylinder; the prompt suggests a starting point. The starting cylinder should be one click after the ending cylinder (of the first partition). The first partition ended at cylinder 203; therefore, type **204** and press Enter. The third prompt, Last Cylinder, wants you to supply the size of the partition. We are going to be generous and give it 500MBs. No use being shy!

The notation used (+500M) specifies the size in megabytes. We could have specified it in kilobytes or bytes. Specify whatever disk space you can afford. Don't forget that we are going to dedicate another partition for swap, so don't use all the available space. Leave something in the neighborhood of 20MB.

Next, we create our 20MB swap partition, `/dev/hda3`.

```
Command (m for help): n
Command action
   e   extended
   p   primary partition (1-4)
Partition number (1-4): 3
First cylinder (1682-1700):  1682
Last cylinder or +size or +sizeM or +sizeK (474-683):   +20M
```

Now we redisplay the partition table to see what we have. Jot down the partition sizes.

```
Command (m for help): p
Disk /dev/hda: 16 heads, 38 sectors, 1700 cylinders
Units = cylinders of 1700 * 512 bytes

    Device Boot   Begin    Start     End   Blocks   Id  System
 /dev/hda1    *       1        1     203   61693     6  DOS 16-bit >=32M
 /dev/hda2          204      204     473   82080    83  Linux native
 /dev/hda3          474      474     507   10336    83  Linux native
```

Notice that the swap partition is type "Linux native." It needs to be "Linux swap." Issue the **t** (type) command:

```
Command (m for help): t
Partition number (1-4): 3
Hex code (type L to list codes): 82
```

Hex 82 is the code for a Linux swap. Type **82** and press the Enter key.

Because we are now done, we need to tell fdisk to write the information and exit. Type **w** to write the changes.

Quit the fdisk program. Disregard the message from fdisk to reboot—there is no reason to.

And now—the fun part!

At the shell prompt, type **setup** and press Enter:

```
# setup
```

The installation program fires up and a colorful menu window is displayed with nine available options.

Just to be sure, select KEYMAP to verify that the U.S. keyboard is selected. If asked if you want to proceed to ADDSWAP, answer Yes.

Next on the list is the ADDSWAP option. The program scans for a Linux swap partition. The program asks if you want to use the swap partition for swap space. Answer Yes. The program formats the swap and activates it. A confirmation window is displayed, specifying completion; press Enter to continue.

A window is displayed, asking if you want to continue to the TARGET section. Press Enter to continue. A list of partitions is displayed. The program wants to know the partition in which to install Linux. Select Linux Native using the arrow keys and select OK. Setup asks if you want to format the partition. The options are Quick and Check. Select Quick, unless you think there are problems with your hard disk (bad blocks), and select OK.

Setup displays the Inode Density window, prompting for your choice of formatting density. The choices are 4096, 2048, and 1024. I always recommend that you choose 2048 or 1024. Why? Well, if you end up installing most of the Linux packages (disk set) and specify a density of 4096, you could run out of inodes. Choose an inode density and select OK.

Setup will now format the root Linux partition.

Next, the Select Other Linux Partition for /etc/fstab window is displayed. The current Linux native partition is marked as In Use. Do not select this partition. If you don't need to select other Linux partitions, choose Cancel. The Done Adding Linux Partitions window is displayed, prompting for confirmation. Press the Enter key.

If you have any DOS FAT partitions, you can make them visible to Linux. The Fat Partitions Detected window is displayed. Choose a DOS partition you want to be visible to Linux. Supply a mount point; this is a directory name where you want the DOS partition mounted. When you are finished, highlight the entry and select OK. The Done Adding FAT... window is displayed, awaiting confirmation. Press the Enter key to continue. The Continue to SOURCE window is displayed, awaiting your response. Select Yes.

The next window displays, prompting for the source installation media. Because we are installing from the CD-ROM, choose 1 Slackware CD-ROM.

The Scan for CD-ROM window pops up, providing two choices: Auto or Manual. Choose Auto and select OK. Of course, if you want to be a Linux hipster, select Manual and specify the device.

The Scanning... window is displayed while the setup attempts to find the CD-ROM drive. When the CD-ROM is found, a new window, Choose Installation Type, appears. The available choices are: Slakware, Slaktest, and Custom. Choose the Slakware option.

When you've specified the installation type, the Continue to Select Disk Sets window pops up. Select Yes to continue.

You are now at the SELECT option. This one is important because it is here that you identify the software sets to install. There are quite a few sets (or packages) to maneuver. The list includes: A, AP, D, E, F, K, N, T, TCL, X, XAP, XD, XV, and Y. Select each set that you wish to install. At the very minimum, select the A set. A decent Linux system will consist of A, AP, D, and N. If you want X Windows—and who doesn't?—add X, XAP, and XV sets. For a robust Linux system, put everything on. When you are finished selecting the sets, select OK.

The Select Prompt Mode window is shown, requesting your assistance. The available options are Full, Newbie, Menu, Expert, Custom, and Tagpath. I recommend that you select Menu and press Enter to continue. (If you want to install *everything*, use Full.)

Next, the Selecting Software from Series XXX window is displayed. If you chose Menu mode, you need to select the software from the current set to install. You use the arrow keys and Spacebar to toggle the entries. When you are finished selecting the software, press Enter to continue. The Auto Installing Package window is displayed, showing the status of the installation. This process loops until all sets have been installed.

Disk Set Considerations

In the K set, you may want to deselect the Kernel Source entry because it can take up space. The N set contains the software Samba for Linux/Windows resource sharing—you might want this. See Chapter 15, "Samba: Merging Linux and Windows."

In the X set, you will choose an X-server. In addition to the server you choose, you might want to include the *Generic VGA* X-server. This provides you with a backup in case the other X-server fails to operate. In the XAP set, be sure to select Netscape if you are going to access the Internet.

You will see the Install Linux Kernel window. Your choices are Bootdisk—from Install, CD-ROM—Kernel from CD-ROM, and Floppy. The best choice here is Bootdisk. Why? Because you used that kernel to boot with; if you have gotten this far with no problems, it will work fine as your "permanent" kernel.

Select the Bootdisk option and press Enter. The Install Bootdisk window is displayed. At this point, you need to remove the rootdisk from the floppy drive, re-insert the boot floppy disk into the drive, and select OK. The Copying... window will pop up.

When the kernel is copied, the Make Boot Disk window is displayed, prompting for a boot method. It is wise to make a boot disk, so retrieve the third floppy, insert it into the drive, and select the LILO option.

The Modem Configuration window is displayed. If you are using a modem, select the port to use (the same as under DOS or Windows).

Next, you will see the Screen Font window. You can select from a number of fonts (text mode). Select what you want. The program may ask if you want to make this the default font. Answer appropriately.

The Install LILO window is shown. LILO (Linux Loader) enables you to boot Linux from the hard drive. You can also use LILO to boot other operating systems.

LILO and UMSDOS Installs

It is not recommended to install LILO for UMSDOS installations.

LILO Consideration

Bad things can happen if LILO is not installed correctly. If you are a new Linux user, you might want to boot into Linux using the boot disk that was created previously. You can install LILO in the future with the liloconfig utility.

If you have decided to install LILO, the best choice is Simple. If you are using the OS/2 Boot Manager, the program will add Linux to the Boot Manager menu.

You will need to specify where LILO should be installed. Select the choice MBR if Linux is the only operating system. If you are using a boot manager such as OS/2 Boot Manager or System Commander, select the Linux root partition.

After LILO installation is finished, the Configure Network window is displayed. If you want to set up networking, select Y, otherwise select N. If you choose to install networking, the Enter Hostname window will pop up. Supply a hostname and select OK. The next entry window, Enter Domain Name is displayed; supply the name and select OK. The Loopback Only window is shown. If you don't have a network card, choose Loopback.

At this point, you should see the Mouse Configuration window. Select the entry that pertains to your mouse. Next, the GPM Configuration window is displayed; I suggest that you install GPM support.

If the Sendmail Configuration is displayed, choose SMTP+Bind and select OK. The Timezone window is shown; choose the appropriate time zone for your area.

Whew! The installation is finally complete. The Setup Complete window pops up, telling you that the installation is done. Select OK, and the Slackware Linux Setup menu is shown again. Select Exit and you will be returned to the shell prompt. To reboot, execute the following:

```
# shutdown -r now
```

This command will shut down the system and reboot (-r).

If you decided to boot Linux with a floppy disk, insert the disk; otherwise, wait for Linux to boot from the hard disk. If you are booting from the hard disk, remove any floppy disk that might be in the drive. Also remove the CD-ROM.

When Linux begins boot up, you will see a series of diagnostic messages. Eventually, you will see the login prompt:

```
Welcome to Linux 2.0.35
stimpy login:
```

Log in as root. You need to apply a password to the root account. This is very important. The root account has unbridled privileges to the system. You don't want anyone walking up and logging in as root; they could do damage to the system. Also, it is a good idea to add an account for yourself that does not have root privileges. This can aid in reducing catastrophic errors. The last thing to consider is configuring the X Windows system, if you chose to install it. See Chapter 4, "Installing X Windows," for details. The following dialog shows how to change the root password and add a new user account. See Chapter 3 for more information on these two commands.

```
Welcome to Linux 2.0.35
stimpy login: root
stimpy login: passwd
   New password: *****
   Re-enter new password: *****
   Pasword changed.
stimpy login: useradd newUserName -s /bin/bash
stimpy login:
```

Now that Linux is installed, it's time to get to know Linux. Chapter 3 provides a good foundation of knowledge to maneuver within Linux.

SuSE Linux Installation

SuSE Linux was recently voted "Best System Software" at LinuxWorld in March 1999. It is also the winner of *Linux Journal*'s 1998 Readers' Choice Award for Favorite Linux Distribution. It's easy to see why. This is a well-thought-out product. The installation is easy and painless.

In this section, we will install SuSE Linux release 6.1. This is the most current release (at the time of this writing). Some of the highlighted features of SuSE Linux are Kernel 2.2.5, KDE 1.1 Desktop Environment, GNOME 1.0, XFree86 3.3.3.1, WordPerfect 8, and StarOffice 5.0 Personal Edition. You can see this is a well-rounded package. Not only do you get the Linux operating system, you also get office software. Don't forget, you get everything else you expect from a Linux distribution: image manipulation, programming tools, multimedia, typesetting, networking (workstation and server), editors, and so on and so forth.

In this section, we are going to take a suggestion from the SuSE team and offer a quick install, except that ours will not be as terse as their version. We will make the same assumption that your hard drive has some spare space, an extra partition, or an operating system (currently installed) that you are willing to lose (read: remove). If the answer to these three assumptions is *false*, then you need to prepare your hard drive before proceeding here.

The fips program, which we have discussed in a previous section, can be used to split a single partition into two. Refer to the previous sections "Multiple Operating Systems on One Machine" and "Hard Disk Partitioning" for more details.

When your machine is partitioned and ready for SuSE Linux, go to the following section "Installing SuSE."

Installing SuSE

Insert the SuSE Bootdisk and start your machine. You will see Loading... messages:

```
Loading initdisk.gz ...
Loading linux...
```

The linuxrc program loads up and the first menu to appear is Choose a Language. Use the up and down arrow keys to choose a language, and select OK.

Next, the Kind of Display option pops up. The options are Color or Mono. Choose the appropriate option and select OK. If you choose color, the screen will switch to a color scheme.

The Keyboard Map screen comes into view, allowing you to select a keyboard type. Choose the option that matches your keyboard and select OK.

Next, the Main Menu is shown. The options are as follows:

- Settings
- System Information
- Kernel Modules (hardware drivers)
- Start Installation/System
- End/Reboot

Choose the Start Installation/System option and select OK. The Start Installation/System menu is displayed. The options are as follows:

- Start Installation
- Boot Installed System
- Start Rescue System
- Start Live CD

Choose the Start Installation option and select OK. The Choose Source Media menu will pop up, requesting your attention. Because we assume a CD-ROM installation, pick CD from the options and select OK.

The Loading Data window appears for a moment, then YaST (Yet another Setup Tool) starts. YaST is the menu-driven installation and configuration tool from the SuSE team. This is a very competent tool that eases the installation and configuration process.

The first menu we see is called Type of Installation. Choose the Install Linux from Scratch option.

Next, we get the Select Swap Partition pop-up. If you have set up a swap partition, it will be listed. Also, the option (No Swap Partition) is listed, allowing you to set one up. After a swap partition has been identified, select Continue.

A Confirmation window is displayed, asking if the swap should be initialized and checked before activation. Choose Yes to continue; a Please Wait window is shown while the swap is initialized.

The Partitioning Harddrives window pops up. You have two choices here: Do Not Partition and Partition. Your partitions should already be set; if not, continue on to partition the drive. A Status window is displayed.

The Creating Filesystems window is revealed, waiting for you to specify a mount point. Highlight the partition and press the F4 key. The Mount Point window pops up; choose the file system, such as /, and select Continue. You can also change the inode density.

A Creating Filesystem confirmation window is shown—select Yes to create the filesystem(s).

A Please Wait window is revealed while the filesystems are created. Next, a new window, Reading Description Files, is displayed, which gathers package information for the installation.

The YaST menu is displayed. Select Load Configuration; these are predefined configuration types, such as Network, Development, Almost Everything, and so on. You can choose Change/Create to add or remove packages. One thing to mention is the Applix package. This is a demo; if you want it—fine; otherwise, it takes up more than 200MB.

Free Space Warning
You may see an Information window pop up, informing you that the amount of free space would drop below 5 percent. You don't want your system to drop to this level. You will have to either increase the size of your Linux partition or reduce the number of packages/software to install.

Select the Start Installation menu choice; the Installing Package status window will pop up. Each package is identified as it is being installed. You are also shown the number of packages installed and the remaining count. Don't walk away thinking you can come back later and the installation will be done. With SuSE, you will most likely be prompted to insert CD 2, CD 3, and CD 4. This depends on the packages chosen, but you should still be prepared for CD swapping. You will then proceed to YaST's menu. You will need to select Main Menu and insert CD 1. At the next selection window, Select Kernel, choose 2.2.5 and select Continue.

The Kernel Options menu is shown; select EISE or SCSI, whichever is appropriate for your hardware. For you MicroChannel fans, SuSE is kind enough to supply you with the option MicroChannel Kernel.

The Create a Bootkdisk window is shown. It is always a good practice to create a bootdisk, in case a problem occurs in booting the system in the future.

Next, it's time to configure LILO. Appropriately enough, the Do You Want to Configure LILO window is displayed—select Yes. Press the F4 key to create a new configuration. Enter a configuration name, select Boot Linux, specify the partition to boot, and select Continue. When the LILO installation is accessible, supply any hardware parameters required. At the Where to Install LILO prompt, choose the root partition. You can set a delay; the default delay is 10 seconds. When you are ready, select Continue.

Using a Boot Manager and YaST
If you are using a boot manager application, YaST asks if the root partition should be activated. Select No, and at the Confirmation window, select Continue.

Boot Manager and LILO
If you are using a boot manager application, you may get a Confirmation window, asking if LILO should be installed to the logical or the extended partition. If you are using a boot manager such as OS/2 Boot Manager or System Commander, choose Logical. Next, select Don't Activate Root Partition.

A number of windows are displayed, each requesting that you supply configuration information. First, the Time Zone Configuration must be addressed; select your time zone and Continue. At the next window, you should select Local for the Adjustment of Hardware Clock window, unless you are synched with GMT.

Now, you will need to specify a Hostname and Domain Name. If you are on a network, you may need to speak to your system administrator for these values; otherwise, you can choose any names you like.

At the Configure Loopback window, specify Yes if you are not on a network. For example, if you only dial the Internet, select Yes. If you are on a network, select No. If you do not configure loopback, you will need to enter a number of IP addresses. Check with your system administrator for details.

Next, at the Sendmail Configuration window, specify Single-user Machine and select Continue. The Output of SuSE Configuration window is displayed; select Continue.

The System Must Restart window is displayed. This does not mean that the machine will reboot, but that Linux will restart with the installed kernel and configuration.

You are now solicited for a root password. Then YaST starts again. You are prompted to choose whether you want to Create an Example User. If you want to, choose Yes.

The Setup Modem window is displayed. If you have a modem, choose Yes, and the Modem Configuration menu is shown. Choose the appropriate port and select Continue.

Mouse configuration comes next. Select your mouse type. The Use GPM? window is shown. GPM enables you to cut and paste text from one part of the screen to another or to a virtual screen. If you choose to install GPM, you will need to test it and select the Keep option.

The All Installed Packages Are Initialized window is displayed, awaiting confirmation. Select Continue. If you intend to run the X Windows system, be sure to run Sax, which is used to configure X.

YaST will terminate and services are started. You can now log in and begin working with Linux! It's time to get to know Linux. You can go to Chapter 3, which provides a good foundation of knowledge to maneuver within Linux.

Summary

We covered a lot of important information in this chapter. We began the chapter with an overview of Linux installation.

We went over the hardware requirements of most Linux systems. A System Planning Worksheet is included for your use, providing you with a preplanning checklist. Some of the items covered are CPU, memory, video, and bus architecture. In addition, hard disk partitioning was discussed.

The last section of the chapter covered distribution-specific installations, including Red Hat 6.0, Caldera OpenLinux 2.2, Slackware 4.0, and SuSE 6.1.

3
Using Linux

Hakuna Matata! It means "No worries," for those of you who missed the movie *The Lion King*. If you are a seasoned Linux user, you know what I mean. If you are new to Linux, the intent of the phrase is, "Do not worry—play with the system. Experiment, explore, and above all, don't worry!"

Linux is designed to protect specific parts of its system. You cannot do much damage, unless you log in as root. Be sure to refer to the later section "The Root Account" for details. Even if you do move or delete some special files by mistake, don't worry. The worst that can happen is that you will have to reinstall the system. And that's okay, it will give you more practice with Linux.

Linux Startup

Before you can begin to use your Linux system, it needs to be booted. There is more than one way to boot Linux.

The least intrusive method is booting from the hard disk. This assumes that you have installed Linux as the only operating system and are using the LInux LOader (LILO) to boot. Linux can coexist with other operating systems, but you will have to spend more time setting up for multiboot support and repartitioning the hard disk.

A second method is to use a boot floppy. This one is also easy: Simply insert your Linux boot floppy into the drive and start the computer (or reboot). The only bothersome part is that you have to insert the floppy every time you want to boot Linux. If you have another operating system—DOS, for example—this is a reasonable option for booting Linux, versus setting up multiboot software. In addition, if your hard disk has more than 1,024 cylinders and the Linux boot partition is beyond cylinder 1,024, you might have to use a boot floppy.

Yet another way to boot Linux is from DOS using LOADLIN. This allows you to be working in DOS, and when you are ready to boot Linux, you simply run the LOADLIN program.

There are other ways to boot Linux. One method is the use of boot manager software, such as BootMagic from PowerQuest or System Commander from V Communications. This software is designed to boot multiple operating systems that reside on a single machine. There are also shareware and freeware boot managers for the cost of the time to download. Along these same lines, if you are running Windows NT, you can use its boot loader. Likewise, OS/2's Boot Manager can be used.

Whatever the method, the loader boots Linux, and you begin to see a flurry of initialization messages scroll up your screen. As Linux loads the various drivers, this information is printed to the screen. Interspersed between these messages are other messages that describe the hardware Linux detects and configures. These messages are not to impress, but to provide information. There may be times when you experience problems with Linux—an indication of the problem may show up in this message traffic. As soon as Linux completes its startup sequence, a login prompt will appear, as shown in the following:

```
Red Hat Linux release 6.0 (Hedwig)
Kernel 2.2.5-15 on an i686
stimpy login:
```

The prompt on your screen may not be the same as the one shown here. Different distributions and different versions of Linux will display dissimilar login prompts.

Linux Shutdown

Booting Linux is straightforward and effortless. Shutting down Linux takes some attention on your part. Do not power down or reset the computer when you are finished with Linux because damage to files can result!

If you use IBM OS/2, Microsoft Windows 95/98/NT, or another UNIX-like system, you will find the shutdown process logically the same. Some manual intervention is required to tell Linux to shut down. Linux keeps various system files open while it is running, such as the I-node table and disk memory buffers. If you suddenly reset the system or turn the power off, the file system(s) may become corrupt. During shutdown, Linux will also unmount any mounted file systems.

Another reason to perform a proper shutdown is that active processes need to shut down gracefully. A database manager may have one or more database files open or an FTP process may be transmitting or receiving a file. When you instruct Linux to shut down, the kernel sends a signal (actually two separate signals) to all running processes. The signal tells each process to "finish what you are doing and stop."

If users are logged in to the system, performing a shutdown will allow them to log out. A user can get very frustrated to learn that the 50-page proposal on his screen never was saved to his user directory.

Never Use Switches to Shut Down Linux
Never turn off the power or press the reset switch while Linux is running. The Linux file system requires synchronization to the disk, and both processes and users (if applicable) require notification that the system is going down. Failure to properly shut down Linux can result in damage to the Linux file system.

Shutdown Commands and Procedures

A number of commands (and procedures) are available to properly shut down Linux. These commands and procedures can vary among distributions of Linux. These variances are due in part to the platform rather than to the actual distribution.

The most effective method to use to shut down Linux is the shutdown command. The syntax of the shutdown command allows up to three parameters. You can specify various command-line flags to shutdown, specify an absolute time that the shutdown is to occur, and specify a message that is sent to all users that are logged on. The syntax is as follows:

```
shutdown [flags] time [warning-message]
```

After you have invoked the shutdown command, it executes a number of tasks. Any users that are logged on are notified of the impending shutdown. The logical SIGTERM signal is sent to all running processes, informing them to terminate. Some versions of Linux will then broadcast the SIGKILL signal to any running processes, ensuring that all processes are terminated. And finally, the shutdown command then calls reboot or halt, depending on the command-line flag. For example, the -r flag means "reboot after shutdown," and the -h flag means "halt after shutdown." My typical shutdown is as follows:

```
shutdown -r now
```

This executes the shutdown command, instructing the command to begin the process immediately and to reboot the system when shutdown is complete.

This leads us to two other commands that will shut down a Linux system: reboot and halt. You should use one of these two commands only if you are the sole user on the system.

> **Avoid reboot and halt Commands**
> Do not use the reboot or halt commands to shut down Linux, unless you are the only user logged on to the system.

Most Linux distributions, but not all, support the Ctrl+Alt+Delete procedure to perform a shutdown. Before trying this procedure, though, you should consult the documentation for your distribution to see if it's supported. If the Linux system does not trap the "three-finger-salute," damage can occur to the file system. If your system does support it, pressing Ctrl+Alt+Delete will initiate the shutdown command.

Logging In to Linux

The "Linux Startup" section mentioned that after Linux completes its startup sequence, a login prompt is displayed, as shown in the following:

```
Red Hat Linux release 6.0 (Hedwig)
Kernel 2.2.5-15 on an i686
stimpy login:
```

This is the login prompt as it appears on my system. Your login prompt will undoubtedly look different. The login prompt also appears after you log out of Linux. We will discuss logging out of Linux in the section that follows.

Linux is a multiuser operating system, allowing multiple users to log in to a single machine. Because of this, a way is needed to differentiate all these users—you do not want everyone logging in with the same name. We do this by assigning a *username* for each person requiring access. In addition, a password is associated with each username. Therefore, the login process consists of two steps: providing a username when prompted and then providing the associated password. This concept is the same as an ATM bank card login. You insert the card into the teller machine and it prompts you for your identification code.

For each username, certain information is known to the system. The most important piece of information about you pertains to your privilege level. The privilege level tells Linux what you can do with the system—for example, access to specific directories or limiting the execution of specific applications and commands. Other information is also known, such as the home directory and user shell. For more information concerning user maintenance, refer to Part IV, "System Administration."

So, what about logging in? Go ahead, give it a try. When you see the shell prompt (as shown in the following):

stimpy login:

Type in your assigned username and press Enter. The system prompts you for your password, as shown here:

Password:

Supply your secret password and press Enter. If the system accepts your entries, you should be presented with the shell prompt. You are now in the system and can begin your journey. Before we discuss how to move around in Linux and execute programs, we will discuss logging out of Linux in the following section.

Logging Out of Linux

Logging out of Linux is simple. At the shell prompt, type the command **logout** and press Enter. Alternatively, you can type the command **exit**. Either way, the system cleans up any running processes and then calls the login routine. The login prompt will again be displayed on the screen.

A third method of logging out is the keystroke sequence Ctrl+D (not all systems support this method).

Managing User Accounts

Even if you are the only user on your Linux system, you must still understand user account maintenance. After all, you can have more than one account. Many people do this. Why? Well, each account can represent a different role that you might perform on your system. For example, suppose that you are an applications developer. You might have one username dedicated to development work and another username for office accounting and administrative chores.

In organizations that run UNIX and Linux systems, the *system administrator* is the person responsible for the maintenance of user accounts and the system as a whole. Large corporations may have many system administrators—there are just too many users and systems to keep up with.

This chapter does not delve into the intricacies of system administration duties; that is reserved for Part IV. The goal of this chapter is to provide you with Linux basics.

Creating an Account

One of the first things you should do after your first login is create a user account for yourself. It's not a good idea for you to log in with the root account, even if you are the sole user of the system. Too many bad things can happen when logged in as root. Reinstalling the system after a few days of use is acceptable, but not four months later, after you've got things configured and running just the way you want them.

Some distributions will collect user account information during the installation process. Yet, the majority of Linux distributions do not do this. Even if you set up required user accounts during installation, you should still read this section to familiarize yourself with the process.

To create a new user account, log in as root and at the shell prompt, type the command **useradd adduser [username]** and press Enter. The following is a dialog to add a new user to a Linux system. An optional method of using useradd follows.

stimpy $ useradd newuser

> **Root Required for adduser Command**
> Be sure that you are logged in as root. You will not be able to execute the adduser process unless you are the superuser.

Look closely at the dialog. System prompts are printed with a normal font, and responses to the system are in boldface. First, supply a username to add. Next, supply the user's full name. After the name prompt, the system prompts us for a Group ID for the user (GID). For the purpose of this example, simply press Enter. The next step is that the system retrieves the next available User ID (UID), prompts for a UID, and defaults the entry to the UID it generated. You can change the UID to anything you want, but it is suggested that you take the default UID.

The next prompt requests the home directory for the new user. Each user in a Linux system has a home directory. When you successfully log in to the system, you are automatically taken to your home directory. Linux generates a directory name based on the username chosen. You can change the directory name, but it is recommended that you accept the default—simply press Enter.

The next prompt solicits a shell for the user. A default shell is provided. For now, just accept the default.

The final prompt is the password to associate with the username. The system administrator of most organizations will assign a default password for all new users, such as "password." The account is set so that the password expires on the next login for the user. This way, the user gets to choose her own password and no one else will know.

After you have provided information for all prompts, Linux displays the user information and requests confirmation. If any of the information is not correct, type **n** and press Enter. Otherwise, if the information is correct, type **y** and press Enter.

If you answer **y**, the system creates the user's home directory, plus various subdirectories and files within the home directory, and then updates system files with information about the user. Some Linux distributions display the work in progress and some do not. Eventually, the shell prompt will be displayed again.

The following dialog shows usage for the useradd command. To get its usage, type **useradd** and then press Enter. Newer "versions" of the useradd command are not interactive as previously described.

```
stimpy $ useradd
usage: usermod [-u uid [-o]] [-g group] [-G group,...]
               [-d home [-m]] [-s shell] [-c comment] [-l new_name]
               [-f inactive] [-e expire mm/dd/yy] [-p passwd] name
stimpy $ useradd -s /bin/bash newuser
stimpy $ passwd newuser
```

In this example, you type **useradd -s /bin/bash newuser** and press Enter. Some versions of useradd specify /bin/sh as the shell. Because bash is the more popular shell under Linux, you might have to specify it, as we did here. Here, we specified the username to be *newuser*; be sure to replace it with the actual name of the user. You can also specify a password for the new user. Be forewarned: anyone standing next to you will see the password because you have to type it after the -p switch. You would be better off executing the passwd command after running useradd. If you do supply a password, be sure it is a default password that all new users log in with. Most organizations use "password" as the default. When a user logs in to the system, he can change his password. We discuss passwords in more detail in the following section.

Additional information about user accounts can be found in Chapter 22, "Managing Accounts."

Passwords

Your password is a very important piece of information; therefore, you should never tell anyone your password. Your password is as precious as your ATM bankcard password (otherwise known as PIN). Think about it.

If someone has your bankcard and your password, they could do some damage to your funds. The same holds true for your Linux username and password.

The most important account that must be protected is the root account. It is very important that you apply a password to the root account, no matter whether your system is for one person or hundreds. If you log in as root, the system is open to your every command. Think of it this way: If someone has your ATM bankcard and password, that person could access your account. If that person has the keys to the bank's vault, he could wreak havoc on many accounts.

Most Linux distributions require you to log in as root during installation. Because this default root account has an empty password, the system never prompts for one. Some distributions, however, will prompt you for a root password during the installation process. If you did not supply a password for root during installation, now is the time to change it.

Root Account Must Have a Password!
Always supply a password for the root account. Provide a password that is hard to break and keep the password secure.

All this talk about passwords is a good segue into the structure of a password. Think about this for just a moment. When you are asked for a password, what criteria do you use? Most people use a scheme that they will easily remember. These schemes usually end up as a birthday, their spouse's first name, or their own name spelled backward. There are many others, but you get the picture. These passwords are too easily broken. Through some ingenious social engineering (that is, creative, manipulative conversation), crackers can gain access to a system just by knowing someone that has a user account on the system.

Linux (and UNIX) systems are case sensitive. That is, it is sensitive to upper and lowercase letters. The password dogood is different from the password DoGood. This leads us to a discussion about constructing passwords. The second password, DoGood, is preferred over the first. Most system administrators will recommend interspersing a number within the password. Using our example, we could make the password stronger by added a number to it: Do4Good. You should refrain from appending a number to the end of the password. Many crack programs now iterate words and append the range of single-digit numbers. Refrain from using single words from the dictionary, if possible. Also, avoid choosing a password of fewer than seven characters. Expressions should also be avoided, such as dowhat, although inserting a number and changing to word-caps would help: Do4What. Even with the best password procedure in place, usernames and passwords can be cracked, given enough time.

One last word of advice—if you must write down your password, do not write it on a sticky note and paste it to your desk, monitor, or telephone. At the very least, put it in a secure desk drawer.

Changing Your Password

If you have not read the preceding section, "Passwords," I suggest you do so before proceeding here. Otherwise, let's see what it takes to change a password. The command `passwd` is used to change a password. Remember that users can change only their own passwords; root can change any password. The following demonstrates the dialog for the `passwd` command:

```
stimpy: $ passwd
Changing password for root
Enter new password:
Retype new password:
Password changed.
stimpy: $
```

As you type the new password, you will notice that no characters are echoed to the screen. This is a security feature of the `passwd` command.

The Root Account

The root login allows you free reign on the system. You can delete everything from a single file to a complete filesystem. The root user can start and stop any process. The reason for this is that *someone* has to be able to create new users, remove users, add and remove files, kill processes, add software, change file ownership, and start and stop the system. The downside to this power is that the wrong keystrokes can result in severe damage to the system. Many system administrators can attest to involuntary catastrophes, such as a recursive delete to a filesystem or a system shutdown in the middle of the day.

The root account is reserved for system administrators. The root login should be used only when it is required. System administrators will normally have two logins: the root login and a user (normal) login. This provides a level of protection for both the system and the administrator. Routine tasks are performed using the user login, and system-critical tasks are handled using the root login.

Even if you are the sole user on your Linux home system, you should still create a user account. This helps prevent any mistakes that can take place.

Use the root login only when necessary. When you are done with root-level work, log out and log back in with your user account. You'll be glad you did.

When using the root login, a couple of precautions should be taken. For one, change the root prompt. Use a prompt that is very obvious—something like ROOT!>. Second, think twice about what you are about to do. I recommend this throughout this book. Think about the command you are about to invoke. Think about it again. Verify where you are in the filesystem. Type the command out, but do not touch the Enter key. Verify the command you typed. If everything is acceptable, press Enter.

The root account gives you abundant power—learn to respect it. Protect yourself and your system and use the account only when necessary.

Moving Around in Linux

Something to keep in mind is that Linux is case sensitive; when you type a command at the command line, Linux differentiates between upper and lowercase letters. Linux will interpret the command adduser differently than AddUser. If you type a command and Linux responds with command not found, check the spelling and check the case. Operating systems such as DOS do not care about case sensitivity; you could type **DIR**, **dir**, or **DiR,** and DOS will interpret them all to be the same command. The case sensitivity holds true for file and directory names under Linux.

In this section, we discuss consoles, execution of commands, and environment variables. At the end of this section, you should feel comfortable moving around and using some simple Linux commands. If you are not logged in yet, do so now and let's forge ahead.

Virtual Consoles

Beginning here, you will begin to see the magic of Linux. If you have used DOS, you know that you have a single screen and keyboard dedicated to the computer. The combination of screen and keyboard is called a *console*. DOS sits around, waits for keystrokes, and displays information to the screen. Have you ever been in a DOS program, such as a word processor, and said, "I wish I could open another screen up and go get a listing of that directory"? Well, you can with Linux! Linux (and most UNIX systems) goes beyond the single console limitation and offers virtual consoles.

Linux allows you to have multiple virtual consoles running at the same time. You use the same keyboard and screen, but you use the function keys to switch to the desired virtual console. It's very simple: You keystroke to an available console, log in as usual, and perform whatever tasks are required. You simply toggle between the various virtual consoles that are running.

Limber up your fingers and let's try this. If you have not already logged in, do so now. Next, press the keystroke sequence Alt+F2 (hold down the Alt key and press F2 simultaneously). The "screen" you had disappears, and you should now see a new screen with a login prompt. This is the second virtual console. Let's try another one: hold down the Alt key and, one by one and slowly, press F3, F4, F5, F6, and finally, the F1 key. Did you notice the individual virtual consoles? You should now be back at your first virtual console.

You can even use the virtual consoles during the installation process. Some people switch to the second console, check the amount of free space left on the hard drive, and then switch back to the installation console.

After Linux boots and presents you with a login prompt, that screen is referred to as *tty1* and is the default. You do not have to do anything special to get it; it is the default screen (virtual console) provided by Linux.

Virtual consoles are a powerful feature, indeed. Think of the options. You can be using a word processor, jump to another virtual console and launch a report, and jump to a third console and send off an email.

Virtual consoles demonstrate the multiuser feature of Linux. You may not have thought about it this way, but when you log to another console, you are effectively logging in as another user. Therefore, if you have four virtual consoles running, you have four users logged in to your system!

An alternative to virtual consoles is the use of the Linux X Windows GUI, known as XFree86. X provides a Graphical User Interface (GUI) over Linux. Chapter 5, "Using X Windows," provides details on this GUI.

Shells and Commands

A Linux shell is nothing more than a program that translates the commands you type at the prompt. A shell is sometimes referred to a command interpreter—this is more a common term in the DOS world. The command interpreter in DOS is called COMMAND.COM. In the Linux (and UNIX) world, we refer to the command interpreter as the *shell*. A few shells are available for Linux; we discuss some of these in this section.

Essentially, a shell is an interpreter between you and the Linux system. At a shell prompt, you type commands and press the Enter key; this action submits the command to the shell. The shell interprets the command and, if valid, executes it or submits it to the operating system. If the command submitted is not recognized, an error message is displayed. Not only is the shell an interpreter, it is also an interface to the system. One other interface to Linux is the X Windows system. X Windows is discussed in Chapter 5.

Figure 3.1 is a graphical representation of the Linux kernel, a shell, and a console:

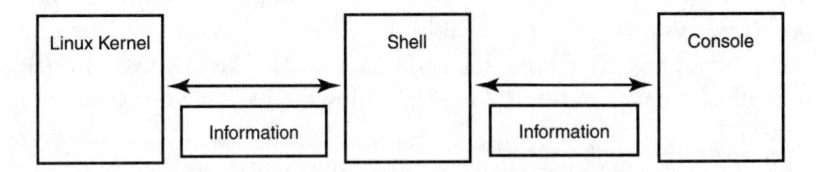

Figure 3.1 Graphical representation of Linux, shell, and console.

When you log in, the system consults your account profile for the shell entry and launches the appropriate shell. The shell runs continuously until you log out. You can change the shell in your account profile with the usermod (moduser) command. Be sure that you provide the complete path to the shell command. You can also change your shell while in Linux; simply type the name of the shell you want to use.

The following example shows how to change the shell for a user account:

```
stimpy $ usermod -s /bin/sh [username]
```

The following shows how to dynamically switch to the Korn shell at runtime. This does not change the specification within your profile:

```
stimpy $ exec pdksh
```

Notice that instead of just typing the shell name at the prompt, the exec command is used.

```
stimpy $ csh
```

You use the exec command to replace the current shell, instead of creating a second process (shell) under the current shell. If you type the shell name alone, as in the previous example, the csh shell will load and execute under the bash shell (if bash is running). When you are done with csh, type **exit,** and the previous shell will resume execution.

Some of the shells that are available for Linux are the Bourne Again Shell (bash), Public Domain Korn Shell (pdksh), zsh, ash, the C shell (csh), and an enhanced version of csh called tcsh. The most popular among Linux users is bash; Linux defaults to this shell for new users. Another shell quickly rising to the surface is pdksh. Not all distributions include all shells listed here.

The shell interprets and executes two types of commands. The first type of command is the built-in command. A built-in is just that: It is a command internal to the shell and only the shell knows how to handle it. The second type of command is called an external command. An external command is a program that resides somewhere within the Linux file system. The shell must find and execute an external command.

A popular use of shells is shell programming, or shell scripting. Shell scripts are very similar to a DOS batch file. A shell script is nothing more than a file that contains a series of built-in and external commands. Shell scripts are executed as an argument to a shell command. For example, to execute a shell script named cleanup, you would type the following:

stimpy $ bash cleanup

Here, a new bash shell is launched, and then it executes the commands found in the file named cleanup.

Let's try a couple of commands and see what happens. First, try the following command:

stimpy $ pwd

The pwd command is a built-in command. This command is used to print the name of the current working directory, as an absolute pathname. Do not confuse this with listing the contents of the current directory; this is a job for the external command ls (lowercase L). The pwd command merely prints the name of the directory in which you currently reside.

The following command can provide some interesting information about a user or users:

stimpy $ finger *username*

Notice that an argument, *username* in this case, is required to successfully execute the finger command. Actually, two arguments can be supplied to the finger command. The syntax of finger is as follows:

finger [*options*] *users*

The finger command (external command) displays information about one or more users. The argument *user* can be either a username (login name) or a first or a last name. If a username is specified, data is printed about that user, including data listed in the .plan and .project files in the user's home directory. If you supplied a first or a last name, information is displayed for all users matching the name. For a list of the available options for finger, refer to the man page. For information on the use of man pages, see the section at the end of this chapter, "Getting Help—The Man Pages."

When you enter a command, the shell performs several tasks. First, it checks to see if the command is a built-in command. The shell checks to see if the command is an *alias* for another command. An alias is a substitute command that you specify to represent another command. If the command is neither a built-in nor an alias, the shell then looks for a program having the specified name. If the shell finds the program, it executes the program, passing any arguments supplied on the command line.

One final note about shells and commands. If the command given is not a built-in command and cannot be found anywhere within the system, an error message will be displayed, as shown in the following sample dialog:

```
stimpy $ thrilling
thrilling: command not found
```

Remember that Linux is a case-sensitive operating system. If you get the preceding error message, be sure to check the spelling and the case.

Executing Commands

Executing a command in Linux, as with other operating systems, requires you to specify a command (and any arguments) and to submit the command.

Commands are carried out a number of ways. When you type a command and press the Enter key, the shell reads and then parses the command line. The shell checks to see if the command is known internally. All shells have a built-in command that it can execute directly. If the command is not an internal command, it checks its alias list for the command. An alias is an assumed name for another command. For example, if you are from the DOS world, you might want to create a command dir that is an alias for ls -al. If the shell finds an alias, it executes the real command. If the command is not an alias, the shell searches the system for an external program file. Remember that Linux is case sensitive, so the name must match exactly. If the command is found, the shell executes it, passing any arguments that are specified. So, you ask, what is an *argument*?

An argument is an option to the specified command. An argument can be many things: a filename, a symbol, another command, a person's name. There can be multiple arguments to a command. Some arguments are optional and some are mandatory. Some arguments, if given, must have arguments of their own. An argument is text given after the command, separated by field separator tokens (space, tab, and so on). The IFS environment variable is used to identify the list of separators. Some examples are discussed next.

The following example demonstrates the cp (copy) command. The syntax for cp is as follows:

```
cp source-filename destination-filename
```

The cp command requires two arguments. If you execute the following:

```
cp myfile.txt
```

cp will print its usage and will not fulfill the request. Here is an example that shows an argument requiring an argument:

```
mount /dev/hda1 /dos -t msdos
```

The mount command is used to attach a filesystem onto a directory. In the previous example, a DOS FAT drive is attached to the /dos directory on the Linux filesystem. The third argument, -t (type of filesystem) requires a filesystem type name. Order of arguments can be important. Using the mount command as an example, the source filesystem must be given before the mount point. The -t is referred to as a *flag* or *option*. Flags are preceded by the dash (-) and are used to modify the command.

The ls command has many options. None of the options are mandatory (that's why they are called options). Options can be appended onto one another or combined. The following is an example using the ls command:

```
stimpy $ ls -AlntF
```

This ls command lists all files (except . and ..), in long format, showing the user and group ID number instead of name, sorting by time modified instead of name, and marks each file entry with a symbol representing its type.

Special symbols can exist within the command line string. Here are a couple of examples:

```
stimpy $ ls -al > files.txt
stimpy # ls -al ¦ more
```

The first example uses the write to redirection symbol (>). The ls command is executed and its output is redirected to the file named files.txt (the listing does not appear on the screen). The second example uses the pipe symbol to connect the programs. The output of one program (left side) is received as input to the second program (right side). Using our previous example, the following will accomplish the same task, but it takes more steps:

```
stimpy $ ls -al > list.tmp
stimpy $ more list.tmp
stimpy # rm list.tmp
```

Now that you know the basics of command execution, let's take a look at recalling previous commands.

Command History

Linux provides a feature that enables you to recall previous commands. More accurately, this is a function of the command shell. The bash shell saves a history of commands in the history list. The number of commands stored is governed by the shell variable named HISTSIZE (under bash). For a more complete discussion of environment variables, see the later section "Environment Variables."

Shells Using Command History
Many shells are available for Linux. Some of these shells do not provide command history functionality—refer to the appropriate documentation for details.

The history list also persists across login sessions, so commands entered in the previous login are available to the current login session. How is this list retained across sessions? Quite simply—in a history file. This history file is normally stored in your home directory. The name of the history file is dependent on the shell that you are using. The filename usually begins with a period, thus hiding the file from directory listings (unless you use the -a or -A switch). For example, if you are using the bash shell, the name of the history file is .bash_history. You can control the name of the history file by using the HISTFILE environment variable under bash.

Commands are recalled from history by using the up and down arrow keys on your keyboard. As you press the up arrow key, previous commands, one by one, are retrieved and displayed at the shell prompt. As you continue to touch the up arrow key, previous commands are displayed until the last command is encountered. Conversely, you can use the down arrow key to move down the history list, retrieving more current commands. So, if you accidentally scoot past a command entry, you can come back to it with the down arrow key.

When the command that you desire is displayed at the shell prompt, simply press Enter to execute it. Or, if required, you can edit the command line. By using the left and right arrow keys, you can maneuver the cursor along the command string. You can use the Backspace and Delete keys to rub out characters, and you can insert new characters into the command string.

Command-Line Editing with bash
Among other shells, bash provides powerful editing of the command-line string. You can use many of the editing features of vi and Emacs. Refer to the bash documentation for details.

You can also see the complete history list at once, using the `history` command. If the number of history entries is beyond the number of screen lines, the list scrolls and you will be unable to see some of the entries. The syntax for the `history` command is as follows:

```
history [#]
```

The optional argument is the number of lines to display from the history list, starting from the most current entry. The following displays the complete list of command entries from the history list:

```
stimpy $ history
1  cd /development/java
2  ls -al
3  cd components
4  ls
5  cd utility
6  make package
7  cp util.jar /production/java/components
8  ls
9  slickedit fill.java
10 javac fill.java
```

The first line is the shell prompt and the `history` command we typed. The lines that follow are the contents of the history list. The following dialog shows the last three entries from the history list (most current last):

```
stimpy $ history 3
9  slickedit fill.java
10 javac fill.java
11 history
```

You may have noticed a slight difference between the entries displayed to the command line and the output of the history list. Each entry within the history list has an associated line number. You can recall a command by using its associated line number. The following dialog demonstrates recalling the `make package` command:

```
stimpy $ !6
stimpy $ make package
```

The exclamation point is called the *bang* character. The bang, when immediately followed by a number, instructs the `bash` shell to retrieve the command associated with the supplied number. Notice that the command is retrieved and placed on the command line, allowing you to edit the command string.

Another nice feature for some of the shells is called *command completion*. The next section discusses this useful feature.

Command Completion

The command completion feature can be useful when typing filenames. When you type one or more characters and press the Tab key, the shell attempts to complete the filename based on the characters you supply.

Linux will do one of three things concerning the template you supply. If multiple files are found matching the template, Linux will supply characters up to the last matching character (of all files found). For example, if we enter **sw** and press the Tab key:

```
stimpy $ sw <Tab>
```

The following is displayed:

```
stimpy $ swap
```

On this system, the files that are found are swapdev, swapon, and swapoff. Your system may find more or less, depending on what was installed.

If Linux finds a unique filename matching the template, it fully completes the filename. To modify the previous example, if we supply the following template:

```
stimpy $ swapd <Tab>
```

Then the following is displayed:

```
stimpy $ swapdev
```

The completion feature becomes quite useful when typing long filenames and directories, especially when typing fully qualified names. The following dialog demonstrates this:

```
stimpy $ cp /prod/java/components/dis <Tab>
```

The command line is updated, as shown in the following:

```
stimpy $ cp /prod/java/components/distrib.jar /pro <Tab>
```

And the following is output:

```
stimpy $ cp /prod/java/components/distrib.jar /prod/java/components/distrib.jar
```

Finally, we alter the second argument and submit the following command:

```
stimpy $ cp /prod/java/components/distrib.jar /prod/java/components/distrib2.jar
```

You will begin to appreciate this feature the more you use it.

Environment Variables

After you log in, Linux creates a number of environment variables for your session. An environment variable is a variable (or alias) that represents some value. These variables may be retained within the shell's or session's environment.

Some environment variables are predefined by the system, some are created by you, and others are created by various processes that execute. Some environment variables exist throughout the life of the current session. Some variables exist only during the execution of a process.

Environment variables that are globally visible are referred to as *exported*. A globally visible variable is one that is seen by all processes within the session. Some variables that are defined by a process are local to the defining process only.

So, what do these environment variables look like? How are they defined? How are they used? Let's begin by answering the first question. We can display the existing environment variables a couple of ways. One way is to use the `env` command, as in the following abbreviated example:

```
stimpy $ env
SHELL=/bin/bash
HOME=/home/mtobler
LOGNAME=mtobler
MAIL=/usr/mail/mtobler
TZ=CST6CDT
PS1=$
```

An environment variable consists of two parts. One is the name of the variable, and the second part is the value. Environment variables are comparable to variables found in most programming languages. The name variable suggests that its value can change—and indeed, the value can change.

A second method of displaying environment variables is to use the `set` command. The `set` command, however, prints all available environment variables. The `env` command lists only the variables that are exported. The `set` command lists all environment variables, exported and local to the shell process. The following is an abbreviated list of variables and their contents using the `set` command:

```
stimpy $ set
SHELL=/bin/bash
HOME=/home/mtobler
LOGNAME=mtobler
MAIL=/usr/mail/mtobler
MAILCHECK=300
TZ=CST6CDT
IFS=
PS2=>
OPTIND=1
PS1=$
```

This list differs from the list on your system. In addition, this list is not a comprehensive one; most listings from a `set` command scroll off the screen.

Let's move on to the second question: How are they defined? Environment variables are defined by specifying a variable name, followed by the assignment operator (=), and then the value of the variable. You need to be cautious, however; if you specify the name of an existing variable, the variable's contents will be overwritten with the new value. As mentioned previously, some variables are predefined by the system when you log in. You can define new environment variables at the command line. We can create a variable named REN to hold the value cat, as shown in the following example:

```
stimpy $ REN=cat
stimpy $
```

To verify that the variables exist, use the set command to see the results:

```
stimpy $ set
SHELL=/bin/bash
HOME=/home/mtobler
LOGNAME=mtobler
MAIL=/usr/mail/mtobler
MAILCHECK=300
TZ=CST6CDT
IFS=
PS2=>
OPTIND=1
PS1=$
REN=cat
```

So, is this environment variable local to the shell's environment, or is it global? Well, we have not exported the variable yet, so it must be local. We can verify this by using the env command, as shown in the following:

```
stimpy $ env
SHELL=/bin/bash
HOME=/home/mtobler
LOGNAME=mtobler
MAIL=/usr/mail/mtobler
TZ=CST6CDT
PS1=$
```

Sure enough, the variable REN does not exist in this list, so it must be local to the shell. Can we change the value of REN? Absolutely! We simply type the name **REN** again and supply a new value, as shown in the following example:

```
stimpy $ REN="a happy cat"
stimpy $
```

And now, let's see if the value of REN has changed. Remember, we have to use the set command:

```
stimpy $ set
SHELL=/bin/bash
HOME=/home/mtobler
LOGNAME=mtobler
MAIL=/usr/mail/mtobler
MAILCHECK=300
TZ=CST6CDT
IFS=
PS2=>
OPTIND=1
PS1=$
REN=a happy cat
```

You can also set the value of an environment variable to the empty string (no value). The variable will continue to exist, but no value is associated. The following dialog demonstrates this:

```
stimpy $ REN=
stimpy $ set
SHELL=/bin/bash
HOME=/home/mtobler
LOGNAME=mtobler
MAIL=/usr/mail/mtobler
MAILCHECK=300
TZ=CST6CDT
IFS=
PS2=>
OPTIND=1
PS1=$
REN=
```

Changing the value of an environment variable allows you to change the behavior of a program. Take notice of the variable MAILCHECK in the previous listing. This variable is used to designate how often to check for new mail. The value shown is in seconds. If we want to increase the value of the mail check from 5 minutes to 10 minutes, we do so as shown in the following example:

```
stimpy $ MAILCHECK=600
stimpy $ set
SHELL=/bin/bash
HOME=/home/mtobler
LOGNAME=mtobler
MAIL=/usr/mail/mtobler
MAILCHECK=600
TZ=CST6CDT
IFS=
PS2=>
OPTIND=1
PS1=$
REN=
```

We can see from the output of set that the variable is now set to the new value.

Another method used to print the contents of an environment variable is to use the echo command. The echo command is used to print the supplied argument to the standard output, followed by a newline character. If you do not supply an argument, a newline is output. The following dialog shows how *not* to display the value of a variable:

```
stimpy $ REN=a happy cat
stimpy $ echo REN
REN
stimpy $
```

What happened? The echo command did as it was told: to print the argument REN. So how do we print the value for REN? We prepend the $ character to the variable's name. Let's try again and see what happens:

```
stimpy $ echo $REN
a happy cat
stimpy $
```

That's better! We have one last question to answer: How are they used? We have seen one example and that was the MAILCHECK environment variable. Another example is the PAGER environment variable. This variable is used by the man command. Some man pages can be very long, often beyond the number of lines that a screen can display. The PAGER variable holds the command that the man command will use to display a screenful of data at a time. The default command man uses is the more command. You could specify the less command as an option. This command allows you to scroll the text up or down—more only displays text from beginning to end.

We've discussed the fact that an environment variable can be either local or exported. Therefore, how do we export a variable that is local? We use the export command, as is shown in the following dialog:

```
stimpy $ REN=a friend of Stimpy
stimpy $ export REN
stimpy $ env
SHELL=/bin/bash
HOME=/home/mtobler
LOGNAME=mtobler
MAIL=/usr/mail/mtobler
TZ=CST6CDT
PS1=$
REN=a friend of Stimpy
```

As you can see, REN is now a part of the exported environment. The variable REN is now available to all processes under this session. Alternatively, we can use the command separator character to collapse two separate command lines onto one. The following shows how:

```
stimpy $ REN=a happy cat; export REN
stimpy $ env
SHELL=/bin/bash
HOME=/home/mtobler
LOGNAME=mtobler
MAIL=/usr/mail/mtobler
TZ=CST6CDT
PS1=$
REN=a happy cat
```

The command separator can be useful to string two or more commands onto the same command line. Be sure to type your commands carefully when using the command separator, or you may get undefined results.

The most important environment variable is the PATH variable. The PATH variable is used whenever the system needs to find a command file. The variable is a colon-separated list of directory paths. For example, your PATH variable may be set as follows:

```
stimpy $ echo $PATH
/usr/bin:/bin:/usr/local/bin
stimpy $
```

If you enter the `finger` command, Linux examines each directory entry in the PATH. If the command is not found in the first entry, it continues to the next entry, and so on and so forth. If the command is found, it is executed. If the command is not found, an error message is displayed.

Using Files and Directories

In this section, we delve into the world of Linux files and directories. An understanding of Linux file systems is very important because everything you do in Linux involves a file system. If you are coming from the DOS or Windows world, some of what you see here will look familiar. This is because the DOS, Windows, and Linux file systems are borne from the UNIX file system. Linux uses a file system to store program files, user email, system files, and library files, among others. It also uses a file system for specialized programming tasks as shared memory.

During the installation process, the directory structure is created and all required files are placed in their proper location. After the installation is done, it is up to you to maintain the file systems.

The important thing to remember about a file system is to think twice before you act on it.

Understanding Files and Directories

Before a file can be stored, a Linux file system with one or more directories must exist. Without a directory, a file would not exist. Following the chicken-and-egg concept, some people will argue that a file is the basic building block, not the directory. After all, a directory is nothing more than a special file that contains filenames and their attributes. Still, directories maintain a logical structure and can be depicted graphically.

Think of the Linux file system as one massive file folder. This single file folder holds many other file folders. A directory can be thought of as file folder. A directory can contain one or more directories and so on.

Files are very specialized because they contain information. Each type of file has its own unique layout. Some files hold structured content—one example is a fixed record length file. With other files, the information contained is random. A word processing file is a good example. The information contained is in no specific order or structure.

All files within a file system must be uniquely identified. This is accomplished by giving a file a name and its location in the file system. The location refers to a directory path where the file is contained. If you have two files with the same name, but they are in different directory paths, they are considered unique.

The term *fully qualified filename* refers to a file's name, with its directory path prepended to the name. For example, if a file is named `sample.cpp` and is contained in the path `/development/projects/billing` (actually stored in the billing subdirectory), the fully qualified filename is `/development/projects/billing/sample.cpp`.

Different types of files are found on a Linux system. The various types of files fall under one of these major categories: ordinary and special files, links, or directories.

Ordinary files consist of executable files (programs), word processing files, shell scripts, database files, and other data files. A majority of your time is spent with ordinary files. If you are a developer, much of your time is spent editing source code files, executing the compiler to produce object files, and running the linker to generate an executable file. All these files—source code, compiler, object, linker, and executable—are ordinary files. If you work in sales, much of your time is spent manipulating spreadsheet files, word processing files, database files, and so on.

How does Linux know the type of a file? What keeps Linux from executing a word processing file? What keeps you from loading an executable file into the Emacs editor? Let's look at a Linux command that will tell us the type of a file. Ironically enough, the name of the command is `file`. The `file` command can be quite useful to help us determine the type of a file. For example, it can tell us if a file is, among others, a (binary) executable, a text file, or a shell script. If the `file` command reports a filename as a binary file, we probably don't want to view it in Emacs. The syntax for the file command is as follows:

`file [switches] file-list`

Refer to the man page for the `file` command to view the available switches. The argument `file-list` is a space-delimited list of files.

Okay, we know how to discover the type of a file. How does Linux know? Well, Linux really knows only two types of files. Either the file is an executable or it isn't. If the execute bit is set for a file, Linux can execute it. If the execute bit is not set, Linux will not attempt to run it. Linux might use the file for some purpose; for instance, the password file is read to verify a user's password.

The execute bit is part of the file access permissions. A number of permission bits are associated with each file. The permission categories are user, group, and other. Permission bits can be set for each category, to include read, write, and execute. Linux maintains these permission bits for each file, yielding a total of nine permission bits. For example, if we want to examine a file, we must have execute and read permissions for the file. The read permission flag designates that we can open a file for read-only. The write bit for a file says that you can open an existing file for write. To create a file, you must have write and execute permission for the directory. To delete a file, you must have write and execute permission for the directory.

Special files fall into two subcategories. The first subcategory is block-special and the second is character-special. Believe it or not, all physical devices are associated with the file system. The keyboard that you use, the console that you look at, and the printer that you print to are all associated with a file in the Linux file system. Most of these special files are found in the /dev directory.

Character-special devices are named as such because they process a stream of bytes, one character at a time. This is in contrast to block-special devices. *Block-special* devices process a block of data at a time. When I say process, I am referring to the reading or writing of data. Hard disks and magnetic drum and tape drives are all block-special devices. It would be very inefficient for these devices to process data one character at a time.

There are other special-device files. One is named /dev/null and the other is a *named pipe*. For /dev/null, anything that is sent to it disappears. If you want to ignore the output of a command, you can redirect output to

/dev/null. You can use /dev/null to create or (completely) truncate a file. To truncate a file to zero (or create one), use the cp (copy file) command, as shown in the following:

```
stimpy $ cp /dev/null ./myfile.txt
stimpy $
```

Because /dev/null has no contents, copying it to another file will set it to zero bytes. Or if the file does not exist, it will be created.

A named pipe is a FIFO (first-in-first-out) buffer. Named pipes are used in special programming situations. A simple example is a server program that accepts requests for service and performs the appropriate action. A named pipe is useful in this type of situation. The server is at the receiving end of the pipe. Any processes that want to send requests attach at the input end of the pipe. More than one process can attach at the input end. As data is fed at the input end, the pipe grows. As the server process reads data, the pipe decreases in size.

A *link* is a very special directory entry. A link is similar to an alias. You can specify that one file is a link to (or points to) another file. Whenever some action is performed on the link, the actual file is operated on. To be sure we are clear on this—a link is not a file; it is a special directory entry that contains the inode number of the linked-to file. So, you ask, what is an inode number?

An *inode number* is a unique identifier that is applied to every file. Think of an inode number as a file's social security number—each file gets a unique number.

There are two types of links: symbolic and hard. *Symbolic* links allow you to link to file without linking to the inode number. A symbolic link can even link to a nonexistent file. Symbolic links can span disks and computers. In other words, a symbolic link can link to a file that exists on another computer. *Hard* links are not as flexible as symbolic links. Hard links can work only on files that are on the same file system. Hard links are direct links to a file's inode number.

The Directory Tree

The directory tree is a way to organize files within directories. The term *directory tree* (or simply tree) is used because the directory structure, when depicted graphically, appears to have a root and branches. A directory tree can be depicted with the root at the top, and the branches growing downward. Alternatively, the root can be at the bottom, with the branches growing upward. A tree can also be shown with the root on the left and the branches growing to the right. Figure 3.2 shows a typical directory tree.

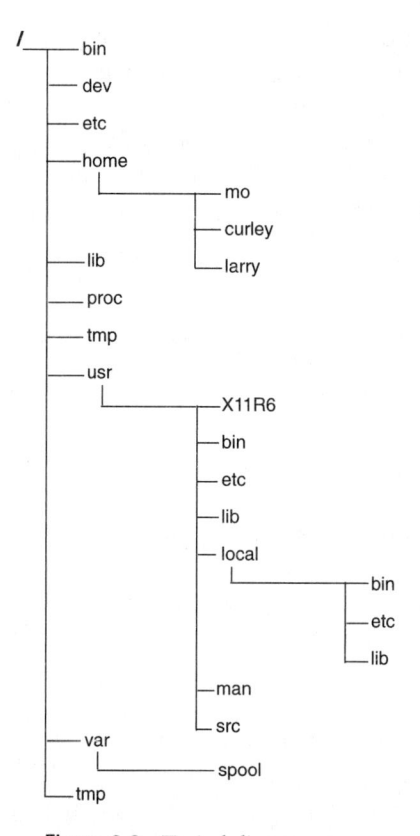

```
/ ─┬─ bin
   ├─ dev
   ├─ etc
   ├─ home ─┬─ mo
   │        ├─ curley
   │        └─ larry
   ├─ lib
   ├─ proc
   ├─ tmp
   ├─ usr ──┬─ X11R6
   │        ├─ bin
   │        ├─ etc
   │        ├─ lib
   │        ├─ local ─┬─ bin
   │        │         ├─ etc
   │        │         └─ lib
   │        ├─ man
   │        └─ src
   └─ var ──┬─ spool
            └─ tmp
```

Figure 3.2 Typical directory tree.

It is important to note that all directory branches start from the root directory. The *root* directory is the main file folder, holding all other directories (folders). If you look at Figure 3.2 again, you will see some important directories, such as /bin, /dev, /etc, /usr, and /var. As you can see, some of these first level directories contain other directories. Moreover, those directories contain other directories, and so on.

The root directory is also known as a *parent* directory. More accurately, the root is the parent of all directories. Each directory has a parent directory. Even root has a parent directory—itself. We use the / character to designate the root directory. All pathnames begin with the slash character, affectionately referred to as *whack*. We also use / to separate the parent and child directories when specifying a path. In the example /usr/local/bin, the directory local is a child of usr and bin is a child of local. We can see the relationship because each name is separated by /.

Each directory contains two special directory entries: . and … The . entry represents the current directory (see the next section) and the .. entry denotes the parent directory. Let's assume that you are in a directory named /development/components and there is a file named Goofy.java. You can refer to that file in a number of ways. For example, suppose that you want to run the head command on Goofy.java. The head command is used to print the first few lines of one or more files. The default number of lines is 10, but you can specify more or less. The following dialog demonstrates some ways we can refer to Goofy.java:

```
stimpy $ head Goofy.java
stimpy $ head ./Goofy.java
stimpy $ head ../components/Goofy.java
stimpy $ head /development/components/Goofy.java
stimpy $ head ../../development/components/Goofy.java
stimpy $
```

The last example is a little extreme. I suspect most people will not specify a path this way. First, you have to know how many levels deep you are, and then specify the complete path. Why not specify the fully qualified name, as shown in the fourth example?

The beginning of this section mentioned that the directory structure is a method of organizing files. Let's examine some of the standard Linux directories.

The root directory (/), as was discussed previously, is primarily used to hold all other directories. It is bad karma to store any file in the root (other than what Linux stores there).

The /bin directory stores binary executable files (programs). The name bin is derived from *binary*. Only Linux system binaries should be stored in this directory. Software (user binaries) that you install is normally stored in another directory.

The /dev directory holds the files that refer to devices. If you recall from the previous section, everything in Linux is a file, and devices (such as a printer) are no exception.

The /etc directory holds Linux-specific configuration files. If you ever have to reconfigure parts of Linux, you may find yourself editing some of these files.

The /home directory contains the home directories for users known to the system. When you log in to the system, you are taken to your home directory, which is found under /home.

The /lib directory is used to hold shared library files. These shared library files contain common function routines used by programs. Library files are referred to as shared because more than one program can access routines found within them. This fact keeps most programs small (and the system smaller) because each program does not have to store those routines.

The /proc directory holds process and kernel runtime information. The information is actually in memory but is accessed through /proc.

The /tmp directory, as you may have guessed, stores temporary files. Most of these temporary files are created by running processes. It is a good idea to visit this directory from time to time to see if any (large) files are left lingering around. The best time to do this is just after logging in to the system.

The /usr directory is used to contain most of the software packages that you install. This directory contains other directories, such as /usr/bin, /usr/etc, /usr/lib, /usr/local, /usr/man, and /usr/src. Let's take a look at these directories.

Executables are stored in /usr/bin (the same as /bin does).

Various configuration files not found in /etc are stored in /usr/etc—mainly configuration files used by the installed software packages.

The /usr/lib directory stores shared library files for the software packages.

The man pages (help files) are stored in /usr/man. The /usr/man directory will also contain a number of directories.

Source code for software can be found in /usr/src. The size of this directory can be quite large if you opt to install source code for all the software packages.

The /usr/local directory is used for nonessential files and programs. The structure of /usr/local will normally be different between UNIX systems. As a rule, however, it will contain /usr/local/bin, /usr/local/etc, and /usr/local/lib.

Files that fluctuate in size can be found in /var. The /var directory typically contains two directories: /var/adm and /var/spool. The /var/adm directory contains system error messages and log files. These files are reviewed and maintained by the system administrator. The /var/spool directory contains files that are used by programs such as news and mail.

Current Working Directory

At any one time, you are located in some directory within the tree. This is referred to as the *current working directory*. Any command that you execute uses the current directory. The pwd command can be used to print the current working directory as a full pathname. The following dialog demonstrates this:

```
stimpy $ pwd
/home/mtobler
stimpy $
```

You can change the current working directory using the `cd` command. This is shown in the following example:

```
stimpy $ cd /bin
stimpy $ pwd
/bin
stimpy $
```

As previously mentioned, many commands use the current working directory. The `ls` command is an example of this. If you execute the command `ls` without specifying a path, it displays the contents of the current directory.

The Home Directory

Every user known to the system has a home directory. User-specific configuration files are stored in a user's home directory. Standard practice dictates that users store their personal files here. When I say personal, I am not necessarily referring to private files, although you can store private files here. If you do, you may want to encrypt files stored there or set special permissions to those directories and files.

Personal files mainly refer to data files specific to a user. For example, any word processing documents that you create should be stored in your home directory. More specifically, they should be stored in a directory under your home directory. For instance, you may store your spreadsheet data files in a directory named `/home/username/spreadsheet`. The directory `username` is substituted for your username.

You can quickly get to your home directory using the `cd` command without an argument. The following dialog shows the command in action:

```
stimpy $ pwd
/usr/local/etc
stimpy $ cd
stimpy $ pwd
/home/mtobler
stimpy $
```

Optionally, you can use the tilde character (~) to specify your home directory. There is no need to use it with the `cd` command, but it might be useful in other situations. Suppose that one of your co-workers has a file that you need. Suzy Cue tells you that the file is named `employees.doc` and is found in her home directory (`scue`). The following is a dialog to use to copy that file to your home directory.

```
stimpy $ cp ~scue/employees.doc ~
stimpy $ pwd
/usr/local/etc
stimpy $ cd
stimpy $ pwd
/home/mtobler
stimpy $
```

As you start working with various software packages, be sure to organize your home directory to match each package. If you store all files you work with only in your home directory, it can become very cluttered!

Some Basic Commands

We have covered a lot of ground so far concerning Linux. Much of this information provides a good, basic understanding of Linux. Among other things, we learned how to start up, shut down, log in and out, and create user accounts. We also learned about environment variables, files and directories, shells, command completion, and virtual consoles.

With this basic knowledge, it is time to turn our attention to some basic commands. The sections that follow investigate how to move around in Linux, how to view the contents of a directory, how to create and delete directories and files, and how to get help.

One thing to keep in mind, as we discussed previously: Linux is a case-sensitive operating system. For example, the two files help and Help are unique names under Linux. If you try to change to the directory /Usr, you most likely will get an error that the directory does not exist. What you meant to type was **/usr**.

Moving Around in the Linux Directory System

Moving around from directory to directory is a common task in Linux. If every file were stored in a single directory, you would never have to move around. The fact is, though, that Linux maintains a directory tree and you will eventually have to move about.

We briefly touched on the cd command in previous sections. It is short for *change directory*. The syntax for cd is

cd [dir]

If you do not provide any arguments to cd, it changes the current directory to be your home directory. If dir is a valid directory, cd changes the current directory to dir.

The argument to cd can be either .. or .. Remember that .. is the current directory's parent and . is the current directory itself. If you are in the root, then issuing the command cd .. changes the current directory to the root, because root is the parent of itself.

86 Chapter 3 Using Linux

The following are some examples of the `cd` command:

```
stimpy $ pwd
/usr/local/etc
stimpy $ cd ..
stimpy $ pwd
/usr/local
stimpy $ cd ~
stimpy $ pwd
/home/mtobler
stimpy $ cd /
stimpy $ pwd
/
stimpy $ cd ..
stimpy $ pwd
/
stimpy $ cd
stimpy $ pwd
/home/mtobler
stimpy $ cd /
stimpy $ pwd
/
stimpy $ cd ../home/mtobler.
stimpy $ pwd
/home/mtobler
stimpy $
```

If you are coming from the DOS world, be sure to use the / (slash) character as a file and directory separator. Linux uses the \ (backslash) character to continue a command on the next line.

Viewing a Directory's Contents

In Linux (and UNIX), the command to view the contents of a directory is `ls`, which is short for list. A directory list contains both files and directories. This command is similar to the DOS command `dir`. In fact, most Linux systems define `dir` to be an alias for `ls`. The syntax for `ls` is as follows:

```
ls [options] [names]
```

The `ls` command has many switches (or options)—too numerous to list here. Refer to the man page for `ls`. Some examples follow.

The following lists the status of /bin:

```
stimpy $ ls -ld /bin
```

List the files in the current directory, listing the oldest first:

```
stimpy $ ls -rt *
```

List all files in the current directory, in long format:

```
stimpy $ ls -al *
```

Depending on the shell, you can get a directory listing in color. The differing colors represent the different types of files. For example, green represents executable files.

Creating New Directories

Okay, you need to start organizing your personal data files. You need to store them in your home directory. You have determined that you will need five directories: spreadsheet, database, documents, source, and timesheet. You know the directories you need, but how do you create a directory? You use the `mkdir` command. This is similar to the DOS command `md`. The syntax for `mkdir` is

```
mkdir [options] directories
```

The `mkdir` command creates one or more directories. You must have write permission (for the parent directory) to create a directory. Let's see how we can use the `mkdir` command:

```
stimpy $ cd
stimpy $ pwd
/home/mtobler
stimpy $ ls
name.txt
stimpy $ mkdir spreadsheet
stimpy $ ls
name.txt
spreadsheet
stimpy $ mkdir database documents source
stimpy $ ls
database
documents
name.txt
source
spreadsheet
stimpy $ mkdir timesheet
stimpy $ ls
database
documents
name.txt
source
spreadsheet
timesheet
stimpy $
```

If you recall, a directory is not like a file; it does not contain data, other than a list of files and directories. When you create a directory with `mkdir`, what actually happens is that Linux creates a new entry in the current directory's list.

Deleting Files and Directories

Inevitably, you will discover files and directories that you no longer require. Help is on the way. Linux offers two commands—one for deleting files and one for deleting directories. Let's start with deleting files.

The rm (short for remove) command is used to delete one or more files. For the command to succeed, you must have write permission for the directory containing the file(s) and the named file(s). The rm command has several options; check the man page for details. The syntax is as follows:

rm [options] files

Two common options available are -r and -d. The -r option is used to recursively remove the contents of a directory. If the name given is a directory (instead of a file), remove the contents of the directory, including subdirectories, and then the named directory.

> **Never Use -r Switch with rm Command**
> Using -r is a very dangerous option. You can inadvertently remove a complete directory tree and its contents. Stop and think twice before executing rm with the -r option.

You can use wildcards to delete files with rm. The following will remove all files in the current directory:

stimpy $ rm *

Always think about the directory you are in—you may not be where you think you are. Many people have fallen victim to this situation. You *think* the current directory is /devel/util and want to remove all files there. You execute the command:

stimpy $ rm *

You press Enter and suddenly realize you are still in /usr/bin! Sorry, there is no way to unerase files. As a precaution, you can use the -i option to rm—this option puts the rm command into interactive mode. For each file to be deleted, rm asks the user for y/n confirmation.

You can also use the wildcard character to specify a filename template for deletions. The following is an example:

stimpy $ rm swi*

In this instance, rm will remove all files that begin with the character sequence swi. The opposite can be achieved:

stimpy $ rm *ity

In this example, all files that end with ity will be removed.

A second, albeit strange, method of deleting files exists. Many Linux veterans will ask, "Why?" How about, "because you can." Here it is—deleting a file using /dev/null:

```
stimpy $ mv myfile.txt /dev/null
```

We will discuss the mv (move) command in a section that follows.

Let's take a look at removing directories. The command to do this is rmdir (remove directory).

The syntax for rmdir is as follows:

```
rmdir [options] directories
```

The named directories are removed from the parent. The directories to be removed must be empty. As previously shown, rm -r can be used to remove a directory and its contents in one fell swoop. The following is a dialog to remove a user's home directory that no longer uses the system:

```
stimpy $ cd ~gbye
stimpy $ ls
names.txt
accounting.xls
company.doc
employees.dbf
stimpy $ rm *
stimpy $ cd ..
stimpy $ rmdir gbye
rmdir: gbye: directory not empty
stimpy $
```

A user's home directory contains files that begin with a period (.). Any files that begin with . are not displayed with ls. You should use the option -al to see all files in a directory.

As with the /dev/null trick with files, you can also remove directories with this unorthodox method:

```
stimpy $ cd ~gbye
stimpy $ ls
names.txt
accounting.xls
company.doc
employees.dbf
stimpy $ cd ..
stimpy $ mv gbye /dev/null
stimpy $
```

> **Avoid -r Switch with rm**
> Unfortunately, there is no way to undelete files or directories. Think twice before you execute the command
> rm -r *.

Viewing Files

We can use a number of methods to view a file. One command that is at our disposal is more. The syntax for more is

`more [options] files`

The more command has a number of options available. Be sure to check the man page for the available options. more will output the contents of files, one screenful at a time. If you press the Spacebar, the next screen of text is displayed. The following is an example of the more command:

`stimpy $ more .profile`

As an alternative, you can use the command less. Most people, including me, will tell you that less is more than more. Here is the syntax for less:

`less [options] files`

The syntax is the same, but the options available for less significantly dwarf more. The options and commands available for less could span pages in a book. Be sure to check the man page for more on less.

Another command that can be used to view a file is head. We have seen this command in a previous section in this chapter. Here is the syntax:

`head [options] files`

There is one caveat: head is primarily used to view the first few lines in a file, the default being 10 lines. The fact remains, though, that it is a command to view a file. You can, however, use the -c or -n options to control the number of lines in a file. The following is an example of head:

`stimpy $ head -5000 install.txt`

This example will print the first 5,000 lines from the file install.txt. Alternatively, you can do this:

`stimpy $ head -c 5k install.txt`

This example duplicates the previous example. The k refers to 1KB blocks.

Another command that displays the contents of a file is cat. The one drawback to cat is that text will scroll up off the screen if the file contains more lines that the screen has. The syntax for cat is as follows:

`cat [options] files`

The cat command (concatenation) is useful when you want to append data to a file. See the man page for additional information.

Copying Files

You will find it necessary to copy a file from one directory to another. Alternatively, you might want to duplicate a file. The cp (copy) command is used to copy a file to another. The syntax for cp follows:

```
cp [options] file1 file2
cp [options] files directory
```

The first form copies `file1` to `file2`. Be careful: If `file2` exists, it will be overwritten. If the destination is a directory, the source file(s) are copied to the directory, and the source file(s) retain their names.

Moving Files

From time to time, you will need to move a file from one location to another. The mv (move) command is used to move a file to another location. The syntax for mv follows:

```
mv [options] source target
```

The mv command moves source to target. Be careful: If target exists, it will be overwritten. The mv command can be useful if you want to rename a file. The following dialog demonstrates the use of mv:

```
stimpy $ cd ~
stimpy $ ls
names.txt
stimpy $ mv names.txt ..
stimpy $ ls
stimpy $ ls ..
names.txt
stimpy $ mv ../names.txt .
stimpy $ ls
names.txt
stimpy $ mv names.txt names
stimpy $ ls
names
stimpy $
```

The first example moves the file to the current directory's parent. That fact is verified by the ls command. The next example moves the file from the parent directory back to the current directory. The last example demonstrates using the mv command to rename a file.

The mv command can also be used on directories. Use the command as you would on files. If the source is a directory and the target is an existing directory, the source is moved as a subdirectory of target. When mv is used on a directory, the directory and its complete contents are moved, too.

Getting Help—The Man Pages

We close this chapter by discussing the Linux help system, known as *man* (manual) pages.

If you need help with a Linux command, you can use man to view documentation. The syntax for man is as follows:

man [*options*] [*section*] [*title*]

The content of each man page has a very well-defined format. One trait of a man page is that it is terse. Another is that it is more technical than explanatory. These two traits, when combined, can make for obscure reading. Don't worry though, the more you use Linux and the man pages, the more you will come to appreciate their usefulness.

From a previous section, "Virtual Consoles," you may recall that you can switch to another screen session using the keystroke sequences Alt+F2, Alt+F3, and so on. If you get in a bind on the default screen and need help, switch to another virtual console and call up man. This way, you do not disrupt any work in progress on the default console.

Summary

We've come to the end of this chapter. It has been a long but fruitful road. We covered a lot of Linux ground. This chapter is probably most important for newcomers to Linux. It provides a good base of knowledge for using and maneuvering through Linux.

This chapter discussed many items, including startup and shutdown, logging in and out, manipulating user accounts and passwords, maneuvering files and directories, and basic commands used to manipulate files and directories.

At this point, you should feel very confident when tooling around in Linux.

4
Installing X Windows

MANY PEOPLE EXPECT THEIR OPERATING SYSTEMS to provide a Graphical User Interface (GUI) to the underlying system. Considering the power of computers today, there is no reason to use a command-line interface. The Macintosh popularized the GUI and showed that computer illiterate people can actually be productive using a computer. The magic behind this productivity is the GUI environment layered on top of the operating system.

In the UNIX world, the X Windows System is the graphical environment of choice. Developed at the Massachusetts Institute of Technology (MIT), X can be found on virtually every UNIX system to date. Linux is no exception. Linux uses a version of X named XFree86.

XFree86 is a freely available implementation of X Windows for Linux, System V/386, 386BSD, and other PC UNIX systems. The network product is known as X11. This allows an application on one machine to display to another machine.

In this chapter, we see what it takes to install and configure XFree86. Configuring X can be a breeze or a nightmare. The hardware of the machine and the version of Linux and XFree86 determine whether it is hard or easy. By far, I highly recommend that you obtain the most current release of Linux and XFree86. The newer releases are more powerful, flexible, and most important—stable.

You will be at an advantage if you know some basic Linux commands. If you have read Chapter 3, "Using Linux," you are equipped with the basic commands required. Installing and configuring X will require that you edit various text files. Any simple text editor will do.

XFree86 is available in two releases: v2.x and v3.x. Because significant defects are present in v2.0, I recommend that you not use it. The time and effort you expend may not be reflected at runtime. In addition, don't even consider any version prior to 2.0. Trying to get any version from 2.0 and earlier will be frustrating and difficult.

XFree86 Defined

XFree86 is a powerful windowing environment for Linux and other PC-oriented UNIX systems. The X Windows System, a GUI designed for UNIX, was developed at MIT. The first X Windows release, X11R1, was available in 1987.

A group of developers (David Wexelblat headed the team) formed the XFree86 Team in 1992 to develop XFree86, a freely redistributable implementation of the X Windows system. Consequently, the XFree86 Project was founded in 1994 and had two purposes. First was to continue research and development of XFree86 for the public. The second purpose was to obtain membership in the X Consortium.

The X Consortium is an organization that was formed to define and create a standardized UNIX windowing environment. MIT and IBM, among other organizations, are working members of the X Consortium.

The XFree86 Project, as a member of the X Consortium, was allowed free reign to information on upcoming releases of X. This gave them an advantage because they had release information before the public.

The most current version of XFree86 to date is release 3.3.3.1, which is based on X Windows Release 6 (X11R6.4). At the time of this writing, most commercial distributions of Linux are shipping with the 3.3.3 release. The June 1999 Slackware 4.0 release contains version 3.3.3.1 of XFree86.

X consists of a number of components, all working together to produce the graphical environment. At the top of the heap is the window manager. The window manager controls the appearance of windows and their widgets, such as buttons, menus, and scrollbars. Another important component is the X Network Protocol (XNP); it provides the protocol for network communications. Tied closely to XNP is Xlib, which is a function library that implements XNP. The core window system provides the core services required by the other components.

Installing XFree86

Most CD-ROM distributions of Linux contain the binary distribution of XFree86. It is also available from a number of FTP sites, such as sunsite.unc.edu. The current version of XFree86 is 3.3.3.1 and is the version shipping with the majority of Linux distributions.

I recommend that you install the version from the Linux distribution. The vendor may have special install scripts to satisfy file dependencies. However, this should not preclude you from downloading the current version of XFree86. For more information, you can visit the XFree86 Project Web site at http://www.xfree86.org.

Hardware Requirements

One of the most important hardware components relating to X is the video adapter. Before installing X, be sure you consult the documentation for your video adapter. Locate the "specification" section—it contains the information required by X. The chip set is the most important item you will need to know. If the documentation does not reveal the chip set used, the SuperProbe program (bundled with X) can be used to detect the chip set. A word of warning—SuperProbe can lock up the video system.

Be sure to consult the XFree86 release notes for a complete list of chip sets supported. You will find README files for the various chip sets— one for each chip set. These README files provide detailed information concerning the support of each chip set.

The minimum machine to run Linux and XFree86 is an 80486. To run X comfortably, you should have at least 16MB of RAM installed. The general rule here is the more RAM, the better. You can use a virtual disk to make up for a lack of physical RAM, but swapping is an input/output (I/O) intensive process. Disk I/O is the most significant bottleneck on a system. You may find technical papers that tell you XFree86 can run in 8MB of physical RAM with no problem. Some will even tell you 4MB of physical RAM! Don't be taken by these recommendations. Experience is the best teacher, as they say, and I am here to tell you that 16MB is the minimum; 32MB is preferred.

> **Memory Consideration for XFree86**
> You can run XFree86 on a Linux system with 16MB of virtual memory, but you will be disgruntled. The comfortable minimum is 16MB of physical memory, or you will experience lackluster performance. If you anticipate heavy X use, you should have 32MB of physical RAM.

To install a standard XFree86 configuration, including X server, basic fonts, libraries, and standard X utilities, requires about 60MB of disk space. If you are a developer and are brave enough to tackle X programming, you will require roughly 200MB of disk space.

Chip Sets

The following chip sets are supported by XFree86 release 3.3.3. Note that chips marked with an asterisk (*) have either limited support, or drivers for them are not actively maintained.

- Ark Logic—ARK1000PV, ARK1000VL, ARK2000PV, ARK2000MT
- Alliance—AP6422, AT24
- ATI—18800, 18800-1, 28800-2, 28800-4, 28800-5, 28800-6, 68800-3, 68800-6, 68800AX, 68800LX, 88800GX-C, 88800GX-D, 88800GX-E, 88800GX-F, 88800CX, 264CT, 264ET, 264VT, 264GT, 264VT-B, 264VT3, 264GT-B, 264GT3 (this list includes the Mach8, Mach32, Mach64, 3D Rage, 3D Rage II, and 3D Rage Pro)
- Avance Logic—ALG2101, ALG2228, ALG2301, ALG2302, ALG2308, ALG2401
- Chips & Technologies—65520, 65525, 65530, 65535, 65540, 65545, 65546, 65548, 65550, 65554, 65555, 68554, 69000, 64200, 64300
- Cirrus Logic—CLGD5420, CLGD5422, CLGD5424, CLGD5426, CLGD5428, CLGD5429, CLGD5430, CLGD5434, CLGD5436, CLGD5440, CLGD5446, CLGD5462, CLGD5464, CLGD5465, CLGD5480, CLGD6205, CLGD6215, CLGD6225, CLGD6235, CLGD6410, CLGD6412, CLGD6420, CLGD6440, CLGD7541(*), CLGD7543(*), CLGD7548(*), CLGD7555(*)
- Cyrix—MediaGX, MediaGXm
- Compaq—AVGA
- Digital Equipment Corporation—TGA
- Epson—SPC8110
- Genoa—GVGA
- IBM—8514/A (and true clones), XGA-2
- IIT—AGX-014, AGX-015, AGX-016
- Matrox—MGA2064W (Millennium), MGA1064SG (Mystique and Mystique 220), MGA2164W (Millennium II PCI and AGP), G100, G200
- MX—MX68000(*), MX680010(*)

- NCR—77C22(*), 77C22E(*), 77C22E+(*)
- NeoMagic—2200, 2160, 2097, 2093, 2090, 2070
- Number Nine—I128 (series I and II), Revolution 3D (T2R)
- NVidia/SGS Thomson—NV1, STG2000, RIVA128, Riva TNT
- OAK—OTI067, OTI077, OTI087
- RealTek—RTG3106(*)
- Rendition—V1000, V2x00
- S3—86C911, 86C924, 86C801, 86C805, 86C805i, 86C928, 86C864, 86C964, 86C732, 86C764, 86C765, 86C767, 86C775, 86C785, 86C868, 86C968, 86C325, 86C357, 86C375, 86C375, 86C385, 86C988, 86CM65, 86C260
- SiS—86C201, 86C202, 86C205, 86C215, 86C225, 5597, 5598, 6326
- 3Dlabs—GLINT 500TX, GLINT MX, Permedia, Permedia 2, Permedia 2v
- Trident—TVGA8800CS, TVGA8900B, TVGA8900C, TVGA8900CL, TVGA9000, TVGA9000i, TVGA9100B, TVGA9200CXR, Cyber9320(*), TVGA9400CXi, TVGA9420, TGUI9420DGi, TGUI9430DGi, TGUI9440AGi, TGUI9660XGi, TGUI9680, ProVidia 9682, ProVidia 9685(*), Cyber 9382, Cyber 9385, Cyber 9388, 3DImage975, 3DImage985, Cyber 9397, Cyber 9520
- Tseng—ET4000AX, ET4000/W32, ET4000/W32i, ET4000/W32p, ET6000, ET6100
- Video 7/Headland Technologies—HT216-32(*)
- Weitek—P9000, P9100
- Western Digital/Paradise—PVGA1
- Western Digital—WD90C00, WD90C10, WD90C11, WD90C24, WD90C24A, WD90C30, WD90C31, WD90C33

SuperProbe

If the documentation for your video card is unavailable, you can still determine the chip set your card uses. The SuperProbe program attempts to determine the chip set and other information about your video card. SuperProbe is found in the /usr/X11R6/bin directory. It can execute on various bus architectures, such as ISA and EISA.

98 Chapter 4 Installing X Windows

> **Using SuperProbe**
> SuperProbe is notorious for locking up the system. This is the result of SuperProbe probing various registers of the video card. If your video card documentation is available and the chip set is listed, there is no reason to run SuperProbe.

To execute SuperProbe, type the following and press Enter:

`stimpy $ SuperProbe`

Be sure to record the output from SuperProbe. The information it provides is used during configuration.

You can solicit SuperProbe to list known video devices. The following demonstrates this:

`stimpy $ SuperProbe -info`

If you think that you are not getting the information you are after, you can execute SuperProbe in verbose mode, as shown in the following example:

`stimpy $ SuperProbe -verbose`

Because the list can get lengthy, it is better if you redirect the output of SuperProbe to a file. The following shows how to execute SuperProbe and redirect its output:

`stimpy $ SuperProbe -verbose > sp.out`

Before you execute SuperProbe, you should terminate any programs that are not required. If SuperProbe hangs the system and applications are running, their associated data files could become corrupt. Also, be sure that all users are logged off the system.

X Servers

The default server is found in /etc/X11 and is named "X." This is actually a link to the server-specific XF86_xxx file that is found in /usr/X11R6/bin. The following is a list of available servers:

- XF86_SVGA—Super-VGA server. Contains accelerated support for Cirrus 542{0,2,4,6,8,9}, 543{0,4} and Western Digital 90C3{1,3} and Oak Technologies Inc. OTI087 chip sets, unaccelerated for the rest of the supported chip sets.
- XF86_Mono—(S)VGA monochrome, optionally Hercules or other monochrome hardware support is linked in.
- XF86_VGA16—Generic VGA 16-color server.
- XF86_S3—S3 accelerated server.

- XF86_Mach32—ATI Mach32 accelerated server.
- XF86_Mach64—ATI Mach64 accelerated server.
- XF86_Mach8—ATI Mach8 accelerated server.
- XF86_8514—8514/A accelerated server.
- XF86_P9000—P9000 accelerated server.
- XF86_AGX—AGX accelerated server.
- XF86_W32—ET4000/W32 and ET6000 accelerated server.

You should check the server file that /etc/X11/X is linked with. If invalid, relink to the proper XF86_xxx file.

Be sure to check the man pages. Each server has an associated man page that provides a wealth of information, such as chip set support and specific configuration options.

Checking for a Previous Installation

Your system may indeed already have XFree86 installed on it. During installation, you are offered the opportunity to select various packages to install. One of them is the XFree86 system. One method to verify whether XFree86 is installed is to try and start it up. The following example shows how to start up X:

```
stimpy $ startx
```

If you are immediately returned to the shell prompt, the XFree86 system probably doesn't exist.

Another method to check the existence of XFree86 is to check the contents of the /usr/X11R6/bin directory. If the directory does not exist, the X will have to be installed.

What if you find the directories and discover that they are full of files? It may be that XFree86 is not configured properly. You might want to jump to the later section "Configuring XFree86." After you have completed the configuration, try to run X.

If none of these options work, you probably need to install the XFree86 system. This section is dedicated to that purpose.

I recommend that you install the version from the Linux distribution CD-ROM. The vendor has no doubt gone to great lengths to automate the process. This helps to reduce errors and reduce the possibility of system damage.

However, this should not preclude you from downloading the current version of XFree86. For more information, you can visit the XFree86 Project Web site at `http://www.xfree86.org`.

Manual Install

First, you need to acquire the complete XFree86 system. The installation in this section assumes the XFree86 3.3.2 release. The most current version of XFree86, at the time of this writing, is the 3.3.3.1 release.

The preferred media is CD-ROM or floppy media. If you have access to either one, it will make life a little easier.

The next option, if the CD-ROM or the floppy isn't available, is to download the package via FTP. A good place to start is at the XFree86 Project (`http://www.xfree86.org`) Web site. Be sure to view the README files found on the FTP site. They will guide you to the proper directories and specify the files you need to download.

It might be a good idea to go to the doc directory and download the documentation. In particular, get the following files: `QuickStart.doc`, `README`, `README.Linux`, `README.Config`, and `RELNOTES`. Read them and become familiar with the requirements and the process. When you are ready, return to the FTP site to get the binaries (and whatever else you want). Refer to the `RELNOTES` file in the binary release directory. It will provide you with the files you require. By the way, be forewarned that the release directory contains at least 30MB worth of files.

The basic steps to manually install XFree86 are the following:

- Acquire the XFree86 distribution.
- Create directories and run preinstallation script.
- Extract the distribution.
- Run post-installation script and configure the system.

The steps are rather easy; it's the attention to detail that is important. Let's forge ahead and get XFree86 on the system. One thing before we get started: This text will not specify the files you will require from the distribution. It is assumed that you have read the appropriate `RELNOTE` file.

The binaries for 3.3.2 can be obtained either as a full release or as an upgrade. The upgrade is good only if you have the 3.3.1 release. We are assuming you are not upgrading. Place the compressed files into the `/var/tmp` directory.

Because you are installing from scratch, create the directory `/usr/X11R6`. Next, extract the required files that have the extension .tgz.

> **X11R6 Directory Location**
> If you don't have enough space on /usr, create the X11R6 directory elsewhere and create a symbolic link to the new directory.

Next, you need to execute the preinstallation script. It checks your system and reports any discrepancies. It is quite possible that you will have to install other system components before you can continue with the X installation. The following dialog demonstrates the procedure:

```
stimpy $ cd /usr/X11R6
stimpy $ sh /var/tmp/preinst.sh
```

The installation utility cannot be executed as shipped. You will have to set to execute bit on the file. First, ensure that the extract file exists in the same directory as the X332*.tgz files. The following sets the file for execution:

```
stimpy $ chmod 755 extract
```

The extract program is designed to unpack the .tgz files (they are gzipped tar files). Extract has been built specifically for the purpose of extracting and installing XFree86.

> **Warning**
> Do not use any other extraction program to unpack the XFree86 distribution.

The following dialog demonstrates the commands to execute for extracting the binaries:

```
stimpy $ cd /usr/X11R6
stimpy $ /var/tmp/extract /var/tmp/X332*.tgz
```

The last step in the process is to execute the post-installation script after the files have been extracted. The dialog that follows shows what to do:

```
stimpy $ cd /usr/X11R6
stimpy $ sh /var/tmp/postinst.sh
```

This final suggestion goes against the grain of Linux and UNIX, but it might be a good idea to reboot the system after all the steps have been performed. If you are feeling lucky, proceed to the section that follows.

Configuring XFree86

After XFree86 is installed on your system, you will have to configure it. Configuring XFree86 can be a time-consuming task. At certain points in the configuration, you may have to guess at a requested value. If the value guessed is incorrect, you have to keep trying until it is correct. You may have a unique video card that requires tweaking of the configuration files. By the way, this can happen with other operating systems.

On the other hand, configuring XFree86 can be a snap. Your video hardware is completely supported—no special tweaking is required. You install XFree86, configure it, and execute it immediately.

Manual configuring XFree86 can be done. Indeed, many veteran Linux users do this. Granted, you may need to open a configuration file and do some editing. Don't let this alarm you; sometimes it is the way to complete the configuration process.

Two programs can help set up the XF86Config file: xf86config and XF86Setup. XF86Setup is a GUI program that uses an X server and utilizes the mouse. In contrast, the xf86config program is a text-mode program, yet it provides the same functionality. In the event that XF86Setup cannot run, xf86config is always available. Who said a text-mode program isn't useful?

We will first examine the use of the xf86config program. The xf86config program is the least intrusive in getting the job done. It is possible that XF86Setup will not work and may even blank your screen, forcing you to reset the video.

If you would rather use XF86Setup instead of xf86config, move on to the later section "The XF86Setup Program." You do not need to run both programs—just one or the other.

The xf86config Program

A utility program, xf86config, is provided to create the XF86Config file. The XF86Config file is normally found in the /usr/X11R6/lib/X11 directory. It can be stored elsewhere, but /usr/X11R6/lib/X11 is the well-known location. xf86config likes to save XF86Config to the /etc directory; be sure you copy it to /usr/X11R6/lib/X11.

The xf86config program displays a screen of information at a time, prompting you for a response. Simply type the response and press Enter.

The following information is required:

- Mouse type, documentation, and the port that it is attached to
- Graphics (video) card documentation and specifications: chip set, amount of video memory, and dot clocks available or clock chip used (if programmable)
- Ramdac type (for some servers)
- Monitor documentation and specifications

One last thing: You must log in as root to successfully execute the xf86config program.

The following is the Welcome screen. All you need to do here is press Enter:

```
This program will create a basic XF86Config file, based on menu selections you make.

The XF86Config file usually resides in /usr/X11R6/lib/X11 or /etc. A sample XF86Config file
is supplied with XFree86; it is configured for a standard VGA card and monitor with 640x480
resolution. This program will ask for a pathname when it is ready to write the file.

You can either take the sample XF86Config as a base and edit it for your configuration, or
let this program produce a base XF86Config file for your configuration and fine-tune it.
Refer to /usr/X11R6/lib/X11/doc/README.Config for a detailed overview of the configuration
process.

For accelerated servers (including accelerated drivers in the SVGA server), there are many
chip set and card-specific options and settings. This program does not know about these. On
some configurations some of these settings must be specified. Refer to the server man pages
and chip set-specific READMEs.

Before continuing with this program, make sure you know the chip set and amount of video
memory on your video card. SuperProbe can help with this. It is also helpful if you know
what server you want to run. Press Enter to continue, or Ctrl-C to abort.
```

This first prompt provides some information that you should verify. For the most part, you can just press Enter.

The second prompt is mouse selection. A menu is presented, providing a number of choices. The screen is shown in the following:

```
First specify a mouse protocol type. Choose one from the following list:
 1.  Microsoft compatible (2-button protocol)
 2.  Mouse Systems (3-button protocol)
 3.  Bus Mouse
 4.  PS/2 Mouse
 5.  Logitech Mouse (serial, old type, Logitech protocol)
 6.  Logitech MouseMan (Microsoft compatible)
 7.  MM Series
 8.  MM HitTablet
 9.  Microsoft IntelliMouse

If you have a two-button mouse, it is most likely of type 1, and if you have a three-button
mouse, it can probably support both protocol 1 and 2. There are two main varieties of the
latter type: mice with a switch to select the protocol, and mice that default to 1 and
require a button to be held at
Boot time to select protocol 2. Some mice can be convinced to do 2 by sending a special
sequence to the serial port (see the ClearDTR/ClearRTS options).
Enter a protocol number:
```

Select the choice that best represents your mouse. If you are using a serial mouse and don't see your brand, choose the Microsoft option. You may need to choose (1) or (6) for some of the newer Logitech mice.

The program continues with mouse options, specifically prompting for ChordMiddle and Emulate3Buttons.

```
Please answer the following question with either 'y' or 'n'.
Do you want to enable ChordMiddle?

You have selected a two-button mouse protocol. It is recommended that you enable
Emulate3Buttons. Please answer the following question with either 'y' or 'n'.
Do you want to enable Emulate3Buttons?

Now give the full device name that the mouse is connected to, for example /dev/tty00. Just
pressing enter will use the default, /dev/mouse.
Mouse device:
```

If you have a two-button mouse, you can use the Emulate3Buttons option to simulate a three-button mouse. To simulate the middle button, you press the two buttons simultaneously.

Next, you are prompted for the mouse device. The default displayed, /dev/mouse, works 99 percent of the time. Press the Enter key to accept /dev/mouse. Some Logitech mice and trackballs require the ChordMiddle to be "y" to activate the middle mouse button.

The next prompt asks if you require special key bindings.

```
Beginning with XFree86 3.1.2D, you can use the new X11R6.1 XKEYBOARD extension to manage the
keyboard layout. If you answer 'n' to the following question, the server will use the old
method, and you have to adjust your keyboard layout with xmodmap.
Please answer the following question with either 'y' or 'n'.
Do you want to use XKB?
```

If you are not sure, you probably don't need it. You will normally answer **n** to this prompt, unless, of course, you need the feature. If you enable it, the left Alt key is assigned Meta (or ESC) and the right Alt key is moved to ModeShift.

The next dialog requests the type of keyboard you are using.

```
The following dialogue will allow you to select from a list of already preconfigured
keymaps. If you don't find a suitable keymap in the list, the program will try to combine a
keymap from additional information you are asked then. Such a keymap is by default untested
and may require manual tuning. Please report success or required changes for such a keymap
to XFREE86@XFREE86.ORG for addition to the list of preconfigured keymaps in the future.
Press Enter to continue, or Ctrl-C to abort.

List of preconfigured keymaps:
  1  Standard 101-key, US encoding
  2  Microsoft Natural, US encoding
  3  KeyTronic FlexPro, US encoding
  4  Standard 101-key, US encoding with ISO9995-3 extensions
  5  Standard 101-key, German encoding
```

```
 6  Standard 101-key, French encoding
 7  Standard 101-key, Thai encoding
 8  Standard 101-key, Swiss/German encoding
 9  Standard 101-key, Swiss/French encoding
10  None of the above
Enter a number to choose the keymap.
```

You will almost always choose number 1. If you are using any of the new keyboards, such as the Microsoft Natural or KeyTronic FlexPro, be sure you select those rather than the Standard 101-key selection.

It is the next prompt that makes people nervous. This is understandable—your monitor can be damaged if the settings are incorrect. Bear in mind, though, that not all monitors will be affected if incorrect settings are given.

At this point, you should have your monitor documentation in hand.

```
Now we want to set the specifications of the monitor. The two critical parameters are the
vertical refresh rate, which is the rate at which the whole screen is refreshed, and most
importantly the horizontal sync rate, which is the rate at which scanlines are displayed.
The valid range for horizontal sync and vertical sync should be documented in the manual of
your monitor. If in doubt, check the monitor database /usr/X11R6/lib/X11/doc/Monitors to see
if your monitor is there.
Press Enter to continue, or Ctrl-C to abort.
```

This prompt is preparing you for the screen that follows. It is purely informational. Press Enter to continue—a list of monitors will be displayed. The following screen shows this message:

```
You must indicate the horizontal sync range of your monitor. You can either select one of
the predefined ranges below that correspond to industry-standard monitor types, or give a
specific range. It is VERY IMPORTANT that you do not specify a monitor type with a
horizontal sync range that is beyond the capabilities of your monitor. If in doubt, choose a
conservative setting.

hsync in KHz; monitor type with characteristic modes
 1  31.5; Standard VGA, 640x480 @ 60 Hz
 2  31.5 - 35.1; Super VGA, 800x600 @ 56 Hz
 3  31.5, 35.5; 8514 Compatible, 1024x768 @ 87 Hz
           interlaced (no 800x600)
 4  31.5, 35.15, 35.5; Super VGA, 1024x768 @ 87 Hz
           interlaced, 800x600 @ 56 Hz
 5  31.5 - 37.9; Extended Super VGA, 800x600 @ 60 Hz,
           640x480 @ 72 Hz
 6  31.5 - 48.5; Non-Interlaced SVGA, 1024x768 @60 Hz,
           800x600 @ 72 Hz
 7  31.5 - 57.0; High Frequency SVGA, 1024x768 @ 70 Hz
 8  31.5 - 64.3; Monitor that can do 1280x1024 @ 60 Hz
 9  31.5 - 79.0; Monitor that can do 1280x1024 @ 74 Hz
10  31.5 - 82.0; Monitor that can do 1280x1024 @ 76 Hz
11  Enter your own horizontal sync range
Enter your choice (1-11):
```

Scan the list for your monitor. The list spans multiple screens, so you may have to move through the list to find your monitor. When you find your monitor, double-check the model number against your documentation. In a pinch, you can also look at the back of your monitor for the specification plate. Select the appropriate monitor entry and press Enter. Choose number 11 if you need to enter the values manually.

The next prompt engages you for the vertical sync range. Again, refer to your monitor manual for these specifications. The following screen shows this message:

```
You must indicate the vertical sync range of your monitor. You can either select one of the
predefined ranges below that correspond to industry-standard monitor types, or give a
specific range. For interlaced modes, the number that counts is the high one (e.g. 87 Hz
rather than 43 Hz).
 1   50-70
 2   50-90
 3   50-100
 4   40-150
 5   Enter your own vertical sync range
Enter your choice:
```

Enter the appropriate sync values and press Enter. If you need to manually enter the vertical sync values, choose number 5.

Next, xf86config prompts you for monitor identification, such as make and model. These descriptive strings are written to the configuration file to act as identification tags. These are only for people reading the file while editing it. The X system does not use this data. The following screen shows this message:

```
You must now enter a few identification/description strings, namely an identifier, a vendor
name, and a model name. Just pressing enter will fill in default names. The strings are
free-form, spaces are allowed.
Enter an identifier for your monitor definition:
Enter the vendor name of your monitor:
Enter the model name of your monitor:
```

You can supply any text string. You can even leave these entries blank.

The next prompt is for video card selection. xf86config wants to know if you want to view a list of video cards.

```
Now we must configure video card specific settings. At this point you can choose to make a
selection out of a database of video card definitions. Because there can be variation in
Ramdacs and clock generators even between cards of the same model, it is not sensible to
blindly copy the settings (e.g. a Device section). For this reason, after you make a
selection, you will still be asked about the components of the card, with the settings from
the chosen database entry presented as a strong hint.
```

```
The database entries include information about the chip set, what server to run, the Ramdac
and ClockChip, and comments that will be included in the Device section. However, a lot of
definitions only hint about what server to run (based on the chip set the card uses) and are
untested.

If you can't find your card in the database, there's nothing to worry about. You should only
choose a database entry that is exactly the same model as your card; choosing one that looks
similar is just a bad idea (e.g. a GemStone Snail 64 may be as different from a GemStone
Snail 64+ in terms of hardware as can be).
Do you want to look at the card database?
```

Because it is easier to select from a list, answer **y**. You will have to refer to your video card documentation—you might need to know the chip set your card uses.

```
0   2 the Max MAXColor S3 Trio64V+      S3 Trio64V+
    1   928Movie                         S3 928
    2   AGX (generic)                    AGX-014/15/16
    3   ALG-5434(E)                      CL-GD5434
    4   ASUS 3Dexplorer                  RIVA128
    5   ASUS PCI-AV264CT                 ATI-Mach64
    6   ASUS PCI-V264CT                  ATI-Mach64
    7   ASUS Video Magic PCI V864        S3 864
    8   ASUS Video Magic PCI VT64        S3 Trio64
    9   AT25                             Alliance AT3D
   10   AT3D                             Alliance AT3D
   11   ATI 3D Pro Turbo                 ATI-Mach64
   12   ATI 3D Xpression                 ATI-Mach64
   13   ATI 3D Xpression+ PC2TV          ATI-Mach64
   14   ATI 8514 Ultra (no VGA)          ATI-Mach8
   15   ATI All-in-Wonder                ATI-Mach64
   16   ATI Graphics Pro Turbo           ATI-Mach64
   17   ATI Graphics Pro Turbo 1600      ATI-Mach64
Enter a number to choose the corresponding card definition.
Press Enter for the next page, q to continue configuration.
Your selected card definition:
```

Scan the list of cards and choose the selection that matches your card. Again, the list will span many pages of screens. If you cannot find your card listed, look for a card that has the same chip set that is listed in your documentation.

Next, xf86config asks for an X server to be used. The safest choice here is choice 5. This is the server that is recommended for the video card's chip set.

```
Now you must determine which server to run. Refer to the man pages and other documentation.
The following servers are available (they may not all be installed on your system):

   1   The XF86_Mono server. This a monochrome server that
       should work on any VGA-compatible card, in 640x480
       (more on some SVGA chip sets).
```

continues ▶

Chapter 4 Installing X Windows

continued

```
 2  The XF86_VGA16 server. This is a 16-color VGA server
    that should work on any VGA-compatible card.
 3  The XF86_SVGA server. This is a 256 color SVGA
    server that supports a number of SVGA chip sets.
    On some chip sets it is accelerated or supports higher
    color depths.
 4  The accelerated servers. These include XF86_S3,
    XF86_Mach32, XF86_Mach8, XF86_8514, XF86_P9000,
    XF86_AGX, XF86_W32, XF86_Mach64, XF86_I128 and XF86_S3V.

These four server types correspond to the four different "Screen" sections in XF86Config
(vga2, vga16, svga, accel).
 5  Choose the server from the card definition, XF86_S3.
Which one of these screen types do you intend to run by default (1-5)?
```

You can choose any of the other options if you feel confident that your choice is the correct one. If it turns out the server doesn't work, you can just execute xf86config again and change the server. Again, the safest choice is the preselected option, 5.

Hang in there, we are just about done.

The next prompt is setting the symbolic link. The default is to set it in `/var/X11R6/bin`.

```
The server to run is selected by changing the symbolic link 'X'. For example, 'rm
/usr/X11R6/bin/X; ln -s /usr/X11R6/bin/XF86_SVGA /usr/X11R6/bin/X' selects the SVGA server.
Please answer the following question with either 'y' or 'n'.
Do you want me to set the symbolic link?
```

Your answer here should be **y**.

The program continues, asking how much RAM your video card has.

```
Now you must give information about your video card. This will be used for the "Device"
section of your video card in XF86Config.

You must indicate how much video memory you have. It is probably a good idea to use the same
approximate amount as that detected by the server you intend to use. If you encounter
problems that are due to the used server not supporting the amount memory you have (e.g. ATI
Mach64 is limited to 1024K with the SVGA server), specify the maximum amount supported by
the server.
How much video memory do you have on your video card:
 1  256K
 2  512K
 3  1024K
 4  2048K
 5  4096K
 6  Other
Enter your choice:
```

Enter the appropriate value and press Enter.

> Again, you are prompted to provide some descriptive text to identify your video card. Type any text you think is appropriate and press Enter.

```
You must now enter a few identification/description strings, namely an identifier, a vendor
name, and a model name. Just pressing enter will fill in default names (possibly from a card
definition).
Your card definition is Number Nine FX Motion 771.
The strings are free-form, spaces are allowed.

Enter an identifier for your video card definition:
You can simply press enter here if you have a generic card, or want to describe your card
with one string.
Enter the vendor name of your video card:
Enter the model (board) name of your video card:
```

> The next prompt requests the RAMDAC and clock settings. The X server can probe the values when you start X.

```
Especially for accelerated servers, Ramdac, Dacspeed, and ClockChip settings or special
options may be required in the Device section.
The RAMDAC setting only applies to the S3, AGX, W32 servers, and some drivers in the SVGA
servers. Some RAMDAC's are auto-detected by the server. The detection of a RAMDAC is forced
by using a Ramdac "identifier" line in the Device section. The identifiers are shown at the
right of the following table of RAMDAC types:
    1  AT&T 20C490 (S3 and AGX servers, ARK driver)   att20c490
    2  AT&T 20C498/21C498/22C498 (S3, autodetected)   att20c498
    3  AT&T 20C409/20C499 (S3, autodetected)          att20c409
    4  AT&T 20C505 (S3)                               att20c505
    5  BrookTree BT481 (AGX)                          bt481
    6  BrookTree BT482 (AGX)                          bt482
    7  BrookTree BT485/9485 (S3)                      bt485
    8  Sierra SC15025 (S3, AGX)                       sc15025
    9  S3 GenDAC (86C708) (autodetected)              s3gendac
   10  S3 SDAC (86C716) (autodetected)                s3_sdac
   11  STG-1700 (S3, autodetected)                    stg1700
   12  STG-1703 (S3, autodetected)                    stg1703
Enter a number to choose the corresponding RAMDAC.
Press Enter for the next page, q to quit without selection of a RAMDAC.
```

> Supply the appropriate choice, if you know it. Otherwise, press q. This prompt is displayed if you chose an accelerated X server.
>
> The next prompt requests a Clockchip setting.

```
A Clockchip line in the Device section forces the detection of a programmable clock device.
With a clockchip enabled, any required clock can be programmed without requiring probing of
clocks or a Clocks line. Most cards don't have a programmable clock chip. Choose from the
following list:
    1  Chrontel 8391                                  ch8391
    2  ICD2061A and compatibles (ICS9161A, DCS2824)   icd2061a
    3  ICS2595                                        ics2595
    4  ICS5342 (similar to SDAC, but ,,,)             ics5342
    5  ICS5341                                        ics5341
```

continues ▶

continued

```
 6  S3 GenDAC (86C708) and ICS5300 (autodetected)s3gendac
 7  S3 SDAC (86C716)                              s3_sdac
 8  STG 1703 (autodetected)                       stg1703
 9  Sierra SC11412                                sc11412
10  TI 3025 (autodetected)                        ti3025
11  TI 3026 (autodetected)                        ti3026
12  IBM RGB 51x/52x (autodetected)                ibm_rgb5xx
Just press Enter if you don't want a Clockchip setting.
What Clockchip setting do you want (1-12)?
```

At this point, you can just press the Enter key if you don't want a Clockchip setting. Otherwise, enter the appropriate number.

We move on to the X -probeonly prompt.

```
For most configurations, a Clocks line is useful since it prevents the slow
and nasty sounding clock probing at server start-up. Probed clocks are
displayed at server startup, along with other server and hardware
configuration info. You can save this information in a file by running
'X -probeonly 2>output_file'. Be warned that clock probing is inherently
imprecise; some clocks may be slightly too high (varies per run).
At this point I can run X -probeonly, and try to extract the clock information
from the output. It is recommended that you do this yourself and add a clocks
line (note that the list of clocks may be split over multiple Clocks lines) to
your Device section afterwards. Be aware that a clocks line is not
appropriate for drivers that have a fixed set of clocks and don't probe by
default (e.g. Cirrus). Also, for the P9000 server you must simply specify
clocks line that matches the modes you want to use. For the S3 server with
a programmable clock chip you need a 'ClockChip' line and no Clocks line.
You must be root to be able to run X -probeonly now.

The card definition says to NOT probe clocks.
Do you want me to run 'X -probeonly' now?
```

Some monitors shouldn't be probed—look for text on this screen that hints at a "no probe" (this example shows it in action). Some cards can be damaged when probed, so watch for the hint. If you're feeling nervous here, answer **n**. Only two more prompts and we are done.

The next prompt is soliciting you for monitor resolutions. You can dynamically change the display resolution while X is running. You can switch from 640×480 to 1024×768 to 1196×768 to 1280×1024, if your video hardware supports them.

```
For each depth, a list of modes (resolutions) is defined. The default
resolution that the server will start-up with will be the first listed
mode that can be supported by the monitor and card.
Currently it is set to:
"640x480" "800x600" "1024x768" "1280x1024" for 8bpp
"640x480" "800x600" "1024x768" for 16bpp
"640x480" "800x600" for 24bpp
```

```
                "640x480" "800x600" for 32bpp
Note that 16, 24 and 32bpp are only supported on a few configurations.
Modes that cannot be supported due to monitor or clock constraints will
be automatically skipped by the server.
 1  Change the modes for 8pp (256 colors)
 2  Change the modes for 16bpp (32K/64K colors)
 3  Change the modes for 24bpp (24-bit color, packed pixel)
 4  Change the modes for 32bpp (24-bit color)
 5  The modes are OK, continue.
Enter your choice:
```

You can simply accept the defaults or spend some time now defining the modes you want.

We finally made it! The last prompt asks if you want to save the configuration file.

```
I am going to write the XF86Config file now. Make sure you don't accidentally
overwrite a previously configured one.
Shall I write it to /etc/XF86Config?
```

Answer **y** and press Enter to save; otherwise, answer **n**.

The file is written (or it is not) and you are returned to the shell prompt. The last bit of output is the sign-off screen:

```
File has been written. Take a look at it before running 'startx'. Note that the XF86Config
file must be in one of the directories searched by the server (e.g. /usr/X11R6/lib/X11) in
order to be used. Within the server press ctrl, alt and '+' simultaneously to cycle video
resolutions. Pressing ctrl, alt and backspace simultaneously immediately exits the server
(use if the monitor doesn't sync for a particular mode).
```

Okay, you've been waiting for this moment. If you are ready to test out X, type **startx** and press Enter. Just for fun, you might want to jump over to the /etc directory and examine the XF86Config file. Without the xf86config program, you would have to create this file yourself.

The XF86Setup Program

The XF86Setup is a graphical utility program used for configuring the XFree86 environment. It is an option to the xf86config program, as detailed in the previous section. You can run the XF86Setup program from a text-mode console or from within a running X session.

You can use the XF86Setup program to perform initial Xfree86 setup or to alter an existing configuration.

The real difference between XF86Setup and xf86config is that the former is a graphical interface, whereas the latter is text mode. The XF86Setup program actually uses an XFree86 server for display. Another advantage with using XF86Setup is that you can do some testing of the configuration to be sure your settings are correct.

The following shows the usage syntax for XF86Setup:

```
XF86Setup [-sync] [-name appname ] [-nodialog] [--arg ...]
XF86Setup [-sync] [-name appname] [-script] [-display display]
         [-geometry geometry] filename [ [ -- ] arg ... ]
```

Table 4.1 details the available arguments to XF86Setup.

Table 4.1 **Available XF86Setup Options**

Option	Description
-sync	Turn on synchronization for all communication with an X server.
-name appname	Use appname as the window name.
-display display	Specify the display to talk to.
-nodialog	Do not use the Dialog program for text-mode user interaction. Normally XF86Setup will use the Dialog program if it is found in the user's PATH; otherwise, a simple text interface is used.
-geometry geomspec	Specify the initial geometry for the window.
-script	Look for the specified filename in the scripts directory instead of searching the user's PATH (if the filename doesn't specify a path).

As mentioned previously, you can launch XF86Setup from a text-mode console or from within an X session. Either way, from a console prompt, run the command XF86Setup. Figure 4.1 shows the initial XF86Setup window.

At the bottom of the window, you will notice three buttons: Abort, Done, and Help. The Abort button allows you to abort any changes you have made and exit the program. The Done button allows you to finalize your installation and save all changes you have made. Help is used to call up the help system for the XF86Setup program.

Across the top of the window, a number of buttons are available to choose from—all pertaining to configuration options. The button options are Mouse, Keyboard, Card, Monitor, Modeselection, and Other. The Mouse button is used to identify and configure the mouse. The Keyboard button allows you to modify the keyboard and identify its type. The Card button is used to identify the video card and its settings. The Monitor button allows you to alter the settings for your video monitor. The Modeselection button is for configuring the video modes that your card and monitor can support. Finally, the Other button includes options such as whether you can kill the X server and allowing video mode switching (among other options).

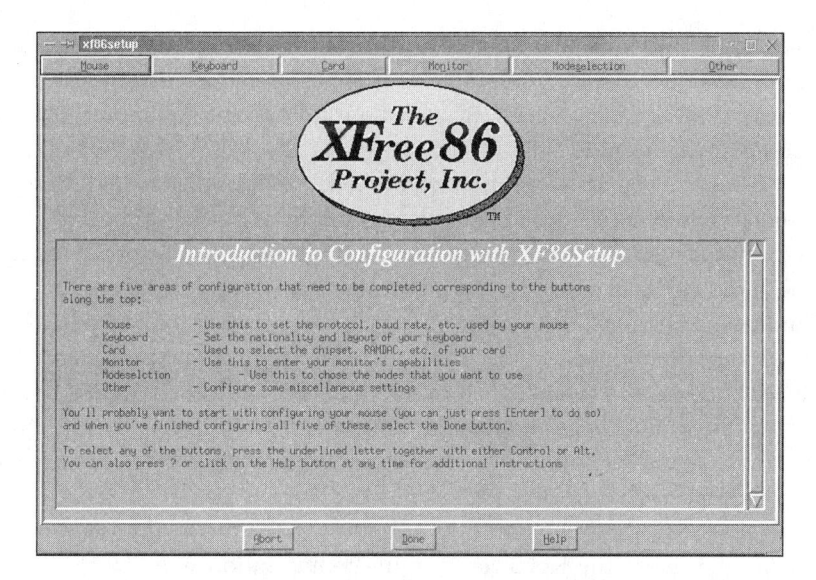

Figure 4.1 The XF86Setup initial window.

Let us take each configuration option in turn, beginning with the Mouse option. Figure 4.2 shows the configuration window for Mouse options.

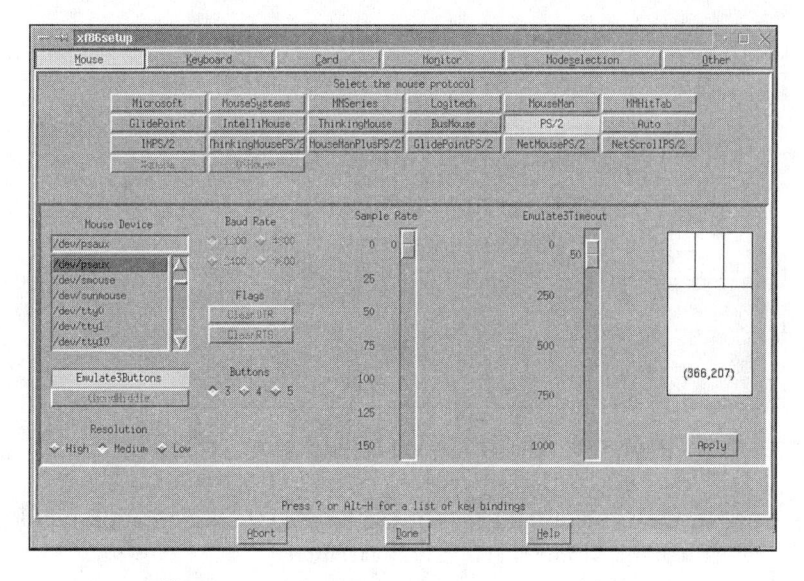

Figure 4.2 The XF86Setup Mouse setup window.

Across the top of the configuration window are the options for the various mouse vendors. Choose the one that is appropriate for your mouse product. The option here may be as easy as choosing PS/2 for any mouse that uses the PS/2 mouse port.

Under the vendor section, along the left, are options for the mouse port, Emulate3Buttons, ChordMiddle, and Resolution. Just left of center (under the vendor section), we find the Baud Rate, Flags, and Buttons. Moving to the right, you will see slider bar adjustments for SampleRate and Emulate3Timeout. To the right of these slider bars is a top view of a mouse displaying the mouse-cursor coordinates. The appropriate mouse buttons will appear highlighted when actual mouse buttons are pressed. Below the mouse you will see the Apply button. This button allows you to apply any changes you have made. Be sure to check the changes you have made before selecting the Apply button.

Next, select the Keyboard option button at the top of the window. Figure 4.3 shows the Keyboard options configuration window.

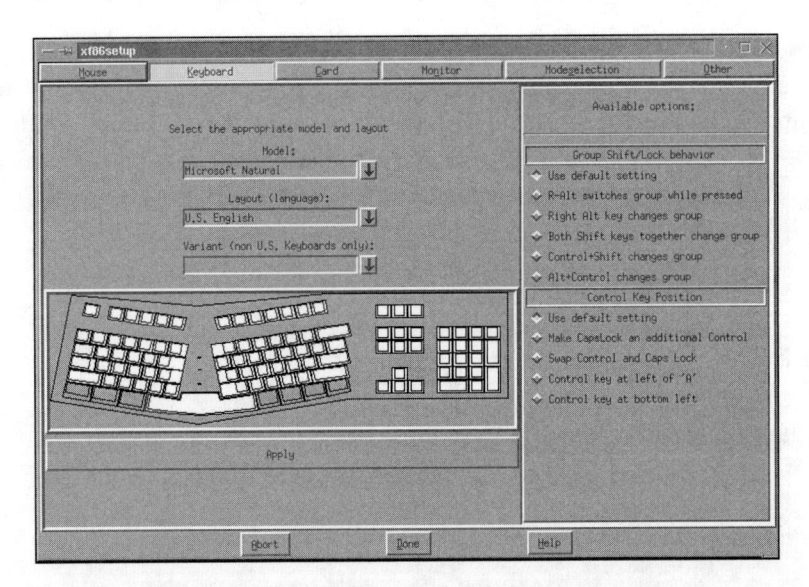

Figure 4.3 The XF86Setup Keyboard setup window.

Starting at the left half (and top) of the Keyboard configuration window, you see selections for Model, Layout, and Variant.

The Model drop-down box allows you to select from the various keyboard manufacturers and their styles of keyboards. The Layout option is used to select the language for the keyboard, such as U.S. English or Canadian.

At the right side of the configuration window, you will find options for Shift/Lock Behavior and Control Key Position. These options are used to further personalize the keyboard to suite your taste. When you have everything just right, select the Apply button found under the keyboard graphic (at the left side).

Next, click the Card button option at the top of the window. Figure 4.4 shows the configuration window for your video card.

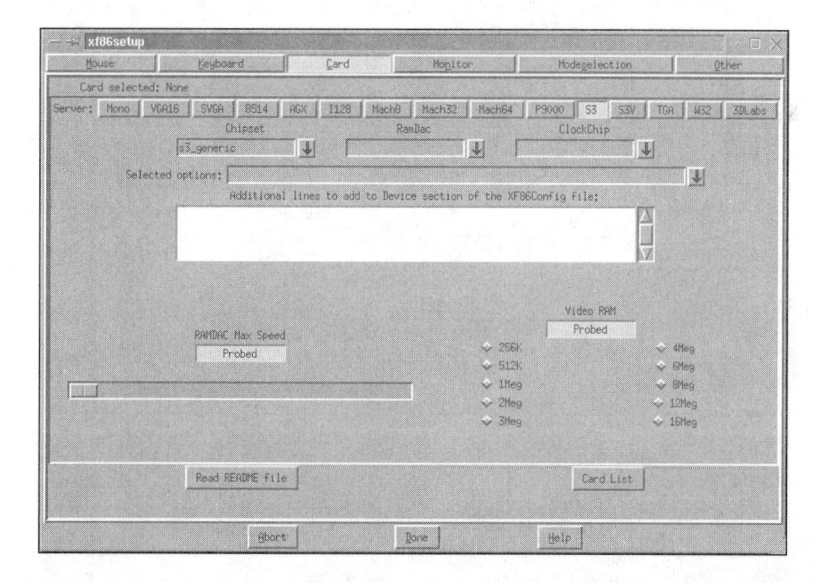

Figure 4.4 The XF86Setup Card setup window.

You can specify many options on this window for your video card. The options available are the X server to use, chip set, RamDac, ClockChip, RamDAC Max Speed, and the amount of Video RAM on the video card. You can even add lines for the Device section in free-form. Refer to the " The XF86Config File" section that follows for more information.

We have just three more options to choose from. The next option that might require adjustment is the Monitor section. Select the Monitor button to display its configuration window. Figure 4.5 shows this window.

At the top of the configuration window, we see the data entry fields for Horizontal and Vertical sync rates. You can enter these values free-form, if you know the ranges. Alternatively, you can select one of the prebuilt value ranges from the choices displayed within the graphical monitor shown in the middle of the configuration window.

Chapter 4 Installing X Windows

After you have selected the correct sync ranges for your monitor, the next option is the Modeselection button. Selecting this button will display the Modeselection configuration window, as shown in Figure 4.6.

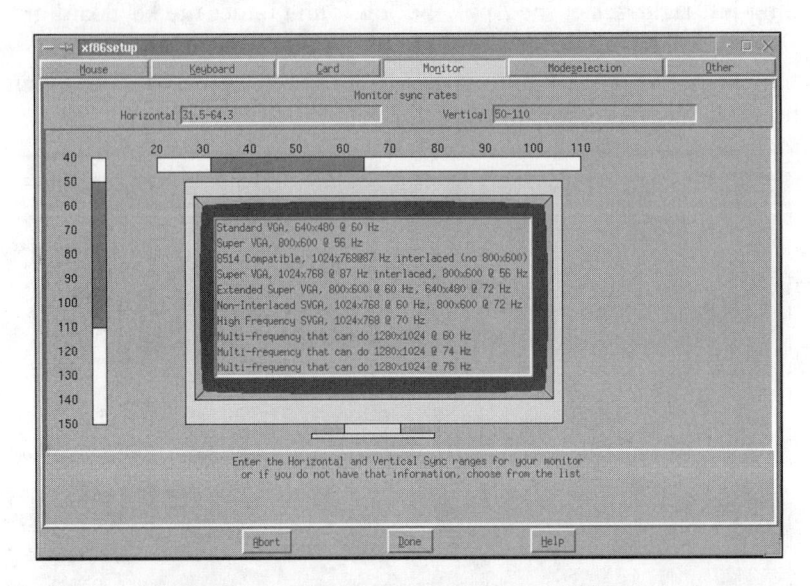

Figure 4.5 The XF86Setup Monitor setup window.

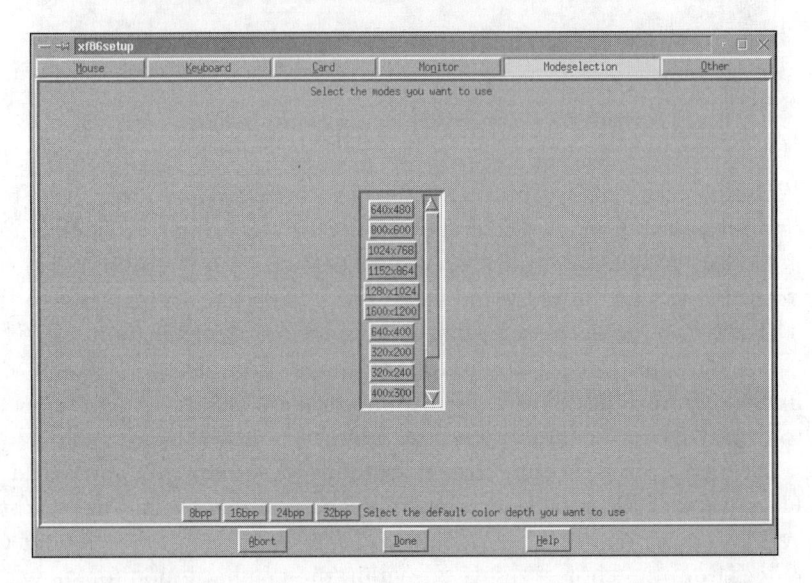

Figure 4.6 The XF86Setup Modeselection setup window.

In this configuration window, you can select the monitor resolution and color depth for your monitor. You can cycle through the selected modes while running the X server. Click the modes you want in your configuration. You can also select the default color depth the server starts with.

Last, but not least, we can configure other miscellaneous settings with the Other button. Selecting this button displays the window shown in Figure 4.7.

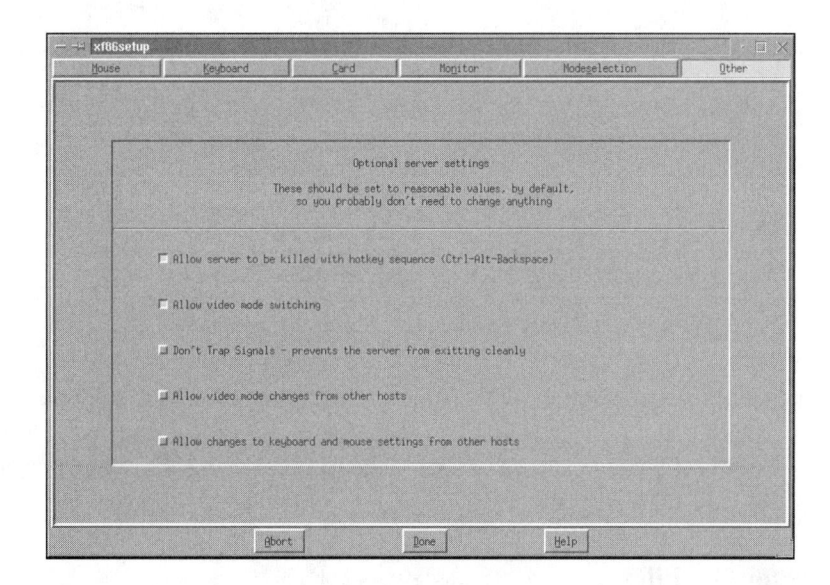

Figure 4.7 The XF86Setup Other setup window.

You can configure for various options not covered at the other windows. These settings are various X server settings that you can change to suit your needs. Most of the options here are already preconfigured to meet the needs of most people. Check the XF86Config man page for more information.

After you have set all the options that you require, you need to select the Done button at the bottom of the XF86Setup window. The window shown in Figure 4.8 will then be displayed.

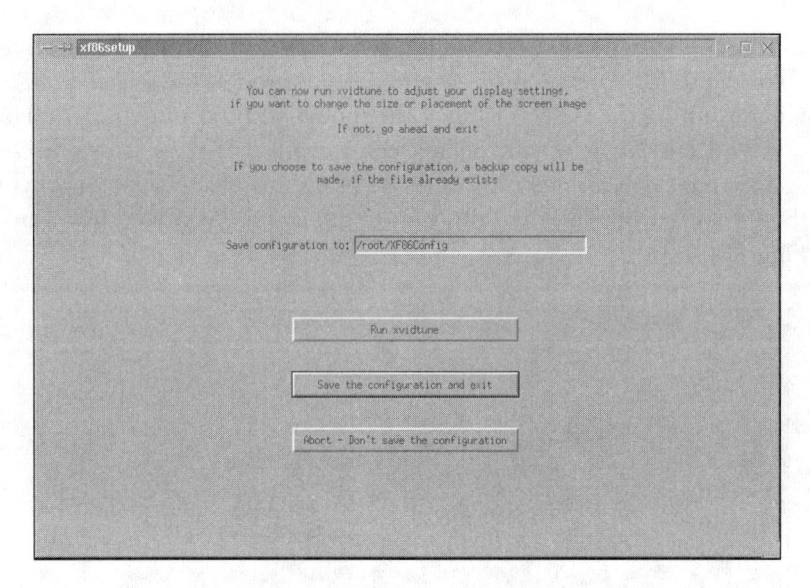

Figure 4.8 The XF86Setup Save Configuration window.

At this point, you can save the settings as you have applied them, you can abort your changes, or you can run xvidtune to adjust the display settings. The xvidtune module allows you to make minute changes to your horizontal and vertical sync settings.

The XF86Config File

The XF86Config file is normally found in the /etc directory. The XF86Config file contains values that the X server uses to configure the X session. For example, you can find information on the horizontal and vertical frequency timings, the mouse type and protocol, the location of font files, and so on.

The XF86Config file contains several sections, such as Keyboard, Monitor, and Pointer. You can find a sample XF86Config file, XF86Config.sample, in /usr/X11R6/lib/X11.

To get a head start, you should copy this to /usr/X11R6/lib/X11/XF86Config and edit that file to meet your configuration. You can refer to the XF86Config man page for Section information. It is advantageous to print a hard copy of the XF86Config man page. You can refer to this while editing the file.

The `XF86Config` file contains the following sections:

- **Files.** Identifies font and RGB paths.
- **Modules.** Optional; defines dynamically loadable modules.
- **ServerFlags.** Sets global server flag options.
- **Keyboard.** Defines the keyboard.
- **Pointer.** Defines the pointer device, normally the mouse.
- **Monitor.** Defines the monitor(s) to the server.
- **Device.** Defines the video hardware.
- **Screen.** Defines how the monitor and video hardware should be used.

The chapter sections that follow describe each of the `XF86Config` file sections in detail. Be sure to check the man page for the `XF96Config` file for additional information.

Files Section

If XFree86 is installed in the default directories, this section will not require changes. This section contains a list of filenames that specify font files that XFree86 uses. The following is a sample File section from a `XF86Config` file:

```
#****************************************************
# Files section. This allows default font and
# rgb  paths set
#****************************************************
Section "Files"

# The location of the RGB database. Note, this is
# the name of the file minus the extension (like
# ".txt" or ".db"). There is normally no need
# to change the default.

    RgbPath     "/usr/X11R6/lib/X11/rgb"

# Multiple FontPath entries are allowed (which are
# concatenated together), as well as specifying
# multiple comma-separated entries in one FontPath
# command (or a combination of both methods)
#
# If you don't have a floating point coprocessor
# and emacs, Mosaic or other programs take long
# to start up, try moving the Type1 and Speedo
# directory to the end of this list (or comment
# them out).
#
```

continues ▶

continued

```
    FontPath    "/usr/X11R6/lib/X11/fonts/misc/"
    FontPath    "/usr/X11R6/lib/X11/fonts/75dpi/:unscaled"
#   FontPath    "/usr/X11R6/lib/X11/fonts/100dpi/:unscaled"
#   FontPath    "/usr/X11R6/lib/X11/fonts/Type1/"
#   FontPath    "/usr/X11R6/lib/X11/fonts/Speedo/"
    FontPath    "/usr/X11R6/lib/X11/fonts/75dpi/"
#   FontPath    "/usr/X11R6/lib/X11/fonts/100dpi/"

# For OSs that support Dynamically loaded modules,
# ModulePath can be used to set a search path for
# the modules. This is currently supported for
# Linux ELF, FreeBSD 2.x and NetBSD 1.x. The
# default path is shown here.

#   ModulePath "/usr/X11R6/lib/modules"
EndSection
```

Your Files section will likely be different from the previous example. If you selected all available fonts, your list will be longer.

The RGB entry defines the path location to the RGB database. You should never have to modify the RGB entry.

If you decide to add other font packages, be sure to add the file(s) to one of the FontPath directories. You also have the option to create appropriate directories and add those paths to the Files section.

Modules Section

A sample of the Modules section follows:

```
#********************************************
# Module section — this is an optional
# section which is used to specify which
# dynamically loadable modules to load.
# Dynamically loadable modules are currently
# supported only for Linux ELF, FreeBSD 2.x
# and NetBSD 1.x. Currently, dynamically
# loadable modules are used only for some
# extended input (XInput) device drivers.
#********************************************
# Section "Module"
# This loads the module for the Joystick driver
# Load "xf86Jstk.so"
#
# EndSection
```

ServerFlags Section

The following is a sample ServerFlags section from the XF86Config file:

```
# ***********************************************
# Server flags section.
# ***********************************************
```

```
Section "ServerFlags"

# Uncomment this to cause a core dump at the spot
# where a signal is received. This may leave the
# console in an unusable state, but may provide a
# better stack trace in the core dump to aid in
# debugging
#     NoTrapSignals

# Uncomment this to disable the <Crtl><Alt><BS>
# server abort sequence This allows clients to
# receive this key event.
#     DontZap

# Uncomment this to disable the <Crtl><Alt><KP_+>
# /<KP_-> mode switching sequences. This allows
# clients to receive these key events.
#     DontZoom

# Uncomment this to disable tuning with the xvidtune
# client. With it the client can still run and fetch
# card and monitor attributes, but it will not be
# allowed to change them. If it tries it will receive
# a protocol error.
#     DisableVidModeExtension

# Uncomment this to enable the use of a non-local
# xvidtune client.
#      AllowNonLocalXvidtune

# Uncomment this to disable dynamically modifying
# the input device (mouse and keyboard) settings.
#      DisableModInDev

# Uncomment this to enable the use of a non-local
# client to change the keyboard or mouse settings
# (currently only xset).
#      AllowNonLocalModInDev
EndSection
```

Normally, you will not have to worry about this section. This section identifies a number of flags used by the X server.

If NoTrapSignals is set and the operating system issues a signal to the X server, the X server will produce a core dump. If you are doing X development, this could be useful if you are having problems.

The keyboard combination Ctrl+Alt+Backspace is quite useful when using X. You may have had to use this keystroke to back out of a hung X server. Oddly enough (or maybe not), this is one of the first keystrokes many new X users execute. If you start X for the first time and you end up staring at a blank screen, use this keystroke to terminate the X server. If DontZap is uncommented, Ctrl+Alt+Backspace will be unavailable. I suggest that you keep DontZap commented.

Keyboard Section

The Keyboard section contains options that describe the keyboard associated with the console. This section also describes special features that XFree86 must address. The following is a sample Keyboard section:

```
# **************************************************
# Keyboard section
# **************************************************
Section "Keyboard"
    Protocol    "Standard"

# when using XQUEUE, comment out the above line,
# and uncomment the following line
#    Protocol    "Xqueue"

    AutoRepeat    500 5
# Let the server do the NumLock processing. This
# should only be required when using pre-R6 clients
#    ServerNumLock

# Specify which keyboard LEDs can be user-controlled
# (eg, with xset(1))
#    Xleds       1 2 3

# To set the LeftAlt to Meta, RightAlt key to
# ModeShift,  RightCtl key to Compose, and
# ScrollLock key to ModeLock:

#    LeftAlt     Meta
#    RightAlt    ModeShift
#    RightCtl    Compose
#    ScrollLock  ModeLock

# To disable the XKEYBOARD extension,
# uncomment XkbDisable.
#    XkbDisable

# To customize the XKB settings to suit your keyboard,
# modify the lines below (which are the defaults).
# For example, for a non-U.S.keyboard, you will
# probably want to use:
#    XkbModel    "pc102"
# If you have a US Microsoft Natural keyboard, you can use:
#    XkbModel    "Microsoft"
#
# Then to change the language, change the Layout setting.
# For example, a German layout can be obtained with:
```

```
#     XkbLayout       "de"
# or:
#     XkbLayout       "de"
#     XkbVariant      "nodeadkeys"
#
# If you'd like to switch the positions of your
# capslock and control keys, use:
#     XkbOptions      "ctrl:swapcaps"

# These are the default XKB settings for XFree86
#     XkbRules        "xfree86"
#     XkbModel        "pc101"
#     XkbLayout       "us"
#     XkbVariant      ""
#     XkbOptions      ""

    XkbKeymap       "xfree86(us)"
EndSection
```

For a majority of XFree86 installations, the defaults for this section can be left as is. The default keyboard is the U.S. 101-key keyboard and standard mappings.

Pointer Section

The Pointer section contains options that pertain to a pointing device, usually the mouse. The mouse is heavily used in X, as with any other GUI-based operating system. You should not have to alter this section after you have defined your device unless you install a new pointing device. The following is a sample Pointer section:

```
# **********************************
# Pointer section
# **********************************

Section "Pointer"
    Protocol    "Microsoft"
    Device      "/dev/mouse"

# When using XQUEUE, comment out the above two
# lines, and uncomment the following line.

#   Protocol   "Xqueue"

# Baudrate and SampleRate are only for some
# Logitech mice

#   BaudRate    9600
#   SampleRate          150
```

continues ▶

continued

```
# Emulate3Buttons is an option for 2-button
# Microsoft mice Emulate3Timeout is the
# timeout in milliseconds (default is 50ms)
    Emulate3Buttons
    Emulate3Timeout    50

# ChordMiddle is an option for some 3-button
# Logitech mice

#    ChordMiddle
EndSection
```

If you don't find your mouse type, you might want to try the Microsoft or Logitech choices—one of these options should work. The newer Logitech mice utilize the MouseMan protocol and older mice use the Microsoft protocol. If you use one of the newer Logitech mice, try Logitech first.

If you are using a mouse from another vendor, start with the Microsoft option or refer to the mouse documentation for more details.

The Device option refers to the port that the mouse uses. If you are using a PS/2 mouse, don't specify the bus mouse. Many people get tripped up by selecting the bus mouse option. A bus mouse is packaged with an associated card that the mouse attaches. As with a serial device, you will have to identify the IRQ that the bus mouse uses.

As a last resort, you can watch the startup messages when Linux boots up to see if it detects a mouse. If detected, Linux displays information about the mouse. The startup messages provide a wealth of information beyond the mouse, so remember this little trick.

If you are fortunate enough to have a three-button mouse, you don't have to worry about the Emulate3Buttons entry (unless the entry is not commented). If you use a two-button mouse and wish to have the functionality of a three-button mouse, uncomment the Emulate3Buttons entry. To simulate the action of the center button, you press both buttons at the same time—this may take some practice. Most operating systems outside of the Linux/UNIX world do not utilize the third button. Many UNIX software packages can use the third button, so you should enable Emulate3Buttons.

ChordMiddle is an entry mostly dedicated to Logitech mice. There is no simple answer when this entry is required. As with many other things with Linux, you simply try it one way; if it works, great! If not, try another option. If you have a Logitech mouse, comment out ChordMiddle. If the mouse exhibits erratic behavior, uncomment the ChordMiddle entry.

Monitor Section

The Monitor section sets the attributes for a video monitor. More than one Monitor section can be in the XF86Config file. Why is this? You can have more than one monitor attached to your system. Or you may want to maintain multiple hardware configurations.

The Monitor section is one of the most important sections in XF86Config and is very critical to the success of running XFree86. In addition, improper entries in this section can cause damage to your system. If modification to this section is not required, leave it alone! Only experienced users need apply. If adjustments are required, do so with utmost caution. As I have said elsewhere in this book, think twice before doing anything.

The following is a sample Monitor section:

```
# **************************************
# Monitor section
# **************************************
# Any number of monitor sections may be present
Section "Monitor"
    Identifier  "Dell 17"
    VendorName  "Dell"
    ModelName   "17"

# HorizSync is in KHz unless units are specified.
# HorizSync may be a comma separated list of discrete values, or a
# comma separated list of ranges of values.
# NOTE: THE VALUES HERE ARE EXAMPLES ONLY. REFER TO YOUR MONITOR'S
# USER MANUAL FOR THE CORRECT NUMBERS.
    HorizSync   31.5, 35.15, 35.5

#   HorizSync 30-64          # multisync
#   HorizSync 31.5, 35.2     # multiple fixed sync frequencies
#   HorizSync 15-25, 30-50   # multiple ranges of sync frequencies

# VertRefresh is in Hz unless units are specified.
# VertRefresh may be a comma separated list of discrete values, or a
# comma separated list of ranges of values.
# NOTE: THE VALUES HERE ARE EXAMPLES ONLY.  REFER TO YOUR MONITOR'S
# USER MANUAL FOR THE CORRECT NUMBERS.
    VertRefresh 50-100

# Modes can be specified in two formats. A compact one-line format, or
# a multi-line format.
# These two are equivalent
#    ModeLine "1024x768i" 45 1024 1048 1208 1264 768 776 784 817 Interlace
#    Mode "1024x768i"
#       DotClock      45
#       Htimings      1024 1048 1208 1264
```

continues ▶

```
continued

#         Vtimings        768 776 784 817
#         Flags           "Interlace"
#     EndMode

# This is a set of standard mode timings. Modes that are out of monitor spec
# are automatically deleted by the server (provided the HorizSync and
# VertRefresh lines are correct), so there's no immediate need to
# delete mode timings (unless particular mode timings don't work on your
# monitor). With these modes, the best standard mode that your monitor
# and video card can support for a given resolution is automatically
# used.
# 640x400 @ 70 Hz, 31.5 KHz hsync
Modeline "640x400"       25.175 640  664  760  800   400 409 411 450
# 640x480 @ 60 Hz, 31.5 KHz hsync
Modeline "640x480"       25.175 640  664  760  800   480 491 493 525
# 800x600 @ 56 Hz, 35.15 KHz hsync
ModeLine "800x600"       36     800  824  896 1024   600 601 603 625
# 1024x768 @ 87 Hz interlaced, 35.5 KHz hsync
Modeline "1024x768"      44.9  1024 1048 1208 1264   768 776 784 817 Interlace
```

Identifier provides a logical name to associate with this Monitor section. You can provide any name you like for the Identifier. The Identifier is used in other parts of the XF86Config file to refer to a specific Monitor section.

VendorName and ModelName are also identifiers. They do not participate in monitor configuration.

The HorizSync entry identifies appropriate horizontal sync frequencies (in KHz) for the monitor. For multisync monitors, a range of values is appropriate. Optionally, you can specify several ranges, delimited by a comma. For fixed-frequency monitors, you must supply a series of single values.

Next, we find the VertRefresh entry. This is used for specifying the vertical refresh frequencies (in KHz) for the monitor. As with the HorizSync entry, the values can be expressed as a range of values or as a list of discrete values.

Moving down the Monitor section, we come upon the ModeLine entries. The ModeLine entry specifies the various resolution modes for the monitor. One ModeLine entry exists for each resolution identified. A ModeLine can be specified as a one-line or a multiline format. Both are shown in the previous sample. The format is as follows:

```
ModeLine modename DotClock Htimings (4) Vtimings (4) Flags
```

The modename attribute is an identifier that refers to the associated resolution mode within other sections of XF86Config. The DotClock is the driving clock frequency (specified in MHz) that is associated with the resolution mode. The Htimings and Vtimings are a series of four numbers expressed in KHz.

Numerous files can be useful in determining these values. The two files `modesDB.txt` and `Monitors` may contain ModeLine information appropriate for your monitor. Additionally, the `VideoModes.doc` provides descriptions for determining the ModeLine values for each resolution.

Device Section

A Device section describes a video card. You can have as many Device sections as required; just be sure that each section has a unique name.

```
# Any number of graphics device sections may be present
# Standard VGA Device:
Section "Device"
    Identifier "Generic VGA"
    VendorName "Unknown"
    BoardName  "Unknown"
    Chipset    "generic"
#   VideoRam   256
#   Clocks     25.2 28.3
EndSection

# Device configured by xf86config:
Section "Device"
    Identifier  "NumberNine771"
    VendorName  "NumberNine"
    BoardName   "FX771"
    # VideoRam    2048
    # s3RefClk  16
# Use Option "nolinear" if the server doesn't start up correctly
# (this avoids the linear framebuffer probe). If that fails try
# option "nomemaccess".
# Refer to /usr/X11R6/lib/doc/README.S3, and the XF86_S3 man page.
    Ramdac      "normal"
    # Insert Clocks lines here if appropriate
EndSection
```

We do not detail the Device section. We recommend that you refer to the extensive documentation (`/usr/X11/lib/X11/doc`) and the man pages.

Screen Section

The Screen section combines a Monitor and a Device entry to determine which resolution and color depth should be used. The identifier names from the Monitor and Device sections are used to refer to the specific entry. The following keywords (and their associated servers) are used for Driver entries in the Screen section:

- Accel—For the XF86_S3, XF86_Mach32, XF86_Mach8, XF86_8514, XF86_P9000, XF86_AGX, and XF86_W32 servers
- SVGA—For the XF86_SVGA server

- VGA16—For the XF86_VGA16 server
- VGA2—For the XF86_Mono server
- Mono—For the non-VGA monochrome drivers in the XF86_Mono and XF86_VGA16 servers

The Screen section example that follows contains a number of entries, each on a separate line. Each entry specifies some element of the screen display. The Driver entry determines which X server this screen is associated with. Refer to the section "X Servers" for a list of servers. The server keywords previously shown are used to access the servers. The following example shows a Screen section:

```
#****************************************
# Screen sections
#****************************************
# The Color SVGA server
Section "Screen"
    Driver      "svga"
    Device      "Generic VGA"
    #Device     "NumberNine771"
    Monitor     "Dell 17"
    Subsection "Display"
        Depth       8
        #Modes "1280x1024" "1024x768" "800x600" "640x480"
        ViewPort    0 0
        Virtual     320 200
        #Virtual    1280 1024
    EndSubsection
EndSection

# The accelerated servers (S3, Mach32, Mach8, 8514,
# P9000, AGX, W32, Mach64)
Section "Screen"
    Driver      "accel"
    Device      "NumberNine771"
    Monitor     "Dell 17"
    Subsection "Display"
        Depth       8
        Modes       "1280x1024" "1024x768" "800x600" "640x480"
        ViewPort    0 0
        Virtual     1280 1024
    EndSubsection
    Subsection "Display"
        Depth       16
        Modes       "640x480" "800x600" "1024x768"
        ViewPort    0 0
        Virtual     1024 768
    EndSubsection
    Subsection "Display"
```

```
        Depth       24
        Modes       "640x480" "800x600"
        ViewPort    0 0
        Virtual     800 600
    EndSubsection
    Subsection "Display"
        Depth       32
        Modes       "640x480" "800x600"
        ViewPort    0 0
        Virtual     800 600
    EndSubsection
EndSection
```

Each server can have an associated Screen section to use if the corresponding server is successfully started.

After the Driver entry, we find the Device and Monitor entries. These entries identify the video card and the monitor that are associated with this definition. These entries refer to entries in the Device and Monitor sections using the named identifiers. Refer to the Device and Monitor sections for more details.

If the ColorDepth is not specifically identified during startup, the DefaultColorDepth specifies the color mode to use. You will notice that a Display subsection is associated with ColorDepth. The Depth entry identifies the color depth that correlates with the subsection. You can choose a color depth of 8, 16, 24, or 32.

Next, we find an entry that defines the resolutions. Its identifier is Modes. The identifiers are quoted resolutions, separated by a space. The server selects each resolution in turn (left to right) and looks for an appropriate Modeline found in the Monitor section. If a match is found, the server starts up the interface at that resolution. You can dynamically change to another resolution using the keyboard sequence Ctrl+Alt+Key, if more than one resolution is available.

The last two lines of the subsection are ViewPort and Virtual. The ViewPort entry specifies coordinates of the upper-left corner of the virtual desktop. The ViewPort entry is valid only if Virtual is set. The Virtual entry is used to identify the size of the virtual desktop. To understand the concept, imagine a mural painted on a wall. In your hand you hold an empty picture frame; imagine that you can view the mural only through this picture frame. As you move the picture frame on the mural, you are able to see other parts of the mural. As you move the mouse to the edge of the screen, the viewport "slides" over the virtual desktop.

If your video card has insufficient RAM to implement a virtual desktop, you can switch to a window manager that supports a virtual desktop. A good example of this is fvwm window manager. The difference with fvwm is that any window that is not in view will not use any video RAM. When a window is brought onscreen, fvwm will write the contents of the window into video RAM.

Summary

Getting XFree86 up and running can be a daunting task. In this chapter, we covered many aspects of installing and configuring XFree86. We discussed required hardware, such as chip sets, memory, and hard disk space.

The SuperProbe program attempts to identify information about a video card. Most people use SuperProbe to identify the chip set being used by the card.

Installing XFree86 manually really isn't an involved task, as we discovered. More time is spent in acquiring the XFree86 distribution than in installing it.

The xf86config program is used to create the XF86Config file. The XF86Config file describes many configuration options, such as monitor, screen, device, and keyboard definitions.

5
Using X Windows

IN THIS CHAPTER, WE WILL EXPLORE the wonderful world of X Windows. X is more than just a pretty face—it is a portal through which you use Linux. You are about to discover the absolute magic of X. No other operating system offers such GUI potential.

Most Linux distributions come with a complete implementation of X known as XFree86, a freely distributable version of X. Some distributions are also shipping KDE (K Desktop Environment). Two notable distributions, Red Hat and SuSE, include the GNOME environment in their package.

X can be a nightmare or a dream come true. A nightmare, you ask? Well, you have to understand that X is infinitely configurable. Many options and many window managers are available to choose from, making it difficult to stay satisfied.

Besides networking, X is one Linux tool that must be configured correctly to be usable. Watch out, though; after you get it working and learn the power of X, you will be hooked forever!

We assume that you have installed the XFree86 window system on your Linux system. This chapter discusses the use of X under Linux. Some of the topics we cover are navigation, window managers, and specific applications.

Overview of the Graphical Environment

Figure 5.1 is a snapshot of a KDE 1.1 desktop running under SuSE 6.1 Linux. You will find KDE to be a very powerful graphical environment. KDE is shipped with other distributions as well, such as Red Hat, Slackware, and Caldera.

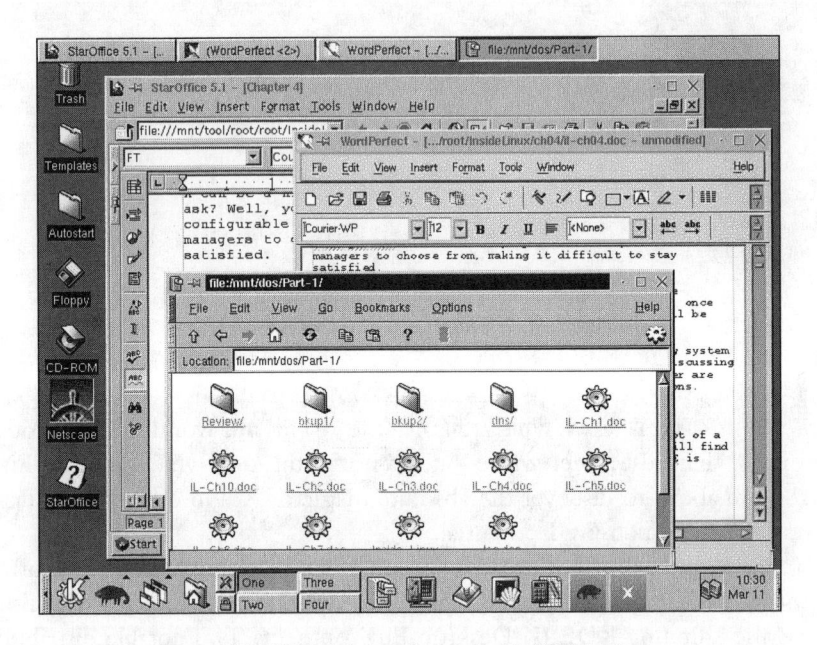

Figure 5.1 KDE 1.1 snapshot under SuSE 6.1 Linux.

If you are familiar with GUI environments on other operating systems, the screen should look familiar. On the left side of the desktop, there are icons. The first one is the Trash icon—as you delete files, they are deposited here. Just be sure to use the Move to Trash command. You can recover deleted files from the trash. The Templates folder icon contains skeleton files that can be used to create a new file of a specific type. For example, a URL template can hold a URL address. The Autostart folder icon is used to automate the execution of applications when the desktop starts up. It goes beyond that, too; if you have a document in Autostart, the associated application will start up and open the document. If a directory is stored in Autostart, it will be opened up. Be careful, though; any documents and applications in the directory will be started, too!

The Desktop

The portion of the screen that is occupied by applications is the desktop. Icons that represent files or programs also can be laid on the deskop. In Figure 5.1, three programs are running on the desktop: two popular word processing programs and the KFM file manager. KFM is one of many file managers that you can execute and use for file management under KDE.

The Taskbar

At the top of the screen in Figure 5.1 is a horizontal bar called the taskbar. When you execute an application, a button representing the application appears. You will notice that the taskbar has four buttons. The fourth button, file:/dos/Part-1/, is depressed, meaning that the application (KFM) has focus. KFM's title bar is blue in color and its window is in the foreground. Compare KFM's window to the other two windows: The other windows are obscured by KFM, and their title bars are gray. To make an application current (in focus), you can either click the window or you can click the window's button in the taskbar.

The Panel

The horizontal bar at the bottom of the screen is known as the *panel*. The panel serves a number of purposes. First, it houses various icons that can represent files, programs, or menus. You can add new icons to the panel or remove existing icons. You can add new items or remove existing items from any of the menus that reside on the panel. Second, you can control the window session from the panel, such as performing a log out or locking the screen. Take a close look at the panel, just left of center in Figure 5.1. You will see four buttons labeled One, Two, Three, and Four. These correspond to the four (independent) virtual screens. You do not see this functionality with some operating systems' GUI environments. The intent of virtual desktop is to reduce screen clutter. Here's how it works: You click One and start an application. Next, you click Two and start your second application on that screen. You can continue this process as you see fit. You can have up to eight virtual desktops to organize your running applications. Each virtual desktop is independent of the others.

Navigating X

As with any other graphical environment, X allows input from the keyboard and the pointing device. Most people use a mouse as their pointing device, but other devices can be used, such as a light pen or trackball (among other types). The mouse (or other pointer) is the optimal navigation tool. You can use the keyboard, but navigation is easier with a mouse.

You engage the environment by moving the mouse, pointing at some widget, and clicking. For example, if you need to make a window current, move the pointer onto the window and click. This is not the case with all X Window managers. With some window managers, merely moving the mouse over a window makes it current.

The Main Menu

Menu navigation is fairly intuitive with X. Most objects have an associated pop-up menu by means of the right mouse button. If you right-click the desktop, a pop-up (floating) menu appears. On the panel in KDE, the far left button, when clicked, will expose the main menu. Other menus pull up from icons on the panel. Figure 5.2 shows the KDE desktop with the main menu exposed.

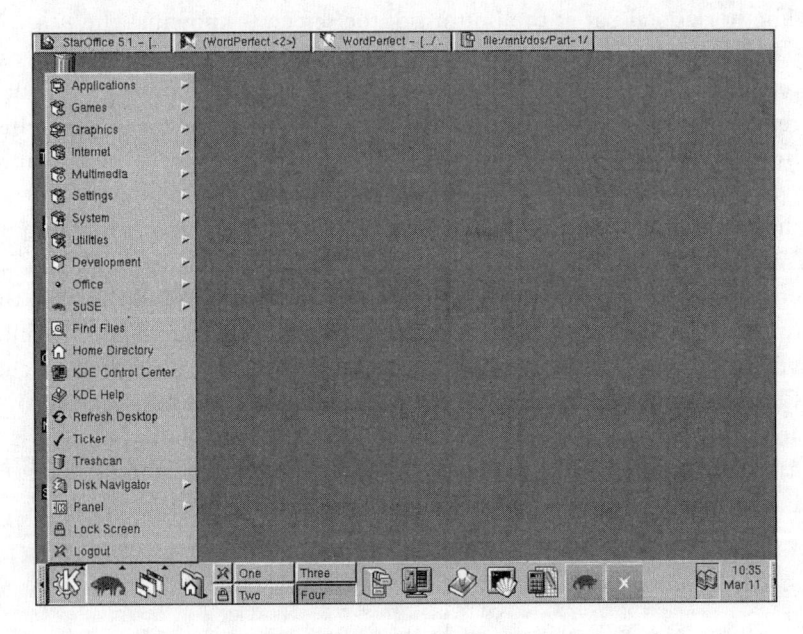

Figure 5.2 KDE desktop with the main menu exposed.

A wealth of applications and utility programs are contained in this menu. So much, in fact, that you might get dizzy. Of course, the quantity depends on the packages (or disk sets) you chose during installation. With some operating systems' system menus, the logical categorization of applications is by application name. On the KDE desktop, applications are categorized by functionality. This functionality can be very beneficial for a beginner (or an intermediate) Linux user. This allows the user to search for an application that can fulfill the task at hand.

The Menus Do Not Show Everything!
Many more programs and script commands are available than those shown on the menus. Most of the ones shown on menus are utilities and programs used by system administrators, software developers, and advanced users. Most of these applications use a command-line interface.

Experimentation is your best teacher, as well as this book. Peruse the various levels of menus; see what is available to you. If you find an application you are unsure of, use the Help system. Better yet, launch the program and see what happens!

Before we get too deep into the use of KDE, we need to discuss some X basics. After all, KDE is only one graphical environment you can use.

Window Managers

I have used the term *window manager* without actually defining it. Contrary to what some people might say, the X Windows system does not define a window manager. The window manager sits between the X Windows system and the user. The display of windows (size/position), scrollbars, and other window decorations are controlled by the window manager. You have complete control over the look and feel of your X environment. The reason we have so many window managers is because of the individualistic mentality of most Linux users. Be happy that you have a choice.

Choosing a window manager can be difficult. If you are not well-informed, choosing the wrong window manager can result in an unpleasant interface. A lean-and-mean window manager for a Linux power user would be inadequate for a Linux beginner. At the same time, a window manager that is infinitely configurable may be overwhelming for a beginner. You have to find a window manager with the right balance for your needs. Let's examine a few window managers and how they might be useful. Some of the window managers we will discuss are AfterStep, CDE, Enlightenment, fvwm, fvwm95, GNOME, KDE, olwm, olvwm, and twm.

AfterStep

AfterStep is a window manager that is modeled after the NEXTSTEP environment. The original intent of AfterStep was to mimic NEXTSTEP's look and feel, but it has diverged over time. The two primary goals of the AfterStep developers are stability and a minimal drain on memory.

Common Desktop Environment (CDE)

The Common Desktop Environment is a commercial GUI environment. It is considered to be a standard environment to be used under many flavors of UNIX. Hewlett-Packard, IBM, and Sun Microsystems (among others) are jointly involved in the design and implementation of CDE. Appropriately enough, CDE is available on UNIX systems, such as HP-UX, AIX, and Sun Solaris (among others). CDE is also available for Linux.

Enlightenment

Enlightenment is fast, stable, and intensely configurable. It offers 100-percent compliance to the GNOME environment. What is unique about Enlightenment is that you can create peculiar window shapes. Users are able to define the smallest of window details.

Because Enlightenment is still in the development stage, it can exhibit erratic behavior. If you consider the possibilities, however, it might be worth the effort to get Enlightenment up and running. Red Hat utilizes Enlightenment to support GNOME, Red Hat's default environment. A bit of trivia: The author of Enlightenment (Rastermann) used to work for Red Hat.

fvwm

The fvwm window manager is derived from and improves on twm. Robert Nation developed fvwm, which was considered to be *the* window manager to use. Other window managers have followed in fvwm's footsteps, such as fvwm2 and fvwm95. fvwm provides a virtual desktop, supplying multiple desktops to the user. Each desktop can be larger than the physical screen—you use the mouse to "move" the current desktop behind the screen. Think of the desktop as a wall mural and your screen as a picture frame. The picture frame acts as a portal into the mural. You use the mouse to move the mural about the frame, bringing windows into view.

The fvwm window manager also introduces the sticky window concept. This allows you to anchor a window to a specific coordinate on the physical screen. As you scroll around on the desktop, any sticky windows stay put.

fvwm95

The fvwm95 window manager is based on fvwm2 (which is based on fvwm). Much of the functionality of fvwm2 is retained; the majority of the changes involve the look and feel. The fvwm95 window manager is an attempt to emulate the graphical environment of a popular operating system (which will remain nameless). Enough said.

GNOME

GNOME stands for GNU Network Object Model Environment. The goal is to provide a freely distributable, user-friendly desktop. Because GNOME is not a complete window manager, it will require one, such as Enlightenment. Red Hat uses GNOME as the default graphical environment and utilizes Enlightenment as the base window manager.

If you are using GNOME and decide to change window managers, be sure it is GNOME aware. GTK+ is the GUI toolkit used for GNOME applications, providing a consistent look and feel. Also unique to GNOME applications is the utilization of CORBA (Common Object Resource Broker Architecture). This allows GNOME components (applications) seamless interoperability, regardless of the machine on which they are executing. CORBA also allows applications written in different languages to seamlessly communicate.

KDE

The intent of the K Desktop Environment is similar to GNOME's—to provide a desktop environment with a consistent look and feel across applications. KDE is also similar to GNOME in that it requires a window manager. Applications packaged in KDE include a file manager, an integrated help system, a window manager, and a configuration utility for the display.

LessTif

LessTif is a clone of OSF/Motif. It consists of a window manager, a widget set, and UIL implementation.

olwm

The olwm window manager is derived from the Open Look Window Manager from Sun's Open Windows graphical interface.

olvwm

The olvwm window manager is equivalent to olwm with the addition of a virtual desktop. This desktop is larger than the physical screen. The olvwm also supports XPM pixmaps and GIF images, displayed as icons and for menu type images.

twm

The classic window manager from MIT, which features shaped windows and title bars, icon management, macro functions, and much more.

Exploring the Graphical Environment

We begin our GUI travels with KDE, a popular graphical environment that is included with a few distributions. You have already seen some examples in this chapter. This section shows you some of the basic utilities, such as system navigation, dial-up connectivity, and desktop customization, to name a few. By the way, KDE recently won "Innovation of the Year" at the CeBIT'99 conference. The next section follows up with an overview of GNOME.

KDE

You can start KDE from the command line or have the system start it up automatically, after boot up. To start up the KDE environment, you use the startx command. This assumes, of course, that KDE is the default window manager. The syntax is as follows:

startx [[client] options] [-- [server] options

The startx command is normally a shell script that is used to start up the X Window system. In a pinch, you can do the following to start up KDE:

stimpy $ startx
stimpy $

Some systems are set so that you can start KDE with the kde command, as in the following:

stimpy $ kde &
stimpy $

The rule of thumb is to execute the startx command. Figure 5.3 shows KDE after it has initialized.

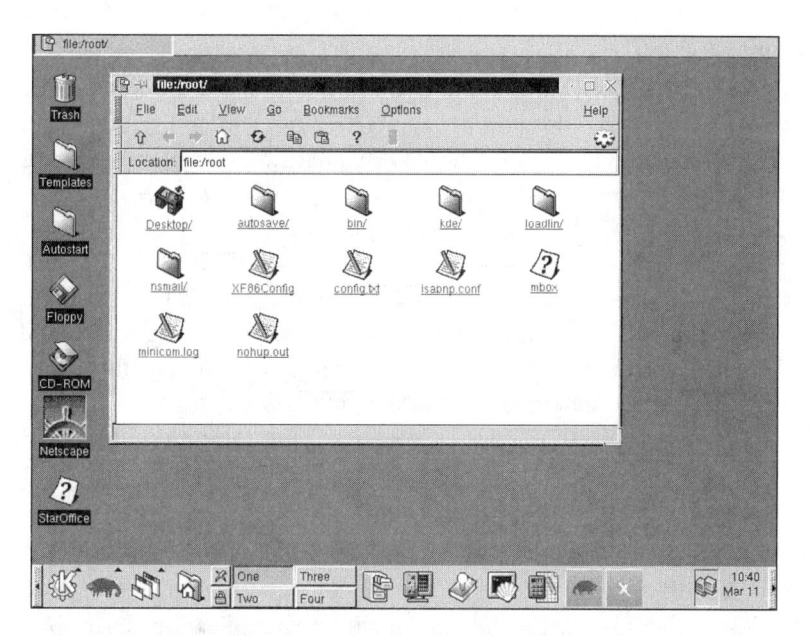

Figure 5.3 The KDE environment after startup.

The horizontal bar spanning the top of the screen is the taskbar. The panel is the horizontal bar that spans the bottom of the screen. The desktop, basically, is everything else on the screen. The desktop is where you arrange your running programs and icons. The following sections provide a quick review of these three areas.

KDE Taskbar

When you execute an application, a button representing the application appears. The button's text displays the name of the application. You can scan the taskbar to see any applications that are running. You can also click an application's button to make it current. This is a quick way to switch to another running program. Figure 5.3 shows that kfm, the KDE file manager, is the sole application running on the desktop and is represented in the taskbar.

As applications are launched, the taskbar begins to fill with buttons. If you continue to launch applications and the taskbar fills, the buttons will be resized (shrunk) to accommodate new buttons.

KDE Panel

The KDE panel provides a number of services. First, it houses various icons that represent files, programs, or menus. You can add and remove icons and menus from the KDE panel. The KDE panel is a convenient repository to hold your frequently used commands. This provides you with a central point from which to execute your favorite commands.

The KDE panel is also home to the virtual desktop panel. The default location is on the left side of the KDE panel. The KDE panel defaults the number of virtual desktops to four. You can have up to eight virtual desktops represented on the panel, configurable through the KDE control center. We discuss virtual desktops in a section that follows.

You can get a pop-up "hint" if you hover the mouse pointer over a KDE panel icon. Look at Figure 5.3 again; you will see a pop-up hint with the text KDE control center.

KDE Main Menu

To expose the KDE main menu, you click the application starter button found on the panel at the extreme left. The main menu is shown in Figure 5.4. By the way, some versions of KDE offer a humorous pop-up hint—hover the mouse pointer over the application starter button.

You will notice that the menu maintains a set of application categories, such as Applications, Games, Settings, and so forth. This is rather intuitive, grouping programs based on their functionality. If you look closely, you will see that Find Files is currently selected.

Two menu items should be of immediate interest to you. The KDE control center is used to modify the look of KDE's interface. You can alter colors, the placement and style of window adornments, sound, and the screen saver, just to name a few. The Logout menu item will shut down the current KDE window session and return to the previous system state.

Virtual Desktops

With KDE, the days of "window noise" are over. What do I mean by window noise? This occurs when you have too many windows open on your desktop. It's as if the windows are fighting for screen real estate. Some operating systems have one desktop on which to place application and file windows. With KDE (and other window managers), you have the option of specifying two or more virtual desktops.

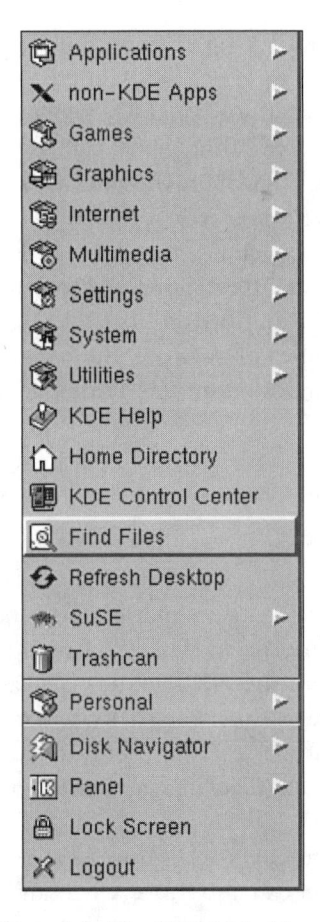

Figure 5.4 The KDE Main Menu.

Virtual desktops provide a way to organize your application windows. For example, you could have your Internet dialer program and browser in one virtual desktop, a word processor in another, and a file manager and terminal shell running in a third. Using virtual desktops reduces window clutter (noise) and enables you to manage your productivity.

You can use the mouse or keyboard to switch from one desktop to another. With the mouse, you simply click the appropriate desktop button on the panel. With the keyboard, use Ctrl+F1 through Ctrl+F8 to display the corresponding desktop. You can keystroke Ctrl+Tab to cycle through the desktops.

Each virtual desktop has an associated name. The default names are One, Two, Three, Four, and so on. You can change these names to better fit your needs. Click the virtual desktop button until a cursor appears (once or twice should do it), backspace to erase, and then type the new name. You can also change the name(s) from the Kpanel Configuration window. Move your mouse onto an empty area of the panel, right-click, and select Configure. Click the desktop's tab page, then click the appropriate desktop name field, and change the name. Alternatively, you can get to the KPanel Configuration window from the Main Menu: Select Settings, Applications, and Panel. While you are at the KPanel Configuration/Desktops tab page, you can also increase or decrease the number of virtual desktops. Use the Visible slider bar to choose the number of desktops you want.

You can move a window from one virtual desktop to another. Click the Window Control menu (at the extreme left on the window's title bar), select To Desktop, and then choose a virtual desktop. If you specified a virtual desktop other than the current one, the current window will disappear.

KDE Sticky Window

Virtual desktops help to reduce window noise and help manage your productivity. A situation may occur when you want a window to exist on every desktop. You might want the X Clock or Calculator to be visible no matter which desktop is current. Enter the sticky window. On the left side of a window's title bar you will see a push pin. To anchor the window to the screen, click the push pin. Clicking the pin again releases the sticky state of the window.

In the previous section, you read how to move a window from one desktop to another. You can also move a window using the push pin. Select the desktop that contains the window you want to move. Anchor the window with the push pin. Switch to the desktop where you want the window. Finally, click the push pin and the window now resides in the current desktop.

KDE Desktop Configuration

Something that has been stressed about KDE and other window managers is configurability. Using KDE's control center, you can change the look and feel of KDE.

You can launch the control center a couple of ways. An icon for the control center can be found on the panel—the icon is a monitor with a green card overlaid. To aid your search, you can use the mouse pointer to view the pop-up tips for each icon. You can also start the KDE control center from the main menu (via the application starter button). Figure 5.5 shows the control center.

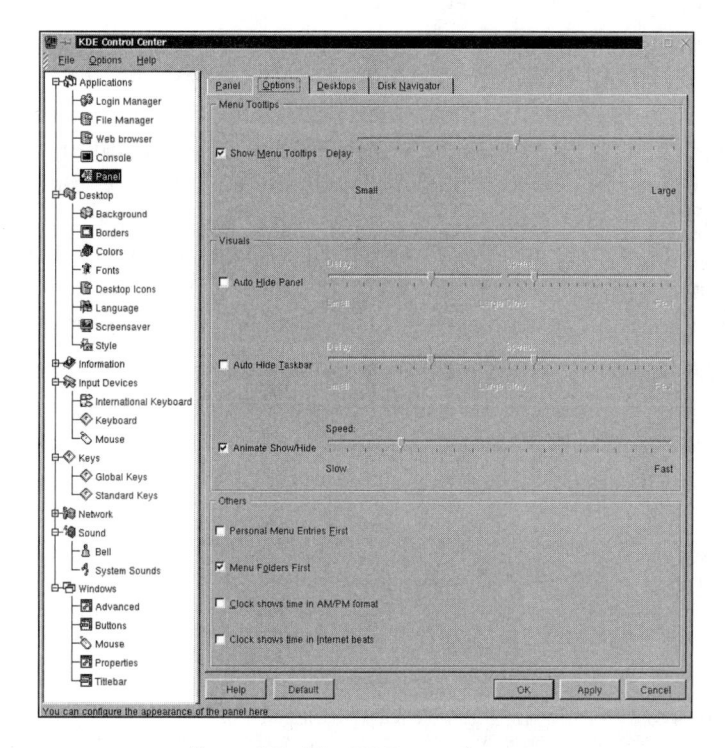

Figure 5.5 The KDE control center.

You will notice that the control center is divided into two panes. The left pane shows a tree view for the major configuration modules. They are called modules because they are actually individual programs. If you open the main menu (via the application starter button) and select Settings, you will see the same modules listed. From the Settings menu, you can launch any of the modules singly. Using the control center allows a central point from which to configure all aspects of KDE. Each module will display its options in the right pane of the control center.

In Figure 5.5, all modules have been expanded except two: Information and Network. The Information module displays read-only data about your machine's hardware and Samba and X Windows status. The Network module holds the Talk Configuration module. The Panel module is currently running in the right pane with the Options tab page displayed.

At the lower portion of the right pane, you will see five buttons: Help, Default, OK, Apply, and Cancel. You use Help to get information about the current module panel. Default restores the factory default settings to the current module panel. OK applies any module changes you have made and closes the module panel. Apply also applies module changes but leaves the module panel visible so that you can continue to make changes. Using Apply is a way to test any changes you are curious about. The Cancel button closes the current module panel without applying changes.

The following is a list of the modules and a description for each:

- **Applications.** Contains the supplemental KDE application and its associated settings, such as the panel and kfm (KDE file manager).
- **Desktop.** You can change various aspects of the desktop, such as background color or wallpaper, window borders, window colors, window style, and so on.
- **Information.** Displays read-only data about your machine's hardware and Samba and X Windows status.
- **Input Devices.** Holds keyboard and mouse settings.
- **Keys.** Contains configuration for key bindings (shortcut keystrokes).
- **Network.** Contains settings for the network.
- **Sound.** You can view/modify sound settings for your system.
- **Windows.** Settings for window adornments and functionality, such as the title bar buttons (inclusion and placement), reactions to mouse events, and so on.

> **Always Apply Changes**
> If you make changes to a module, be sure to select OK or Apply before switching to another module configuration; otherwise, you will lose those changes.

Modify a Desktop Setting

The first change most people make to their desktop is the background. Let's be consistent with everyone else and change the KDE background.

First, execute the KDE control center. You can find its icon on the panel—it's represented by a monitor with a green card superimposed. You can also find the control center on the main menu—choose the Application Starter button, then choose the KDE control center item. Click the plus sign (+) next to the desktop module and click Background. Your KDE control center should look like Figure 5.6.

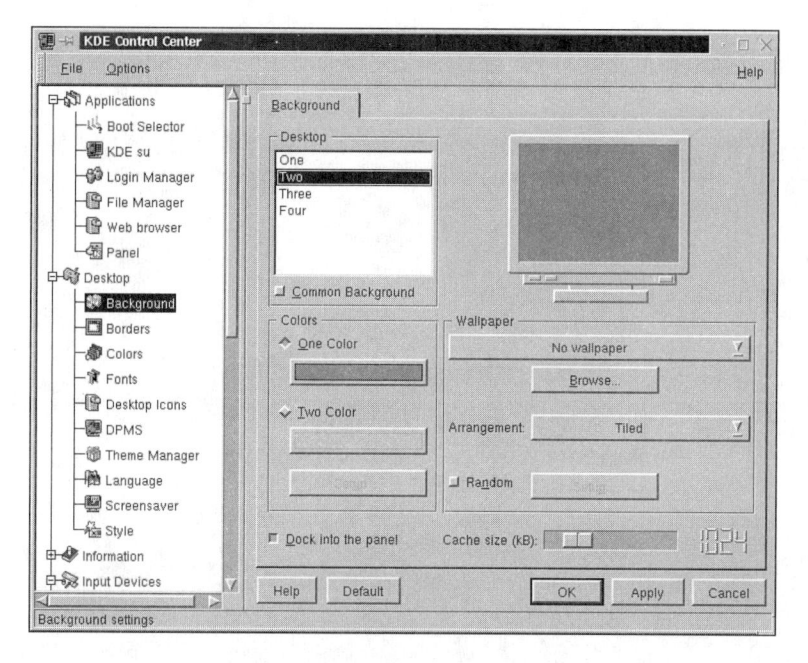

Figure 5.6 The KDE control center with Background selected.

The default background for KDE is blue. Let's make the background something interesting and utilize a bitmap image. Notice that there are three group boxes: Desktop, Colors, and Wallpaper. We will be working in the Wallpaper group box. The first field in the group box is the background drop-down list. If you have not already changed the wallpaper, the current setting is No Wallpaper. Select liquid_helium.jpg or whatever suits your fancy. Click the Apply button to see the effect on the desktop. Remember, if you click the OK button, the desktop module will close. Use Apply to check the result of your change—if you do not like the change, you can select something else. Figure 5.7 shows the result of the background wallpaper change. Your desktop will appear different if you selected some other background wallpaper.

As you move through the wallpaper choices, the resulting change is shown on the sample "monitor" on the Background tab page. You can click the Wallpaper drop-down box and then use the up or down arrow keys to cycle through the wallpaper choices. When you are satisfied with the wallpaper, click OK. Finally, select File, Exit to quit the KDE control center application.

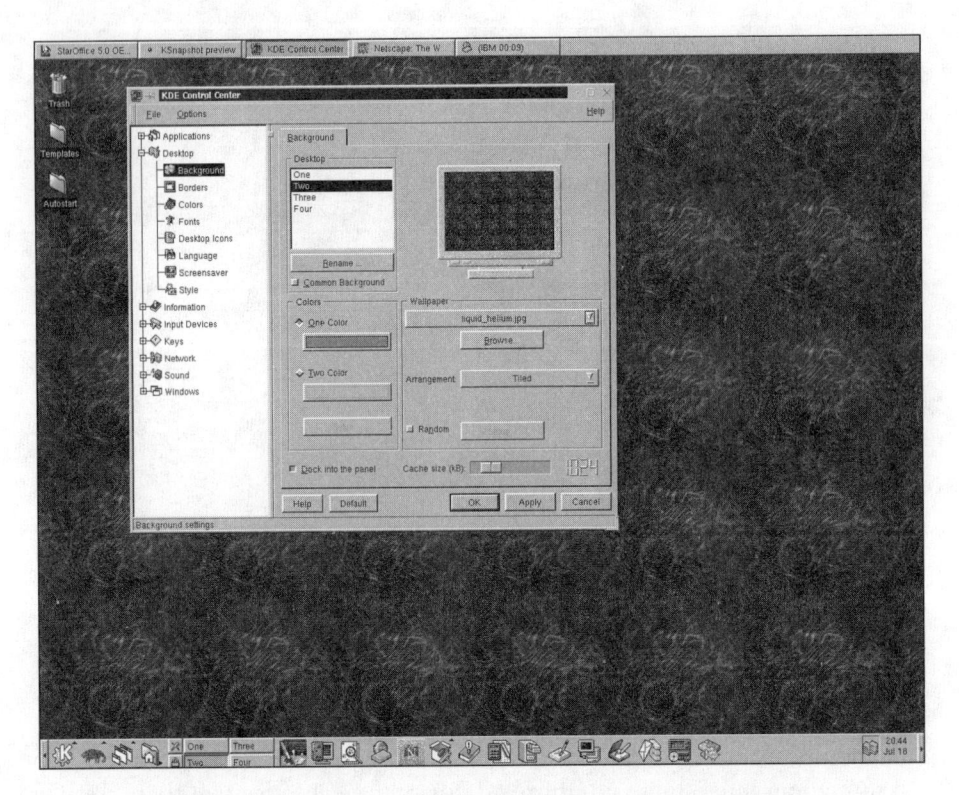

Figure 5.7 KDE desktop with new background wallpaper applied.

Customizing the Panel

If you find yourself executing a command frequently, you can add its icon to the panel. As an experiment, let's add the Font Manager icon to the panel. Click the Application Starter button and then select Panel, Add Application, System, and Font Manager. The icon will show up on the panel. Click the icon to test it out; the KDE Font Manager window will display. You can also drag an icon to the panel. As an example, click and hold the Template icon (on the desktop), drag the icon onto a blank portion of the panel, and release the button.

Suppose that you want to move the icon to another location on the panel. This is very simple to do—place the mouse pointer on the icon, right-click, and select Move. Slide the mouse to the new location and click to anchor the icon. The mouse pointer does not have to be on the panel to move the icon.

As a final exercise, let's remove the icon from the panel. Place the mouse pointer on the icon, right-click, and select Remove. The icon vanishes from the panel.

Right-clicking an icon reveals its context-sensitive menu. You should note that not every icon has a context-sensitive menu. Experimentation will be your best teacher.

By the way, the background wallpaper change affects only the current virtual desktop. If you want the background wallpaper to be applied to all virtual desktops, click the Common Background check box in the Desktop group.

Extreme KDE Customization—Themes

A *theme* is a collection of settings that alters the look and feel for windows (and its adornments), menus, backgrounds, and so on.

The themes URL for KDE is http://kde.themes.org/. This site has a gallery of screenshots that show the available themes. Changing a window manager theme is somewhat involved. The easiest way to change a theme is to use a shell script, such as ktinstall (Dmitry Zakharov) or ktheme_perl (Matt Herbert). These utilities can be found at the preceding URL. The customization described in this section assumes the use of ktinstall.

First, open a kvt window session; change to your home directory, and then change to the .kde directory. The following dialog shows this:

```
stimpy $ cd ~/.kde
stimpy $
```

Next, move the *.tar.gz file that contains the theme from the download directory to the ~/.kde directory. The remainder of this section assumes the Swing_Metal theme. The following dialog shows the move procedure:

```
stimpy $ mv /tmp/Swing.Metal.tar.gz ./
stimpy $ ls -al
total 923
drwxr-xr-x   3 root     root         1024 Jul 18 21:45 .
drwx--x--x  10 root     root         2048 Jul 18 21:52 ..
-rw-r--r--   1 root     root       665153 Jul 17 15:38 KDE_Ocean.tar.gz
-rw-r--r--   1 100      root         1393 Dec  1  1998 README
-rw-r--r--   1 root     root       215870 Jul 17 15:35 Swing_Metal.tar.gz
-rwxr-xr-x   1 100      root        36579 Dec  1  1998 ktinstall
drwxr-xr-x   7 root     root         1024 Jul 14 22:59 share
stimpy $
```

Before you install the new theme, be sure to record and archive the current theme. The following dialog shows how this is done, utilizing ktinstall:

```
stimpy $ ktinstall -m Default
Theme name [Default]:
Save panel position and size (y/n)? [y]: y
Include sounds (y/n)? [y]: y
```

continues ▶

Chapter 5 Using X Windows

continued

```
Number of wallpapers (1-8)? [4]:
Readme file [none]:
Done
stimpy $
```

Finally, you install the new theme, as the following dialog demonstrates. Be prepared for some screen flicker as the install script automatically reinitializes KDE.

```
stimpy $ ./ktinstall Swing_Metal.tar.gz
Saving configuration files...
Installing Swing_Metal...
kpanel: waiting for windowmanager
Done.
Stimpy $
```

Figure 5.8 shows the results:

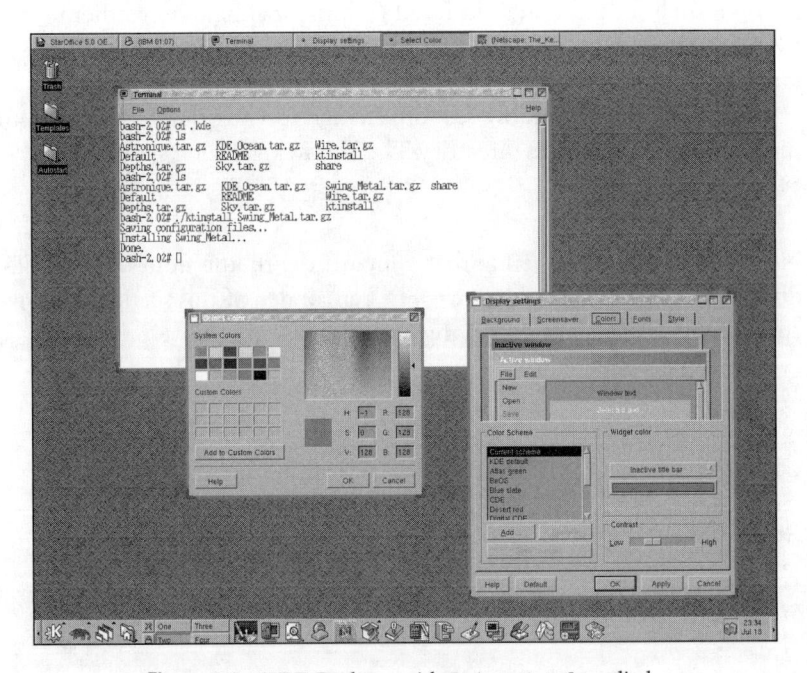

Figure 5.8 KDE Desktop with `Swing_Metal` applied.

If you do not like the results of the new theme, you can use the uninstall feature of ktinstall. The following example shows the syntax:

```
stimpy $ ./ktinstall -u
```

> **Warning**
> When using the ktinstall script to install or uninstall a theme, leave your mouse and keyboard alone until the script has finished.

Launching Applications

As mentioned previously in this chapter, you can launch applications and expose windows in a number of ways.

The panel at the bottom of the screen houses application icons. Click the application of choice.

You can also execute an application from the main menu. The main menu is exposed when you click the application starter button found at the extreme left on the panel. The application starter button is adorned with a large "K."

Another method to launch an application is to execute the keystroke sequence Alt+F2, which opens the command window. Type in a command and press Enter. If found, the command will run. Try it: Press Alt+F2, type **xedit** into the command window, and press Enter. The xedit program window should display.

Command-Line Window

In addition to executing a command using its icon, you can open up a terminal window. The KDE terminal window is called *kvt* and provides you with a Linux command-line window. You can find kvt on the panel and the Main Menu. On the panel, look for an icon that looks like a workstation with a pop-up window.

To execute kvt via the main menu, click the application starter button, go to Utilities, and then Terminal. The kvt window appears and a command-line shell is offered.

You can do anything with kvt that you can do with a standard console shell, plus much more.

KDE File Management

File management, using any operating system, is a daily task for most people. Files are downloaded and must be moved. Directories are scanned for files that must be edited. Temporary directories must be purged. Files are copied from one drive to another. Directories and files are renamed. The list of options is virtually endless.

150 Chapter 5 Using X Windows

So, how does KDE help us out? Bundled with KDE is a file manager called kfm (KDE file manager). You can launch kfm in one of several ways. First, you can click the home directory icon (a folder with a house) on the panel. A second method is to choose home directory, which is found on the main menu. You can also execute kfm using the command window (Alt+F2) or from a command shell window, such as kvt. Figure 5.9 shows a kfm window.

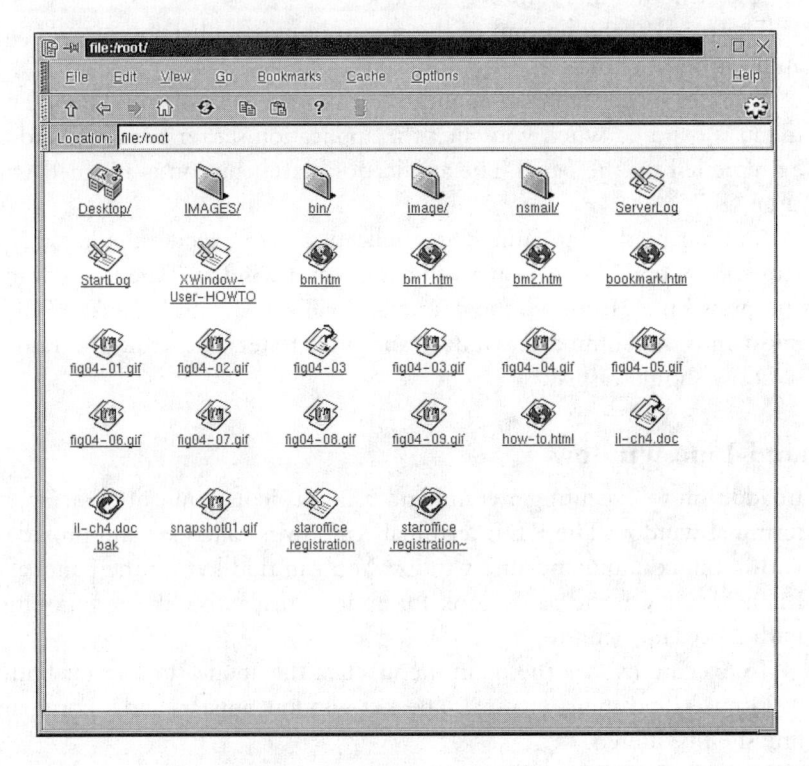

Figure 5.9 The KDE file manager (kfm) window.

You can start kfm with the -d option to keep kfm from opening your home directory (this is the default behavior).

Navigating with kfm

An icon that looks like a folder is a directory. Other file types have associated icons that specify their types. If you look again at Figure 5.9, you will notice a number of file types and their corresponding icons.

Opening Directories and Files

To open a directory, click the folder. The contents of the selected folder are shown. The up arrow button on the toolbar (just under the menu) will go to the parent directory. This is synonymous with the cd .. command at a shell prompt. The left and right arrow buttons are history buttons.

You can also type directly into the Location bar. kfm supports http, FTP, and file protocols. Any of these protocols can be specified when identifying a filename to open. You can use kfm as a Web browser! Figure 5.10 proves the point.

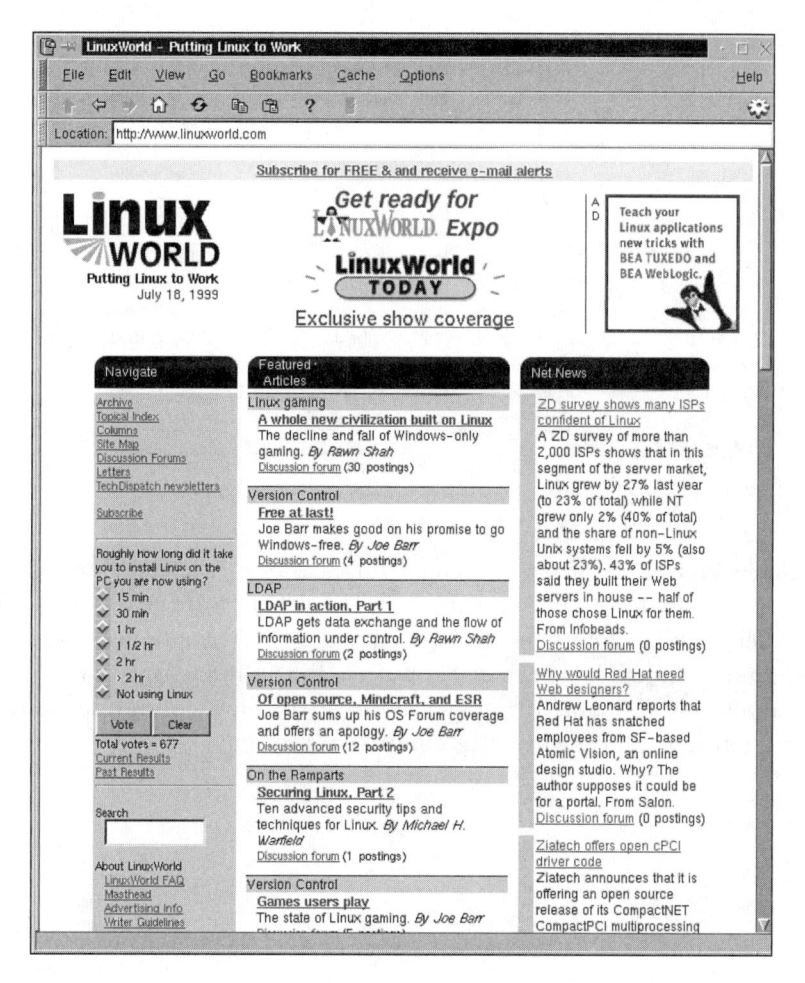

Figure 5.10 The KDE file manager displaying a Web page.

Notice the http protocol specification in the Location bar. Hot links are fully supported, as well as graphics.

Figure 5.11 shows kfm in FTP mode.

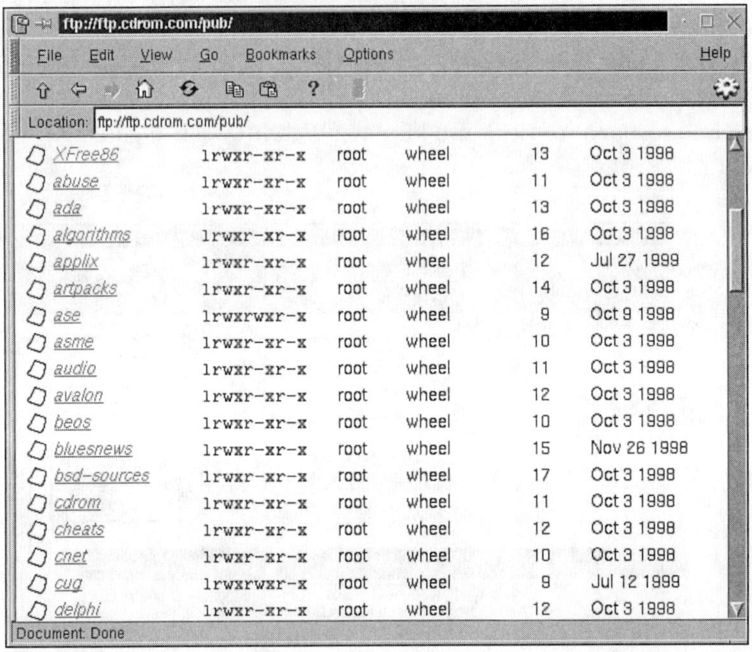

```
ftp://ftp.cdrom.com/pub/                                           _ □ ×
File   Edit   View   Go   Bookmarks   Options                         Help

Location: ftp://ftp.cdrom.com/pub/

  XFree86        lrwxr-xr-x    root    wheel    13   Oct 3 1998
  abuse          lrwxr-xr-x    root    wheel    11   Oct 3 1998
  ada            lrwxr-xr-x    root    wheel    13   Oct 3 1998
  algorithms     lrwxr-xr-x    root    wheel    16   Oct 3 1998
  applix         lrwxr-xr-x    root    wheel    12   Jul 27 1999
  artpacks       lrwxr-xr-x    root    wheel    14   Oct 3 1998
  ase            lrwxrwxr-x    root    wheel     9   Oct 9 1998
  asme           lrwxr-xr-x    root    wheel    10   Oct 3 1998
  audio          lrwxr-xr-x    root    wheel    11   Oct 3 1998
  avalon         lrwxr-xr-x    root    wheel    12   Oct 3 1998
  beos           lrwxr-xr-x    root    wheel    10   Oct 3 1998
  bluesnews      lrwxr-xr-x    root    wheel    15   Nov 26 1998
  bsd-sources    lrwxr-xr-x    root    wheel    17   Oct 3 1998
  cdrom          lrwxr-xr-x    root    wheel    11   Oct 3 1998
  cheats         lrwxr-xr-x    root    wheel    12   Oct 3 1998
  cnet           lrwxr-xr-x    root    wheel    10   Oct 3 1998
  cug            lrwxrwxr-x    root    wheel     9   Jul 12 1999
  delphi         lrwxr-xr-x    root    wheel    12   Oct 3 1998
Document: Done
```

Figure 5.11 The KDE file manager using the FTP protocol.

Under kfm's View menu, the long format has been selected, showing a listing similar to the `ls -al` command. The default format (or view) is Icon. Other views are Short and Text (no graphics). Other options under the View menu are Show Hidden Files, Show Tree, and an interesting one—Show Thumbnails. If the file is a graphical image, the file's icon is displayed as a thumbnail graphic. Figure 5.12 confirms this magic.

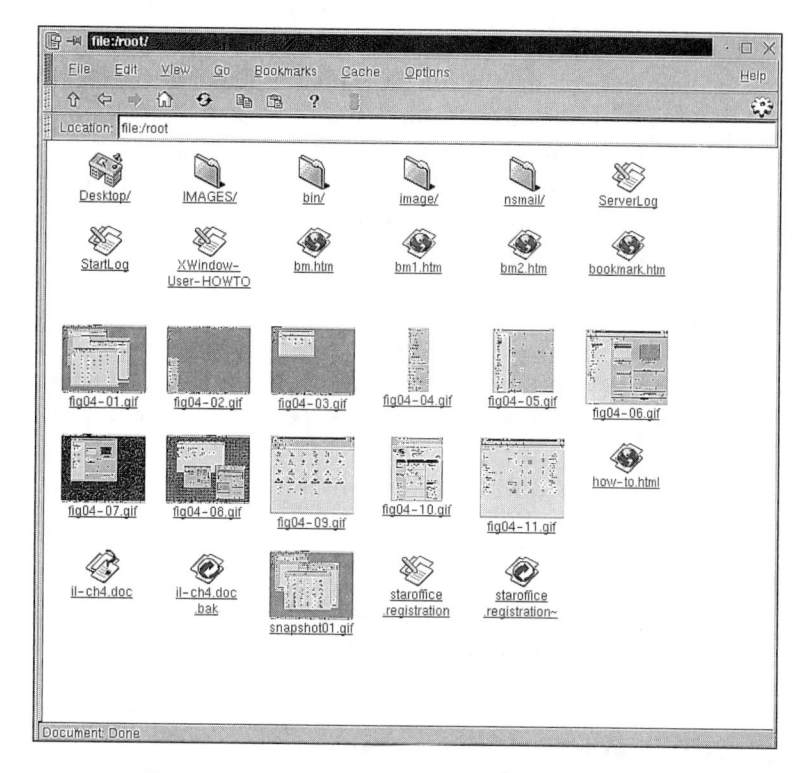

Figure 5.12 The KDE file manager in thumbnail view.

The downside to the thumbnail view is that it takes a little longer to display a directory (if graphical files are present).

With kfm, you can also view the contents of zip and tar files. Just click the archive file.

Copy, Move, and Link

If you need to move, copy, or create a file link, click a file, drag the icon to the destination, and release. A pop-up menu offers the choices Copy, Move, or Link. A link created by kfm is a soft link rather than a hard link.

You can drag the file from kfm to the desktop or to another kfm window. To open a second kfm window, select File, New Window. With this technique, you can browse to the destination (second kfm) and drag files from one kfm window to another.

Bookmarks

If you are familiar with the bookmark feature of Web browsers, kfm's bookmarks should not surprise you. To the uninitiated, a bookmark is an anchor to some file entity. If you bookmark a directory, for example, the next time you select the bookmark, kfm will display the directory's contents. If a file is bookmarked, it is opened with the appropriate application. You can bookmark any file by right-clicking the file and selecting Add to Bookmarks.

File History

Found under kfm's Cache menu, you will see the Show History option. If you choose Show History, you see a list of URL entries, representing local, http, and FTP filenames. Basically, the History list shows where you have been.

To go to a location listed in the History list, simply click the URL of choice.

File Properties

To display the properties of a file, right-click the file and select Properties. If you have proper rights, you can rename the file and change any number of attributes for User, Group, and Others.

Mounting a Device

A common task in Linux is the installation of software and updates to a Linux system using a CD-ROM. You might also mount a CD-ROM on a daily basis, accessing the data stored there. You could put the entry in the /etc/fstab file to automatically mount the device at boot up. With CD-ROMs and floppy disks, however, you must mount to read the media and unmount it to remove it. You must perform this cycle every time you want to read another CD-ROM or floppy. In this section, we create a desktop icon to automate the process of mounting and unmounting a CD-ROM.

The first step is to click the Templates icon on the desktop. The KDE file manager executes and displays the contents of the Templates folder.

The second step involves dragging the Device icon onto the desktop. Click and hold the Device icon, drag it onto the desktop, and release the mouse button. A pop-up menu appears; select Copy. You should now have an icon named Device on your desktop.

The next step is to modify the attributes of the Device icon. Click the new Device icon and choose Properties from the pop-up menu. The Properties dialog box is displayed. Figure 5.13 shows the General tab page.

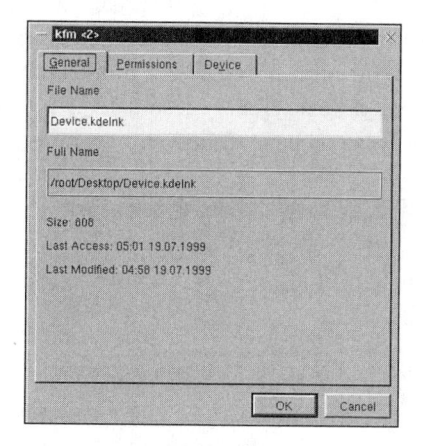

Figure 5.13 The General tab for Device Properties.

Change the filename to **CD-ROM.kdelnk**. Next, select the Device tab on the Properties dialog box. Figure 5.14 shows the Device tab page.

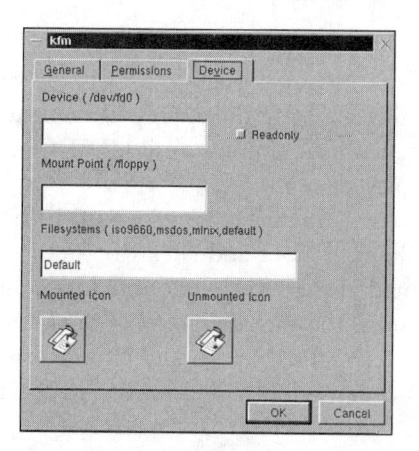

Figure 5.14 The Device tab for Device Properties.

For the Device field, you need to supply the name of the device that is associated with your CD-ROM drive. On my machine it is /dev/hdc. The device for your machine may be different. Be sure to click the Read-only check box if your CD-ROM is a read-only device (most are). Next, type the mount point for the CD-ROM. This can be any directory you have created for mounting the device. You might have a directory named /cdrom or /mnt/cdrom on which to mount your physical CD-ROM device. In the Filesystems field, type **iso9660**. Next, click the Mounted Icon button and select the Mounted icon from the list—its name is `cdrom_mount.xpm`. Finally click the Mounted Icon button and select the Unmounted icon from the list—its name is `cdrom_unmount.xpm`. Figure 5.15 is a snapshot of the Device tab page filled in—the correct icons are shown here.

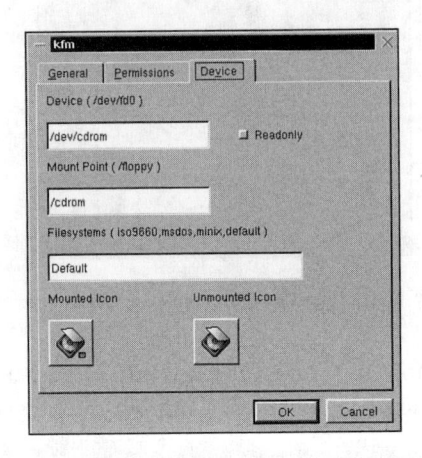

Figure 5.15 The Device tab for Device Properties (filled in).

After all fields are filled in with the appropriate entries, click the OK button. The Device icon should now read CD-ROM, and the Unmounted icon should be displayed.

To test out the new icon, open the CD-ROM drive door and insert a CD-ROM disc. Close the door and click the (new) CD-ROM desktop icon. The icon should change to the mounted icon and a kfm window should display, showing the root directory of the CD-ROM. When you are done, right-click the CD-ROM icon and choose Unmount. You can now open the CD-ROM drive door and remove the disc media.

Printer Setup

In the previous section, you set up a CD-ROM device icon on the desktop to mount and unmount a CD-ROM device. You can do the same thing for a printer. To print files, you drag and drop files onto the desktop Printer icon. Follow along as we create a Printer icon.

The first step is to single-click the Templates icon on the desktop. The KDE file manager will execute and display the contents of the Templates folder.

Next, drag the Program icon out onto the desktop. Click the Program icon, drag it onto the desktop, and release the mouse button. A pop-up menu appears; select Copy. You should now have an icon named Program on your desktop.

The third step is to modify the attributes of the Program icon. Right-click the new Program icon and choose Properties from the pop-up menu. The Properties dialog box is displayed. Figure 5.16 shows the General tab page.

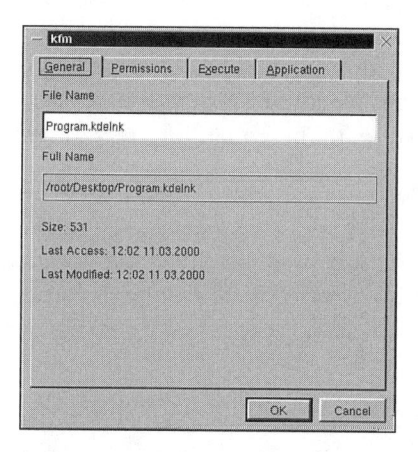

Figure 5.16 The General tab for Program Properties.

Change the filename to **Printer.kdelnk**. Next, select the Execute tab page on the Properties dialog box and enter **lpr %f** for the Execute field. The following snapshot, Figure 5.17, shows the Execute tab page.

Figure 5.17 The Execute tab for Program Properties.

Click the "cog" icon to select a printer icon from the list. More than one printer icon may be available—select the one that appeals to you.

Click the OK button to save the changes and dismiss the dialog box. You can test out your new Printer icon by dragging a file and dropping it on the icon.

GNOME

GNOME can be launched manually from the command line, or you can instruct the system to start it automatically after system initialization. To start up the GNOME environment, as with most other window managers, use the `startx` command. We assume that you have set up GNOME to be the default window manager. The syntax for `startx` is as follows:

```
startx [ [client] options] [ -- [server] options
```

The `startx` command is, as a rule, a shell script and is used to start the X Windows system and subsequently, the window manager. You can start up GNOME as demonstrated in the following dialog:

```
stimpy $ startx
stimpy $
```

Figure 5.18 shows GNOME after it has initialized.

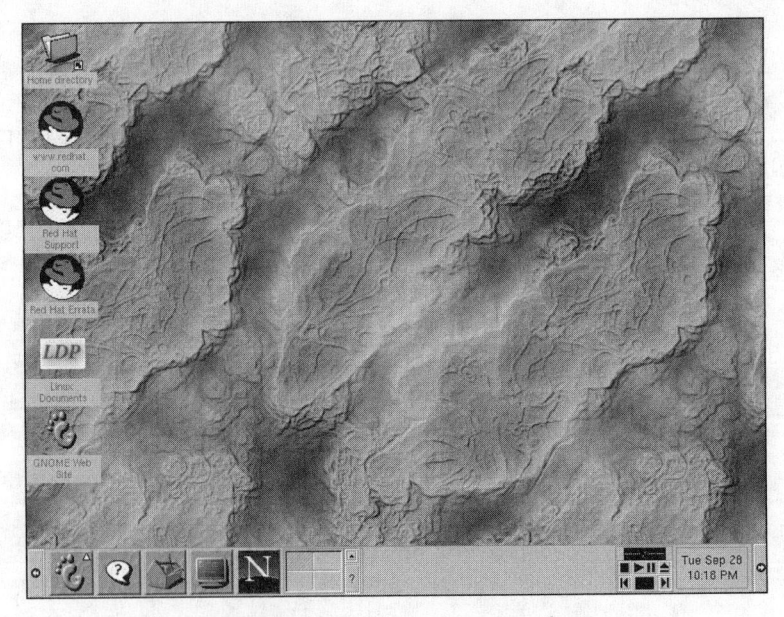

Figure 5.18 The GNOME environment after startup.

Considering that GNOME is highly configurable, the previous figure may not look the same as your GNOME display. The horizontal bar at the bottom of the display is called the GNOME panel. The GNOME panel houses menus and other icons called *applets*. An applet is nothing more than a program that resides on the GNOME panel. Take a look at the far right of the GNOME panel; this particular applet is the GNOME panel clock, showing the date and time.

All the space above the GNOME panel is referred to as the desktop, as it is in KDE and most other window managers. In the previous figure, you can see a number of icons, such as Home Directory, Linux Documents, and GNOME Web Site, on the left edge of the desktop. These icons refer to various URLs. You can place assorted objects on the desktop. For example, if you place a directory object on the desktop and double-click that object, the GNOME file manager executes and the respective directory contents are displayed. Other objects, such as programs or data files, can be placed on the desktop. If you double-click a data file, its associated application executes and the data file is opened. You should consider the desktop as a place where you put your most-used applications, data files, and directories.

Take another look at the GNOME panel (the bar at the bottom) in Figure 5.18. Just to the right of the five icons, you will see what is called the GNOME pager. The pager shows four small windows, arranged and viewed (logically) as a window pane. The pager shows any running applications and their desktop locations. To the right of the pager is the Task List—the Task List shows any running applications for the current virtual display.

In the sections that follow, we discuss the GNOME panel, the pager, and the desktop in more detail.

GNOME Panel

The GNOME panel provides a number of services. First, it houses various icons that represent files, programs, or menus. You can add and remove icons from the panel, as well as menus. The panel is a convenient repository to hold your frequently used commands. This provides you with a central point from which to execute your favorite commands.

The GNOME panel also houses the pager. The default location for the pager is normally in the center of the panel. The GNOME panel defaults the number of virtual desktops to four. You can have up to eight virtual desktops represented on the panel, configurable through the GNOME control center. We discuss the pager and virtual desktops in more detail in the later section "GNOME Pager and Virtual Desktops."

Pop-up "hints" are available if you hover the mouse pointer over any of the panel icons. Figure 5.19 shows a pop-up hint in action for the Netscape icon.

Figure 5.19 A pop-up hint in action.

The GNOME main menu icon is found on the panel. It is located at the extreme left on the panel and it looks like a bare foot. You have to be cautious when describing the (physical) location of applets on the GNOME panel—you can move any applet along the panel, effectively changing its location. In the next section, we discuss the GNOME main menu.

GNOME Main Menu

To expose the GNOME main menu, click the application starter button found on the panel at the extreme left. The main menu is shown in Figure 5.20.

GNOME 161

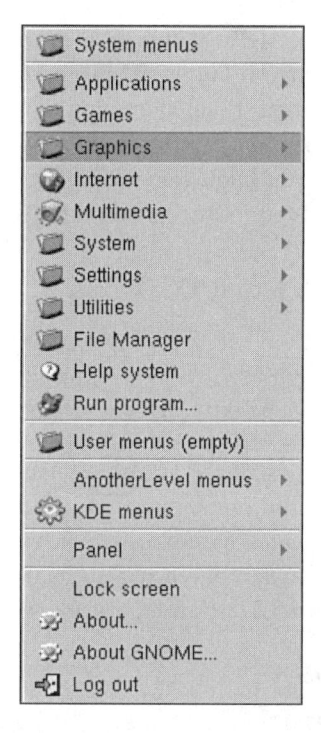

```
System menus
Applications       ▶
Games              ▶
Graphics           ▶
Internet           ▶
Multimedia         ▶
System             ▶
Settings           ▶
Utilities          ▶
File Manager
Help system
Run program...
User menus (empty)
AnotherLevel menus ▶
KDE menus          ▶
Panel              ▶
Lock screen
About...
About GNOME...
Log out
```

Figure 5.20 The GNOME main menu.

As with menus from other window managers, we see various submenus containing options that are logically organized. For example, if you select the Games menu, a pop-up menu will display, showing a list of games that are installed (if you installed them, that is) and are ready to be executed.

Take note of the menu item Log Out. This option will stop the current GNOME graphical interface and return you to the (text mode) command prompt. At the Really Log Out dialog box, you can choose to Log out, Halt, or Reboot. If you choose Log Out, you will be returned to the command prompt. The Reboot choice will shut down GNOME, return to the command prompt, and then initiate a reboot sequence. The Halt option will shut down GNOME, return to the command line, and execute the `halt` command. You can restart GNOME, as described earlier, by executing the `startx` command.

One of the first menu items you will want to execute can be found under the Settings submenu. The item is titled GNOME control center and executing this command will allow you to modify your GNOME environment. It is similar in operation to the KDE control center—you can change the background color or image, add new themes, adjust sound events, and change keyboard settings, among other options.

The GNOME Pager and Virtual Desktops

The GNOME environment offers a way to organize your running applications using the pager. The pager provides you with the ability to place (or execute) applications within a specific virtual desktop. The two main areas of the pager are the virtual desktop area and the application area. The virtual desktop area shows all the available virtual desktops, and the application area contains any running applications. The desktop area depicts the individual desktops as panes within an encompassing frame. The application area displays each application name within its own rectangle, to the right of the desktop area. Figure 5.21 shows the pager in action.

Figure 5.21 The GNOME pager.

Virtual desktops provide you with the capability to organize running applications. For example, you might run your office application on one virtual desktop, a file manager and terminal shell on a second desktop, and a Web browser on a third desktop. Virtual desktops allow you to better manage your productivity, and they help to reduce window clutter.

The mouse and keyboard can be used to switch from one virtual desktop to another. To switch to another virtual desktop using the mouse, click the appropriate virtual desktop on the pager's application area. With the keyboard, you use Alt+F1 through Alt+F*xx* (*xx* is the maximum number of desktops) to display the corresponding desktop. For example, Alt+F3 displays the third virtual desktop on the pager.

The default behavior for the GNOME pager is to show running tasks only for the current virtual desktop. You can change this behavior by opening the GNOME pager settings configuration window. To bring up this window, place the mouse on the pager's application area, right-click, and then select Properties. When the GNOME pager settings window appears, select the Tasklist tab page. Figure 5.22 shows the Pager Settings window.

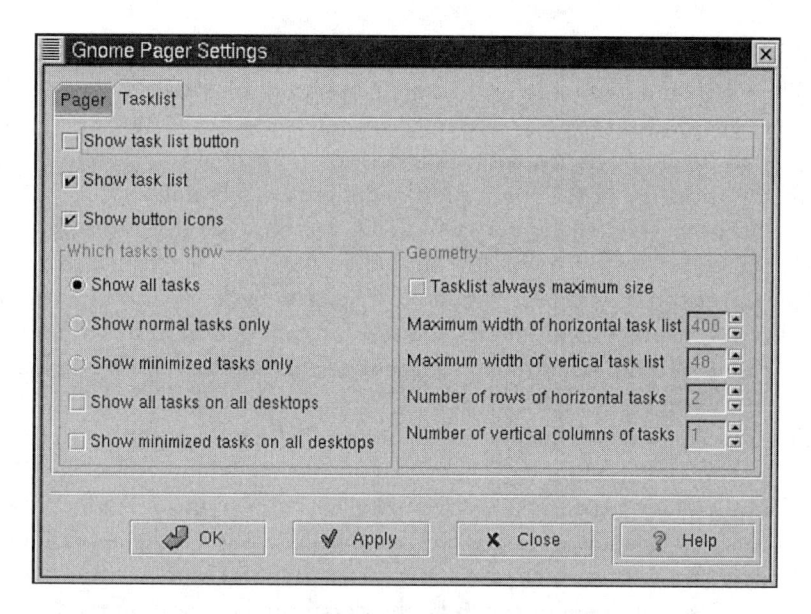

Figure 5.22 The GNOME Pager Settings window.

To show all tasks running, select (check) both Show All Tasks on All Desktops and Show Minimized Tasks on All Desktops. These check boxes are found under the Which Tasks to Show section. When you are finished, click the OK button. Now all running tasks, no matter which virtual desktop they are running on, will show up on the application view of the pager.

You can move an application window from one virtual desktop to another. To do so, click the Window Control menu (at the extreme left on the window's title bar), select Desktop, and then choose a virtual desktop. If you specify a virtual desktop other than the current one, the window will disappear. You should note that the individual desktops are not named—you move it to another desktop by specifying the direction of the new desktop (right, left, above, below).

The pager is also the home to application icons; these are housed on the pager's Quicklaunch area. The Quicklaunch area spans the section from the left edge of the pager to the left of the desktop area. Refer to Figure 5.21; you will see five launchers consisting of the Main Menu, Help, GNOME Configuration Tool, Terminal emulation program, and Netscape Communicator. You can launch these applications by clicking the appropriate applet icon.

GNOME Sticky Window

There may be times when you want an application's window to be visible on all virtual desktops. For example, you might want a clock or a chat program to be visible no matter which desktop is current. You do this by changing the stickiness of the application's window. Let's give it a try.

Select the Main Menu, select Utilities, and then select GNOME DiskFree. The DiskFree window should be displayed, showing a usage dial for each partition you have mounted. Click the System button (at the upper-left of the window) and select the Stick/Unstick option. You will notice that the title bar of the window no longer shows its color, even if you click the title bar. Now, click each virtual desktop to see the effect. You will notice that DiskFree's window stays visible and in the same position.

The previous section explained how to move a window from one desktop to another. Using the stickiness feature allows you to move a window from one desktop to another. Select the desktop that contains the application window you want to move. Select the Stick/Unstick option from the window's System menu. Switch to the desktop where you want the window to reside. Finally, select the Stick/Unstick option again from the window's System menu. The window should now reside within the current desktop.

GNOME Desktop Configuration

Something unique to Linux window managers is their configurability. GNOME is no exception; you can change the look and feel of GNOME using the GNOME control center.

The control center can be launched in a couple of ways. An applet icon exists on the panel—the icon simply portrays a wooden toolbox with tools. You can use the mouse pointer to view the pop-up tips for each icon to help you find the applet. You can also start the GNOME control center from the Settings menu option on the main menu. Figure 5.23 shows the control center.

The control center is divided into two separate panes. The left pane consists of a tree view for the major configuration modules, or *capplets*. These capplets are actually individual programs, serving a specific purpose. Your control center may have more or fewer capplets than what is shown in the previous figure. The right pane is the work area. This is where the capplet displays its configuration options. Because each capplet is really an individual program, you can launch each one individually. You can find the individual capplets on the Settings menu. In addition to the option GNOME control center, you will see Desktop, Multimedia, and so on. For example, if you want to alter the mouse settings, select the main menu, Settings, Peripherals, and then Mouse. This will execute the control center and expose the Mouse capplet.

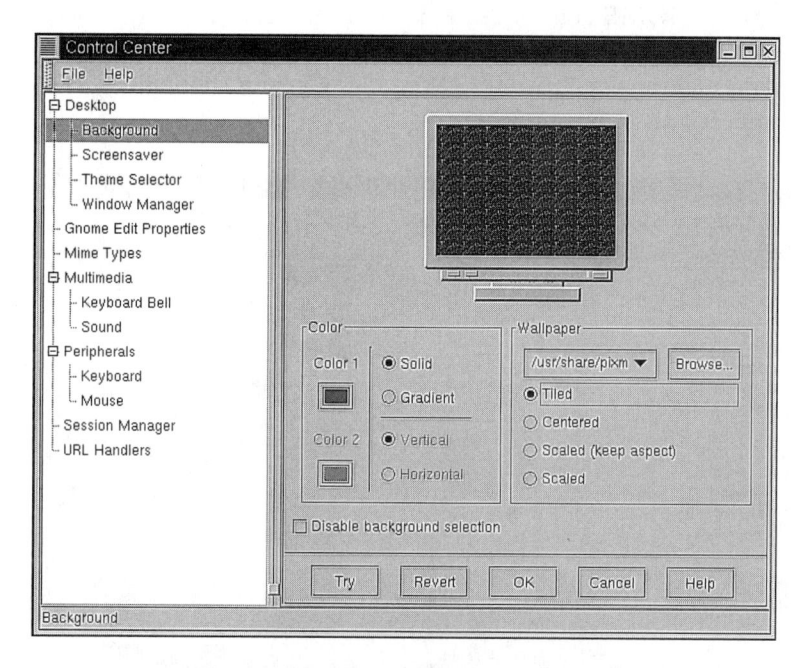

Figure 5.23 The GNOME control center.

Figure 5.23, all modules have been expanded to show their respective choices. Notice that the Background option (under Desktop) is currently selected. In the workspace (right panel), you will see the options for Background configuration. You can select a color as either a solid or a gradient—or use a bitmap to paint wallpaper as the background.

At the lower portion of the right pane, you will see five buttons: Try, Revert, OK, Cancel, and Help. Use Help to get information about the current capplet. Revert is used to restore the factory default settings for the current capplet. OK applies any capplet configuration changes and closes the capplet panel (but not the control center). Try also applies capplet changes, but leaves the capplet panel visible so you can continue to make changes. You use Try as a way to test any changes you have made. The Cancel button closes the current module panel without applying changes.

Be sure to peruse all the capplets available. Experiment with each capplet to see the changes that can be executed.

Modify a Desktop Setting

Most people like to personalize their background. As an exercise, let's change the GNOME background.

If the GNOME control center is not running, run it now. When the control center is displayed, open the desktop section and select the Background capplet. Your GNOME control center should look like the one shown in Figure 5.24.

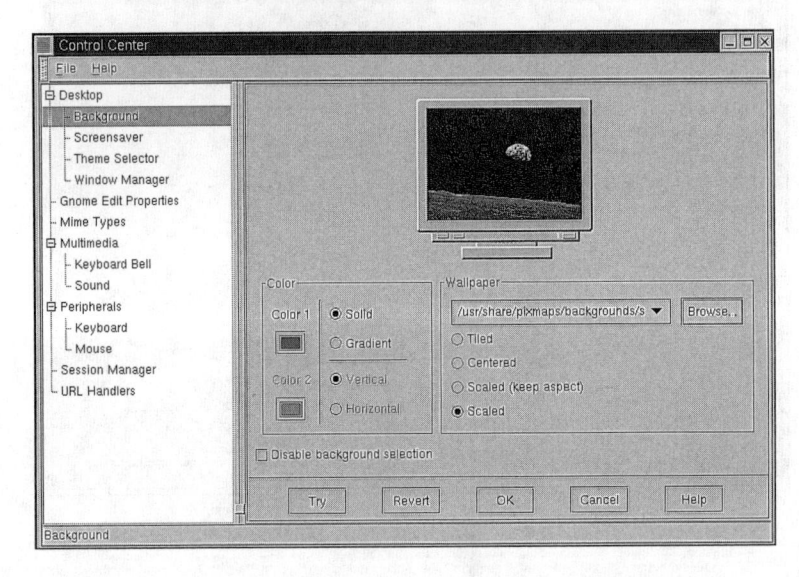

Figure 5.24 The GNOME control center with Background selected.

Let's change the background to something interesting and utilize a bitmap image. In the section titled Wallpaper, click the Browse button. The default location for the bitmaps is in /usr/share/pixmaps/backgrounds and its subdirectories. Find a bitmap that is appealing to you and click the OK button to dismiss the Wallpaper Selection dialog box. Figure 5.25 shows the changes made on my system.

As you select the various wallpaper choices, the resulting change is shown on the sample monitor on the Background workspace panel. When you are satisfied with your new wallpaper, click the OK button. To close the control center, select File, and then Exit.

Be sure to experiment with the other capplets found on the control center; after all, Linux is about personal customization.

Figure 5.25 The GNOME desktop with new background wallpaper applied.

Customizing the Panel

The GNOME panel comes equipped with its own configuration tool, as do other parts of GNOME. This section demonstrates some configuration options for the panel.

First things first. Place the mouse on a blank area of the panel, right-click, and then select Global Properties. This executes the Global Panel Configuration dialog box, as shown in Figure 5.26.

The Miscellaneous tab page is currently displayed, showing its options. As an example, let's change the applet padding value. Applet padding determines the amount of space that separates each applet on the panel; the default is 3. Change the slider to 10 and click the Apply button. Notice the change that has taken effect; more white space is between each applet on the panel. Before continuing, you might want to return the padding to its default value.

Some GNOME users like to lock their applets in place on the panel. You can do this by selecting the Free Movement option button within the Movement section (Miscellaneous tab page). If this option button is selected, you will be unable to move the applets along the panel.

You might also visit the Animation tab page. This page enables you to alter the animation effects for the panel. You can also turn the feature off by unchecking the Enable Animations check box.

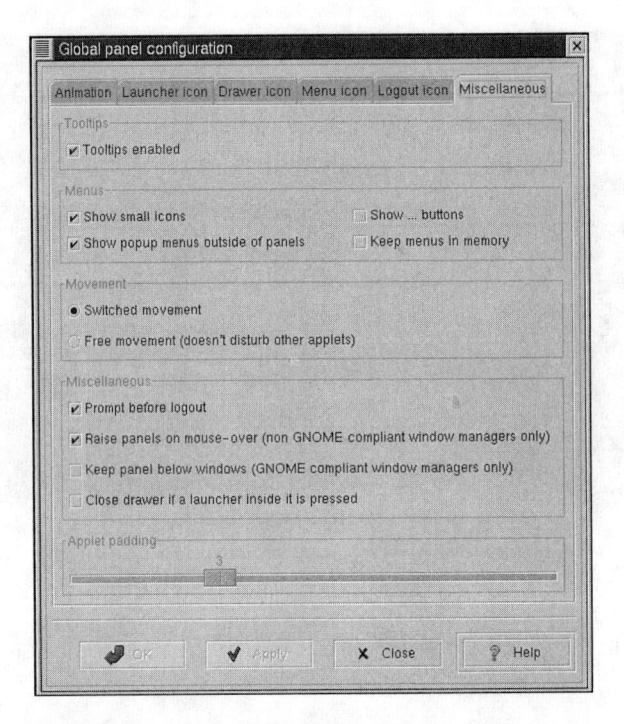

Figure 5.26 The Global Panel Configuration dialog box.

Launching Applications

Applications can be launched in several ways. You can select an application icon from the GNOME main menu, from an application applet on the panel, from the Run Program dialog box, or from a terminal window.

You can execute an application from the GNOME main menu. To expose the main menu, click the main menu button found at the extreme left on the panel (the main menu button is a stylized foot).

The GNOME panel at the bottom of the screen houses application applet icons. Click the application applet to execute it.

You can also execute an application using the Run Program dialog window. Run Program is a simple dialog box, requiring only a program name and a mouse click on the Run button. From the main menu, select Run Program. The Run Program dialog box should display. Next, type **gdiskfree** into the text box and click the Run button. The GNOME DiskFree application window should display and the Run Program dialog box should disappear. Select File, and then Exit to close the DiskFree application.

Command-Line Window

You can also execute an application from a GNOME terminal window. The GNOME terminal window command is simply named GNOME Terminal. It provides you with a graphical Linux command-line window. You can find the GNOME Terminal on the panel and on the main menu. On the panel, look for an icon that looks like a monitor. You can find the GNOME Terminal on the Utilities menu via the main menu.

You can, of course, do anything from within the GNOME Terminal that you can do with a standard console shell.

GNOME File Management

It seems that a day does not pass without performing various file-management tasks. This is not specific to Linux—other operating systems offer various forms of file management. You need a way to manipulate files and directories, such as create, delete, and move.

GNOME provides a graphical file manager named gmc. The GNOME file manager can be executed from the main menu or from a GNOME terminal window by executing the command gmc at the command prompt. Additionally, you can execute gmc using the Run Program command from the main menu. Figure 5.27 shows the GNOME file manager.

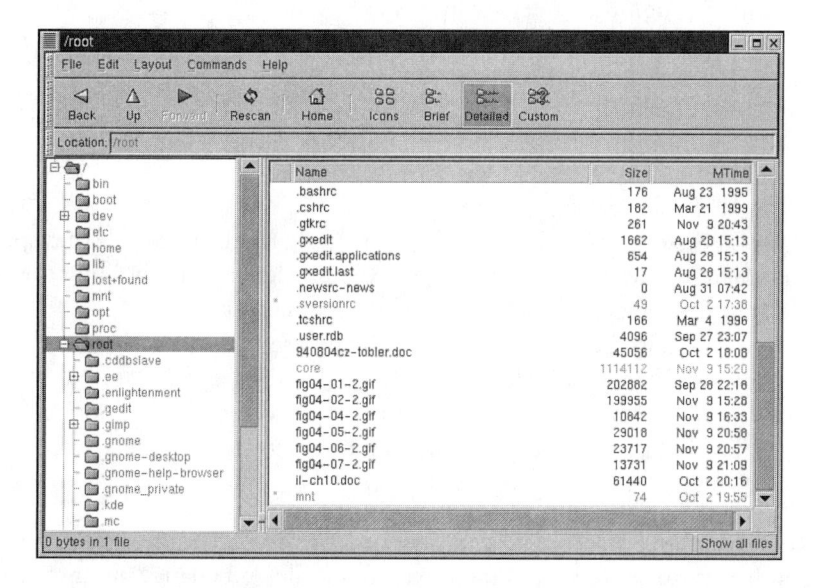

Figure 5.27 The GNOME file manager (gmc) window.

You might be curious about the GNOME file manager command being named gmc. It is called gmc because it is the GNOME edition of the Midnight Commander file manager.

Navigating with GNOME File Manager

As can be expected, a folder icon represents a directory. If the file manager is in Icon view, other file types will have an associated icon. If the file manager is in List (Brief, Detailed, or Custom) view, files are represented textually.

The GNOME file manager contains two navigation windows. The left pane contains the tree view and the right pane contains the directory view. The default directory view for gmc is the Icon view, and it displays icons for each type of file. You can also switch the file manager into List view, either Brief, Detailed, or Custom. Each of these is a list view, showing different levels of detail for the contents of the current directory. In these list views, you can also click any of the column tiles, such as Size, to sort the view.

Opening Directories and Files

In the tree-view pane, you can open a directory by clicking the plus (+) sign and close a directory by clicking the minus (–) sign.

To open a directory in the Directory pane, double-click the folder you want to open. The contents of the selected folder are shown on the right panel. You can use the Back and Up icons, found on the toolbar, to move back up through the directory hierarchy.

You can also type a directory name directly into the Location bar. Click in the Location bar and type the directory entry you require.

The GNOME file manager also supports the FTP protocol. You can specify any valid FTP address and filename to open.

Copy, Move, and Link

If you need to move, copy, or create a file link, right-click a file and specify the operation desired. You can move a file by clicking and holding the source file and then dragging it to the destination directory.

You can drag the file from gmc to the desktop or to another gmc window. To open a second gmc window, select File and Create New Window. With this technique, you can browse to the destination (the second gmc) and drag files from one gmc window to another.

File Properties

To display the properties of a file, right-click the file and select Properties. If you have proper rights, you can rename the file and change any number of attributes for User, Group, and Others.

Summary

This chapter covered a lot of territory concerning X Windows, specifically on the K Desktop Environment. The various parts of the display were covered, including the panel, the desktop, the main menu, and the taskbar.

We discussed a few of the more popular window managers, such as AfterStep, CDE, Enlightenment, fvwm, fvwm95, GNOME, KDE, olwm, olvwm, and twm.

Next, we covered KDE in detail. KDE is a popular window manager that is included with most Linux distributions. You read how to manipulate virtual desktops and configure the desktop. How to add a new theme to KDE was covered, enabling you to change the look and feel of your KDE.

Launching applications and file management using kfm were covered. Finally, we added two icons, CD-ROM and Printer, to the desktop to help automate reading CD-ROM discs and printing files, respectively.

We also looked at the GNOME environment in detail. GNOME is highly configurable and is considered the newest generation of graphical environments for Linux.

GNOME consists of the panel, which houses menus and other icons known as applets (not to be confused with Java applets). GNOME also consists of the desktop—the area of the screen where running applications reside. The GNOME pager and virtual desktops were discussed.

We also discussed sticky windows and desktop configuration for GNOME. A window that is "sticky" will continue to be displayed in every virtual desktop. Next, the GNOME control center was covered, showing how to configure the environment.

Launching applications under GNOME was discussed, describing several ways to execute applications under the GNOME environment. Finally, we closed the chapter by discussing directory and file management using the GNOME file manager.

II

Configuration

6 Network Configuration

7 Hardware Configuration

6

Network Configuration

WE HAVE A SIMPLE CHALLENGE BEFORE US. Although configuring the network is an easy task, it does require some organization and forethought. A number of configuration files and variables are available to work with. We also have to consider that different distributions configure the network differently. This chapter deals with various aspects of network configuration specifically aimed at TCP/IP.

Linux utilizes TCP/IP (Transmission Control Protocol/Internet Protocol) to enable networking support. The Internet, as well as many corporate local area networks, uses TCP/IP as the networking protocol. Linux is very well-suited for networking. You can set up a small network in your home with just two computers, a couple of network cards, wire, and Linux. You can also connect your Linux-driven computer to the Internet, thus gaining access to a world of information (literally). Linux is also effective in the corporate environment, hosting hundreds of connections.

In this chapter, we take a closer look at networking with TCP/IP, including hardware requirements, network configuration files, and utility commands that are useful for troubleshooting and maintenance.

TCP/IP Overview

Linux fully supports the complete implementation of the TCP/IP protocol suite. This enables very effective networked systems. TCP/IP consists of many protocols, not just one. You may have heard or read about some of these protocols. The following is a brief list:

- **File Transfer Protocol (FTP).** For file transfer between systems.
- **Internet Protocol (IP).** Specifies network addresses and packet format definition and routing.
- **Routing Information Protocol (RIP).** Used by routers.
- **Simple Mail Transport Protocol (SMTP).** For email.
- **Simple Network Management Protocol (SNMP).** For remote network management.
- **Transmission Control Protocol (TCP).** Connection-oriented data transfer (reliable).
- **User Datagram Protocol (UDP).** For connectionless data transfers (unreliable).

Each of the TCP/IP protocols serves a specific purpose. All the individual protocols utilize the TCP/IP protocol architecture to transmit and receive packets of data. TCP/IP is a flexible and powerful protocol suite because each protocol is individually focused. TCP/IP is, by far, the most widely used network protocol.

The TCP/IP protocol suite is considered a four-layer network model. The four layers are application, transport, network, and link.

The link layer consists of hardware and software, in the form of network cards and cabling (or wiring) and drivers. Each of these components contributes to the physical implementation of the network.

The network layer provides the implementation of packet routing. The responsibility here is to move the packets of data from one endpoint to the other.

The transport layer is responsible for controlling the flow of data between the two endpoints. Normally, one endpoint is the client utilizing the services of the server. TCP or UDP facilitates the transport layer. TCP provides reliable transmission of data, whereas UDP is unreliable.

The application layer consists of software that implements the lower layers to provide specific functionality. For example, FTP is a program that is specifically used to transfer files and SMTP is used (specifically) for handling electronic mail.

The following sections describe the two individual protocols that make up the base functionality of TCP/IP.

Internet Protocol (IP)

This protocol identifies the routing and format of data packets, known by IP as datagrams. The format of the datagrams includes information such as source and destination addresses, header length, and type of service. All the work required to move a datagram from one endpoint to the other is accomplished by IP.

IP is a data delivery service that is both connectionless and unreliable. Unreliable means that if packets are somehow lost, there is no guarantee of retransmission. Connectionless is synonymous with stateless—IP handles each datagram independently of other datagrams. Moreover, IP does not guarantee sequence of delivery of datagrams. For example, if datagrams 1 and 2 are transmitted in said order, datagram 2 may arrive before datagram 1. Why? It is quite possible that datagram 1 will take a different route than datagram 2. The receiver has no way of knowing that the datagrams are out of sequence.

Transmission Control Protocol (TCP)

TCP utilizes IP (network layer) to carry the packets of data (byte stream) from source to destination. TCP is reliable; this means it guarantees delivery of the packets. Furthermore, TCP guarantees that the order of the packets received is the same as the order sent. To deliver on the guarantee, retransmission of packets may be required. The basic steps are the following: Establish a connection, transmit the data packets, and close the connection.

With TCP, the sender and receiver first establish a connection. After the connection is confirmed, data packets can be transmitted. The send side sets a timer upon transmission of the data stream. If the sender does not receive an acknowledgment when the timer expires, the packet is re-sent. After all data is sent, the connection is closed. The sender and receiver are comparable to a client and server system.

IP Addresses

For two systems to communicate, each must have a unique network address. Think of it this way: If everyone on your street had the same address, wouldn't people have a hard time finding you? Like a house, a Linux system must be uniquely identifiable to the rest of the network.

For TCP/IP-oriented networks, the address is called the *IP address*. TCP/IP uses a 32-bit address and is expressed as four octets. An example of an IP address is 198.137.240.91 (currently, the White House address). Each distinct octet has meaning—an IP address is not simply a number that is sequentially assigned. One portion of the address specifies the network address and the other portion designates the host address of the network. Using our example, the 198.137.240 portion refers to an address of a Class C network, and the 91 portion refers to the host.

If you are part of an internal network, with no connection to the Internet, you can use any network addresses to suit your needs. However, if your network participates in the Internet, your IP addresses are assigned by the Network Solutions, Inc. (NSI) at http://www.networksolutions.com. The addresses are assigned by NSI depending on the size of the network. The following list shows the distribution of network addresses:

- **Class A.** For networks 1.0.0.0 through 126.0.0.0. The first octet houses the network address. The remaining portion (24 bits) is dedicated to the host address, providing up to 16,777,214 hosts.
- **Class B.** Network addresses range from 128.0.0.0 to 191.255.0.0 and are identified in the first two octets. This provides 16,383 networks and 65,534 hosts for each network.
- **Class C.** This class is represented by the range 192.0.0.0 through 223.255.255.0. The first three octets identify the network address, supplying more than 2 million networks and 254 hosts for each.
- **Classes D, E, F.** Any addresses falling within the range 224.0.0.0 to 254.0.0.0 are for experimentation, development, or are reserved for the future.

You should know about a number of special addresses. Each of these provides for special use on the local machine and for networks at large.

If you proofread the preceding list, you know that the address 127.x.x.x is not included. This is known as the loopback address and is used as a network for the local machine. Any network traffic is simply looped back to the local machine. The loopback interface is quite useful for network diagnostics and communicating to servers located on the local machine.

Two other types of special addresses are called directed and limited broadcasts. A *directed* broadcast sends a message to all nodes within the specified network. Using our dotted address example 198.137.240.91, you would use 198.137.240.255 to broadcast a message to all nodes on the specified network. A *limited* broadcast is used to broadcast to the local network. This is achieved using 255.255.255.255 for the IP address.

Getting the "this network" address is achieved using zero for the host address portion. If we use the White House dotted address 198.137.240.91, then 198.137.240.0 is used to get this network.

To represent this node on a network, we use the all zeros (0.0.0.0) IP address. This can be useful if a node is required to discover its IP address, because many nodes do not have a static IP address. For example, to refer to node 91 on the local network, you specify 0 for the network portion and specify the node: 0.0.0.91.

If you are connecting to the Internet via your ISP (by dial-up), then your IP address will be assigned to you dynamically. In other words, the server to which you connect extracts an IP address from an available pool and assigns that to your system. In this case, you do not need to specify an IP address.

The Network Mask and Network Address

If we need to "hide" the portion of the IP address, we use a netmask. Why would you want to do this? Using a netmask allows us to get to the network portion of an IP address.

For example, to get the network portion for the IP address 198.137.240.14, we use a netmask of 255.255.255.0. The network portion is revealed by logically ANDing the IP address with the netmask address. The result is that the host portion is zeroed out of the IP address, leaving the network portion available. This allows you to subdivide an IP network into several subnetworks.

You can determine the mask to use by parsing the IP address and scanning each IP Class address range. Therefore, for a Class A IP address, the first octet identifies the network. The network portion for a Class B address constitutes the first two octets, and so on. The following illustrates this:

IP Address	Netmask	Host Address
Class A 94.122.44.12	255.0.0.0	0.122.44.12
Class B 188.202.14.18	255.255.0.0	0.0.14.18
Class C 200.180.28.14	255.255.255.0	0.0.0.14

Name Server Address

The domain name system (DNS) is responsible for mapping (or converting) host names to Internet addresses. This is important because the majority of us use a pseudonym instead of the actual IP address of a host. For example, it is easier to remember (and type) www.whitehouse.gov instead of the 198.137.240.91 dotted address to get the White House Web site.

Your network administrator can supply you with the address of the name server(s) used on your network. If you use a dial-up service to access the Internet, your ISP can supply you with the name server addresses.

Gateway Address

A computer that resides on two networks is called a gateway. The gateway's responsibility is to transport packets between the two disparate networks.

Consult with your system administrator if you require a gateway address. If you are using loopback, a gateway address is not required.

Hardware Requirements

To plug your Linux machine into a TCP/IP network (utilizing ethernet), you will require an ethernet card. The following is a partial list of the more common cards that Linux supports:

- 3Com—EtherLink 3c503, 3c503/16, 3c507, and 3c509
- Novell—NE1000, NE2000, NE1500, and NE2100
- Western Digital—WD80x3 series of cards

You can find a comprehensive list in the Hardware HOWTO. In addition, you can find more information concerning Ethernet and Linux in the Ethernet HOWTO.

As mentioned previously, you should refer to the Ethernet and Hardware HOWTOs because a wealth of information concerning network cards is available. Equally important are the sections that deal with suboptimal network cards. A number of cards will work with Linux, but in the end, you will experience erratic behavior or suffer poor performance. For example, supposed NE1000 and NE2000 clones will give you grief. If you are shopping for a card, refer to the Linux documentation before finalizing your purchase.

At a minimum, Linux can be set up for networking sans networking hardware. This is easily achieved using what is known as *loopback* mode. Quite simply, this is a network connection that is looped back to itself. A number of Linux programs require loopback.

The Serial Line Internet Protocol (SLIP) and Point-to-Point Protocol (PPP) are supported by Linux to provide dial-up network connectivity. If you are using Linux at home and have an ISP, for example, you can use SLIP or PPP with your modem to gain access to the Internet. For more detailed information, refer to Chapter 13, "Dial-Up Networking Services: SLIP and PPP."

Linux also supports other types of network cards, such as ARCnet and token ring. Additionally, other network protocols are supported besides TCP/IP, including IPX and AppleTalk. In this chapter, we address only Ethernet and TCP/IP.

Configuring TCP/IP

In this section, we begin the journey of TCP/IP configuration. You will need to know several items, such as your machine's hostname and IP address. Beginning with the next section, a brief overview is provided, which is followed by a section dedicated to the TCP/IP configuration files.

TCP/IP Configuration Overview

To quickly summarize, you need to know the following when configuring TCP/IP:

- **Hostname.** Your machine's name on the network.
- **IP address.** Your machine's dotted address on the network.
- **Broadcast address.** The address to use when sending messages to all nodes on a network.
- **Domain name.** The name of the domain to which your machine belongs.
- **Netmask.** The network mask used for your network.
- **Name server address.** The address of the name server(s) that service your network.
- **Gateway address.** The address of the gateway machine, if applicable.

If you are dialing to an ISP for access to the Internet, your ISP can supply you with the required documents detailing this information.

Although network configuration is rather easy, it requires some forethought. You must visit and modify a number of configuration files. IP addresses must be exact, and pseudonyms must be verbatim.

Most Linux distributions provide a network configuration application (text or graphical mode) to ease maintenance of the configuration files. This could be the install or setup program. For Slackware, you use Setup; for SuSE Linux, you use YaST. The following lists some distributions and their associated configuration program:

Distribution	Tool
Caldera OpenLinux 2.2	Lisa
Red Hat 6.0	Linuxconf
Slackware 4.0	Setup or manual file editing
SuSE Linux 6.1	YaST

Configuration Files

This section provides an overview of the network configuration files. We provide an overview of each file, describing its responsibility. Examples are provided and discussed.

We assume that the networking software is installed on your Linux system. If not, you must install it first before continuing here.

Most Linux distributions store the network configuration files in the /etc directory. It is possible that your distribution stores its TCP/IP configurations files elsewhere. If you do not find the files in /etc, you might try /usr/etc or /usr/etc/inet. At the very least, you could locate the files with the find command. Check the find man page for details. If you cannot find any of the files, you probably don't have network support installed.

> **Fictitious Names and Addresses**
> This chapter provides sample network configuration files. Unless otherwise noted, the names and IP addresses used are fictitious.

The /etc/HOSTNAME (/etc/hostname) File

The /etc/HOSTNAME file is used to house the complete name of the host. This file should contain only one line and that line must be the machine's name.

A number of applications read from this file, especially network-oriented applications. System startup scripts might also read the /etc/HOSTNAME file. Note that in some distributions, the filename is in lowercase, as in /etc/hostname.

Most distributions provide the hostname command to display the current name of the system. The syntax for the command is as follows:

```
hostname [option] [nameOfHost]
```

You can specify several options, such as displaying the NIS domain name or the IP addresses of the host. A user with proper privileges can change the hostname by supplying the nameOfHost argument. The following shows two sample dialogs for the hostname command:

```
devel24 $ hostname
devel24.cartoon.com
...
stimpy $ hostname
stimpy
stimpy $
```

Some versions of hostname print the machine name only, without the domain name. The second dialog in the previous example shows this. If this is the case, consult the man page for printing the complete name.

The /etc/hosts File

This file contains IP address entries and their associated hostname—each entry on its own line. The entries found within the /etc/hosts file are, as a rule, dedicated to the local machine. Other entries may be in this file, such as the gateway and the name server addresses. The hostname-to-IP address mapping (for name resolution) should be found only in the name server's files, not in the /etc/hosts file.

The following is a sample of an /etc/hosts file. Two entries are listed. The first is the loopback entry, and the second is the actual machine name and IP address.

```
# hosts        This file describes a number of hostname-to-address
#              mappings for the TCP/IP subsystem. It is mostly
#              used at boot time, when no name servers are running.
#              On small systems, this file can be used instead of a
#              "named" name server.
# Syntax:
# IP-Address   Full-Qualified-Hostname  Short-Hostname
127.0.0.1     localhost
253.10.123.33 stimpy.cartoon.com       stimpy
```

If you are not on an actual network and are using loopback only, you should see only the localhost entry. Each entry (line) can have three column items separated by a space or tab. The first column item is the IP address of the host. The second item is the fully qualified name of the host. The third column item is a short name (or nickname) for the host—usually just the hostname portion of the fully qualified name. You can place comments into the file and begin with the # character. You can have more than one nickname listed.

If your machine does not participate on a network or if your machine is a standalone with dial-up access, the sole entry will be localhost.

If no name server is on your network, this file should contain an entry for every machine on the network you want to access. The following sample demonstrates the use of /etc/hosts for resolving machines on a local network:

```
# hosts  This file describes a number of
#  hostname-to-address mappings for the TCP/IP
#  subsystem. It is mostly used at boot time,
#  when no name servers are running. On small
#  systems, this file can be used instead of a
#  "named" name server. Syntax:
# IP-Address   Full-Qualified-Hostname  Short-Hostname
127.0.0.1     localhost
253.10.123.33 stimpy.cartoon.com    stimpy    michaelj
253.10.123.35 ren.cartoon.com                 ren       billj
253.10.123.22 daffy.cartoon.com               daffy     paulc
253.10.123.25 bugs.cartoon.com                bugs      franks
253.10.123.31 coyote.cartoon.com    coyote    jimmyw
```

Notice that each entry has multiple nicknames, ensuring that you can refer to each machine by different names.

> **Setup /etc/hosts for Boot Up**
> If you are configuring a machine to act as a DNS server, the /etc/hosts file should contain entries for vital machines that the DNS must access. This is because during boot up, DNS functionality is unavailable.

Like the other network configuration files, /etc/hosts is editable with any ASCII-oriented editor.

The /etc/networks File

The /etc/networks file is functionally similar to the /etc/hosts file. The /etc/networks file contains a list of network names and their respective IP addresses. This allows remote networks to be referenced by name instead of by an IP address.

The route command uses this file. An entry must exist for every network that must be connected. If you recall, the IP address is divided into two portions. The first portion designates the network, and the second designates the host on the network. When specifying the IP address in the /etc/networks file, only the network portion (of the IP address) is required. You can zero out the node portion of the address. The following shows the syntax for the route command:

```
route [option] [command]
```

The route command is used to manually alter the routing tables used by the system. This is usually handled by the routed command. Check the route man page for more details.

In the sample /etc/networks file that follows, notice that the first column entry is the pseudonym and the second column identifies the IP address. This contradicts the order in the /etc/hosts file.

```
# networks     This file describes a number of
# netname-to-address mappings for the TCP/IP
# subsystem. It is mostly used at boot time,
# when no name servers are running.
Loopback       127.0.0.0
Localnet       165.11.0.0
Firstnet       163.122.0.0
Secondnet      161.224.0.0
Thirdnet       165.55.0.0
# End.
```

At a minimum, the localnet and loopback entries should exist, even if you are connecting to an ISP only through a dial-up connection.

The /etc/host.conf File

This file designates how hostnames are to be resolved. The file must contain two lines, as shown in the following example:

```
# /etc/host.conf
# Automatically generated on Fri Jul 9 13:46:19
# /etc/localtime 1999.
# PLEASE DO NOT EDIT THIS FILE!
# Change variables (NAME SERVER + YP_SERVER) in /etc/rc.config instead.
#
order hosts bind
multi on
```

The order entry designates the sequence in which the search must take place. In this example, the resolver will first check the /etc/hosts file for names to look up; if unsuccessful, the resolver will go to the name server for name resolution.

The multi entry, if on, determines whether a machine listed in /etc/hosts can have multiple IP addresses. The argument to multi can be on or off.

The /etc/resolv.conf File

The /etc/resolv.conf file ordinarily contains two entries. One entry specifies the IP address of the name server (the name is not identified). The second entry specifies the domain name, preceded by the *domain* tag. A third entry can be specified, *search*, and identifies the domain to search. This file is used by the resolver library.

```
domain cartoon.com
search cartoon.com
name server 216.168.74.2
name server 216.168.64.2
```

As shown in the example, you can specify more than one name server. Each name server entry must be on a line by itself. Any of the name servers can be queried to resolve the name.

The rc Files

The rc files, otherwise known as *run command* files, are located in the /etc/rc.d directory. As the system boots up, the init program reads various files in the /etc/rc.d directory. Several daemon processes are started at this time, such as cron and sendmail. These processes are identified in files found in the /etc/rc.d directory. In addition to process startup, the TCP/IP network is configured using files found in /etc/rc.d and, potentially, in its subdirectories.

Linux distributions that follow the System V Init boot process use the /etc/rc.d structure. BSD Init stores the boot files in the /etc directory. System V Init is (slowly) being adopted as the standard method for boot up of Linux systems. Newer distributions of Linux reflect the System V functionality.

The directory structure of /etc/rc.d consists of various subdirectories, such as /etc/rc.d/init.d, /etc/rc.d/rc0.d, /etc/rc.d/rc1.d, /etc/rc.d/rc2.d, and so on. Each directory contains scripts to start up or shut down a specific runlevel.

Within the /etc/rc.d/init.d directory are a number of scripts. Each script file is responsible for starting up a specific service, such as nfs or sendmail. In addition, script files may be used to switch to another runlevel.

The system performs several tasks at boot up. When the kernel boots up, it launches the *init* process. The init process is a program that normally resides in the /sbin directory, but can be found elsewhere. The kernel will look for init in well-known places and will run the first one found. The shell script rc.sysinit (in /etc/rc.d), is executed by init. The /etc/rc.d/rc.sysinit script performs necessary system initialization. Finally, if the rc.serial script exists, rc.sysinit will execute it.

The next thing init does is run all scripts for the current runlevel. As mentioned previously, /etc/rc.d contains subdirectories such as /etc/rc.d/init.d, /etc/rc.d/rc0.d, /etc/rc.d/rc1.d, /etc/rc.d/rc2.d, and so on. Each subdirectory corresponds to a specific runlevel. For example, /etc/rc.d/rc5.d contains the scripts necessary to bring up (or shut down) the X Windows System, and /etc/rc.d/rc3.d contains scripts to boot Linux into full multiuser mode. Finally, init runs the rc.local script found in the /etc/rc.d directory.

The /etc/inittab file contains a significant amount of information concerning boot up and shutdown. If you want to examine the details of Linux booting, check this file. The following is a sample /etc/inittab file from Red Hat:

```
# inittab       This file describes how the INIT process should set up
#               the system in a certain run-level.
#
# The run-levels used by COL are:
#   0 - halt (Do NOT set initdefault to this)
#   1 - Single-user mode (including initialization of network interfaces,
#       if you do have networking)
#   2 - Multiuser, (without NFS-Server and some such)
#       (basically the same as 3, if you do not have networking)
#   3 - Full multiuser mode
#   4 - unused
#       (should be equal to 3, for now)
```

```
#    5 - X11
#    6 - reboot (Do NOT set initdefault to this)
#
# Default run-level.
id:3:initdefault:

# System initialization.
si::sysinit:/etc/rc.d/rc.modules default
bw::bootwait:/etc/rc.d/rc.boot

# What to do in single-user mode.
~1:S:wait:/etc/rc.d/rc 1
~~:S:wait:/sbin/sulogin

l0:0:wait:/etc/rc.d/rc 0
l1:1:wait:/etc/rc.d/rc 1
l2:2:wait:/etc/rc.d/rc 2
l3:3:wait:/etc/rc.d/rc 3
l4:4:wait:/etc/rc.d/rc 4
l5:5:wait:/etc/rc.d/rc 5
l6:6:wait:/etc/rc.d/rc 6
# Normally not reached, but fallthrough in case of emergency.
z6:6:respawn:/sbin/sulogin

# Trap CTRL-ALT-DELETE
ca:12345:ctrlaltdel:/sbin/shutdown -t3 -r now

# Action on special keypress (ALT-UpArrow).
kb::kbrequest:/bin/echo "Keyboard Request--edit /etc/inittab to let this work."

# When our UPS tells us power has failed, assume we have a few minutes
# of power left. Schedule a shutdown for 2 minutes from now.
# This does, of course, assume you have power installed and your
# UPS connected and working correctly.
pf::powerfail:/sbin/shutdown -h +5 "Power Failure; System Shutting Down"

# If battery is fading fast -- we hurry...
p1::powerfailnow:/sbin/shutdown -c 2> /dev/null
p2::powerfailnow:/sbin/shutdown -h now "Battery Low..."

# If power was restored before the shutdown kicked in, cancel it.
po:12345:powerokwait:/sbin/shutdown -c "Power Restored; Shutdown Cancelled"

# Run gettys in standard run-levels
1:12345:respawn:/sbin/getty tty1 VC linux
2:2345:respawn:/sbin/getty tty2 VC linux
3:2345:respawn:/sbin/getty tty3 VC linux
4:2345:respawn:/sbin/getty tty4 VC linux
5:2345:respawn:/sbin/getty tty5 VC linux
6:2345:respawn:/sbin/getty tty6 VC linux
# Run xdm in run-level 5
x:5:respawn:/usr/bin/X11/xdm -nodaemon
```

Regardless of the distribution, you can find the origin of the boot process in the /etc/inittab file. Open the inittab file and look for an entry that resembles one of the following:

```
si::sysinit:/etc/rc.d/rc.modules default
...or...
si::sysinit:/etc/init.d/boot
```

The entry in your inittab may look different; the previous are just two of many examples. The sysinit line identifies the script file to use for booting. This boot script file is similar to the AUTOEXEC.BAT file used by DOS. This script alone is not the sole contributor to booting the system—this script will call other scripts and programs.

The following shows two distributions and their respective configuration and boot script files:

Distribution	Configuration	Initialization
Slackware	/etc/rc.d/rc.inet1	/etc/rc.d/rc.inet2
Red Hat	/etc/rc.d/init.d/network	/etc/rc.d/rc3.d/*

Red Hat uses the System V Init directory structure to house the scripts that start up system services. With Red Hat, the actual system configuration files are in /etc/sysconfig. The files found in the subdirectories of /etc/rc.d are merely links to the files in /etc/rc.d/init.d.

Most current distributions provide a utility program to allow you to configure the network interfaces (among other system configurations). Some examples follow:

Distribution	Tool
Red Hat 6.0	Linuxconf
SuSE Linux 6.1	YaST
Caldera OpenLinux 2.2	Lisa

For casual users, you should use these utilities. If you are an up-and-coming system administrator, you will want to work manually, in addition to the tools. The following lists some distributions and their associated configuration programs:

Distribution	Configuration Program
Red Hat	/usr/bin/netcfg
Slackware	/sbin/netconfig

The rc files for the Slackware distribution follow a different organization. The Slackware rc files are executed by init (at boot up) and are found in the /etc/rc.d directory. The files rc.inet1 and rc.inet2 are used to configure

TCP/IP. The rc.init1 file configures IP addresses and routing information (among other parameters). The TCP/IP daemons are started up by way of the rc.inet2 file. The following is a sample /etc/inittab file from Slackware. Compare this to the Red Hat /etc/inittab shown previously:

```
# inittab       This file describes how the INIT process should set up
#               the system in a certain run-level.
# Version: @(#)inittab  2.04  17/05/93  MvS
#       2.10 02/10/95 PV
#       3.00 02/06/1999 PV
# Author: Miquel van Smoorenburg, <miquels@drinkel.nl.mugnet.org>
# Modified by: Patrick J. Volkerding, <volkerdi@ftp.cdrom.com>
# These are the default runlevels in Slackware:
#   0 = halt
#   1 = single-user mode
#   2 = unused (but configured the same as runlevel 3)
#   3 = multiuser mode (default Slackware runlevel)
#   4 = X11 with XDM
#   5 = unused (but configured the same as runlevel 3)
#   6 = reboot
# Default runlevel. (Do not set to 0 or 6)
id:3:initdefault:

# System initialization (runs when system boots).
si:S:sysinit:/etc/rc.d/rc.S

# Script to run when going single user (runlevel 1).
su:1S:wait:/etc/rc.d/rc.K

# Script to run when going multiuser.
rc:2345:wait:/etc/rc.d/rc.M

# What to do at the "Three Finger Salute."
ca::ctrlaltdel:/sbin/shutdown -t5 -rf now

# Runlevel 0 halts the system.
l0:0:wait:/etc/rc.d/rc.0

# Runlevel 6 reboots the system.
l6:6:wait:/etc/rc.d/rc.6

# What to do when power fails (shutdown to single user).
pf::powerfail:/sbin/shutdown -f +5 "THE POWER IS FAILING"

# If power is back before shutdown, cancel the running shutdown.
pg:0123456:powerokwait:/sbin/shutdown -c "THE POWER IS BACK"

# If power comes back in single-user mode, return to multiuser mode.
ps:S:powerokwait:/sbin/init 3

# The getties in multiuser mode on consoles and serial lines.
# NOTE NOTE NOTE adjust this to your getty or you will not be
```

continues ▶

continued

```
#  able to login !!
# Note: for 'agetty' you use linespeed, line. for 'getty_ps'
# you use line, linespeed and also use 'gettydefs'
c1:1235:respawn:/sbin/agetty 38400 tty1 linux
c2:1235:respawn:/sbin/agetty 38400 tty2 linux
c3:1235:respawn:/sbin/agetty 38400 tty3 linux
c4:1235:respawn:/sbin/agetty 38400 tty4 linux
c5:1235:respawn:/sbin/agetty 38400 tty5 linux
c6:12345:respawn:/sbin/agetty 38400 tty6 linux

# Serial lines
#s1:12345:respawn:/sbin/agetty 19200 ttyS0 vt100
#s2:12345:respawn:/sbin/agetty 19200 ttyS1 vt100

# Dialup lines
#d1:12345:respawn:/sbin/agetty -mt60 38400,19200,9600,2400,1200 ttyS0 vt100
#d2:12345:respawn:/sbin/agetty -mt60 38400,19200,9600,2400,1200 ttyS1 vt100

# Runlevel 4 used to be only for an X-window system, until we discovered
# that it throws init into a loop that keeps your load avg at least 1 all
# the time. Thus, there is now one getty opened on tty6. Hopefully no one
# will notice. ;^)
# It might not be bad to have one text console anyway, in case something
# happens to X.
x1:4:wait:/etc/rc.d/rc.4
# End of /etc/inittab
```

The Slackware distributions runs the /etc/rc.d/rc.M to go into multiuser mode.

```
#!/bin/sh
# rc.M      This file is executed by init(8) when
#           the system is being initialized for one of
#           the "multiuser" run levels (i.e.,
# Version:  @(#)/etc/rc.d/rc.M  2.02  02/26/93
# Author:   Fred N. van Kempen, <waltje@uwalt.nl.mugnet.org>
#   Heavily modified by Patrick Volkerding <volkerdi@ftp.cdrom.com>
# Tell the viewers what's going to happen...
echo "Going multiuser..."

# Screen blanks after 15 minutes idle time.
/bin/setterm -blank 15

# If there's no /etc/HOSTNAME, fall back on this default:
if [ ! -r /etc/HOSTNAME ]; then
 echo "darkstar.example.net" > /etc/HOSTNAME
fi
# Set the hostname.  This might not work correctly if TCP/IP is not
# compiled in the kernel.
/bin/hostname `cat /etc/HOSTNAME | cut -f1 -d .`

# Initialize the NET subsystem.
if [ -x /etc/rc.d/rc.inet1 ]; then
```

```
    . /etc/rc.d/rc.inet1
    . /etc/rc.d/rc.inet2
  else
    if [ -x /usr/sbin/syslogd ]; then
      /usr/sbin/syslogd
      sleep 1 # Prevents a race condition with SMP kernels
      /usr/sbin/klogd
    fi
    if [ -x /usr/sbin/lpd ]; then
      /usr/sbin/lpd
    fi
fi
```

You will notice that the system checks for the existence of the /etc/rc.d/rc/inet1 script file. If the script file exists, it is executed. Additionally, the /etc/rc.d/rc/inet2 script file is executed. The /etc/rc.d/rc/inet1 initializes important network parameters for the system, whereas the /etc/rc.d/rc/inet2 script launches network daemons. The following is a sample /etc/rc.d/rc.init1 file:

```
#! /bin/sh
# rc.inet1    This shell script boots up the base INET system.
# Version:    @(#)/etc/rc.d/rc.inet1    1.01    05/27/93
HOSTNAME=`cat /etc/HOSTNAME`
# Attach the loopback device.
/sbin/ifconfig lo 127.0.0.1
/sbin/route add -net 127.0.0.0 netmask 255.0.0.0 lo

# IF YOU HAVE AN ETHERNET CONNECTION, use these lines below
# to configure the eth0 interface. If you're using only loopback
# or SLIP, don't include the rest of the lines in this file.

# Edit for your setup.
IPADDR="127.0.0.1"        # REPLACE with YOUR IP address!
NETMASK="255.255.255.0"       # REPLACE with YOUR netmask!
NETWORK="127.0.0.0"    # REPLACE with YOUR network address!
BROADCAST="127.0.0.255"       # REPLACE with YOUR broadcast address, if you
                              # have one. If not, leave blank and edit below.
GATEWAY=""    # REPLACE with YOUR gateway address!

# Uncomment the line below to configure your ethernet card.
/sbin/ifconfig eth0 ${IPADDR} broadcast ${BROADCAST} netmask ${NETMASK}

# If the line above is uncommented, the code below can also be uncommented.
# It sees if the ethernet was properly initialized, and gives the admin some
# hints about what to do if it wasn't.
if [ ! $? = 0 ]; then
  cat << END
Your ethernet card was not initialized properly. Here are some reasons why this
may have happened, and the solutions:
1. Your kernel does not contain support for your card. Including all the
   network drivers in a Linux kernel can make it too large to even boot, and
```

continues ▸

continued

```
        sometimes including extra drivers can cause system hangs. To support your
        ethernet, either edit /etc/rc.d/rc.modules to load the support at boottime,
        or compile and install a kernel that contains support.
  2. You don't have an ethernet card, in which case you should comment out this
        section of /etc/rc.d/rc.inet1. (Unless you don't mind seeing this error...)
END
fi
# Older kernel versions need this to set up the eth0 routing table:
KVERSION=2.2
if [ "$KVERSION" = "1.0" -o "$KVERSION" = "1.1" \
 -o "$KVERSION" = "1.2" -o "$KVERSION" = "2.0" -o "$KVERSION" = "" ]; then
 /sbin/route add -net ${NETWORK} netmask ${NETMASK} eth0
fi
# Uncomment this to set up your gateway route:
if [ ! "$GATEWAY" = "" ]; then
 /sbin/route add default gw ${GATEWAY} netmask 0.0.0.0 metric 1
fi
# End of rc.inet1
```

The important entries here are IPADDR, NETMASK, NETWORK, BROADCAST, and GATEWAY. You will need to supply the appropriate values for these entries. Your system administrator will have the values required for your network.

The following is a partial listing for the /etc/rc.d/rc.init2 file:

```
#!/bin/sh
# rc.inet2     This shell script boots up the entire INET system.
#  Note, that when this script is used to also fire
#  up any important remote NFS disks (like the /usr
#  distribution), care must be taken to actually
#  have all the needed binaries online _now_ ...
# Author:     Fred N. van Kempen, <waltje@uwalt.nl.mugnet.org>
# Modified for Slackware by Patrick Volkerding <volkerdi@slackware.com>
# Some constants:
NET="/usr/sbin"
IN_SERV="lpd"
LPSPOOL="/var/spool/lpd"

# If we see IPv4 packet forwarding support in the kernel, we will turn it on.
# This was the default for 2.0.x kernels, but with recent kernels it must be
# activated through a file in /proc. IPv4 packet forwarding support is
# required if you plan to use your Linux machine as a router or firewall.
# If you don't want your Linux machine to forward packets, change the 1 below
# to a 0.
IPV4_FORWARD=1
if [ -f /proc/sys/net/ipv4/ip_forward ]; then
  if [ "$IPV4_FORWARD" = "1" ]; then
    echo "Activating IPv4 packet forwarding..."
    echo 1 > /proc/sys/net/ipv4/ip_forward
  else
    echo "Disabling IPv4 packet forwarding..."
    echo 0 > /proc/sys/net/ipv4/ip_forward
  fi
```

```
fi
...
# The 'echo' below will put a carriage return at the end
# of the list of started servers.
echo
# Done!
```

The rc.inet1 script configures the basic network interface to include your IP and network address and routing table information. The path of a datagram packet is determined by information contained in the routing table. The packet is examined for the destination IP address and is compared to entries in the routing table. When a match is found, the packet is forwarded on to the destination machine (which may not be the ultimate destination). On small networks, the routes can be defined statically. For larger networks, dynamic routing is employed. The ifconfig and route programs are used to configure the network interface and the routing table, respectively. The ifconfig program is used to configure a network device interface. Quite simply, it associates an IP address with an interface. The syntax for ifconfig is as follows:

```
ifconfig [interface address-family parameters addresses]
```

You will find an ifconfig entry in the /etc/rc.d/rc.inet1 file shown previously:

```
/sbin/ifconfig lo 127.0.0.1
```

This line configures the loopback interface with the specified IP address. A few lines down in the file, you will see the following line:

```
/sbin/ifconfig eth0 ${IPADDR} broadcast ${BROADCAST} netmask ${NETMASK}
```

This line configures the interface (eth0) associated with the ethernet card in your machine. Don't forget, you must supply values for the IPADDR, NETMASK, NETWORK, BROADCAST, and GATEWAY variables.

You will also find references to route in the /etc/rc.d/rc.inet1 file, such as the following:

```
if [ ! "$GATEWAY" = "" ]; then
  /sbin/route add default gw ${GATEWAY} netmask 0.0.0.0 metric 1
fi
```

The TCP/IP command, route, is used to dynamically manipulate the routing tables. The syntax for route is:

```
route [option] [command]
```

Two commands can be specified to route: add and del. The add command to route will add a route to the routing table. Conversely, del is used to remove a route from the routing table. If you execute the route command without any arguments, the routing table is printed. Here's a snippet from the /etc/rc.d/rc.inet1 file, showing route in action:

```
# Attach the loopback device.
/sbin/ifconfig lo 127.0.0.1
/sbin/route add -net 127.0.0.0 netmask 255.0.0.0 lo
```

In this example, the route is executed with the command add. The IP address and netmask are associated with the loopback device and are added to the routing table. The -net argument specifies that the address is a network address, not a host address. The following is a minimal /etc/rc.d/rc.init1 file and should work. Be sure to edit the appropriate entries:

```
#! /bin/sh
HOSTNAME=`cat /etc/HOSTNAME`
# Attach the loopback device.
/sbin/ifconfig lo 127.0.0.1
/sbin/route add -net 127.0.0.0 netmask 255.0.0.0 lo
# Edit for your setup.
IPADDR="127.0.0.1"          # REPLACE with YOUR IP address!
NETMASK="255.255.255.0"     # REPLACE with YOUR netmask!
NETWORK="127.0.0.0"         # REPLACE with YOUR network address!
BROADCAST="127.0.0.255"     # REPLACE with YOUR broadcast address, if you
                            # have one. If not, leave blank and edit below.
GATEWAY=""          # REPLACE with YOUR gateway address!

# Uncomment the line below to configure your ethernet card.
/sbin/ifconfig eth0 ${IPADDR} broadcast ${BROADCAST} netmask ${NETMASK}
/sbin/route add -net ${NETWORK} netmask ${NETMASK} eth0
# End of rc.inet1
```

As mentioned previously, the /etc/rc.d/rc.inet2 script fires up various daemon servers that TCP/IP uses. Check the /etc/rc.d/rc.inet2 file for the following lines:

```
# Start the INET SuperServer:
if [ -f ${NET}/inetd ]; then
  echo -n " inetd"
  ${NET}/inetd
else
  echo
  echo "WARNING:  ${NET}/inetd not found."
  echo -n "Continuing daemon loading: "
fi
```

Your script may not look exactly like this example, but what is important is that inetd is started. inetd is a TCP/IP daemon that listens to various ports for incoming requests for connections. When a request arrives, inetd services the request by spawning the appropriate server. An example might be a remote FTP request; `inetd` will spawn the ftpd daemon to handle the request. In a pinch, the following (minimal) `/etc/rc.d/rc.inet2` file should work:

```
#!/bin/sh
# Some constants:
NET="/usr/sbin"

# Start the SYSLOGD/KLOGD daemons:
if [ -f ${NET}/syslogd ]; then
  echo -n " syslogd"
  ${NET}/syslogd
  sleep 1 # prevent syslogd/klogd race condition on SMP kernels
  echo -n " klogd"
  ${NET}/klogd
fi

# Start the INET SuperServer:
if [ -f ${NET}/inetd ]; then
  echo -n " inetd"
  ${NET}/inetd
else
  echo
  echo "WARNING: ${NET}/inetd not found."
  echo -n "Continuing daemon loading: "
fi

# # Start the NAMED/BIND name server:
# if [ -f ${NET}/named ]; then
#   echo -n " named"
#   ${NET}/named -u daemon -g daemon
# fi

# Start the ROUTEd server:
if [ -f ${NET}/routed ]; then
  echo -n " routed"
  ${NET}/routed -g -s
fi
# end
```

Note that lines associated with the `named` daemon are commented out. If you need its services, be sure to uncomment the appropriate lines.

Testing the Network

You will need to reboot Linux after the network is configured. When the system is up and running, you can use the `netstat` and `ping` commands to examine various aspects of your TCP/IP network.

Most system administrators turn to the netstat command when troubleshooting a network system. The netstat command provides a wealth of information. Of course, you can use netstat just to check the status of the network—its use is not restricted to troubleshooting. The following is the syntax for the netstat command:

netstat [*options*]

There are a number of options to netstat, such as displaying the routing table and listing TCP socket connections. The following shows a sample dialog with the netstat command. All the following examples are from a machine that is connected to the Internet via PPP using a dial-up connection:

```
stimpy $ netstat -t
Active Internet connections (w/o servers)
Proto Recv-Q Send-Q Local Address          Foreign Address         State
tcp        1      0 slip-32-101-245-24:1076 206.132.58.226:www     CLOSE_WAIT
tcp        0      0 slip-32-101-245-24:1075 216.32.5.210:www       CLOSE
tcp        1      0 slip-32-101-245-24:1073 206.132.58.226:www     CLOSE_WAIT
tcp        1      0 slip-32-101-245-24:1071 206.132.58.226:www     CLOSE_WAIT
```

The -t option to netstat displays TCP socket information, both connected and listening.

```
netstat -r
Kernel IP routing table
Destination     Gateway         Genmask         Flags MSS Window  irtt Iface
32.97.113.138   *               255.255.255.255 UH      0 0          0 ppp0
loopback        *               255.0.0.0       U       0 0          0 lo
default         32.97.113.138   0.0.0.0         UG      0 0          0 ppp0
```

The -r option to netstat shows the kernel routing table. This example shows the system connected to the Internet using PPP.

```
netstat -i
Kernel Interface table
Iface  MTU Met   RX-OK RX-ERR RX-DRP RX-OVR   TX-OK TX-ERR TX-DRP TX-OVR Flg
lo    3924   0      24      0      0      0      24      0      0      0 LRU
ppp0  1500   0     630      5      0      0     634      0      0      0 OPRU
```

To show statistics for network interfaces, use the -i option to netstat. The previous dialog demonstrates this.

```
netstat
Active Internet connections (w/o servers)
Proto Recv-Q Send-Q Local Address          Foreign Address         State
tcp        1      0 slip-32-101-245-24:1067 my2.netscape.com:www   CLOSE_WAIT
tcp        1      0 slip-32-101-245-24:1066 my2.netscape.com:www   CLOSE_WAIT
Active UNIX domain sockets (w/o servers)
```

```
Proto RefCnt Flags      Type       State         I-Node Path
unix  1      [ ]        STREAM     CONNECTED     1944   @000000ac
...
unix  1      [ ]        STREAM     CONNECTED     2011   /tmp/.X11-unix/X0
unix  1      [ ]        STREAM     CONNECTED     1952   /dev/log
...
unix  1      [ ]        STREAM     CONNECTED     37     /dev/log
```

The `netstat` command, without any options given, shows the active network connections.

```
netstat -o
Active Internet connections (w/o servers)
Proto Recv-Q Send-Q Local Address           Foreign Address        State       Timer
tcp      1      0  slip-32-101-245-24:1076  206.132.58.226:www     CLOSE_WAIT  off
tcp      0      0  slip-32-101-245-24:1075  216.32.5.210:www       CLOSE       on2
tcp      1      0  slip-32-101-245-24:1073  206.132.58.226:www     CLOSE_WAIT  off
tcp      1      0  slip-32-101-245-24:1071  206.132.58.226:www     CLOSE_WAIT  off
Active UNIX domain sockets (w/o servers)
Proto RefCnt Flags      Type       State         I-Node Path
unix  1      [ ]        STREAM     CONNECTED     1944   @000000ac
...
unix  1      [ ]        STREAM     CONNECTED     2011   /tmp/.X11-unix/X0
unix  1      [ ]        STREAM     CONNECTED     1952   /dev/log
...
unix  1      [ ]        STREAM     CONNECTED     37     /dev/log
```

The `-o` option expands the default `netstat` output to include timer state expiration.

The `ping` command is used to confirm that a host is online. Use `ping` sparingly, however, because it can impose a load on the network. Most system administrators of large networks hide `ping` from the average user, reserving its use for the administrator. The following sample dialogs demonstrate the use of the `ping` command.

Example 1:

```
stimpy $ ping -c 10 localhost
PING localhost (127.0.0.1): 56 data bytes
64 bytes from 127.0.0.1: icmp_seq=0 ttl=255 time=0.401 ms
64 bytes from 127.0.0.1: icmp_seq=1 ttl=255 time=0.247 ms
64 bytes from 127.0.0.1: icmp_seq=2 ttl=255 time=0.242 ms
64 bytes from 127.0.0.1: icmp_seq=3 ttl=255 time=0.254 ms
64 bytes from 127.0.0.1: icmp_seq=4 ttl=255 time=0.256 ms
64 bytes from 127.0.0.1: icmp_seq=5 ttl=255 time=0.257 ms
64 bytes from 127.0.0.1: icmp_seq=6 ttl=255 time=0.257 ms
64 bytes from 127.0.0.1: icmp_seq=7 ttl=255 time=0.267 ms
64 bytes from 127.0.0.1: icmp_seq=8 ttl=255 time=0.248 ms
64 bytes from 127.0.0.1: icmp_seq=9 ttl=255 time=0.253 ms
--- localhost ping statistics ---
10 packets transmitted, 10 packets received, 0% packet loss
round-trip min/avg/max = 0.242/0.268/0.401 ms
```

Example 2:
```
stimpy $ ping -c 10 www.internic.org
ping: unknown host: www.internic.org
```

Example 3:
```
stimpy $ ping -c 10 www.internic.net
64 bytes from 198.41.0.6: icmp_seq=0 ttl=255 time=210 ms
64 bytes from 198.41.0.6: icmp_seq=1 ttl=255 time=180 ms
64 bytes from 198.41.0.6: icmp_seq=2 ttl=255 time=240 ms
64 bytes from 198.41.0.6: icmp_seq=3 ttl=255 time=250 ms
64 bytes from 198.41.0.6: icmp_seq=4 ttl=255 time=291 ms
64 bytes from 198.41.0.6: icmp_seq=5 ttl=255 time=190 ms
64 bytes from 198.41.0.6: icmp_seq=6 ttl=255 time=261 ms
64 bytes from 198.41.0.6: icmp_seq=7 ttl=255 time=180 ms
64 bytes from 198.41.0.6: icmp_seq=8 ttl=255 time=201 ms
64 bytes from 198.41.0.6: icmp_seq=9 ttl=255 time=200 ms
--- localhost ping statistics ---
10 packets transmitted, 10 packets received, 0% packet loss
round-trip min/avg/max = 180.0/220.3/291.0 ms
```

In the first sample, we are "pinging" the local machine addresses as localhost. You should always get a positive response; if not, you do not have loopback set up for localhost (maybe you've given the local machine another name).

In the second sample, we attempt to ping the host www.internic.org, for which we receive an unknown host message from the ping command. This message could mean that the host really does not exist. If the site does exist, it could be that name resolution has failed for one reason or another.

In the third sample, we ping the host named www.internic.net. This query proves to be successful, as shown by the response packets.

Summary

In this chapter, we covered the TCP and IP protocols, which provide the basic mechanism to the remainder of the TCP/IP protocol suite. TCP/IP is a four-layer network model, consisting of application, transport, network, and link. In addition, TCP/IP is not just one protocol, but many. The IP protocol is connectionless and unreliable, whereas TCP is connection oriented, reliable, and guarantees packet delivery.

You discovered that IP addresses consist of two parts—the network address and the host address—and are specified as four octets. The number of octets that make up the network address is dependent on the Class rating of the IP address.

The netmask is used to retrieve the host address portion from an IP address.

The name server address designates the DNS server, responsible for mapping host names to Internet address. The gateway address defines a machine that is used to transport packets between two networks.

We discussed TCP/IP configuration, discussing both ethernet and dial-up connections. The various configuration files are shown and explained. We also know that these files and their locations vary among Linux distributions. The important ones to remember are `/etc/HOSTNAME`, `/etc/hosts`, `/etc/networks`, `/etc/host.conf`, `/etc/resolv.conf`, and the rc files. The first file to examine is `/etc/inittab` because this file directs all booting operations. From there, you can drill down the other networking scripts.

Lastly, we looked at two tools, `netstat` and `ping`, that can be used to troubleshoot and obtain the status of a network.

7

Hardware Configuration

HARDWARE UNDER LINUX IS A MUCH-DISCUSSED TOPIC. The most popular question I am asked is, "Will Linux run on my hardware?." This is a very broad question. You cannot refer to your computer as one piece of hardware, because it is composed of many hardware components. You must think about each individual hardware component, determine if it is supported, and assess how it fits into the overall picture.

This chapter discusses various hardware topics, ranging from the mouse to the video card.

Overview

Years ago, Linux enjoyed very limited hardware support. This was due in part to the narrow scope of hardware to choose from. For example, the two-button mouse was the de facto standard for a pointing device. Video hardware consisted of a VGA (and Super-VGA) video card and supporting monitor. Keyboards were limited to 83- and 101-key keyboards. Popular hard drives used the IDE interface. Modems came in external and internal non-operating-system-specific versions. The hardware list nowadays, though, is vast, proprietary, and diverse.

Motherboards come in all shapes and sizes, consisting of both proprietary and "open" chip sets. The are a number of styles, such as ISA, MCA, and PCI.

Video card offerings are incredibly diverse and proprietary. This one area seems to be the most difficult to marry with Linux. At a minimum, Linux works with any video card running in text mode. The difficult part is when you switch to graphics mode to use a graphical windowing system (XFree86).

The two-button mouse is not the only popular pointing device in use. There are trackballs, touch pads, pen pads, writing pads, and joysticks, to name a few.

Keyboards come in a variety of styles, such as 83-key, 128-key, "natural," DVORAK, Internet, and others. The Internet-style keyboard is in the new generation of keyboards that are mainly targeted at specific operating systems. These keyboards have dedicated buttons to launch your browser, email program, CD controls, and so on.

Hard drives are now available in various interfaces. There are IDE, EIDE, SCSI, ATA, Ultra-ATA, and others. And it is not just the drive you have to consider; the controller is an important consideration also.

Modems are following the same path as keyboards—they are available in versions that are operating-system-specific. This makes communicating with the device more difficult from other operating systems such as Linux and DOS.

Many machines come with sound systems that are more powerful and sophisticated than many home music systems. This makes sound support an important consideration for most users. Fortunately, the standard seems to be SoundBlaster, which most sound cards support.

Many other hardware devices are as important as the devices just discussed, such as printers and plotters, scanners, removable drives, CD-ROMs and CD-writers (or burners), tape drives, and many more.

The following sections discuss some of the more popular hardware in use today.

Hard Drives

This is one area where Linux enjoys robust support of hardware. Linux supports most hard drive interface standards, such as MFM, RLL, IDE, EIDE, ESDI, and SCSI.

If you're upgrading your system with a newer hard disk, be sure to use a hardware solution. If your system BIOS has a 2GB limit and you want to add a larger hard drive, be sure to use (add) a controller with an onboard BIOS. Many hard drives come with software drivers to support hard disks beyond 2GB, but these drivers can be used with only specific operating systems.

MFM and RLL Interface

Linux supports standard MFM and RLL controllers. These interfaces have not been offered in years, but they exist in older machines on which Linux can run.

If your system utilizes one of these controllers, be sure to use the ext2fs filesystem. Additionally, be sure that the "block checking" option is set when formatting the disk.

IDE and EIDE Interfaces

Both the IDE and Enhanced IDE (EIDE) interfaces are supported. You can have up to two IDE interfaces, with two devices on each interface.

You can also use ESDI controllers emulating the ST-506 interface. Older 8-bit XT controllers will also work.

Ultra-ATA Controllers

Most Ultra-ATA 33 and 66 controllers are supported. These controllers are commonplace among the newer systems.

This is the controller of choice for users wanting to upgrade their 2GB-limit computers. For example, you can install most Ultra-ATA controllers to support drives over 2GB. These controllers will coexist with the machine's built-in IDE controller. These controllers are also backward-compatible with (E)IDE drive types.

Unfortunately, some of these controllers do not support ATAPI CD-ROM drives on their interface, so you will have to utilize an existing IDE interface to use this type of CD-ROM drive.

SCSI Controllers

When shopping for a SCSI controller, be sure you read the fine print. You might think you are getting a good deal, but the SCSI controller you just purchased might interface only to a CD-ROM drive. You are better off using an (E)IDE interface and drive(s).

Your best bet is to find one of the Adaptec SCSI controllers, because most of them are supported. Many other fine SCSI controllers are also supported:

- Adaptec: AVA-1502E, AVA-1505, AVA-1515, AVA-1825, AHA-1510, AHA-152x, AHA-154x, AHA-174x, AHA-274x, AHA-274xT, AHA-284x, AHA-2910B, AHA-2920, AHA-2920C, AHA-2930(U/U2), AHA-2940, AHA-2944D, AHA-2950, AHA-3940, AHA-3950, AHA-3985

Chapter 7 Hardware Configuration

- Always: IN2000
- AMD: AM53C974
- AMI: Fast Disk
- BusLogic: FlashPoint, BT-920, BT-932, BT-950, BT-952
- Compaq: Smart Array 2
- DPT: PM2001, PM2012A
- DPT: Smartcache/SmartRAID Plus, III, and IV
- DTC: 3180, 3280, 329x
- Future Domain: TMC-16x0, TMC-3260, TMC-8xx, TMC-950, TMC-1800, TMC-18C50, TMC-18C30, TMC-36C70
- Initio: INI-9090U, INI-9100, INI-9200, INI-9400, INI-9520, INI-A100, INIC-950
- Iomega: PPA3 parallel port SCSI Host Bus Adapter
- Media Vision: Pro Audio Spectrum 16 SCSI
- Mylex: A Series: BT-742A, BT-542B; C Series: BT-946C, BT-956C, BT-956CD, BT-445, BT-747C, BT-757C, BT-757CD, BT-545C, BT-540CF; S Series: BT-445S, BT-747S, BT-747D, BT-757S, BT-757D, BT-545S, BT-542D, BT-742A, BT-542B; W Series: BT-948, BT-958, BT-958D
- NCR: 5380 cards, 53C400, 53C406a, 53C7x0, 53C810, 53C815, 53C820, 53C825, 53C860, 53C875, 53C895
- Qlogic: FASXXX and FASXX card family; IQ-PCI, IQ-PCI-10, IQ-PCI-D
- Quantum: ISA-200S, ISA-250MG
- Seagate: ST-01 and ST-02
- SIIG: Ultrawide SCSI Pro
- SoundBlaster: 16 SCSI-2
- Tekram: DC-390, DC-390
- Trantor: T128, T128, T228
- UltraStor: 14F, 24F, 34F
- Western Digital: WD7000

Some known controllers are not supported:

- Adaptec: AHA 2940UW Pro, AAA-13x RAID Adapter, AAA-113x Raid Port Cards, AIC-7810
- NCR chip 53C710
- Most non-Adaptec DTC boards

Modems

All external modems connected to a standard serial port should work under Linux. Also, most (non-"Wintel") internal modems utilizing a standard serial interface should work.

Be very cautious and read the fine print if you purchase an internal modem. If the box says something like "Designed specifically for the Windows *xx* operating system," move on to the next modem. These modems are designed to be used with drivers and software that will run only under those operating systems. You will have difficulty getting one of these modems to operate properly under Linux.

If you must have a fax modem, be sure that the software provided can be run under Linux. The fax software must be used to drive these devices. The efax program available for Linux can be used with Class I and Class II fax modems. You should always choose at least a Class II fax modem.

The Aztech MDP3858 56.6 modem is reportedly unsupported, so be cautious if you contemplate purchasing this modem.

As mentioned previously, most every external modem with a serial interface will work under Linux. You might spend a few extra dollars (to pay for the case), but it is well worth the cost to avoid the headaches inflicted by internal modems. One nice feature of external modems are status lights, which provide feedback about the modem. Additionally, if your modem becomes locked up or operates erratically, you can reset it by cycling the power. An internal modem gets its power from the computer, so a reset would involve cycling the computer's power.

Be sure to check out the later section "Serial Ports" for more information.

Mouse

Most two- and three-button mice are supported. The following is a list of mice that are supported by Linux:

- Microsoft: Serial mouse, busmouse
- Mouse Systems: Serial mouse

- Logitech: Mouseman serial mouse, serial mouse, busmouse
- ATI: XL Inport busmouse
- C&T: 82C710
- Almost any PS/2-interface mouse

Alpha and beta drivers are available for some of the newer mice, but they are not listed here because they tend to cause erratic behavior.

You should be able to use the touch-pad-type devices, as long as they support a mouse protocol.

Most Logitech mice implement the Microsoft mouse protocol, so they are supported. You can also emulate three-button actions, even if the mouse has only two buttons.

Peripheral Computer Interface (PCI)

The PC has seen many bus architectures over the years. Personally, I have owned or used machines employing these various architectures.

Back in the PC's early days, the architecture was ISA, as either 8- or 16-bit, and running at 8 Mhz. Some machines are still available with this architecture. They are known for being inexpensive, yet very slow. The good news is that many cards are still available for ISA.

Next we saw the Micro Channel Architecture (MCA), which was introduced by Big Blue (IBM). MCA (16- and 32-bit) was a good architecture found on IBM PS/2 machines, but it never achieved mass consumption. Expansion cards were always hard to find, as they are today. If you need to find an expansion card for one of these machines, you will have to attend a "computer swap meet."

EISA is another architecture introduced during the MCA era. It offers a 32-bit path and is rather expensive to support (expansion card support). Its design was marketed to the server market rather than to the desktop user. As with the MCA, you will have a hard time finding expansion cards for an EISA-enabled machine.

The VESA Local Bus (VLB) is a 32-bit bus based on the 486 architecture. This architecture is relatively inexpensive, and expansion card support is good. Be cautious of early machines with VLB, because erratic behavior at higher bus speeds is commonplace.

The current standard is the PCI Local Bus, which offers 32-bit support (64-bit support will arrive soon). PCI is inexpensive and fast, and it enjoys a vast array of expansion card support. An advantage of the PCI architecture is that it is not dependent on the installed processor.

Video Cards

It was not too long ago that Linux offered limited support for video. Text mode has always been supported, because most video adapters and monitors offered a least common denominator for text. The challenge came when running in graphics mode—specifically, running the XFree86 windowing system. XFree86 servers were limited in their support for high-resolution output. When you could get XFree86 to run, memory leaks were commonplace, or the video would crash or lock up. You had to spend a lot of time tweaking your XF86Config file, and you had to be intimately familiar with the capabilities of your monitor and video card, such as horizontal and vertical sync rates.

Many video cards are fully supported, and support for other cards is being added on a monthly basis. Many video cards are supported at the chip set level. For example, many cards utilizing the S3 chip set are supported, such as ELSA Winner 1000 Pro and 2000 Pro, and Number Nine GXE64 and GXE64Pro. Other cards from Diamond, Orchid, and STB (among others) are also fully supported. The (current) S3 Server supports these chip sets: 732, 764, 765, 775, 785, 801, 805, 864, 868, 911, 924, 928, 964, 968, and M65.

The Tseng chip sets—ET3000, ET4000, ET4000/W32, and ET6000—are supported by XFree86. Also, support for the accelerated features of the ET4000/W32, W32i, W32p, and ET6000 is provided by the SVGA driver.

This section could go on and on about all the various incarnations of chip set and video card combinations (not to mention monitor settings). A good place to turn for this information is the /usr/X11R6/lib/X11/doc directory. In this directory, you will find many important files. Here is a dump of the directory under SuSE (6.3) Linux:

```
-rw-r--r--   1 root     root        63218 Dec 23  1996 AccelCards
-rw-r--r--   1 root     root         9596 Jun 25  1999 BUILD
-rw-r--r--   1 root     root         8266 Jun 25  1999 COPYRIGHT
-rw-r--r--   1 root     root        21859 Dec 23  1996 Devices
-rw-r--r--   1 root     root        48786 Jul 31  1997 Monitors
-rw-r--r--   1 root     root        25202 Jun 25  1999 QuickStart.doc
-rw-r--r--   1 root     root        34745 Aug 17  1999 README
-rw-r--r--   1 root     root         3528 Aug 17  1999 README.3DLabs
-rw-r--r--   1 root     root        23311 Jun 25  1999 README.Config
-rw-r--r--   1 root     root         1731 Jun 25  1999 README.DECtga
-rw-r--r--   1 root     root         4188 Oct 18  1996 README.DGA
-rw-r--r--   1 root     root         3011 Jun 25  1999 README.I128
-r--r--r--   1 root     root         6470 Nov  6 08:55 README.LinkKit
-rw-r--r--   1 root     root         6500 Jun 25  1999 README.Linux
-rw-r--r--   1 root     root         7063 Jun 25  1999 README.MGA
lrwxrwxrwx   1 root     root           11 Jan  8 11:36 README.Mach32 -> READ.Mach32
```

continues ▶

Chapter 7 Hardware Configuration

continued

```
lrwxrwxrwx   1 root     root           11 Jan  8 11:36 README.Mach64 -> READ.Mach64
-rw-r--r--   1 root     root         2315 Jun 25  1999 README.NVIDIA
-rw-r--r--   1 root     root         8006 Aug 18  1999 README.Oak
-rw-r--r--   1 root     root        17469 Jun 25  1999 README.P9000
-rw-r--r--   1 root     root         2173 Nov  6 08:57 README.Rage128
-rw-r--r--   1 root     root        28405 Jun 25  1999 README.S3
-rw-r--r--   1 root     root        12064 Aug 17  1999 README.S3V
-rw-r--r--   1 root     root         8300 Jun 25  1999 README.SiS
-rw-r--r--   1 root     root         3391 Jun 25  1999 README.Video7
-rw-r--r--   1 root     root         9760 Jun 25  1999 README.W32
-rw-r--r--   1 root     root        10285 Jun 25  1999 README.WstDig
-rw-r--r--   1 root     root        26390 Jun 25  1999 README.agx
-rw-r--r--   1 root     root         2132 Jun 25  1999 README.apm
-rw-r--r--   1 root     root        10196 Jun 25  1999 README.ark
-rw-r--r--   1 root     root        25555 Jul  5  1999 README.ati
-rw-r--r--   1 root     root        38784 Jun 25  1999 README.chips
-rw-r--r--   1 root     root        43450 Jun 25  1999 README.cirrus
-rw-r--r--   1 root     root         3808 Jun 25  1999 README.clkprog
-rw-r--r--   1 root     root         2707 Jun 25  1999 README.cyrix
-rw-r--r--   1 root     root         5538 Jun 25  1999 README.epson
-rw-r--r--   1 root     root         3532 Jun 25  1999 README.i740
-rw-r--r--   1 root     root         2301 Nov  6 08:57 README.i810
-rw-r--r--   1 root     root        24292 Jul  5  1999 README.mouse
-rw-r--r--   1 root     root         4920 Jun 25  1999 README.neo
-rw-r--r--   1 root     root         3666 Aug 17  1999 README.rendition
-rw-r--r--   1 root     root         8184 Jun 25  1999 README.trident
-rw-r--r--   1 root     root        49035 Jun 25  1999 README.tseng
-rw-r--r--   1 root     root        21116 Aug 17  1999 RELNOTES
-rw-r--r--   1 root     root         1708 Dec 23  1996 ServersOnly
-r--r--r--   1 root     root        43725 Nov  6 08:55 VGADriver.Doc
-rw-r--r--   1 root     root        63594 Jun 25  1999 VideoModes.doc
-rw-r--r--   1 root     root         5291 Jul  5  1999 xinput
```

Numerous README files were excluded from this list to save space. The README files are available for Rage128, agx, cyrix, trident, 3DLabs, MGA, S3, apm, epson, tseng, Config, Mach32, S3V, ark, i740, DECtga, Mach64, SiS, ati, i810, DGA, NVIDIA, Video7, chips, mouse, I128, Oak, W32, cirrus, neo, LinkKit, P9000, and WstDig. I leave it to your interpretation as to which chip set the name refers to. For example, WstDig refers to the Western Digital chip sets.

You should read the README file that is appropriate for your video card. You can use the information provided to validate the settings for the XF86Config configuration file.

You should also read the Monitors file for any important information about video monitors in general. It also contains manufacturer-specific information that you can use in configuring your system.

The Devices file contains configuration settings for many popular video cards. Be sure to check here for your card. You might find your card here and not have to concern yourself with experimenting with the configuration.

You should also check out the AccelCards file, which contains important information concerning accelerated video cards.

If you are thinking of purchasing a new video card, you should narrow your search to two or three cards. Next, check the appropriate files listed in this section for each of the cards to help determine the best card to use.

XFree86 Checklist

You should have the following information ready before you attempt to configure XFree86. Be sure your documentation pertains to the hardware you are using. You can actually damage a monitor if the settings are incorrect. You should have the following information available:

- The manufacturer and model of your video card. Be sure you know the card's model name. You might even look at the card itself for validation. You should also know the graphics chip set, RAMDAC, and clock chip.
- The amount of RAM your video card has installed. Look at the card, at the card's documentation, or on the video board itself.
- Determine if the video card is VGA-compatible. Most cards these days are (unless you are running an old monochrome [single-color] card).
- Get all the specifications for the video monitor, which consists of horizontal and vertical sync rate(s). Be absolutely sure that the settings you provide are within the monitor's limits, or the monitor could be damaged.
- Determine the name, type, and protocol for your mouse.

XFree86 Configuration

Three tools are available on most distributions of Linux: xf86config, XF86Setup, and xvidtune. The first two are used to perform comprehensive configuration for the XFree86 system—they cover the mouse, video card, monitor, and so on. The xvidtune program is used to tweak the video output. Some distributions might have their own proprietary setup programs. Refer to the distribution-specific documentation for more details.

The configuration utility that has been around the longest is xf86config. It's considered the least common denominator. The xf86config utility is a text-based, line-oriented program, allowing you to get XFree86 up and running with a minimum of fuss. Granted, you do have to know a little more about your system settings, but other configuration programs might not be workable (at least initially). Personally, I can configure XFree86 and have it running in less time using xf86config than I can using the other utilities.

XF86Setup is a graphically-oriented utility for configuring XFree86. Many people prefer to use it, but there are instances in which XF86Setup will not work. If you have a nonstandard (VGA) card or an unusual video monitor, XF86Setup might not run, or the video output might be skewed and unreadable. You option then is to drop back to xf86config.

The xvidtune utility utilizes a graphical interface and is used after your XFree86 system is running. You use this program to tweak the video mode output. For example, in 800×600 mode, the image on-screen might be "off-center," so you would use xvidtune to "move" the output.

Serial Ports

The long-standing input/output port is the RS-232 port. Although newer machines are equipped with the USB port, this section addresses the RS-232 port, because it is the most widely used serial interface.

The physical connection for RS-232 utilizes either 9 or 25 pins. On the PC side, it is a male connector. Older machines exhibit the 25-pin connector, whereas newer machines offer a 9-pin connector as standard. Most machines come with two serial ports, commonly referred to as COM1 and COM2. The term "COM*x*" is heavily used in the DOS and Windows world and is a logical reference rather than an absolute name.

There is more to a serial port than just the number of pins. Other devices work in harmony to ensure reliable serial communications. One device is the Universal Asynchronous Receiver-Transmitter (UART) chip, which is responsible for the majority of the workload. The intent here is not to dissect the serial port piece by piece, but to provide a high-level overview.

The serial port's notoriety is based on modem connectivity. The word *modem* means *modulator-demodulator*. The real work done by a modem, besides maintaining a connection, is to perform analog-to-digital (and back) conversion. The modem converts the digital data to an analog signal, which is then transmitted across the wire to the receiving modem. The receiving modem then converts the analog signal back to digital form.

Many other devices can be connected to the serial port besides a modem. Devices such as printers, video terminals, mice, and other computers are just a few common devices. Although it's fairly inefficient, two computers can be *networked* using serial connections. Artisoft's LANtastic network operating system offers the serial interface as an optional network connection.

Internal modems come with their own onboard serial port, which is where a majority of conflicts arise. Most of these internal modems default the serial port to COM1 or COM2, which is what the computer's built-in serial ports use.

Serial Port Naming

The first thing we need to do is get rid of the logical naming convention of "COM*x*." We are using Linux, so we need to use the correct names.

As with every other device on a Linux system, the serial port is a device, each with a corresponding entry in the /dev directory. For example, the first serial port on a Linux system is represented by /dev/ttyS0 (zero, not the letter O), the second serial port is /dev/ttyS1, and so on. One thing to keep in mind is that the existence of a device entry in /dev does not mean that the *real* device exists. For example, /dev/ttyS0 through /dev/ttyS23 exist on my system, even though the machine has only two serial ports.

You should also keep in mind that /dev/ttyS0 does not necessarily refer to the *absolute* first serial port. It can refer to the third serial port you added using a multipurpose expansion card. The setserial command is used to associate a /dev/ttySxx file to the actual serial device. The setserial command only makes the connection; it does not set the addresses and IRQ for the serial device. This is done using jumpers on the card, through software, or using Plug-n-Play (PNP).

During installation, some Linux distributions create a /dev/modem device, which is actually a symbolic link to the actual /dev/ttySxx entry. This allows you to refer logically to the modem (serial) port as /dev/modem rather than trying to remember the real name. Also, if your mouse is a serial interface mouse, you probably will have the /dev/mouse device as a symbolic link to the appropriate serial device. If you use these symbolic names, be sure to adjust them if the actual link changes.

Serial Configuration

With serial configuration, everything starts with the hardware. You must know the addresses and IRQ settings for each of the serial ports in use on your machine. You can obtain this information via your BIOS configuration or through identification using a software program. If you are using an expansion card with serial ports, you might check the jumper settings.

Be cautious about the bootup messages displayed about serial devices—the information might not always be correct. The messages *might* be accurate, but do not depend on them to be. If you are using settings based on the startup messages and the serial device does not work, the information should be considered suspect. If you cannot see the messages (they do scroll quickly), try running the `dmesg` command after bootup. The following was cut and pasted from the output of the `dmesg` command:

```
...
Adding Swap: 34236k swap-space (priority -1)
Serial driver version 4.27 with HUB-6 MANY_PORTS MULTIPORT SHARE_IRQ enabled
ttyS00 at 0x03f8 (irq = 4) is a 16550A
ttyS01 at 0x02f8 (irq = 3) is a 16550A
...
```

In this instance, the output is correct. Although this particular machine offers PNP, it is disabled, and all devices are hard-coded (manually configured) in the BIOS. Personally, I have found that PNP causes more problems than it solves (even for operating systems that are supposed "experts" with PNP).

For IRQ settings, Linux accepts only what it is told about the serial device. Linux does not probe for IRQ values from a serial port. The following list shows the IRQ values for a normally equipped PC:

- IRQ 0: Timer channel 0
- IRQ 1: Keyboard
- IRQ 2: Cascade for controller 2
- IRQ 3: Serial port 2
- IRQ 4: Serial port 1
- IRQ 5: Parallel port 2, sound card
- IRQ 6: Floppy diskette
- IRQ 7: Parallel port 1
- IRQ 8: Real-time clock
- IRQ 9: Redirected to IRQ2
- IRQ 10: Not assigned
- IRQ 11: Not assigned
- IRQ 12: Not assigned
- IRQ 13: Math coprocessor
- IRQ 14: Hard disk controller 1
- IRQ 15: Hard disk controller 2

The serial ports normally assigned to ttyS0 and ttyS2 use IRQ 4, and ports assigned to ttyS1 and ttyS3 use IRQ 3. Although this is a rule of thumb, do not take it to heart. You can see that there are not a lot of extra IRQ slots available for use.

The following list shows the addresses normally used for the standard (four) serial ports:

- ttyS0: Address 0x3f8
- ttyS1: Address 0x2f8
- ttyS2: Address 0x3e8
- ttyS3: Address 0x2e8

You can output the contents of /proc/interrupts, as shown in the following dialog:

```
stimpy $ cat /proc/interrupts
           CPU0
    0:     5461793         XT-PIC  timer
    1:      103302         XT-PIC  keyboard
    2:           0         XT-PIC  cascade
    3:      270309         XT-PIC  serial
    8:           2         XT-PIC  rtc
   10:       76802         XT-PIC  ide0, ide2
   12:      183043         XT-PIC  PS/2 Mouse
   13:           1         XT-PIC  fpu
   15:           4         XT-PIC  ide1
  NMI:           0
stimpy $
```

As you can see, the serial device in use is utilizing IRQ 3. This output shows the IRQ values and the associated devices that are in service.

You should also check out the /etc/rc.d/serial file, which is a script file that is executed at bootup. You can discover some of the inner workings of serial detection with this file.

You can experiment with other IRQ values if you want. Just be certain that you configure the device and then configure within Linux. Stay away from IRQs 1, 6, 8, 13, and 14, because they are used by the system.

Check your distribution of Linux, because it might offer a setup utility to configure the system's serial ports. Figure 7.1 shows the menu option to configure the modem device using SuSE's YaST tool.

214 Chapter 7 Hardware Configuration

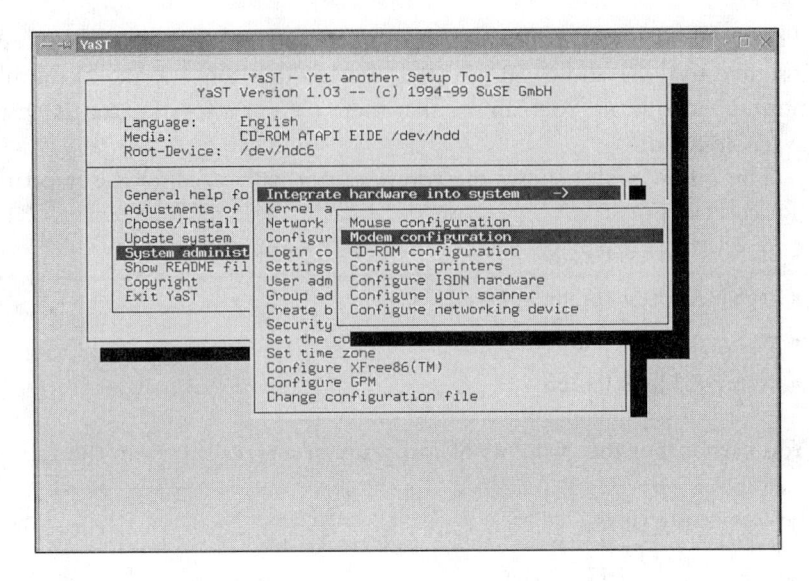

Figure 7.1 SuSE YaST tool: Configuring a modem.

Invoking this menu selection reveals the Modem Configuration screen, shown in Figure 7.2.

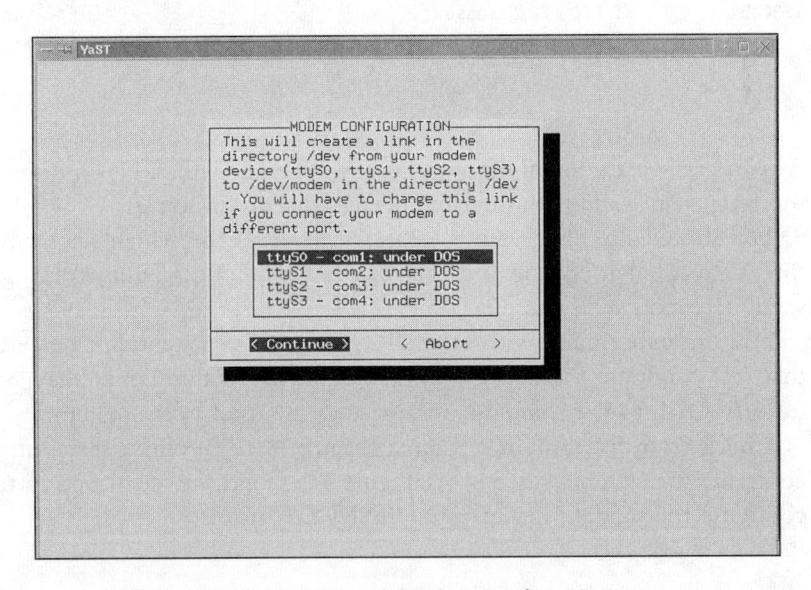

Figure 7.2 SuSE YaST tool: Modem Configuration screen.

You should note that this option is setting the modem configuration (association) to a specific serial port.

Figure 7.3 shows Red Hat's Linuxconf utility program. In this figure, the Linuxconf tool is displayed, showing the Modem Configurator tab, which allows you to assign your modem to a specific serial port.

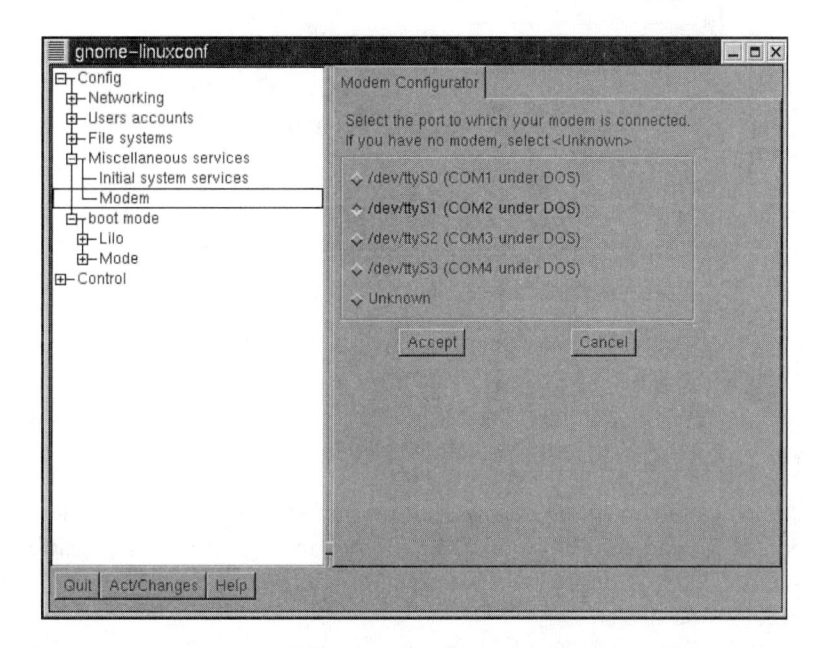

Figure 7.3 Red Hat's Linuxconf utility: Configuring a modem.

Finally, within TurboLinux, you can use the TurboHW configuration tool to assign your modem to a specified serial port, as shown in Figure 7.4.

You should note that these tools are used to set the modem configuration (association) to a specific serial port.

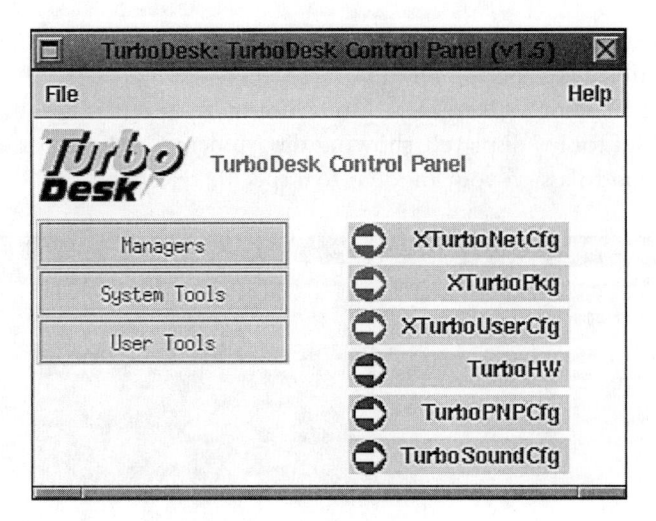

Figure 7.4 TurboDesk control panel: TurboHW option.

Sound Cards

The PC's built-in speaker is not discussed in this section. This section addresses sound card support under Linux running on the Intel platform.

Table 7.1 provides a list of sound cards that are supported by the Linux kernel sound driver.

Some of the items listed are not manufacturer-specific, but are chip set-specific. This allows you to run the sound card regardless of the manufacturer. Of course, just because your sound card uses an identified chip set does not mean it will work. You should also note that many sound card manufacturers change their cards to use different chip sets.

Table 7.1 **Sound Cards Supported by Linux**

Manufacturer	Model(s)
Acer	FX-3D
Any	AD1816- and AD1816A-based cards
ATI	Stereo F/X
Audio Excel	DSP 16

Sound Cards

Manufacturer	Model(s)
Chip sets	ESC614, ESS1688, ESS1788, ESS1868, ESS1869, ESS1887, ESS1888, ESS688, ES1370, ES1371
CMI8330	Chip set
Compaq	Deskpro XL onboard sound
Corel	Netwinder WaveArtist
Crystal	CS423x
Ensoniq	AudioPCI (ES1370), AudioPCI 97 (ES1371), SoundScape
Gallant	SC-6000, SC-6600
Gravis	Ultrasound, ACE, Max
Highscreen	Sound-Booster 32 Wave 3D
HP	Kayak
IBM	MWAVE
Interface	6850 UART MIDI Interface
Logitech	Sound Man 16, SoundMan Games, SoundMan Wave
MAD16 Pro OPTi chip sets	82C928, 82C929, 82C930, 82C924
Media Vision	Jazz16
MediaTriX	AudioTriX Pro
MiroSOUND	PCM12
Mozart	OAK OTI-601
OPTi	82C931
Orchid	SW32
Pinnacle	MultiSound
Pro Audio	Spectrum 16, Audio Studio 16
ProSonic	16
Roland	MPU-401 MIDI interface
S3	SonicVibes
SoundBlaster	1.0, 2.0, 16, 16ASP, 32, 64, AWE32, AWE64, PCI 128, Pro, Vibra16, Vibra16X
Terratec	Base 1, Base 64
TI	TM4000M notebook
Turtle Beach	Maui, Classic, Fiji, Hurricane, Monterey, Pinnacle, Tahiti, Maui, Tropez, Tropez+

continues ▶

Table 7.1 **Continued**

Manufacturer	Model(s)
VIA	Chip sets
VIDC	16-bit sound
Yamaha	OPL2, OPL3, OPL3-SA1, OPL3-SA2, OPL3-SA3, OPL3-SAx, and OPL4 sound chips

You should note that competing manufacturers claim to be SoundBlaster compatible but are not. However, if the card uses SoundBlaster chip sets, it is quite possible that the sound card will work with the SoundBlaster driver. For other cards, try the MAD16 or MSS/WSS drivers.

SoundBlaster

Some distributions of Linux utilize the sndconfig utility. You might want to use this first. If it does not work or the utility is not available, this section should be of some help.

As with any hardware device, you must set up the device itself and then tell the BIOS and operating system about the device. Some of the older (and some new) sound cards are configured using jumpers or switches. Check the documentation for details. Basically, you set the DMA, IRQ, and addresses, just to name a few. When you have established these settings, be sure to record them before installing the card.

If you want to use the PNP support provided by Linux, be cautious. Full support for PNP is not in the current version of Linux (now 2.2). Look for the isapnp utility on your system. If it isn't available, you might find it at your Linux distributor's site.

The pnpdump utility is used to probe all ISA PNP cards, dumping resource data to standard output. The dump from pnpdump is in a form expected by isapnp. However, you must uncomment the appropriate. Alternatively, you can use the -c switch to pnpdump. This switch tells pnpdump to attempt safe settings for the devices. You can redirect the output to an `isapnp.conf` file, used by the isapnp utility. Be sure to check the man page for each of these utilities for more information.

As soon as all the settings are appropriate for the sound card, ensure that the isapnp utility is executed at system startup. The following dialog shows the sequence of executions and the results:

```
stimpy $ pnpdump -c > /etc/isapnp.conf
stimpy $ isapnp /etc/isapnp.conf
IRQ 0 in use
```

Sound Cards 219

```
IRQ 1 in use
IRQ 2 in use
IRQ 3 in use
IRQ 8 in use
IRQ 10 in use
IRQ 12 in use
IRQ 13 in use
IRQ 15 in use
Board 1 has Identity c3 00 00 58 8d 45 00 8c 0e:  CTL0045 Serial No 22669 [checksum c3]
CTL0045/22669[0]{Audio           }: Ports 0x220 0x330 0x388; IRQ5 DMA1 DMA5 ---
 Enabled OK
CTL0045/22669[1]{Reserved        }: Port 0x100; --- Enabled OK
CTL0045/22669[2]{WaveTable       }: Port 0x620; --- Enabled OK
CTL0045/22669[3]{Game            }: Port 0x200; --- Enabled OK
CTL0045/22669[4]{StereoEnhance   }: Port 0x108; --- Enabled OK
stimpy $
```

If you're using a PNP card, sound support should be installed as a loadable kernel module versus compiling support into the kernel. Why? Upon bootup, the kernel is loaded before the card is configured, so the settings for the card are not known.

Next you need to check for the existence of the sndstat device file. The following dialog shows the execution of ls to check on the status:

```
stimpy $ ls -al /dev/snd*
lrwxrwxrwx   1 root     root          16 Jan  8 11:26 /dev/snd -> /proc/asound/dev
crw-rw-rw-   1 root     audio     14,  6 Nov  8 13:48 /dev/sndstat
stimpy $
```

Table 7.2 lists the sound device files found in the /dev directory.

Table 7.2 **Sound Device Files Found in /dev**

File	Description
/dev/audio	Usually linked to the device file /dev/audio0
/dev/audio0	Device-compatible with the Sun workstation, supporting only u-law encoding
/dev/audio1	Second audio device
/dev/dsp	Usually linked to the device file /dev/dsp0
/dev/dsp0	First device for digital sampling
/dev/dsp1	Second device for digital sampling
/dev/mixer	Usually linked to the device file /dev/mixer0
/dev/mixer0	First sound mixer
/dev/mixer1	Second sound mixer
/dev/music	Sequencer interface (high-level)

continues ▶

Table 7.2 **Continued**

File	Description
/dev/sequencer	MIDI, FM, and GUS access (low-level)
/dev/sequencer2	Usually linked to the device file /dev/music
/dev/midi00	First raw MIDI port
/dev/midi01	Second raw MIDI port
/dev/midi02	Third raw MIDI port
/dev/midi03	Fourth raw MIDI port
/dev/sndstat	Shows the status of the sound driver

You can load the sound kernel module manually using one of two commands: insmod or modprobe. The following dialog demonstrates the use of each:

```
stimpy $ insmod sound
stimpy $
stimpy $ modprobe -a sound
stimpy $
```

Finally, you are ready to test everything. Note that you might have to reboot your system to engage the sound support, especially if you have compiled a new kernel for sound support. The following dialog shows you how to send a sound file to devices:

```
stimpy $ cat dspfile >/dev/dsp
stimpy $ cat effects.au >/dev/audio
stimpy $
```

Alternative Sound Drivers

A very popular sound driver system is the Open Sound System (OSS) driver from 4Front Technologies. This is a commercial package that is available on some distributions of Linux (check your documentation for details). This package allows for easier configuration, plus it supports more sound cards. The downside is that you have to pay for this system. You can get an evaluation copy from http://www.opensound.com.

Another option is the Advanced Linux Sound Architecture (ALSA), which can be used to replace the kernel drivers. Here are ALSA's goals:

- Create a fully modularized sound driver that supports kerneld and kmod
- Create the ALSA Kernel API, which surpasses the current OSS API
- Maintain compatibility with most OSS/Lite binaries

- Create the ALSA Library (C, C++), which simplifies ALSA application development
- Create the ALSA Manager, an interactive configuration program for the driver

You can find the ALSA system at http://www.alsa-project.org.

Summary

In this chapter, we covered some of the more popular hardware devices that are used under Linux. Many of these devices are required, such as a hard drive or video monitor. Others are optional, such as a modem or sound card. Yet support is expected for these "optional" devices. Let's face it: In this day and age, who wants to use his or her system without an Internet connection or some music?

The chapter began with an overview of hardware devices, including some history. Next, we jumped into a discussion of hard drives, including controller cards. Some of the interfaces available are MFM, RLL, IDE, EIDE, ESDI, and SCSI. Remember, if you are upgrading your system with a newer hard disk (larger than 2GB), and your system BIOS has a 2GB limit, be sure to use a hardware solution. Choose a controller that has an onboard BIOS; stay away from software solutions provided by the hard disk manufacturers.

Next, we covered the mouse, including mice with serial and PS/2 interfaces. The next section briefly discussed PCI support.

The following section covered video output and, more specifically, support for a graphical interface. Be sure to check the information provided in the /usr/X11R6/lib/X11/doc directory. The discussion then led to three tools available on most Linux distributions: xf86config, XF86Setup, and xvidtune. The xf86config and XF86Setup utilities provide overall configuration of the XFree86 system. The xvidtune program is used to tweak the video output.

Next, we covered the serial port, discussing device naming and configuration. You should ensure that your serial port(s) are configured with the proper IRQs and addresses so that your Linux system can properly communicate with the devices. Many Linux systems provide utility programs to help with the configuration of serial devices, such as modems.

The last section provided information concerning the installation and configuration of sound cards, with a focus on the SoundBlaster family. The steps are easy, involving setting up and installing the card, using the PNP utilities (if required), identifying the sound card to Linux, and executing tests to verify the setup.

III

Linux Services

8 Email Services: SMTP and POP

9 File Transfer Protocol (FTP)

10 Domain Name Service (DNS)

11 Network Information Service (NIS)

12 Network File Service (NFS)

13 Dial-Up Networking Services: SLIP and PPP

14 UNIX-to-UNIX Copy Program (UUCP)

15 Samba: Merging Linux and Windows

16 Apache Web Server

17 Internet News Service

18 Print Services

8

Email Services: SMTP and POP

YEARS AGO, WE MIGHT HAVE WONDERED what we would do without the postal system. Even today, we might ask ourselves the same question. However, there are many other options for transporting correspondence from one place to another besides the postal system.

Without a doubt, the most popular option for transporting correspondence is the Internet email system. This chapter discusses both the client and server side of the email equation.

Overview

By far, the easiest and most efficient method for sending and receiving correspondence is by Internet email. You are not restricted to sending text only. You can attach files of all types to an email message, from a simple text file to a large binary graphics file.

The most common type of attachment is the word processing document file. Prospective candidates send their résumés via email at the request of employers and recruiters. Software and source code are also transmitted using the Internet email system. Proposals, pictures, presentations, spreadsheets, and many other file types are transferred.

The popularity of email makes sense for a number of reasons. Efficiency is a major factor in the decision about mode of transport. As soon as you send an email, within minutes (or seconds) it is with the recipient. (Of course, this is not always the case. The travel time depends on the network bandwidth and traffic.)

Another reason for the popularity of email is convenience. Like me, you might be up at 3:00 in the morning working. As soon as you are finished, you can pack up the document and send it off. There's no need to wait for some office to open its doors for business. As a recipient, you can start your email program and check incoming email at any time. If you are out sick or on vacation, your email will just pile up, waiting until you decide to read it.

This chapter explores the use of email from the client side and from the server side. In the next several sections, terminology is introduced, and then we will proceed to the use of some mail clients. Subsequent sections deal with the server end of the email picture, providing insight into the installation, configuration, and maintenance of an email server.

Comprehending Electronic Mail

In order to fully understand an electronic mail system, you need to get a grasp on the terminology and concepts. It seems that every Linux topic lives in its own world, and each world has its own glossary.

The topic of email is no different. It comes with its own glossary, some of which we will cover in the following sections. We will also look at the concepts and mechanics of electronic mail.

Mailbox

A mailbox is a repository for storage of email messages. The repository can be implemented as one large text file, a binary file, or a combination of the two. Other implementations are proprietary ISAM (Indexed Sequential Access Method) files, or a combination of directories and files.

The implementation is not necessarily important, but you should understand that a mailbox exists somewhere.

Electronic Mail Components

There is a saying that goes "A picture is worth a thousand words." With that said, Figure 8.1 is provided as a means of explaining the email process without too many words.

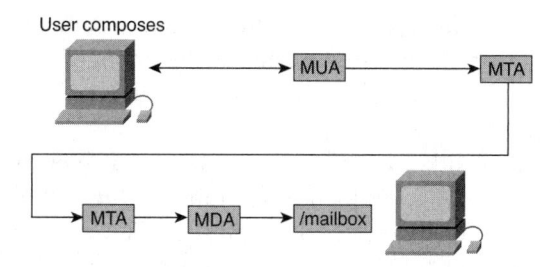

Figure 8.1 An email processing model.

As you can see, the email processing model is broken down into three components: the Mail User Agents (MUA), Mail Transfer Agents (MTA), and Mail Delivery Agents (MDA). Each of these components has a specific task. They are described in the next three sections.

In a nutshell, the user composes an email message using the MUA, and then the MUA passes the email message to the MTA. The MTA transmits the email message to the destination MTA. Finally, the destination MTA passes the email message to the MDA, and the MDA places the email message in the recipient's mailbox.

Mail User Agent (MUA)

There are three elements to the electronic mail system. The first of the three, the MUA, is the interface that a user interacts with to manipulate email messages. This is the software, or program, that you use to compose, transmit, view, print, sort, and delete email messages.

You are not restricted to using a single MUA—you are free to jump among them if you want. Be cautious about doing this, however, because most MUA mailbox formats are different. This means that you cannot point each MUA at a single mailbox and expect the MUA to read it.

Some examples of mail user agents are mailx, elm, mutt, mh, zmail, exmh, Netscape, Kmail, and others. We will discuss these programs in later sections.

Mail Transfer Agent (MTA)

The second element of an email system is the MTA. The job of the MTA is to transfer messages from one machine to another.

After you have composed a message and clicked the Send button, the MUA passes the email message to an MTA, which transmits the message to another MTA. The email message may continue this routing. The receiving MTA may transmit the email to another MTA, and so on.

An MTA does not interpret an email message for content. You do not use an MTA to compose and read email. Oddly enough, it is quite possible to transmit an email message directly to an MTA, but we will not discuss that here.

The MTA is the workhorse of the email system. The email that you create would never make it to its destination without the functionality of an MTA. Fortunately, you do not have to understand the MTA in order to use email. However, knowing that an MTA exists and knowing how it works is helpful in understanding the big picture of running an email system. The most popular mail transfer agent is *sendmail*.

Mail Delivery Agent (MDA)

The third element in an email system is the MDA. The job of the MDA is to take an email message given to it from the receiving MTA and place the email into the destination mailbox.

The separation of duties among the three components provides for a cohesive system, whereby each component has a specific and well-defined job. The MTA is concerned with transmission and protocol details; the MDA is concerned with the actual delivery of an email message to the recipient.

Email Message Header and Body

An email message is comprised of two sections: the header and the body.

The header consists of a number of items, including the author, recipient(s), date and time of creation, and so on. Here is the format for each field in the header:

```
From: Joe Schmoe js@afakemail.net
To: AnotherJoe Schmoe ajs@sillyend.net
...
```

Basically, the format is of the form *key: value* pairs. There is a key name, a colon (:), and a value. Some fields are required, and some are optional.

The body of the email message is the content of the email. It does not make much sense to send an email with a blank body. There are situations in which this is acceptable, but for the most part, you send an email message because you have something to say. The body of the email is separated from the header using a blank line.

```
Received: from mail-faker-3.strnge.net [123.123.556.454]
    by in12.weldonpew.net id 5235234.5423-3 ; Tue, 22 Feb 2000 23:23:23 +0000
Received: from unknown-111-43.sillyone.com.
    (unknown-101-88.sillyone.com [656.343.333.343] (may be forged))
    by mail12-weldonpew.net with ESMTP id FDRE4343 for <mtobler@ibm.net>;
    Tue, 22 Feb 2000 15:21:34 -0800 (PST)
```

```
From: tom_whodoneit@afakemail.net
Received: from stimpy (unknown-2-3.sillynet.net [434.545.434.233]) by
    unknown-432-43.sillyone.net  with SMTP id FDRE4343 for <mtobler@ibm.net>;
    Tue, 22 Feb 2000 15:21:33 -0800 (PST)
To: mtobler@ibm.net
Date: Tue, 22 Feb 2000 14:19:00 -0800
Subject: membership
Message-ID: <msg434343.abc-defg43.53553c33@sillynet.net>
Organization: Sillynet
MIME-Version: 1.0
Content-Type: text/plain; charset=us-ascii
Content-Transfer-Encoding: 8bit
Content-ID: <msg434343.abc-defg43.53553c33@sillynet.net>
X-Gateway: FunnGateWIse 2.0 for PewterHalt
X-Mozilla-Status: 8003
X-Mozilla-Status2: 00000000
X-UIDL: 78904-32103093.34

Hi Michael,
I would like to join HJUG. I want to attend Wednesday's
meeting. Could you tell what I have to do.

Thanks, Tom
```

A blank line always separates the headers from the body. The body contains the information the sender is trying to communicate. The "message" as most people think of it is really the body of the message.

Simple Mail Transfer Protocol (SMTP)

The MTAs communicate and transmit email messages using the SMTP protocol. SMTP is not the only protocol used. For example, the UNIX-to-UNIX Copy Program (UUCP) is also used to transfer email traffic. However, SMTP is by far the most widely used protocol to move email traffic over TCP/IP.

SMTP Envelope and Body

The SMTP protocol employs the concept of an *envelope* and *body*, similar in concept to an email's header and body. For SMTP, its body is the complete email message.

The SMTP envelope is similar to an email's header. It contains information such as the originator and recipient addresses. If there are delivery problems, SMTP can return the email to the originator and (possibly) the error condition.

MUA Programs

This section briefly describes some common MUA programs. As mentioned, an MUA is the user interface program a person uses to manipulate email messages.

mailx

The mailx program is a simple, line-oriented program developed at the University of California at Berkeley. It has a command syntax that is suggestive of ed (editor), with lines replaced by messages. mailx can be found on most distributions of Linux.

elm

If you are looking for a mail user agent that is screen-oriented, check out the elm program. It was developed at Hewlett-Packard and submitted to the public domain a number of years ago. The public-domain version of elm provides MIME support. elm is provided on most distributions of Linux.

mutt

The mutt program is a descendant of elm. It embraces many of elm's commands but is considered more powerful and configurable.

The mutt user agent can support POP3 or IMAP and provides support for MIME and PGP. You can find the mutt home page at `http://www.mutt.org`. You can find mutt on most distributions of Linux.

exmh

A Tcl/Tk mail user agent known as exmh was created by Brent Welch (previously with Xerox PARC and Sun).

Netscape

If you have the Netscape Communicator package, you will find Messenger, a full-featured MUA that provides MIME support. Messenger is also used as a Usenet newsreader client program. Messenger is described later.

Emacs rmail/smail

The Emacs editor can be used to compose, send, receive, and read email messages.

In smail mode, you can use Emacs to compose and send email messages. If you are an Emacs user, this can be an advantage because the interface is familiar.

Using rmail mode, you can utilize Emacs to read email. You probably do not want to use rmail, because it converts your inbox to a format unknown to other email user agents. You can, however, get vm, which is a mail reader designed for Emacs.

BSD mail

For a simple, line-oriented email client, you can use the mail program. This program originated from the BSD Mail program, which was designed to be used on TTY terminals. I use this one to quickly purge mail coming from cron and other system daemons. You can also use it to send email notifications from within system administration scripts.

Using MUAs

In this section, we will explore the use of two mail user agents: KDE's Kmail and Netscape's Messenger. The programs' interfaces are similar, yet the features of each are different.

KDE Kmail

The K Desktop Environment (KDE) includes a mail client called Kmail. It is a very useful email client, providing a graphical user interface. The Kmail program was developed by David Rugge and Markus Wuebben.

To execute Kmail, go to the KDE main menu and select the Internet, Mail client menu option. If this is the first time you have executed Kmail, you will see the dialog box shown in Figure 8.2.

Figure 8.2 Kmail creating the Mail mailbox.

This dialog box is merely telling you that the Mail directory could not be found and it will create it. Kmail creates the Mail directory in your home

Chapter 8 Email Services: SMTP and POP

directory. The Mail directory contains various mail files, such as inbox, outbox, sent-mail, and trash.

Figure 8.3 shows the Settings dialog box. If this is the first invocation of Kmail, this dialog box appears automatically. Otherwise, you select the File, Settings menu option.

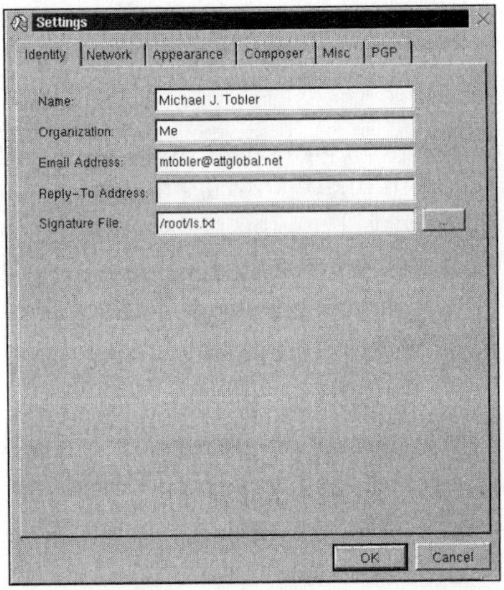

Figure 8.3 Kmail's Settings dialog box, Identity tab.

The Settings dialog box has six tabs: Identity, Network, Appearance, Composer, Misc, and PGP. At a minimum, you should visit the Identity and Network tab pages and provide the information required. The information you provide will allow you to send and receive email.

To begin sending and receiving email, you will have to change only the settings on the Identity and Network tabs.

On the Identity tab page (refer to Figure 8.3), you should provide your full name, organization (if applicable), email address, reply-to address, and signature file.

Figure 8.4 shows the Network tab page. On this tab page, you should specify the method of mail transmission, either Sendmail or SMTP. If Sendmail is selected, be sure to supply the fully-qualified path to the program. If you select SMTP, supply the name of the SMTP server you will send to. Next, you have to configure the Incoming Mail section on the Network tab. You need to have at least one account set up so that you can receive email messages. Click Add to create a new account.

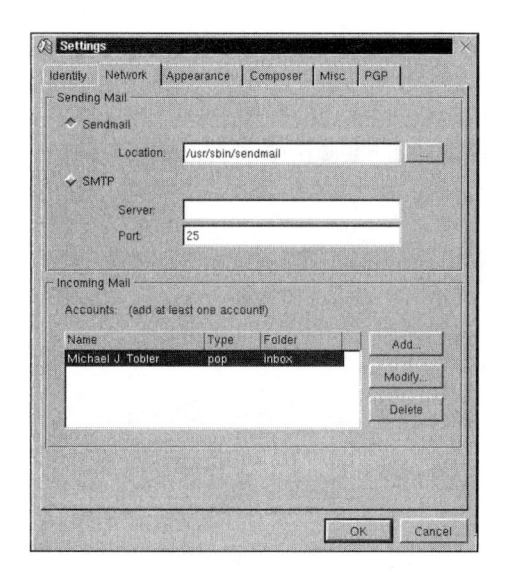

Figure 8.4 Kmail's Settings dialog box, Network tab.

The Configure Account dialog box is shown in Figure 8.5. In this dialog box, you need to supply your name, login account name, password (optional), the mail host, and the port to use. Optionally, you can select from a number of radio buttons and choose where you want to store mail. If you leave the Password field empty, whenever Kmail goes to retrieve mail, it will prompt you for your password.

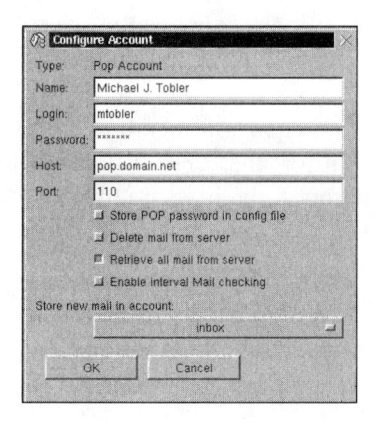

Figure 8.5 Kmail's Configure Account dialog box.

Chapter 8 Email Services: SMTP and POP

Figure 8.6 shows the Kmail Mail Reader window. It consists of three panes, a menu bar, and a toolbar. The three panes are Folders, Headers, and Message. The Folders pane is located in the upper-left portion of the Mail Reader window. The Headers pane is located in the upper center of the window, and the Message pane is located under the Headers pane.

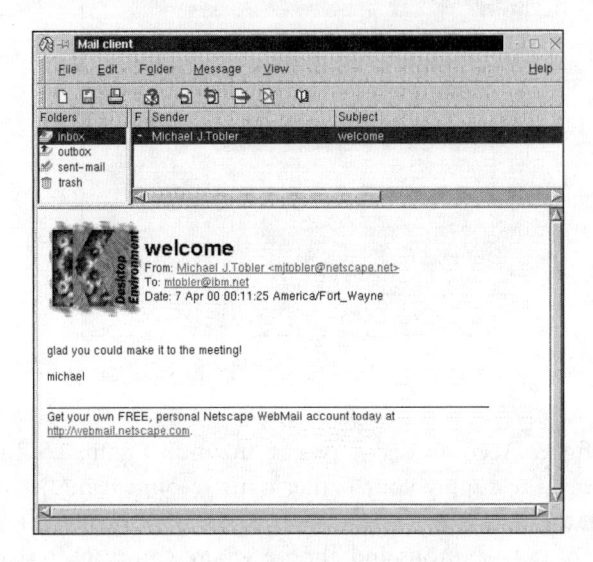

Figure 8.6 Kmail's Mail Reader window.

The Folders pane contains message folders or mailboxes. Click a folder to select it. Any messages that are contained in the folder will appear in the Headers pane.

The Headers pane shows a list of header information, such as Sender, Subject, and Date. If you click a header, the associated message is displayed in the Message pane. To sort messages, click the column to sort on.

The Message pane shows the header and body of the selected message (in the Headers pane). The message can be scrolled using the Page Up and Page Down keys, or line-by-line using the up and down arrow keys. The following list describes the keyboard keys you can use to browse messages:

- N: Next message
- P: Previous message
- +: Next unread message
- -: Previous unread message

When you are ready to receive mail, select the File, Check mail menu option. If you did not supply a password in the configuration window, you will see the Please Set Password and Username dialog box, shown in Figure 8.7.

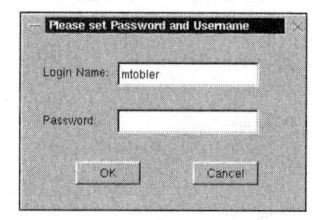

Figure 8.7 Kmail's Please set Password and Username dialog box.

This dialog box is displayed so that you can supply your password for retrieving mail from the server. Be sure to change the username if required. At the same time that this window is displayed, the Retrieving Messages window is displayed, showing the current state of message retrieval. The Retrieving Messages window is shown in Figure 8.8.

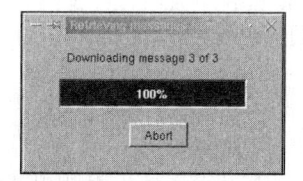

Figure 8.8 Kmail's Retrieving messages window.

This window is a status window, showing you the current progress of message retrieval. Various messages are displayed, depending on the state of retrieval. When all messages have been retrieved, the window disappears.

To compose a new email message, select the File, New Composer menu option. Figure 8.9 shows the Kmail Composer window. If you did not specify a signature file in the configuration window, Kmail will prompt you for a signature file every time you compose an email. If you are not interested in a signature file, select the File, Settings menu option. Click the Composer tab and unselect the Automatically Append Signature radio button. Finally, click the OK button to dismiss the dialog box.

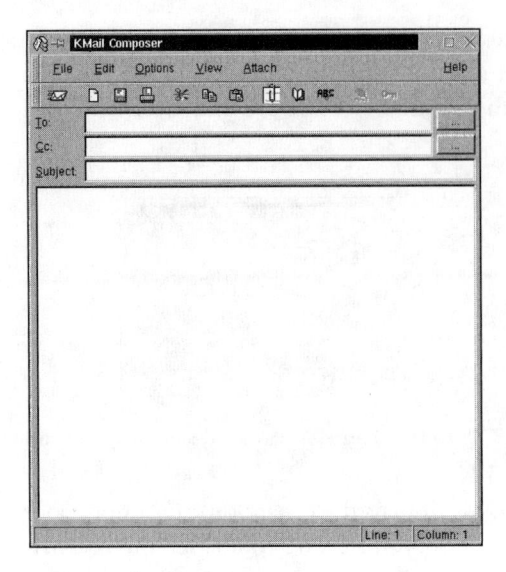

Figure 8.9 Kmail's Composer window.

You use the Kmail Composer window to compose your email and send it when finished. Fill in the appropriate fields in the Composer window to complete your email. The ellipsis (...) buttons to the right of the To: and Cc: fields invoke the address book, allowing you to select addresses from the list. When you have completed the message, click the Send icon (the envelope) on the toolbar, or select the File, Send (or Send Later) menu option.

The Kmail address book allows you to store commonly used email addresses. To invoke it, select the File, Addressbook menu option. The address book is shown in Figure 8.10.

After the file has been attached, it appears in the Attachments pane found at the bottom of the Composer window.

There are many other fine features found in the Kmail program. Be sure to select the Help menu to read about Kmail's various features.

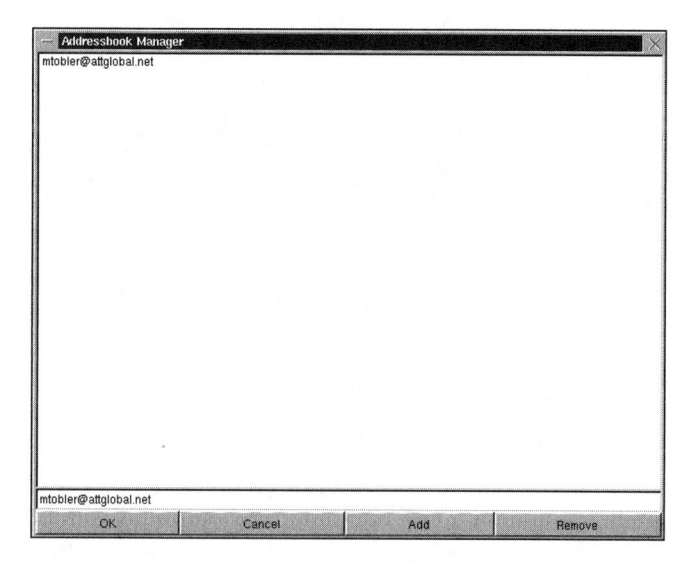

Figure 8.10 Kmail's Addressbook in the other fields.

Netscape Messenger

The Netscape Communicator package includes a mail client called Messenger. It is a very versatile and capable email client, provided through a graphical user interface. Communicator is included on most distributions of Linux. It can also be downloaded for the cost of connect time.

There are a number of ways to invoke Messenger. From a command window, you can execute Netscape with the `mail` option, as shown in the following dialog:

```
stimpy $ netscape -mail &
stimpy $
```

This starts the Messenger application, and the `&` returns a command prompt. A second option is to execute Messenger from the Communicator option on the Netscape browser pull-down menu. Other options on the Communicator menu are Composer, Navigator, and Radio, to name just a few.

A third option is to set up an icon and place it on the desktop or a graphical environment panel or make it a system menu option. The easiest way to set this up is to find the Netscape Navigator (browser) icon, make a copy of it, and then change the path (or shortcut) to read `netscape -mail` instead of `netscape`.

238   Chapter 8   Email Services: SMTP and POP

After you have invoked Messenger, you will see the application window, shown in Figure 8.11.

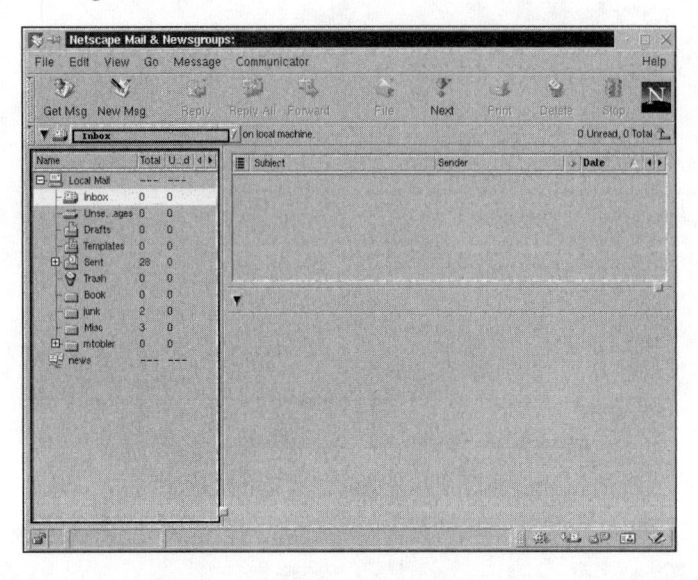

Figure 8.11   Netscape Messenger window.

The Messenger window is divided into three panes. You can customize the way you view the Messenger window using the View, Show menu option. From here, you can display or hide each of the following:

- Message toolbar
- Location toolbar
- Messages
- Folders

The Folder pane is located on the left side of the Messenger window. This pane houses a tree view, showing the hierarchy of folders. The email messages are stored in these folders. The default folders are shown in Figure 8.11. You are free to add or delete folders as you wish. However, it is not recommended that you delete any of the default folders.

The Header (or Thread) pane is located at the top right of the window. This pane is a list of messages that are found in the currently selected folder (in the Folder pane). Information shown (columns) includes Subject, Sender, and Date, among others. This list is scrollable, allowing you to browse the message headers. To read the content of a message, you select the associated message header.

The Message pane shows the message header and body (or text or content) that is currently selected in the Header pane. This pane is also scrollable, allowing you to read messages that span many lines. Figure 8.12 shows the Messenger window in action.

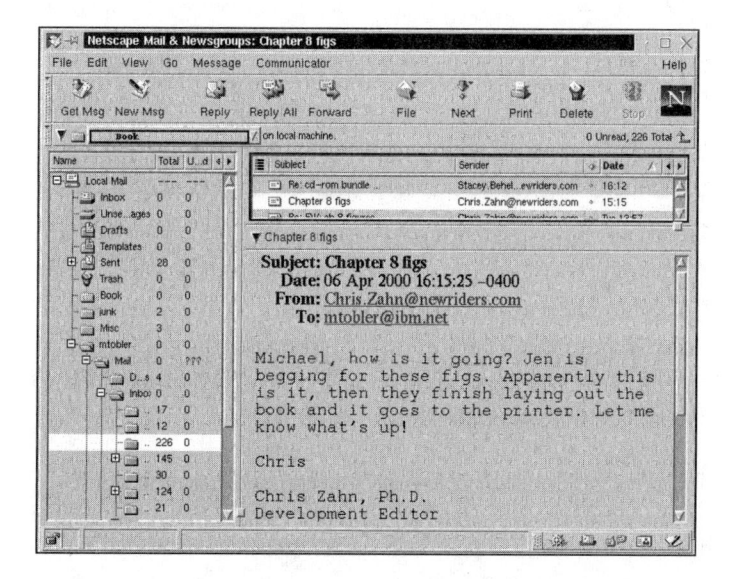

Figure 8.12 Netscape Messenger displaying an email message.

From this point, you can reply to, forward, move, delete, print, or save a mail message. In order to enable the transmitting and receiving of email, you have to adjust some entries in the Preferences dialog box. Select the Edit, Preferences menu option, and then open the Mail & Newsgroups tree view on the left side. At a minimum, you should visit the Identity and Mail Servers options. Figure 8.13 shows the Identity settings pane.

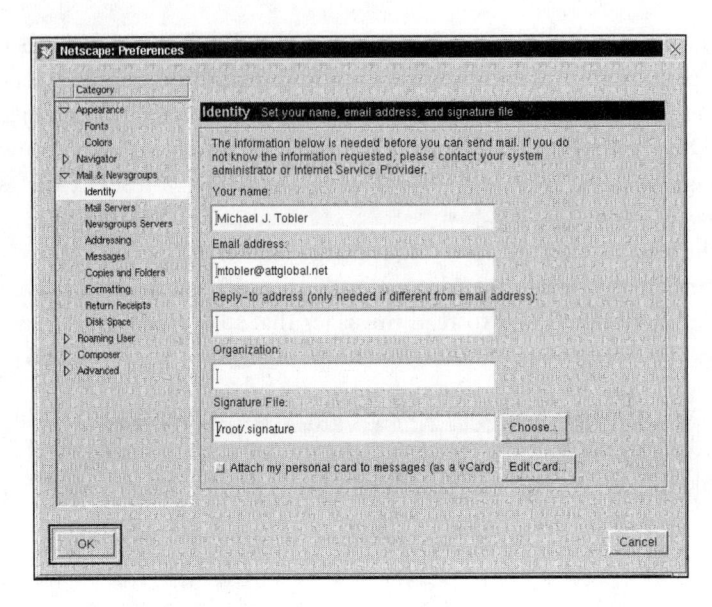

Figure 8.13 Netscape Messenger, Preferences dialog box, Identity pane.

You should supply your full name, email address, reply-to address, organization, and signature file. The first two options are the most important.

The second group of configuration options that need to be set are found in the Mail Servers pane, shown in Figure 8.14.

Figure 8.14 Netscape Messenger, Preferences dialog box, Mail Servers pane.

A number of options need to be set. The Incoming Mail Servers section requires information. In addition, you should set the appropriate data for the Outgoing Mail Server section. If you want to, you can change the location of the local mail directory. Be sure to provide the appropriate settings. Your ISP (or system administrator) can provide you with the information required.

When you are ready to receive mail, select the File, Get New Messages menu option. You will see the Netscape Password window, waiting for you to enter your password, as shown in Figure 8.15.

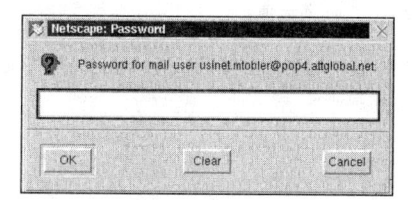

Figure 8.15 Netscape Password window.

This window is displayed so that you can supply your password for retrieving mail from the server. After you have supplied your password, a status window appears, displaying the current state of message retrieval. When all the messages have been retrieved, the window disappears.

To compose a new email message, you can click the New Msg icon on the toolbar, select the Message, New Message menu option, or press Ctrl+M. The Messenger Compose window is displayed, as shown in Figure 8.16.

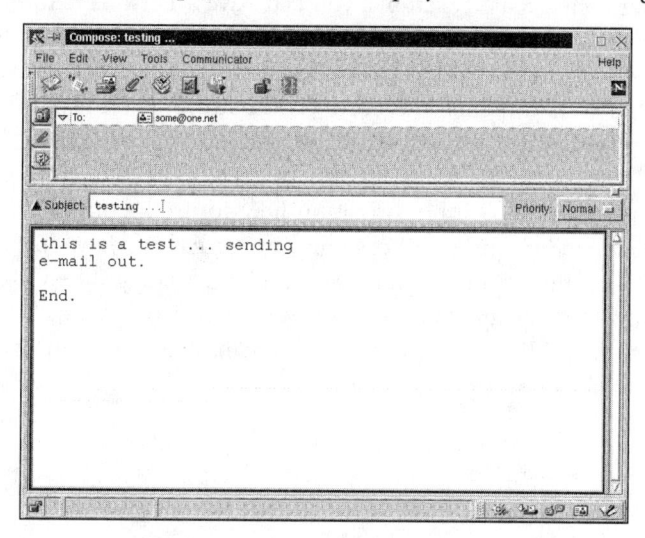

Figure 8.16 Netscape's Compose window.

Chapter 8 Email Services: SMTP and POP

You can select email addresses from the Address Book by selecting the Communicator, Address Book menu option. Figure 8.17 shows Messenger's Address Book window.

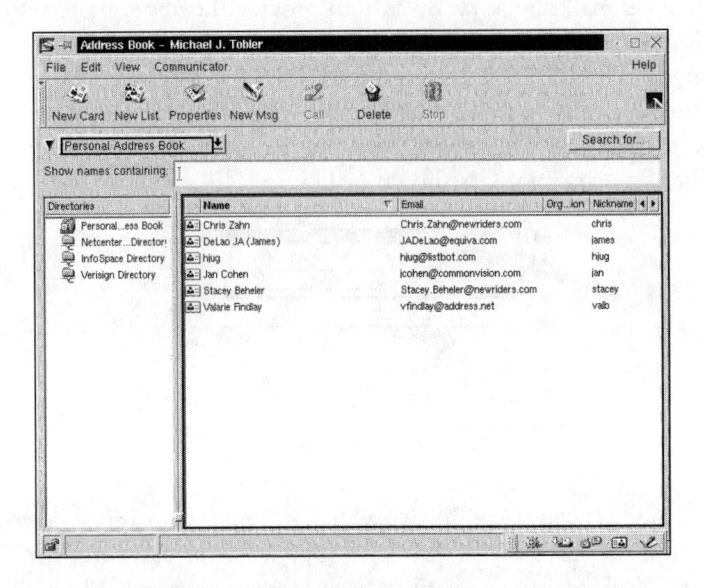

Figure 8.17 Netscape Messenger's Address Book window.

The Address Book allows you to manipulate contact information. In the left pane are various directories to help you organize your address book, such as classifying contacts. For example, you can have a Personal and Professional contact list. In the right pane are the contacts for the currently selected directory. You use the Address Book to add, edit, remove, and organize your contacts. If you click the New Card button or select the File, New Card menu option, the Netscape Card window is displayed, as shown in Figure 8.18.

You can provide useful information here for each contact, such as full name, email address, title, and organization, to name a few. There are two other tabs on this window: Contact and Conferencing. The Contact window allows you to enter information such as address; work, home, and fax phone numbers; and a URL entry. The Conferencing tab is used in conjunction with Netscape's Conference software.

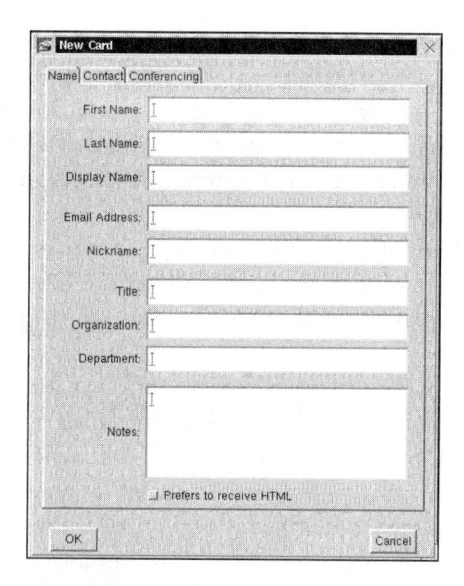

Figure 8.18 Netscape Messenger's Card window.

To attach a file to an email, simply click the tab on the far left that has a paper clip. Place the mouse in the blank area of the tabbed page, right-click, and select Attach File from the pop-up menu. A file browser window is displayed. Simply navigate to the directory, and select the file to attach. When you have the file selected, click the Attach button. The file will be listed on the Attachment tab page. You can now click the Address tab to continue adding recipients.

The third tab page allows you to request a return receipt, make the email encrypted, use uuencode, and other options.

In addition to email functionality, Netscape Messenger can be used as a Usenet newsreader. Be sure to check the online help system and documentation provided with Communicator.

The sendmail Package

If you want a true MTA muscle machine, the BSD sendmail package is what you need. It has been around for quite a while and has endured the test of time. Most Linux distributions include it on their CD-ROM, and it gets installed during the installation process.

On the flip side, sendmail has traditionally been a bear to comprehend and configure. Yet, as it has matured over time, it has become an easier package to deal with. The configuration system has improved quite a bit, hiding much of the tweaking that was required in the past. Some distributions provide a preconfigured sendmail system, allowing you to install the package "out of the box."

The sendmail system transmits a message to one or more recipients, routing the message over the necessary networks. The sendmail system does provide forwarding as required to deliver email messages to the correct destination.

As mentioned previously, sendmail is not a user interface program. Its job is to deliver email messages. If no flags are specified to sendmail, it will read from the standard input up to an end-of-file or a line consisting of only a single period. When this condition is satisfied, sendmail sends a copy of the message to the addresses identified. Local email addresses are identified in a lookup file and aliased appropriately. To prevent aliasing, precede the address with a backslash (\) character.

Table 8.1 lists the options for sendmail.

Table 8.1 **Parameters for sendmail**

Parameter	Description
-B*type*	Sets the body type to *type*. Values are 7BIT or 8BITMIME.
-ba	Uses ARPANET mode. Input lines must end with CR-LF, plus all messages must be generated with a CR-LF at the end. Additionally, the From: and Sender: fields should have the sender's name.
-bd	Runs as a daemon process, requiring Berkeley IPC. sendmail connection requests.
-bD	The same as -bd, except that it runs in the foreground.
-bh	Prints the host status database.
-bH	Purges the host status database.
-bi	Initializes the alias database.
-bm	Delivers mail normally.
-bp	Prints the queue listing.
-bs	Uses RFC821 SMTP protocol.
-bt	Tests address mode. Reads addresses and provides verbose parsing. Used for debugging configuration tables.

Parameter	Description
-bv	Verifies names only. Used for validating users and mailing lists.
-C*file*	Uses the alternative configuration file specified by *file*.
-d*X*	Sets the debugging level to that specified by *X*.
-F*fullname*	Sets the sender's name.
-f*name*	Sets the name of the *from* person (originator). This option can be used by trusted users.
-qI*substr*	Limits the processing jobs to those having *substr* of the queue ID.
-qR*substr*	Limits processed jobs to those containing *substr* of the recipients.
-qS*substr*	Limits processing jobs to those containing *substr* of the sender.
-R *return*	Sets the return amount of the message if the message bounces (is returned). The parameter can be full to return the entire message or hdrs to return the header portion.
-r*name*	An alternative and obsolete form of the -f flag.
-t	Reads the message for recipients.
-U	Initial user submission. Should be set only when called from a user agent.
-V *envid*	Sets the original envelope id. Propagates across SMTP to servers that support DSNs.
-v	Verbose mode.
-X *logfile*	Logs traffic in and out of mailers in the file specified by *logfile*.
--	Stops processing command flags.

Note that the -q option can be specified in a number of ways. Here are the two most common:

```
/usr/sbin/sendmail -q
/usr/sbin/sendmail -bd -q2h
```

The first invocation specifies that sendmail should process its queue and then exit. The second invocation tells sendmail to run as a daemon and process its queue every two hours.

sendmail Options

In addition to the parameters, a number of options may be set. As a rule, these are used only by a system administrator. An option can be set on the command line with the -o flag or the -O flag, or in the sendmail configuration file. Table 8.2 details the options.

Table 8.2 **Options for sendmail**

Option	Description
AliasFile=*file*	Uses the alternative alias file identified.
HoldExpensive	Does not initiate a connection for mailers considered expensive to connect to.
CheckpointInterval=*N*	Checks the queue file every *N* successful deliveries. The default is 10. Avoids excessive duplicate deliveries.
DeliveryMode=*x*	Sets the delivery mode to *x*: i = interactive, b = background delivery, q = queue only, and d = deferred.
ErrorMode=*x*	Sets error processing to mode *x*: m = mail back the error message, w = write back the error message, p = print errors on the terminal, q = throw away error messages, and e = do special processing for BerkNet.
SaveFromLine	Saves UNIX-style From lines at the front.
MaxHopCount=*N*	The maximum number of times a message is allowed to hop before a determination is made that the message is in a loop.
IgnoreDots	A period on a line by itself is *not* a message terminator.
SendMimeErrors	Sends error messages in MIME format.
ConnectionCacheTimeout=*timeout*	Sets the connection cache timeout.
ConnectionCacheSize=*N*	Sets the connection cache size.
LogLevel=*n*	Sets the log level.
MeToo	Sends to me if I am in an alias expansion.
CheckAliases	Validates the right side of aliases if the newaliases command is being used.
OldStyleHeaders	The message may have old-style headers.

Option	Description
QueueDirectory=*queuedir*	Identifies the queue message directory.
StatusFile=*file*	Saves statistics in the specified file.
Timeout.queuereturn=*time*	Sets the timeout on undelivered messages in the queue to the specified time.
UserDatabaseSpec=*userdatabase*	If set, *userdatabase* is queried to obtain forwarding information.
ForkEachJob	Forks each job during queue runs.
SevenBitInput	Strips messages to 7 bits.
EightBitMode=*mode*	Sets the handling of 8-bit input to 7-bit destinations to one of the following: m = convert to 7-bit MIME format, p = pass as 8 bits, and s = bounce the message.
MinQueueAge=*timeout*	Sets how long a job must sit in the queue between attempts to send it.
DefaultCharSet=*charset*	Sets the default character set used for 8-bit data.
DialDelay=*sleeptime*	Sleeps for *sleeptime* seconds and tries again if the connection fails.
NoRecipientAction=*action*	Sets the behavior if there are no recipient headers.
MaxDaemonChildren=*N*	Sets the maximum number of children that an incoming SMTP daemon allows to spawn.
ConnectionRateThrottle=*N*	Sets to *N* the maximum number of connections per second to the SMTP port.

Configuring sendmail

Current implementations of sendmail for Linux are available as a binary distribution. As mentioned previously, most distributions of Linux install sendmail during installation (if you selected the package for installation). Be sure to visit your distribution's Web site for a prebuilt package. Otherwise, you can download the sendmail (source) package, unpack it, and execute the make linux command at the command line.

As with anything else related to Linux (and UNIX), you want to get things configured with a minimum of effort and with some level of accuracy.

Obtaining sendmail

Most modern distributions of Linux include the sendmail package. Be sure to check your distribution media if sendmail is not installed. In a pinch, you can try the `which` command to see if the sendmail executable exists, as shown in the following dialog:

```
stimpy $ which sendmail
/usr/sbin/sendmail
stimpy $
```

The `which` command found the sendmail executable in the /usr/sbin directory. In contrast, the following dialog demonstrates the use of the `which` command to locate the sendmail executable. Since sendmail exists on this system, half the battle is getting the sendmail system up and running. Most of the work is in verifying the configuration files.

```
stimpy $ which sendmail
which: no sendmail in (/sbin:/usr/sbin:/usr/local/sbin//root/bin:/usr/local/bin:/usr/
bin:/usr/X11R6/bin:/bin:/usr/lib/java/bin:/var/lib/dosemu:/usr/games/bin:/usr/games:/
opt/gnome/bin:/opt/kde/bin:/usr/openwin/bin:/usr/lib/pgsql/bin:/opt/pilotsdk/bin)
stimpy $
```

In this dialog, you can see that the `which` command could not find sendmail in the usual locations. This does not mean that sendmail does not exist on your system. You can perform an exhaustive search using the `find` command, as shown in the following dialog:

```
stimpy $ find / -name sendmail -print
/etc/permissions.d/sendmail
/sbin/init.d/sendmail
/usr/doc/packages/sendmail
/usr/doc/susehilf/raw_whatis/sendmail
/usr/sbin/sendmail
/usr/lib/sendmail
/usr/share/sendmail
stimpy $
```

Checking the distributions of Linux on my system—Red Hat 6.1, SuSE 6.3, Slackware 7.0, and TurboLinux 6.0—reveals the sendmail executable in the /usr/sbin directory. The one exception, Caldera 2.3, places the sendmail executable in the /usr/libexec/sendmail directory.

If you do not have sendmail installed, and the package is not available on your distribution media, you can download the sendmail package from the ftp://ftp.sendmail.org FTP site. You will find the sendmail package available as a compressed tar file (*.Z) and a gzipped tar file (*.gz). It is recommended that you download the gzipped package, because it is smaller in size, thereby making the download quicker.

Building the sendmail Package

First of all, you need to unpack the source distribution. This is easily achieved using the `tar` command, as shown in the following dialog:

```
stimpy $ tar -xzvf sendmail.x.x.x.tar.gz
stimpy $
```

The *x.x.x* represents the version of sendmail you are using. The current version is 8.10.0, making the name of the file `sendmail.8.10.0.tar.gz`.

A number of directories are created, and all required files are extracted and placed in their appropriate directory. As with any other package to be built, you should first examine the README file(s). In a nutshell, the process is as follows:

1. Read any relevant README files. They will point you to other files that are important.
2. Create any necessary site configuration build files, as noted in `devtools/Site/README`.
3. Execute the `Build` script found in the `./sendmail` directory.
4. Change to the `cf/cf` directory, and use the `cp` command to create a new `*.mc` file from the generic `platform.mc` file provided. Finally, execute `Build` *filename*.cf.
5. Copy *filename*.cf to the `/etc/mail/sendmail.cf` directory. Finally, install the sendmail executable by executing `Build install`.

The following dialog demonstrates some of the initial operations required:

```
stimpy $ pwd
/tmp/sendmail-8.10.0
stimpy $ cd devtools/Site
stimpy $ cp ../OS/Linux ./site.Linux.m4
stimpy $ cd ../..
stimpy $ pwd
/tmp/sendmail-8.10.0
stimpy $
```

All of these commands place the Linux-specific site file in the expected directory. Next, we need to build the package, or sendmail executable. The following dialog demonstrates this:

```
stimpy $ pwd
/tmp/sendmail-8.10.0
stimpy $ ./Build
Making all in:
/tmp/sendmail-8.10.0/libsmutil
Configuration: pfx=, os=Linux, rel=2.2.13, rbase=2, rroot=2.2, arch=i586, sfx=
```

continues ▶

continued

```
Using M4=/usr/bin/m4
Creating ../obj.Linux.2.2.13.i586/libsmutil using ../devtools/OS/Linux
...
...
cc -o vacation  -L../libsmdb -L../libsmutil  vacation.o ...
groff -Tascii -man vacation.1 > vacation.0 || cp vacation.0.dist vacation.0
make[1]: Leaving directory `/tmp/sendmail-8.10.0/...
stimpy $
```

The script to execute is `Build` (shown in bold text), which is found in the base sendmail directory, shown as `sendmail-8.10.0` in this example. Building the package is quite easy because most of the hard work is handled by the `Build` script file. The `Build` message output is quite extensive, much more than what is revealed in the preceding dialog. The complete build process should take no longer than a couple of minutes.

To confirm the successful build of the sendmail binary, you can execute sendmail as shown in the following dialog:

```
stimpy $ ./sendmail -d0.1 -bt < /dev/null
Version 8.10.0
 Compiled with: LOG MATCHGECOS MIME7TO8 MIME8TO7 NAMED_BIND NETINET
                NETUNIX NEWDB QUEUE SCANF SMTP USERDB XDEBUG
/etc/mail/sendmail.cf: line 0: cannot open: No such file or directory
stimpy $
```

The next step is to create the `.cf` file for the Linux platform. This process is detailed in the following section.

Building the .cf File

For construction of the `.cf` file, the `Build` script executes the m4 macro processor, which uses an `.mc` file as input.

When the sendmail command first executes, it reads a configuration file named `sendmail.cf`, found in the `/etc/mail` directory. Proper configuration of this file can be an overwhelming task. Fortunately, there are tools that can make this task much easier. This section briefly discusses the creation of the `sendmail.cf` file.

To begin the configuration process, we will utilize the talents of the `Build` script file. The following dialog demonstrates the steps required for building the `.cf` file:

```
stimpy $ pwd
/tmp/sendmail-8.10.0
stimpy $ cd cf/cf
stimpy $ ls -al *.mc | grep linux
-rw-r--r--   1 103     103       800 Sep 24 17:48 generic-linux.mc
stimpy $ cp generic-linux.mc linux.mc
```

The sendmail Package

```
stimpy $ ./Build linux.cf
Using M4=/usr/bin/m4
rm -f linux.cf
/usr/bin/m4 ../m4/cf.m4 linux.mc > linux.cf || ( rm -f linux.cf && exit 1 )
chmod 444 linux.cf
stimpy $
```

From the base sendmail directory, we change to the cf/cf directory, which contains .mc and .cf files for a number of platforms. Next, you need to make a copy of the supplied .mc file as a local working copy. As shown in the dialog, we named it linux.mc, but you can give the file any name you want. Finally, we execute the Build script, passing the name of the target file (which is linux.cf in this dialog).

The following listing shows the contents of the generic linux.mc file used to build the linux.cf file:

```
# This is a generic configuration file for Linux
#
divert(0)dnl
VERSIONID(`$Id: generic-linux.mc,v 8.1 1999/09/24 22:48:05 gshapiro Exp $')
OSTYPE(linux)dnl
MAILER(local)dnl
MAILER(smtp)dnl
```

You must specify an OSTYPE so that platform-specific items are properly configured, such as the pathname for status files, flags required for the local mailer, and other items. Just be sure it is set to linux.

MAILER(...) defines the mailers (delivery agents) you want sendmail to support. The local mailer is always included automatically. You should be aware that the MAILER(...) declarations should occur at the end of the configuration (.mc) file. Additionally, the MAILER(smtp) entry should always precede the MAILER(uucp) entry, if applicable.

Table 8.3 lists the MAILER options.

Table 8.3 **Options for MAILER**

Option	Description
local	The local and prog mailers. You should always include these, unless you relay mail to another site.
smtp	The Simple Mail Transfer Protocol (SMTP) mailer.
uucp	The UNIX-to-UNIX Copy Program mailer.
usenet	Usenet (network news) delivery.
fax	Facsimile transmission.
pop	Post Office Protocol.
procmail	An interface to procmail.

continues ▶

Table 8.3 Continued

Option	Description
mail11	The DECnet mail11 mailer. Useful only if you have the mail11 program.
phquery	The phquery program.
cyrus	The cyrus and cyrusbb mailers.

It is truly amazing to see the outcome from the previous build process. Look again at the contents of the linux.mc file, consisting of five instructional lines. The resulting linux.cf file consumes 1,165 lines of text! The following output shows snippets from various sections of the file:

```
# temporary file mode
O TempFileMode=0600
# match recipients against GECOS field?
#O MatchGECOS=False
# maximum hop count
#O MaxHopCount=17
# location of help file
O HelpFile=/etc/mail/helpfile
...
#   Format of headers    #
##########################
H?P?Return-Path: <$g>
HReceived: $?sfrom $s $.$?_($?s$¦from $.$_)
   $.$?{auth_type}(authenticated)
   $.by $j ($v/$Z)$?r with $r$. id $i$?u
   for $u; $¦;
   $.$b
H?D?Resent-Date: $a
H?D?Date: $a
H?F?Resent-From: $?x$x <$g>$¦$g$.
H?F?From: $?x$x <$g>$¦$g$.
H?x?Full-Name: $x
# HPosted-Date: $a
# H?l?Received-Date: $b
H?M?Resent-Message-Id: <$t.$i@$j>
H?M?Message-Id: <$t.$i@$j>
...
# short circuit local delivery so forwarded email works
R$=L < @ $=w . >    $#local $: @ $1    special local names
R$+ < @ $=w . >     $#local $: $1      regular local name
...
```

Examine the last couple of lines—they look fairly cryptic. Actually, they are simple compared to some of the other rules (and definitions) found in the file.

Once the `linux.cf` file is ready, it needs to be copied to the `/etc/mail` directory. The following dialog demonstrates how to do this:

```
stimpy $ pwd
/tmp/sendmail-8.10.0/cf/cf
stimpy $ cp ./linux.cf /etc/mail/sendmail.cf
stimpy $
```

The last step is to install the new sendmail executable. If you are replacing a current installation, be sure to save the binary, just in case the new version does not work as expected. The following dialog shows how to back up the current binary and then install the newly built binary:

```
stimpy $ pwd
/tmp/sendmail-8.10.0
stimpy $ which sendmail
/usr/sbin/sendmail
stimpy $ cp /usr/sbin/sendmail /usr/sbin/sendmail.orig
stimpy $ ./Build install
Making all in:
/mnt/tool/root/root/sm/sendmail-8.10.0/libsmutil
Configuration: pfx=, os=Linux, rel=2.2.13, rbase=2, rroot=2.2, arch=i586, sfx=
Making in ../obj.Linux.2.2.13.i586/libsmutil
...
...
Making in ../obj.Linux.2.2.13.i586/mailstats
make[1]: Entering directory `/mnt/tool/root/root/sm/sendmail-8.10.0/obj.Linux.2.2.13.i586/mailstats'
install -c -o bin -g bin -m 555 mailstats /usr/sbin
stimpy $ sendmail -d0.1 -bt < /dev/null
Version 8.10.0
Compiled with: LOG MATCHGECOS MIME7TO8 MIME8TO7 NAMED_BIND
     NETINET NETUNIX NEWDB QUEUE SCANF SMTP USERDB XDEBUG

============ SYSTEM IDENTITY (after readcf) ============
     (short domain name) $w = ren
 (canonical domain name) $j = ren.stimpy.net
        (subdomain name) $m = stimpy.net
             (node name) $k = ren
========================================================

ADDRESS TEST MODE (ruleset 3 NOT automatically invoked)
Enter <ruleset> <address>
stimpy $
```

The output from the `Build` script spans many lines (about 100 on my system). Besides installing the executable, other chores are accomplished, such as the creation of directories and the installation of man pages. Notice the last command executed in the preceding dialog. We executed this in a previous dialog to test the build of the sendmail binary.

You are now ready to fire up the sendmail system.

Executing sendmail

The sendmail program is normally executed as a daemon process. The following dialog demonstrates its execution:

```
stimpy $ sendmail -bd -q1h
stimpy $ ps x | grep sendmail
 5766 ?     S    0:00 sendmail -bd -q1h
stimpy $
```

The `-bd` switch tells sendmail to execute as a daemon (background) process. The `-q1h` switch tells sendmail to check the mail queue once every hour. The `ps x ...` command shows that the sendmail process is indeed running.

Be sure to refer to Tables 8.1 and 8.2 for a description of command-line switches and options for the `sendmail` command.

Summary

This chapter covered the client and server aspects of electronic mail. An overview was provided, describing the intent and use of electronic mail.

Next, terminology was covered, including terms such as *mailbox, MTA, MUA,* and *MDA.* The basic structure of the client/server email model was described, including a figure to provide a visual perspective.

The mail user agent (MUA) is the interface that a user interacts with to manipulate email messages. The job of the mail transfer agent (MTA) is to transfer messages from one machine to another. The third component, the mail delivery agent (MDA), takes an email message given to it from the MTA and places the email in the appropriate destination mailbox.

An email message consists of a header and a body. The header contains addressing information that is used to route the message to its recipient(s). The body of the email is the textual portion, which is the content of the email.

Next we covered MUAs, the email client programs that are utilized by users to manipulate their email messages. Some well-known MUAs include elm, pine, Kmail, and Netscape Messenger, to name just a few.

The KDE Kmail MUA program was covered, including figures to visually present the tool and its use. The basic operation of the tool was covered. The Netscape Messenger MUA program was also covered, highlighting some of the tool's basic features.

Finally, we discussed the sendmail package and provided details concerning the creation and installation of the configuration file and the sendmail executable.

9

File Transfer Protocol (FTP)

As you know, TCP/IP is actually a suite of protocols. In this chapter, we take a look at one protocol, the File Transfer Protocol (FTP). FTP is one of the most widely used protocols on the Internet.

In the next section, we begin our discussion of FTP by providing an overview of FTP. In the sections that follow, we see what it takes to set up and use FTP.

FTP Overview

As mentioned previously, FTP is the most widely used protocol on the Internet. Why? Well, most of the traffic on the Internet involves the transferring of files. The World Wide Web just might catch up and pass up FTP in terms of bandwidth consumed, but until then, FTP remains the king.

FTP is available for just about every operating system. You will find it available for every flavor of UNIX and, of course, Linux. And, believe it or not, it is available for various types of Windows. Make no mistake, FTP was born under UNIX. FTP is implemented with varying degrees of user interface. The most common is the command-line interface. The easy-to-use interface is the windowed interface, providing the capabilities of drag-and-drop file transfers. Most browsers, such as Netscape Navigator, provide the capability to invoke FTP functionality through its interface.

The FTP service provides both client and server functionality. Therefore, if you want merely to upload and download files from remote sites, all you need is the client facilities—this chapter addresses those needs. Moreover, if you are ready to provide the functionality of FTP services to external users, this chapter is for you. By providing FTP services, external users will be able to connect to your site to upload and download files.

What are the capabilities of the File Transfer Protocol? Specifically, you can upload files from one computer to another, and you can do the reverse—you can download files from one machine to another. Directory facilities are also available, allowing you to create directories, change from one directory to another, remove directories, and list the contents of a directory.

File manipulation is also available, including the capability to delete a file from the remote system and to rename a file. You cannot execute programs, however, because FTP's sole mission in life is to transfer files. To use the facilities of FTP, the remote machine must provide FTP server capabilities, and the local machine must provide client FTP facilities. The FTP client initiates a connection to the FTP server, whereby the two ends negotiate the link.

Most FTP sites allow both registered and anonymous user connections. A logon sequence is required whether you are a registered user or an anonymous user. The logon sequence is the same as a Linux logon: You (or your FTP client software) provide a username and then a password. Sites allowing anonymous access allow anyone to obtain an FTP connection. This is accomplished by supplying the username anonymous and providing the email address as the password. A registered user will, as a rule, have more privileges than an anonymous user. The following dialog demonstrates a logon to a fictitious site, and then help is called up, showing a list of available FTP commands.

```
stimpy $ ftp ftp.bugs.net
Connected to ftp.bugs.net
220 ftp FTP server Wed Mar 11 13:01 CST 1999 ready.
User (ftp.bugs.net): anonymous
331 guest login ok, send complete email address for password
password: *****
230- Welcome to The Bugs FTP site
ftp>
ftp> help
Commands may be abbreviated. Commands are:
!               delete          literal         prompt          send
?               debug           ls              put             status
append          dir             mdelete         pwd             trace
ascii           disconnect      mdir            quit            type
bell            get             mget            quote           user
binary          glob            mkdir           recv            verbose
```

```
bye           hash          mls           remotehelp
cd            help          mput          rename
close         lcd           open          rmdir
ftp>
```

Not all sites offer anonymous FTP access. You will be informed of that fact during logon or when you attempt to access the FTP site. You will see a message similar to the following:

```
Login failed, User "anonymous" is unknown.
```

In the sections that follow, first we summarize the FTP options and commands and then we proceed on to the use of FTP.

FTP Commands

In this section, a listing of the FTP startup options and commands are summarized. We follow the summary with a more detailed explanation of the most commonly used options and commands.

Table 9.1 lists the options to FTP. These options may be specified at the command line or within the command interpreter.

Table 9.1 **Summary of FTP Options**

Option	Description
-v	The verbose option, which forces FTP to show every response coming from the remote server. It also reports on the transfer statistics.
-n	Keeps FTP from using the autologin feature after connecting.
-i	Turns off interactive prompting during multiple file transfers. If prompting is on, the FTP program displays the filename and asks if you want to download it.
-d	Enables debugging. See the debug entry in Table 9.2.
-g	Disables file name globbing. See the glob entry in Table 9.2.

The client host with which FTP is to communicate may be specified on the command line. If this is done, FTP immediately attempts to establish a connection to an FTP server on that host; otherwise, FTP enters its command interpreter and awaits instructions from the user. When FTP is awaiting commands from the user, the prompt ftp> is provided to the user. The commands shown in Table 9.2 are recognized by FTP:

Table 9.2 **Summary of FTP Commands**

Command	Description
![command [args]]	Invoke an interactive shell on the local machine. If there are arguments, the first is taken to be a command to execute directly, with the rest of the arguments as its arguments.
$ macro-name [args]	Invoke the macro specified. Arguments are passed to the macro.
account [passwd]	Supply a supplemental password that the remote system requires to access any resources after login. If the argument is not supplied, the user is prompted for a password.
append local-file [remote-file]	Append the local file to the file on the remote machine.
ascii	Toggle the file transfer type to ASCII.
bell	Toggle to sound a bell after each file transfer completes.
binary	Toggle the file transfer type to binary.
bye	Close the current FTP session and exit the FTP interpreter.
case	When case is enabled, the file names on the remote with letters in uppercase are written in the local directory with lowercase letters.
cd remote-directory	Change the remote machine's current working directory.
cdup	Change the remote machine's current working directory to the parent of the current working directory.
chmod mode file-name	Alter the permission of the remote file filename to mode.
close	Close the current FTP session and return to the FTP command interpreter.

FTP Commands

Command	Description
cr	Toggle carriage return stripping for any ASCII type file transfer.
delete remote-file	Delete the remote file named remote-file.
debug [debug-value]	Toggle debugging mode.
dir [remote-directory] [local-file]	List the directory remote-directory and (optionally) output the content in local-file.
disconnect	Synonym for close.
form format	Change the file transfer form to format.
get remote-file [local-file]	Transfer file remote-file and store it locally. If the local file name is not provided, it will inherit the name the way that it exists on the remote machine.
glob	Toggle the expansion of a file name for the commands mdelete, mget, and mput. If globbing is off, file name arguments are not expanded.
hash	Toggle hash-sign printing (on/off) for each data block transferred.
help [command]	Output provides information about the available commands or the meaning of command. If no argument is given, all available commands are output, otherwise descriptive text is given for command.
idle [seconds]	Set the remote server inactivity timer to seconds. If seconds is not provided, the current inactivity timer is displayed.
lcd [directory]	Change the local machine's working directory. The user's home directory is used if a directory is not specified.
ls [remote-directory] [local-file]	Print a listing of the contents of a directory on the remote machine.
macdef macro-name	Define a macro.
mdelete [remote-files]	Delete the remote-files identified.
mdir remote-files local-file	Similar to dir, except multiple remote files may be specified.
mget remote-files	Download the specified remote-files. If wildcards are given, they are expanded.

continues ▶

Table 9.2 **Continued**

Command	Description
mkdir *directory-name*	Create a directory on the remote machine.
mls *remote-files local-file*	Similar to nlist, except multiple remote files can be specified.
mode [*mode-name*]	Toggle the file transfer mode to mode-name.
modtime *file-name*	Display the last modification time for remote file-name.
mput *local-files*	Upload the files specified. If wildcards are provided, expand the names.
newer *file-name*	Get a file if the modification time on the remote system is more current than the local file.
nlist [*remote-dir*][*local-file*]	Display a file list in a directory on the remote machine. If remote-directory is not identified, the current working directory is used.
nmap [*inpattern outpattern*]	Set or unset the filename mapping mechanism.
ntrans [*inchars outchars*]]	Set or unset the character translation mechanism.
open host [*port*]	Attempt to connect to the identified host using the optional port.
prompt	Toggle interactive prompting during multiple file transfers.
proxy *ftp-command*	Invoke an FTP command on a secondary connection.
put *local-file* [*remote-file*]	Upload a file from the local machine to the remote machine.
pwd	Display the current working directory on the remote machine.
quit	Synonym for bye.
quote *arg1 arg2* ...	Send the argument list to the remote FTP server.
recv *remote-file* [*local-file*]	Synonym for get.
reget *remote-file* [*local-file*]	Performs similar to get, except if local-file exists (and is smaller), the transfer is continued from the apparent point of failure.

Command	Description
remotehelp [*command-name*]	Get help from the remote FTP server.
remotestatus [*file-name*]	Display the status of the remote machine.
rename [*from*] [*to*]	Rename the `from` file to name `to`.
reset	Purge the reply queue.
restart *marker*	Recommence the following `get` or `put` at the identified marker.
rmdir *directory-name*	Delete directory-name on remote machine.
runique	Toggle the storing of local files and use unique names.
send *local-file* [*remote-file*]	Synonym for `put`.
sendport	Toggle using `PORT` commands to establish a connection for a data transfer.
site *arg1 arg2* ...	Send the identified arguments to the remote FTP server.
size *file-name*	Display the remote file-name's size.
status	Display the current FTP status.
struct [*struct-name*]	Set structure for file transfer to `struct-name`.
sunique	Toggle remote machine file storage using unique filenames.
system	Display the operating system type on the remote machine.
tenex	Set the file transfer type to `TENEX`.
trace	Toggle packet tracing.
type [*type-name*]	Set the file transfer type to `type-name`. If `type-name` is not identified, print the type.
umask [*newmask*]	Set the remote `umask` on to `newmask`.
user *user-name* [*password*][*account*]	Identify yourself to the remote FTP server.
verbose	Toggle verbose mode—if on, all responses are displayed.
? [*command*]	Synonym for `help`.

The number of commands for FTP can seem overwhelming. Yet, if you consider the number of commands available under Linux, this list is rather small. Most users only use a handful of commands, specifically the commands that deal with uploading, downloading, and maneuvering through the directory hierarchy.

Table 9.3 lists the environment variables that FTP may use during a session.

Table 9.3 **Environment Variables Used by FTP**

Environment Variable	Description
HOME	For default location of a .netrc file, if one exists.
SHELL	For default shell used by FTP.

The usage for FTP is as follows:

```
ftp [option] [host]
```

You can specify the FTP host to connect with on the command line. The FTP program attempts to connect with the FTP server on the host identified on the command line. If you do not specify a host, the FTP program immediately goes into command mode. This allows you to submit commands interactively with the FTP program. The following dialog demonstrates using FTP with a specified hostname:

```
stimpy $ ftp ftp.bugs.net
Connected to ftp.bugs.net
220 ftp FTP server Wed Mar 11 16:22 CST 1999 ready.
User (ftp.bugs.net): anonymous
331 guest login ok, send complete email address for password
password: *****
230- Welcome to The Bugs FTP site
ftp> quit
stimpy $
```

The FTP prompt is the > character; at this point, FTP is sitting, patiently awaiting your next command.

FTP Transfer Commands

Because FTP signifies the transferring of files, we will now discuss the commands dedicated for the movement of files. In the sections that follow, we discuss each type of transfer.

File Commands for Downloading

The most common of the commands concerns the downloading of one or more files. As a rule, most people running the FTP client program are interested in getting one or more files from a remote site (or sites). The get command is used to download a single file from the remote site. The usage for get is shown here:

```
get remote-file [local-file]
```

At the FTP command prompt, you type **get** and specify the file to download as the argument. If you do not specify a filename to use locally, the remote filename is used. You can specify the filename to use locally. The file is stored in the current directory on your machine.

The second command dedicated to retrieving files from a remote system is mget. This command is used to download one or more files from the remote system to your machine. You can use wildcards with the mget command. For example, if you want to get all files with an extension of .txt, you would execute the command as shown in the following dialog:

```
ftp> mget *.txt
```

Each file found on the remote machine that matches the wildcard would be transferred to your machine.

The recv command is a synonym for the get command. The syntax for recv is as follows:

```
recv remote-file [local-file]
```

You can use either of the commands to perform a file download. Note that not every version of the FTP client will support all receive commands.

File Commands for Uploading

The opposite of downloading files, of course, is uploading files. From time to time, you will find the need to send a file or files to a remote machine. The put command is used to upload a single file to the remote site. The usage for put is shown here:

```
put local-file [remote-file]
```

The put command allows you to send a file that is stored on your machine to the remote FTP machine. If the argument remote-file is not specified, the local filename is used in naming the remote file. At the FTP command prompt, you type **put** and specify the filename to upload as the argument (to put). The following dialog demonstrates the put command:

```
ftp> put document.txt
```

The second command, mput, is dedicated to sending files from your machine to the remote system. This command is used to upload one or more files from your local machine to the remote site. You can use wildcards with the mput command. For example, if you want to transmit all files with the extension of .txt, you execute the mput command as shown in the following dialog:

```
ftp> mput *.txt
```

Each file found on your machine that matches the wildcard will be transmitted to the remote site. You might also be interested to know that send is a synonym for the put command. The syntax for send is as follows:

```
send local-file [remote-file]
```

Not every version of the FTP client program supports all the transmit commands. Some of the more primitive FTP programs will support only the minimum of commands to facilitate file transfer.

Supplemental Commands for File Transfer

In this section, we cover some of the commands that are used to supplement a file transfer. For example, you can change the file transfer mode or have FTP show the status of the transfer.

You use the status command to show the current state of the FTP session. The following dialog shows the status for an FTP session that has just been started.

```
ftp> status
Not connected.
Type: ascii; Verbose: On; Bell: Off; Prompting: On; Globbing: On
Debugging: Off; Hash mark printing: Off
ftp>
```

The following dialog shows the status of the local FTP session after connecting to a remote site.

```
ftp> status
Connected to metalab.unc.edu.
Type: binary; Verbose: On; Bell: Off; Prompting: On; Globbing: On
Debugging: Off; Hash mark printing: Off
ftp>
```

The command prompt is used as a toggle, alternately turning interactive mode on or off. During a multiple file transfer (mget or mput), a prompt is presented to the user, requesting confirmation for file transfer. The following dialog demonstrates this:

```
ftp> mget *
200 Type set to A.
mget ATAPI-FAQ? n
mget AfterStep-FAQ/AfterStep-FAQ? N
ftp>
```

This is useful if you have a number of files to download and you want to exclude a limited number.

The `hash` command is used to display the current status of a file transfer. If `hash` is toggled on, a hash mark is printed for every block transferred. Your FTP program will identify the size of the block when you turn `hash` on. The following dialog shows the execution of the `hash` command.

```
ftp> hash
Hash mark printing On (2048 bytes/hash mark).
ftp>
```

For this version of FTP, a hash mark will be displayed for every 2048 bytes transmitted. The following dialog shows a file transfer in action, with hash turned on.

```
ftp> get ATAPI-FAQ
200 PORT command successful.
150 Opening ASCII mode data connection for ATAPI-FAQ (10615 bytes).
####
226 Transfer complete.
10813 bytes received in 1.15 seconds (9.39 Kbytes/sec)
ftp>
```

The `ascii` and `binary` commands are used to toggle the file type for the ensuing transfer. Issuing either command will set the type of transfer to be ASCII or binary file type. This command is especially important depending on the operating systems involved. The following dialog shows the use of the `binary` and `ascii` commands.

```
ftp> binary
200 Type set to I.
ftp> ascii
200 Type set to A.
ftp>
```

It is always a good idea to keep the mode set to binary. Beware, however, that every time you start your FTP program, you may have to reset it to binary mode because most FTP programs start up in ASCII mode. If you transfer a binary file using ASCII file mode, the destination file will be corrupted.

Using FTP

In this section, we examine some dialogs that demonstrate the use of FTP. The dialog presented is an actual dialog with an existing site. This will allow you to connect to the same site, if you want, and perform the same dialog (or one similar to it).

In the previous section, we mentioned that you can specify the host to connect to on the `ftp` command line, as shown in the following example:

```
stimpy $ ftp ftp.bugs.net
```

You can also specify a connection to an FTP host while sitting at the FTP command-line prompt. In the dialog that follows, we will demonstrate all ftp usage from within the FTP command interpreter. Follow along as we connect to and perform some routine ftp tasks.

Be sure that you have established a connection to the Internet. If you are hard-wired on a local area network that is tied to the Internet, you are ready to go. If you require dial-up connectivity, do so at this time.

The first thing that you must do is start up the FTP client program. As shown previously, we merely execute the ftp command, as shown in the following:

```
stimpy $ ftp
ftp>
```

The FTP command prompt is displayed, patiently awaiting a command from us. An interesting site with lots of good Linux information can be found at METALAB. To be more specific, this is the home of the Linux Documentation Project (LDP). The World Wide Web URL for the LDP is http://metalab.unc.edu/linux. A wealth of information can be found here, but we are not discussing Web browsers and surfing the WWW. We are here to cruise an FTP site and do some work.

The next thing you have to do is to connect to the FTP site. This is accomplished using the open command to the ftp command interpreter. Here is our current dialog:

```
ftp> open ftp.metalab.unc.edu
Connected to helios.metalab.unc.edu.
220-
220-                    Welcome to UNC's MetaLab FTP archives!
220-                 at the site formerly known as sunsite.unc.edu
220-
220-You can access this archive via http with the same URL.
220-
220-example:    ftp://metalab.unc.edu/pub/Linux/ becomes
220-             http://metalab.unc.edu/pub/Linux/
220-
220-For more information about services offered by MetaLab,
220-go to http://metalab.unc.edu
220-
220-   We're using wu-ftpd. You can get tarred directories if you issue
220-the following command:
220-
220-     get dirname.tar
220-
```

```
220- You can also get gzipped or compressed tarred directories by
220-following the .tar with .gz or .Z, respectively.
220-
220-Have suggestions or questions? Please mail ftpkeeper@metalab.unc.edu.
220-
220 helios.oit.unc.edu FTP server (Version wu-2.5.0(1) Tue Aug 31 15:21:58 EDT 1999) ready.
Name (ftp.metalab.unc.edu:root):
```

Now that we have established a connection to the FTP site, we will need to log in to gain access to the FTP site. Before you log in to an FTP site, be sure to read the information provided on the welcome screen. Notice that information is given concerning the history of this site, some URL addresses for accessing the site, and information regarding the downloading of files.

Next, the server asks us to log in to the site with the following prompt:

```
Name (ftp.metalab.unc.edu:root):
```

Because it is always a good idea to appease the login gods, we will log in as user anonymous, as shown in the following dialog:

```
220 helios.oit.unc.edu FTP server (Version wu-2.5.0(1) Tue Aug 31 15:21:58 EDT 1999) ready.
Name (ftp.metalab.unc.edu:root): anonymous
331 Guest login ok, send your complete email address as password.
Password:
230-
230-              Welcome to UNC's MetaLab FTP archives!
230-           at the site formerly known as sunsite.unc.edu
230-
230-You can access this archive via http with the same URL.
230-
230-example:    ftp://metalab.unc.edu/pub/Linux/ becomes
230-            http://metalab.unc.edu/pub/Linux/
230-
230-For more information about services offered by MetaLab,
230-go to http://metalab.unc.edu
230-
230-  We're using wu-ftpd. You can get tarred directories if you issue
230-the following command:
230-
230-    get dirname.tar
230-
230-  You can also get gzipped or compressed tarred directories by
230-following the .tar with .gz or .Z, respectively.
230-
230-Have suggestions or questions? Please mail ftpkeeper@metalab.unc.edu.
230-
230 Guest login ok, access restrictions apply.
Remote system type is UNIX.
Using binary mode to transfer files.
ftp>
```

Notice that when you enter your password, no characters are displayed. Most FTP sites merely require that you use your email address as the password, as is requested here. Notice, too, that another welcome screen is displayed. Not all FTP sites that you visit will be this verbose. Still other FTP sites will be more long-winded with their information.

Okay, we are logged in and ready for action. First off, it is always a good idea to know where you are. A good place to start is with the `ls` command. This command is the same as the one found in Linux—it displays the contents of the current directory. The difference is that the directory contents that are displayed are from the remote machine. The following dialog demonstrates this:

```
ftp> ls
200 PORT command successful.
150 Opening ASCII mode data connection for /bin/ls.
total 33208
dr-xr-xr-x   9 root     other         512 Aug 13 13:58 .
dr-xr-xr-x   9 root     other         512 Aug 13 13:58 ..
-r--r--r--   1 root     other    33955712 Oct 18 02:44 IAFA-LISTINGS
lrwxrwxrwx   1 root     other           7 Jul 15  1997 README -> WELCOME
-rw-r--r--   1 root     other         659 Sep 01 15:52 WELCOME
dr-xr-xr-x   2 root     other         512 Jul 15  1997 bin
dr-xr-xr-x   2 root     other         512 Jul 15  1997 dev
dr-xr-xr-x   2 root     other         512 Jul 18  1997 etc
drwxrwxrwx  10 ftp      20           4608 Sep 19 19:48 incoming
lrwxrwxrwx   1 root     other          13 Jun 04  1998 ls-lR -> IAFA-LISTINGS
dr-xr-xr-x  17 root     root          512 Jun 08 11:43 pub
dr-xr-xr-x   3 root     other         512 Jul 15  1997 unc
dr-xr-xr-x   5 root     other         512 Jul 15  1997 usr
226 Transfer complete.
ftp>
```

A number of files and directories are here. Notice that the default output shows detail similar to the Linux command (and option) `ls -al`. We can see file permission and type, file owner, group, file size, date/time stamp, and the file's name. The file named WELCOME is displayed when you change to the directory.

The files that are of interest to us are within the pub (public) directory. Therefore, your next assignment is to change to that directory. The `cd` command is used to perform this feat, the same as it does in Linux. The dialog that follows demonstrates the use of the `cd` command:

```
ftp> cd pub
250 CWD command successful.
ftp> ls
200 PORT command successful.
150 Opening ASCII mode data connection for /bin/ls.
total 51
```

```
dr-xr-xr-x   17 root     root          512 Jun 08 11:43 .
dr-xr-xr-x    9 root     other         512 Aug 13 13:58 ..
drwxrwsr-x   25 901      1002         1024 Oct 18 14:26 Linux
drwxr-xr-x   10 root     other         512 Feb 10  1999 UNC-info
drwxr-xr-x   10 root     other         512 May 06 01:01 X11
drwxr-xr-x   34 root     root         1024 Feb 10  1999 academic
drwxr-xr-x    9 root     other         512 Apr 03  1996 archives
drwxr-xr-x   27 root     root         1024 Aug 02 10:55 docs
drwxr-xr-x   15 root     other         512 Jun 23  1998 electronic-publications
lrwxrwxrwx    1 root     other          12 Dec 22  1998 ggi -> packages/ggi
drwxr-xr-x  169 root     other       25088 Oct 18 01:32 gnu
drwxr-xr-x    5 root     bin           512 Aug 10 17:00 languages
lrwxrwxrwx    1 root     other           5 Jun 08 11:43 linux -> Linux
drwx--x--x    2 root     root         8192 Nov 20  1998 lost+found
drwxr-xr-x    7 root     other         512 Feb 27  1997 micro
drwxr-xr-x   20 root     other        1024 Nov 08  1998 multimedia
drwxr-xr-x   24 root     root         1024 Oct 12 10:57 packages
lrwxrwxrwx    1 root     other          16 Jul 18  1997 solaris -> packages/solaris
drwxr-xr-x    5 root     bin           512 Jul 20 09:35 sun-info
drwxr-xr-x    3 root     staff         512 Jan 21  1995 talk-radio
226 Transfer complete.
ftp>
```

As you can see, the cd command is successful—the FTP server explicitly acknowledges that fact. In the previous dialog, we invoked the ls command to show the contents of the pub directory. This output further establishes that we have moved to another directory.

Next, if you scan the directory contents, you see a directory named linux. This directory is actually a link to the directory named Linux. Because this is where you want to be, issue the cd command to the Linux directory, as is done in the following dialog:

```
ftp> cd Linux
250 CWD command successful.
ftp> ls
200 PORT command successful.
150 Opening ASCII mode data connection for /bin/ls.
total 6226
-rw-rw-r--    1 347      1002         2899 Aug 16 13:27 !INDEX
-rw-rw-r--    1 347      1002         6390 Sep 19 21:18 !INDEX.html
-rw-rw-r--    1 347      1002         4008 Aug 16 13:27 !INDEX.short.html
...
-rw-rw-r--    1 347      1002           73 Jun 08 15:14 How-do-I-get-Linux
-rw-rw-r--    1 754      1002       226388 Oct 18 14:25 NEW
-rw-rw-r--    1 754      1002       337245 Oct 18 14:25 NEW.html
drwxrwsr-x    2 347      1002         1024 Jul 12 17:05 NEW.logs
-rw-rw-r--    1 root     1002          479 Feb 10  1999 README
drwxrwsr-x   26 347      1002         1024 Jul 15 17:02 apps
drwxrwsr-x   30 347      1002         1024 Oct 05 10:06 distributions
drwxrwsr-x   13 347      1002         1024 Jun 24 14:18 docs
drwxrwsr-x   31 347      1002         1024 Feb 10  1999 system
```

continues ▶

continued

```
drwxrwsr-x   13 347      1002         1024 Sep 21 14:40 utils
-rw-rw-r--    1 347      1002          788 Oct 13 12:20 welcome.html
226 Transfer complete.
ftp>
```

As you may have noticed, we have issued the `ls` command here after the `cd` command. The complete directory contents have been scaled down to reduce page clutter (notice the ... in the list). Notice the files beginning with the name !INDEX.... These files contain the (current) directory listing with descriptions for each file. One file is a text-only version of the list and the other two files are HTML formatted versions of the list. Another file that should be of interest to you is the README file; you should read this file because it may provide special instructions for the current directory.

Next, we need to change to the docs directory—this is our next directory destination. The dialog that follows shows the interaction required.

```
ftp> cd docs
250-README for docs
250-
250-What you'll find here: documents and information about Linux
250-
250-
250 CWD command successful.
ftp> ls
200 PORT command successful.
150 Opening ASCII mode data connection for /bin/ls.
total 52
-rw-rw-r--    1 670      1002         1272 Jun 06 23:41 !INDEX
-rw-rw-r--    1 670      1002         2857 Jun 06 23:41 !INDEX.html
-rw-rw-r--    1 670      1002         2197 Jun 06 23:41 !INDEX.short.html
drwxrwsr-x   13 347      1002         1024 Jun 24 14:18 .
drwxrwsr-x   25 901      1002         1024 Oct 19 00:55 ..
-rw-rw-r--    1 670      1002        17982 Sep 05  1992 COPYING
lrwxrwxrwx    1 347      1002           24 Apr 05  1999 FAQ -> faqs/Linux-FAQ/Linux-FAQ
lrwxrwxrwx    1 root     other          20 Apr 05  1999 HARDWARE -> HOWTO/Hardware-HOWTO
drwxrwxrwx    6 670      1002         4096 Oct 17 21:58 HOWTO
lrwxrwxrwx    1 root     other          16 Apr 05  1999 INFO-SHEET -> HOWTO/INFO-SHEET
lrwxrwxrwx    1 root     other          17 Apr 05  1999 LDP -> linux-doc-project
drwxrwsr-x    2 670      1002          512 Feb 10  1999 LJ
lrwxrwxrwx    1 root     other          18 Apr 05  1999 LSM -> linux-software-map
lrwxrwxrwx    1 root     other          14 Apr 05  1999 META-FAQ -> HOWTO/META-FAQ
-rw-r--r--    1 root     1002           79 Feb 10  1999 README
drwxrwsr-x    6 670      1002          512 Feb 10  1999 Raven
drwxrwxrwx    8 670      1002          512 Jun 11 10:59 faqs
drwxrwsr-x    3 670      1002          512 Sep 01  1998 fhs
lrwxrwxrwx    1 347      1002            3 Apr 05  1999 fsstnd -> fhs
```

```
drwxrwsr-x   2 670      1002         1024 Feb 10  1999 historic
lrwxrwxrwx   1 root     other            5 Apr 05  1999 howto -> HOWTO
drwxrwsr-x  10 670      1002          512 Jul 24 07:14 linux-announce.archive
drwxrwsr-x  11 670      1002          512 Oct 05 17:07 linux-doc-project
drwxrwsr-x   5 670      1002         1024 Oct 16 01:47 linux-journal
drwxrwsr-x   2 670      1002          512 Aug 30 03:08 linux-software-map
lrwxrwxrwx   1 root     other           13 Apr 05  1999 man-pages -> LDP/man-pages
drwxrwsr-x   7 670      1002          512 Sep 02  1997 old
226 Transfer complete.
ftp>
```

Finally, we change to the faqs directory—this is our final destination. Follow along, as shown in the next dialog.

```
ftp> cd faqs
250-README for docs/faqs
250-
250-What you'll find here: Linux FAQs
250-
250-
250 CWD command successful.
ftp> ls
200 PORT command successful.
150 Opening ASCII mode data connection for /bin/ls.
total 137
drwxrwxrwx   8 670      1002          512 Jun 11 10:59 .
drwxrwsr-x  13 347      1002         1024 Jun 24 14:18 ..
-rw-rw-r--   1 670      1002        10615 Feb 06  1996 ATAPI-FAQ
drwxrwxr-x   2 670      1002          512 Dec 07  1998 AfterStep-FAQ
-rw-rw-r--   1 670      1002        27559 Dec 02  1998 BLFAQ
lrwxrwxrwx   1 347      1002           19 Apr 05  1999 FAQ -> Linux-FAQ/Linux-FAQ
drwxrwxr-x   2 670      1002          512 Jun 06 23:43 Ftape-FAQ
-rw-rw-r--   1 670      1002        37134 Dec 02  1998 GCC-SIG11-FAQ
-rw-rw-r--   1 670      1002         2802 Jun 18  1997 Joe-Command-Reference
drwxrwxr-x   2 670      1002          512 Feb 10  1999 Linux-FAQ
drwxrwxr-x   2 670      1002          512 Feb 10  1999 PPP-FAQ
-rw-r--r--   1 root     other           57 Feb 10  1999 README
-rw-rw-r--   1 670      1002        42072 Dec 02  1998 SMP-FAQ
drwxrwxr-x   3 670      1002          512 Feb 10  1999 Threads-FAQ
lrwxrwxrwx   1 root     other           25 Apr 05  1999 Wine-FAQ -> ../../ALPHA/wine/Wine.FAQ
lrwxrwxrwx   1 347      1002            9 Apr 05  1999 linux-faq -> Linux-FAQ
-rw-rw-r--   1 670      1002          118 Feb 11  1999 new.gif
-rw-rw-r--   1 670      1002          317 Feb 11  1999 next.gif
-rw-rw-r--   1 670      1002          317 Feb 11  1999 prev.gif
drwxrwxr-x   2 670      1002          512 Feb 10  1999 security
-rw-rw-r--   1 670      1002          316 Feb 11  1999 toc.gif
-rw-rw-r--   1 670      1002          150 Feb 11  1999 updated.gif
226 Transfer complete.
ftp>
```

Now that we are in the destination directory, we scan its contents for a file to download. The SMP-FAQ looks like it should be a good read, so we will download that file to our machine. You say you cannot remember the command to download a file? To help jog your memory, you can use the ? or the help command to display the available FTP commands. The dialog that follows shows the result of issuing the help command.

```
ftp> ?
Commands may be abbreviated. Commands are:

!           debug       mdir        sendport    site
$           dir         mget        put         size
account     disconnect  mkdir       pwd         status
append      exit        mls         quit        struct
ascii       form        mode        quote       system
bell        get         modtime     recv        sunique
binary      glob        mput        reget       tenex
bye         hash        newer       rstatus     tick
case        help        nmap        rhelp       trace
cd          idle        nlist       rename      type
cdup        image       ntrans      reset       user
chmod       lcd         open        restart     umask
close       ls          prompt      rmdir       verbose
cr          macdef      passive     runique     ?
delete      mdelete     proxy       send
ftp>
```

Scanning the list, you will see the get command; this is the command that you use to download a file from the remote system to your local machine. The following dialog shows how to use the get command to download the SMP-FAQ file.

```
ftp> get SMP-FAQ
local: SMP-FAQ remote: SMP-FAQ
200 PORT command successful.
150 Opening BINARY mode data connection for SMP-FAQ (42072 bytes).
226 Transfer complete.
42072 bytes received in 7.02 secs (5.9 Kbytes/sec)
ftp>
```

The first command tells the remote system to send the file named SMP-FAQ to your local machine. The FTP server checks for the existence of the file and your permissions to obtain it. The next line acknowledges the name of the file for both sides of the transfer. The fourth line is displayed when the transfer is initiated. The line specifies the transfer mode (text or binary), the file name being transferred, and the size of the file in bytes. After the file has finished its journey, the message Transfer Complete is displayed, and the line that follows shows the transfer statistics. Finally, the FTP command prompt is displayed, waiting for your next instruction.

The following dialog shows how to obtain help for a specific command:

```
ftp> help cdup
cdup            change remote working directory to parent directory
ftp>
```

This dialog shows how to employ the built-in help system. In addition to querying for the available FTP commands (as shown in a previous dialog), you can get help on a specific command. The previous dialog demonstrates obtaining help for the `cdup` command. Although the message is not detailed, it is sufficient to understand the command. Refer to the `ftp` man page for more information on the available commands.

Finally, we close our working example with the dialog that follows:

```
ftp> close
221-You have transferred 42072 bytes in 1 files.
221-Total traffic for this session was 53632 bytes in 5 transfers.
221-Thank you for using the FTP service on helios.oit.unc.edu.
221 Goodbye.
ftp>
```

The `close` command is used to sever the connection to the remote host. Effectively, you are logged off and the connection is broken. In this dialog, the remote system displays statistical information regarding the connection, such as the number of files transferred and the total number of bytes transferred. As a token gesture, the remote system signs off, telling you Thanks... and Goodbye.

Although the connection is closed, you are still in the FTP environment; you can issue another `open` command and visit another FTP site. We close this section by demonstrating the use of the `quit` command. This command shuts down the FTP client and returns you to the parent shell prompt. The following dialog shows the finale:

```
ftp> quit
stimpy $
```

The sample dialog session detailed previously is a good starting point for you to begin your FTP adventures.

Configuring an FTP Server

In the previous sections, we covered the use of FTP with respect to the client side. We now look to see what it takes to set up an FTP server. This will allow other users to connect to your machine, upload, and download files.

One of the first decisions you have to make is whether you want to allow anonymous access or restrict your site to a user-login system. Either way, you have to configure a few items on your system and get the FTP daemon running. You have to focus on your file system and apply restrictions so that users do not wreak havoc upon it.

The second step in this process is to determine an FTP site name. This should be a logical name—do not use a machine name, because this has security and maintenance implications. As far as maintenance goes, moving the server to another machine will prove to be difficult. Decide on a logical name and have it refer to the actual machine on which the FTP server resides. The template for an FTP site name follows:

`ftp.domainName.domainType`

If you are serving up HTTP, you probably want to use the same name as the HTTP domain name. For example, if your HTTP URL is `www.mydomain.net`, you should name your FTP site `ftp.mydomain.net`. This provides a level of consistency for users accessing your site. Most Internet-savvy people instinctively prefix `ftp` to the domain name and domain type. For example, if I am visiting the site named `http://www.metalab.unc.edu`, I intuitively type **`ftp://ftp.metalab.unc.edu`** to access that domain's FTP site (try it yourself).

If you have DNS running, setting up for the alias is fairly easy. Simply provide an entry in the database, similar to the following example:

```
ftp     IN      CNAME     machine.mydomain.net
```

This will ensure that if you have to change the machine that facilitates FTP services, you have to change only the database entry.

Configuring the FTP Daemon: `ftpd`

There are two ways to (automatically) invoke the FTP daemon. The first is through the facilities of `inetd`, and the second is through the `rc` files. If your FTP site is the main target of external users, startup via the `rc` files is preferred. Otherwise, the easiest and more (system) efficient method is to use `inetd` facilities.

Using `inetd` is quite simple—the `inetd` daemon monitors the FTP port (21) for any activity. If the activity is a packet request for an FTP connection, `inetd` will spawn the FTP daemon `ftpd`.

You should check the file `/etc/inetd.conf` for a valid FTP entry. The following is an extract from an actual `/etc/inetd.conf` file:

```
# standard services.
ftp      stream   tcp     nowait    root    /usr/sbin/ftpd    ftpd
#
```

The `ftpd` daemon allows a number of options to be specified when it is invoked. Table 9.4 shows a list of the common options available.

Table 9.4 **Summary of Options for the `ftpd` Daemon**

Option	Description
-A	Allows only anonymous FTP connections or accounts in the `/etc/ftpchroot` file. Other connection requests are refused.
-d	Debugging is enabled. Information is written to `syslog`.
-D	The `ftpd` daemon will detach from the terminal and become a daemon. It will accept connections on the FTP port and fork child processes appropriately to service them.
-h	The FTP server will use high port ranges for any passive connections.
-l	Each FTP session is logged using `syslog`.
-M	Enables multi-homed mode.
-S	The `ftpd` daemon will log anonymous transfers to `/var/log/ftpd`.
-U	Every concurrent session is logged to `/var/run/utmp`, whereby commands such as `who` can be utilized for query.

continues ▶

276 Chapter 9 File Transfer Protocol (FTP)

Table 9.4 **Continued**

Option	Description
-T	Timeout period—the maximum period allowed for requests.
-t	The timeout period for inactivity.
-u mask	Alters the umask to mask. The default is 027.

Be sure to check the ftpd man page for your distribution; the options for your distribution may be different. Verify that a daemon process is specified to handle FTP requests. This will be identified in the /etc/inetd.conf file.

The following is an extract from an /etc/inetd.conf file from the SuSE 6.2 Linux distribution. The difference here is that SuSE specifies that inetd should launch the tcpd daemon versus the ftpd daemon. The tcpd daemon is a control facility for the various Internet services.

```
# These are standard services.
#
ftp     stream  tcp     nowait  root /usr/sbin/tcpd wu.ftpd -a
# ftp   stream  tcp     nowait  root /usr/sbin/tcpd proftpd
# ftp   stream  tcp     nowait  root /usr/sbin/tcpd in.ftpd
#
```

The tcpd program can monitor requests such as telnet, finger, ftp, exec, tftp, and talk. When a request comes in, the inetd daemon runs the tcpd program versus the actual server process. Then, tcpd logs the request, performs required housekeeping, and then runs the appropriate server process.

As you can see, this sample includes optional entries (that are commented out) to start up the tcpd daemon. Your file may look similar to this or the previous sample—ensure that an ftp line is not commented out.

Directory Structure for FTP

Setting up an FTP directory structure is a simple procedure. The simplest tree structure consists of a dedicated file system designated for FTP. A straightforward example is to use /usr/ftp or other similar name. Whatever the root path is does not matter; it is the file structure and contents below the root path that is of concern.

A number of directories are required for FTP servicing. The minimum structure consists of bin, dev, etc, lib, and pub. The use of each directory corresponds to its use within Linux.

The bin directory contains any commands required to support your FTP services. The minimum requirement here is the ls command. The full pathname will be /usr/ftp/bin, using our previous example. Some other command files you might want in /usr/ftp/bin are compress, gzip, and tar.

The dev directory holds a copy of the /dev/zero file. The ld.so file and, ultimately, the ls command will use /usr/ftp/zero, as is usual. The exception to this is on the newer Linux distributions. To test this, do not copy /dev/zero to /usr/ftp/dev; connect and run ls and see what happens. Be sure to read the lib description that follows for additional information. If you do need to copy /dev/zero, be sure to use the mknod command. You might also require the tcp and udp files in the /usr/ftp/dev directory.

Next, you will need to copy the passwd file into the /usr/ftp/etc directory. Follow this up by copying the group file. Both of these files can be found in the /etc directory. Open each file into your favorite editor and remove all entries except anonymous, ftp, and bin. Next, replace all passwords with an asterisk. Using an asterisk for the password entry will disallow user access to the account.

The lib directory is the next directory you need to create. You will place the /lib/libc.so.*XXX* file into the /usr/ftp/lib directory. Be sure to copy the actual version file (replacing the *XXX*), such as libc.so.4, libc.so.4.7.6, or libc.so.6. Your version number will probably be different than what is listed here. Before copying the file, log in to the site and issue the ls command to see whether ls requires the libc.so.*XXX* file.

Lastly, you need to create the pub directory. This directory is a very important one because this is why your users are coming to your FTP site. You can create any number of directories under /usr/ftp/pub as necessary for organizational purposes. As a minimum, you might create the directories upload (or incoming), docs, utils, and any other directories that you see fit.

Within each of the directories under /usr/ftp/pub, you should have a README file that describes what the current directory is used for. You might also have a CONTENTS file that lists the directory contents and a description of each file.

Directory Permissions

Setting up the permissions for the directory structure is quite simple. You will not want your anonymous users perusing your Linux system—doing so will inevitably be catastrophic. So, how do you keep users from going outside of the FTP sandbox? You use the chroot command. The syntax for chroot follows:

chroot newRootDir [*command*]

The command effectively changes the root directory for the command specified. If no command is specified, command is taken to be the user's shell. The chroot command is used to change the root directory to one other than /. Using our example, if you set the root to be /usr/ftp for anonymous users, all directory-manipulation commands will be relative to the /usr/ftp directory. If the user executes a command such as cd /pub, the user's current directory will actually be /usr/ftp/pub.

In the previous section, I suggested that you create an upload or incoming directory. This directory is where your users can upload files to the FTP site. If you are allowing upload functionality, you will have to provide execute and write permission on that directory. Common practice dictates that you review any files uploaded to this directory. After you have determined the validity of a file, you can move it somewhere within the pub directory structure for other users to access. If you do not want users to get files from the upload (incoming) directory, be sure to remove read permissions.

The balance of the directory structure should be set to execute and read for the anonymous accounts. The chmod command is used to perform this magic. Check the chmod man page for more details.

Configuring FTP Logins

In a previous section, you created your directory structure and placed various files within the hierarchy. If you are allowing anonymous access, you need to verify that appropriate entries exist in the /usr/ftp/etc/passwd and /usr/ftp/etc/ group files for user anonymous.

In the /usr/ftp/etc/group file, be sure to create a unique group entry for anonymous FTP accounts.

In the /usr/ftp/etc/passwd file, create any anonymous user entries that you require. The two most common are the user names ftp and anonymous.

Verifying the FTP Setup

The test is quite simple—it is a matter of connecting to the system and exercising various commands. You should try to maneuver through other parts of your Linux file system. Try to execute various Linux commands. You should also attempt to copy, move, and delete files. Before doing this, you should put some "dummy" text files around the filesystem that you can test with.

I suggest using the previous section titled "Using FTP" as a guideline. Using a second machine, log in to the new FTP site and exercise its functionality and organization.

Summary

In this chapter, we covered the use of the File Transfer Protocol (FTP). After the "FTP Overview" section, we examined FTP commands that are available. You learned that not all the commands detailed are available in every FTP client program.

The file transfer commands were discussed, including file download, file upload, and supplemental commands. The section "Using FTP" provided a real-world dialog of a client FTP session.

Finally, we closed the chapter by demonstrating the configuration of an FTP server so that users can access your own FTP site.

10
Domain Name Service (DNS)

DNS IS CHIEFLY RESPONSIBLE FOR MAPPING (converting) hostnames to Internet addresses. Sounds simple enough, but there is more to it than that.

A lot of people don't really like to work with numbers—except for mathematicians and engineers, I suppose. But for the rest of us, pseudonyms are preferred. For example, to get to the Web site of the White House, would you rather specify www.whitehouse.gov or 198.137.240.91? You might know the dotted address now, but by tomorrow you will have forgotten it. Even if you could remember that IP address, just how many can you memorize?

Enter the Domain Name System, sometimes called Domain Name Service. To reduce confusion, let's just call it DNS. DNS provides two types of lookup. One is a hostname lookup and the other is a reverse lookup. The first type results in an IP address if given a hostname. The second, reverse lookup, provides a hostname if given an IP address.

DNS is a distributed database of hostnames and IP addresses. Why distributed? It's because not every Internet site houses all mappings. That would be like putting all your eggs into one basket. Each organization within the Internet is responsible for its own database content. One system on the Internet can query another system for hostname or IP address information. The protocol that facilitates this communication is—you guessed it—DNS.

This chapter explains setting up and maintaining a DNS system.

DNS Overview

In the Internet's beginning, mapping hostnames to IP addresses was a simple function and was easy to maintain. The /etc/hosts file was used for this purpose, as it still is today. As new hosts came onto the Internet landscape, you simply added the hostname and its associated IP address. In those early days, adding ten or twenty new host addresses was a routine task. Yet that routine task can be time consuming for a system administrator.

As time passed and the Internet began to grow, the task of maintaining the /etc/hosts file became unwieldy. Another issue is the sheer size of the /etc/hosts file. Imagine a host file with hundreds and hundreds of entries. A better method of maintaining and performing host-to-IP-address mapping needed to be developed.

Sun Microsystems developed a solution called the Network Information System (NIS), also known as the Yellow Pages. The master host maintains the /etc/hosts file, allowing any client (host) to obtain the /etc/hosts file as required. NIS is really effective only with small- to medium-sized local-area networks.

For the Internet, the Network Information Center (NIC) implemented a similar scheme. A single database of hostnames and addresses was hosted by the NIC. All Internet sites had to download this master hosts file from the NIC. Imagine the load that was realized by the NIC servers as remote machines logged in to download, via FTP, the newest hosts file.

To resolve these issues, a new system was required. That system is known as the Berkeley Internet Domain System (BIND) and is synonymous with DNS. Actually, BIND is an implementation of DNS that includes the resolver and name server. The DNS system is described by a number of Request For Comments (RFCs). A good source for RFC lookup and retrieval can be found at http://www.cis.ohio-state.edu/hypertext/information/rfc.html.

With Linux (and UNIX) applications, the resolver is accessed using two library functions, gethostbyaddress and gethostbyname. The first library function, gethostbyaddress, returns a hostname if given an IP address. The second function, gethostbyname, performs the inverse: given a hostname, it returns an IP address. The resolver communicates with the name server (called named) to perform the actual mapping. If you are a software developer, this is important to know because you must have an IP address before establishing a connection using TCP. Technically, the resolver is not an application or a system, but is the collection of library functions that requests the mapping.

Each DNS is responsible for host information within its area of responsibility, or zone. In addition, each DNS maintains information about other DNS entities and their zones. At the root is the NIC, which maintains the top-level domains, called organizational domains in this book. Figure 10.1 provides a graphical representation of the organizational domains.

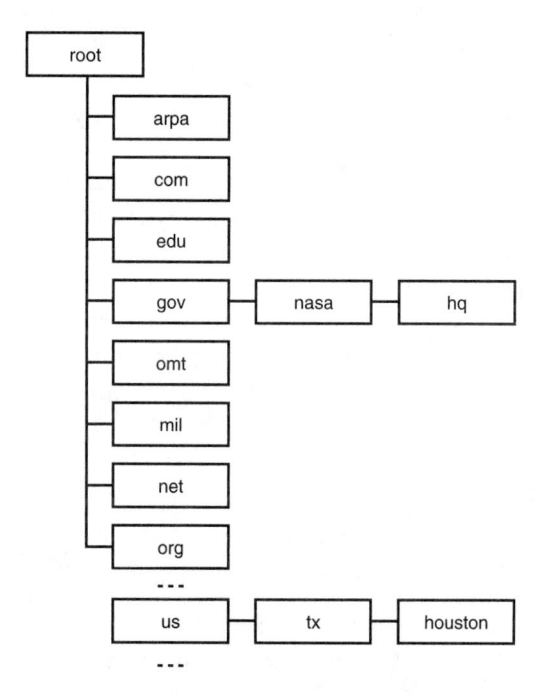

Figure 10.1 Top-level DNS.

Take note of the top-level domains that are connected to the root node. The root node, by the way, is actually unnamed; I've named it only as a point of reference. You have undoubtedly seen HTTP and FTP sites with some of these domains. Most people think that these top-level domains are exclusive to the United States; many people do not realize that a U.S. ("us") domain exists. Take a look at the example provided in the previous diagram; us.tx.houston is an actual site (at the time of this writing). Try it out—enter the following URL into your favorite browser: http://www.houston.tx.us.

This brings up a point about the organizational domains. To set the record straight, .gov and .mil are the only two organizational domains that are bound to the United States. The other organizational domains, such as .com and .org are not specific to the United States; many non-U.S. entities use them. Popular among non-U.S. entities is appending second-level (under top-level) domains. One well-known one is .co.uk, which relates to commercial entities within the United Kingdom (UK).

Domain names are not case sensitive; you can supply a domain name in uppercase, lowercase, or mixed case letters. A domain name consists of an individual domain name from a different level; each domain level is delimited by a period. Look again at the previous figure. Notice that the levels are maintained as a hierarchy—but in reverse when compared to the Linux file system. With the file system, the root is the start of a pathname, whereas the root is the end node in a fully qualified domain name.

A fully qualified domain name (FQDN) is a complete domain name that ends with a period. If the terminating period is absent from the domain name, the domain name is not fully qualified and requires completion.

Table 10.1 describes the organizational domains as shown in the previous figure. The special case (four letter) domain, *arpa*, is required for mapping an address to a name. The two-letter domains are designated as country codes. These country codes are derived from the International Standards Organization (ISO) 3166 standard.

Table 10.1 **Organizational Domains and Descriptions**

Organizational Domain	Description
com	Commercial organization
edu	Educational organization
gov	U.S. government organization
int	International organization
mil	U.S. military
net	Network organization
org	Other organization

How is a name resolved and an IP addressed revealed, based on a domain name? Most people do not know, or even care, how a Web page appears when they type www.whitehouse.gov; they just want the page to display. But for us, it is helpful to know just how a name is discovered and the IP address returned. For each top-level domain, a master name server exists. When a domain name inquiry is made, the request goes to a root server to return the address of a master name server for the top-level domain. A DNS server performs this inquiry.

DNS Overview

After we have that address, the DNS server contacts a master name server and requests the name server responsible for the domain name we are requesting.

Next, DNS uses the name server's address, contacts that server, and requests the server's address that maintains the requested domain name. Finally, this last name server resolves the name and returns an IP address.

This process may seem time consuming and bandwidth intensive, but it is actually quite efficient—and also quite clever. One feature of DNS is result caching. If a mapping is obtained, it is cached for subsequent queries, thereby reducing "manual" lookups by DNS.

Let's look at an example to see how this works. Figure 10.2 graphically depicts the dialog. This diagram is a Unified Modeling Language (UML) sequence diagram. The entities are listed horizontally at the top of the diagram. Each entity has a vertical line associated with it; this vertical line is known as the entity's lifeline. A horizontal line that "connects" two lifelines can be an event, a process, or some other functionality. These events are shown as a sequence of events over time. The first event in the sequence is always at the top, with subsequent events progressing to the bottom of the diagram.

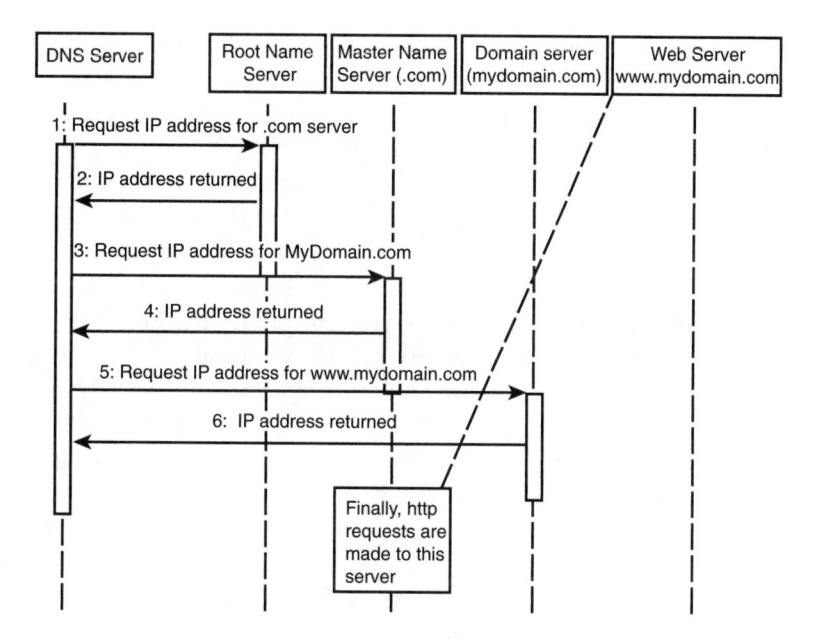

Figure 10.2 DNS and name server dialog.

Suppose you need the address for www.mydomain.com. The DNS server interrogates the root server for the IP address of the server that handles the .com domain. That IP address is returned to the DNS server. Next, the DNS server asks the master name server for the IP address for the domain server responsible for mydomain.com; the IP address is then returned. Finally, the mydomain.com name server is interrogated for the IP address for www.mydomain.com server.

As mentioned previously, the NIC is responsible for the top-level domains, whereas other entities are responsible for zones within the lower-level domains. The word "zone" has appeared in this chapter without a clear definition. A zone is a branch (or subtree) within the DNS tree. A majority of the zones branch from the second-level domain from the DNS tree. In Figure 10.1, a subtree zone might be found at the nasa.gov domain. Each zone is maintained by the organization responsible for the zone. Furthermore, each zone can be divided into one or more smaller zones. How these zones are logically organized is determined by the responsible organization. A zone can represent a business unit, such as a department, or by graphical region, such as an organizational branch.

Using our fictitious domain, www.mydomain.com, we can divide this domain into zones based on departments. For example, the zone named sales.mydomain.com can represent the sales department and research.mydomain.com can represent the research and development department. Each host machine within each zone will have its name prepended to the domain name. For example, if the research and development department has a host named stimpy, the domain name is stimpy.research.mydomain.com. A domain includes all hosts within the (entire) organization, whereas a zone includes only the hosts within the zone's area of responsibility. Organizationally, responsibility can be delegated from the root administrator to a zone administrator. Therefore, the administrator for research.mydomain.com is responsible for the host stimpy.research.mydomain.com and any other hosts within the administrator's zone of responsibility.

After a zone is established, name servers must be provided to support that zone. These name servers maintain a domain name space. The domain name space contains information concerning hosts and information about those hosts. The information contained in a domain name space persists in a database and is manipulated by a name server. Redundancy is provided for by the use of multiple name servers. A primary name server and at least one secondary name server is required (there can be many secondary name servers). The primary name server and secondary name server(s) must be independent of each other in the event of an outage. They should be on their own (dedicated) machine. This alleviates any DNS downtime if one of the machines fail to run. Another reason you must have more than one name server is because InterNIC requires it before approving your domain name.

The primary name server reads domain name space data from configuration files found on disk. If the configuration files change, such as when a new server is added to the system, a signal (normally SIGHUP) is sent to the primary name server to reread the configuration files. The secondary name server(s) retrieves domain name space data from the primary name server, rather than from disk. The secondary name server(s) polls, on a regular basis, the primary name server for new domain name space data. If the primary name server has new data, the data is transferred to the secondary name server(s).

An important feature of DNS is information caching. If a name server obtains a mapping, that mapping is cached for subsequent queries. Caching can be turned off for a name server, but it is highly recommended that caching be enabled.

DNS Configuration

The easiest way to set up DNS is to use your ISP's DNS server(s), if available. You could also set up a hybrid, in which you let the ISP maintain the primary name server and your organization maintains the secondary name server(s).

Of course, this chapter is about setting up DNS, not delegating responsibility to another party. By setting up DNS at your domain, you maintain complete control over your internal network. An advantage to maintaining DNS internally is that of better performance. Response is quicker with an internal DNS because an ISP's DNS works hard to serve many sites besides yours.

A number of files will need to be examined and possibly edited, such as /etc/host.conf and /etc/resolv.conf. These files are standard ASCII files and can be edited with any text editor. As with most other Linux configuration files, configuration entries exist on a separate line and individual fields are delimited by a space or a tab.

Setting Up the /etc/host.conf File

Begin DNS setup by checking and possibly modifying the /etc/host.conf file. Other files may or may not be used, depending on entries found in the /etc/host.conf file. For example, if the bind argument is not given for the order entry, the /etc/resolv.conf file is not used.

Environment variables may be used to override any settings for the resolver. We will take a look at these environment variables after discussing the options to the /etc/host.conf file.

A number of options are available for use in the /etc/host.conf file. Each option is specified on a separate line within the file. You can use comments in the file; their use is recommended to clarify the intent of the options. A comment is identified with the # character, beginning in the first position of a line. The options available for the /etc/host.conf file are alert, multi, nospoof, order, reorder, and trim.

The alert option can have one of two arguments specified: either on or off. If the argument is on, a log entry is generated using the syslog facility if an attempt is made to spoof an IP address. What is spoofing? Spoofing occurs when a machine uses an IP address as an alias for another IP address (or domain name). If the option is off, no logging is performed.

The multi option can also have one of two arguments: either on or off. If multi is on, a host can have more than one IP address in the /etc/hosts file. This will apply to host queries only and is not actually used for DNS queries.

The nospoof option also accepts the on or off arguments. If the argument to nospoof is on, spoofing is prohibited. For example, if a name is returned for an IP address, the name is resolved and compared to the IP address given. If the argument to nospoof is off, spoofing is not prevented.

The order option specifies the order in which names are resolved. The arguments can be bind, hosts, or nis. The bind argument specifies that DNS is to be used to resolve a name. The argument hosts is specified so that the /etc/hosts file is queried for resolution. The nis argument specifies that the NIS protocol is to be used for resolution.

The arguments to the reorder option are on or off. If the option is on, the resolver will try to reorder the host addresses, percolating local addresses to be first on the list. The reordering is performed for all methods of lookup.

And lastly, the trim option specifies that the domain name should be removed before an /etc/hosts query is executed. The argument to trim is a domain name such as stimpy.com. The advantage here is that only the hostname has to be put into the /etc/hosts file. The following is a sample /etc/host.conf file:

```
#
# /etc/host.conf
#
# Generated on Wed Jul 14 22:41:24 /etc/localtime 1999.
#
order hosts bind
```

DNS Configuration

```
# do not allow spoofing
nospoof on
# log any spoofing attempts
alert on
multi on
# end of /etc/host.conf
```

In this sample /etc/host.conf file, we can see that the /etc/hosts file is first queried for name resolution. If the name is not resolved, DNS is used to resolve the name. Spoofing is not allowed and any attempt to spoof is logged using the syslog facility. The multi option is set to on because the /etc/hosts file contains multiple IP address entries for a host.

> **Supply a Host Argument**
> The hosts argument should always be supplied to the order option. This ensures that the /etc/host file is interrogated for name resolution, even if the DNS server goes down.

Environment Variables

The following bulleted list describes the environment variables that can be used to override settings provided in the /etc/host.conf file.

- **RESOLV_HOST_CONF.** This variable is used to change the filename for the configuration file that is to be used, instead of the default name of /etc/host.conf.

- **RESOLV_SERV_ORDER.** This setting overrides any arguments to the order keyword found in the /etc/host.conf file.

- **RESOLV_SPOOF_CHECK.** If this option is set, it overrides the nospoof option in the /etc/host.conf file. The valid arguments are off to disable spoof checking, warn to engage spoof checking and include warning, and warn off to provide spoof checking yet disable the warning functionality.

- **RESOLV_ADD_TRIM_DOMAINS.** Same as the trim option to /etc/host.conf; it contains a list of domains to trim. This list does not override the list found in /etc/host.conf, but extends that list.

- **RESOLV_OVERRIDE_TRIM_DOMAINS.** Same as the trim option to /etc/host.conf; it contains a list of domains to trim. This list overrides the list specified in /etc/host.conf.

- **RESOLV_MULTI.** This environment variable overrides the multi option found in the /etc/host.conf file.

- **RESOLV_REORDER.** This option, if available, overrides the reorder option in the /etc/host.conf file.

Setting Up the `/etc/resolv.conf` File

If the `bind` argument has been specified to the `order` option (in `/etc/host.conf`), you will have to modify the `/etc/resolv.conf` file. If the `bind` argument is not specified, DNS is effectively disabled. Review the `/etc/host.conf` to be sure that the `bind` argument is specified on the order line.

The `/etc/resolv.conf` file is used to control the order and the method by which names are resolved. The search order and the name servers to contact are specified in this file.

Several options are available to the `/etc/resolv.conf` file. Each option requires one or more arguments. The options available are `domain`, `nameserver`, and `search`. We will examine each of the options in turn.

The `domain` option is used to specify the domain name for the given host. The following is a sample domain option:

```
domain mydomain.com
```

The argument to the `nameserver` option simply specifies a name server to use for name resolution. This entry is, in my opinion, the most important option in `/etc/resolv.conf`. The argument is specified as an IP address. You can have more than one `nameserver` line in the `/etc/resolv.conf` file. The following is a snippet from a fictitious `/etc/resolv.conf` file showing three `nameserver` entries:

```
nameserver 199.13.255.122
nameserver 199.13.255.124
nameserver 199.13.255.126
```

The name servers (host) are queried in the order given, so be sure to specify the most dependable name server(s) first. If nothing else, you should have at least one `nameserver` entry in the `/etc/resolv.conf` file. As soon as the first name server responds to a host query, the search stops at that point. Not only will the search stop if a host is resolved, the search will also stop if a name server returns a `host not found` message.

For the `search` option, one or more arguments can be specified, each separated by a space or a tab. Each argument is a domain name to be tried for name resolution. These domains are appended to the hostname to attempt resolution. The following search line is taken from a fictitious `/etc/resolv.conf` file:

```
search research.mydomain.com sales.mydomain.com mydomain.com
```

If the search option is not specified in the /etc/resolv.conf file, a search is conducted starting with the local domain name and then traversing parent domains up to and including the root. If a domain name is not supplied for the domain option, a call to the library function getdomainname is made by the resolver.

Setting Up named (BIND 4.x)

In this section, you set up the name server. This server is called named, pronounced "name-dee." The named server reads its configuration file when starting; this file and others are found in the /etc and /var directories. The named server is a daemon process and is (normally) launched at system startup and continues to run until a shutdown is initiated.

Some of the files involved with named are briefly described in the following list:

- **/etc/named.boot.** The name server configuration that is read when named starts.
- **/etc/named.pid.** An ASCII file that contains the process ID of named. Older systems will write to this file (rather than the /var/run/named.pid).
- **/var/run/named.pid.** An ASCII file that contains the process ID of named. Newer systems will write to this file (rather than the /etc/named.pid).
- **/var/tmp/named_dump.db.** Contains a dump of the named server database.
- **/var/tmp/named.run.** Contains debugging information for named.
- **/var/tmp/named.stats.** Contains statistical data for named server.

You can initiate named in two ways. One way is to start it directly, supplying any arguments required. The named server program is ordinarily found in the /usr/sbin directory. The server will start up by reading the /etc/named.boot file and any other configuration files specified therein. After the server has started, it writes its process ID to the named.pid file (found in the /var/run directory). A second method of starting the named server is to use ndc, which is the control interface to the named daemon. You can use ndc to send various commands to the name server, such as start, stop, restart, status, and so on. I discuss these two methods of starting up named later in this section.

Before you start up the named daemon, you need to visit the /etc/named.boot file and alter its contents. In the next section, you modify this file.

Configuring the /etc/named.boot File

The /etc/named.boot is the boot file read by the named server. In this section, you look at the various options that can be specified in this file. As with other Linux configuration files, each option is specified on its own line. Comments can be used and are denoted with the semicolon character.

The following is a sample /etc/named.boot file:

```
; Sample /etc/named.boot file for the domain "my.domain.edu".
; ns = name server
; All relative file names can be found in this directory.
directory /var/named

; All information is read from the file "/var/named/my.domain.file".
; IP -> hostname translation is done by ".../my.domain.file.rev".
primary         my.domain.edu           my.domain.file
primary         168.192.in-addr.arpa    my.domain.file.rev

; If you have further child zones and you are not a secondary ns for them,
; specify a stub here:
;stub subzone.my.domain.edu 192.168.2.1 subzone.stub

; Use the following entries, if you want to use this as a secondary server.
; The primary server is contacted from time to time for the most recent
; information. "my.domain.file.bak" is used as starting file at boot time until
; the primary ns has been contacted (and in case the primary ns is down).
; You should then also put this host into the "NS" part of the primary ns.
secondary       my.domain.edu           192.168.7.7     my.domain.file.bak
secondary       168.192.in-addr.arpa    192.168.7.7     my.domain.file.rev.bak
primary .                               localhost
primary 127.in-addr.arpa                127.in-addr.arpa
cache . root.cache

; if you have further name servers, which might have more information cached.
; A good choice here is the ns, which is authoritative for the zone above you.
forwarders 192.168.7.5 192.168.7.7 192.168.68.11
; If you enable "slave", it will ask one of the "forwarders" to fetch the
; correct answer. This will lead to more complete "forwarding" ns
slave
```

A few options are very important—primarily cache, directory, forwarders, primary, secondary, and slave. I discuss these six important options first and then take a look at some of the other options that are available. The following list provides a brief explanation for the first six options:

- **cache.** Provides information to named for caching. The cache option requires two arguments: a domain name and a filename. The primary use of the cache option is to specify information such as the location of root domain servers.

- **directory.** This option designates the directory in which the zone files exist. The default directory is /var/named.

- **forwarders.** The argument to this option is a list of addresses. If name resolution information is not found in the cache, the servers specified in this list are queried by named.
- **primary.** The arguments to this option are a domain name and a filename, which declares the (authoritative) local server for the named domain. This option declares that the (specified) file contains authoritative data for the (domain) zone.
- **secondary.** The arguments to this option are a domain name, an address list, and a filename. The local server is declared as a secondary master server for the specified domain.
- **slave.** This option specifies that the (local) name server is merely a slave server. Requests for name resolution are forwarded to the servers that are listed in the forwarders option.

For the cache option, the root domain name is normally specified as the domain argument. A file with the name root.cache, normally found in /var/named, contains information that is placed in the backup cache. This cache is used only for hints to find the root servers. Multiple cache files can be specified. You should always have a cache option specified in the /etc/named.boot file. The cache option tells named to load the root server data from the named.ca file. The named.ca file maintains root name server information.

Retrieving the root.cache File

The root.cache file should be retrieved from FTP.RS.INTERNIC.NET at predefined intervals because the list changes periodically.

The directory option provokes the server to change its working directory to the directory specified. This can be critical for proper $INCLUDE file processing. Remember, files specified in the /etc/named.boot file can be specified as relative to this directory.

The forwarders option identifies IP addresses for servers that can execute recursive queries for other servers. If the boot file contains one or more forwarders entries and if no data is in the cache, a server sends queries to the forwarders first. One by one, each forwarder is queried for resolution until a reply is received or the forwarders list is depleted. If the forwarders list is depleted, the server operates as if the forwarders option did not exist. However, if a server is in forward-only mode, only those servers listed in the forwarders list are queried.

For the `primary` option, the second argument specifies the filename containing the authoritative data for the zone specified by the first argument. If you refer to the previous sample, `/etc/named.boot`, the first `primary` option specifies that the `my.domain.file` contains the authoritative data for the `my.domain.edu` domain.

A secondary server will attempt to retrieve authoritative data from the primary server, rather than getting the data from files. For this reason, it is important that at least one primary server must be given. A server will continue to contact each server until it receives the zone database. After this happens, the data is stored in the backup file (the third argument). The zone data is retrieved from the backup if no primary server responds.

The `slave` option exists only for backward compatibility. The `slave` option is identical to the options, `forward-only` directive to the `named` daemon. This option causes a server to query only the servers in the `forwarders` list. Machines that do not have access to the Internet will be set up as slaves.

The following options are also available but, unlike the six options previously covered, are not considered minimally required. Let's take a quick look at some of the other available options.

The `include` option specifies that the cited (include) file should be processed as though the file's contents were embedded at the point of the `include` option. This is similar to the `#include` directive as used in the C and C++ languages. The `include` option expects a single argument—the filename to include.

The `limit` option is used to alter the internal limits of BIND. Values for the `limit` argument can be specified as either kilobytes (k), megabytes (m), or gigabytes (g). For example, a number followed by the letter m specifies the limit in megabytes. The `datasize` argument specifies the size of the process data that is controlled by the Linux kernel. The `transfers-in` argument specifies the maximum number of named-xfer subprocesses that BIND will invoke and maintain. The `transfers-per-ns` argument designates the maximum amount of zone transfers that can be introduced to a remote name server. The maximum number of file descriptors available to BIND is specified with the `files` argument.

The `sortlist` option specifies networks that are favored or other networks. Queries for host addresses from local network hosts can expect responses in the following order: local network addresses, sort list addresses, and finally, other addresses.

The `check-names` option, when set, tells BIND to check for names in primary or secondary zone files. BIND will also check in response messages during recursion. If the check is unsuccessful, BIND generates one of three failures. If a zone cannot be loaded or the response failed caching, a `fail`

DNS Configuration

message is generated. If a `warn` is generated, an entry is written to the system log files. The third type, `ignore`, tells BIND to disregard an invalid name and process it normally.

The following is a sample `/var/named/root.cache` file:

```
; This file holds the information on root name servers needed to
; initialize cache of Internet domain name servers
; formerly NS.INTERNIC.NET
.                          3600000    IN   NS    A.ROOT-SERVERS.NET.
A.ROOT-SERVERS.NET.        3600000         A     198.41.0.4
; formerly NS1.ISI.EDU
.                          3600000         NS    B.ROOT-SERVERS.NET.
B.ROOT-SERVERS.NET.        3600000         A     128.9.0.107
; formerly C.PSI.NET
.                          3600000         NS    C.ROOT-SERVERS.NET.
C.ROOT-SERVERS.NET.        3600000         A     192.33.4.12
; formerly TERP.UMD.EDU
.                          3600000         NS    D.ROOT-SERVERS.NET.
D.ROOT-SERVERS.NET.        3600000         A     128.8.10.90
; formerly NS.NASA.GOV
.                          3600000         NS    E.ROOT-SERVERS.NET.
E.ROOT-SERVERS.NET.        3600000         A     192.203.230.10
; formerly NS.ISC.ORG
.                          3600000         NS    F.ROOT-SERVERS.NET.
F.ROOT-SERVERS.NET.        3600000         A     192.5.5.241
; formerly NS.NIC.DDN.MIL
.                          3600000         NS    G.ROOT-SERVERS.NET.
G.ROOT-SERVERS.NET.        3600000         A     192.112.36.4
; formerly AOS.ARL.ARMY.MIL
.                          3600000         NS    H.ROOT-SERVERS.NET.
H.ROOT-SERVERS.NET.        3600000         A     128.63.2.53
; formerly NIC.NORDU.NET
.                          3600000         NS    I.ROOT-SERVERS.NET.
I.ROOT-SERVERS.NET.        3600000         A     192.36.148.17
; temporarily housed at NSI (InterNIC)
.                          3600000         NS    J.ROOT-SERVERS.NET.
J.ROOT-SERVERS.NET.        3600000         A     198.41.0.10
; temporarily housed at NSI (InterNIC)
.                          3600000         NS    K.ROOT-SERVERS.NET.
K.ROOT-SERVERS.NET.        3600000         A     198.41.0.11
; temporarily housed at ISI (IANA)
.                          3600000         NS    L.ROOT-SERVERS.NET.
L.ROOT-SERVERS.NET.        3600000         A     198.32.64.12
; temporarily housed at ISI (IANA)
.                          3600000         NS    M.ROOT-SERVERS.NET.
M.ROOT-SERVERS.NET.        3600000         A     198.32.65.12
; End of File
```

You are ready to start `named` and see how things run. In the next section, you see how to start and communicate with `named`.

Starting and Talking to named

As mentioned earlier in this chapter, named can be started in one of two ways. The daemon can be started directly, using its executable name. The second way to invoke named is by use of ndc. This section reviews these two methods of booting named. It also explores the use of signals to manipulate named when it is running.

When named is started without any arguments, the daemon first reads its configuration file (/etc/named.boot), reads any other configuration file(s) specified, and then begins listening for queries. The following is the usage for named:

named [-d debuglevel] [-p port#[/localport#]] [{-b} bootfile] [-q] [-r]

Various arguments can be specified to named. Table 10.2 describes the available arguments to named:

Table 10.2 **Options for Starting named**

Option	Description
-b	Use this option to specify a boot configuration file to read.
-d	Use this option to print debugging information. A number that is specified after the d switch determines the level of messages generated.
-p	This option tells named to use nonstandard port numbers. The getservbyname will return the default port number. Two port numbers, separated by a slash, can be specified. The first port is used when contacting remote servers. The second argument is the service port for the local instance of named.
-q	Use this option to trace all incoming queries.
-r	This option turns off recursion for the server. Responses come only from primary or secondary zones. The options no-recursion option in the /etc/named.boot file is the preferred method of turning off recursion over this command-line option.

You can also start the named daemon using the ndc executable. The ndc command is the control interface to the named daemon. The ndc command enables you to perform administrative tasks interactively with named, providing feedback during debugging. You can specify a number of options to ndc. Table 10.3 shows the options:

Table 10.3 **Options for the ndc Command**

Option	Description
status	This option displays the status of named as displayed by the ps command.
dumpdb	This option forces named to dump the current database and the cache to the /var/tmp/named_dump.db file.
reload	This option forces named to verify serial numbers for primary and secondary zones and then to reload any that have changed.
stats	This option causes named to do a dump of its statistics to the /var/tmp/named.stats file.
trace	Executing this option invokes named to increment the tracing level by one. If the tracing level is nonzero, trace information is written to the /var/tmp/named.run file. More detailed tracing information is provided by higher tracing levels.
notrace	This option effectively causes named to reset the tracing level to zero. This results in the closing of the /var/tmp/named.run file.
querylog	This option invokes named to toggle the query logging feature on or off. If on, every query will be logged with the syslog facility. Be cautious because this option causes the log files to increase significantly (and quickly).
start	This option starts up the named daemon.
stop	This option stops named.
restart	This option causes named to be killed and restarted.

The following dialog demonstrates the use of ndc to start up the named daemon and then check on its status:

```
bash-2.02# ndc start
Name Server Started
bash-2.02# ndc status
 3595  ?  S    0:00 named
bash-2.02#
```

The following dialog shows the result of the dumpdb option to ndc and the contents of the resultant /var/tmp/named_dump.db file. Note that the IP addresses shown have been changed to protect the innocent.

```
bash-2.02# ndc dumpdb
Dumping Database
bash-2.02# cat /var/tmp/named_dump.db
; Dumped at Thu Jul 15 16:40:23 1999
;; ++zone table++
;; --zone table--
; Note: Cr=(auth,answer,addtnl,cache) tag only shown for non-auth RR's
```

continues ▶

continued

```
; Note: NT=milliseconds for any A RR which we've used as a nameserver
; --- Cache & Data ---
; --- Hints ---
$ORIGIN .
.           3600    IN      NS      A.ROOT-SERVERS.NET.     ;Cl=0
            3600    IN      NS      B.ROOT-SERVERS.NET.     ;Cl=0
            3600    IN      NS      C.ROOT-SERVERS.NET.     ;Cl=0
            3600    IN      NS      D.ROOT-SERVERS.NET.     ;Cl=0
            3600    IN      NS      E.ROOT-SERVERS.NET.     ;Cl=0
            3600    IN      NS      F.ROOT-SERVERS.NET.     ;Cl=0
            3600    IN      NS      G.ROOT-SERVERS.NET.     ;Cl=0
            3600    IN      NS      H.ROOT-SERVERS.NET.     ;Cl=0
            3600    IN      NS      I.ROOT-SERVERS.NET.     ;Cl=0
            3600    IN      NS      J.ROOT-SERVERS.NET.     ;Cl=0
            3600    IN      NS      K.ROOT-SERVERS.NET.     ;Cl=0
            3600    IN      NS      L.ROOT-SERVERS.NET.     ;Cl=0
            3600    IN      NS      M.ROOT-SERVERS.NET.     ;Cl=0
$ORIGIN ROOT-SERVERS.NET.
K           3600    IN      A       198.356.0.11            ;Cl=0
L           3600    IN      A       18.32.412.12            ;Cl=0
A           3600    IN      A       212.422.10.4            ;Cl=0
M           3600    IN      A       164.320.164.12  ;Cl=0
B           3600    IN      A       164.98.10.107   ;Cl=0
C           3600    IN      A       192.33.14.12            ;Cl=0
D           3600    IN      A       128.8.100.90            ;Cl=0
E           3600    IN      A       142.403.230.10  ;Cl=0
F           3600    IN      A       142.16.16.441   ;Cl=0
G           3600    IN      A       142.412.36.4            ;Cl=0
H           3600    IN      A       198.663.2.53            ;Cl=0
I           3600    IN      A       162.636.148.17  ;Cl=0
J           3600    IN      A       168.414.10.100  ;Cl=0
bash-2.02#
```

The ndc command provides a simplified interface to the named daemon. You can achieve the same results utilizing signals to named. Let's take a look how we can do this.

You utilize the kill command to transmit a signal to the daemon. The kill command can be used to send a specified signal to any Linux process, not just to named. You should always specify the signal to send. If you do not specify a signal, kill will send the TERM signal by default. Table 10.4 shows the signals that can be sent to the named daemon.

Table 10.4 **Signals to the named Command**

Signal	Description
SIGHUP	Sending this signal causes named to read the named.boot file and then reload the database.
SIGINT	If named gets this signal, it will dump the current database and cache to /var/tmp/named_dump.db. This is the same as the dumpdb option to ndc.
SIGIOT	This signal is synonymous with the ndc stats option. Statistical data is dumped into the /var/tmp/named.stats file (data is appended).
SIGSYS	If the server is compiled with profiling, a profiling dump is made to the /var/tmp directory.
SIGTERM	This signal causes the server to dump the contents of the primary and secondary database files. Useful if you want to save modified data at shutdown.
SIGUSR1	Turns on debugging and increments the debug level. This is the same as the trace option to the ndc command.
SIGUSR2	This is the same as the notrace option to the ndc command. This signal turns off debugging.
SIGWINCH	This signal toggles the logging of incoming queries using the syslog facility. This signal is synonymous with the querylog option to ndc.

The following dialog demonstrates sending the SIGINT signal to the daemon. Before you can send the signal, however, you must first get the process ID for the named process. We show the results of the signal by displaying the contents of the /var/tmp/named_dump.db file.

```
bash-2.02# ps -ax | grep named
 3796 ?  S    0:00 named
bash-2.02# kill -SIGINT 3796
bash-2.02# cat /var/tmp/named_dump.db
; Dumped at Thu Jul 15 17:21:13 1999
;; ++zone table++
;; --zone table--
; --- Cache & Data ---
; --- Hints ---
$ORIGIN .
.           3600    IN      NS      A.ROOT-SERVERS.NET.     ;Cl=0
            3600    IN      NS      B.ROOT-SERVERS.NET.     ;Cl=0
            3600    IN      NS      C.ROOT-SERVERS.NET.     ;Cl=0
            3600    IN      NS      D.ROOT-SERVERS.NET.     ;Cl=0
            3600    IN      NS      E.ROOT-SERVERS.NET.     ;Cl=0
            3600    IN      NS      F.ROOT-SERVERS.NET.     ;Cl=0
```

continues ▸

continued

```
          3600    IN    NS    G.ROOT-SERVERS.NET.    ;Cl=0
          3600    IN    NS    H.ROOT-SERVERS.NET.    ;Cl=0
          3600    IN    NS    I.ROOT-SERVERS.NET.    ;Cl=0
          3600    IN    NS    J.ROOT-SERVERS.NET.    ;Cl=0
          3600    IN    NS    K.ROOT-SERVERS.NET.    ;Cl=0
          3600    IN    NS    L.ROOT-SERVERS.NET.    ;Cl=0
          3600    IN    NS    M.ROOT-SERVERS.NET.    ;Cl=0
$ORIGIN ROOT-SERVERS.NET.
K         3600    IN    A     198.41.0.11       ;Cl=0
L         3600    IN    A     198.32.64.12      ;Cl=0
A         3600    IN    A     198.41.0.4        ;Cl=0
M         3600    IN    A     198.32.65.12      ;Cl=0
B         3600    IN    A     128.9.0.107       ;Cl=0
C         3600    IN    A     192.33.4.12       ;Cl=0
D         3600    IN    A     128.8.10.90       ;Cl=0
E         3600    IN    A     192.203.230.10    ;Cl=0
F         3600    IN    A     192.5.5.241       ;Cl=0
G         3600    IN    A     192.112.36.4      ;Cl=0
H         3600    IN    A     128.63.2.53       ;Cl=0
I         3600    IN    A     192.36.148.17     ;Cl=0
J         3600    IN    A     198.41.0.10       ;Cl=0
bash-2.02#
```

After `named` is started, you can check out its operation by using the `nslookup` command. The `nslookup` command is used to query Internet domain names. At a command prompt, simply execute `nslookup`. After `nslookup` starts, it will display its command prompt: >. If you need help, type **help** at the `nslookup` prompt and help text will be displayed. The following dialog demonstrates a domain name lookup:

```
> www.whitehouse.gov
Server:   some.dnsserver.com
Address:  665.122.864.244

Non-authoritative answer:
Name:      www.whitehouse.gov
Addresses: 198.137.240.91, 198.137.240.92
>
```

The `Non-authoritative answer:` text with the response indicates that the DNS found the domain name in the cache, rather than going out on the Internet and querying servers directly.

You have been running `nslookup` in interactive mode. The `nslookup` command offers a command prompt whereby you submit commands and receive feedback. You can continue this dialog until you are finished. When you are finished using `nslookup`, you can use the `exit` command to quit the program and return to the shell prompt. The `nslookup` command can also be executed in noninteractive mode. In noninteractive mode, you simply invoke `nslookup` with required parameters, and `nslookup` will return information to the standard output. Check the man page for `nslookup` for complete details about the command.

To further assist in debugging `named`, you can examine the `/var/log/messages` (or `/usr/adm/messages`) file to check for any problems. If you invoke `named` manually (for testing), you can execute the `tail` command against the `/var/log/messages` file. The following dialog demonstrates this:

```
bash-2.02# ndc start
Name Server Started
bash-2.02# tail -3 /var/log/messages
Aug 19 23:33:06 stimpy named[851]: starting
Aug 19 23:33:06 stimpy named[851]: cache zone "" loaded (serial 0)
Aug 19 23:33:06 stimpy named[852]: Ready to answer queries.
bash-2.02#
```

Notice that we instructed the `tail` command to print only the last three lines in the file. In addition to checking the `/var/log/messages`, you can check the debug file named `/var/tmp/named.run` (on newer Linux systems).

Summary

In this chapter, we explored the use of the Domain Name Service (DNS). You learned that DNS is used to map hostnames to Internet addresses. This enables you to type logical names such as `www.whitehouse.gov`, instead of the actual address in dotted notation, as in `198.137.240.91`.

The setup and configuration of DNS was covered next. You can avoid the hassle of setting up your own DNS by using your ISP's DNS servers, if available. Otherwise, the information provided in the "DNS Configuration" section should get you up and running. Various configuration files and environment variables must be checked to be sure they are properly set—these items were covered in detail.

The name server, `named`, was covered next. The details of configuring `named`'s configuration files and starting up the daemon were covered. The daemon can be started in one of two ways. You can start it directly, supplying required arguments, or you can use `ndc`, the control interface to the `named` daemon. Configuration files, such as `/etc/named.boot`, were also covered.

Finally, we discussed the details of starting the `named` daemon and communicating with it. Communicating with the `named` daemon by using signals allows us to query its status and manipulate the running daemon. For example, you can send `named` the SIGTERM signal, and the server will dump the contents of the primary and secondary database files.

11

Network Information Service (NIS)

THE NETWORK INFORMATION SERVICE (NIS) provides the functionality of a distributed database system to contain various configuration files. Normally, these configuration files are stored locally and must be propagated to other machines as changes are made. A common use, for example, is to store the /etc/password file in NIS and provide a global access point for all hosts on the network.

This chapter explains what it takes to get NIS up and running, including installation and configuration.

Overview

The popularity of a distributed computing environment is growing rapidly. This type of network configuration presents many challenges. One challenge is the maintenance and distribution of shared configuration files. Some examples of these are the /etc/passwd, /etc/group, and /etc/hosts files. The challenge is not about the modification and upkeep of these files, but rather the distribution of the information contained in these files. Adding a single user to the system is not much of a chore, but making that new information available to other hosts on the network could take some effort. Consistency is the key to a properly managed network. Any changes made to a system configuration file, /etc/passwd for example, must be consistently communicated to all hosts.

Every day, Linux systems are being integrated into the networks of organizations of every size and shape. In some cases, Linux systems are being used as application and Web servers, DNS servers, and workstations. Because of this, it is important that Linux systems become seamless members of an organization's network.

The NIS addresses the challenges of dealing with a distributed computing network—namely, that of distributing network configuration files such as /etc/passwd. Because Linux is becoming an integral part of most organizational networks, it is important that Linux provide NIS functionality to those network communities.

The system that predated NIS was YP, or Yellow Pages, from Sun. The name was changed to NIS because British Telecom PLC maintains a registered trademark in the United Kingdom for the name "Yellow Pages." Much of the terminology you will encounter, such as ypserv and ypbind, were carried forward to NIS.

As mentioned previously, NIS consists of a distributed database that contains information normally stored in host files, such as the /etc/passwd, /etc/shadow, /etc/group, and /etc/host files. NIS provides for a centralized facility for managing this information. You maintain the information at one central server, the NIS server. Other hosts using NIS on the network obtain the information stored at the NIS server on an as-needed basis. Some of the common files that are handled by NIS are shown in the following list:

- **/etc/aliases.** Aliases and mailing lists for the mail system
- **/etc/bootparams.** Provides information about diskless nodes
- **/etc/ethers.** Provides MAC to IP mappings
- **/etc/group.** Provides group access information
- **/etc/hosts.** Provides IP address to hostname mappings
- **/etc/netgroup.** Network group definitions used by NIS
- **/etc/netmasks.** IP network masks
- **/etc/networks.** Network addresses
- **/etc/passwd.** Provides user access information
- **/etc/protocols.** Provides network protocol and number mappings
- **/etc/rpc.** Provides RPC numbers
- **/etc/services.** Provides port number to TCP/IP mappings

You are not required to set NIS to support all these files. It is up to you to decide which files should be maintained using NIS. Additionally, you can use NIS to maintain information in other files.

The general rule is to use NIS for storing information that has no host-specific data. Notice that the /etc/fstab file is not mentioned in the previous bulleted list. Why? This is because the /etc/fstab file contains information about filesystems and mount points found on hosts within a network. This file is specific to the host that it is associated with. It would be difficult to maintain filesystem information with NIS. This should not preclude you, however, from using NIS for storage and identification of general data.

Beginning with the next section, we begin our journey into the concepts, installation, and usage of NIS.

The NIS Model

NIS is modeled after the client/server model. The client/server model has shown itself to be an efficient and well-proven solution for many software systems. The request-and-response concept is well documented and understood. Software systems built on the client/server can be built rather quickly and can be tuned for peak efficiency.

The host portion of NIS maintains the data files, which are called *maps*. As can be expected, the client portion of the NIS system is the requester. The NIS system is built with a hierarchical structure of servers. This helps ensure that the system is scalable and that the workload can be distributed with ease. Figure 11.1 provides us with a graphical representation of NIS.

The master server sits at the top of the hierarchy. The master owns the maps. Branching from the master are slave servers. These slaves help to relieve the load from the master. NIS clients can request NIS information without having to worry about whether to communicate with a master server or slave server. The master server is responsible for all map updates and distribution to slaves. If a change has taken effect, the server is responsible for ensuring that all slaves are updated. Although an NIS slave server can service a request from an NIS client, the slave server's maps are read-only; the slave can not update its maps. This ensures that map modifications happen only at the master server.

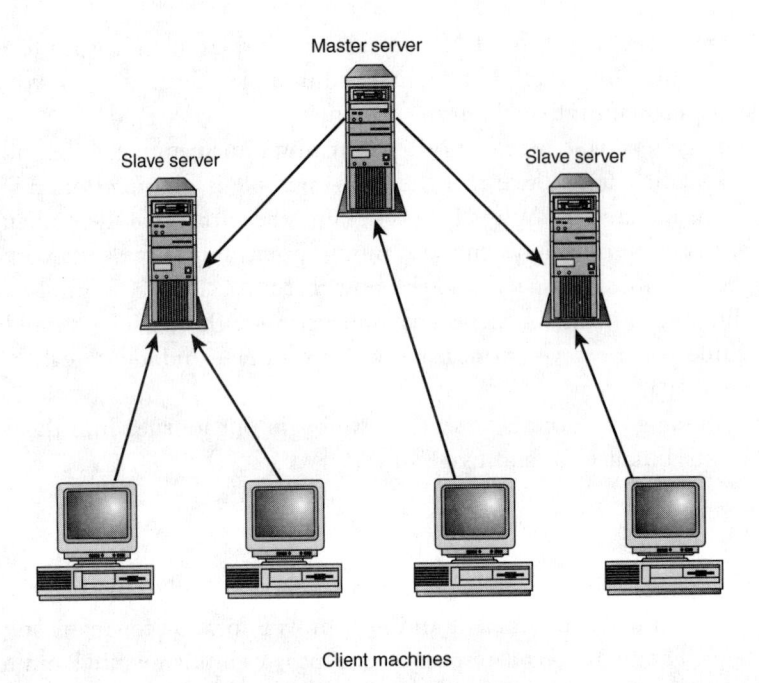

Figure 11.1 NIS system structure.

A simple example demonstrates the concepts of the NIS system. The /etc/passwd file should be familiar to most Linux users, especially those people playing the role of administrator. Remember that the /etc/passwd file is used to contain usernames and their associated passwords. (The exceptions are systems that utilize shadow passwords. In this configuration, the password is actually stored in the /etc/shadow file). Information besides the username and password is contained in the /etc/passwd file, but I am trying to keep the example simple. Any client that requires username verification will normally read from the /etc/passwd file. If the system is executing NIS, the request goes to the NIS server for the desired information. It does not matter whether the request is handled by the master server or a slave server. The information is gathered from the passwd map and sent back to the client.

What about adding a new user, you ask? Or you might need to delete a user or modify the settings for a user. At the master server, you modify the passwd file as required. After you have made the necessary changes, you rebuild the NIS maps. Remember, all this happens at the master server. After the maps have been updated, they must be distributed to the slave servers. This happens rather quickly and seamlessly.

Structuring NIS

Do not burden yourself with an NIS system in which the configuration data is simple and fairly static. In other words, it might be a waste of resources to use NIS to maintain maps of information that scarcely change. For example, not much advantage exists in using NIS to maintain the /etc/shells or /etc/protocols files.

When thinking about the implementation of NIS, you need to consider how information is partitioned within the network. This analysis must be done from an organizational level, rather than from the scope of network itself. Think about how the organization is partitioned. Are the departments intertwined (physically or logically) within the organization, or are they separate? It is probably safe to say that most organizations logically and physically partition their departments. The accounting department may occupy the northwest corner of the floor or might occupy three floors of the organization's building.

NIS provides the concept and implementation of what is called a *domain*. An NIS domain follows the concept of a network domain—it is used to logically group related units. If your organization is large, implementing NIS domains for organizational units probably makes sense. For example, you might dedicate an NIS domain for the accounting department, a domain for the exploration department, and a domain for the research department.

In actuality, an NIS domain declares and maintains a set of NIS maps. NIS clients are not precluded from obtaining information from NIS servers outside their domain. However, it makes more sense to partition the domains so that network traffic is minimized. For example, NIS clients in the exploration domain communicate primarily with NIS servers in the exploration (NIS) domain. If only four exploration engineers (and computers) are within the department, you should not create an NIS domain because the resources and maintenance effort do not offset the advantages of using NIS.

Naming NIS Domains

Establishing NIS domain names is a simple task. Some administrators find themselves wanting to be creative with respect to names. Although this might be cute when establishing hostnames, the same might not make sense for NIS domain names. If you have decided that the exploration department requires its own NIS domain, it probably does not make sense to use the name "ipswitch" for the domain name. No sense of association exists with the two organizational entities. Using the name "exploration" for the domain name makes sense. Even the name "explore" makes more sense than "ipswitch."

In organizations that require subdepartmental organization, you may need to partition the NIS domains accordingly. For example, within the exploration department might be the oil exploration and natural gas exploration subdepartments. If the breadth of machines warrants the additional domains, you might partition NIS domains using oil.exploration and gas.exploration as domain names. Notice the use of dotted notation for the subcategory naming.

> **NIS and DNS Domain Names**
> Be sure to refrain from choosing an NIS domain name that matches the DNS domain name. Using the same name can create a security risk.

NIS Server Allocation

No hard-and-fast rules determine the number of NIS servers to implement; there are many factors to consider. The physical network structure can be a determining factor, as well as the amount of predicted NIS traffic. Machine hardware can play into the factoring because many machines run much slower than others.

User profiles can play into the NIS server partitioning. A user profile, in this sense, is the type of user and the type of (computer) work performed. For example, a user who spends a lot of time at the console utilizing command-line utilities to perform work consumes more NIS resources than a user working with a spreadsheet or word processor.

Given that the server and client hardware are on equal footing, the ratio can be in the neighborhood of one server per 30 clients. If the client hardware is faster, increase the number of NIS servers (slave servers). If the server hardware is faster, you might bump the ratio to one server per 40 clients.

If you have determined that you need only one NIS server, you should be sure you implement two NIS servers. One server will be the master server and the other will be a slave server. Using two machines provides the system with a backup in case the master server fails for some reason. Some administrators say, "For every master server, there shall be a slave server."

Configuring NIS

Configuring NIS is a simple task. Organization is the key to success when setting up the NIS servers and NIS clients. This section covers the tasks required to enable an NIS master server, NIS slave server, and NIS client. For demonstration purposes, the text assumes that only one domain name will be used for the NIS system.

Configuring the NIS Master Server

For this chapter, it is assumed that you have partitioned your domain names, that you have the available NIS server machines, and that there will be only one NIS server and one NIS domain. Your first task is to name the NIS domain on the NIS server. The `domainname` command is used to set the domain name for the selected NIS server. The following dialog demonstrates the use for the `domainname` command:

```
stimpy $ domainname admin
stimpy $
```

On some Linux distributions, the `nisdomainname` and `ypdomainname` commands are synonymous with the `domainname` command. In some cases, these two commands are aliases for the `domainname` command. Invoking the `domainname` command without a name (no argument) will reveal the current domain name being used.

Some distributions of Linux will execute the `domainname` command at system startup. You can check the `/etc/rc.d` directory for the startup files containing calls to the `domainname` command. For example, for version 6.3 of SuSE Linux, the `/etc/rc.d/boot` file contains the following snippet to set the NIS domain name:

```
# set hostname and domainname
#
test -n "$FQHOSTNAME" && {
  ECHO_RETURN=$rc_done
  echo -n Setting up hostname
  hostname ${FQHOSTNAME%%.*} || ECHO_RETURN=$rc_failed
  echo -e "$ECHO_RETURN"
}
test -n "$YP_DOMAINNAME" && {
  ECHO_RETURN=$rc_done
  echo -n Setting YP up domainname
  domainname $YP_DOMAINNAME || ECHO_RETURN=$rc_failed
  echo -e "$ECHO_RETURN"
} || domainname ""
# set and adjust the CMOS clock
...
```

After setting the hostname, the domain name is set to the appropriate value. Setting the domain name, even if you are not using NIS, will do no harm.

For Red Hat Linux version 6.1, the domain name is set in the `/etc/rc.d/rc.sysinit` startup file. The following is a snippet from the file showing the call to the `domainname` command.

```
# Set the NIS domainname
if [ -n "$NISDOMAIN" ]; then
  action "Setting NIS domainname $NISDOMAIN" domainname $NISDOMAIN
```

continues ▶

continued

```
else
  domainname ""
fi
...
```

For the Slackware Linux distribution, the domain name is set in the /etc/rc.d/rc.inet2 startup file. The following is a snippet from the file showing the call to the `domainname` command:

```
# # First, we must set the NIS domainname. NOTE: this is not
# # necessarily the same as your DNS domainname, set in
# # /etc/resolv.conf! The NIS domainname is the name of a domain
# # served by your NIS server.
#
if [ -r /etc/defaultdomain ]; then
  nisdomainname `cat /etc/defaultdomain`
fi
# # Then, we start up ypbind. It will use broadcast to find a server.
if [ -d /var/yp ] ; then
  echo -n " ypbind"
 ${NET}/ypbind
fi
# # If you are the NIS master server for the NIS domain, then
# # you must run rpc.yppasswdd, which is the RPC server that
# # lets users change their passwords.
if [ -x ${NET}/rpc.yppasswdd ]; then
  echo -n " yppasswdd"
 ${NET}/rpc.yppasswdd
fi
...
```

For TurboLinux version 4.0, the domain name is set in the /etc/rc.d/rc.sysinit startup file (as in Red Hat). The following is a snippet from the file showing the call to the `domainname` command:

```
# Set the NIS domain name
if [ -n "$NISDOMAIN" ]; then
  domainname $NISDOMAIN
else
  domainname ""
fi
...
```

Now that the domain name has been established for the server, the next step is to validate the various administrative files. For every file, examine each entry for validity and remove any unwanted or expired entries. It is imperative that you have only the entries that your system will require. Doing this will ensure that the NIS map files contain only valid information. This will also ensure that your system is less susceptible to security violations.

Some of the files that you should visit and validate are shown in Table 11.1.

Table 11.1 **Files Maintained by NIS**

File	Description
/etc/aliases	Provides aliases and mailing lists for the mail system.
/etc/bootparams	Provides information about diskless nodes.
/etc/ethers	Provides MAC to IP mappings.
/etc/group	Provides group access information.
/etc/hosts	Provides IP address to hostname mappings.
/etc/netgroup	Identifies network group definitions used by NIS; this is specific to NIS.
/etc/netmasks	Provides IP network masks.
/etc/networks	Identifies network addresses.
/etc/passwd	Provides user access information.
/etc/protocols	Provides network protocol and number mappings.
/etc/rpc	Provides RPC numbers.
/etc/services	Provides port number to TCP/IP mappings.
/etc/shadow	Provides password information for user account. Not all systems employ shadow password functionality.

All these files may not be supported by your distribution of Linux; be sure to check the documentation for details. Notice that the /etc/netgroup file is used by NIS; you should know that it is NIS specific and is not a part of the stock of administrative configuration files.

Be sure to verify that any commands and directory paths are correct. Verify that all usernames have an associated password. You may have to consult the /etc/shadow file for this if your system uses shadow passwords. Ensuring that each account has a password will help in the fight against security breaches through NIS. If you will be using NIS to maintain other organizational-specific files, you should also ensure that these files are up to date.

Executing the `ypinit` Command

After you have determined that all your administrative files are up to date, the next action is to build the NIS maps. This is performed using the

ypinit command. The `ypinit` command is used to build and install the NIS database. The following shows the usage for the `ypinit` command:

```
ypinit [-m] [-s master_name]
```

The `ypinit` command accepts two options, which are `-m` and `-s master_name`. The `-m` switch is used to identify that the local host is the NIS master. Because you are at the master server, you must execute `ypinit` with the `-m` switch. The following dialog demonstrates the invocation.

```
stimpy $ ypinit -m
stimpy $
```

The `-s master_name` option is used if you are at a slave server. It is used to set up the slave server with the map files from the master server.

When the `ypinit` command executes, it builds the domain directory named /var/yp. Some versions may build the directory /etc/yp, so be sure to browse around the directory tree for the directory. The domain directory is created for the default domain.

After the domain directory exists, the `ypinit` command generates the administrative maps necessary for your system and places those maps in the domain directory (/var/yp).

For example, the following dialog shows the current state of NIS (on my system) before executing the `ypinit` command. This is for a SuSE 6.3 Linux system. The YaST utility was first used to install both the ypserver and ypclient packages from the CD-ROM media.

```
stimpy $ /var/yp
Makefile   nicknames   ypmake.conf.sample
stimpy $ ls -al
total 20
drwxr-xr-x   2 root    root        1024 Feb  7 10:22 .
drwxr-xr-x  18 root    root        1024 Feb  7 10:22 ..
-rw-r--r--   1 root    root       13980 Nov  8 14:36 Makefile
-rw-r--r--   1 root    root         185 Nov  8 14:36 nicknames
-rw-r--r--   1 root    root        1114 Nov  8 14:36 ypmake.conf.sample
stimpy $
```

I have not discussed the files that you see in the /var/yp directory. They are important, however, because they contribute to the build process.

The /var/yp/nicknames file is a translation table for NIS maps. This file contains a list of aliases and the associated NIS maps. Each line contains a single entry. The following shows the contents of the file shown in the previous dialog:

```
stimpy $ cat nicknames
passwd     passwd.byname
group      group.byname
```

```
networks    networks.byaddr
hosts       hosts.byname
protocols   protocols.bynumber
services    services.byname
aliases     mail.aliases
ethers      ethers.byname
stimpy $
```

This is the default content for the file on this SuSE system. The ypmake.conf.sample is provided as a template for creating a true ypmake configuration file. Continuing with our efforts, the following dialog demonstrates the execution of the ypinit command on this system. In addition, other commands are executed (bold text) to show the results of the ypinit command. The domain name created on this system is admin.

```
stimpy $ domainname admin
stimpy $ domainname
admin
stimpy $ /usr/lib/yp/ypinit -m
At this point, we have to construct a list of the hosts which will run NIS
servers. ren.stimpy.net is in the list of NIS server hosts. Please continue to add
the names for the other hosts, one per line. When you are done with the
list, type a <control D>.
    next host to add: ren.stimpy.net
    next host to add:
The current list of NIS servers looks like this:

ren.stimpy.net

Is this correct? [y/n: y] y
We need some minutes to build the databases...
Building /var/yp/admin/ypservers...
Running /var/yp/Makefile...
make[1]: Entering directory `/var/yp/admin'
Updating passwd.byname...
failed to send 'clear' to local ypserv: RPC: Program not registered
Updating passwd.byuid...
failed to send 'clear' to local ypserv: RPC: Program not registered
Updating group.byname...
failed to send 'clear' to local ypserv: RPC: Program not registered
Updating group.bygid...
failed to send 'clear' to local ypserv: RPC: Program not registered
Updating rpc.byname...
failed to send 'clear' to local ypserv: RPC: Program not registered
Updating rpc.bynumber...
failed to send 'clear' to local ypserv: RPC: Program not registered
Updating services.byname...
failed to send 'clear' to local ypserv: RPC: Program not registered
Updating netid.byname...
failed to send 'clear' to local ypserv: RPC: Program not registered
make[1]: Leaving directory `/var/yp/admin'
```

continues ▶

continued

```
stimpy $
stimpy $ ls -al
total 22
drwxr-xr-x   3 root     root        1024 Feb  7 11:15 .
drwxr-xr-x  18 root     root        1024 Feb  7 10:22 ..
-rw-r--r--   1 root     root       13980 Nov  8 14:36 Makefile
drwxr-xr-x   2 root     root        1024 Feb  7 11:16 admin
-rw-r--r--   1 root     root         185 Nov  8 14:36 nicknames
-rw-r--r--   1 root     root        1114 Nov  8 14:36 ypmake.conf.sample
-rw-r--r--   1 root     root          15 Feb  7 11:15 ypservers
stimpy $
stimpy $ cat ypservers
ren.stimpy.net
stimpy $
stimpy $ ls -al admin
total 148
drwxr-xr-x   2 root     root        1024 Feb  7 11:16 .
drwxr-xr-x   3 root     root        1024 Feb  7 11:15 ..
-rw-------   1 root     root       12443 Feb  7 11:16 group.bygid
-rw-------   1 root     root       12448 Feb  7 11:16 group.byname
-rw-------   1 root     root       13287 Feb  7 11:16 netid.byname
-rw-------   1 root     root       12454 Feb  7 11:16 passwd.byname
-rw-------   1 root     root       12452 Feb  7 11:16 passwd.byuid
-rw-------   1 root     root       16335 Feb  7 11:16 rpc.byname
-rw-------   1 root     root       14210 Feb  7 11:16 rpc.bynumber
-rw-------   1 root     root       30012 Feb  7 11:16 services.byname
-rw-------   1 root     root       12369 Feb  7 11:16 ypservers
stimpy $
```

The first map that ypinit creates is the ypservers map, found in the /var/yp directory. This is verified as a result of the ls -al command. The /var/yp/ypservers map file contains a list of hosts that will run as NIS servers.

A new directory, /var/yp/admin, is created as a result of the ypinit command. The contents of this domain directory are new NIS maps. For every domain name that exists, a directory reflecting that name will exist within the /var/yp directory. Within each domain directory will be a number of map files.

If you refer to the previous dialog, you will notice that the ypinit command queried for a list of hosts that will run NIS servers. The hosts are not required to be running at the time of executing ypinit but should be active NIS servers when it is appropriate. The contents of the /var/yp/ypservers file are also shown in the dialog.

Executing `ypserv`—The Master Server Process

After the `ypinit` command has completed its execution, you can start the NIS master server in one of two ways. You can reboot the system, which is not a productive choice (this is reserved for the Windows operating systems). The second method is to start the server manually, which is quite easy (this is reserved for Linux and UNIX operating systems). The usage for the `ypserv` command is shown as follows.

```
ypserv [-b] [-d [path]] [-p port]
```

Table 11.2 lists the options that are available to the `ypserv` command.

Table 11.2 **Options for the `ypserv` Command**

Option	Description
-d --debug [path]	This option is used to execute the server in debug mode. Normally, ypserv reports errors using the syslog facility. The ypserv command will not run as a daemon with this option set. The optional parameter *path* defines the directory that ypserv should use, instead of /var/yp.
-b --dns	If the host is not found in the hosts maps, use this option to query the DNS for host information.
-p --port port	This option specifies the port that ypserv should bind to.
-v --version	This option prints the version number and exits.

The following dialog demonstrates the execution of the `ypserv` command.

```
stimpy $ ypserv
stimpy $
stimpy $ ps x
...
 1880 tty1    S    0:00 /opt/Office51/bin/soffice.bin
 5390 tty1    S    0:05 kvt -T ption Terminal -icon kvt.xpm -miniicon kvt.xpm
 5391 pts/0   S    0:00 bash
 5702 ?       S    0:00 ypserv
stimpy $
```

Not much to it—all operations should be this easy! The `ps x` command is executed to verify the existence of the `ypserv` daemon. Notice that it is running as a background process because there is no controlling terminal.

Normally, the `ypserv` daemon is executed at system startup. The process continues to run on an NIS server machine that maintains a complete NIS database. At startup, or when the process receives the SIGHUP signal, `ypserv` will parse the `/etc/ypserv.conf` file for configuration information.

The `ypserv.conf` Configuration File

The `ypserv.conf` file is a typical Linux configuration file that contains options for `ypserv`. The file is normally found in the `/var/yp` directory but may also be found in the `/etc` directory. It also contains a list of rules for host and map access for the `ypserv` and `rpc.ypxfrd` daemons. The `ypserv` and `rpc.ypxfrd` daemons will read this file at startup or if they receive a SIGHUP signal. There should be only one entry per line. If the entry is an option line, the format is as follows:

`option: [yes | no]`

If the entry is an access rule, the format is as follows:

`host:map:security:mangle[:field]`

If any rules exist, they are tried one at a time. If a match is not found, access to a map is allowed. Table 11.3 lists the options available to the `ypserv.conf` file.

Table 11.3 **Options for the `ypserv.conf` File**

Option	Description
dns	If this option is specified, the NIS server will query nameserver for hostnames that are not found in the hosts.* maps. The default is *no*.
xfr_check_port	This option tells the NIS master server that it must run on a port less than 1024. The default is yes.

Table 11.4 describes the fields used for the access rules.

Table 11.4 **Field Descriptions for Access Rules in `ypserv.conf`**

Option	Description
host	IP address. Wildcards are allowed. Examples are 131.234. = 131.234.0.0/255.255.0.0, and 131.234.214.0/255.255.254.0.
map	Identifies the name of the map, or you can use an asterisk for all maps.
security	The choices are: none, port, deny, and des. The option none always allows access. Mangle the passwd field if so configured; default is not to mangle. The option port allows access if the port is less than 1024. If mangle is not set, do not allow access. If mangle is yes, allow access and mangle the passwd field. The option deny is used to deny access to this map. The option des requires DES authentication.

Option	Description
mangle	The possible values are yes or no. If yes, the field entry is mangled.
field	Determines the field that should be mangled. The default is the second field.

Mangle

Some of the options mentioned in Table 11.4 use the term *mangle*. This means the field is replaced by *x* if the port check reveals that the request originated from an unprivileged user.

Do not rely on the access rules to provide robust security. The access rules might slow down a cracker, but they will not stop him.

Creating a Slave Server

In this section, you will see what it takes to set up an NIS slave server. The one prerequisite is that you have the master server running before creating any slave servers.

Initializing a slave server is as easy as setting up a master server. The `ypinit` command is executed to perform the setup. The difference between setting up a master and a slave is determined by the `ypinit` option used. To create a slave, the `-s` option is used and the master server is specified.

To begin, you should be at the machine that will act as the slave server. If you have not named the server using the `domainname` command, you should do so now. Remember, to execute the command you simply provide the name as an argument to the command, as shown in the following sample dialog. You should be logged in as the root user to execute these commands.

```
stimpy $ domainname slaveName
stimpy $
```

Now that the name is set, it is time to execute the `ypinit` command. Remember, the master server must be running to execute the `ypinit` command for the slave. The following dialog demonstrates an attempt to create a slave server on the master, even after changing the name with the `domainname` command.

```
stimpy $ /usr/lib/yp/ypinit -s admin
The host specified should be a running master NIS server, not this machine.
stimpy $
```

The following dialog demonstrates the use of `ypinit` for the slave server.

```
stimpy $ /usr/lib/yp/ypinit -s ren
stimpy $
```

One other thing—the master server named as the argument must be accessible from the slave server. The directory structure is created and the map files are built from the master server's map files.

Setting Up an NIS Client Using `ypbind`

To enable an NIS client, you will have to have one or more servers running the NIS `ypserv` daemon. Be sure that an NIS server is running; otherwise, you run the risk of the client machine hanging.

Setting up an NIS client is straightforward. The concept is that the client binds itself to a server using—you guessed it—the `ypbind` command.

```
ypbind [-broadcast | -ypset | -ypsetme] [-p port] [-f configfile]
       [-no-ping] [-broken-server] [-debug]
ypbind -c [-f configfile]
ypbind --version
```

When `ypbind` starts up or receives the SIGHUP signal, it parses the `/etc/yp.conf` file. The `ypbind` command then attempts to use the entries found in the file for its binding.

The `ypbind` command removes itself from the controlling terminal, as all good daemons do, and uses `syslog()` for logging errors and warnings.

The `ypbind` process consists of a master process and a slave process. The master services RPC requests, asking for binding information. The slave process is used to initialize the bind, and it validates it periodically. If a failure occurs, the bind is invalidated and the process is retried.

The `ypbind` command searches for a server on the NIS domain, and then stores that information in a binding file. The binding file usually resides in the `/var/yp/binding` directory. The name for the binding file is customarily `[domainname[.[version]`. It is possible to have several files because an NIS client can be bound to more than one domain.

Table 11.5 describes the options for the `ypbind` command. Please note that the `ypbind` command in some Linux distributions does not support all options listed.

Table 11.5 **Options for the `ypbind` Command**

Option	Description
`-broadcast`	This option is used to send a broadcast for information required to bind to an NIS server.
`-ypset`	This option allows a root user from any remote machine to change the binding for a domain using the `ypset` command. The default is that no one can change the binding. Be cautious because this is an unsecure option.

Option	Description
-ypsetme	This option is the same as -ypset, but only root is allowed to change the binding.
-c	This option tells ypbind to check the configuration file for syntax errors and exits.
-debug	This option invokes ypbind in debug mode, keeping ypbind from running in the background. Additionally, ypbind will write error messages and debug output to standard error.
-broken-server	This option is used to tell ypbind to accept answers from servers running on an illegal port number. Avoid this option if you can.
-no-ping	This keeps ypbind from checking whether the binding is alive; it is used with dial-up connections to prevent ypbind from keeping the connection open.
-f configfile	This option tells ypbind to use configfile.
-p port	This is used to specify the port that ypbind will bind to. This allows you to use router filter packets to the NIS ports.
--version	This option prints the version number and exits.

For some versions of ypbind, after a bind has been established, ypbind will transmit YPPROC_DOMAIN requests to the NIS server at 20-second intervals. If ypbind does not get a response (or the server responds that it does not have this domain any longer), ypbind will seek out a new NIS server. If ypbind finds a server that responds faster, ypbind switches to the faster server. You can tell ypbind to use network broadcasts to find a new server. This is an insecure method. Rather, you should give ypbind a list of known, secure servers. In this case, ypbind sends a ping to all servers and binds to the first one that answers.

Additional NIS Commands and Files

The NIS system offers a number of commands beyond what has been discussed thus far. Some of the commands discussed in this section may or may not be available on your Linux distribution.

The ypwhich Command

The ypwhich command is used to return the name of the NIS server or the map master. The usage for ypwhich is as follows:

```
ypwhich [ -d domain ] [ -Vn ] [ hostname ]
ypwhich [ -d domain ] [ -t ] -m [ mname ]
ypwhich -x
```

The `ypwhich` command returns the name of the NIS server that is supplying NIS services to the NIS client. The NIS server might also be the master for a map. If you invoke the command without any arguments, the value returned is the NIS server for the local machine. If you specify a hostname, that host machine will be queried to discover the NIS master that is being used.

Table 11.6 describes the available options for the `ypwhich` command.

Table 11.6 **Options for the `ypwhich` Command**

Option	Description
-d *domain*	Specifies a domain other than the default.
-t	Inhibits the map nickname translation.
-m *mname*	Locates the master NIS server for a map. A hostname cannot be specified in this option. The *mname* can be a map name or the nickname for a map.
-x	Displays the map nickname translation table.
-Vn	Prints the version of `ypbind` and exits.

The `ypcat` Command

The `ypcat` command is used to print the values for all keys in an NIS database. The usage for the command is as follows:

```
ypcat [ -kt ] [ -d domain ] mapname
ypcat -x
```

The `ypcat` command is used to print the values for all keys from the NIS database specified by the identified `mapname`. The `mapname` identified can be a map name or a map nickname.

The options available to the `ypcat` command are listed in Table 11.7.

Table 11.7 **Options for the `ypcat` Command**

Option	Description
-d *domain*	Identifies a domain other than the default.
-k	Displays the map keys. Useful with maps in which the values are null or the key does not exist as part of the value.
-t	Inhibits map nickname translation.
-x	Displays the map nickname translation table and exits.

The ypmatch Command

The ypmatch command is used to print the values of one or more keys from an NIS map. The usage for the ypmatch command follows:

```
ypmatch [ -kt ] [ -d domain ] key ... mapname
ypmatch -x
```

The ypmatch command prints the values of one or more keys from the NIS database. This is specified by the identified mapname. The mapname may be a map name or a map nickname.

The options available to the ypmatch command are shown in Table 11.8.

Table 11.8 **Options for the ypmatch Command**

Option	Description
-d domain	Specifies a domain other than the default.
-k	Displays the map keys. Useful with maps in which the values are null or the key does not exist as part of the value.
-t	Inhibits map nickname translation.
-x	Displays the map nickname translation table and exits.

The yppoll Command

The yppoll command returns the version and master server of an NIS map. The usage for the yppoll command is shown in the following:

```
yppoll [ -h host ] [ -d domain ] mapname
yppoll
```

Two options are available for the yppoll command. These options are as follows:

- **-h host.** Ask the NIS server for information about mapname. If the host is not identified, the server polled will be the default server returned by the ypwhich command.
- **-d domain.** Specify a domain other than the default.

The ypxfr Command

The ypxfr command is used to transfer an NIS database from a remote server to a local host. The usage for the ypxfr command is as follows:

```
ypxfr [-f] [-c] [-d target domain] [-h source host] [-s source domain]          [-C
↪taskid
program-number ipaddr port] [-p yp_path ] mapname ...
```

The `ypxfr` command is used to copy an NIS database from an NIS server to the local host. Normally, the `ypxfr` command is executed by the `ypinit` command or by the `ypserv` command when `ypserv` receives a request from `yppush` for a map transfer.

A temporary map is created in the `/var/yp/[domainname]` directory. The file is populated with the map entries and retrieves map parameters. The original version of the map is replaced with the temporary map if the transfer succeeded.

For all maps, you have an NIS master server, which maintains a canonical copy of the NIS map; all the other servers, the NIS slaves, copy the new version of the map from the master whenever an update is made. Normally, you have one NIS master for all maps.

The `ypxfr` command is used most often where several NIS servers (master and slaves) are in use. The `ypxfr` command is executed as a cron job. If the data for a map is fairly static, updating once a day should be sufficient. For other highly dynamically changing files, you may want to set cron to run `ypxfr` every hour or two.

The `ypxfr` command offers a number of options, which are described in Table 11.9.

Table 11.9 **Options for the ypxfr Command**

Option	Description
-f	This option forces a map transfer. The `ypxfr` command will not transfer a map if the copy on the NIS master is the same as the local host.
-c	This option specifies that the `clear current map` request should not be sent to `ypserv` running on the local host. You should use this flag when invoking `ypxfr` via `ypinit`. You can also use this flag if `ypserv` is not running locally. If the option is not specified under either of these two conditions, then `ypxfr` will complain that it can not communicate to the local `ypserv`.
-d *domain*	This option specifies a domain other than the default.
-h source *host*	This option obtains the map from host. If *host* is not specified, the `ypxfr` command requests the name of the master from the NIS service, to try to get the map from there.

Option	Description
-s source domain	This option identifies a source domain to transfer a map from.
-C taskid program# ipaddr port	This option is used only by the ypserv command. When ypserv executes ypxfr, ypxfr is registered as program#; should call the yppush process at the host with ipaddr; is listening on port; and waiting for a response to taskid.
-p yp_path	This option changes the directory for the maps to yp_path/[domainname] rather than the default of /var/yp/[domainname].
mapname	This option specifies the names of the map(s) to transfer.

The yppush Command

The yppush command is used to force distribution of modified NIS databases. The usage for the command is as follows:

yppush [-d domain] [-t timeout] [-p # parallel jobs] [-h host] [-v] mapname ...

The yppush command is used to copy the updated NIS maps from the master to the slave servers within an NIS domain. This command is normally invoked from the /var/yp/Makefile file after the master databases have been modified. Be sure to check the Makefile for the NOPUSH=True rule. If this line exists, you must comment it out. To determine the slave servers that must be updated, the yppush command compiles a list from the ypservers NIS map. The destination host can be specified on the command line.

The yppush command offers a number of options, which are described in Table 11.10.

Table 11.10 **Options for the yppush Command**

Option	Description
-d domain	This option is used to specify a domain. The default is to use the NIS domain for the local host. You must specify the domain name for the local host if the domain name is not set.
-t timeout	This option is used as a timeout flag, interpreted in seconds. The value determines the number of seconds that yppush waits for a response from a slave server. If no response is received, yppush tries another NIS server.

continues ▶

Table 11.10 **Continued**

Option	Description
`-p # parallel jobs`	This option directs `yppush` to send the multiple map transfer request in parallel, rather than submitting the request serially (the default).
`-h` *host*	This option specifies transfer of a map to the identified host. Multiple hosts can be specified using multiple instances of this option.
`-v`	This option tells `yppush` to print debugging messages as it executes.

Summary

This chapter discussed the installation and use of the Network Information Service (NIS). NIS provides a distributed database system containing various system administration files.

An overview of NIS was discussed; you learned that NIS was originally named the Yellow Pages (YP). Because of trademark issues, the name was changed to NIS.

Some of the files that NIS traditionally houses are found in the /etc directory and are named `aliases`, `bootparams`, `ethers`, `group`, `hosts`, `netgroup`, `netmasks`, `networks`, `passwd`, `protocols`, `rpc`, and `services`.

The NIS model is a client/server model. The host portion of NIS maintains data files known as *maps*. The client side sends requests to the server, soliciting information identified in the map files.

Configuring an NIS master server is accomplished using the `ypinit` command. This command is also used to initialize a slave server. The slave server maps are populated from the master server(s).

The `ypserv` daemon is the server process used to handle requests coming from NIS clients. An NIS client uses the `ypbind` daemon to attach to a server, thereby submitting a request to the bound server.

The chapter concludes with a section detailing some of the miscellaneous NIS commands. The commands covered are `ypwhich`, `ypcat`, `ypmatch`, `yppoll`, `ypxfr`, and `yppush`. The `ypwhich` command returns the name of the NIS server. The `ypcat` command prints the values for all keys in an NIS database. The `ypmatch` command prints the values of one or more keys from an NIS map. The `yppoll` command returns the version and master server for a map. To transfer an NIS database from a remote server to a local host, use the `ypxfr` command. Finally, the `yppush` command forces distribution of modified NIS databases.

12

Network File Service (NFS)

THE NETWORK FILE SYSTEM (NFS) is a popular and widely used protocol for file sharing. Many organizations use NFS to serve up users' home directories. This allows users to roam about and use more than one machine; thus, each user will have access to his or her home directory.

Overview

As mentioned previously, NFS is a protocol for the sharing of files. NFS was originally developed and released in 1985 by Sun Microsystems. Sun Microsystems advertises an installed base of eight million NFS systems. NFS has come to be a very robust solution and runs on many platforms.

The growth of NFS in the PC arena the last few years is attributed to the growth of Linux and other PC-based operating systems. NFS is also enjoying fast growth in the workstation and server markets. Some of the highlighted features of NFS are the following:

- NFS maintains the scalability required to support small to large enterprise networks.
- An automatic mounting facility provides continuous and transparent access to files.
- NFS Version 3, which is a new version of the NFS protocol, is designed to increase scalability and performance.
- Quick access to information is provided by local disk caching.

- NFS implements centralized administration, thereby reducing the effort required to perform your routine administration tasks.
- Some NFS systems provide support for diskless and dataless client systems.
- NFS has an open architecture. However, this creates security risks—this architecture is understood by crackers.

NFS is implemented as a client/server architecture supporting the sharing of files. The NFS system is available on a wide range of heterogeneous platforms, from mainframes to the PC. Another plus is that NFS is an open standard. This means that you do not have to worry about proprietary mechanisms or rely on a single vendor to provide products, updates, or technical support. NFS is even defined in a number of RFCs and is part of X/Open Common Application Environment.

You can obtain the source code for NFS and can license it from SunSoft. You can also obtain the written specification for free by downloading it from the Internet. The current advertisement says that more than 300 organizations have licensed NFS technology. Many products to enhance NFS are available for most operating system platforms.

Table 12.1 lists some of the vendors that provide solutions for NFS.

Table 12.1 **Vendors Providing NFS Support**

Vendor	Operating System(s)
Amdahl	UTS
Apple	A/UX
BSDI	UNIX
Cray	UNICOS
DEC	Ultrix, VMS
Dell	SVR4
FTP Software	DOS, Windows, OS/2
Frontier Technology	DOS, Windows
Hewlett-Packard	HP-UX
Hummingbird	UNIX, Windows
IBM	AIX, MVS
Intel	UNIX
ICL	UNIX
Net Manage	DOS, Windows

Vendor	Operating System(s)
Nixdorf	TOS 35
Novell	Netware
OSF	OSF1
Santa Cruz Operation (SCO)	SCO UNIX
SunSoft	Solaris, DOS, Windows
Silicon Graphics	IRIX
Process Software	VMS
Texas Instruments	TI SVR3.2
TGV	VMS

When a directory (or file) is shared using NFS, that directory (or file) appears to be a part of the local filesystem, rather than the one on the remote system. NFS is not restricted to large networks within an organization. You could set up your own network of Linux machines, using NFS to share files and directories. For example, you might have your main server located in a large closet, attic room, or basement. Using NFS, you can share all the files and directories that exist on that server to all the other machines in your house. The files and directories appear to be local to the machine you are using, rather than on the remote server. Of course, NFS must reach across the network to obtain information on the files, but all this trafficking is done transparently.

Although NFS can be used with various networks, it is optimally designed for the TCP/IP protocol. NFS is found more often on networks running TCP/IP, mainly because of the popularity of TCP/IP today. But because NFS is such a popular file-sharing protocol, implementations of it can be found on heterogeneous operating systems. Refer to Table 12.1 to review the list of vendors and operating systems.

Under Linux and UNIX, the NFS system is employed in a peer-to-peer mode. This provides a kind of AC/DC perspective: Your machine can be running as an NFS server sharing files to other clients, plus your system can act as an NFS client obtaining shares from other NFS servers—and this can happen simultaneously.

The Network File System is easily implemented, even on your home network. You have nothing to fear with NFS. The only thing required on your part, as with anything else, is time. Just because NFS is running on your corporate network does not mean that you cannot get it running on your two-machine network at home. After you get it running, you will wish you had done it sooner.

NFS Design and Architecture

Because NFS is based on a client/server architecture, it naturally consists of a client program and the server program. There is also the protocol that allows the client and server to communicate their requests. You will see how NFS servers share their filesystems and how the clients can access these shared filesystems.

If you have ever mounted a local filesystem, the concept of NFS will be easy to understand. Even if you have never mounted a filesystem, do not fret—it will come easily.

Basically, the NFS server exports a file or directory, making it visible to NFS clients. The NFS client simply mounts the requested filesystem.

The mechanism of mount is that of incorporating the remote filesystem with the local filesystem. A specialized service that is available for the client side is the *automounter*. The automounter provides the capability to automatically mount and umount (unmount) a filesystem when that filesystem is required. If you are familiar with the *mtools* package, consisting of commands such as mdir and mcopy, you are familiar with automount functionality. When you insert a DOS floppy and execute the mdir command, the command first mounts the floppy, and then accesses the floppy's directory structure through the local (mounted) directory, and finally, mdir executes umount on the floppy.

NFS Protocol

The NFS protocol is composed of remote procedures that provide clients the capability to manipulate files and directories on remote machines (NFS servers) as if those files were local. The NFS protocol provides the routines necessary for a client to send a request for a file or directory operation. The server accepts this request and attempts to execute the request. Whether the request succeeds or fails, a response is returned to the client making the request. In the case of failure, an error value is returned. In the case of success, the results appropriate for the execution of the request are returned to the client.

Various file operations are available in the NFS protocol, such as read, rename, mkdir (make directory), and write.

Using the NFS protocol routines, clients send requests for file operations to servers, and servers respond by attempting to perform the operation (provided the user has proper permission) and then sending back successful results or error values. The NFS protocol includes a full spectrum of file operations, including mkdir, read, rename, and write.

Error Recovery

One of the design goals for the NFS protocol is swift error recovery. Each of the NFS calls identifies the arguments necessary to execute that procedure call. This clearly provides two benefits of NFS. The first benefit is that NFS can gracefully and quickly recover from any failure, be it network or system. The second benefit allows for painless administration.

Transport Independence

NFS is not associated with any transport protocol. This results in a file-sharing system that is transport independent. The NFS architecture is designed so that any future protocols can carry NFS traffic. A few protocols are in use today, such as User Datagram Protocol (UDP) and Transmit Control Protocol (TCP).

Protocol independence is achieved using a Remote Procedure Call (RPC) layer; the NFS protocol is actually implemented on top of the RPC transport technology. This implies that the NFS calls are implemented in terms of RPC calls. NFS also utilizes the External Data Representation (XDR), which further aids in NFS being machine and language independent. XDR is a standard for the description and encoding of data. It is used for transferring data between disparate computer architectures. A language is used to describe data formats in XDR—it can be used only to describe data.

NFS Client

An NFS server exports files and directories, thereby allowing NFS clients to gain access to those resources. The NFS client simply mounts the remote filesystem to a local resource, such as a directory. This results in the remote filesystems being an integral part of the local Linux filesystem. Figure 12.1 visually demonstrates a mounted filesystem.

A service called the *automounter* provides functionality to automatically mount a filesystem and then unmount it when an operation is complete. The automounter is an NFS client-side enhancement, reducing the manual tasks of mounting and unmounting a remote filesystem.

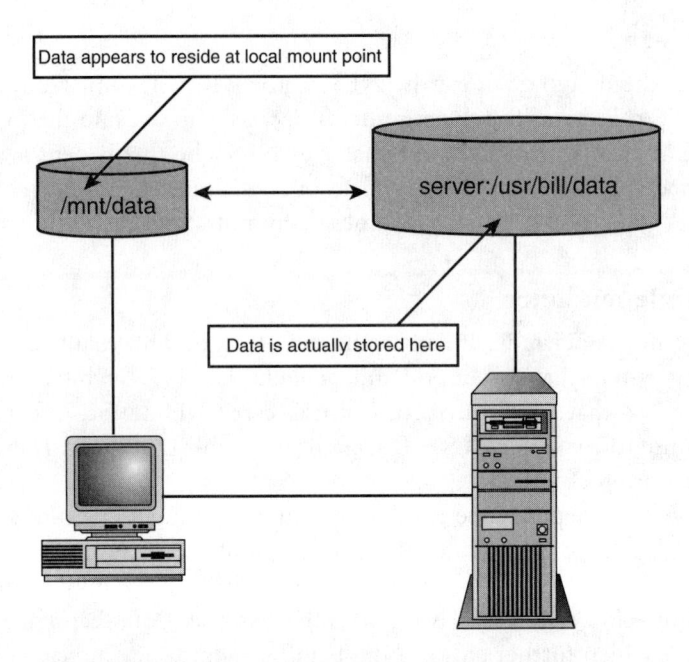

Figure 12.1 A remote filesystem mounted on a local directory.

The Automounter and NFS Namespace

The automounter must perform its magic somehow. The magic I am talking about is the capability to mount a filesystem and then later unmount the filesystem. The magic behind all this is called a map. The automounter uses maps to make the proper mounting associations. A map describes the association of the local pathname with the remote filesystem. The local pathname is actually called a mount point, or simply, mount. It is called a mount point because it is the "point" at which you "mount" a remote filesystem. The NFS namespace is the aggregation of mount points.

A client maintains a mount point for each remote filesystem the client wishes to access. All accesses to the remote filesystem are made through the local mount point. The NFS system transparently shields the user from specifics of the remote filesystem. Referring to Figure 12.1, you can see that the mount point for the client is /mnt/data and the remote filesystem is the server:/usr/bill/data directory path.

Both paths represent a root (start point), each from a different perspective. For the server side, the server:/usr/bill/data directory path is the starting point given to the NFS client. The client may only traverse down the hierarchy. For the client, the /mnt/data directory represents the logical start point for filesystem traversal. The word *logical* is used because you are not traversing a filesystem on your system.

The key to NFS administration, if you consider automounter maps, is the maintenance of the automounter maps. The automounter maps should be stored in a central and well-known location. The Network Information Service (NIS), if available, can be used for this purpose. Otherwise, you can utilize the facilities of the Linux system files for map storage.

Purpose of the Automounter

The automounter has some amount of intelligence. As mentioned previously, the automounter automatically mounts remote filesystems as required. If a user is trying to access a filesystem that is not currently mounted, the automounter will attempt to mount the filesystem. The automounter uses information in the map to execute the mounting. The automounter will also automatically unmount a filesystem that has been idle for some time. I use *idle* here to mean a filesystem that has not been accessed over a period of time. You can set the minimum timeout for the automounter for automatic unmounting; the default is five minutes. If you set the timeout to zero, automatic unmounting is disabled.

The automounter is actually a collection of individual components. Each of these components is critical to the success of the automounter.

As can be expected, a daemon process is required and is called `automountd`. This daemon is the real workhorse, because it is the process that handles all the requests to the NFS server daemon process (`nfsd`).

The second component is the `automount` command. The `automount` command is used to configure mount points for `autofs`. The `automount` command works using a base mount point and map, and uses this combination to automatically mount filesystems when they are accessed in any way.

The third component is `autofs`, which is implemented as a virtual filesystem. The `autofs` command is used to control the `automount` daemons that are running on your Linux system; normally, `autofs` is executed at system boot.

The following discussion describes the sequence of events for a "generic" automount start up—I will discuss `automount` as it applies to Linux. The `automount` command is executed at system start up. Next, `automount` reads the master configuration file named `auto.master`. After this point, if a user attempts to access a filesystem identified as a mount point, the `autofs` daemon calls on the services of the `automount` daemon, requesting that it mount the filesystem. The operation performed by the user can be something as simple as the `cd` or `ls` command.

Next, the `automount` daemon tries to establish a conversation at the server side with `nfsd`, the NFS daemon. A lookup is performed in `/etc/mnttab`, searching for the requested path, `server:/usr/bill/data` using our example. After the path has been verified, the filesystem is mounted to the proper mount point—`/mnt/data`, using our example. Thus, the namespace is updated to include the new mount.

NFS Server

The NFS server has a fairly straightforward job—its focus is to provide access to its filesystems by NFS clients within the network. The NFS server makes the filesystems available to the world by exporting the filesystem(s). An exported filesystem is one that has been exported by the server and is available for access by NFS clients within the network.

At system startup, a configuration file is read that contains information for exporting filesystems. Basically, the configuration file contains entries for each filesystem that is exported. The following list identifies the fields for each export entry:

- The directory pathname that is to be exported
- A list of client machines that will access the exported filesystem
- Access restrictions that might be required

Both daemon processes, `mountd` and `nfsd`, after execution, sit and wait for requests (filesystem accesses) from NFS clients.

NFS and Linux

This section explores the world of NFS specific to the Linux operating system. After all, other operating systems are out there, and you want to be able to utilize those filesystems. You also want to share the filesystems found on your Linux systems, if that is a requirement.

Linux is a natural choice for NFS support. You can use your Linux system as an NFS client, mounting remote filesystems (that are available) to your local filesystem. You can also offer your Linux system as an NFS server, allowing Linux clients to mount filesystems offered by your NFS server. Considering that Linux implements NFS in peer-to-peer mode, you can have the best of both worlds. Your Linux system can run as an NFS server sharing files to NFS clients, and your system can operate simultaneously as an NFS client.

You should be sure to read the following section on security. As you know, NFS is a protocol for file sharing, which can create security issues. NFS is an open architecture that is known and understood by crackers; therefore, NFS offers another door through which crackers can gain access to your system. With all this said, let us begin our journey.

Setting Up an NFS Server

You might be tasked with NFS server administration at your organization, or you may want to set up an NFS server on your home network. Either way, proper organization and a clear understanding of the maintenance aspects of NFS will allow you to get NFS up and running with a minimum of hassle.

NFS offers a number of benefits to users:

- You can keep administrative data on one central host, relieving you of having to replicate those files to multiple machines.
- User data can all be stored on one central host, allowing users to be mobile. Users can move about the organization or outside the doors and continue to access their data transparently. If you are using NIS, your users can also log in to any system and gain access to their data.
- You can store application and system data that consumes large amounts of disk space on a central host. This reduces maintenance chores, and it allows your users to gain access as required.

Basically, setting up an NFS server requires some quick file manipulation and ensuring that the required daemons are started. As mentioned previously, NFS sits on top of the RPC mechanism, so you have to be sure that the RPC components are properly set up.

Preconditions

Our journey to set up NFS will take us through a universal technique. Most all NFS systems follow the same pattern for setup and execution.

If you are unfamiliar with what NFS is and its architecture, I recommend that you read the earlier sections of this chapter. NFS is not rocket science, but an understanding of its functionality is beneficial.

The NFS Portmapper

The RPC server registers with the `portmapper` daemon on startup. The portmapper obtains the port numbers on which the RPC server will listen for incoming requests. This relieves the portmapper from having to listen on the ports. The portmapper is an RPC service and acts as an intermediary for RPC clients.

When an RPC client requires the services of the RPC server, it contacts the portmapper at a well-known IP port (port 111) to ascertain the RPC server's port number. Optionally, the client may request that the portmapper contact the RPC server on behalf of the client. The portmapper is indeed an important part of the RPC mechanism. If the portmapper ceases to exist (crashes, for example), RPC clients will be unable to contact RPC servers such as NIS and NFS.

The portmapper goes beyond the functionality it provides within the NFS terrain. The portmapper is also responsible for *RPC broadcasts*, which are requests that are transmitted to all RPC servers handling a specific RPC service. In these situations, the portmapper is contacted to transmit the broadcast to the RPC servers on behalf of the requester. This is done because hosts must know the port numbers (of the RPC servers) to deliver the broadcast. The problem is that RPC servers are not always at well-known addresses.

On Linux, the portmapper is named portmap or rpc.portmap and is normally found in the /usr/sbin directory. It is rare indeed, but possible, that it is named rpcbind on your distribution.

After you have the name of the portmapper, you need to fire it up. For now, you can invoke it by hand at the Linux command line. The following dialog demonstrates the action:

```
stimpy $ portmap
stimpy $
```

Now that is an uneventful dialog, to say the least. To ensure that the portmapper is running, you can do a couple of things. One is to use the trusty ps command to confirm the portmapper's existence. The following dialog demonstrates two techniques to use ps to discover the existence of the portmapper.

```
stimpy $ ps ax
...
 359 tty1    SN   0:05 kscd -caption CD Player -icon kscd.xpm
3348 tty1    SN   0:04 kvt -T ption Terminal -icon kvt.xpm -miniicon kvt.xpm
3349 pts/0   SN   0:00 bash
3475 ?       SN   0:00 portmap
3476 pts/0   RN   0:00 ps ax
...
stimpy $ # ps ax | grep portmap
3475 ?       SN   0:00 portmap
3480 pts/0   SN   0:00 grep portmap
stimpy $
```

In the first example, the ps command is executed, listing all processes. You will have to look through all the entries to find the portmapper entry. In the second example, the `grep` command is utilized to ferret out the portmapper entry from the process listing; sometimes it is worth the extra keystrokes.

The second technique to check for the existence of the portmapper is to use the `rpcinfo` command. This command is used to report RPC information. The following dialog demonstrates the use of the `rpcinfo` command to discover the existence of available RPC services.

```
stimpy $
stimpy $ rpcinfo -p
 program vers proto port
 100000  2  tcp   111  portmapper
 100000  2  udp   111  portmapper
stimpy $
```

As you can see, the portmapper is running on this system. Both the `ps` command and `rpcinfo` command confirm the portmapper's existence. If the portmapper is not running, the output from `rpcinfo` will resemble the following dialog.

```
stimpy $ rpcinfo -p
rpcinfo: can't contact portmapper: RPC: Remote system error - Connection refused
stimpy $
```

For now, you started the portmapper by hand, but you will want to automate this task whenever the system boots. You can adapt the `rc` scripts to invoke the RPC portmapper at system start up. Your Linux distribution determines the directory location of the rc files. Some of the well-known locations are the /etc/init.d, /etc/rc.d/init.d, or /etc/rc.d directories.

If the `rpcinfo -p` failed to report successfully, but the portmapper exists in the `ps ax` listing, you need to consult the /etc/hosts.allow and /etc/hosts.deny files. The reason that `rpcinfo` might be reporting failure is because all access to the portmapper is governed by the entries in the /etc/hosts.allow and /etc/hosts.deny files. For a more detailed explanation, you should check out the man page for the `tcpd` daemon command. A man page may also exist on your distribution for hosts_access(5) (man 5 hosts_access). This man page goes into great detail about the two files previously mentioned.

Another option for invoking the portmapper is to use the `rpc` command, if available. Normally, this file is found in the /etc/rc.d/init.d directory. Some Linux distributions may locate the file in the /etc/init.d directory. If you do not have a man entry for the `rpc` command, and the `which` command does not reveal the file, you can execute *find* to locate the command. The following dialog demonstrates the use of the `rcp` command:

```
stimpy $ rpcinfo -p
 program vers proto port
 100000  2  tcp   111  portmapper
```

continues ▶

336   Chapter 12 Network File Service (NFS)

continued

```
 100000 2 udp 111 portmapper
stimpy $ ./rpc stop
Shutting down RPC services          done
stimpy $ rpcinfo -p
rpcinfo: can't contact portmapper: RPC: Remote system error - Connection refused
stimpy $ ./rcp start
stimpy $ Starting RPC portmap daemon           done
stimpy $ rpcinfo -p
 program vers proto port
 100000 2 tcp 111 portmapper
 100000 2 udp 111 portmapper
stimpy $
```

The following shows the rpc script.

```
#
. /etc/rc.config
base=${0##*/}
link=${base#*[SK][0-9][0-9]}

test $link = $base && START_PORTMAP=yes
test "$START_PORTMAP" = yes -o "$NFS_SERVER" = yes ¦¦ exit 0
if test -x /sbin/portmap ; then
 PORTMAP=/sbin/portmap
else
 PORTMAP=/usr/sbin/portmap
fi
return=$rc_done
case "$1" in
 start)
     checkproc $PORTMAP && {
       killproc $PORTMAP 2> /dev/null
       echo -n "Re-"
  }
     echo -n "Starting RPC portmap daemon"
     startproc $PORTMAP ¦¦ return=$rc_failed
     /bin/sleep 1
  if test "$NFS_SERVER_UGID" = yes; then
     if test -x /usr/sbin/rpc.ugidd ; then
    startproc /usr/sbin/rpc.ugidd  ¦¦ return=$rc_failed
   fi
  fi
     echo -e "$return"
     ;;
 stop)
     if test -x /usr/sbin/rpc.ugidd ; then
       killproc -TERM /usr/sbin/rpc.ugidd  ¦¦ return=$rc_failed
     fi
     echo -n "Shutting down RPC services"
     killproc -TERM $PORTMAP ¦¦ return=$rc_failed
     echo -e "$return"
     ;;
 restart¦reload)
```

```
            $0 stop && $0 start ¦¦ return=$rc_failed
            ;;
    status)
        status="OK"
        if test "$NFS_SERVER_UGID" = yes; then
          checkproc /usr/sbin/rpc.ugidd ¦¦ status="rpc.ugidd down"
        fi
            checkproc $PORTMAP && echo "OK" ¦¦ echo "portmapper down"
            ;;
    *)
            echo "Usage: $0 {start¦stop}"
            exit 1
esac
test "$return" = "$rc_done" ¦¦ exit 1
exit 0
```

Remember, many scripts are specific to a Linux distribution, so this script may not work on your distribution. In all likelihood, the rpc command (script or otherwise) exists on your system.

The /etc/exports File

The /etc/exports file is important and should not be overlooked. The content of this file determines the filesystems that the NFS server allows clients to mount. The syntax for the file is as follows:

directory   [*option*, ...]

Each line contains a mount point (directory) and a list of machine (host) names that are allowed to mount the filesystem. Optionally, a parenthesized list of mount parameters may follow a machine name. Any blank lines are ignored and a # character signifies a comment in the file. An entry can span multiple lines using a \ (backslash) character. The following is a sample /etc/exports file:

```
# a sample /etc/exports file ...
/               rooty(rw) boss(rw,no_root_squash)
/devel          devel(rw)
/usr            *.local.domain(ro)
/pub            (ro,insecure,all_squash)
/pub/private         (noaccess)
```

The first line exports the entire filesystem to machines rooty and boss. The third entry demonstrates using wildcard hostnames. The fourth line exports the public FTP directory (/pub) to all hosts, invoking requests under the nobody account. The insecure option allows clients with NFS that don't use a reserved NFS port. The last entry (noaccess) denies all access (to NFS clients) to the /pub/private directory.

The mapping options are given in the parentheses, such as rw and insecure. A hostname can be prefixed to the option, thereby associating the option to the host. Table 12.2 lists the available mapping options.

Table 12.2 **Mapping Options for the /etc/exports File**

Option	Description
root_squash	This option is a security feature denying the super user on the specified hosts any access rights; it does this by mapping requests from uid 0 on the client to uid 65534 (should be associated with the user nobody) on the server. This does not apply to uids that might be as sensitive, such as *bin*.
no_root_squash	This option turns off root squashing. Mainly used for diskless clients.
squash_uids and squash_gids	This option specifies a list of uids (or gids) that are subject to anonymous mapping. A valid list of IDs looks like squash_uids=0-15,20,25-50
all_squash	This option is used to map all uids and gids to the anonymous user. Useful for NFS-exported public FTP directories, news spool directories, and so on.
map_daemon	This option turns on dynamic uid and gid mapping. Each uid in an NFS request will be translated to the equivalent server uid, and each uid in an NFS reply will be mapped the other way round.
map_static	This option enables static mapping, specifying the name of the file that describes the uid/gid mapping: map_static=/etc/nfs/foobar.map.
map_nis	This option enables NIS-based uid and gid mapping.
anonuid and anongid	These options are used to explicitly set the uid and gid of the anonymous account. This is useful for PC/NFS clients, in which you might want all requests to appear to be from one user.

You can specify the NFS clients in several ways. Table 12.3 shows the various formats.

Table 12.3 **NFS Client Formats**

Format	Description
single host	Commonly used format. You can specify a host using an abbreviated name that is recognized by the resolver, a fully qualified domain name, or an IP address.
netgroups	NIS netgroups may be identified as @group. The host part of all netgroup members is extracted, and then added to the access list.
wildcards	The hostnames can contain the * and ? wildcard characters. Can be used to make the exports file more compact. Example: `*.foo.edu` matches all hosts in the `foo.edu` domain. However, these wildcards do not match dots in a domain name. Thus, the preceding pattern does not include hosts such as `www.cs.foo.edu`.
IP networks	Directories can be exported to all hosts on an IP (or sub) network simultaneously. You do this by specifying the IP address and netmask pair as address/netmask.

If no machine name is given, any machine is allowed to import (or mount) the filesystem within the limits set by the options.

If you have made any modifications to the /etc/exports file while the NFS system is running, you should shut down the daemons and restart them.

The `mountd` and `nfsd` Daemons

The `mountd` daemon is the RPC-specific mount daemon. The `nfsd` daemon is an NFS server daemon that accepts RPC requests from clients. These two daemons complete the circuit for the NFS server side. Before you start up these daemons, however, you will need to verify and possibly modify the /etc/exports file. If you have not examined the /etc/exports file, you should read the previous section so that you can verify the file. This file must be valid because both the `mountd` and `nfsd` daemons read it.

When you feel comfortable that the /etc/exports file is in order, it is time to fire up the `mountd` and `nfsd` daemons. The `mountd` daemon should be invoked first, and then the `nfsd` daemon. The following dialog demonstrates this:

```
stimpy $ mountd
stimpy $ nfsd
```

Again, nothing spectacular here. As with the portmapper, you can verify the existence of the two daemons with the `ps` command and the `rpcinfo` command. The following dialog shows how to query for daemons:

```
stimpy $ ps ax
...
 328 tty1    SN   0:00 /opt/Office51/bin/soffice.bin
 359 tty1    SN   0:07 kscd -caption CD Player -icon kscd.xpm
3475 ?       SN   0:00 portmap
3927 tty1    SN   0:05 kvt -T ption Terminal -icon kvt.xpm -miniicon kvt.xpm
3928 pts/0   SN   0:00 bash
3951 tty1    SN   0:45 /opt/netscape/netscape
3960 tty1    SN   0:00 (dns helper)
4131 ?       SN   0:00 mountd
4134 pts/0   SWN  0:00 [nfsd]
4137 pts/0   RN   0:00 ps ax
stimpy $ rpcinfo -p
 program vers proto port
 100000   2   tcp   111  portmapper
 100000   2   udp   111  portmapper
 100005   1   udp   915  mountd
 100005   1   tcp   917  mountd
 100005   2   udp   920  mountd
 100005   2   tcp   922  mountd
 100005   3   udp   925  mountd
 100005   3   tcp   927  mountd
 100003   2   udp  2049  nfs
stimpy $
```

As you can see, the listing from the `ps ax` command shows that the two daemons (`mountd` and `nfsd`) are running. To further verify their existence, the `rpcinfo -p` command is executed. You can see by the output that the portmapper is running, that `mountd` is running and responsible for a number of ports, and that the `nfs` daemon is also executing.

Many Linux distributions offer a script to help ensure that all the RPC and NFS server daemons are started and invoked in the correct order. The RPC script is customarily named `rpc` and should be found in the /etc/rc.d/init.d directory. Some Linux distributions store the script in the /etc/init.d directory. The syntax for the command is shown in the following dialog:

```
stimpy $ cd /etc/rc.d/init.d
stimpy $ ./rpc
Usage: ./rpc {start|stop}
stimpy $ ./rpc start
Starting RPC portmap daemon ... done
stimpy $
```

Additionally, most distributions provide an `nfs` script, and it is found in the `/etc/rc.d/init.d` directory. Some distributions of Linux may store the script in the `/etc/init.d` directory. The following shows the usage for the `nfs` script.

```
stimpy $ ./nfs
Usage: ./nfs {start|stop|status|reload|restart}
stimpy $
```

Notice that the usage shows the options to start and stop the daemons. You also have the option to check the status of, reload, and restart the daemons. The `restart` option automatically executes the `stop` option first, and then invokes the `start` option. The `reload` option is synonymous with the `start` option in most distributions. The following shows a sample `nfs` script.

```
#
. /etc/rc.config
nfs=no
while read where what type options rest ; do
 case "$where" in
      \#*|"") ;;
      *) case "$options" in
           *noauto*) ;;
           *) if test "$type" = "nfs" ; then
                nfs=yes
                break
              fi ;;
         esac
 esac
done < /etc/fstab
case `uname -r` in
 0.*|1.*|2.0.*) RPCSTATD="" ; RPCLOCKD="" ;;
 *)
   test -x /usr/sbin/rpc.kstatd && RPCSTATD=/usr/sbin/rpc.kstatd
   test -x /usr/sbin/rpc.klockd && RPCLOCKD=/usr/sbin/rpc.klockd
   ;;
esac
return=$rc_done
case "$1" in
 start|reload)
     test "$nfs" = "yes" || exit 0;
     test -n "$RPCLOCKD" && startproc $RPCLOCKD
     test -n "$RPCSTATD" && startproc $RPCSTATD
     echo -n "Importing Network File System (NFS)"
     mount -at nfs || return=$rc_failed
     sleep 1
     ldconfig -X 2>/dev/null
     echo -e "$return"
     ;;
 stop)
     test "$nfs" = "yes" && echo -n "Remove Net File System (NFS)"
```

continues ▶

continued

```
        umount -at nfs &
        sleep 2
        test "$nfs" = "yes" && echo -e "$return"
        ;;
    restart)
        $0 stop && $0 start || return=$rc_failed
        ;;
    status)
        mount -t nfs | while read from x point rest ; do
         echo -e "$from\033[50G$point"
        done
        ;;
    *)
        echo "Usage: $0 {start|stop|status|reload|restart}"
        exit 1
esac
test "$return" = "$rc_done" || exit 1
exit 0
```

As mentioned previously, `mountd` is the mount daemon and `nfsd` is the NFS server daemon. On your distribution, the daemons may be named `rpc.mountd` and `rpc.nfsd`. Be sure to check the documentation for your Linux distribution.

Remember, the portmapper must be invoked and running before the `mountd` and `nfsd` daemon.

Exporting Filesystems

There is no broadcast of available filesystems by the server to NFS clients. The NFS server maintains a list of exported filesystems and the restrictions that are applicable for each export, called the filesystem table. When a mount request is received from an NFS client, the NFS server checks the request against its filesystem table. If the filesystem is in the list and the restrictions are satisfied, the server permits the mount.

The filesystem table and the contents of the `/etc/exports` file can be different. The NFS server creates the filesystem table from the contents of the `/etc/exports` file at the time that it initializes. The filesystem table is not updated by the NFS server unless the system is rebooted or the `exportfs` command is executed.

The `exportfs` command is used to maintain the table of exported filesystems. On some Linux distributions, the table exists as the `/var/lib/nfs/xtab` file. Unfortunately, not all Linux distributions have the `exportfs` command installed. If you do not have one, you can create a script to perform the logic. The following demonstrates the minimum for the script:

```
#!/bin/bash
killall -HUP /usr/sbin/rpc.mountd
killall -HUP /usr/sbin/rpc.nfsd
```

Be sure that the command name for each daemon is correct for your Linux distribution and that the directory path is appropriate. The HUP signal is sent to the daemons, effectively telling them to reinitialize. The net effect is that the /etc/exports file is read from disk by the NFS server and the filesystem table is regenerated.

For some Linux distributions, the `rcnfsserver` command can be executed to update the filesystem table if changes have been applied to the /etc/exports file. A man page may not exist for this command, so do not count on using that method for verification of `rcnfsserver`. For example, for the installed version of SuSE Linux 6.3 (on my machine), no man entry exists for `rcnfsserver`, but executing the `which` command reveals the file's existence, as shown in the following dialog:

```
stimpy $ man rcnfsserver
No manual entry for rcnfsserver
stimpy $ which rcnfsserver
/usr/sbin/rcnfsserver
stimpy $ rcnfsserver
Usage: /usr/sbin/rcnfsserver {start|stop|status|reload|restart}
stimpy $
```

Another method of updating the filesystem table is to stop and start the daemons using the `nfs` command. The following dialog demonstrates this:

```
stimpy $ cd /etc/rc.d/init.d
stimpy $ nfs stop
stimpy $ nfs start
stimpy $
```

If the `restart` option is available for the `nfs` command, you can invoke the command that way, as in the following dialog. The previous section, "The `mountd` and `nfsd` Daemons," discusses the `nfs` command in more detail.

```
stimpy $ cd /etc/rc.d/init.d
stimpy $ nfs restart
stimpy $
```

Before you create any script to force a reread of the /etc/exports file, check to see if either the `exportfs` or `rcnfsserver` command exists.

Using the NFS Client

There is not much to using an NFS client. The only requirements are that an NFS server is running, that at least one filesystem exists to mount, and the proper restrictions are satisfied.

You use the mount command to import a filesystem. This is what the term "NFS client" refers to. The mount command is used to execute a request to the NFS Server for importing a remote filesystem. The basic usage for the mount command is shown in the following:

```
mount -t type device dir
```

This tells the system to attach (or mount) the filesystem found on device (device), which is of type type, at the dir directory. Conversely, you use the umount command to unmount (or detach) the filesystem. The following dialog demonstrates the use of the mount command to import an NFS filesystem:

```
stimpy $ mount -t nfs sillyhost:home/bill /home/bill
```

Some distributions of Linux prefer that you execute the mount command with the -F option, as shown in the following dialog:

```
stimpy $ mount -F nfs sillyhost:home/bill /home/bill
```

Be sure to check the mount man page for the proper syntax for your Linux distribution.

To enforce that the system mounts an nfs filesystem at boot, you should edit the /etc/fstab file as usual. You should ensure that the -t nfs type is specified. In the following dialog, the contents of the /etc/fstab file shows an entry to mount an nfs type filesystem.

```
stimpy $ cat /etc/fstab
/dev/hda7      swap      swap      defaults    0    0
/dev/hda6      /         ext2      defaults    1    1
/dev/hdc       /cdrom    iso9660   ro,noauto,user,exec 0 0
/dev/hda5      /mnt/rh   ext2      defaults    1    1
/dev/fd0       /flop     auto      noauto,user 0    0
sillyhost:home/bill /home/bill nfs rsize=8192,wsize=8192,timeo=14,intr 0 0
none           /proc     proc      defaults    0    0
```

Using our previous example, the sillyhost... entry will be automatically mounted at system boot. This sample should work for most all Linux distributions. You should always check the documentation for your distribution to be certain.

You can also easily mount a filesystem by specifying the mount point, if the device is listed in the /etc/fstab file. For example, referring to the previous /etc/fstab sample, if you want to mount the /dev/hda5 device, you simply issue the mount command as shown in the following dialog:

```
stimpy $ mount /mnt/rh
stimpy $
```

Because the entry exists in the /etc/fstab file, all the proper parameters are available to mount the device to the identified mount point.

From here, all you do is access the filesystem as you normally would with any mounted filesystem.

The mount Command

The following section details the mount command. The mount command, these days, consists of many options. I hope to clarify the usage for mount.

The official usage for the mount command is shown as follows:

```
mount [-hV]
mount -a [-fFnrsvw] [-t vfstype]
mount [-fnrsvw] [-o options [,...]] device | dir
mount [-fnrsvw] [-t vfstype] [-o options] device dir
```

As you can see, four variant usages exist for the mount command, each one for a specific application.

All UNIX and Linux files are organized within a filesystem that is a hierarchical tree starting at /, known as *root*. This is not to be confused with the *root user*. Normally, the filesystem consists of more than one device; the mount command is used to import (or attach) these devices to the root filesystem. To unmount a filesystem, you use the umount command.

The most common form of usage for mount is as follows:

```
mount -t type device dir
```

This execution mounts the *device* device of type -t *type* onto the *dir* directory. The local directory (mount point) becomes the root of the mounted device.

Ironically, four usages for the mount command do not perform a device mount. They are as follows:

```
mount -h
mount -V
mount [-t type]
mount
```

The first form prints only help text associated with the mount command. The second form displays the version of mount and exits. The third form of mount lists all the filesystems of the type identified that are mounted. The last form lists all the filesystems that are mounted.

The form of the identified device is a block special device by filename. Some examples are /dev/hdc for a CD-ROM and /dev/fd0 for a floppy disk. Another example is /dev/hdb11 representing the tenth logical drive on the second IDE hard drive or /dev/hda5 representing the fourth logical drive on the first hard disk (these do exist on my system). You are not restricted to identifying a device as previously shown. You can also identify devices as some.domain.name:/directoryName.

You can add devices that are continually mounted at boot to the /etc/fstab file. The /etc/fstab file can be helpful in several ways. If an entry for a device exists in the file, you can mount it manually by specifying only the device or the mount point. The following example demonstrates this. The first dialog shows an entry in the /etc/fstab file:

```
stimpy $ cat /etc/fstab
...
/dev/hda5      /mnt/rh     ext2      defaults     1    1
...
```

Assuming that the /dev/hda5 entry exists as shown, you can mount the device onto the /mnt/rh directory by issuing one of the two following mount commands:

```
stimpy $ mount /dev/hda5
stimpy $ mount /mnt/rh
```

You do not need to specify the device type, device, and mount points because this information is already specified in the /etc/fstab file. Customarily, the superuser (root) is the only user that can execute the mount command. With the /etc/fstab file, however, you can use the user option, allowing anyone to mount the corresponding device. You should know that only the user that mounted the device is allowed to unmount the device. If you want any user to be able to unmount a device, you should use the users option rather than the user option.

Options for mount

A whole host of options are available for the mount command. In this section, I explore the options available, providing descriptions for each. Table 12.4 outlines the various options available to you.

Table 12.4 **Options for the `mount` Command**

Option	Description
-V	Show the version.
-h	Show a help message.
-v	Verbose mode.
-F	This option will fork an individual invocation of mount for each device. The advantage is speed. If you are mounting NFS devices, the timeouts will be concurrent. The downside is that the order of mounts is arbitrary.
-f	This option is a sort of "test" (or fake) mode. If you are having problems with mount, this option acts as a debugger (use with the -v option).
-n	Perform the mount and exclude writing the entry in /etc/mtab.
-s	Mainly used for the Linux autofs-based automounter. This tells mount to allow for awkward mount options versus failing.
-r	Mount the filesystem as read-only; synonymous with the -o ro option.
-w	Mount the filesystem as read/write; synonymous with -o rw. This is the default.
-L label	Mount the partition possessing the specified label.
-U uuid	Mount the partition possessing the specified uuid.
-t vfstype	This option identifies the filesystem type. The currently supported filesystem types are (shown in linux/fs/filesystems.c) adfs, affs, autofs, coda, coherent, devpts, ext, ext2, hfs, hpfs, iso9660, minix, msdos, ncpfs, nfs, ntfs, proc, qnx4, romfs, smbfs, sysv, ufs, umsdos, vfat, xenix, xiafs. The *coherent sysv*, and *xenix* types are equivalent. Both the coherent and xenix types will be removed sometime in the future.
-o	Options are specified with a -o flag, using a comma to separate the options. The options are: - atime—Update the inode access time for every access; the default. - auto—Specify that the mount is acceptable with the -a option. - defaults—Use the default options, which are rw, suid, dev, exec, auto, nouser, and async.

continues ▶

Table 12.4 **Continued**

Option	Description
	- `dev`—Interpret character or block special devices.
	- `exec`—Allow execution of binaries.
	- `noatime`—Do not allow updates to the inode access times on the filesystem.
	- `noauto`—The filesystem can only be explicitly mounted.
	- `nodev`—Do not interpret character or block special devices.
	- `noexec`—Disallow the execution of binaries on the mounted filesystem.
	- `nosuid`—Disallow set-user-id or set-group-id bits to occur.
	- `nouser`—Prohibit a non-root user to mount the filesystem; this is the default.
	- `remount`—Used to attempt a remount of an already mounted filesystem. Used to change the mount flags for a filesystem.
	- `ro`—Mount the filesystem as read-only.
	- `rw`—Mount the filesystem as read/write.
	- `sync`—Synchronize I/O to the filesystem.
	- `user`—Permit an ordinary user to mount the filesystem; implies the options `noexec`, `nosuid`, and `nodev`.

The man page for the `mount` command provides more level of detail for filesystem-specific mounts. Be sure to refer to it for any special needs you may have.

Optimizing NFS on Low-Bandwidth Connections

So many variables are at work when you analyze network activity that a whole chapter can be written about it. This section touches on only three options for adjusting the performance of NFS on low-bandwidth connections. The section is short and sweet to keep things simple.

Admittedly, the NFS protocol is a sluggish protocol. Therefore, if you throw NFS over a sluggish line such as a modem or ISDN line, expect poor performance. Some of the TCP/IP protocols, such as FTP, are quicker than NFS. The advantage to using NFS is that you do not have to copy files back and forth as you do with FTP. You access the mounted filesystems as if they were native to the machine.

You will have to adjust the NFS parameters to allow its use over sluggish lines. If you do not adjust the settings, NFS will report errors. First, you should refrain from using the soft mount option, because timeouts will begin to surface. Using the hard mount option will force retries. Two other options need to be altered: `retrans` and `timeo`.

The format for `retrans` is `retrans=n`, in which *n* is a number. This number represents the number of times to repeat a request before the request is aborted.

The format for `timeo` is `timeo=n`, in which *n* is a number. This number represents the RPC timeout period in tenths of a second. The default value is vendor specific, normally ranging from 5 to 10 tenths of a second. Under Linux, the default value is 7 tenths of a second. If a reply does not occur within the time identified by *timeo*, a minor timeout has occurred. At this time, the `timeo` value is doubled and the request is re-sent. This process continues until the `retrans` count is reached. If the client does not receive a reply, a major timeout has occurred.

What, then, is the general rule? You should concentrate on varying the `timeo` value versus the `retrans` option. Increasing the `retrans` value will generate more requests to the NFS server, which creates a load on the server. Generally, doubling the `timeo` value will solve timeout issues.

Summary

In this chapter, you explored the use of the Network File System (NFS), beginning with an overview of NFS, developed by Sun Microsystems, which advertises an installed base of about eight million systems. NFS is a protocol used for file sharing.

NFS consists of a client program and the server program. The NFS server responsibility is to export a file or directory. The NFS client then mounts the required filesystem.

Next, I discussed the NFS client, including the automounter. The automounter, which is a client-side enhancement, provides the functionality to automatically mount a filesystem. When the operation is complete, the automounter unmounts the device.

The NFS server was discussed next. The role of the NFS server is to make filesystems available by exporting them. I then covered setting up the NFS server, including the `portmapper`, `mountd`, and `nfsd` daemons. The `/etc/exports` file was covered, which contains the filesystems that the NFS server can export to clients.

The NFS client was covered, consisting of the `mount` command. The success of the `mount` command is dependent on a running NFS server and a filesystem that can be mounted. Finally, the `mount` command was discussed in a fair amount of detail.

13

Dial-Up Networking Services: SLIP and PPP

LINUX PROVIDES TWO PROTOCOLS for serial-line connectivity. Specifically, connectivity is through a modem, whether it is an asynchronous, an ISDN, or a synchronous modem. The two protocols are Serial Line Internet Protocol (SLIP) and Point-to-Point (PPP). Both protocols provide the functionality to establish connectivity with a remote system. The connection is made to an Internet service provider (ISP) or through a gateway.

The first part of this chapter focuses on the SLIP protocol. The last part of the chapter examines PPP in detail.

Serial Line Internet Protocol (SLIP)

In this first section, we examine SLIP in detail. Although PPP is the more widely used dial-up protocol, SLIP continues to be a contender and is supported by most public and private ISPs.

We begin the SLIP journey with a brief overview and then jump into the configuration and use of SLIP.

SLIP Overview

The only hardware requirements for SLIP are a serial port with a FIFO buffer and a modem. If you are using an older computer—an 80286 (or compatible), for example, you may want to check your serial port UART chip set. At a minimum, you want to have a 16550 UART.

SLIP supports the TCP/IP protocols over a serial line, whether it's over a dial-up phone line or a dedicated leased line. You should contact your ISP to obtain the configuration requirements for SLIP connectivity with their system. Configuring SLIP is a fairly straightforward task, and you should be up and running with a minimal amount of fuss.

Logically, the network for a SLIP connection consists of only two machines: the SLIP server (provided by your ISP) and the SLIP host, which is your end. We refer to SLIP as a point-to-point network connection because only two endpoints are within the network. Think of SLIP (and PPP) in the same light as the phone system. You pick up your receiver and dial the destination phone number. When your party answers at the other end of the line, a network connection is established. This is also considered a point-to-point connection. If either end disconnects, the network connection is broken.

When a connection is established from the host to the server, a logon sequence is initiated to verify your identity. After the verification process is complete, the server furnishes an IP address for your host. This IP address can either be dynamic or static. If the address given to your host is a static address, that address is the same every time you establish a SLIP connection. If your SLIP server provides for dynamic IP addresses, every time you establish a SLIP connection your host will receive a different IP address. The SLIP server will output the IP addresses (among other data) that are assigned for the current session. The Dial-Up IP Protocol (dip) program can capture the dynamic IP address and configure the SLIP driver automatically. The dip program is used to simplify connectivity to the SLIP server. We discuss the use of dip in a section that follows.

Some information that you must have available, if you're using a dial-up connection, includes the ISP's phone number, the authentication type, whether your ISP provides static or dynamic IP addresses, the ISP domain name, the DNS address list, whether the ISP uses a default gateway or a static gateway, and the maximum connection speed provided by the ISP. If your ISP is using static IP addressing, you will need the IP address assigned to your host. Also, if your ISP is using a static gateway, be sure to obtain the address for it.

Beginning with the next section, we discuss the specifics of SLIP configuration under Linux.

SLIP Preflight Checklist

Setting up your Linux system to enable SLIP is fairly easy. SLIP configuration is a one-time setup; you should not have to change any of your settings unless you switch to another service provider or your service provider's configuration changes.

In the following sections, we discuss the prerequisites that must be addressed before jumping into the actual use and setup of SLIP. We also examine the various configuration files and requirements of TCP/IP networking to enable SLIP.

Verifying the Loopback Interface

The loopback interface, sometimes called the dummy interface, is used to provide an IP address for your machine, provided that the only network interface you are using is SLIP or PPP. Also, some applications require the loopback interface in order to run. In addition, other TCP/IP services require an IP address to be functional. If your machine is part of a real ethernet network, the loopback interface is not required.

The loopback interface is specified by the network name lo—that is, LO is lowercase. To activate the loopback interface, the `ifconfig` command is used. The IP address that is designated for loopback is 127.0.0.1; this is an address designated by the InterNIC as reserved for no entity. The syntax for the `ifconfig` command is

```
ifconfig interface [aftype] options ¦ address ...
```

To enable the lo interface with the address 127.0.0.1, you invoke the `ifconfig` command, as shown in the following dialog:

```
stimpy $ ifconfig lo 127.0.0.1
```

This will execute `ifconfig` and its result will be to assign the IP address 127.0.0.1 to the loopback address. You can obtain the status of any active interfaces by invoking `ifconfig` without any arguments. Check the man page for `ifconfig` for a complete rundown of options. The following shows the output of an `ifconfig` inquiry:

```
stimpy $ ifconfig
lo        Link encap:Local Loopback
          inet addr:127.0.0.1  Mask:255.0.0.0
          UP LOOPBACK RUNNING  MTU:3924  Metric:1
          RX packets:25 errors:0 dropped:0 overruns:0 frame:0
          TX packets:25 errors:0 dropped:0 overruns:0 carrier:0
          collisions:0 txqueuelen:0
ppp0      Link encap:Point-to-Point Protocol
          inet addr:32.100.174.75  P-t-P:32.96.116.18  Mask:255.255.255.255
          UP POINTOPOINT RUNNING NOARP MULTICAST  MTU:1500  Metric:1
          RX packets:15 errors:0 dropped:0 overruns:0 frame:0
          TX packets:17 errors:0 dropped:0 overruns:0 carrier:0
          collisions:0 txqueuelen:10
stimpy $
```

The `ifconfig` command responds that two interfaces are active: lo and ppp0. Next, you should verify the contents of your /etc/hosts file for the loopback entry. The following is the contents of an /etc/hosts file:

```
# hosts        This file describes a number of hostname-to-address
#              mappings for the TCP/IP subsystem. It is mostly
#              used at boot time, when no name servers are running.
#              On small systems, this file can be used instead of a
#              "named" name server.
# IP-Address   Full-Qualified-Hostname   Short-Hostname
127.0.0.1      localhost
```

The name is not necessarily important as long as you map the corresponding interface name to the logical hostname.

Verifying /etc/resolv.conf File

The /etc/resolv.conf file is used for name resolution. Entries found in this file designate a DNS server and its associated IP address. More than one DNS server can be specified in this file. As mentioned previously, your ISP can provide you with the DNS server(s) and their associated IP address. The following is sample output from a /etc/resolv.conf file:

```
# /etc/resolv.conf
nameserver 165.87.194.244
nameserver 165.87.201.244
```

The /etc/resolv.conf file identifies the DNS servers that the resolver can contact to resolve hostnames.

You can also set up your Linux to use DNS locally. Many Linux power users do this because it can cut down on name-resolution traffic from your host to the server (and vice versa). Doing this will provoke your DNS to cache DNS lookups, thereby decreasing accesses to the remote DNS for name resolution.

Setting Up SLIP

As mentioned previously, SLIP is used to establish a network connection between two machines: the server (remote machine) and the host (your machine). SLIP is so firmly entrenched that most ISPs support the protocol.

A number of variations of SLIP exist, most notably CSLIP. CSLIP is a compressed version of SLIP that utilizes the Van Jacobson header-compression algorithm on outbound IP packets. The result is increased throughput, especially for interactive network sessions. Before implementing CSLIP, check with your ISP because most ISPs do not support CSLIP.

Although SLIP is easy to configure and use, the core mechanism can seem complicated. For most distributions of Linux, the SLIP driver is an integral part of the kernel. This provides faster response and is more efficient. A special tty line discipline, SLIPDISC, is used to convert the specified serial line to SLIP mode. Under this discipline, the serial line cannot be used for any other purpose, other than to communicate with SLIP-aware applications. Effectively, any non-SLIP applications are blocked from using the device when SLIP is active.

To establish a SLIP network connection, a pair of programs are utilized, specifically slattach and dip. You cannot use a generic communications application to dial up a remote SLIP server and establish a network connection. Both slattach and dip are used collectively to initiate and establish a SLIP network connection on a serial device using special system calls. The `slattach` command is used to convert a specified serial line to SLIP mode. Subsequently, the `dip` command is used to establish the network connection, login negotiation, and to initiate the SLIP connection on the serial line.

Using `slattach`

The following shows the syntax for the `slattach` command:

```
slattach [option] [-c command] [-p protocol] [-s speed] [tty]
```

Several options are available, such as enabling debug output and operating in quiet mode. Check the slattach man page for more details.

The -c *command* switch is used to execute the specified command after the line is hung up (disconnected). This can be utilized to run one or more scripts or to automatically maintain (reestablish) a network connection if the line was severed.

The -p *protocol* switch identifies the protocol to use for the serial line. For many versions of slattach, the default value is cslip (compressed SLIP). Other values that can be specified are adaptive (adaptive CSLIP/SLIP), kiss (a special protocol used to communicate with AX.25 packet radio terminal node controllers), ppp (Point-to-Point Protocol), slip (standard SLIP), and tty. The tty argument is used to return the serial device back into normal serial operation. Do not use the ppp argument to establish a PPP network connection, because PPP requires the pppd daemon to be active on the specified serial line. The adaptive option leaves it to the kernel to decide the type of SLIP protocol that the remote end uses.

The -s *speed* switch simply designates a line speed to be used for the serial device.

The following dialog switches /dev/cua3 to assume SLIPDISC line discipline and then attaches the device to the next active SLIP network interface:

```
stimpy $ slattach /dev/cua3 &
stimpy $
```

This assumes that the modem is on /dev/cua3. If no active SLIP connections exist, the line is attached to sl0 (that's SL0, not S10). The second SLIP connection will be attached to sl1, and so on. Most Linux kernels support up to eight simultaneous SLIP links.

As mentioned previously, the default protocol for slattach assumes CSLIP. The following dialog demonstrates invoking slattach to use normal SLIP:

```
stimpy $ slattach -p slip /dev/cua3 &
stimpy $
```

If you're not sure which protocol option to use (SLIP or CSLIP), it is recommended to use adaptive because this leaves the decision to the kernel.

You may have noticed in the dialogs that the ampersand (&) is used to put slattach into the background. Obviously, if you are invoking slattach from a terminal, you will want that terminal back. Otherwise, slattach will rob the terminal until such time that slattach is terminated. You can terminate slattach using the kill command—simply use the ps command to locate the process ID for slattach.

The slattach command is not specific to SLIP. You can use slattach to enable other TCP/IP protocols such as KISS and PPP.

Using `ifconfig` and `route`

After we have a SLIP connection and we have associated our serial device for SLIP usage, we must configure the network interface. This is done the same as with any other (normal) network connection. The two commands we use for this purpose are ifconfig and route.

The ifconfig command is used to configure the network interfaces. It is used at boot time to set up the required interfaces. The ifconfig command can be used from the command line, which is usually done only during debugging or testing, or during system tuning. If you execute ifconfig with no arguments, ifconfig shows the status of any active interfaces. If a single interface argument is given, it displays the status of the given interface only; if a single -a argument is given, it displays the status of all interfaces, even those that are down. If you recall from the earlier section "Verifying the Loopback Interface," we used ifconfig to configure the loopback interface. We repeat the syntax here to jog your memory:

```
ifconfig interface [aftype] options | address ...
```

The route command is used to manipulate the IP routing table. The core functionality of route is to set up the static routes to specific hosts or networks via an interface. This interface should have already been configured with the `ifconfig` command. To add a route to the table, use the following syntax for `route`:

```
route [-v] [-A family] add [-net¦-host] target [netmask Nm] [gw Gw] [metric N] [mss M]
➥[window W] [irtt I]
[reject] [mod] [dyn] [reinstate] [[dev] If]
```

To delete a route from the table, use the following syntax for `route`:

```
route [-v] [-A family] del [-net¦-host] target [gw Gw] [netmask Nm] [metric N] [[dev] If]
```

After control of the line is in possession of the SLIP driver, the network interface will have to be configured. You configure the network interface using the `ifconfig` and `route` commands. Let's assume that the host is `stimpy` and we dialed a server with the name `ren`. The following dialog shows the commands to execute:

```
stimpy $ ifconfig sl0 stimpy pointopoint ren
stimpy $ route add ren
stimpy $
```

As you can see, the first command configures the (first serial) interface as a point-to-point link to `ren`. The second command, route invocation, adds the machine `ren` to the routing tables. Some implementations of Linux may require that you identify the device (with the `dev` option) to the `route` command.

To take down the interface, use the same commands but in reverse order. For example, you first execute `route` to remove the entries from the routing tables. Second, you execute `ifconfig` to take down the serial interface. Finally, you need to terminate the `slattach` process. You can run the `ps` command to locate the process ID for the running `slattach` process and then issue the `kill` command to terminate it. For example, the following dialog demonstrates the commands to execute and the order in which to execute them:

```
stimpy $ route del ren
stimpy $ ifconfig sl0 down
stimpy $ ps a ¦ grep slattach
 4918   p1 S    0:00 slattach /dev/cua1
stimpy $ kill 4918
stimpy $
```

In the next section, we take a look at the `dip` command, which is the Dial-Up IP Protocol driver.

Using dip for SLIP Automation

Looking back on the last sections, you are probably thinking, "Getting connected is fairly easy, but I'd like to automate that whole process." Well, that is what computers are all about, right? And Linux offers just the program for you; the program is called the Dial-Up IP Protocol (dip).

In this section, we explore the use of dip and how it can help with automating the SLIP process. The `dip` command supports the processing of a `chat` script, allowing you to specify a command-response dialog to help with dialing, connecting, and the login process. You can also include commands to automate the setup of the SLIP network interface and establish entries to the kernel routing tables.

The following shows the syntax for `dip`, in its most general form:

`dip [options ...] [script file]`

A lot of supporting information is given in this section for the `dip` command. A sample `dip` script is supplied at the end of the section, preceded by a variables list and a command list. But first, Table 13.1 lists the most common command-line arguments to `dip`.

Table 13.1 **Common `dip` Command Arguments**

Switch	Description
-a	Prompt for username and password.
-i	Act as a dial-in server.
-k	Kill the `dip` process that has locked the specified tty device or the most recent invocation of `dip`.
-l *line*	Indicate the line to be killed.
-m *mtu*	Set the Maximum Transfer Unit (MTU); the default is 296.
-p *proto*	Set the line protocol to be one of these: SLIP, CSLIP, SLIP6, CLSIP6, PPP, or TERM.
-t	Run `dip` in test (interactive or command) mode.
-v	Set verbose mode. This enables debug output to include echoing of each line of the script.

As you can see, `dip` can also be used as a dial-in server, as represented by the -i switch. The `dip` command can also be invoked in interactive mode (or command mode), as designated by the -t switch. This allows you to participate in the dial-up and login process, allowing you to record the prompts and responses required to establish a modem connection. You can then use the results and establish a script file to automate the process.

Table 13.2 lists the commands supported by dip. Simply type the command, plus any required arguments, and press Enter. These commands can be included in a chat script or executed while you are in command mode:

Table 13.2 **Common dip Commands**

Command	Description
label:	Defines a label.
beep [times]	Beeps on user's terminal [times] times.
bootp [howmany [howlong]]	Uses the BOOTP protocol to fetch both local and remote IP addresses.
Break	Sends a BREAK.
chatkey keyword [code]	Allows you to add to dip's modem response words.
config [interface¦routing][pre¦up¦down¦post]	Stores interface configuration {arguments...} parameters.
databits 7¦8	Sets the number of data bits.
dec $variable [decrement-value¦$variable]	Decrements a variable; the default is 1.
Default	Instructs dip to set the default route to the remote host it connected to.
dial phonenumber [timeout]	Transmits the string in the init variable as the modem initialization string and then dials the specified number. The default timeout is 60 seconds. Dip will parse any strings returned by the modem and will set $errlvl accordingly. The standard codes are as follows: 0—OK, 1—CONNECT, 2—ERROR, 3—BUSY, 4—NO CARRIER, 5—NO DIALTONE. You can change or add to these with the chatkey command.
echo on¦off	Enables or disables the display of modem commands.
exit [exit-status]	Exits script leaving established [C]SLIP connection intact and dip running.
flush	Flushes input on the terminal.

continues ▶

Table 13.2 **Continued**

Command	Description
get $variable [value|ask|remote [timeout_value| $variable]]	Gets the value for a specified variable. If the second parameter is ask, a prompt is printed and the appropriate value is read from standard input. If the second parameter is remote, the value is read from the remote machine. Otherwise, the second parameter is a constant or another variable that will supply the value.
goto label	Transfers control to the specified label within the chat script.
Help	Prints a list of commands.
if expr goto label	Tests a result code. The expr must have the form $variable op constant where op is one of the following: ==, !=, <, >, <=, or >=.
inc $variable [increment-value\|$variable]	Increments the specified variable. The default increment value is 1.
init init-string	Sets the initialization string to the indicated string (default is AT E0 Q0 V1 X4). Note that the initialization string is sent before the dialing command is issued.
mode [SLIP|CSLIP|SLIP6|CSLIP6|PPP|TERM]	Sets the line protocol.
modem modem-name	Sets the type of modem.
netmask xxx.xxx.xxx.xxx	Indicates the netmask address to use.
onexit	Executes the specified command upon dip's exit. Works like the shell command, but is executed (only) when dip finishes. The onexit command that is executed is the last one encountered; any previous onexit commands are replaced by the new ones.

Command	Description
parity E¦O¦N	Sets the type of parity.
password	Prompts for a password and transmit it.
proxyarp	Requests Proxy ARP to set.
print $variable	Prints the contents of some variable.
psend command [arguments]	Sends the output of specified command to the serial driver, optionally passing arguments to command. The UID is reset to the real UID before running command.
port tty_name	Sets the name of the terminal port to use. (The path /dev/ is assumed.)
quit	Exits with nonzero exit status.
reset	Resets the modem. Does not work properly on several modems.
securidfixed fixedpart	Stores the fixed part of the SecureID password.
securid	Prompts for the variable part of the password generated by the ACE System SecureID card. The fixed part of the password must already have been stored using a secureidf command. The two parts are concatenated and sent to the remote terminal server.
send text-string	Sends a string to the serial driver.
shell command [parameters]	Executes command through the default shell (obtained from the shell variable) with parameters as the command-line arguments. dip variable substitution is performed before executing the command. If you don't want a parameter beginning with a $ to be interpreted as a dip variable, precede it with a \.

continues ▶

Table 13.2 **Continued**

Command	Description
skey [timeout ¦ $variable]	Tells dip to look for an S/Key challenge from the remote terminal server. dip then prompts the user for the secret password, generates the response, and sends it to the remote host. The optional parameter timeout sets how long dip is to wait to see the challenge. $errlvl is set to 1 if the skey command times out. If skey successfully sends a response, $errlvl is set to 0. Requires S/Key support to be compiled in.
sleep time-in-secs	Waits some time.
speed bits-per-sec	Sets port speed (default is 38400). Note that the actual speed associated with 38400 can be changed using setserial(8). Also, you should tell port's real speed here because dip takes care of the set_hi and such bits by itself. Also, don't be afraid, if you told the speed 57600 and it reports back 38400. Everything's okay, the proper flags were applied, and the real port speed will be what you told it to be— that is, 57600.
stopbits 1¦2	Sets the number of stop bits.
term	Enters a terminal mode.
timeout time-in-sec	Sets timeout. This defines the period of inactivity on the line, after which dip will force the line down and break the connection (and exit).
wait text [timeout_value ¦ $variable]	Waits for some string to arrive.

The following table lists the special variables that can be used within a script file. Some of these variables can be set with a value and some are read-only; all variables can be read for their contents. Note that the variable names are lowercase and must begin with a dollar sign. Table 13.3 briefly describes each variable's purpose.

Table 13.3 **Variables for a `dip` Chat File**

Variable	Description
$errlvl	Holds the result of the previous command
$locip IP	Number of local host in dotted quad notation
$local	Fully qualified local hostname
$rmtip IP	Number of remote host in dotted quad notation
$remote	Fully qualified remote hostname
$mtu	Maximum Transfer Unit (maximum number of bytes that are transferred at once)
$modem	Modem type (at present, the only valid value is HAYES)
$port	Name of the terminal port to use
$speed	Transfer rate between the local host and the modem, in bits/sec

Something to note: `dip` will resolve any hostname to its IP address if you supply the hostname in the `local` and `remote` special variables.

Sample `dip` Script

The following is a sample `dip` script:

```
# bugs.dip
#
top:
# define the name for connection."ren.stimpy.net"
get $local ren.stimpy.net
# set up the remote end "bugs.bunny.net"
get $remote bugs.bunny.net
# set up the  netmask 255.255.255.0
netmask 255.255.255.0
# define the serial port and speed.
port cua02
speed 38400
# clean up the modem (reset it)
reset
flush
# if your modem doesn't respond properly to
# the previous "reset", then comment out
# the reset or delete it altogether. then
```

continues ▶

continued

```
# uncomment the following two lines.
# send ATZ\r
# wait OK 3
# set the initialization string for modem, then dial
get $init ATQ0V1E1X4
dial 123-4567
if $errlvl != 0 goto modem_ERR
wait CONNECT 60
if $errlvl != 0 goto modem_ERR

# if we got to here, we're connected ...
# ... log in to the remote system
login:
  sleep 2
  send \r\n\r\n
  wait ogin: 10
  if $errlvl != 0 goto login_ERR
  send THE_USERNAME\n
  sleep 2
  wait word: 10
  if $errlvl != 0 goto pswrd_ERR
  send THE_PASSWORD\n

log-success:
# we're logged in, now wait for prompt
  wait SOMETEXT 15
  if $errlvl != 0 goto prompt_ERR

# if we've gotten here, then we've completed
# all tasks required for SLIP connectivity
fini:
  # set up SLIP
  get $mtu 296
  # Ensure execution of route
  default
  print CONNECTED $locip == $rmtip
  mode CSLIP
  goto exit
#
prompt_ERR:
  print Time out waiting for login prompt
  goto error
#
login_ERR:
  print Time out waiting for logon
  goto error
#
pswrd_ERR:
  print Time out waiting for password prompt
  goto error
```

```
#
modem_ERR:
  print Problem with the modem
  goto general_ERR
#
general_ERR:
  print Could not connect with the remote system
  quit 1
exit:
  exit
```

This sample script can be used to connect to bugs.bunny.net by invoking dip with the script name as its argument:

`# dip bugs.dip`

After successfully connecting to bugs and CSLIP has been engaged, dip will detach itself from the terminal and become a daemon process (or background process). Recall that if you invoke dip with the -k switch, dip will kill the dip process that has locked the specified tty device or the most recent invocation of dip. The following dialog demonstrates this:

`# dip -k`

Let's take a look at the script file. The first statement in the script is a get command, which actually sets a variable to the specified value. In this script, the first statement, $local, is set to ren.stimpy.net. The second statement sets the variable $remote to bugs.bunny.net. Those lines follow:

```
get $local ren.stimpy.net
# set up the remote end "bugs.bunny.net"
get $remote bugs.bunny.net
```

The next line is the netmask statement; this statement and the next four statements (through reset) configure the terminal and reset the modem. You may experience a problem with the reset command; this command does not work with all modems. If you do have problems, either comment out the reset statement or remove the line altogether. Next, uncomment the two lines that read as follows:

```
# send ATZ\r
# wait OK 3
```

The statement following the reset statement, flush, purges any modem strings that may exist in the (receive) buffer. This ensures that no extraneous strings are in the buffer when the login sequence executes.

The wait statement instructs dip to wait for the string specified as the first argument to wait. The second argument specifies a timeout as a number of seconds; if the string is not detected within the timeout range, the $errlvl variable is set to 1. The $errlvl variable is checked for success; if it is nonzero, the previous statement failed and we branch out to the appropriate error section. The following excerpt demonstrates the sequence:

```
wait ogin: 8
if $errlvl != 0 goto login_ERR
```

The concluding commands that are executed after the login is successful are `default`, which makes the SLIP link the default route to all hosts, and `mode`, which enables SLIP mode on the line and configures the interface and routing table for you. The next command, `goto exit`, routes the execution of the script around the error statements that follow.

The following section of the script deals with exceptional conditions. Each label is used to deal with a specific error (exceptional) condition. A message is printed and then a `goto` statement is used to branch to the generic error message routine. Notice that the `modem_ERR:` section does not require a `goto` statement; it could just fall through to the `general_ERR` statement. The reason we use a `goto` statement is that we may need to add another error statement. If you insert the new statement after `modem_ERR`, you might forget to include the `goto` statement.

```
prompt_ERR:
  print Time out waiting for login prompt
  goto general_ERR
#
login_ERR:
  print Time out waiting for logon
  goto general_ERR
#
pswrd_ERR:
  print Time out waiting for password prompt
  goto general_ERR
#
modem_ERR:
  print Problem with the modem
  goto general_ERR
#
general_ERR:
  print Could not connect with the remote system
  quit 1
```

The last statement in the script is `exit`, which is used as an unconditional egress of the script. The SLIP connection remains valid and dip continues to run. If you recall, the command `dip -k` is used to kill the running dip process.

Remember to provide the script filename as an argument to the `dip` command. If you do not provide the filename extension, `dip` assumes an extension of .dip.

Utilizing dip for Static IP Connectivity

This section addresses using dip to establish a SLIP connection when the IP addresses for the local and remote are well-known (static). The following script is generic in nature and can be modified for your use.

```
# static.dip
top:
get $local some.local.name
get $remote some.remote.name
netmask 255.255.255.0
# set up the modem
port cua02
speed 38400
reset
flush
# if your modem doesn't respond properly to
# the previous "reset", then comment out
# the reset or delete it altogether. then
# uncomment the following two lines.
# send ATZ\r
# wait OK 3
# set the initialization string for modem, then dial
get $init ATQ0V1E1X4
dial 123-4567
if $errlvl != 0 goto modem_ERR
wait CONNECT 60
if $errlvl != 0 goto modem_ERR
login:
  sleep 2
  send \r\n\r\n
  wait ogin: 10
  if $errlvl != 0 goto login_ERR
  send USER_NAME\n
  sleep 2
  wait word: 10
  if $errlvl != 0 goto pswd_ERR
  send USER_PASSWORD\n

log-success:
# we're logged in, now wait for prompt
  wait CONFIRMATION_TEXT 15
  if $errlvl != 0 goto prompt_ERR

# if we've gotten here, then we've completed
# all tasks required for SLIP connectivity
fini:
  # set up SLIP
  get $mtu 296
  default
  print CONNECTED $locip == $rmtip
  mode CSLIP
  goto exit
```

continues ▶

continued

```
#
prompt_ERR:
  print Time out waiting for login prompt
  goto error
#
login_ERR:
  print Time out waiting for logon
  goto error
#
pswd_ERR:
  print Time out waiting for password prompt
  goto error
#
modem_ERR:
  print Problem with the modem
  goto general_ERR
#
general_ERR:
  print Could not connect with the remote system
  quit 1
exit:
  exit
```

It is acceptable to use dotted-quad addresses for the `get $local` and the `get $remote` statements, but as always, you should specify the machine names because dip will resolve the names to IP addresses automatically.

After name resolution, dip will perform its magic of dialing, connecting, log in, and finally, switching the line into SLIP mode and configuring the routing tables.

In the section that follows, we will take a look at dip usage for dynamic IP connectivity.

Utilizing dip for Dynamic IP Connectivity

This section demonstrates the use of dip to establish a SLIP connection when the IP address is not known for the local and remote machines. The `dip` command will capture the IP addresses through the serial line after connectivity is established. The following sample script file demonstrates the functionality required:

```
# dynamic.dip
top:
# set up the modem
port cua02
speed 38400
reset
flush
# if your modem doesn't respond properly to
```

```
# the previous "reset", then comment out
# the reset or delete it altogether. then
# uncomment the following two lines.
# send ATZ\r
# wait OK 3
# set the initialization string for modem, then dial
get $init ATQ0V1E1X4
dial 123-4567
if $errlvl != 0 goto modem_ERR
wait CONNECT 60
if $errlvl != 0 goto modem_ERR
login:
  sleep 2
  send \r\n\r\n
  wait ogin: 10
  if $errlvl != 0 goto login_ERR
  send USER_NAME\n
  sleep 2
  wait word: 10
  if $errlvl != 0 goto pswd_ERR
  send USER_PASSWORD\n
  get $remote remote 10
  if $errlvl != 0 goto remote_ERR
  get $local local 10
  if $errlvl != 0 goto local_ERR

log-success:
# we're logged in, now wait for prompt
  wait CONFIRMATION_TEXT 15
  if $errlvl != 0 goto prompt_ERR

# if we've gotten here, then we've completed
# all tasks required for SLIP connectivity
fini:
  # set up SLIP
  get $mtu 296
  default
  print CONNECTED $locip == $rmtip
  mode CSLIP
  goto exit
#
prompt_ERR:
  print Time out waiting for login prompt
  goto error
#
login_ERR:
  print Time out waiting for logon
  goto error
#
pswd_ERR:
  print Time out waiting for password prompt
  goto error
```

continues ▶

continued

```
#
modem_ERR:
  print Problem with the modem
  goto general_ERR
#
remote_ERR:
  print Time out getting remote IP address
  goto error
#
local_ERR:
  print Time out getting local IP address
  goto error
#
general_ERR:
  print Could not connect with the remote system
  quit 1
exit:
  exit
```

In this script, the modem is set up and initialized. Next, the remote SLIP server is dialed and a connection is established. After the username and password have been submitted and verified, the remote and local IP addresses are captured by the `dip` command. The `dip` command does this by examining the incoming data for anything that looks like an IP address. The `dip` command will time out after 10 seconds if it cannot find an IP address. Finally, if everything passes inspection, `dip` switches the line into SLIP mode and configures the routing tables.

Running `diplogin` as a SLIP Server

Using dip to act as a SLIP server is relatively easy. The basic course of attack is to set up the various configuration files and then execute the `diplogin` command.

You need to create an account for each user that will need SLIP connectivity to your system. You will also need to add an entry for every user to the `/etc/diphosts` configuration file.

Define Account Entry in `/etc/passwd`

First, you need to supply an entry in the `/etc/passwd` file for each user requiring SLIP service. Be sure to define `diplogin` as the login shell for each user entry in the `/etc/passwd` file. The following is a sample entry:

```
stimpy:x:1000:100:Stimpson J. Cat:/home/stimpy:/user/sbin/diplogin
```

In this sample, after stimpy has logged in, the login program sets the current directory to the home directory specified in the `/etc/passwd` file, which is `/home/stimpy`. Next, the `diplogin` command is executed, which is a symbolic link to the dip command (dip is run in input mode). Finally, the dip command scans the /etc/diphosts file for the identified username.

Define Username Entry in /etc/diphosts

Each user must be described in the /etc/diphosts file. The following is the template for an /etc/diphosts entry:

```
user : password : remote host : local host : netmask : comments : protocol,MTU
```

The first field, *user*, is the user name. The entry here must match the logged in user.

The second field permits you to define an encrypted password for the user. If this field is not the null (empty) string, dip will display a prompt and the user must supply a password. If the special entry s/key is specified, then S/Key authentication will be enforced. Note that dip must be compiled with the S/Key option enabled.

The third field of the entry specifies the name of the remote host. This entry may also be the actual IP address. If the entry is a hostname, name resolution will take place using the name server or the /etc/hosts file.

The fourth field identifies the name of the local host. Like the third field, this may be the actual IP address. If the entry is a name, then name resolution will take place using the name server or the /etc/hosts file.

The fifth field identifies the netmask and must be in dotted notation. If this field is empty, as in this sample entry that follows, the address 255.255.255.0 is used.

The sixth field is merely used for commentary—it can contain any text. The dip command will not try to interpret the entry.

The seventh field contains comma-separated flags. Possible flags are as follows:

```
SLIP - use the SLIP protocol.
CSLIP - use the Compressed SLIP protocol.
SLIP6 - use the SLIP6 protocol.
CSLIP6 - use the Compressed SLIP6 protocol.
PPP - use the PPP protocol.
number - defines the MTU parameter of this connection.
```

You must specify one of the first five entries, a comma, and finally specify the MTU required.

The following is a sample entry from an /etc/diphosts file for the user named stimpy.

```
stimpy::stimpynet:localHost::Stimpson J. Cat:SLIP,296
```

This specifies that stimpy is the username. A password prompt is displayed and awaits user input. The remote host name is stimpynet and the localhost is named localHost. The netmask is not identified, so the address 255.255.255.0

is used. The text `Stimpson J. Cat` only provides additional information for the reader of the file. The protocol to use is SLIP, with an MTU value of 296.

Execute `diplogin`

After `dip` locates the correct line entry for the user, `dip` sets the terminal into raw mode and sets up the serial line to the defined SLIP protocol. Finally, after the line is enabled, routing table entries are defined to complete the connection.

The `dip` command then continues to run in the background until the connection is dropped. After the line drops, the entries are removed from the routing table, and the line is returned to normal mode.

Starting with the next section, we begin our journey with Point-to-Point Protocol.

Point-to-Point Protocol (PPP)

As was mentioned in the opening of the previous section, Linux provides two protocols for serial-line connectivity: Serial Line Internet Protocol (SLIP) and Point-to-Point Protocol (PPP). Both SLIP and PPP provide facilities to establish connectivity with a remote system. PPP is a protocol that was developed after SLIP and is now the preferred protocol over SLIP for serial-line connectivity.

PPP Overview

PPP is a more powerful and robust protocol than SLIP. It provides features and capabilities that are lacking with SLIP. You should always prefer PPP to SLIP when establishing a network connection over a serial line.

The hardware requirements for PPP are the same as for SLIP; a serial port with a FIFO buffer and a modem are all that is required.

PPP is used to support the TCP/IP protocols over a serial connection, whether it's over a dial-up phone line (or ISDN), a null modem cable, a telnet link, or a dedicated leased line.

At the lower levels, PPP is divided into two parts: the High-Level Data Link Control (HDLC) and the Link Control Protocol (LCP). HDLC defines the ground rules for the structure of the PPP frames. This allows the frame to contain packets from protocols other than IP. A field within the frame identifies the protocol type. In addition to handling IP datagrams, PPP can also use Van-Jacobson (VJ) header compression. Effectively, this compresses the TCP packets, allowing increased performance.

At a higher level, PPP functionality is also split into two parts: the HDLC and the pppd daemon. The pppd daemon delivers the LCP, support for user authentication, and the Network Control Protocols (NCP) for establishing the IP Control Protocol (IPCP).

Beginning with the next section, we discuss the specifics of PPP configuration under Linux.

PPP Preflight Checklist

This section outlines the prerequisites that must be addressed before jumping into the actual use and setup of PPP.

Some prerequisites are obvious, and others require explanation. The following list identifies the requirements for PPP usage:

- PPP support is available, either as a loadable module or statically.
- The PPP software is installed on your system.
- Your Linux system provides TCP/IP support.
- You have a modem installed on a known serial port.
- You have gathered the following information from your ISP to support PPP connectivity. Be prepared, some ISP support staff do not understand PPP and what is required for PPP connectivity, especially if the ISP is Microsoft influenced. Yet other ISPs can provide excellent support, both verbally and with written documentation. The following is a list of attributes you should acquire from your ISP for PPP connectivity:
    - The phone number to the ISP.
    - If using static IP assignment, you will need the IP address for your machine. Otherwise, you will be using dynamic IP assignment.
    - Does the remote server use PAP/CHAP? If so, you will need to obtain the ID and SECRET entries required for connecting to the ISP. Normally, these entries are your username and password.
    - The Domain Name Service (DNS) server address(es) for hostname resolution.

If PPP is not installed on your system, you should refer to the distribution documentation. To install support, running the installation program provided with your Linux distribution should install the necessary components for PPP use. For example, with RedHat, use RPM to install the package that supports PPP. Under SuSE Linux, you can use YaST to install the PPP package. For Caldera OpenLinux, you can use the KPackage program to install RPM-compatible packages.

You can easily check for the existence of PPP support using the `dmesg` command. You can invoke it as shown in the following dialog:

```
stimpy $ dmesg | grep PPP
PPP: version 2.3.3 (demand dialing)
PPP line discipline registered.
PPP BSD Compression module registered
PPP Deflate Compression module registered
stimpy $
```

You will need to visit a number of configuration files to enable PPP; these will be examined in sections that follow.

Verify DNS Support

After the PPP connection is established, your Linux machine will need to use the facilities of hostname resolution—resolving hostnames into their respective IP addresses. Your ISP should provide you with the names of its DNS servers. After you have this information, you need to provide entries in the /etc/resolv.conf and /etc/hosts.conf files.

The /etc/resolv.conf file is used for name resolution. Entries found in this file designate a DNS server and its associated IP address. More than one DNS server can be specified in this file. As mentioned previously, your ISP can provide you with the DNS servers and their associated IP addresses. The following is sample output from an /etc/resolv.conf file:

```
domain the-isp.domain.name
nameserver 19.265.15.5
nameserver 19.265.15.10
```

Your ISP will have one or more DNS servers; be sure to enter all DNS servers and their respective IP addresses.

You can also set up your Linux to use DNS locally. Many Linux power users do this because it can cut down on name-resolution traffic from your host to the server (and vice versa). Doing this will provoke your DNS to cache DNS lookups, thereby decreasing accesses to the remote DNS for name resolution.

The following is a sample entry from an /etc/host.conf file:

```
order hosts,bind
multi on
```

The first line tells the resolver to query information (resolution) from the /etc/hosts file. If resolution is not found there, the resolver queries the DNS server(s).

Using PPP

To establish a PPP network connection, a pair of programs are utilized, specifically chat and pppd. In the next section, we discuss the chat program. The pppd program is discussed in the section that follows.

Using chat

The chat program provides the automation required to establish a connection between your local machine and the remote PPP server. The objective of chat is to establish the connection between the local pppd and the remote's pppd process. The syntax for chat is as follows:

```
chat [options] scriptFile
```

Table 13.4 lists the options available for chat. Be sure to refer to the man page for chat for more detailed information.

Table 13.4 **Common chat Options**

Switch	Description
-f chat file	Read the chat script from the chat file. Multiple lines are permitted in the file. To separate strings, use the space or the tab character.
-t timeout	Set a timeout for receipt of the expect string. If the expect string is not received within the timeout period, reply string is not transmitted.
-r report file	Set the filename for report string output.
-e	Echo will be enabled when chat starts up. The ECHO keyword can be used to subsequently toggle echoing on and off. Output is to stderr.
-v	Verbose mode will be enabled when chat starts up. The chat program will log both text received from the modem and output strings to the modem, plus the state of chat. See the -s flag for logfile options.
-V	The chat script is executed in stderr verbose mode. The chat program will output all dialog to the stderr device.
-s	Use stderr. All log messages will be sent to stderr.
-S	Do not use the SYSLOG for logging. Normally, error messages are sent to SYSLOG. If -S is used, neither log messages from -v nor error messages are not sent to SYSLOG.

continues ▶

Table 13.4 Continued

Switch	Description
-T *phone number*	Pass in a string, normally a phone number, that is substituted for the \T meta-character in a send string.
-U *phone number*	Pass in a string, normally a phone number, that is substituted for the \U meta-character in a send string.
script	If a script is not specified with the -f option in a file, the script is submitted to the chat program.

As mentioned previously, two programs are used to establish PPP connectivity: chat and pppd. With SLIP connectivity, we have to use only the dip program. Unfortunately, pppd does not provide for dial-up and logging facilities.

The chat program implements UUCP-style chat script functionality. In a nutshell, a chat script consists of alternating expect-send string sequences, separated by spaces. Optionally, subexpect-subsend string pairs can be used, separated by a dash. The following example demonstrates this:

```
ogin:-BREAK-ogin: ppp ssword: myPswd
```

We will now break down and analyze what is happening in this script. The first line tells chat to expect the string ogin:. If chat does not receive the login prompt within the timeout period, chat will send a BREAK to the remote end and again will wait for the string ogin:. If ogin: is received, the break is not transmitted.

When the login prompt is received (ogin:), chat will send the string ppp and wait for the string ssword:. If the prompt is received, chat will transmit the password myPswd. You should note that a carriage return character is sent immediately after the reply string.

Chat scripts are fairly straightforward. The previous script is not a comprehensive one because it does not include the expect-send strings required to perform modem initialization, dial-up, and the login dialog. The following demonstrates a more comprehensive script, from start to finish.

```
stimpy # chat -v '' ATZ OK ATDT1234567 CONNECT '' ogin:-BREAK-ogin: ppp word: stimpy3
```

The chat program anticipates that the first string is an expect string, but because the modem won't expel text before we have sent something to it, the empty string ("") is specified as the (first) expect string. The first send string is ATZ, which is a modem reset for Hayes-oriented modems. Next, we expect to see the string OK as a response to the reset command. We follow up by submitting the dial command and the phone number to dial. The chat program then waits for the CONNECT string to return from the modem. The empty string is transmitted because we want to wait only on the login prompt. Finally, the login sequence is executed as shown in the previous example.

You have probably noticed that most `expect` strings are not complete words. For example, instead of expecting the string `Login`, the string `ogin:` is used. Or, instead of expecting `Password`, the string `word:` is identified. The main reason to do this is expectation of the incoming text. It is possible that instead of `Login`, the text string is actually `login` (with a lowercase l). Or, instead of `Password`, the text string is actually `password` (with a lowercase p). You have to think about these seemingly insignificant details when developing chat scripts. Even if you are positive that your PPP server is sending `Password`, nothing prevents them from changing the text string. Suffice it to say that standard practice dictates using the few letters of the expect string.

The chat program offers a number of escape sequences. Table 13.5 lists the escape sequences offered by chat. Any of the escapes can be in the `send` string.

Table 13.5 **Escape Sequences for chat**

Switch	Description
`''`	Expects or sends the null (empty) string. Although no characters are transmitted, the implied return character is still sent.
`\b`	Represents a backspace character.
`\c`	Suppresses the newline character at the end of the reply string. Use this to send a string without a trailing return. It must be at the end of the send string.
`\d`	Delays for one second.
`\K`	Inserts a BREAK
`\n`	Sends a newline (linefeed) character.
`\N`	Sends the null character.
`\p`	Pauses for 1/10 of a second.
`\q`	Suppresses writing the string to SYSLOG.
`\r`	Sends or expects a carriage return.
`\s`	Represents a space character in the string.
`\t`	Sends or expects a tab character.
`\\`	Sends or expects a backslash character.
`\ddd`	Used to represent an ASCII character using the equivalent octal digits.

continues ▶

Table 13.5 **Continued**

Switch	Description
^C	Substitutes the sequence with the control character represented by C.

Some of the escape sequences may not be identified in the expect string. Be sure to consult the man page for chat for more information.

We need to touch on the subject of security. Executing the chat program with the script dialog is subject to inspection by other users on the system. Anyone can execute the ps -ef command sequence and view the complete command line. You say you have not tried these switches to the ps command? Try it now to see the results. So, how do you deflect any users from examining the chat script? The solution is rather simple—you put the chat dialog into a file and then tell chat to use the contents of the file for the dialog. Referring back to Table 13.1, you will see that using the -f switch and supplying the script file as an argument will instruct chat to use the file's contents for the chat dialog. The following demonstrates the syntax:

```
stimpy $ chat -f chat_script_filename
```

It is also easier to modify and maintain a script within a file, rather than modifying the command line. You cannot identify a chat file (with -f) and specify a chat dialog on the command line, because they're mutually exclusive. The following is a sample chat script file:

```
'' ATZ
OK ATDT1234567
CONNECT ''
ogin:-BREAK-ogin: ppp
word: stimpy3
```

The expect-send pairs reside on the same line. This makes maintenance and troubleshooting much easier.

It is always good to expect potential failure and to be able to recover from it. You can specify that a script should be aborted if some failure is detected. For example, chat cannot determine the difference between CONNECT and BUSY; chat does not know that the string BUSY is considered an exceptional condition. So, how do you inform chat of exceptional conditions? You do this by specifying abort strings.

The chat keyword ABORT is used to specify an abort sequence. The following sample script demonstrates the use of ABORT:

```
ABORT BUSY
ABORT 'NO CARRIER'
'' ATZ
OK ATDT5551212
CONNECT ''
```

The chat will abort execution of the script if it detects any of the identified ABORT sequences as an expect string.

Using pppd

The pppd command is the Point-to-Point Protocol Daemon. The syntax for pppd is as follows:

pppd [tty_name] [speed] [options]

Table 13.6 lists the more common options for the pppd command.

Table 13.6 **Common Options for pppd**

Option	Description
asyncmap <map>	Sets the async character map to <map>. The map describes that control characters cannot be successfully received over the serial line.
auth	Specifies that the peer is required to authenticate itself before network packets can be sent or received.
connect script	Uses the executable or shell command specified by script to set up the serial line.
crtscts	Uses hardware flow control (RTS/CTS) on the serial port.
defaultroute	Adds a default route to the system routing tables.
disconnect script	Runs the executable or shell command specified by script after pppd has terminated the link.
escape xx,yy,...	Causes the characters to be escaped on transmission. The characters escaped are specified as hex numbers, delimited by commas.
file *name*	Reads the options from file *name*.
lock	Uses UUCP-style lock file for the serial device to ensure exclusive access to that device.
mru *n*	Sets the MRU value to *n*. The minimum value is 128 and the default is 1500.
mtu *n*	Sets the MTU value to *n*.
passive	Specifies that the passive option be used in the LCP.
debug	Enables connection debugging facilities.
local	Does not use the modem control lines; ignores the state of CD (Carrier Detect) and pppd will not change the state of DTR.

continues ▶

Table 13.6 **Continued**

Option	Description
login	Utilizes the system password database for authenticating the peer using PAP. Also, records the user in the system wtmp file.
modem	Uses the modem control lines, which is the default. The pppd command will wait for the CD from the modem to be asserted when opening the serial device, and it will drop the DTR when the connection is terminated.
netmask n	Sets the interface netmask to n.
nodetach	Doesn't detach from the controlling terminal.
xonxoff	Uses software flow control (that is, XON/XOFF) on the serial port.

Be sure to refer to the man page for pppd for an exhaustive list of commands available.

Option Files for pppd

After pppd executes and before it scans the arguments on the command line, it scans a number of configuration files for default options. These files contain any of the valid command-line arguments. Comments can be included in the files and are delineated by the # sign.

One file is the options file and is found in the /etc/ppp directory. This file is always searched and parsed when pppd first executes. It is accepted practice to use this file for any global defaults. Doing this can help with any potential security issues that could arise. For example, you could specify that PAP authentication be used from the peer; to do this, you include the auth option in the /etc/ppp/options file. The user cannot override this option. The following is an excerpt from a sample /etc/ppp/options file:

```
# /etc/ppp/options
# The name of this server.
name <host>
# Enforce the use of the hostname
usehostname
# If no local IP address is given,
# noipdefault
# Specify which DNS Servers the incoming
# Win95 or WinNT Connection should use
#ms-dns 192.168.1.1
#ms-dns 192.168.1.2
# enable this on a server that already
# has a permanent default route
#nodefaultroute
# Increase debugging level (same as -d). The
```

```
# debug output is written to syslog LOG_LOCAL2.
debug
# Require the peer to authenticate itself before
# allowing network packets to be sent or received.
noauth
# Use hardware flow control (i.e. RTS/CTS) to
# control the flow of data on the serial port.
crtscts
# Specifies that pppd should use a UUCP-style
# lock on the serial device
lock
# Use the modem control lines.
modem
# Set the MRU
#mru 542
# Set the MTU  to n
#mtu <n>
# Set the interface netmask to <n>, a 32 bit netmask in "decimal dot"
# notation (e.g. 255.255.255.0).
netmask 255.255.255.0
# Don't fork to become a background process
nodetach

# Specifies that pppd should disconnect
# if the link is idle for n seconds.
idle 600
# ---<End of File>---
```

A second file that is read after the /etc/ppp/options file is parsed is .ppprc. This file is found in the user's home directory. Users have the ability to establish their own sets of default options by merely supplying the required options in the file.

Script Files for pppd Connections

In this section, we introduce a set of scripts to help automate log-in and PPP startup. After these files are set up, you have to execute only a single command to establish a PPP connection. The following files are used for version 2.1.2 of PPP:

```
/usr/sbin/pppd
/etc/ppp/options
/ etc/ppp/ppp-on
/ etc/ppp/ppp-off
```

For version 2.2 of PPP, we add a third file to the list, as shown in the following:

```
/usr/sbin/pppd
/etc/ppp/options
/etc/ppp/ppp-on
/etc/ppp/ppp-off
/etc/ppp/ppp-on-dialer
```

The following is a sample ppp-on script. You should use this script file no matter whether you are using version 2.1.2 or 2.2 of PPP.

```sh
#!/bin/sh
# Script to initiate a PPP connection.
# Change as required.
TELEPHONE=123-4567        # The telephone number to the remote
ACCOUNT=theAccount        # Account name
PASSWORD=thePassword      # Password to use
LOCAL_IP=0.0.0.0          # Local IP address1; if dynamic = 0.0.0.0
REMOTE_IP=0.0.0.0         # Remote IP address; usually 0.0.0.0
NETMASK=255.255.255.0     # Netmask, if required
# Export
export TELEPHONE ACCOUNT PASSWORD
# Location of the script which dials the phone and logs
DIALER_SCRIPT=/etc/ppp/ppp-on-dialer
# Initiate the connection
exec /usr/sbin/pppd debug /dev/ttySx 38400 \
$LOCAL_IP:$REMOTE_IP connect $DIALER_SCRIPT
```

You will have to modify the ppp-on script; the script previously shown is really a template. Starting from the top and moving down, you first have to supply the proper phone number to your ISP. Next, the ACCOUNT field is your username that is registered with your ISP. The field that follows ACCOUNT, PASSWORD, is the password you use for login purposes. You may need to alter the following lines:

```
DIALER_SCRIPT=/etc/ppp/ppp-on-dialer
...
exec /usr/sbin/pppd debug /dev/ttySx 38400
```

If your pppd executable and ppp-on-dialer file exist in a different directory path, you will need to change those paths in the script file.

Next, a sample ppp-on-dialer script is supplied as follows:

```sh
#!/bin/sh
#
/usr/sbin/chat -v                        \
    TIMEOUT         3                    \
    ABORT           '\nNO CARRIER\r'     \
    ABORT           '\nNO ANSWER\r'      \
    ABORT           '\nBUSY\r'           \
    ''              \rAT                 \
    'OK-+++\c-OK'   ATH0                 \
    TIMEOUT         60                   \
    OK              ATDT$TELEPHONE       \
    CONNECT         ''                   \
    ogin:--ogin:    $ACCOUNT             \
    sword:          $PASSWORD
```

The ppp-on-dialer script file contains the actual dialog that is required to dial up and log in to the remote PPP server. In this sample, three ABORT sequences are identified; be sure to add any other abort sequences you may require. Check your modem manual for any exceptional conditions (error strings) that may need to trigger an abort sequence. Also, pay close attention to the value for the TIMEOUT variable—you may need to extend this time.

Finally, a sample ppp-off script is supplied as follows:

```sh
#!/bin/sh
# Find device to kill.
if [ "$1" = "" ]; then
DEVICE=ppp0
else
DEVICE=$1
fi
# If the ppp0 pid file exists, then it's running
if [ -r /var/run/$DEVICE.pid ]; then
kill -INT `cat /var/run/$DEVICE.pid`
# If kill didn't work, then no process
# is running for this pid
if [ ! "$?" = "0" ]; then
rm -f /var/run/$DEVICE.pid
echo "ERROR: Deleted pid file"
exit 1
fi
#
echo "Terminated PPP link: $DEVICE"
exit 0
fi
#
# ppp not running
echo "ERROR: Invalid PPP link: $DEVICE"
exit 1
```

This last script is used to shut down PPP in a graceful fashion. You should not have to alter this file.

And now, the moment of truth. After you have made all the required adjustments to the scripts, it is time to execute and test for success. First, you need to execute the ppp-on script file, as the following dialog demonstrates:

```
stimpy $ ppp-on &
stimpy $
```

The trailing ampersand (&) puts the execution of the script into the background and returns the command prompt.

Testing the PPP Scripts

At the end of the previous section, we executed the ppp-on script. An effective method of debugging the fruits of our labor is to examine the /var/log/messages file (or /var/adm/messages). You use the tail command to reveal the last messages written to the log. In the example that follows, I have requested an extract of the previous 200 messages written to the log file. I have parsed out only the lines that pertain to the PPP dialog.

```
stimpy $ tail -200 /var/log/messages
Oct 11 04:24:26 stimpy pppd[13718]: pppd 2.3.5 started by root, uid 0
Oct 11 04:24:26 stimpy pppd[13718]: Using interface ppp0
Oct 11 04:24:26 stimpy pppd[13718]: Connect: ppp0 <--> /dev/modem
Oct 11 04:24:26 stimpy pppd[13718]: sent [LCP ConfReq id=0x1 <asyncmap 0x0> ...
Oct 11 04:24:26 stimpy pppd[13718]: rcvd [LCP ConfAck id=0x1 <asyncmap 0x0> ...
Oct 11 04:24:26 stimpy pppd[13718]: rcvd [LCP ConfReq id=0x1 <mru 1500> ...
Oct 11 04:24:26 stimpy pppd[13718]: sent [LCP ConfAck id=0x1 <mru 1500> ...
Oct 11 04:24:26 stimpy pppd[13718]: sent [PAP AuthReq id=0x1 user="user" ...
Oct 11 04:24:29 stimpy pppd[13718]: sent [PAP AuthReq id=0x2 user="user"
Oct 11 04:24:32 stimpy pppd[13718]: sent [PAP AuthReq id=0x3 user="user"
Oct 11 04:24:34 stimpy pppd[13718]: rcvd [PAP AuthAck id=0x3 ""]
Oct 11 04:24:34 stimpy pppd[13718]: Remote message:
Oct 11 04:24:34 stimpy pppd[13718]: sent [IPCP ConfReq id=0x1 <addr 0.0.0.0>]
Oct 11 04:24:34 stimpy pppd[13718]: sent [CCP ConfReq id=0x1 <deflate 15>...
Oct 11 04:24:34 stimpy pppd[13718]: rcvd [IPCP ConfReq id=0x2 <addr 32.96 ...
Oct 11 04:24:34 stimpy pppd[13718]: sent [IPCP ConfRej id=0x2 <compress VJ ...
Oct 11 04:24:35 stimpy pppd[13718]: rcvd [IPCP ConfNak id=0x1 <addr 32.100 ...
Oct 11 04:24:35 stimpy pppd[13718]: sent [IPCP ConfReq id=0x2 <addr 32.100 ...
Oct 11 04:24:35 stimpy pppd[13718]: rcvd [CCP ConfRej id=0x1 <deflate 15> ...
Oct 11 04:24:35 stimpy pppd[13718]: sent [CCP ConfReq id=0x2]
Oct 11 04:24:35 stimpy pppd[13718]: rcvd [IPCP ConfReq id=0x3 <addr 32.96 ...
Oct 11 04:24:35 stimpy pppd[13718]: sent [IPCP ConfAck id=0x3 <addr 32.96 ...
Oct 11 04:24:35 stimpy pppd[13718]: rcvd [IPCP ConfAck id=0x2 <addr 32.100 ...
Oct 11 04:24:35 stimpy pppd[13718]: local  IP address 32.100 ...
Oct 11 04:24:35 stimpy pppd[13718]: remote IP address 32.96 ...
Oct 11 04:24:35 stimpy pppd[13718]: rcvd [CCP ConfAck id=0x2]
Oct 11 04:24:35 stimpy pppd[13718]: rcvd [CCP ConfReq id=0x4 < 04 02>]
Oct 11 04:24:35 stimpy pppd[13718]: sent [CCP ConfRej id=0x4 < 04 02>]
Oct 11 04:24:35 stimpy pppd[13718]: rcvd [CCP ConfReq id=0x5]
Oct 11 04:24:35 stimpy pppd[13718]: sent [CCP ConfAck id=0x5]
Oct 11 04:24:41 stimpy pppd[13718]: rcvd [IPCP ConfReq id=0x6 <addr 32.96 ...
Oct 11 04:24:41 stimpy pppd[13718]: sent [IPCP ConfReq id=0x3 <addr 0.0.0.0>]
Oct 11 04:24:41 stimpy pppd[13718]: sent [IPCP ConfAck id=0x6 <addr 32.96 ...
Oct 11 04:24:41 stimpy pppd[13718]: rcvd [IPCP ConfNak id=0x3 <addr 32.100.175.196>]
Oct 11 04:24:41 stimpy pppd[13718]: sent [IPCP ConfReq id=0x4 <addr 32.100 ...
Oct 11 04:24:41 stimpy pppd[13718]: rcvd [IPCP ConfAck id=0x4 <addr 32.100 ...
Oct 11 04:24:41 stimpy pppd[13718]: local  IP address 32.100 ...
Oct 11 04:24:41 stimpy pppd[13718]: remote IP address 32.96 ...
stimpy $
```

As you can see, the PPP dial-up and login is successful. Your output from the log file will no doubt look different from that shown previously. If the results from your connection are successful, congratulations! Execute your favorite browser and surf to your heart's content.

When you have finished your surfing, issue the `ppp-off` command (script). The following is the output from the log file after disconnecting:

```
Oct 11 04:38:59 stimpy pppd[13718]: Terminating on signal 15.
Oct 11 04:38:59 stimpy pppd[13718]: sent [LCP TermReq id=0x2 "User request"]
Oct 11 04:38:59 stimpy pppd[13718]: Hangup (SIGHUP)
Oct 11 04:38:59 stimpy pppd[13718]: Modem hangup
Oct 11 04:38:59 stimpy pppd[13718]: Connection terminated.
Oct 11 04:38:59 stimpy pppd[13718]: Exit.
stimpy $
```

Tracing through the `/var/adm/messages` file allows you to see just where you might be having problems.

Summary

In this chapter, we discovered that the Serial Line Internet Protocol (SLIP) is used to provide dial-up network connectivity between your local machine and a remote host.

We learned that a number of prerequisites must be fulfilled in order to utilize SLIP. For hardware, a serial port with a FIFO buffer and a modem are the only requirements. TCP/IP networking must be enabled and the SLIP package must be installed. The loopback interface must be configured and enabled. The `/etc/resolv.conf` should have entries for any DNS servers for name resolution.

To establish a SLIP network connection, slattach and dip are used. Both slattach and dip are used collectively to initiate and establish a SLIP network connection.

After the SLIP connection is established, the network interface is configured with the `ifconfig` and `route` commands.

We also learned that the `dip` command can be used to automate the SLIP process. The `dip` command supports scripting, automating the command-response dialog used for dialing, connecting, and the login process. Commands can be included in the script to automate the SLIP network interface and to establish entries in the routing tables.

In this chapter, we also discussed what it takes to get connected using PPP.

A number of prerequisites are required to utilize PPP. A serial port with a FIFO buffer and a modem are the hardware requirements for PPP. TCP/IP networking must be enabled and the PPP package must also be installed. The `dmesg` command can be used to verify the existence of the PPP software. Entries for name resolution must exist in the `/etc/resolv.conf` and `/etc/hosts.conf` files. Your ISP can provide this information for you.

We learned that the `chat` command is used to automate the PPP dial-up and login process. The `chat` command supports scripting, automating the expect-send dialog used for dialing, connecting, and the login process. The `pppd` command is the Point-to-Point Protocol Daemon.

We examined the various script files required for instantiating a PPP session, namely: `ppp-on`, `ppp-on-dialer`, and `ppp-off`.

Finally, we found that we can examine the `/var/log/messages` file (or `/var/adm/messages`) to help in debugging our PPP connectivity.

14

UNIX-to-UNIX Copy Program

UNIX-TO-UNIX COPY PROGRAM (UUCP) IS ONE of the long-standing and established protocols within the TCP/IP suite. The primary use of UUCP is to facilitate the transport of email between systems.

Beginning with the next section, we begin our UUCP journeys by providing an overview of UUCP. In the sections that follow, we discuss the requirements to set up and use UUCP between your machine and other machines.

UUCP Overview

UUCP is one of the most widely used TCP/IP protocols on the Internet and has been around a long time. The UUCP package was developed at AT&T Bell Labs in the mid '70s. The focus was (and still is) on providing a simple network protocol for the transfer of files and email over standard dial-up phone lines.

A few implementations of UUCP are available for various flavors of UNIX and Linux. In addition, implementations of UUCP can be found for other operating systems, such as DOS and Mac OS. Despite the diversity of platforms and operating systems, the UUCP systems are quite compatible. A standard UUCP that can be used as a baseline product does not exist.

Two strains of UUCP are in use today: Taylor UUCP and HoneyDanBer (HDB) UUCP. HDB is also called Basic Networking Utilities (BNU). The two strains (and variations of those) of UUCP vary mostly with respect to installation and configuration. For the traditional UNIX user, HDB is usually the choice. The choice among Linux users seems to be the Taylor strain. Most distributions allow you to install either version, or both, if you have the patience and nerves to do so.

In this chapter, we discuss both strains so that you can take advantage of both, if the mood strikes you. After you have read this chapter and sailed both UUCP waters, you can strike out on your own and try other strains and implementations.

Basic UUCP Configuration

Most new users to UUCP feel overwhelmed by the configuration process. If you approach the configuration for both UUCP strains in a stepwise fashion, the process will be a smooth one. The good news is that you can use Taylor on your end and HDB on the remote end, and both will communicate properly. The difference is in the setup.

For both versions, the stage is set under the directory /usr/lib/uucp. From this base directory, things start to change rapidly between the two strains. The subdirectories and the contents of those subdirectories are where the two strains diverge. For some newer versions of Taylor, the directory that contains the configuration files is /etc/uucp.

Be sure to read the appropriate section for the strain of UUCP you want to use. If you try to force a Taylor configuration onto HDB implementation, nothing will work properly (and vice versa).

The next section addresses the configuration of Taylor UUCP because most Linux users use that implementation. The configuration of HDB UUCP follows immediately thereafter. After we have covered the configuration of UUCP, whether it is Taylor or HDB, the sections that follow address the use of UUCP. But first, let us be sure our UUCP is configured properly.

Configuration: Taylor UUCP

As mentioned in the previous section, the UUCP road to configuration starts at the /usr/lib/uucp directory.

Some newer versions of Taylor store the configuration files in the /etc/uucp directory path. A quick way to discover whether your Taylor UUCP uses /etc/uucp or /usr/lib/uucp is to create a sys file and place it in one of the directories. Next, run the uuchk command; if it reports No systems, move the file to the other directory and rerun the uuchk command. It should display the system(s) defined. If your system does use /etc/uucp instead of /usr/lib/uucp, be sure to adjust the directory references identified in this chapter accordingly.

Table 14.1 shows the configuration files and a brief description of each.

Table 14.1 **Taylor UUCP Configuration Files**

File	Description
/usr/lib/uucp/call	This file contains the log name and password for any identified remote systems.
/usr/lib/uucp/config	This is the most important of configuration files. Most of the basic configuration parameters are set in here.
/usr/lib/uucp/dial	This file contains information for the dialers.
/usr/lib/uucp/dialcodes	This file maintains a list of translations for representative dialcodes.
/usr/lib/uucp/password	The password file contains log names and passwords for remote systems that will dial your machine.
/usr/lib/uucp/port	This file contains the details pertaining to each port for dial out.
/usr/lib/uucp/sys	This file details the remote systems and the required instructions to contact them.

Check Initial Configuration

Before we begin our journey of file configuration in more detail, let us discuss a supporting executable to help determine the state of our UUCP configuration. The command uuchk, executed without any parameters or options, reveals some information about your UUCP setup. The following dialog demonstrates this:

```
stimpy # uuchk
Spool directory /var/spool/uucp
Public directory /var/spool/uucppublic
Lock directory /var/lock
Log file /var/spool/uucp/Log
Statistics file /var/spool/uucp/Stats
Debug file /var/spool/uucp/Debug
Global debugging level
uucico -l will strip login names and passwords
uucico will strip UUCP protocol commands
Start uuxqt once per uucico invocation
uuchk: no systems found
stimpy #
```

As you can see, some revealing bits of information are provided. For this system, we can see that the spool directory is at the /var/spool/uucp directory. The last line tells us that no systems are defined for dial out. Your output may be different than what is shown previously.

Before we leave this section, execute the uuchk command and direct the output to a file. This way, you have a record of the UUCP configuration before you make any changes. In the later section "Verify the Configuration," you will reexecute the uuchk command and compare the outputs.

Configuration File: config

The first file we want to visit is the /usr/lib/uucp/config file. If this file does not exist, use an ASCII editor to create the file. If you have no other entry in this file, you should at least identify your machine name to UUCP. The following is a snippet from a /usr/lib/uucp/config file:

```
stimpy # more config
nodename        stimpy
stimpy #
```

The line entry consists of two parts. The first part is the keyword nodename and the second part is the name of your machine. If you are creating this file for the first time, enter the nodename keyword, then whitespace, and then the machine name. Whitespace can be a space or a tab, but it is usually a tab.

The name you choose for your UUCP system does not have to reflect the actual machine name for your Linux system. Some people prefer to identify their UUCP name as something different than the Linux machine name. For some people, consistency is important, so those people name their UUCP system the same as their Linux system name (as I did). One thing to remember is that the name you identify in the /usr/lib/uucp/config file must be the same as the name expected for any remote UUCP systems you connect with. If the name is incorrect, a connection will not be established.

Other entries can exist in the /usr/lib/uucp/config , but for now, save the file and exit out of your editor. I will describe some of the other entries (such as identification of the spool directory) that can exist in this file.

Configuration File: sys

The next file that you should examine is the /usr/lib/uucp/sys file. This file contains information about remote systems that you want to connect and interact with. Without this file, you will not be able to contact any remote systems. The following is a snippet from a /usr/lib/uucp/sys file:

```
# sys file:
# default parameters ...
protocol-parameter G packet-size 1024
# remote entries:
#
system    ren
time Any
phone 123-456-7890
port      portOne
speed     57600
chat "" \r\c ogin:-BREAK-ogin:-BREAK- \L word: \P
#
system    toastMan
call-login *
call-password *
time Any
phone 456-789-0123
port      portOne
speed     57600
chat "" \r\c ogin:-BREAK-ogin:-BREAK- \L word: \P
...
```

This file contains all the remote systems that you need to establish a connection with. For each remote system identified, be sure the parameters required to dial and establish a connection (to the remote site) are correct.

Take a look at the third line in the file, which is shown here again:

`protocol-parameter G packet-size 1024`

Any configuration entries that occur before the first system line are considered default configuration values. These default values are used by all system entries. The defaults can be overridden within the individual system entries. As a rule, protocol parameters and other similar configuration options are set in the defaults section.

The sample sys file shown previously contains two remote system entries: ren and toastMan. The line entries that follow the system entry are the parameters required to establish a connection to the identified site. For example, the phone number to connect to ren is 123-456-7890; the connection speed is 57600 baud, and UUCP will use the logical port named portOne. We will discuss the /usr/lib/uucp/port file in just a moment.

The remote system is identified by the system keyword. This name must be the actual name of the remote UUCP system. If you use a logical name, when your UUCP system dials and connects with the remote system, the verification process will fail. System names are traded by both ends of the UUCP connection during negotiation. Thus, if the system being called does not match the name presented, failure will occur.

You can have only one system name in the sys file. There may be times when you would like to have multiple configurations for a single site; if this is the case, you can utilize the functionality of *alternates*. We will discuss the `alternates` keyword in a moment.

The `time` keyword is used to restrict the times that the remote system can be contacted. In this sample sys file, the argument to time is Any, which means that you can dial that system at any time, day or night. Why would it be important to designate time restrictions? It might be that the remote system is available only during specific hours and on specific days of the week. Or you might want to dial the system during off-peak hours to save on long-distance charges.

Next, the `phone` keyword is used to identify the phone number to dial to reach the remote site. You can include any special dialing sequences and tokens before and after the phone number. This allows you to access an outside line, disable call waiting, or insert pauses as appropriate.

The `port` keyword is used to identify the serial port to use for the remote connection. This is not the actual device as found on your Linux system. The port name identified here is a logical name (or alias) for an entry in the /usr/lib/uucp/port file, which is covered in the next section.

If you use a direct connection between the two machines, you will want to identify the logical port name in the /usr/lib/uucp/sys file. The name can be any logical name you like, such as directPortOne. Be sure to provide the proper entry in the /usr/lib/uucp/port file, which is covered in the section that follows.

The modem speed is determined by the `speed` keyword. This is the maximum speed to which the serial line is set. This should be set to the maximum allowed by the modem.

The `chat` keyword contains the sequence of instructions to establish the connection. This is the "conversation" that is held between the two UUCP endpoints after a modem connection is established. This is sometimes called the login chat sequence. The logic follows the expect-send pattern of tokens as is used by other TCP/IP protocols (SLIP and PPP come to mind). In other words, an expect string is anticipated and a send string is transmitted. This alternating sequence of expect and send pairs is never deviated from. The chat script that follows is taken from the sample sys file shown previously.

```
chat "" \r\c ogin:-BREAK-ogin:-BREAK- \L word: \P
```

This chat is interpreted as follows: Expect nothing from the remote system (empty string) and send a carriage return character, followed by $#$#. Next, expect the string ogin: and respond with the login name, which is designated by the token \L. The dash character after the ogin: string means, "if you do not see the ogin: string after the timeout period, send a BREAK character." The next expect string is word:—the password is sent to the remote system, which is designated by the token \P.

You probably noticed that the words (strings) to expect are not complete. In other words, the strings Login: and Password: are not specified, but rather ogin: and word: are to be expected. Why is this, you ask? Well, one system may send the string Password: whereas another system might send password:. Also, the possibility exists that garbage characters are introduced into the data stream. Therefore, the best answer in these situations is to specify some least common denominator for a string.

The dash character is referred to as a *subchat*. The subchat is used to identify a response if the main expect fails. If the (main) string expected is seen, the subchat is not executed.

One last note concerning any strings that are sent: The carriage return character is automatically sent after any string that is transmitted.

Configuration File: port

The /usr/lib/uucp/port configuration file contains all the identified port(s) to be used by UUCP. If you recall from the previous sys section, the port (for some systems) is identified using a logical port name rather than the device name. This allows you to change the actual port without having to disturb the sys file. The following is a snippet from a typical port file.

```
# designation for portOne
port       portOne
device     /dev/cua0
type       modem
speed      57600
dialer     Hayes
# designation for portTwo
port       portTwo
device     /dev/cua1
type       modem
speed      115200
dialer     Hayes
```

This snippet is fairly straightforward. Notice that there are two port entries: portOne and portTwo. You can name the ports any name that you like. The key to a proper name is whether it properly represents the port designation. Some other names that are easy to remember are serialOne, serialTwo, comOne, comTwo, and so on.

Some administrators use numbers mixed with the alpha names. Personally, I find that can sometimes become confusing. A good example is the logical port name serial1. You have to look really hard to see that the last character is the number 1 and not the lowercase letter L. I find that it is better to explicitly spell out any numeric portion. Another option is to use the underscore character to precede the numeric portion. For example, instead of naming the port **serialEleven**, you could write it as **serial_11**. In the end, you should do whatever is most comfortable for you and your system.

As mentioned previously, the `port` keyword is used to uniquely identify the logical port. You can use whatever name you like, as long as the port name designated in the sys file can be found in the port file.

The `device` keyword is used to identify the hardware device. The argument to the device keyword should be a path designation to the serial device.

The `type` keyword identifies the hardware device that controls the data stream. The device identified in the sample snippet is modem.

If you use a direct connection between the two machines, you need to identify a logical port name in the *port* line and specify the *type* to be "direct." You can use any logical name you like, such as `directPortOne`.

The speed of the line and the maximum speed allowed is determined by the keyword *speed*. The speed should be a value that is enumerated for the device. For example, acceptable speeds for serial lines would be 300, 1200, 2400, 4800, 9600, 19200, and so on.

The keyword `dialer` refers to a dialer entry in the `/usr/lib/uucp/dial` file; this entry initializes the device identified by the `type` keyword. In other words, the dialer named `Hayes` contains entries for modem initialization, dialing commands, and so forth. The dial file, which contains one or more dialer entries, is discussed in the later "Configuration File: `dial`" section.

Configuration File: `call`

The `/usr/lib/uucp/call` file contains an entry, consisting of a login and password, for each identified remote system that you poll. The following provides a simple example:

```
ren uName pSwd
```

This identifies `ren` as a remote system that is polled. The username `uName` is used for login purposes and the password is `pSwd`.

Configuration File: `dial`

The dial file contains entries for the dialers. Each dialer entry is used to specify how a modem is to dial the phone. The dialer is identified by a logical name. A chat script is associated with the dialer. The following sample demonstrates a typical entry in the dial file.

```
# the Hayes dialer
dialer    Hayes
chat      "" ATZ OK ATE0V1X4&C1 OK ATDT\T CONNECT
```

As you can see, a dialer entry is straightforward. The most you should be concerned with is the chat script. You should have a good understanding of the modem and its AT command set. If the modem does not implement the Hayes AT command set, you will need to apply the proper command(s) in the chat script.

In the previous example, the dialer is identified using the logical name Hayes. Because chat scripts begin with an expect string, the empty string is specified (the modem will not speak arbitrarily). Next, the ATZ command is sent to the modem to reset it. After the modem is reset, it responds with the string OK. Next, the modem initialization string ATE0V1X4&C1 is sent to the modem, setting the modem to a known state. Again, the OK string is expected back from the modem. The next string send is the AT dial string. The token sequence \T is replaced with the telephone number identified in the sys file. The final expect string in the chat is CONNECT.

Most Hayes modems return the connection speed as part of the CONNECT string (if configured properly). For example, if the two modems establish a connection at 9600 baud, the string returned is CONNECT 9600. For this chat script, the only concern is that a connection is established—not the speed of the connection. For this reason, only the CONNECT string is expected. You can, however, check for specific connect strings if that is a requirement.

Configuration File: dialcodes

The file /usr/lib/uucp/dialcodes maintains a list of translations for representative dialcodes.

Configuration File: password

The file /usr/lib/uucp/password contains the log names and passwords for any remote systems that dial your system. The format is as follows:

```
# uuguest-login-name      password
bbunny                    bunnyPass
```

In the previous example, bbunny is the remote username and the associated password is bunnyPass.

Verify the Configuration

One last thing to check is the ownership of the files you have created. For example, the following dialog shows the effects of file ownership after creating the required files:

```
stimpy # ls -al
total 468
drwxr-xr-x   2 root   root      1024 Oct 25 01:05 .
drwxr-xr-x  58 root   root      7168 Oct 13 23:17 ..
```

continues ▶

Chapter 14 UNIX-to-UNIX Copy Program (UUCP)

continued

```
-rw-r--r--   1 root   root        16 Oct 24 23:54 config
-rw-r--r--   1 root   root       324 Oct 25 01:05 sys
-rwxr-xr-x   1 root   root     66444 Jul 22 19:24 uuchk
-r-sr-sr-x   1 uucp   uucp    223308 Jul 22 19:24 uucico
-rwxr-xr-x   1 root   root     72640 Jul 22 19:24 uuconv
-rwxr-xr-x   1 root   root       319 Jul 22 19:24 uusched
-r-sr-sr-x   1 uucp   uucp    100224 Jul 22 19:24 uuxqt
stimpy #
```

Notice the files owned by root. The files in this directory require ownership by the uucp user. To fix this problem, you issue the chown command. The following sample dialog shows how to do this:

```
stimpy # chown uucp.uucp *
stimpy #
```

The chown command is used to change the user and group ownership of one or more files. The first argument to chown is the user and group, and the second argument is the file or files that require ownership modification. For more information about the usage of chown, check its man page.

Because we want to change ownership for both the owner and the group, we identify the owner name, a period (.), and then the group name. Because we want all the files in the directory to have the same owner name and group, we provide the all-files wildcard. The following dialog bears the fruits of our labor:

```
stimpy # ls -al
total 468
drwxr-xr-x   2 root   root      1024 Oct 25 01:05 .
drwxr-xr-x  58 root   root      7168 Oct 13 23:17 ..
-rw-r--r--   1 uucp   uucp        16 Oct 24 23:54 config
-rw-r--r--   1 uucp   uucp       324 Oct 25 01:05 sys
-rwxr-xr-x   1 uucp   uucp     66444 Jul 22 19:24 uuchk
-r-sr-sr-x   1 uucp   uucp    223308 Jul 22 19:24 uucico
-rwxr-xr-x   1 uucp   uucp     72640 Jul 22 19:24 uuconv
-rwxr-xr-x   1 uucp   uucp       319 Jul 22 19:24 uusched
-r-sr-sr-x   1 uucp   uucp    100224 Jul 22 19:24 uuxqt
stimpy #
```

As you can see, file ownership is now set to uucp.

To verify the changes you have made, execute the uuchk command as you did in a previous section. The following dialog demonstrates this:

```
stimpy $ uuchk
Local node name stimpy
Spool directory /var/spool/uucp
Public directory /var/spool/uucppublic
Lock directory /var/lock
Log file /var/spool/uucp/Log
Statistics file /var/spool/uucp/Stats
Debug file /var/spool/uucp/Debug
```

```
Global debugging level
uucico -l will strip login names and passwords
uucico will strip UUCP protocol commands
Start uuxqt once per uucico invocation

System: ren
 When called using any login name
 Call out using port portOne at speed 9600
 The possible ports are:
 *** There are no matching ports
 Phone number 123-456-7890
 Chat script "" \r\c ogin:-BREAK-ogin:-BREAK- \L word: \P
 Chat script timeout 10
 Chat script incoming bytes stripped to seven bits
 At any time may call if any work
 May retry the call up to 26 times
 May make local requests when calling
 May make local requests when called
 May send by local request: /
 May send by remote request: ~
 May accept by local request: ~
 May receive by remote request: ~
 May execute rnews rmail
 Execution path /bin /usr/bin /usr/local/bin /usr/lib/news /usr/lib/news/bin
 Will leave 50000 bytes available
 Public directory is /var/spool/uucppublic
 Will use any known protocol
stimpy $
```

The uuchk output should be different than what was captured in the earlier section titled "Check Initial Configuration." If the output is the same, you should examine the output from uuchk. Are you storing the configuration files in the proper directory? Are you using the correct configuration filenames? You should also check the contents of the various configuration files to be sure that you are using the proper keywords.

If you examine the previous output of uuchk closely, you will notice the message *** There are no matching ports. If we take a look at both the /usr/lib/uucp/sys and /usr/lib/uucp/port files, we will see the problem. First, the /usr/lib/uucp/sys file is output and then the /usr/lib/uucp/port file.

```
stimpy $ cat sys
# sys file:
# remote entries:
#
system   ren
time any
phone 123-456-7890
port     portOne
speed    9600
chat ""  \r\c ogin:-BREAK-ogin:-BREAK- \L word: \P
stimpy $
```

Next, we show the /usr/lib/uucp/port file:

```
# designation for portOne
port     portOne
device   /dev/cua0
type     modem
speed    57600
dialer   Hayes
# designation for portTwo
port     portTwo
device   /dev/cua1
type     modem
speed    115200
dialer   Hayes
stimpy $
```

The problem is obvious: in the /usr/lib/uucp/sys file, the speed identified is 9600, whereas in the /usr/lib/uucp/port file, the speed identified for portOne is 57600 baud. Assume the /usr/lib/uucp/sys file has been changed to reflect the speed of 57600. The following is the output from uuchk after the applied changes.

```
bash-2.03# uuchk
Local node name stimpy
Spool directory /var/spool/uucp
Public directory /var/spool/uucppublic
Lock directory /var/lock
Log file /var/spool/uucp/Log
Statistics file /var/spool/uucp/Stats
Debug file /var/spool/uucp/Debug
Global debugging level
uucico -l will strip login names and passwords
uucico will strip UUCP protocol commands
Start uuxqt once per uucico invocation

System: ren
 When called using any login name
 Call out using port portOne at speed 57600
 The possible ports are:
  Port name portOne
   Port type modem
   Using port name as device name
   Speed 57600
   Carrier available
   Hardware flow control available
   Dialer Hayes
    Chat script "" ATZ OK ATE0V1X4&C1 OK ATDT\T CONNECT
    Chat script timeout 60
    Chat script incoming bytes stripped to seven bits
    Wait for dialtone ,
    Pause while dialing ,
    Carrier available
    Wait 60 seconds for carrier
```

```
Phone number 123-456-7890
Chat script "" \r\c ogin:-BREAK-ogin:-BREAK- \L word: \P
Chat script timeout 10
Chat script incoming bytes stripped to seven bits
At any time may call if any work
May retry the call up to 26 times
May make local requests when calling
May make local requests when called
May send by local request: /
May send by remote request: ~
May accept by local request: ~
May receive by remote request: ~
May execute rnews rmail
Execution path /bin /usr/bin /usr/local/bin /usr/lib/news /usr/lib/news/bin
Will leave 50000 bytes available
Public directory is /var/spool/uucppublic
Will use any known protocol
stimpy $
```

You will notice that all of the issues concerning the port have been resolved. The uuchk command is very useful in determining any problems that might occur with UUCP and its configuration files. Use uuchk whenever you suspect a problem with UUCP.

Configuration: HoneyDanBer (HDB) UUCP

The most current implementation of UUCP is HoneyDanBer (HDB). HDB UUCP is more prevalent among UNIX systems and can also be found for Linux. If Taylor UUCP is your UUCP implementation of choice, configuring HDB UUCP might seem confusing. However, after you learn the format, configuring HDB is quite painless.

A number of files have to be visited. Table 14.2 lists the files involved.

Table 14.2 **HoneyDanBer UUCP Configuration Files**

File	Description
/usr/lib/uucp/Devices	This file describes the devices that participate in connecting with remote systems.
/usr/lib/uucp/Dialers	This file contains the chat script required to dial and establish a connection with a remote system.
/usr/lib/uucp/Permissions	This file maintains the permission settings that are required for file handling at the remote and local machines.

continues ▶

Table 14.2 **Continued**

File	Description
/usr/lib/uucp/Systems	The Systems file contains information about the remote systems and other attributes relating to each system.

You will recall that the /usr/lib/uucp/sys file, under Taylor UUCP, maintains the name of the system and is used to identify itself to the remote system. With HDB UUCP, a configuration file is not used to identify the local system, but relies on the execution of the hostname command to set the name. The syntax for the hostname command is as follows:

```
stimpy $ hostname [options][name of host]
```

You invoke the hostname command using the -s option and supplying the name of your host machine, as shown in the following sample:

```
stimpy $ hostname -s goofBall
```

Let us now take a look at each of the HDB configuration files in turn, beginning with the /usr/lib/uucp/Systems file.

Configuration File: Systems

Each of the remote systems that you wish to connect with, or allow a connection with your machine, is found in the /usr/lib/uucp/Systems file. Each line in the file describes a single remote system. The line consists of multiple attributes, each separated by whitespace. The format for a system entry is as follows:

```
remoteSystem schedule device speed phoneNumber logScript
```

The *remoteSystem* attribute designates the remote system name. As with Taylor UUCP, you must be sure the name is correct because the name is validated during login negotiation.

The *schedule* refers to days and times that the remote system can be contacted. The entries here are similar to the format that Taylor UUCP allows.

The *device* attribute identifies the device that is used to contact the remote systems. This entry must correspond to an entry in the /usr/lib/uucp/Devices file.

If you want to identify a direct connection between the remote and the local machine, a logical name such as directPortOne can be used. Be sure to provide a device entry in the Devices file. A description of the Devices file follows this section.

Basic UUCP Configuration

The *speed* identifies the allowable speed or speeds that can be used for the connection. This value should correspond to the enumerated values allowed for the identified `device`.

The *phoneNumber* attribute identifies the phone number that is used to dial the remote system. Any dial modifiers can be specified here if you so desire. If you modify the dialing sequence, you should specify this in the `/usr/lib/uucp/Dialers` file. For example, if you need to disable call waiting when dialing any remote site, this should be specified in the Dialers file. If you do not specify the call-waiting string in the Dialers file, you will have to prefix each phone number with the string.

The *logScript* is the typical `expect-send` dialog that is used with other TCP/IP protocols utilizing a chat script, such as SLIP and PPP. A response (string of text) is expected from the remote end and the send entry is transmitted in response. The focus of this script is for login purposes only. Modem initialization and dialing is not specified in this script.

The following is a sample entry from a `/usr/lib/uucp/Systems` file:

```
rabbit Any ACU 28800 123-456-7890 ogin: uucp sword: pswd
```

The remote system is identified as `rabbit`. The remote system can be contacted at any time (24 hours/day, 7 days/week). The acronym ACU stands for Automatic Calling Unit and is an entry found in the `/usr/lib/uucp/Devices` file. The phone number to dial is `123-456-7890`. Finally, the login script is interpreted as follows: wait for the string `ogin:` and respond by sending the string `uucp`. Next, wait for the string `sword:` from the remote system and respond by transmitting the string `pswd`. Notice that the complete word is not specified for the expect string. This is common practice with chat scripts. You can never be sure if the expect string is `Password:` or `password:`, so I suggest that you reduce the word to a known string.

Configuration File: `Devices`

Next in the relationships among HDP configuration files, we come to the `/usr/lib/uucp/Devices` file. As mentioned previously, the Devices file is used to describe the available devices that are used to contact the remote systems. The structure of the Devices file is the same as it is in the Systems file. Each line designates a different device, and each line consists of multiple attributes, each separated by whitespace. The following shows the syntax for a device entry:

```
device ttyLine dialerLine speed dialer
```

The `device` is the logical name that uniquely identifies the actual device. If you have identified a device in the Systems file, a matching entry (device) should be in the Devices file.

The ttyLine attribute identifies the actual device, such as /dev/modem, that facilitates establishing a connection to the remote system.

The dialerLine entry is obsolete now, but it is retained for backward compatibility.

The attribute speed is used to identify the maximum speed that is used to establish a connection. This should match an enumerated value that is understood by the device.

Configuration File: Dialers

Next, the dialer entry in the /usr/lib/uucp/Dialers file identifies an entry found in the /usr/lib/uucp/Dialers file. It can also be used to identify a command file that is used to handle the initialization and dialing. The following is a sample device entry:

```
ACU modem - 28800 USR288
```

The device is identified as ACU. The tty line to be used is /dev/modem and can utilize a line speed of (up to) 28800 baud. Because the dialerLine attribute is obsolete, a dash is used for its entry. The dialer entry is identified by the logical name USR288. A corresponding entry can be found in the /usr/lib/uucp/Dialers file. This leads us to the configuration of the Dialers file.

As with the Systems and Devices files, the /usr/lib/uucp/Dialers file contains one or more unique entries, each on a separate line. The fields for each entry are separated by whitespace. The following shows the syntax for a Dialer entry:

```
dialer translate chatScript
```

The attribute *dialer* is the logical name of the Dialer entry. The dialer attribute (in Dialer) matches the dialer entry found in the /usr/lib/uucp/Devices file.

The *translate* keyword specifies the conversion of tokens to (other) tokens or commands that are understood by the device.

Finally, the *chatScript* is the standard expect-send script dialog that is used to initialize and dial the modem. The following is a sample entry from a /usr/lib/uucp/Dialer file:

```
USR288 -, "" ATZ OK\r \EATDT\T\r CONNECT
```

The logical name for this dialer is USR288 and matches an entry in the /usr/lib/uucp/Devices file previously shown. A dash is interpreted as comma, which translates to a pause by the modem. Next, the chat script is encountered. The first expect is the empty string, so the first send string is the modem reset AT command. The modem should send the string OK in response to the reset command. The AT dial string is sent to the modem followed by the telephone number identified in the /usr/lib/uucp/Systems file. The token \T is replaced with the actual telephone number. Finally, the string CONNECT is expected.

Configuration File: `Permissions`

The last configuration file we need to examine is the /usr/lib/uucp/ Permissions file. This file is used to identify the permissions concerning file transfer and remote execution of commands. The following is a sample Permissions file:

```
MACHINE=bunny LOGNAME=bugs \
READ=/var/spool/uucp \
WRITE=/var/spool/uucp \
SENDFILES=yes REQUEST=yes \
COMMANDS=/bin/rmail:/bin/rnews
#
MACHINE=duck LOGNAME=daffy \
READ=/var/spool/uucp:/var/spool/uucp/uucppublic:/files \
WRITE=/var/spool/uucp:/var/spool/uucppublic \
SENDFILES=yes REQUEST=yes \
COMMANDS=/bin/rmail:/usr/bin/rnews
```

In this sample, you can see that two remote systems are described: bunny and duck. For the sake of consistency, each entry in the Permissions file consumes only a single line in the file. Here, the backslash character (\) is used as a line-continuation identifier. Most people administrating UUCP follow this convention because breaking the entry into multiple lines makes it more readable.

The attribute named MACHINE identifies the remote machine, which is named bunny and the login is bugs. The attribute READ identifies a list of one or more directories that files can be read from. Likewise, the WRITE attribute is used to identify the list of (one or more) directories where files are written. The SENDFILES attribute states whether the remote site can send files to your site; the values for SENDFILES are yes or no. Like SENDFILES, the REQUEST attribute specifies whether the remote site can request files from your site; again, the values are yes or no. The attribute COMMANDS contains a list of one or more commands that the remote system is allowed to execute on your machine.

A UUCP Session

In the previous two sections, we covered the configuration of two strains of UUCP: Taylor and HoneyDanBer. Each strain diverges significantly with respect to configuration filenames and the structure and content of those files. Despite these differences of configuration, the outward functionality of Taylor and HDB UUCP is the same. In other words, a Taylor UUCP system can connect to and communicate with an HDB UUCP system, and vice versa.

Overview of the uucp Command

When you think about the intent of UUCP—to copy one or more files from one machine to another—the outward functionality required is minimal. This means that the uucp application is uncomplicated. The following shows the syntax for UUCP's main command, uucp:

```
uucp [options] source-file  destination-file
uucp [options] source-file ...  destination-directory
```

The first form copies the `source-file` to the `destination-file`. Using the second form copies all the files specified as `source-file` ... to the `destination-directory`. The `source-file` can be a pathname relative to the uucp directory if the file is on the local machine. If the file is on the remote machine, the syntax for the pathname identification is of the following form:

```
system!path
```

This form of pathname specification consists of the remote machine name and the pathname of the file, using the ! character as a separator. You can also transfer a file from a source destination to your local machine via a second remote machine (sort of a middleman machine). This can be specified as follows:

```
system1!system2!pathname
```

Any pathname identified with the ~ character by itself will begin relative to the UUCP public directory. Be careful, however; some systems may interpret a lone ~ as relative to the local home directory of the current user. If this is the case, you must quote the ~ character. Any pathname that has the following form will begin relative to the `named-user`'s home director:

```
~named-user
```

The uucp command can be invoked at any time to transfer a file. If the UUCP system is not running, the file is queued until a connection with the remote system is established. This implies that the copy is not initiated immediately. If a connection is not currently established, the `uucico` command is invoked to transfer the file(s).

Table 14.3 provides a description for each `uucp` command. Be sure to check the `uucp` man page for more information.

Table 14.3 **Descriptions for `uucp` Command Options**

Option	Description
-c	If specified, the local source files are not copied to the spool directory. The files must be processed by `uucico` before they are removed, or the copy will fail.
-C	If this option is specified, the local source files are copied to the spool directory.
-d	This option, when supplied, creates the necessary directories when performing a copy.
-f	If specified, the copy is aborted if any required directories do not exist.
-g *grade*	Specifies a grade to be set for the file-transfer command. Highest grade jobs are executed first. The grades run from high to low, using the following list: 0–9, A–Z, and a–z.
-m	Uses the mail system to report on the completion or failure of a file transfer.
-n *user*	Sends mail to the user on the remote system to report on the completion or failure of a file transfer.
-r	This option only queues the file for transfer at a later time; the `uucico` daemon is not started immediately.
-j	Using this option will print out the jobid to the standard output. You can use this jobid to cancel a job later.
-W	If you specify this option, the remote relative path-names are not prefixed to the current directory.
-x *type*	Specifies specific debugging types to be enabled. The following are typical debugging types: `abnormal`, `chat`, `config`, `execute`, `handshake`, `incoming`, `outgoing` `uucp-proto`, `port`, `proto`, and `spooldir`.
-I *file*	Identifies the configuration file to be used.
-v	Displays the version information.
--help	Shows help for the `uucp` command.

UUCP Scripts

Both strains of UUCP, Taylor and HDB, provide expect-send scripting for the purposes of login. In Taylor UUCP, login scripting is specified in the /usr/lib/uucp/sys file; in HDB UUCP, scripting is specified in /usr/lib/uucp/Systems file. The expect string is specified in the same manner for either Taylor or HDB UUCP. The send string is also treated in the same logical manner for both strains.

Login scripting is critical to the success of a connection. If your machine cannot log in to the remote system, file transfer will never happen. If you are using direct descendants of Taylor or HDB UUCP, you should not have a problem. If you are using a special distribution (proprietary) of UUCP, you will have to examine the documentation provided by the package.

Script logic in UUCP implements the typical expect-send string pairs found in other TCP/IP protocol packages, such as the Point-to-Point Protocol (PPP). The first string in a script is always the string of text to be expected. The second string of text in a script is the text to be transmitted in response to the expect string. These expect-send text pairs continue to alternate until the end of script is encountered. A typical login script, in its simplest form, follows:

```
ogin: jqpublic sword: pswd3
```

A majority of UUCP sites require only this dialog to establish a connection. As is common practice, the expect strings are shortened to compensate for UUCP login inconsistencies. One system might send Password and another system might send password.

Table 14.4 briefly describes the escaped characters that are allowed in a chat script.

Table 14.4 **UUCP Escaped Character Descriptions**

Option	Description
\\	Transmits (a single) backslash (\) character for both send and receive
\c	Specifies that the carriage return character should not be sent
\d	Pauses the script for one second
\p	Pauses the script for less than one second
\n	Transmits the newline character
\r	Transmits the carriage return character
\s	Transmits the space character
\t	Transmits the (horizontal) tab character

The `\s` sequence allows you to embed a space in either the expect or the send string. Normally, a space character delimits the expect-send pair. The sample dialog that follows appears okay, but a problem exists:

```
ogin: user name sword: pswd
```

The intent here is to expect the string `ogin:` and then send the string `user name`. Next, the string `sword:` is expected and the string `pswd` is sent in response. The way this script is really executed is as follows: the first expect string is `ogin:` and the string `name` is sent in response. Next, the text `name` is expected and the text `sword:` is sent in response. Finally, the script interpreter will wait for the string `pswd`, which never comes.

Logically, the script should bomb out at the second expect string `name`. Technically, however, the login will most likely fail when the remote end receives the login name of `user`. Suffice it to say that this script will not work.

To fix this script, the `\s` is inserted between `user` and `name`, as the following corrected script demonstrates:

```
ogin: user\sname sword: pswd
```

Notice that two expect-send pairs are now in the script, which is what we want. If the expect string `ogin:` is received, the string `user name` is transmitted. Lastly, if the text `sword:` is detected, the text `pswd` is transmitted in response.

If the remote UUCP is not transmitting a login prompt, you can send a BREAK or carriage-return character to initiate a dialog. The following scripts show how this can be done:

```
ogin:-BREAK-ogin: userName sword: pswd
...
"" \r\p ogin: userName sword: pswd
```

The first sample script specifies an expect string of `ogin:`, as usual. If that string is not detected within the timeout period, the subscript is executed. The subscript consists of the BREAK and the subsequent expect string of `ogin:`. The dash (-) character is used to introduce a subscript. Thus, the script waits for `ogin:`; if that string is not received, a BREAK character is sent to the remote site to invoke a response. Next, the script waits for the (expect) string `ogin:`.

The second sample script waits for the empty string, which provokes the script to immediately continue to the send string. The send string consists of a carriage-return character, followed by a one-second pause. This pause allows some time to pass so that the remote end has time to respond to the carriage-return character. When the remote end receives the carriage-return character, it normally responds with a getty (login) process.

Sample uucp Dialogs

The following dialog demonstrates the use of the uucp command to transfer a file from the remote machine to the local machine. The file is given a new name on the local machine.

```
stimpy $ uucp daffy!quack.txt myquack.txt
```

The remote machine name and filename are identified as the first argument to the uucp command. The machine name and filename are delineated by the bang (!) character. The first name encountered is the machine name, followed by the bang character, and finally the filename. The second argument to the uucp command is the filename to use for the local copy.

The next dialog shows how to transfer a file from your local machine to the remote machine:

```
stimpy $ uucp myfile.txt goofy\!/usr/spool/uucppublic
```

In the previous example, the local file named myfile.txt is transmitted to the remote machine named goofy. The file is stored in the directory path /usr/spool/uucppublic on the machine named goofy.

In the sample that follows, a file is transferred from a remote machine to the local machine via a second machine. The file is given a new name on the local machine.

```
stimpy $ uucp goof!ball!someFile.txt newFile.txt
```

The previous dialog transfers the file someFile.txt from the machine named goof through the (intermediary) machine named ball, finally arriving at the local machine with the file name of newFile.txt.

The following dialog will capture a file from a remote system to the local system, including email confirmations:

```
uucp -m -nbbunny daffy!quack.txt myquack.txt
```

After the transfer is complete, mail is sent to the user named bbunny on the remote machine and to dduck on the local machine. Note that mail is sent whether the transfer failed or succeeded.

UUCP Status

As mentioned previously, if you invoke the uucp command to transfer files or mail, the transfer may not happen immediately. For example, if you invoke uucp to transfer a file at 8:00 a.m., and the remote system cannot be called until 8:00 p.m., the transfer will not take place for twelve hours. So, how do you keep up with the transfer queue, especially if you are transferring many files to many destinations? You use the uustat command to query the status of UUCP transfer(s). The syntax for uustat follows:

uustat [options ...]

If you want to check the status of your uucp jobs, invoke the uucp command without any arguments. Table 14.5 lists the options available to the uustat command.

Table 14.5 **Descriptions for the uustat Command**

Option	Description
-a	Display all file(s) in the transfer queue.
-e	Display all executions in the execution queue.
-s *system*	Display all queued jobs for the named system.
-S *system*	Display all queued jobs queued for all systems, except for the system named.
-u *user*	Display all queued jobs for the named user.
-U *user*	Display all queued jobs for all users, except for the named user.
-c *command*	Display all jobs requesting the named command.
-C *command*	Display all jobs requesting a command other than the named command.
-y *hours*	Display all jobs queued younger than the number of hours supplied.
-o *hours*	Display all jobs queued that are older than the number of hours supplied.
-k *jobid*	Kill the named job.
-r *jobid*	Rejuvenate (renew) the identified job.
-q	Display status of queued commands for all remote systems.
-m	Display status for conversations of all remote systems.
-p	Display status of processes that have locks on systems and ports.
-i	Prompt the user for each job in list to kill that job.
-K	Kill all jobs listed.
-R	Rejuvenate (renew) each job.
-M	For each job listed, generate an email to the UUCP administrator.
-N	Send an email to the user requesting the job.
-W *comment*	Include a comment in mail sent.

continues ▶

Table 14.5 **Continued**

Option	Description
-x *type*	This option specifies the types of debugging information, which are abnormal, chat, config, execute, handshake, incoming, outgoing, port, proto, spooldir, and uucp-proto.
-I *file*	Use the identified configuration file.
-v	Display the version information.

If you wish to kill a queued job that you have submitted, issue the uustat command, as follows:

```
stimpy $ uustat -k 43
```

If you are logged in as root (or superuser), you can kill any UUCP queued job(s); otherwise, you can kill only your queued job(s). This holds true for all uustat options utilizing kill functionality.

If you want to check on the status of all uucp jobs, you invoke the uustat command, as shown in the following example:

```
stimpy $ uustat -a
```

This will show all uucp jobs that are queued, no matter who initiated the job.

Summary

We began this chapter with an overview of the UNIX-to-UNIX Program (UUCP). We learned that the two strains of UUCP are Taylor and HoneyDanBer. Taylor UUCP is the predominate strain used under Linux, and HDB is preferred among UNIX enthusiasts.

The first part of the chapter covered the configuration of Taylor UUCP, followed by HDB UUCP. Some of the major differences between the two are directory paths, names for the configuration files, and the contents of those configuration files.

The uuchk command is used to verify the configuration of UUCP and can be used for either Taylor or HDB strains.

Under Taylor UUCP, the important configuration files are /usr/lib/uucp/config, /usr/lib/uucp/port, and /usr/lib/uucp/sys. The sys file identifies remote systems, the port file contains information pertaining to logical-to-physical port mapping, and the config file contains basic configuration parameters. Some of the other files are /usr/lib/uucp/call, /usr/lib/uucp/dial, /usr/lib/uucp/dialcodes, and /usr/lib/uucp/password.

With HoneyDanBer UUCP, the configuration files are `/usr/lib/uucp/Devices`, `/usr/lib/uucp/Dialers`, `/usr/lib/uucp/Permissions`, and `/usr/lib/uucp/Systems`. The Devices file contains logical port name to physical port name mapping, Dialers maintains information about dialer configuration, the Permissions file contains information about login, and the Systems file contains information pertaining to remote UUCP systems.

In the latter part of the chapter, we discussed usage of the `uucp` command, including UUCP chat scripts. And finally, we provided an overview and examples of the use of the `uustat` command, which provides status information about UUCP.

15

Samba: Merging Linux and Windows

WHETHER WE LIKE IT OR NOT, Linux (and UNIX) must coexist with the Windows suite of operating systems. The phrase "Windows suite of operating systems" refers to all flavors of Windows, such as Windows 3.xx, Windows 9x, Windows NT, Windows 2000, and so on. When I refer to Linux, I am talking about most distributions of Linux and UNIX in general.

The fact remains that at some point in your use of Linux, you will want to integrate into a network consisting of Windows machines. Alternatively, it might be that you are running a Linux network and you want to add Windows machines to the mix. Enter Samba.

Samba is a suite of Linux applications that speak a protocol called Server Message Block (SMB). Samba runs on UNIX platforms but speaks natively to Windows clients. This chapter explores the world of Samba, including its installation, configuration, and operation.

Overview

Quite simply, Samba allows Linux and Windows machines to coexist on the same network. Resources can be shared, giving Windows users seamless access to Linux resources without a hassle. A Windows user can access file and print services without knowing those services are offered by Linux.

Samba is not restricted to the intermingling of Linux and Windows machines. Other operating systems can speak the SMB protocol. IBM's OS/2 supports SMB, supplying file and print sharing. Commercial SMB products are available for other operating systems, such as Macintosh and variants of UNIX. The Samba suite has been ported to a number of platforms, including AmigaOS, Novell Netware, and VMS.

Here are some of the services offered by Samba:

- The sharing of filesystems, whether they exist on a server or a client workstation. Thus, you can share a Linux filesystem with a Windows client, or you can share a Windows filesystem with a Linux client.
- The sharing of printers, whether they are on a server or a client workstation. Thus, you can share a Linux printer with a Windows client, or you can share a Windows printer with a Linux client.
- The authentication of clients (users).
- Providing name resolution, such as WINS resolution.

The most compelling reason to use Samba seems to be the sharing of file and printer resources. At least initially, most administrators want this feature. Once Samba is installed and running, and the administrator discovers Samba's other capabilities, he or she is eager to implement these other features.

Samba also provides the ability to secure file and print resources through password authorization. It does this through the use of two modes of validation—*share mode* and *user mode* authentication and authorization.

In share mode, a single password is associated with a resource, such as a printer. The password must be supplied by any user who needs access to the printer. As you can imagine, this method is not desirable from a security point of view.

With the user mode of validation, each user has his or her own identity, consisting of a username and password. This allows the system administrator to allow or deny the user access to resources.

Samba was introduced by Andrew Tridgell of Canberra, Australia. Back in 1991, he encountered the issue of having to mount a UNIX disk to his DOS machine. The issue was specific to an application that required the NetBIOS (Network Basic Input Output System) interface. NetBIOS is software that provides an interface between software and network hardware. In order to allow a disk to be shared over a network, functionality was added to DOS, allowing disk I/O to be redirected to NetBIOS. Microsoft added this sharing protocol, which became SMB.

To resolve his issue, Tridgell reverse-engineered the SMB protocol using a packet sniffer. This allowed him to create a file-sharing server that ran on the UNIX machine. From the DOS side, the UNIX system appeared to be a normal PC server. Another issue arose for Tridgell: A company claimed that the name "SMB" was trademarked. He decided to take a UNIX approach to things. He used the grep command to search the dictionary for words that would closely match "SMB." Quite possibly, the dialog might have looked like this:

```
stimpy $ grep -i 's.*m.*b' /usr/dict/words
```

Here are some of the responses this search found:

```
salmonberry
samba
scramble
scrambled
```

It was obvious what the new name had to be: Samba.

Microsoft has pushed a Request For Comment (RFC) for the latest incarnation of SMB, known as the Common Internet File System (CIFS). CIFS, at its core, is SMB all over again.

The Samba suite consists of a number of components. As you might expect, a number of daemons run in the background, awaiting requests from clients. One of these daemons is named smbd. It provides file and print services to clients. The smbd daemon handles share mode and user mode authentication and authorization. Another daemon is nmbd; it provides NetBIOS name resolution and browsing.

For the client side of things, the smbclient program implements an interface that is similar to the FTP client. This program is used to access SMB shares found on other SMB servers, such as a filesystem on Windows NT. smbclient also allows you to access a remote Windows printer from your Linux system.

The Samba suite also consists of a number of utility programs, each providing special functionality. The testparm utility is designed to validate the smb.conf configuration file. The testprns utility is used to test printers that are defined in the printcap file. The smbstatus utility lists current connections to the smbd server. The nmblookup utility permits a Linux system to execute NetBIOS name queries. The smbpasswd utility permits you to change SMB passwords on both Samba and Windows NT servers. The following sections discuss these utilities in more detail.

Obtaining and Installing Samba

You should always check your Linux distribution to see if Samba is provided. For the most popular distributions, the most current version of Samba is included. Installing Samba from your distribution's CD-ROM is much simpler and might have enhancements to more tightly integrate with the distribution.

If you do not have Samba on your distribution CD-ROM, you should check the vendor's Web site for a current version of Samba. One reason for checking is that most vendors provide a click-n-go installation for packages within their distribution. This makes for easier and effortless installations and updates. Also, most vendors stay current with the most popular packages. For example, the current version of Samba at its home site is 2.06, and the version distributed by SuSE Linux is the same. If you want to get to the real source of Samba, you should surf to the Samba home page at http://www.samba.org.

You can download Samba as a binary package or as a build package. Samba binaries are available for many popular platforms. You can download the binary packages via http from the Samba home site. Several mirror sites also offer the packages. Keep in mind that the latest version of Samba might not be available for every platform. Downloading the binary package allows you to install and run Samba without having to build the sources first. A quick visit to the Samba binary download page reveals releases for Caldera, Debian, Red Hat, Slackware, SuSE, and TurboLinux distributions. Be sure to check the version for your distribution before downloading. For example, the most current version of SuSE is 6.3, but the Samba binary listed is for version 6.1.

The Samba package can also be downloaded using the CVS source code control system. The advantage of this method is that you can update your sources any time with just a single command. You should visit the Samba home page for more information on fetching the CVS sources.

Checking for the Existence of Samba

It is quite possible that Samba is already installed on your system. If you are not sure, you can check for its existence as shown in the following dialog. Each command invocation is highlighted in bold text.

```
stimpy $ smbclient
Usage: smbclient service <password> [options]
Version 2.0.6
        -s smb.conf            pathname to smb.conf file
        -B IP addr             broadcast IP address to use
        -O socket_options      socket options to use
        -R name resolve order  use these name resolution services only
```

```
        -M host                   send a winpopup message to the host
...
stimpy $ smbd -V
Version 2.0.5a
stimpy $ nmbd -V
Version 2.0.5a
stimpy $
```

In this dialog, a check is first made for the smbclient program. As mentioned previously, the smbclient program implements a simple FTP-like (command-line) client. The second command invoked is the smbd daemon with the -v switch. The smbd daemon provides file and print services to SMB clients. The last command invocation is to the nmbd daemon, which provides NetBIOS name resolution and browsing.

Another interesting test is to execute the testparm utility, which allows you to test the smb.conf configuration file. If you successfully executed the commands just shown, you should execute testparm like this:

```
stimpy $ testparm
Load smb config files from /etc/smb.conf
Processing section "[homes]"
Processing section "[printers]"
Loaded services file OK.
ERROR: lock directory /var/lock/samba does not exist
Press enter to see a dump of your service definitions
... <enter key pressed>
# Global parameters
[global]
        workgroup = ARBEITSGRUPPE
        netbios name =
        netbios aliases =
        server string = Samba 2.0.5a
        interfaces =
        bind interfaces only = No
...
        delete readonly = No
        dos filetimes = No
        dos filetime resolution = No
        fake directory create times = No
[homes]
        comment = Heimatverzeichnis
        read only = No
        create mask = 0750
        browseable = No

[printers]
        comment = All Printers
        path = /tmp
        create mask = 0700
        print ok = Yes
        browseable = No
stimpy $
```

On the sixth line, note the error message `ERROR: lock directory /var/lock/samba does not exist`. This is not a significant error. It merely means that the Samba server is not currently running and most likely has never been executed. After executing the smbd daemon, you can check for the directory's existence, as shown in the following dialog:

```
stimpy $ ls -al /var/lock
total 4
drwxrwxr-x   4 root      uucp         1024 Feb  4 01:13 .
drwxr-xr-x  17 root      root         1024 Jan  8 11:38 ..
drwxr-xr-x   3 root      root         1024 Jan  8 11:34 subsys
stimpy $ smbd -D
stimpy $ ls -al /var/lock
drwxrwxr-x   4 root      uucp         1024 Feb  4 01:13 .
drwxr-xr-x  17 root      root         1024 Jan  8 11:38 ..
drwxr-xr-x   2 root      root         1024 Feb  4 01:18 samba
drwxr-xr-x   3 root      root         1024 Jan  8 11:34 subsys
stimpy $ ps x
  PID TTY      STAT  TIME COMMAND
    1 ?        S     0:03 init [2]
    2 ?        SW    0:01 [kflushd]
...
 2792 ?        S     0:00 smbd -D
 2801 pts/0    R     0:00 ps x
stimpy $
```

The first ls command shows that the /var/lock/samba directory does not exist yet. Next, the smbd daemon is invoked. A second invocation of the ls command reveals that the daemon indeed created the /var/lock/samba directory. The last command executed is ps x, which shows that the smbd daemon is indeed running. You might be wondering what the /var/lock/samba directory is used for. The Samba daemons, when they execute, write a file to the directory; this file contains the daemon's process ID. For example, the following dialog shows the PID for the smbd daemon executed in the preceding dialog:

```
stimpy $ ps x
  PID TTY      STAT  TIME COMMAND
    1 ?        S     0:03 init [2]
    2 ?        SW    0:01 [kflushd]
...
 2792 ?        S     0:00 smbd -D
 2802 ?        Z     0:00 [cron <defunct>]
 2824 pts/0    R     0:00 ps x
stimpy $ ls -al /var/lock/samba
total 3
drwxr-xr-x   2 root      root         1024 Feb  4 01:24 .
drwxrwxr-x   4 root      uucp         1024 Feb  4 01:13 ..
```

```
-rw-r--r--    1 root     root            20 Feb  4 01:24 smbd.pid
stimpy $ cat /var/lock/samba/smbd.pid
2792
stimpy $
```

You can use this PID to control the daemons, such as restarting the daemon or terminating it. One word of caution: Do *not* kill the daemons with the SIGKILL (9) signal. This will leave the shared memory area in an unstable state. We will discuss sending signals to the daemons later.

Installing Samba

If Samba does not exist on your system, use the distribution's installation program. Most Linux distributions allow you to run the Linux installation program to install, remove, and update packages.

For example, installing Samba on Red Hat is a simple matter of executing the package manager. The following sample dialog demonstrates executing the rpm command to install the Samba package under Red Hat:

```
stimpy $ rpm -ivh samba-2.06-1.i386.rpm
```

If you are running SuSE Linux, you should execute the YaST tool. From the YaST main menu, select the Choose, Install Packages menu option. Next, select the Change, Create Configuration menu option. The Samba suite is found in the N - Network package. Simply select it, return to the previous menu, and select the Start Installation menu option. YaST will install the Samba suite and configure your system. If you downloaded the Samba package from the SuSE Web site, you can still use YaST to install the package. Again, start YaST and select the Choose, Install Packages menu option. Next, select the Install Packages menu option and browse to the directory where the Samba package resides. Select the Samba package with the Spacebar, and then press the F10 function key to start the installation. Once you have installed the package, the SuSEConfig utility will configure and update your SuSE system.

If you are running TurboLinux, you will use the TurboPkg or XTurboPkg tool. Using these tools, you can install an RPM package from a local filesystem, CD-ROM, or FTP server.

If you are using Caldera's OpenLinux, you can execute the kpackage program from within the KDE. You can find kpackage on the Caldera Open Administration System menu, or you can select Menu, COAS menu and choose the kpackage icon. Figure 15.1 shows kpackage in action.

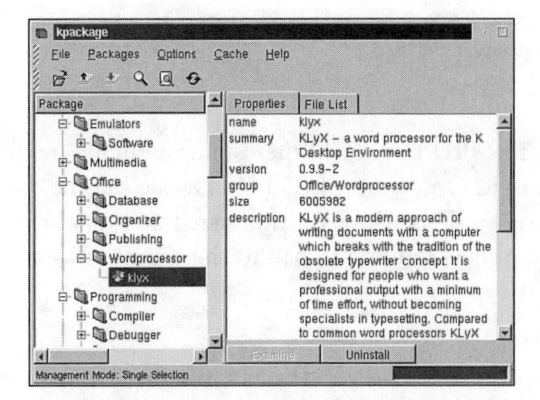

Figure 15.1 The kpackage program running in Caldera OpenLinux.

If you are running the Slackware distribution, you can use the Setup utility to execute the package tool. You can execute Setup from within a graphical shell window or from the text mode shell. Figure 15.2 shows Setup running in a KDE shell window.

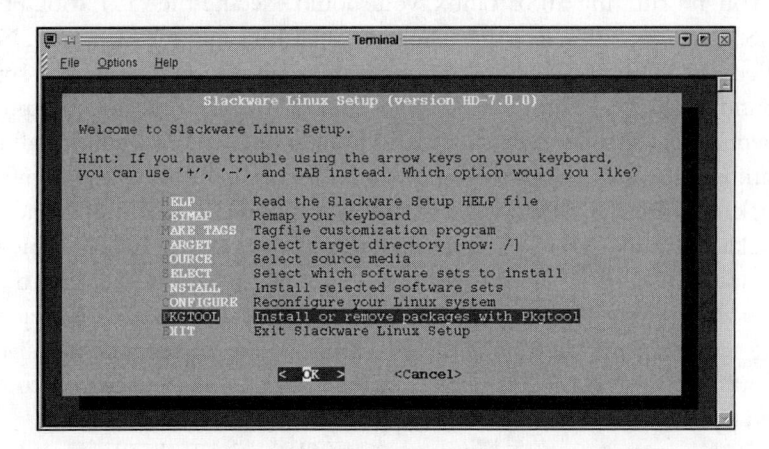

Figure 15.2 The Setup program running in a Slackware KDE window.

If you are using another Linux distribution, be sure to check the documentation for proper package selection and installation. By this time, the complete Samba package should be installed and at least partially configured.

Configuring Samba

A single configuration file, `smb.conf`, completely controls Samba's behavior. For Linux, the configuration file exists in the `/etc` directory. Under most versions of UNIX, however, the configuration file exists in the `/usr/local/samba/lib` directory. If you downloaded the Samba suite, be sure to check the documentation for the configuration file's location.

Configuring for the Samba Web Administration Tool (SWAT)

Two more important steps are required. These steps relate to the use of the Samba Web Administration Tool (SWAT). SWAT, which was added to version 2.0 of Samba, is a browser-based administration tool used to configure Samba. You can use SWAT to set up the Samba server and update its configuration. You can also set up Samba by hand, which many administrators still prefer. If you are new to Samba, there will be less trial and error in setting up Samba if you use SWAT.

The first file you need to check is the `/etc/services` file. You must ensure that there is an entry for the SWAT tool. The following is a snippet from this file:

```
#
# netplan
#
netplan         12000/tcp
#
# swat is the Samba Web Administration Tool
#
swat            901/tcp
#
# Entries for IBM DB2 Database
#
db2cdb2inst1    50000/tcp       # Connection port for DB2 instance db2inst1
db2idb2inst1    50001/tcp       # Interrupt  port for DB2 instance db2inst1
```

Notice the entry for SWAT. If your `/etc/services` file does not have this entry, you will have to add it manually. Fire up your favorite text editor, and add the entry just as it appears here. The `901` specifies the port to use to communicate with SWAT. The `/etc/services` file identifies the available network services and their corresponding port numbers and whether they use TCP or UDP.

Next, you need to check the `inetd.conf` file that is found in the `/etc` directory. The following is a snippet from the `/etc/inetd.conf` file:

```
#
# netbios-ssn    stream    tcp    nowait    root    /usr/sbin/smbd    smbd -l
↪/var/log/samba -s /etc/smb.conf
# netbios-ns     dgram     udp    wait      root    /usr/sbin/nmbd    nmbd
#
# swat is the Samba Web Administration Tool
swat             stream    tcp    nowait.400 root   /usr/sbin/swat    swat
#
# amanda backup server with indexing capabilities
```

The line that begins `swat stream...` is the line you need to verify in your /etc/inetd.conf file. It is quite possible that the entry is there but is commented out (as it was on my SuSE Linux system). If the line is prefixed with a #, simply remove the character. If the line does not exist, be sure to type it exactly as shown in the example.

If you edited the /etc/inetd.conf file, you must tell the inetd daemon to reread this file. You can also reboot the machine, and the changes will take effect. Otherwise, you should issue the HUP signal to the inetd daemon to force the daemon to reread the /etc/inetd.conf file. The following dialog demonstrates this procedure:

```
stimpy $ ps x | grep inet
  124 ?        S      0:00 /usr/sbin/inetd
 3691 pts/0    S      0:00 grep inet
stimpy $ kill -HUP 124
stimpy $
```

First, you execute the ps command, looking for the inetd entry. You can run grep against the ps command to help ferret out the entry. Once you have determined the process ID for the inetd daemon, you can execute the kill command, passing the HUP signal to the daemon. This forces the daemon to reread its configuration file.

The `smb.conf` Configuration File

If you installed Samba from your Linux distribution's CD-ROM, a "default" smb.conf file should exist in the /etc directory. If you downloaded the Samba suite, the installation scripts might not have placed an smb.conf file in the /etc directory. Be sure to check the Samba directory tree for a sample smb.conf file. Be sure to copy it to the directory where Samba expects it.

The smb.conf file is the configuration file for the Samba suite. This file contains runtime configuration information and is designed to be configured and administered by the SWAT utility.

The file consists of *sections* and *parameters*. A section is identified by a name enclosed in square brackets. A section continues until the next section is identified. The following is a sample section:

```
[global]
```

Within each section are one or more parameters, given as key-value pairs, as in the following example:

```
name = value
```

The smb.conf file is line-oriented. In other words, each line represents a comment, section, or parameter. Both section and parameter names are case-insensitive. A comment line can begin with either a semicolon (;) or a hash (#) character. As with other typical UNIX configuration files, the backslash (\) is used as the line-continuation character. The *value* part of an entry can be a string or a boolean value. Valid boolean values are yes or no, 0 or 1, and true or false.

The following is a sample smb.conf file, taken directly from a freshly installed version of Samba (version 2.0.6) on version 6.3 of SuSE Linux.

Listing 15.1 **Sample Samba smb.conf Configuration File**

```
; /etc/smb.conf
; Copyright (c) 1999 SuSE
;
[global]
   workgroup = arbeitsgruppe
   guest account = nobody
   keep alive = 30
   os level = 2
   kernel oplocks = false
   security = user
; Uncomment the following, if you want to use an existing
; NT-Server to authenticate users, but don't forget that
; you also have to create them locally!!!
;   security = server
;   password server = 192.168.1.10
;   encrypt passwords = yes
   printing = bsd
   printcap name = /etc/printcap
   load printers = yes
   socket options = TCP_NODELAY
   map to guest = Bad User
; Uncomment this, if you want to integrate your server
; into an existing net e.g. with NT-WS to prevent nettraffic
;   local master = no
;
; Please uncomment the following entry and replace the
; ip number and netmask with the correct numbers for
; your ethernet interface.
;    interfaces = 192.168.1.1/255.255.255.0
; If you want Samba to act as a wins server, please set
; 'wins support = yes'
   wins support = no
; If you want Samba to use an existing wins server,
; please uncomment the following line and replace
; the dummy with the wins server's ip number.
;    wins server = 192.168.1.1
;
; Do you want samba to act as a logon-server for
; your windows 95/98 clients, so uncomment the
; following:
```

continues ▶

continued

```
;   logon script =%U.bat
;   domain logons = yes
;   domain master = yes
; [netlogon]
;   path = /netlogon
[homes]
   comment = Heimatverzeichnis
   browseable = no
   read only = no
   create mode = 0750
;
; The following share gives all users access to the Server's CD drive,
; assuming it is mounted under /cd. To enable this share, please remove
; the semicolons before the lines
; [cdrom]
;   comment = Linux CD-ROM
;   path = /cd
;   read only = yes
;   locking = no
[printers]
   comment = All Printers
   browseable = no
   printable = yes
   public = no
   read only = yes
   create mode = 0700
   directory = /tmp
; end of file
```

A number of sections are defined in this file. Three special sections are predefined:

- **[global]**. Parameters in this section apply globally to the server. This section also defines default values for other sections in the configuration file.
- **[homes]**. This section allows clients (users) to connect to their home directory.
- **[printers]**. This section works like [homes], but for printers. Users can connect to any printer defined in the /etc/princap file.

Each section in the configuration file, except for the [global] section, describes a shared resource. The shared resource is also referred to as a *share*. The section name, such as [netlogon] or [cdrom], identifies the shared resource. The parameters within the section are used to define the share's attributes.

Variable Substitution

You can set up some of the strings to accept substitutions. The substitution identifier is replaced with an actual value. For example, consider the following entry:

path = /home/%u

If the user who is connected is "daffy," the entry will be finalized like this:

path = /home/daffy

Table 15.1 details the substitutions that are available in Samba.

Table 15.1 **Variable Substitutions for the `smb.conf` File**

Flag	Description
%S	Replaced by the name of the current service, if available.
%P	Replaced by the root directory, if available.
%u	Replaced by the service's username, if available.
%g	Replaced by the primary group name of %u.
%U	Replaced by the session username.
%G	Replaced by the primary group name of %U.
%H	Identifies the home directory of the user %u.
%v	The version of Samba that is running.
%h	Replaced by the Internet hostname that Samba is executing on.
%m	Replaced by the client machine's NetBIOS name.
%L	Replaced by the server's NetBIOS name.
%M	Replaced by the client machine's Internet name.
%N	Extracts the name of the NIS home directory server.
%p	Replaced by the path of the service's home directory.
%R	Replaced by the protocol level as soon as protocol negotiation has finished. The values can be CORE, COREPLUS, LANMAN1, LANMAN2, or NT1.
%d	Extracts the process ID of the current server process.
%a	Replaced by the remote machine's architecture. You should not consider this option 100-percent reliable. Some of the architectures that it recognizes are Samba, Windows for Workgroups, Windows NT, and Windows 95. All others get the value UNKNOWN.
%I	Replaced by the client machine's IP address.
%T	Replaced by the current date and time.

If you are not quite sure of the exact result of some of these substitutions, experiment to validate the outcome. Do not experiment on a production system.

Use of Name Mangling

Samba supports the concept of *name mangling* so that DOS and Windows clients can use files that don't conform to their 8.3 format. The case of filenames can also be set using this feature.

A number of options determine the name-mangling behavior provided by Samba; they are listed in this section. The testparm utility can be used to determine the defaults. Each server can set each of these name-mangling options.

Table 15.2 details the substitutions that are available in Samba.

Table 15.2 **Name-Mangling Options**

Flag	Description
mangle case = yes/no	Used to control whether filenames should be mangled, which are not completely specified by the default case configuration option. The default is no.
case sensitive = yes/no	Used to control whether filenames are case-sensitive. The default is no.
default case = upper/lower	Controls the default case for new filenames. The default is lower.
preserve case = yes/no	Controls whether new files are created with the case that the client uses. Otherwise, they are forced to be the default case. The default is yes.
short preserve case = yes/no	Controls whether new files (created by Samba) should conform to 8.3 syntax. In other words, if filenames are created in upper case or if they are forced to the default case. The default is yes.

The default for version 2.0 of Samba is the same as a Windows NT server—it is case-insensitive but preserves case.

Using SWAT

The Samba Web Administration Tool (SWAT) is used to maintain the smb.conf configuration file. Using the SWAT tool frees you from having to maintain the configuration file by hand. Although some power users would rather edit than click, the majority of administrators find it easier to maintain the `smb.conf` file using SWAT. The interface for SWAT is a Web browser.

You need to edit your `/etc/inetd.conf` and `/etc/services` to allow SWAT to be launched via `inetd`.

As mentioned in the earlier section "Configuring for the Samba Web Administration Tool (SWAT)," you must ensure that your `/etc/services` and `/etc/inetd.conf` files have the proper entries for running SWAT. In the `/etc/services` file, you must have the following entry:

```
swat 901/tcp
```

`/etc/inetd.conf` should have an entry like this:

```
swat stream tcp nowait.400 root /usr/local/samba/bin/swat swat
```

If you have to edit one (or both) of these files, you must send the HUP signal to the `inetd` daemon. The following dialog demonstrates this:

```
stimpy $ ps x ¦ grep inet
  124 ?        S     0:00 /usr/sbin/inetd
 3691 pts/0    S     0:00 grep inet
stimpy $ kill -HUP 124
stimpy $
```

This tells the `inetd` daemon to reread its configuration files.

To execute SWAT, you must first start your Web browser. As soon as the browser is running, you need to connect to `http://localhost:901`. After the browser connects, a dialog box appears, waiting for you to log in for the SWAT session (see Figure 15.3).

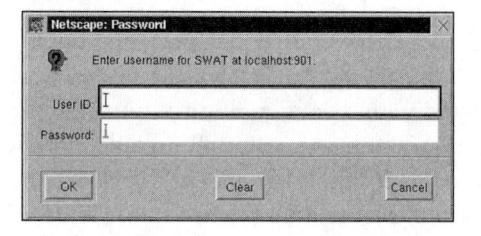

Figure 15.3 SWAT Password dialog box.

You must enter a valid username and password to access the SWAT tool. At this point, you can log in as the root user. Enter the username and password, and then click the OK button (or whatever is applicable for your browser).

428 Chapter 15 Samba: Merging Linux and Windows

> **Executing SWAT Remotely**
> Although you can connect to SWAT from a remote machine, this is not recommended because your username and password would be sent in the clear. You can obtain information on executing SWAT with SSL from the http://www.samba.org Web site.

When you have been authenticated, you see the home page for SWAT, as shown in Figure 15.4.

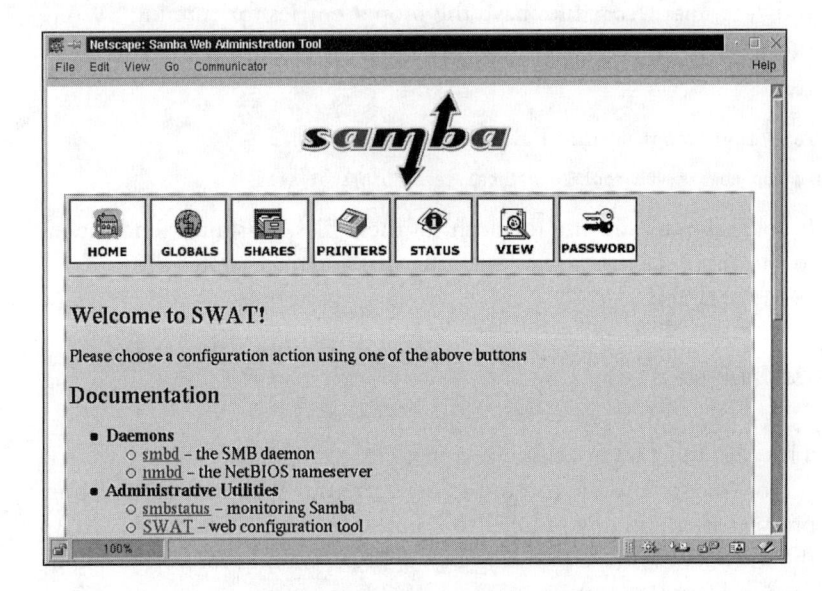

Figure 15.4 SWAT Home page.

This page contains a number of URL links. The buttons at the top of the page are Home, Globals, Shares, Printers, Status, View, and Password. Each button is associated with a configuration action.

As you look down the page, you will notice a number of URL links. These are documentation links, providing a Web interface to Samba's man pages. Although Figure 15.4 doesn't show all the choices, the available documentation links are described in the following list:

- Daemons

    smbd: The SMB daemon

    nmbd: The NetBIOS name server

- Administrative Utilities

    smbstatus: Monitors Samba

    SWAT: Web configuration tool

smbpasswd: Manages SMB passwords

make_smbcodepage: Codepage creation

testparm: Validates your `config` file

testprns: Tests printer configuration

- General Utilities

    nmblookup: NetBIOS name query tool

    smbtar: SMB backup tool

    smbclient: Command-line SMB client

- Configuration Files

    `smb.conf`: Main Samba configuration file

    `lmhosts`: NetBIOS hosts file

    `smbpasswd`: SMB password file

- Miscellaneous

    Samba introduction

    Joining an NT domain

    Changing UNIX permissions using NT

    smbrun: Internal smbd utility

To demonstrate the Web interface to the documentation, Figure 15.5 shows the man page for the `smbd` daemon in HTML format.

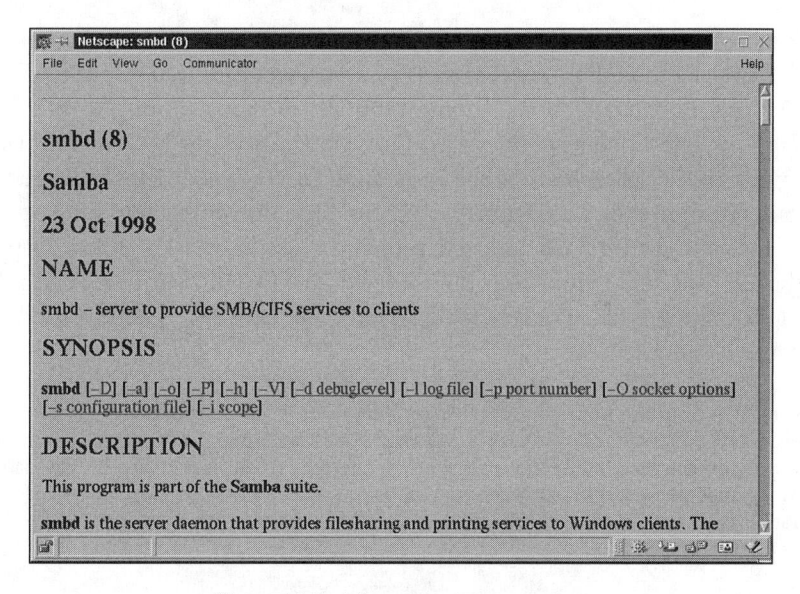

Figure 15.5 The `smbd` (8) man page.

Figure 15.5 verifies that the documentation is formatted in the style of a man page. The Name, Description, Synopsis, and Options (among other optional) sections are provided as you would expect.

To view and modify the global settings for Samba, click the Globals button. Figure 15.6 shows a portion of the Globals page.

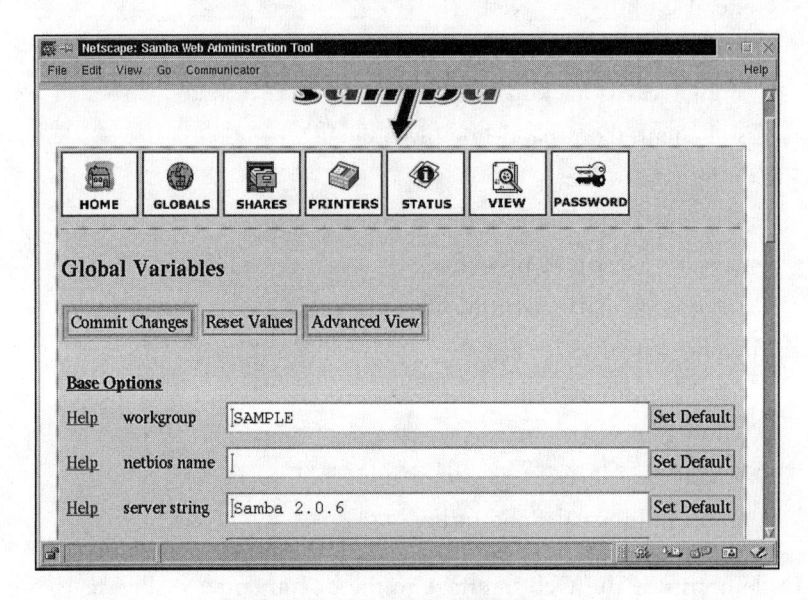

Figure 15.6 The Globals SWAT page.

You can see the first three of four options for the Base Options section of the Globals page. This page consists of seven sections: Base Options, Security Options, Logging Options, Tuning Options, Browse Options, WINS Options, and Locking Options. You can obtain help for each individual option found in each section. For example, if you need help with the netbios name option, shown in Figure 15.6, you click the word Help just to the left of the option name. Clicking Help opens a new browser window, displaying the appropriate section from the smb.conf(8) HTML man page. The following is a snippet taken from the displayed Web page after Help for netbios name was clicked:

```
netbios name (G)
    This sets the NetBIOS name by which a Samba server is known. By default it is the
same as the first component of the host's DNS name. If a machine is a browse server or
logon server this name (or the first component of the hosts DNS name) will be the name
that these services are advertised under.
    See also "netbios aliases".
    Default: Machine DNS name.
```

```
    Example: netbios name = MYNAME
nis homedir (G)
    Get the home share ...
...
```

You will notice a Set Default button to the right of each option. This button automatically sets the default value for the associated field. For example, if you click the Set Default button for the workgroup option in the Base Options section, the value WORKGROUP will be inserted into the text box.

At the top of the Globals page are three other buttons. The button labeled Commit Changes writes any changes you have made to the smb.conf configuration file. The Reset Values button resets all the fields to the values they had before any changes were made. The button labeled Advanced View expands the available configuration options in two ways. First, it adds a number of new sections to the page. Second, it expands the number of individual options for any existing section. For example, the first section, Base Options, expands to offer the following individual options: workgroup, netbios name, server string, netbios aliases, and interfaces. As an example of a new major section, the Protocol Option section appears under the Advanced View page. The Protocol Option section offers a number of individual options, such as protocol, read bmpx, and read raw. You can return to the Basic View by clicking the View button at the top of the page.

The Shares button, when clicked, displays the Shares page, shown in Figure 15.7.

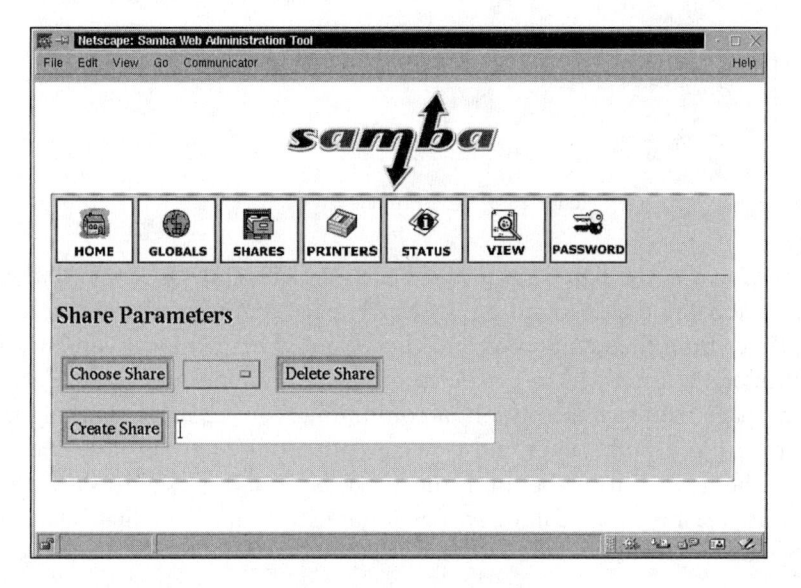

Figure 15.7 The Shares SWAT page.

As shown in the figure, no shares are currently set up. You can create a new share by clicking the Create Share button. The two other buttons on this page are Choose Share and Delete Share. The third field, a combo box, allows you to choose among any available shares and display the settings. If you click Create Share or select a share from the combo box (and click Choose Share), the page will be expanded to show a number of options for the share. There is a Basic View and an Advanced View. The Commit Changes and Reset Values buttons are also available on the Shares page.

If you want to add a printer to be shared, click the Printers button. Figure 15.8 shows the Printers page, which allows you to add a new printer share, modify an existing printer share, or delete an existing printer share.

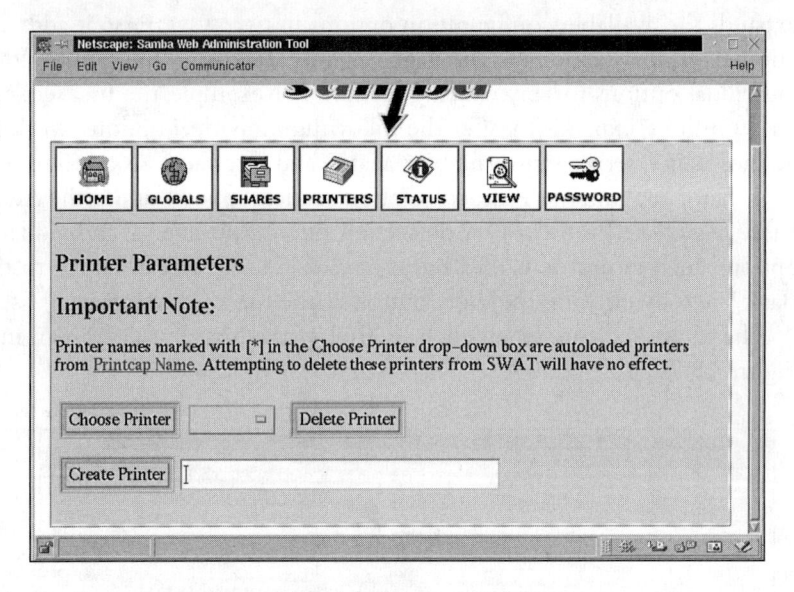

Figure 15.8 The Printers SWAT page.

As shown in the figure, no printer shares are currently selected. All the functionality that is found on the Shares page is available here. If you select a printer from the combo box and click Choose Printer, or if you click Create Printer, the page will be expanded to reveal a number of options. Again, on this page you have the option of committing your changes, resetting the options to default values, and viewing (and modifying) the advanced options.

The next available option is the Status button. It is used to show the current status of the Samba system. Figure 15.9 shows the Status page for Samba.

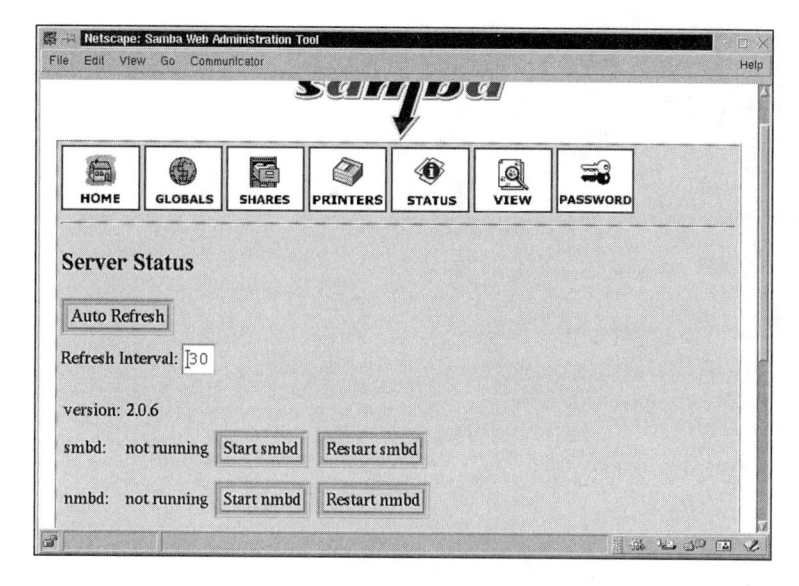

Figure 15.9 The Status SWAT page.

In this figure, the Samba system is not running. The Auto Refresh button is used to set a recursive timer that will automatically refresh the Web page with updated information. The default refresh cycle is every 30 seconds, but you can set it to almost any value. You can also set it to stop refreshing. Use the browser's Refresh button to update the static status page.

A number of other command buttons are available. The Start smbd and Restart smbd buttons are used to start the `smbd` daemon and restart a running `smbd` daemon, respectively. Figure 15.10 shows that the `smbd` daemon is running now that the Start smbd button was clicked.

This page also shows any shares that are enabled. There are a number of sections. The Active Connections section shows any users who are using a share. Some of the fields for this section are PID, Client, IP address, and Date. The Active Shares section shows any shares that are currently enabled. The fields for this section are Share, User, Group, PID, Client, and Date. The last section, Open Files, shows any files that are currently open. The column fields for this section are PID, Sharing, R/W, Oplock, File, and Date.

The View button is used to view the contents of the `smbd.conf` file. The default view is called Normal View, and it shows a brief version of the file. Figure 15.11 shows the View page.

Chapter 15 Samba: Merging Linux and Windows

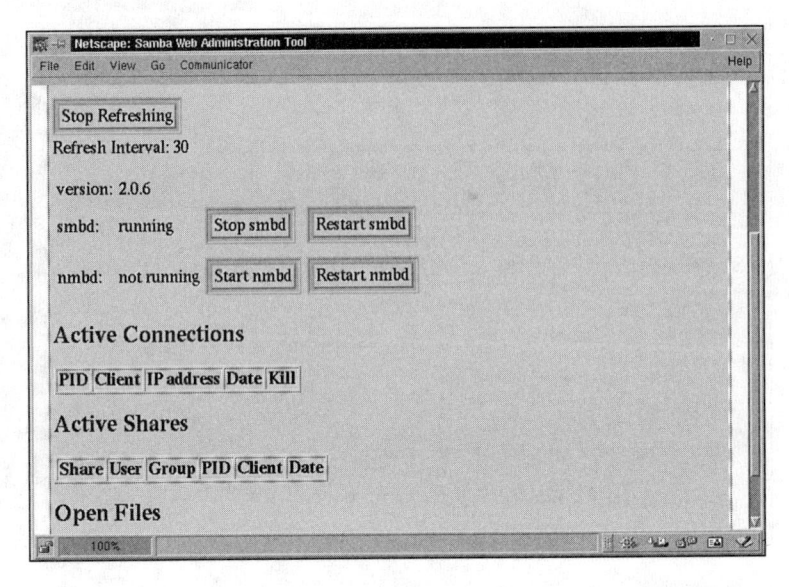

Figure 15.10 The Status SWAT page showing the `smbd` daemon running.

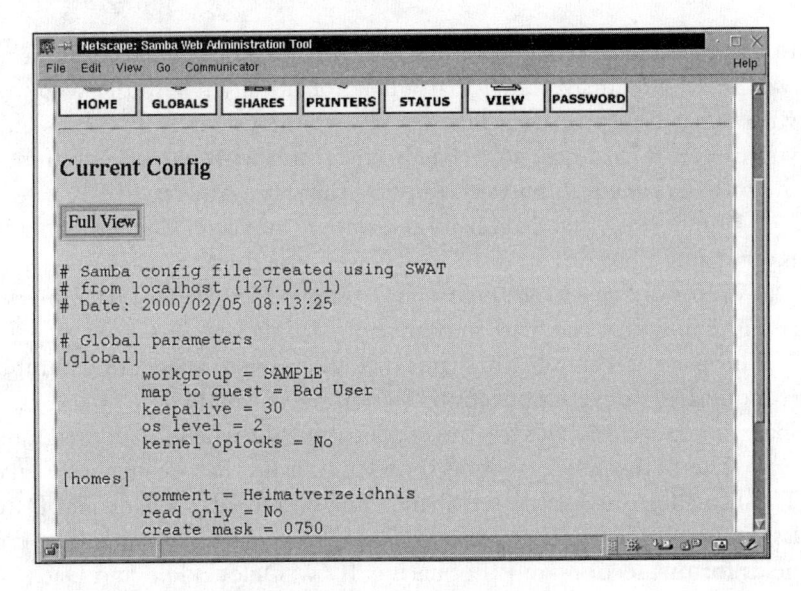

Figure 15.11 The View SWAT page.

You can click the Full View button to expand the listing, which shows the complete contents of the `smbd.conf` configuration file. Figure 15.11 shows the [global] options and some of the [homes] options. If you click the Full View button, the [global] section expands to show more than 200 options. The other sections also expand, and some new sections appear.

The last configuration page is the Password page. You see it when you click the Password button. Figure 15.12 shows a partially obscured Password page.

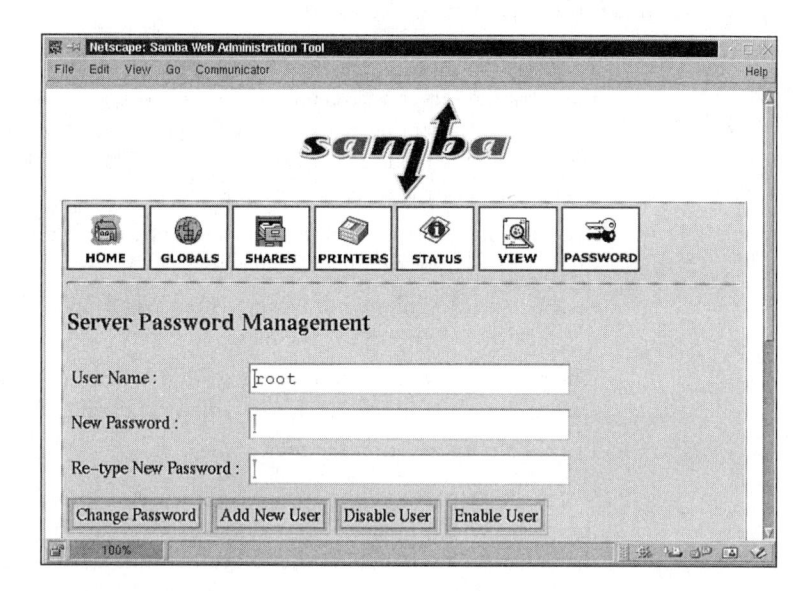

Figure 15.12 The Password SWAT page.

The Password page allows you to maintain the usernames that will be accessing any of the Samba shares.

Executing Samba

Until now, we have been configuring Samba for use. The following sections discuss the execution of the two Samba daemons (which were covered briefly earlier in this chapter).

The `smbd` daemon

The `smbd` daemon provides file and print sharing services. Whenever a client request for a connection comes in, a Samba session is created. This session consists of a copy of the server (`smbd`). This server copy continues to provide services to the client until that client terminates.

The configuration file is reloaded by the server every minute if changes have taken effect. You can force the `smbd` daemon to reread the file by sending the server a `SIGHUP` signal. The reloading of the configuration file is not performed by any server copies that exist for client connections. The client must reconnect in order for changes to be applied.

The `smbd` process can accept a number of options on the command line. Table 15.3 describes these options.

Table 15.3 **Command-Line Options for `smbd`**

Option	Description
`-D`	Executes the server as a daemon. In other words, it runs in the background, accepting requests on the appropriate port. This is the recommended way of executing `smbd`. The default operation is for the server to not operate as a daemon.
`-a`	Specifies that each new connection will append log messages to the log file. This is the default behavior.
`-o`	Specifies that log files will be overwritten when opened. The default is to append to the log files.
`-P`	The passive option, which causes `smbd` to not send out network traffic. This is useful for developers when debugging.
`-h`	Prints help information for `smbd` and exits.
`-V`	Prints the version number for `smbd` and exits.
`-d debuglevel`	Specifies the debug level. The valid range is from `0` to `10`; the default is `0`. The higher the value, the more detailed the messages.
`-l log file`	Specifies that `log file` is the log filename where informational and debug messages from the server will be logged.
`-p port number`	Specifies the port number. The default value is `139`. This port number is the port to use for connection requests from Samba clients.
`-s configuration file`	Specifies the configuration file. See the `smb.conf` (5) man page for more information.
`-i scope`	Specifies a NetBIOS scope that the server uses to communicate with when generating NetBIOS names.

To shut down a user's `smbd` process, you should send the SIGTERM (-15) signal and wait for the process to die on its own. It is not recommended that SIGKILL (-9) be used, except as a last resort. Doing this might leave the shared memory area in an inconsistent state.

You can raise the debug log level for `smbd` by sending the SIGUSR1 signal. The SIGUSR2 signal is used to lower the debug level.

The `nmbd` daemon

The `nmbd` program (the NetBIOS name server) provides NetBIOS-over-IP naming services to Samba clients.

The `nmbd` server understands and responds to NetBIOS (over IP) name service requests, such as those generated by SMBD/CIFS clients (Windows and LanManager clients). The server also engages in browsing protocols, such as those for the Windows Network Neighborhood view.

The `nmbd` server can respond to an SMB/CIFS client that wants to know the IP number for the SMB/CIFS server. If the NetBIOS name is specified for the `nmbd` server, it will respond with the host IP number that it is running on.

The `nmbd` server can be used as a Windows Internet Name Server (WINS) server, meaning it will serve as a WINS database server. The `nmbd` server will create a database from name registration requests from and replies to clients.

The `nmbd` process can accept a number of options on the command line. Table 15.4 describes these options.

Table 15.4 **Command-Line Options for `nmbd`**

Option	Description
-D	Executes the server as a daemon. In other words, it runs in the background, accepting requests on the appropriate port. This is the recommended way of executing `nmbd`. The default operation is for the server to not operate as a daemon.
-a	Specifies that each new connection will append log messages to the log file. This is the default behavior.
-o	Specifies that log files will be overwritten when opened. The default is to append to the log files.
-h	Prints help information for `nmbd` and exits.
-V	Prints the version number for `nmbd` and exits.
-H filename	Identifies the NetBIOS `lmhosts` file, which is a list of NetBIOS names to IP addresses that is loaded by the `nmbd` server. It is used by the name resolution mechanism to resolve NetBIOS name queries required by the server.
-d debuglevel	Specifies the debug level. The valid range is from 0 to 10; the default is 0. The higher the value, the more detailed the messages.

continues ▶

Table 15.4 Continued

Option	Description
-l logfile	Specifies a filename to which operational data from the nmbd server will be logged. The log filename is created by appending the .nmb extension to the specified base name. Some common defaults are /usr/local/samba/var/log.nmb, /usr/samba/var/log.nmb, and /var/log/log.nmb.
-n primary NetBIOS name	Overrides the NetBIOS name Samba uses for itself. This overrides the setting in the smb.conf file.
-p UDP port number	The UDP port number that nmbd responds to name queries on. The default is 137.
-s configuration file	The configuration filename to read. See the smbd.conf man page for more details.
-i scope	Specifies a NetBIOS scope that nmbd uses to communicate with when generating NetBIOS names.

To shut down the nmbd process, you should send the SIGTERM (-15) signal and wait for the process to die. You should not use the SIGKILL (-9) signal, except as a last resort. Using the SIGKILL signal might leave the shared memory area in an inconsistent state.

You can send the SIGHUP signal to nmbd. This causes nmbd to dump the name lists into the file namelist.debug, usually in the var/locks directory. This signal also causes nmbd to dump its server database to the log.nmb file.

You can raise the debug log level for nmbd by sending the SIGUSR1 signal. The SIGUSR2 signal is used to lower the debug level.

Using smbclient

The smbclient program, providing an FTP-like interface, is a Samba client used to access SMB/CIFS shares on servers. Unlike NFS, smbclient does not provide the ability to mount a share on a local directory. The usage for smbclient is as follows:

```
smbclient servicename <password> [-s smb.conf] [-O socket options]
[-R name resolve order] [-M NetBIOS name] [-i scope] [-N] [-n NetBIOS name]
[-d debuglevel] [-P] [-p port] [-l log basename] [-h] [-I dest IP] [-E] [-U username]
[-L NetBIOS name] [-t terminal code] [-m max protocol] [-b buffersize] [-W workgroup]
[-T<c¦x>IXFqgbNan] [-D directory] [-c command string]
```

The smbclient program accepts a number of command-line options. Table 15.5 describes these options.

Table 15.5 **Command-Line Options for smbclient**

Option	Description
servicename	The name of the service you want to use on the server. The service name is of the form //server/service, where server is the NetBIOS name and service is the name of the service offered.
password	The password required to access the service on the server. There is no default password. If a password is not supplied and the -N option is not specified, the client prompts for a password.
-s smb.conf	Identifies the pathname of the smb.conf file.
-O socket options	Used to set the TCP socket options for the client.
-R name resolve order	Allows the user to determine the name resolution services to use when looking up the NetBIOS name of the host to connect to. Available options are lmhosts, host, wins, and bcast. See the smbclient man page for more information.
-M NetBIOS name	Allows you to send messages with the WinPopup protocol.
-i scope	Specifies the NetBIOS scope that the smbclient program will use to communicate with when generating NetBIOS names.
-N	Suppresses the password prompt from the client to the user.
-n NetBIOS name	Allows you to override the hostname.
-d debuglevel	debuglevel is an integer from 0 to 10, or the letter A. The default is 0. The higher this value, the more detail that will be logged.
-p port	The TCP port number to be used when making connections to the server. The default is 139.
-l logfilename	Specifies the base filename (logfilename) where operational data will be logged.
-h	Prints a usage message for the smbclient and exits.
-I IP address	The IP address of the server to connect to.
-E	Causes smbclient to write messages to the standard error stream rather than to the standard output stream.
-U username	Specifies the username to be used by the client to make a connection.

continues ▶

Table 15.5 **Continued**

Option	Description
-L	Allows you to look at the available services.
-t terminal code	Specifies how to interpret filenames coming from the remote server.
-b buffersize	Changes the size of the transmit and send buffer. The default is 65520 bytes.
-W workgroup	Defines the workgroup to connect to, overriding the default workgroup specified in the smb.conf file.
-T tar options	The smbclient program can be used to create tar-compatible files for the files on an SMB/CIFS share.
-D initial directory	Changes to the current directory before starting.
-c command string	A semicolon-separated list of commands that are to be executed instead of prompting from stdin.

The user is provided with an smbclient prompt upon execution of the program. The smbclient command prompt is similar to the following:

```
smb:\>
```

This prompt indicates that the smbclient program is waiting for a command to execute. Each command consists of a command word, optionally followed by command options.

Table 15.6 lists the commands available for the smbclient program.

Table 15.6 **Commands for the smbclient Program**

Command	Description
? [command]	If command is specified, a brief description of the specified command is displayed.
! [shell command]	If specified, a shell is executed locally with the specified shell command.
cd [directory name]	The current working directory on the server is changed to the directory specified.
del mask	A request is made to the server to delete from the current working directory all files matching mask.
dir mask	Used to show a list of files matching mask in the current working directory.

Option	Description
`exit`	Terminates the server connection and exits.
`get remote-file-name [local file name]`	Copies the file called `remote-file-name` from the server to the client.
`help [command]`	The same as the `?` command.
`lcd [directory name]`	The current working directory on the local machine is changed to the directory specified.
`lowercase`	Toggles the lowercasing of filenames. Used with the `get` and `mget` commands.
`ls mask`	Refers to the `dir` command in this table.
`mask mask`	Allows the user to set a mask to be used during recursive operation of the `mget` and `mput` commands.
`md directory name`	The same as the `mkdir` command.
`mget mask`	Copies files matching `mask` from the server to the local machine.
`mkdir directory name`	Creates a new directory on the server.
`mput mask`	Copies files matching `mask` on the local machine to the working directory on the server.
`print file name`	Prints the `file name` file from the local machine to a print service on the server.
`printmode graphics or text`	Sets print mode for binary data or text.
`prompt`	Toggles the prompting for filenames for the `mget` and `mput` commands.
`put local file name [remote file name]`	Copies the file called `local file name` from the client to the server.
`queue`	Displays the print queue.
`quit`	The same as the `exit` command.
`rd directory name`	The same as the `rmdir` command.
`recurse`	Toggles directory recursion for the commands `mget` and `mput`.
`rm mask`	Removes files matching `mask` from the server.

continues ▶

Table 15.6 **Commands for the smbclient program**

Command	Description
`rmdir directory name`	Removes the specified directory from the server.
`tar <c¦x>[IXbgNa]`	Performs a tar operation.
`setmode filename <perm=[+¦\-]rsha>`	A version of the DOS `attrib` command to set file permissions. An example would be `setmode myfile +r` to set `myfile` to read-only.

Summary

In this chapter, we discussed the use of Samba. We began our journey with an overview of Samba. Samba is a suite of applications that can speak the Server Message Block (SMB) protocol. Samba runs on UNIX platforms but can speak to Windows clients natively.

Samba is available on the CD-ROM of most Linux distributions. If it is not available on your distribution, you can obtain it from http://www.samba.org. You can obtain the Samba package as a binary or CVS source distribution.

Samba is configured by a single configuration file named `smb.conf`, which completely controls Samba's behavior. Variable substitution and name mangling were also discussed. You can edit the configuration file manually or use the Samba Web Administration Tool (SWAT). SWAT is a browser-based administration tool used to configure Samba, which ultimately modifies the `smb.conf` file.

Next, we discussed the execution of the Samba daemons, including the `smbd` and `nmbd` daemons. The `smbd` daemon provides file and print services to clients, and `nmbd` provides NetBIOS name resolution and browsing.

Finally, we discussed the smbclient program, which provides an FTP-like interface used to access SMB/CIFS shares on servers.

16

Apache Web Server

IF YOU WANT INFORMATION on the best and most popular Web server on the Internet, you have come to the right place. In this chapter, you take a drive through Apache territory.

This chapter is dedicated to understanding, acquiring, configuring, and using the Apache Web server. We will do in one chapter what many say requires a book—that is, provide the information necessary to install and run Apache.

Apache Overview

Apache has found its place in life as the most popular Web server on the Internet. Apache has held the title since the first part of 1996.

Netcraft (http://www.netcraft.com), a networking consulting company in England is known worldwide for its Web Server Survey (http://www.netcraft.com/survey). In late January 2000, I visited the site to check on the latest results of the survey. The number of developers working on Apache in December 1999 was 5,209,677, which accounted for 54.49 percent of all respondents. Web server usage showed Apache having an installed base of 4,847,992 units, which accounted for 54.81 percent of the respondents. In fact, the Apache Web server is more widely used than all other Web servers combined. Figure 16.1 depicts the statistics graphically.

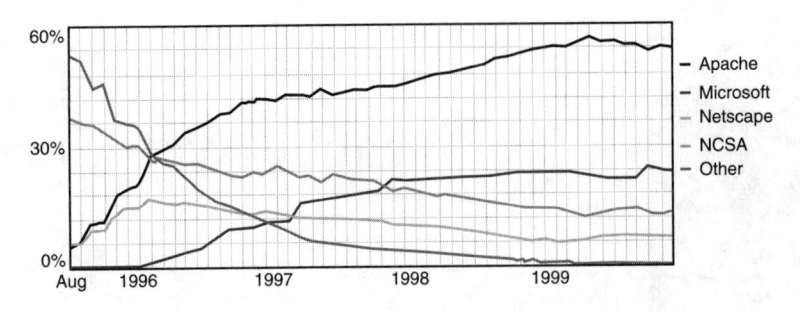

Figure 16.1 The Netcraft Web Server Survey statistics.

Apache is an open-source HTTP server that is available for a variety of desktop and server operating systems, including Linux, A/UX (Apple's UNIX), BSD-based (FreeBSD, and so on), Digital UNIX, HPUX, Solaris, SunOS 4.x, and Windows platforms. The Apache Web server is an efficient and extensible server, providing HTTP services that conform to the current HTTP standards.

The Apache Group does not have any outside sponsors or institutional influence and consists of true server users. These server users are people who make their living running Web servers. These user/developers are empathetic to other server users and strive to provide the functionality suggested by other server users.

Some prominent organizations use (or have switched to) the Apache Web server. Some of these organizations are Hotwired (http://www.hotwired.com), the MIT AI Laboratory (http://www.ai.mit.edu), and the Internet Movie Database (http://www.imdb.com), among others. If you are interested in discovering who is running Apache, an incomplete list of sites is maintained at http://www.apache.org/info/apache_users.html.

You might be interested to know why the name Apache was chosen. Originally, a group of people worked together to provide patches for the NCSA HTTPd Web server version 1.3 (a maintenance release) in early 1995. This group of people became what is known as the Apache Group. After these patches were collected and incorporated, the result was a patchy server—or more appropriately, "A Patchy" server.

Choosing an Apache Package

You may be wrestling with the decision as to what platform on which to run the Apache Web server. You might be reading this book because you want to discover the merits of using Linux. You might be reading this chapter because you have to get Apache up and running at your office. Or you might want to run your own personal Web site on your home machine.

There is really only one true platform choice for running Apache. Collectively, that platform is Linux/UNIX—and more specifically, Linux. After all, this book is about Linux. Your best bet is to pick up a distribution of Linux, such as Caldera's OpenLinux, Slackware, Red Hat, SuSE, or TurboLinux, to name a few. Next, incorporate Apache to provide a secure and robust Web server. Most Linux vendors bundle Apache with their distributions, and some vendors provide server-specific products, such as TurboLinux Server or Red Hat Linux Professional (at a nominal increase in price).

The alternative is to run Apache on some Win32 platform, which really is not an alternative. You can run Apache on Windows 95, Windows 98, and Windows NT, but some security issues exist regarding each of those operating systems. The Windows 95 and Windows 98 platforms have no real security to speak of, especially from a server perspective. Although Windows NT is thought of as a server platform, a number of security holes are well known. Ironically, one security hole is using Linux to gain access to an NTFS drive! The fact is, Windows NT has not stood the test of time as UNIX has.

Using Apache under a Win32 platform might be okay for Web site testing, but if your business relies on reliable and secure Web hosting, put your money on the Linux platform.

Obtaining and Installing Apache

Check the CD-ROM for your Linux distribution to see whether Apache is included. If not, or if you want to have the latest version of Apache, you can obtain the current release from the Apache Software Foundation at http://www.apache.org.

You can download Apache as a binary package or as a build package. The binary distribution of Apache for Linux is available at http://www.apache.org/dist/binaries/linux.

The binary distribution contains the required Apache modules as shared objects. This allows you to enable or disable modules using the LoadModule and AddModule directives within the configuration file without having to recompile the Apache source.

You can obtain a complete Apache distribution that comes with complete source code at http://www.apache.org/dist. Of course, you will have to build the Apache package. This process is not that difficult, given enough time.

As of this writing, the gzipped source package, apache_1.3.9.tar.gz, is 1.4MB. As a contrast, the gzipped binary package for an Intel Pentium machine, `apache_1.3.9-i686-whatever-linux2.tar.gz`, is 2.3MB. It will take you almost twice as long to download the binary version (about 30 minutes using a 28.8 connection), but you will be ready to roll after you unzip the binary package.

In this chapter, I discuss Apache version 1.3, which is the current version as of the writing of this chapter. More specifically, the version detailed here is version 1.3.9 of Apache.

It is quite possible that Apache is installed on your machine. You may have installed it at the time you installed your Linux distribution. You can check for Apache's existence, as shown in the following dialog:

```
stimpy $ httpd -v
Server version: Apache/1.3.9 (Unix)  (SuSE/Linux)
Server built:   Nov  9 1999 02:46:17
stimpy $ httpd -V
Server version: Apache/1.3.9 (Unix)  (SuSE/Linux)
Server built:   Nov  9 1999 02:46:17
Server's Module Magic Number: 19990320:6
Server compiled with....
 -D EAPI
 -D HAVE_MMAP
 -D HAVE_SHMGET
 -D USE_SHMGET_SCOREBOARD
 -D USE_MMAP_FILES
 -D USE_FCNTL_SERIALIZED_ACCEPT
 -D HTTPD_ROOT="/usr/local/httpd"
 -D SUEXEC_BIN="/usr/sbin/suexec"
 -D DEFAULT_PIDLOG="/var/logs/httpd.pid"
 -D DEFAULT_SCOREBOARD="/var/logs/httpd.scoreboard"
 -D DEFAULT_LOCKFILE="/var/logs/httpd.lock"
 -D DEFAULT_XFERLOG="/var/log/access_log"
 -D DEFAULT_ERRORLOG="/var/log/error_log"
 -D TYPES_CONFIG_FILE="/etc/httpd/mime.types"
 -D SERVER_CONFIG_FILE="/etc/httpd/httpd.conf"
 -D ACCESS_CONFIG_FILE="/etc/httpd/access.conf"
 -D RESOURCE_CONFIG_FILE="/etc/httpd/srm.conf"
stimpy $ httpd -t
Syntax OK
stimpy $
```

Notice that there are three invocations (see bolded text in preceding code) of the `httpd` daemon: two requesting version information and the third performing a syntax test. The first variation, `httpd -v`, prints the version of the `httpd` daemon and then exits. The second variation, `httpd -V`, prints the version and build parameters of the `httpd` daemon and then exits. The third invocation, `httpd -t`, tells the `httpd` daemon to run syntax tests on the configuration files only. The program exits after syntax parsing with either a code of zero (`Syntax OK`) or not zero (`Syntax Error`). The following dialog demonstrates this execution:

```
stimpy $ httpd -t
Syntax OK
stimpy $
```

The `httpd` daemon performs a syntax check on the configuration files, provides a report, and then exits. You can see how `httpd` reports success, but what if a problem exists with the configuration file? The following dialog demonstrates this:

```
stimpy $ httpd -t
Syntax error on line 82 of /etc/httpd/httpd.conf:
Invalid command 'PikFile', perhaps misspelled or defined
by a module not included in the server configuration
stimpy $
```

That entry should be `Pidfile`, and it identifies the filename that the daemon will use to write its process ID number to after it has started.

The error reporting only provides FRS (find, report, stop) functionality. The following snippet from the `/etc/httpd/httpd.conf` file contains three errors, one on each line:

```
TerverRoot "/usr/local/httpd"
MockFile /var/lock/subsys/httpd/httpd.accept.lock
SidFile /var/run/httpd.pid
```

The entries should be `ServerRoot`, `LockFile`, and `Pidfile`, respectively. The `httpd` daemon reports only on the first error it encounters; it reports the error and then stops. Thus, you have to fix the `TerverRoot` entry first, and then rerun the `httpd -t` command again to see the second error, and so on.

Beginning the Apache Installation

After you have downloaded the Apache source package, you have to uncompress it and then unarchive it. The compressed file's extension determines the tool you use for decompression. If the extension is .Z, you use the `uncompress` command. If the extension is .gz, you use the `gzip` (or `gunzip`) command.

After the file is decompressed, you need to run the `tar` command to de-archive the contents. Doing this creates a number of directories and places various files in each of those directories.

Chapter 16 Apache Web Server

You can place the `apache_1.3.9.tar.gz` (or whatever version you have) into the `/usr/local/etc/apache` or `/usr/local/apache` directory. From this directory, you decompress and de-archive the contents. The following dialog demonstrates the sequence:

```
stimpy $ gunzip apache_1.3.9.tar.gz
stimpy $ ls -al
total 6107
drwxr-xr-x   2 root      root         1024 Jan 30 10:32 .
drwxr-x---   7 root      root         1024 Jan 30 10:31 ..
-rw-r--r--   1 root      root      6225920 Jan 30 07:38 apache_1.3.9.tar
stimpy $ tar xvf apache_1.3.9.tar
apache_1.3.9/
apache_1.3.9/src/
apache_1.3.9/src/ap/
apache_1.3.9/src/ap/.indent.pro
apache_1.3.9/src/ap/Makefile.tmpl
apache_1.3.9/src/ap/ap.dsp
apache_1.3.9/src/ap/ap.mak
...
apache_1.3.9/icons/small/rainbow.gif
apache_1.3.9/icons/small/transfer.gif
apache_1.3.9/icons/small/unknown.gif
apache_1.3.9/icons/small/uu.gif
apache_1.3.9/logs/
stimpy $
```

Alternatively, you can execute the `tar` command to perform both the unzipping and de-archiving in one step, as shown in the following dialog:

```
stimpy $ tar apache zxvf 1.3.9.tar.gz
apache_1.3.9/
apache_1.3.9/src/
apache_1.3.9/src/ap/
apache_1.3.9/src/ap/ap.dsp
apache_1.3.9/src/ap/ap.mak
...
apache_1.3.9/icons/small/rainbow.gif
apache_1.3.9/icons/small/uu.gif
apache_1.3.9/logs/
stimpy $
```

Personally, I prefer the two-step process because there may be documentation to read before running the `tar` extract.

The important commands are in bold text. The `tar` command displays the name of the directory and file as it is processed. If the filename's extension is .Z, you execute the uncompress command as shown in the following sample dialog:

```
stimpy $ uncompress apache_1.3.9.tar.Z
stimpy $ ls -al
```

```
total 6107
drwxr-xr-x   2 root     root         1024 Jan 30 10:32 .
drwxr-x---   7 root     root         1024 Jan 30 10:31 ..
-rw-r--r--   1 root     root      6225920 Jan 30 07:38 apache_1.3.9.tar
```

Again, you can execute the `tar` command to fulfill both the unzip and de-archive operations in one step.

Building Apache the Easy Way

Either way, the next step is to execute the build process. The first step is to execute the `configure` command supplied in the Apache package. The following dialog demonstrates this:

```
stimpy $ cd apache
stimpy $ ./configure
Configuring for Apache, Version 1.3.9
 + Warning: Configuring Apache with default settings.
 + This is probably not what you really want.
 + Please read the README.configure and INSTALL files
 + first or at least run './configure --help' for
 + a compact summary of available options.
 + using installation path layout: Apache (config.layout)
Creating Makefile
Creating Configuration.apaci in src
Creating Makefile in src
 + configured for Linux platform
 + setting C compiler to gcc
 + setting C pre-processor to gcc -E
 + checking for system header files
 + adding selected modules
 + checking size of various data types
 + doing sanity check on compiler and options
Creating Makefile in src/support
Creating Makefile in src/regex
Creating Makefile in src/os/unix
Creating Makefile in src/ap
Creating Makefile in src/main
Creating Makefile in src/lib/expat-lite
Creating Makefile in src/modules/standard
stimpy $
```

The `configure` command is executed (shown as bold text in the preceding code listing), which then displays a number of status text lines. A number of makefiles are created, along with a number of options for building the source code. The next command you execute is the `make` command, as shown in the following sample dialog:

```
stimpy $ make
===> src
make[1]: Entering directory `/mnt/tool/root/apache/apache_1.3.9'
```

continues ▶

continued

```
make[2]: Entering directory `/mnt/tool/root/apache/apache_1.3.9/src'
===> src/regex
sh ./mkh  -p regcomp.c >regcomp.ih
gcc -I. -I../os/unix -I../include ... -c regcomp.c -o regcomp.o
...
sed <apxs.pl >apxs \
    -e 's%@TARGET@%httpd%g' \
    -e 's%@CC@%gcc%g' \
    -e 's%@CFLAGS@% -DLINUX=2 ... `../apaci`%g' \
    -e 's%@CFLAGS_SHLIB@%%g' \
    -e 's%@LD_SHLIB@%%g' \
    -e 's%@LDFLAGS_MOD_SHLIB@%%g' \
    -e 's%@LIBS_SHLIB@%%g' && chmod a+x apxs
make[2]: Leaving directory `/mnt/tool/root/apache/apache_1.3.9/src/support'
<=== src/support
make[1]: Leaving directory `/mnt/tool/root/apache/apache_1.3.9'
<=== src
stimpy $
```

Various status messages are displayed as the package is being built. The compiler, the assembler, and the linker, among other tools, are executed to produce the Apache package. The process does not take very long at all; I tested the build on a Pentium 166mHz with 96MB RAM, and the build took about 13 minutes. The complete process, including the configuration and build process, consumed approximately 15 minutes total. I tested the configure and build processes under Slackware 7.0, TurboLinux 4.0, Red Hat 6.1, SuSE 6.3, and OpenLinux 2.3 and experienced no problems.

This out-of-the-box procedure is recommended because it is easier and less time consuming than manually configuring and building Apache.

Building Apache the Manual Way

The second method of building the Apache package is to do it manually. Building Apache manually takes a little longer (than the "easy way") and involves more research on your part. The advantage is that you have more control over the configuration and build process. If you want more control, or if you want to learn about the intricacies of Apache, the manual method is the way to go.

To begin the build process, as with any package build, you should examine any README files. The Apache README file suggests that you read the INSTALL file (in the same directory as the README), so let us begin there.

Build Requirements

A concern for any package is the amount of disk space consumed. For Apache, the disk requirement is approximately 12MB of free disk space, but this requirement is only temporary. After the installation is complete, Apache occupies only about 3MB of disk space. The actual amount depends on the modules that have been compiled in the Apache build.

For the compiler, you should be using an ANSI-compliant C compiler. I recommend that you use the GNU C compiler from the Free Software Foundation (FSF). This compiler comes on most distributions of Linux. If you do not have it on your CD-ROM distribution, you can download it for free at http://www.gnu.org. If you do not want to (or cannot) use GCC, be sure that the compiler you use is ANSI compliant.

Apache can load modules at runtime using the Dynamic Shared Object (DSO) support feature. Apache performs this functionality using the dlopen() and dlsym() system function calls. The dlopen() call loads a dynamic library from the named file to the function. If the open is successful, a handle for the dynamic library is returned to the caller. The dlsym() call accepts a handle for a dynamic library and a symbol name, and it returns the address where the symbol is loaded. Unfortunately, the DSO feature is not a portable mechanism, so DSO may not be available on all platforms. Currently, the platforms supporting DSO are Linux, AIX, BSDI, DYNIX/ptx, Digital UNIX, FreeBSD, HPUX, IRIX, Mac OS, Mac OS X Server, NetBSD, OpenBSD, OpenStep/Mach, SCO, Solaris, SunOS, UNIXWare, and ReliantUNIX. Ultrix is not supported.

It is not required, but I recommend that you have a Perl 5 Interpreter available. If the Perl interpreter is not available, the build and installation will still succeed. Some of the support scripts will not be available, such as the apxs and dbmmanage Perl scripts. Perl 5 is the version you want available; if you are not sure how to switch, use the --with-perl option.

Modifying the Configuration File

The next step is to make a copy of the Configuration.tmpl file. You can find this file in the src directory. Copy this file to the file named Configuration. The following sample demonstrates this:

```
stimpy $ cp Configuration.tmpl Configuration
stimpy $
```

The file Configuration.tmpl is a template and should never be modified directly, and a script file (named Configure) actually uses the Configuration file. Do not edit the file named Makefile either, because it is auto-generated by Configure. You edit the Configuration file to select the modules to be included. Additionally, you can set various compiler flags in the Configuration file.

The `Configuration` file has five types of line entries. Like most other Linux configuration files, the comment character is included as a type. The `#` character is used to denote a comment. The second type of entry designates a `Makefile` option. The third type of entry is the `AddModule` entry, which specifies a module to be included. The fourth type is a `Rule` entry, which directs `Configure` to create the `Makefile` file. The fifth entry type is the `%Module` keyword. This defines a module that is to be compiled in, but disabled.

The `Configuration` file is heavily commented; open it up in your favorite editor and take a look at it. The first section is the `Makefile` configuration. The options are described in Table 16.1.

Table 16.1 **Configuration File—Makefile Section**

Flag	Description
EXTRA_CFLAGS	Added to the standard `Makefile` flags for the compiler.
EXTRA_LDFLAGS	Added to the standard `Makefile` flags for the linker.
EXTRA_LIBS	Added to the standard `Makefile` flags as an additional flag for a library.
EXTRA_INCLUDES	Added to the standard `Makefile` flags for identification of include file(s).
EXTRA_DEPS	Added as additional `Makefile` dependencies to external files, such as third-party libraries.
#CC	Settings for the C Compiler—the settings here have priority. The default is that this line is disabled (commented out). If not set, `Configure` attempts to determine the compiler to use.
#CPP	Settings for the C++ Compiler—the settings here have priority. The default is that this line is disabled (commented out). If not set, Configure attempts to determine the compiler to use.
#OPTIM	Optimization flags—the optimization settings here take priority.
#RANLIB	Path to the ranlib program, which generates an index to the contents of an archive and stores it in the archive. (You probably do not need this.)

Most users will not have to bother with the `Makefile` section. `Configure` will try to determine the operating system and compiler and provide the proper settings based on its findings. If `Configure` or the compiler gets quirky, you will probably have to define `CC`, `CPP`, and `OPTIM`.

The `AddModule` section can get fairly detailed. Table 16.2 describes the modules that are available at the time of this writing.

Table 16.2 **Configuration File—AddModule Section**

Module	Description
mod_access	Host-based access control.
mod_auth	User authentication using text files.
mod_auth_digest	MD5 authentication (experimental).
mod_browser	Apache 1.2.* only. Set environment variables based on `User-Agent` strings. Replaced by `mod_setenvif` in Apache 1.3 and up.
mod_cgi	Invoking CGI scripts.
mod_cookies	Up to Apache 1.1.1. Support for Netscapelike cookies. Replaced in Apache 1.2 by `mod_usertrack`.
mod_digest	MD5 authentication.
mod_dir	Basic directory handling.
mod_dld	Apache 1.2.* and earlier. Start-time linking with the GNU `libdld`. Replaced in Apache 1.3 by `mod_so`.
mod_dll	Apache 1.3b1 to 1.3b5 only. Replaced in 1.3b6 by `mod_so`.
mod_env	Passing of environments to CGI scripts.
mod_example	Apache 1.2 and up. Demonstrates Apache API.
mod_expires	Apache 1.2 and up. Apply "Expires:" headers to resources.
mod_headers	Apache 1.2 and up. Add arbitrary HTTP headers to resources.
mod_imap	Imagemap file handler.
mod_include	Server-parsed documents.
mod_info	Server configuration information.
mod_isapi	Windows ISAPI extension support.
mod_log_agent	Logging of user agents.
mod_log_common	Up to Apache 1.1.1. Standard logging in the common logfile format. Replaced by the `mod_log_config` module in Apache 1.2 and up.

continues ▶

Table 16.2 **Continued**

Module	Description
mod_log_config	User-configurable logging replacement for mod_log_common.
mod_log_referer	Logs document references.
mod_mime	Determines document types using file extensions.
mod_mime_magic	Determines document types using "magic numbers."
mod_mmap_static	Maps files into memory for faster serving.
mod_negotiation	Content negotiation.
mod_proxy	Caching proxy capabilities
mod_rewrite	Apache 1.2 and up. Powerful URI-to-filename mapping using regular expressions.
mod_setenvif	Apache 1.3 and up. Set environment variables based on client information.
mod_so	Apache 1.3 and up. Experimental support for loading modules (DLLs on Windows) at runtime.
mod_spelling	Apache 1.3 and up. Automatically correct minor typos in URLs.
mod_status	Server status display.
mod_userdir	User home directories.
mod_unique_id	Apache 1.3 and up. Generate unique request identifier for every request.
mod_usertrack	Apache 1.2 and up. User tracking using cookies (replacement for mod_cookies.c).
mod_vhost_alias	Apache 1.3.7 and up. Support for dynamically configured mass virtual hosting.
/experimental/mod_mmap_static.o	Can make some Web servers faster. However, because it is an experimental module, I recommend that you do not use it. Documentation is not available so as to detract you from enabling it.
mod_vhost_alias.o	Provides support for mass virtual hosting. This is enabled by dynamically changing the document root and CGI directory.
mod_env.o	Sets up environment variables that are passed to CGI and SSI scripts.
mod_log_config.o	Determines the logging configuration.

Module	Description
`mod_log_agent.o`	Optional module for NCSA user-agent logging compatibility. I recommend that you use `access_log`.
`mod_log_referer.o`	Optional module for NCSA referer logging compatibility. I recommend that you use `access_log`.
`mod_mime_magic.o`	Determines a file's type by examining it and comparing the results against a database of signatures—based on the UNIX `file` command.
`mod_mime.o`	Maps filename extensions to content types, encodings, and "magic" type handlers.
`mod_negotiation.o`	Permits content selection based on `Accept*` headers.
`mod_status.o`	Permits the server to display details about its performance and its status. A performance hit is inevitable.
`mod_info.o`	Displays the server's configuration information including modules—useful for debugging.
`mod_include.o`	Translates server-side include statements in text files.
`mod_autoindex.o`	Handles requests for directories that have no index file.
`mod_dir.o`	Handles requests on directories and directory index files.
`mod_cgi.o`	Handles CGI scripts.
`mod_asis.o`	Implements `.asis` file types, allowing embedded HTTP headers at the beginning of a document.
`mod_imap.o`	Handles internal imagemaps.
`mod_actions.o`	Specifies that CGI scripts act as "handlers" for specific files.
`mod_spelling.o`	Tries to correct URL misspellings that users might have supplied—catches the majority of misspelled requests.
`mod_userdir.o`	Selects resource directories using username and a common prefix.
`mod_alias.o`	Provides URL translation and redirection.

continues ▶

Table 16.2 **Continued**

Module	Description
mod_rewrite.o	Permits URI-to-URI and URI-to-filename mapping using a regular expression-based rule-controlled engine.
mod_auth_anon.o	Allows for anonymous-FTP-style username and password authentication.
mod_auth_dbm.o	Work with Berkeley DB files—make sure there is support for DBM files on your system. You may need to adjust EXTRA_LIBS. Should not be used with the mod_auth_db.o module.
mod_auth_db.o	Work with Berkeley DB files—make sure there is support for DBM files on your system. You may need to adjust EXTRA_LIBS. Should not be used with the mod_auth_dbm.o module.
mod_digest.o	Implements HTTP Digest Authentication instead of Basic Auth (less secure).
/experimental/mod_auth_digest.o	Implements HTTP/1.1 Digest Authentication versus Basic Auth (less secure). Although this is a mod_digest update, it is still experimental.
/proxy/libproxy.a	Allows the server to act as a proxy server for HTTP and FTP.
mod_cern_meta.o	Utilizes metainformation files compatible with the CERN Web server.
mod_expires.o	Applies Expires headers to resources.
mod_headers.o	Sets arbitrary HTTP response headers.
mod_usertrack.o	Utilizes Netscape cookies to construct and log click-trails from Netscape cookies. For user tracking only.
modules/example/mod_example.o	Demonstrates the use of the API. Should be used only for testing—*never* use this on a production server.
mod_unique_id.o	Generates unique identifiers for each hit. May not work on all systems.
mod_so.o	Allows adding modules to Apache without recompiling. Currently experimental—supported only on a subset of the platforms.
mod_setenvif.o	Allows you to set environment variables based on HTTP header fields in the request.

Although the modules classified as "experimental" are included in the previous table, I highly recommend that you not include those modules in a production Web server.

Next, let's take a look at rules. The syntax for a rule in the `Configuration` file is shown in the following sample:

```
Rule RULE=value
```

`value` can be either `yes` or `default`. If the value is `yes`, `Configure` performs the rule. If the value is `default`, `Configure` takes a best guess. Table 16.3 describes the current rules.

Table 16.3 **Configuration File—Rules Section**

Rule	Description
SOCKS4	If yes, add the socks library location to `EXTRA_LIBS`, otherwise `-L/usr/local/lib \lsocks` is assumed.
SOCKS5	If yes, add the socks5 library location to `EXTRA_LIBS`, otherwise `-L/usr/local/lib \lsocks5` is assumed.
IRIXNIS	Effective only if you are running SGI IRIX.
IRIXN32	If running a version of IRIX using n32 libraries, `Configure` will use those instead of the o32 libraries.
PARANOID	Introduced in version 1.3. Allows modules to control how `Configure` works. If `PARANOID` is yes, `Configure` will print the code that the modules execute.
EXPAT	Incorporates James Clark's Expat package into Apache. The default is to include it if the `lib/expat-lite/` directory exists.
DEV_RANDOM	Used only when compiling `mod_auth_digest`.
WANTHSREGEX	Apache requires a POSIX regex implementation. Henry Spencer's excellent regex package is included with Apache and can be used.

Be sure to check the documentation included with the Apache package for changes to the Rules section. Be sure to examine the `Configuration` file and set any rules to the appropriate values for your Apache implementation.

Building Apache

After you have the `Configuration` file with the proper settings for your Apache implementation, the next step is to build Apache. Before you execute

Chapter 16 Apache Web Server

the build, however, you need to be sure the configuration is set properly. You do this with the `Configure` command. The following dialog demonstrates this:

```
stimpy $ cd src
stimpy $ ./Configure
Using config file: Configuration
Creating Makefile
 + configured for Linux platform
 + setting C compiler to gcc
 + setting C pre-processor to gcc -E
 + checking for system header files
 + adding selected modules
 + checking size of various data types
 + doing sanity check on compiler and options
Creating Makefile in support
Creating Makefile in regex
Creating Makefile in os/unix
Creating Makefile in ap
Creating Makefile in main
Creating Makefile in lib/expat-lite
Creating Makefile in modules/standard
stimpy $
```

Your output should resemble the previous sample. The `Configure` command is used to create the various `Makefiles` required to build Apache. Finally, you need to build Apache. The following dialog shows how to start the build process:

```
stimpy $ make
===> regex
make[1]: Nothing to be done for `all'.
<=== regex
===> os/unix
gcc -c -I ...
...
<=== modules/standard
<=== modules
gcc -c -I./os/unix -I./include    -DLINUX=2 -DUSE_HSREGEX -DUSE_EXPAT -I./lib/expat-lite
↪modules.c
gcc -c -I./os/unix -I./include    -DLINUX=2 -DUSE_HSREGEX -DUSE_EXPAT -I./lib/expat-lite
↪buildmark.c
gcc    -DLINUX=2 -DUSE_HSREGEX -DUSE_EXPAT -I./lib/expat-lite       \
       -o httpd buildmark.o modules.o libstandard.a main/libmain.a ./os/unix/libos.a
ap/libap.a regex/libregex.a lib/expat-lite/libexpat.a  -lm -lcrypt
stimpy $
```

Various commands are executed from the Makefile. The command that is being executed and the results are displayed to the standard output. After the make has finished, you should have an executable within the src directory named httpd, as shown in the following sample dialog:

```
stimpy $ ls -al
-rwxr-xr-x   1 root      root         673 Jan 30 10:44 apaci
-rw-r--r--   1 161       20          3126 Jan  1  1999 buildmark.c
...
-rw-r--r--   1 root      root         952 Jan 31 00:21 buildmark.o
drwxr-xr-x   2 161       20          1024 Jan 31 00:14 helpers
-rwxr-xr-x   1 root      root      631900 Jan 31 00:22 httpd
drwxr-xr-x   2 161       20          1024 Jan 30 10:44 include
drwxr-xr-x   3 161       20          1024 Jan 30 10:45 lib
drwxr-xr-x   2 161       20          1024 Jan 31 00:21 main
stimpy $
```

As you can see, the build was successful and the Web server is ready to go. It is always an exciting moment to execute an application you have just built, especially an application as important as a Web server! Be forewarned, however, that you could receive an error upon invocation of httpd. The following dialog shows what happened when I executed the httpd server.

```
stimpy $ ./httpd
fopen: No such file or directory
httpd: could not open document config file /usr/local/apache/conf/httpd.conf
stimpy $
```

Obviously, the configuration file httpd.conf is not found in the identified path. The sections that follow continue the Apache configuration process.

Apache Runtime Configuration

As mentioned in the previous section, you will have a binary executable file named httpd, which should be found in the src directory. Optionally, if you downloaded the binary distribution, the Linux httpd binary will already exist. A third option is that Apache is already installed from your Linux distribution. In this section, I assume that you have just built the Apache executable and that you are ready to install and configure it for runtime use.

You can, if you wish, run Apache from the same directory tree in which you built it. The configuration is designed to function in this manner. If you want to run Apache from another tree, you need to create a root directory and move the conf, logs, and icons directories there.

Runtime Configuration Files

Apache utilizes the directives from the three configuration files to initialize and execute. The three configuration files are named `access.conf`, `httpd.conf`, and `srm.conf`; they are found in the `conf` directory. Three template files match each one of these runtime configuration files: `access.conf-dist`, `httpd.conf-dist`, and `srm.conf-dist` found in the `conf` directory. I recommend that you execute the `cp` command, creating the runtime versions of each configuration file. Do not execute the `mv` command to rename the template files because you will have no default files to return to in the future. The following sample dialog demonstrates this:

```
stimpy $ cp access.conf-dist access.conf
stimpy $ cp httpd.conf-dist httpd.conf
stimpy $ cp srm.conf-dist srm.conf
```

Directives can appear in any of these three files. The names used for the files are relative to the server's root, which is set using the `ServerRoot` directive. Optionally, you can set the `ServerRoot` directive using the `-d_serverroot` command-line flag to the `httpd` executable. The Apache configuration files are described in Table 16.4.

Table 16.4 **Configuration Files for Apache**

Option	Description
`conf/httpd.conf`	Contains directives controlling the server daemon's operation. The filename may be overridden with the `-f` command-line flag.
`conf/srm.conf`	Contains the directives controlling the document specifications the server provides to clients. The filename may be overridden with the `ResourceConfig` directive.
`conf/access.conf`	Contains the directives to control access to documents. The filename may be overridden with the `AccessConfig` directive.

In addition to the three configuration files shown in Table 16.4, the server daemon also reads a file containing mime document types. The name of this file is identified by the `TypesConfig` directive. The default name is `conf/mime.types`. This file usually does not need editing.

Next, you must edit each of the configuration files. These files are heavily commented—be sure to leave the comments intact because you may need them in the future. You should pay attention to these comments. If you do not provide the proper settings, the server may not work correctly or may run insecurely.

First edit `conf/httpd.conf`. This configuration identifies general attributes about the server, such as the port number, the user it runs as, and so on.

Next, you should edit the `conf/srm.conf` file. This file is used to set up the root of the document tree. Some examples are server-parsed HTML and internal imagemap parsing.

Finally, edit the `conf/access.conf` file to at least set the base cases of access. You place directives in this file to control access to documents.

The server can be configured at the directory level using the `.htaccess` files. You can place an `.htaccess` file in each directory accessed by the server. Using these files allows some flexibility because it enables you to change behavior while the server is running because these files are read at access time, rather than at startup. The downside, as you may have guessed, is a performance hit that is considerable.

Starting and Stopping the Server

The server executable is named `httpd`. To run this command, you simply invoke it at the command line as you would any other binary. The `httpd` daemon will look for the `http.conf` configuration file on startup. The default location as compiled is `/usr/local/apache/conf/httpd.conf`, but you can change it in one of two ways. The simplest is to execute the `httpd` daemon with the `-f` switch. The following dialog demonstrates this:

```
/usr/local/apache/httpd -f /usr/local/apache/conf/httpd.conf
```

The `config.layout` file can be used to identify various directory paths. A complete list of command-line switches is provided in Table 16.5 in the section that follows.

The `httpd` daemon, as with all Linux daemons, is designed to run as a background process. After you have launched the daemon, the command-line prompt should return. Otherwise, if the daemon experiences any problems with initialization, error messages will be displayed to the standard output.

Most people do not think about it, but you can execute your browser and connect to your local Web server. I occasionally hear the question, "When I start up Netscape and I am not connected to the Internet, I get `Cannot connect` messages from the Netscape browser. How can I eliminate the error windows?" This is quite easy. If you want to start your browser and do not open a local file, supply the URL `http://localhost` to the browser. You might even want to use this URL as your home page setting in Netscape's Preferences/Netscape dialog window. Furthermore, you can associate your Internet home page with the My icon on the Navigation toolbar. That way, you are only one click away from your home page. If you disconnect from your ISP and want to leave Netscape running, you simply click the Home icon to get back to the `localhost` Web server. This eliminates those annoying error windows that Netscape displays every couple of minutes.

As a part of the Web server learning experience, you should record the running processes. Next, execute the server, and then examine the running processes and compare the results with the previous list. In a pinch, you can direct the output from the `ps` command to a file. In any event, you will notice that the server invokes a number of child processes for request handling. The server will run as the root user and the child processes will run as the user identified by the `User` directive in the `http.conf` configuration file.

You should ensure that only the Apache server is using the port that you specified it to use. You should also ensure that the `httpd` daemon is running as the root user if you want to access a port below 1024. The default HTTP port, of course, is port 80. If either of these two is not true, you will probably get an error message that Apache cannot bind to some address.

To decrease security risks, you should set up a new `group` and `user` in `http.conf` to run the server. Most administrators specify the `nobody` user.

Additionally, you can check the `logs` directory for any error log files and review their contents for more details. The file to check is named `error_log`.

Most administrators will want the `httpd` daemon to execute at system startup (boot). This is quite easy—most distributions will default to this configuration if you choose to install Apache during the Linux installation. If you are adding Apache after installing Linux, it is a simple matter of adding an entry for `httpd` to the Linux startup files (such as `rc.local`).

At the other end of the spectrum, you need a way to stop the Apache server. Like other Linux processes, you issue a signal to kill the process. With the Apache daemon, you issue a TERM signal using the `kill` command. You must issue the signal to the parent process, not to a child process. If you kill the child process, the parent merely invokes it again. As previously mentioned, the `httpd.pid` file contains the process ID for the Apache server process. You can `cat` the contents of the file to reveal the PID and then issue the `kill` command. Alternatively, you can use the `cat` command with the `kill` command to reduce the two commands to one. Better yet, you can create a shell script containing the commands required to kill the server. The following dialog demonstrates two options:

```
stimpy $ cat /usr/local/apache/logs/httpd.pid
123
stimpy $ kill -TERM 123
stimpy $
stimpy $ kill -TERM `cat /usr/local/apache/logs/httpd.pid`
stimpy $
```

To simplify matters, you can place the last example in a shell script called `killapache` and just issue the script in the future. Optionally, you can use the `apachectl` runtime control script. This file can be used for manual Apache administration. You can also use `apachectl` to govern the `rc.d` scripts, which control the Apache `httpd` daemon.

Invoking Apache

In this section, the command-line options for the `httpd` daemon are detailed. With Linux and other flavors of Unix, the Apache server is run as a daemon process. This allows the server to run in the background, servicing requests as they arrive.

Alternatively, you can have the `inetd` (Internet) daemon invoke the `httpd` process whenever a request for HTTP service arrives. The `inetd` daemon is executed at boot and listens for connect requests on identified Internet sockets. When a connection is discovered, `inetd` determines which service the socket is associated with and invokes that service. To do this, you need to set the value for the `ServerType` directive.

Table 16.5 details the command-line options for the `http` daemon.

Table 16.5 **Command-Line Options for `httpd`**

Option	Description
-C *directive*	Process the Apache *directive* as if it existed in the configuration file, before reading the configuration files.
-c *directive*	Process the Apache *directive* after parsing the configuration files.
-d serverroot	Set the value for the `ServerRoot` variable to serverroot. It can be overridden in the configuration file with the `ServerRoot` directive. The default is `/usr/local/apache`.
-D name	Define a *name* for use in `IfDefine` directives.
-f config	Execute the commands in the file identified by `config` at startup. If `config` is not prefixed with `/`, it is a relative path to `ServerRoot`. The default is `conf/httpd.conf`.
-L	Print a list of directives combined with expected arguments.
-l	Give a list of all modules compiled into the server, and then exit.
-h	Print a list of the `httpd` options, and then exit.
-S	Show the settings as parsed from the `config` file, and then exit.

continues ▶

Table 16.5 **Continued**

Option	Description
-t	Test the configuration file syntax, but do not start the server. All the configuration files are parsed and interpreted for proper syntax. Also checks the `DocumentRoot` entries.
-T	Test the configuration file syntax, but do not start the server. All the configuration files are parsed and interpreted for proper syntax. Does not check the `DocumentRoot` entries.
-v	Print the `httpd` version and exit.
-V	Print the base version of `httpd` and a list of compile-time settings, and then exit.
-X	Run as single-process mode. Use for debugging purposes—the daemon does not detach from the terminal or fork any child processes.
-?	Print a list of the `httpd` options and exit.

Check the documentation for Apache for more information regarding these command-line options.

Stopping and Restarting the Apache Server

As mentioned previously, you can issue the TERM signal to the `httpd` process to terminate it and its child processes. Two other signals can be sent to the server. In addition to TERM, you can issue the HUP and USR1 signals using the `kill` command. The following dialog shows the invocation of these signals:

```
stimpy $ kill -HUP `cat /usr/local/apache/logs/httpd.pid`
stimpy $ kill -TERM `cat /usr/local/apache/logs/httpd.pid`
stimpy $ kill -USR1 `cat /usr/local/apache/logs/httpd.pid`
stimpy $
```

The HUP signal is used as a `restart` command to the server. Use of the HUP signal in this fashion is not specific to Apache—this is typical among other Linux (and UNIX) processes. The parent process will terminate its children, reread the configuration files, and then execute the child process again.

The TERM signal is used to shut down the server (parent process) and all its child processes. Be sure to give the server time to shut down because it must wait for the children to terminate. After the child processes have terminated, the parent itself terminates.

Finally, the USR1 signal is sent to the server to provide a graceful restart. This signal is similar to the HUP signal. The difference is that the server "informs" the child processes to shut down after requests have been satisfied. After all the child processes have terminated, the server rereads the configuration files and then executes the child processes again.

Apache Log Files

The Apache server utilizes a number of files for logging purposes. The names of these files can be changed through Apache directives.

Apache `httpd.pid` File

When Apache is initializing, it writes its process ID to the `logs/httpd.pid` file. This process ID is the PID for the parent process. The PID is stored so that an administrator can obtain the PID if the server needs to be terminated or restarted.

The filename for PID persistence can be altered with the `PidFile` directive—you might want to consider this for security reasons.

Apache Error Log File

The Apache server logs any error messages to a file named `error_log` in the `logs` directory. The filename can be altered using the `ErrorLog` directive.

Transfer Log

The Apache server logs every request to a transfer file named `access_log` in the `logs` directory. The filename can be altered using the `TransferLog` Apache directive.

Additionally, other log files can be created with the `CustomLog` Apache directive. This enables you to maintain separate transfer logs for different virtual hosts.

Special-Purpose Environment Variables

Typically, environment variables are used by Linux (and UNIX) applications to control their behavior. For example, an application can obtain the current username by examining the environment variable named USER. Table 16.6 describes the environment variables available to Apache.

Table 16.6 **Environment Variables Used with Apache**

Environment Variable	Description
downgrade-1.0	Treats the request as a HTTP/1.0 request.
force-no-vary	Causes any *vary* fields to be removed from the response header before being sent to the client.
force-response-1.0	Forces an HTTP/1.0 response.
nokeepalive	Disables the KeepAlive directive. This addresses a bug found in some versions of Netscape.

Apache's Handler Use

Whenever a file is called, the Apache server maintains internal handlers to perform some action based on the request. The file type (MIME type) is associated with a handler. Most files are handled implicitly, and yet other file types are handled specifically.

Apache can handle files explicitly using filename extensions or location. The advantage is that the handler and type are related with a file.

The Action directive can be used to add a handler. Optionally, you build the handler to the server or within a module. Table 16.7 describes the handlers for Apache.

Table 16.7 **Apache Handlers**

Handler	Description
default-handler	Send the file using the default_handler(), the default handler for static content.
send-as-is	Send the file with HTTP headers.
cgi-script	The file should be treated as a CGI script.
imap-file	Imagemap rule file.
server-info	Obtain information about the server's configuration.
server-parsed	Parse for server-side includes.
server-status	Obtain a report about the server's status.
type-map	Parse for content negotiation.

The following sections detail the corresponding Apache directives for handlers.

AddHandler

The `AddHandler` directive is used to map a filename's extension to a handler name. The directive overrides any mapping that may exist. The following is the syntax for the `AddHandler` directive:

```
AddHandler handler-name extension extension...
```

For example, to treat files with the extension of .cgi as CGI executable scripts, you use the following:

```
AddHandler cgi-script cgi
```

SetHandler

The syntax for the `SetHandler` directive is

```
SetHandler handler-name
```

Effectively, this directive is the same as the `AddHandler` directive, except that the specified `handler-name` is applied to all files within a *directory*, *files*, or *location* section. Optionally, the files can be in the .htaccess directory. For example, if you want a directory to be treated as imagemap rule files, the following entry would be placed in the .htaccess file in the identified directory:

```
SetHandler imap-file
```

All files are treated as imagemap rule files, regardless of their extension.

Summary

In this chapter, we explored the use of the Apache Web server. The chapter began with an overview of Apache, discovering that it is the number-one Web server being used on the Internet.

You can obtain Apache as one of two packages. You can get the binary package, which provides all the binaries required to execute directly. Optionally, you can get the Apache package as a set of source files, allowing you to build the package yourself. Both methods were detailed.

Next, Apache runtime configuration was discussed, covering the various configuration files. The configuration files exist in the conf directory and are named access.conf, httpd.conf, and srm.conf. Sample template files are provided and are named access.conf-dist, httpd.conf-dist, and srm.conf-dist. I recommended that you copy these files and use them as a basis for configuration.

The starting and stopping of the Apache server were covered. The Apache server executable is named httpd and can be invoked with a number of command-line options. These command-line options were detailed.

The use of the HUP, TERM, and USR1 signals was discussed next. These signals are used to communicate to the httpd daemon while it is running. The HUP signal is used as a restart command to the server. The TERM signal is used to shut down the server (parent process) and all its child processes. The USR1 signal is sent to the server to provide a graceful restart.

The Apache log files were covered next, which consist of the httpd.pid, error_log, and access_log files. The httpd.pid file contains the process ID of the currently running daemon. The error_log file is used for logging error messages and the access_log is used to log requests.

Finally, the environment variables and Apache handlers were covered. The environment variables are used to control the behavior of Apache. The AddHandler and SetHandler directives are detailed, in addition to the Apache handlers such as default_handler and server-info.

17

Internet News Service

THE NETWORK NEWS TRANSFER PROTOCOL (NNTP) is designed to transport news articles between collaborating news hosts. NNTP uses TCP and defines an application protocol that is the transport vehicle for Usenet traffic.

This chapter discusses various aspects of Usenet—specifically, the NNTP client and NNTP server.

Overview

Usenet, in a nutshell, is a forum for online discussions. It is a combination of a chat system and an email system. You can connect to a news server, join one or more discussion groups, read new articles, send new articles, and respond to articles.

It is similar to chat in that there are threads of discussion. It is similar to email in that you read articles, send articles, and reply to articles using a program similar to a mail client. With chat, the discussion is in real time, whereas a news discussion is in near-real-time. Although your article might arrive at the news server within seconds, other participants will not see your articles immediately.

Mailing lists predated Usenet as a form of cooperative discussions on the ARPANET. You might be familiar with mailing lists—they still exist today. Usenet is far more popular than mailing lists, at least as indicated by the sheer volume of postings. When considering article volume, Usenet volume is probably equivalent to Internet email volume.

Usenet is a logical network, not a physical one. There is no central governing body that manages Usenet. Usenet is supported by millions of machines on millions of networks across the globe, supporting the hundreds of millions of participant users.

In the simplest explanation, a news server executes on an organization's host, maintaining news articles stored on disk. This news server collaborates with another news server on the Internet, which collaborates with another news server on the Internet, and so on. All of these news servers continually feed each other, radiating articles across the globe.

There is no special requirement to become a part of Usenet. All you need is the hardware, Linux, and the Usenet software required to exchange Usenet news. You have to collaborate with another Usenet site for the exchange of articles. This is as simple as striking an agreement with the site authority to exchange news traffic.

The software that is used for the exchange of Usenet articles is built using the application protocol defined by NNTP. Almost all distributions of Linux include the NNTP software required to both read and distribute Usenet articles. Usenet software has two parts: the client and the server (surprised?). The client software is the user portion that is used to read and post articles to a Usenet newsgroup. The server software is responsible for transferring Usenet news (articles) between news servers.

Historically, Usenet traffic was propagated using UUCP as the transport protocol. As the popularity of Usenet increased, the amount of traffic increased, which exposed the inefficiency of UUCP as the transport protocol. NNTP utilizes TCP/IP and is defined in RFC 977.

Usenet started its life in 1979. Tom Truscott and Jim Ellis, graduate students at Duke University, wanted to craft a way to exchange messages between UNIX computers. It was decided that UUCP would be the transport mechanism. They created a network consisting of three machines. Initially, the traffic was handled by "software," which consisted of a number of shell scripts. This software was eventually rewritten in the C language and made publicly available. This package became what is known as *A News*.

As with most software, A News was written with the intent of handling only a few articles a day. A News became increasingly popular and immediately grew beyond its capabilities.

A couple of programmers at the University of California at Berkeley, Mark Horton and Matt Glickman, rewrote A News. As you might expect, this new version became *B News* and was released in 1982.

In 1987, a new version of B News was written by Geoff Collyer and Henry Spencer. This new release would become (you guessed it) *C News*.

Over the years, C News has had a number of patches—the most current incarnation being the C-News Performance Release.

The Network News Transfer Protocol (NNTP) was introduced in 1986 and is based on network connections. It includes specifications for commands to interactively transfer and retrieve articles.

Many Usenet software packages are based on NNTP. One popular package, from Brian Barber and Phil Lapsley, is nntpd. Another very popular package, Internet News (INN), was developed by Rich Salz. The nntpd package was designed to deliver NNTP capabilities to B News and C News. INN is not just a supplement, but a complete news package. The INN relay daemon can maintain multiple concurrent NNTP links, making this package the popular choice for Usenet hosting.

Basic Usenet Mechanics

In a sense, the components that make up Usenet follow a hierarchical structure. At the lowest level, but probably by far the most important, is the *article*. Without articles, there would be no Usenet. An article is similar in concept to an email document. A number of fields are defined. Each field can (or must) contain data. An article is what is *posted* to one or more newsgroups.

The basic unit of Usenet news is the article. This is a message a user writes and posts to the Internet. In order to enable news systems to deal with it, it is prepended with administrative information called the *article header*. It is very similar to the mail header format laid down in the Internet mail standard RFC 822 in that it consists of several lines of text, each beginning with a field name terminated by a colon, followed by the field's value.

Going up the hierarchical chain, we come to the *newsgroup*. A newsgroup is a forum for online communication with a specified focus or subject matter (topic). A newsgroup has a name associated with it, which (hopefully) identifies the subject matter. The name is a group of individual words, each delineated by a period (.). Each word identifies the newsgroup's hierarchical structure. Let's look at an example to see how the newsgroup name breaks down. A typical example is `comp.os.linux.setup`. The name is broken down from left to right, in contrast to an HTTP URL name. The first name, `comp`, identifies the high-level category *computer*. Next is `os`, which designates the subcategory *operating system*. The third component in the name is `linux`, which identifies the operating system named Linux. The last subname is `setup`, which identifies the exact topic of discussion—setting up Linux.

Here are the top-level categories in Usenet:

- `alt.` Alternative topics. Some `alt.*` groups exist because they are controversial, and others exist because it is easy to create a newsgroup in `alt`.
- `comp.` Computer-related topics.
- `humanities.` Topics relating to humanity, such as philosophy, art, literature, and so on.
- `misc.` A variety of topics that do not fit into one of the other categories.
- `news.` Topics relating to Usenet itself.
- `rec.` Topics relating to hobbies and recreation.
- `sci.` Topics relating to scientific subject matter.
- `soc.` Topics relating to social issues.
- `talk.` Topics designed for ongoing conversations.

This list is not exhaustive by any means. You will realize this if you connect to a news server and download the available newsgroups. You can also go to http://www.deja.com to see a list of available newsgroups.

At the third level is the *news server,* which is responsible for the reception and transmission of articles between servers.

As mentioned earlier, Usenet site owners agree to exchange news; they can exchange whichever newsgroups they want. A site may have a number of local newsgroups that can also be distributed. Each site is free to carry whatever newsgroups it wants.

The act of transferring news from one machine to another is known as *flooding*. Whenever an article is posted to the local news server, it is forwarded to the other Usenet sites on the local host's newsfeed list. An article continues to flow from one Usenet host to the next. A special field in a Usenet article called the `Path:` is used to show the list of hosts that the article has passed through. A news host can examine this field to see if the article has been seen by a host on its newsfeed list. When the article moves through a news host, the host appends its identification to the `Path:` field.

Every Usenet article must have a message identifier. This identifier is used to distinguish the article from others, providing a mechanism for duplicate recognition by the servers and client software. A news server logs the article in a history file for future reference.

The `Distribution` field for an article can be used to restrict an article's transmission. You can specify that an article remain within the local domain.

A news server checks this field. If it discovers the restriction to remain within the domain, the article is not transmitted.

Two schemes are used to move Usenet traffic: batching and ihave/sendme articles. Both have their strengths and weaknesses.

With the *batching* of articles, which is typical among UUCP Usenet systems, articles are collected over time and placed in a single file for transmission. When the time comes to transmit, the file is compressed and sent to its destination. The receiving host is responsible for verifying the articles—that is, it checks for duplicates and so on. Transmission is quicker, but the receiving station has the overhead of processing many articles.

The other method is the *ihave/sendme* protocol. The originator (or source) host gathers a list of available articles and transmits the list to the destination, which is the *ihave* of the protocol. The destination host accepts the list and processes it. The destination host then transmits a *sendme* message, identifying the message IDs to the originator. The downside of this protocol is the amount of overhead for the conversation between the originator and the destination hosts.

The NNTP protocol offers up to three ways to get articles from one machine to another: the active, passive, and interactive modes.

Active mode, commonly referred to as *pushing* the news, is similar to the ihave/sendme protocol. In push (active) mode, the sender relays an article, and the receiver either accepts or rejects the article. The downside of this is that the receiver must check each article presented to it.

Using *passive* mode, which is sometimes called *pulling* the news, the destination host requests from the source host articles from identified newsgroups after a specified date. Once the receiver has all the articles, it checks them against its history file, checking for and discarding duplicate articles.

Interactive mode allows a newsreader (client application) to specify the articles that exist on identified newsgroups.

Using a Usenet Newsreader

Usenet newsreaders come in all shapes and sizes. A good newsreader allows the user to read, post, reply to, save, and print articles. The more sophisticated newsreaders go far beyond these basic activities. Here are some of the newsreaders that are included with most distributions of Linux:

- **pine.** A screen-oriented message-handling tool that works with Internet News and email.
- **tin, rtin.** A full-screen Usenet newsreader. It can read news locally (from /var/spool/news) or remotely (rtin).

- **krn.** KDE graphical newsreader.
- **Netscape.** Provides an integrated newsreader and email client.

At a minimum, you want a newsreader that can connect to the remote news server, subscribe to one or more newsgroups, and then manipulate articles (read, post, and so on) in a selected newsgroup.

The next two sections look at two popular newsreaders: krn and Netscape.

Using krn, the KDE Newsreader

This section looks at krn, the graphical newsreader packaged in the K Desktop Environment. KDE is shipped with most distributions of Linux.

If you have KDE installed, you can find krn by selecting the Internet, News client menu item. Figure 17.1 shows krn after it is executed from the K menu.

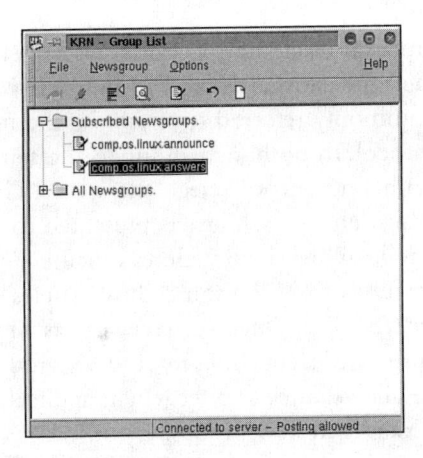

Figure 17.1 KDE's krn newsreader application.

When you execute krn, you will see the groups window, as shown in Figure 17.1. The krn application has a second window, the articles window, which is displayed when you choose a newsgroup from the groups window. We will see an example of the articles window later in this chapter.

You can see that there is a tree view in the main window of the application and that the Subscribed Newsgroups branch is currently expanded. The krn application sports menus and an icon toolbar, providing two ways to execute commands. The File, Connect to Server menu option has been selected. The toolbar reflects this fact because the red plug icon can be selected.

Figure 17.2 shows the krn Group List window with the All Newsgroups tree expanded. The newsgroup `comp.os.linux.networking` is subscribed to—the check mark reflects the subscription status.

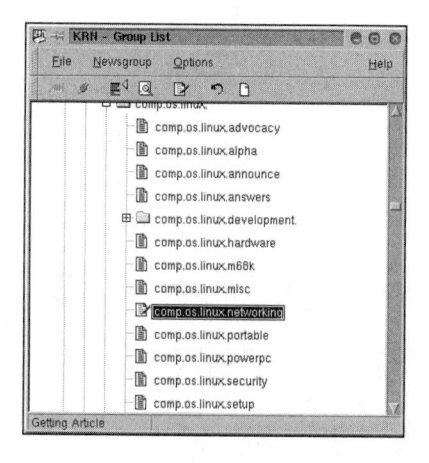

Figure 17.2 The krn newsreader with newsgroup subscribed.

At this point, you could continue subscribing to newsgroups by selecting them in the Group List window. When you have finished, you can collapse the All Newsgroups branch. If you open the Subscribed Newsgroups branch, you should see the newsgroups that you have subscribed to.

To work with articles within a newsgroup, you can double-click the name of the newsgroup in the Subscribed Newsgroups tree. Optionally, you can right-click the newsgroup and select the Open option from the pop-up menu. The articles window will open, and the krn Confirmation dialog box will appear, asking how many articles you want to download. You can request that the download begin from either the oldest or newest articles. Figure 17.3 shows the articles window and the confirmation dialog box.

Specify the number of articles to download, and click the OK button to continue. The krn articles window will capture the articles and display them in the window. Figure 17.4 shows the articles after they have been downloaded.

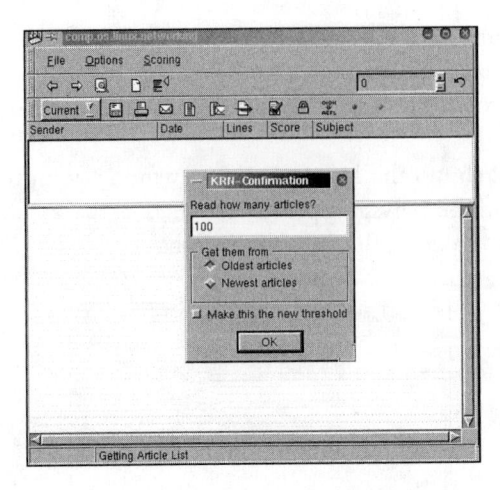

Figure 17.3 krn's articles window and confirmation dialog box.

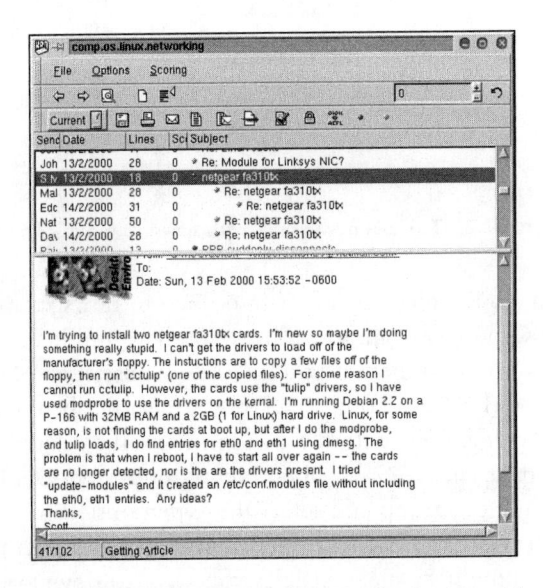

Figure 17.4 krn's articles window populated with articles.

Notice that there are replies to the original article and a reply to the reply. This is shown as an indented hierarchy. To read an article, click the article in the top pane. The article's body will be displayed in the lower pane. To reply to an article, select the File, Post Followup menu option. Figure 17.5 shows the article composition window, ready to accept a reply. When you are ready to send the reply, click the send icon on the toolbar.

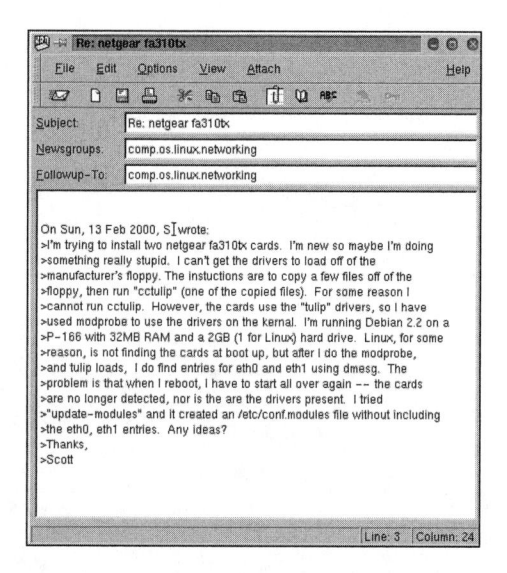

Figure 17.5 krn's article composition window.

You can also post and mail a response to an article. This means that you will draft a response and then post a copy to the newsgroup, and a copy will be emailed to the article's author. You also have the option of *forwarding* an article using email. Other options include printing and saving (to disk) the selected article.

Using krn is as easy as using an email client, and you can be "heard" by millions of people!

Using Netscape's Newsreader

Just about every distribution of Linux comes with Netscape's Communicator product. Within the Communicator suite is an application called Messenger, an email client that doubles as a newsreader. Messenger is quite easy to use. If you happen to be using it for your email client, you will be quite comfortable using it as your newsreader.

You can start Messenger using a desktop icon or at a command prompt. The following dialog shows two ways you can execute Messenger at the

command line to bring up the newsreader. The first invocation brings up
Netscape's Messenger, and the second brings up Netscape's Message Center.

```
stimpy $ netscape -mail &
stimpy $ netscape -news &
stimpy $
```

Optionally, if the Netscape browser (Navigator) is currently executing, you can open Messenger by selecting the Communicator, Messenger menu option. Figure 17.6 shows the Messenger window.

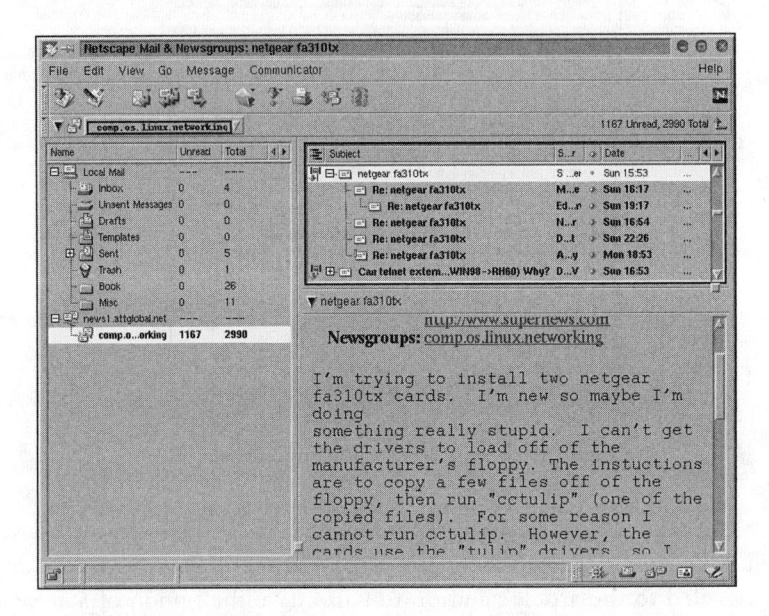

Figure 17.6 Netscape's Messenger (email and newsreader) window.

If you are using Messenger as your email client, Figure 17.6 will look familiar to you. The left pane is the tree view, offering various folders for email, news servers, and their associated newsgroups. Although it's partially obscured, the newsgroup selected in the figure is `comp.os.linux.networking`. As a matter of fact, the selected message thread is the same as in Figure 17.4.

The upper-right pane is the article thread pane. You scroll through the list of articles, selecting articles of interest. In the figure, notice that the selected article contains replies, shown as a hierarchical tree view. You can expand the article's tree by clicking the + icon. Conversely, you can collapse the article tree by clicking the - icon.

The lower-right pane is the article view pane. This is where the body of the article is displayed. You can scroll this area to view the article if necessary.

Basic Usenet Mechanics 479

To subscribe to a newsgroup, right-click the news server listed in the folder tree view and choose the Subscribe to Newsgroups option from the pop-up menu. The newsgroup selection window appears, as shown in Figure 17.7.

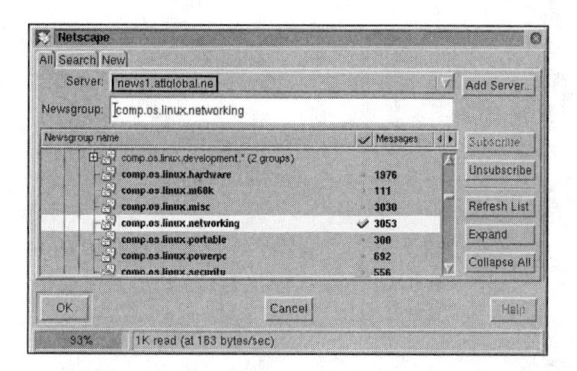

Figure 17.7 Messenger's newsgroup subscription window.

As you can see, `comp.os.linux.networking` is currently selected. A check mark signifies that you have subscribed to the newsgroup. You can select more than one newsgroup in the selection window. When you have selected all the newsgroups you want to join, click the OK button and the selection window will close.

You can now return to the Messenger window. The newsgroups you selected are listed in the folder tree view. Click a newsgroup that you want to participate in. The Download headers window appears, prompting you for the number of articles to download, as shown in Figure 17.8.

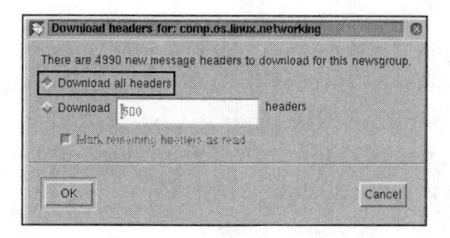

Figure 17.8 Messenger's Download headers window.

You can choose to download all headers or indicate the quantity you want to download. Click the OK button to continue. When all the articles have been downloaded, the article thread pane is populated with the new articles. Figure 17.9 shows the Messenger window, waiting for action.

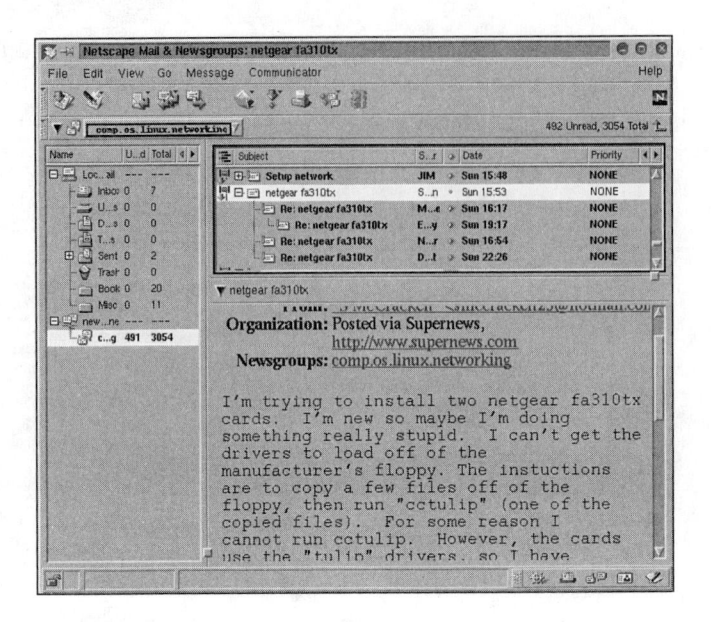

Figure 17.9 Messenger with articles selected for viewing.

At this point, you can select other newsgroups (if you chose more than one), read all unread articles, post new articles, or reply to articles.

To post a new article, select the File, New, New Message menu option. Alternatively, you can click the New message to this newsgroup toolbar icon (a pen on paper). You can also respond to an article. Select the desired article and select the Message, Reply, To Newsgroup menu option. Alternatively, you can select the Reply to the message toolbar icon. The article composition window will be displayed, as shown in Figure 17.10.

The name of the newsgroup is shown in the Newsgroup field, which is similar to the To (or cc:) field when you're composing an email. The Subject field is filled in, and the text of the original article appears. You can choose to write your reply before the original text or after it. Some people inject replies directly into the original text. You might do this if you want to address each point individually.

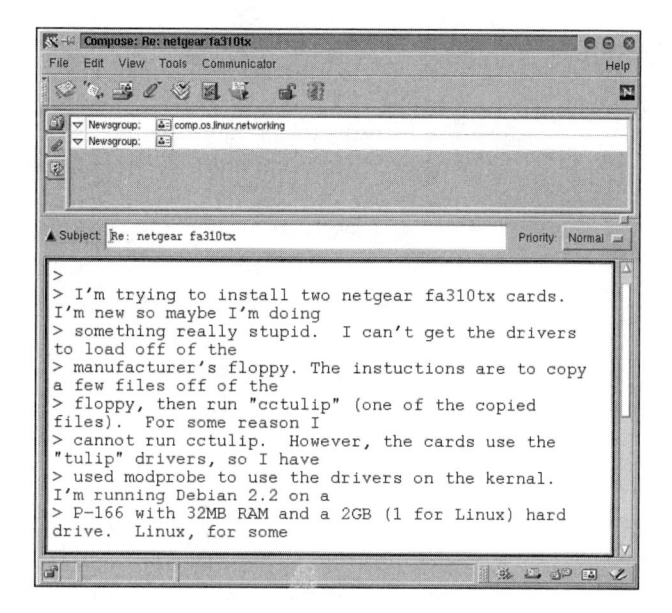

Figure 17.10 Messenger's article composition window.

Common Usenet Terms

Usenet is a world unto itself. You must learn to live within that world if you want to (truly) participate within the newsgroup communities. Methods of communication vary, which is typical when you're conversing with a group of people. An interesting point about Usenet is that anyone in the world can participate. Keep this in mind when you're actively participating. The person you respond to might not be from your culture or even speak your native tongue.

Table 17.1 lists the common Usenet expressions you might require in your terminology arsenal.

Table 17.1 **Common Usenet Terms**

Term	Description
Aahz's Law	The best way to get information on Usenet is not to ask a question, but to post the wrong information.
Boigy's Law	The theory that certain topics in every newsgroup are discussed repeatedly (cyclically), such as every month. Often, the period of the cycle, and the length of the resulting discussion, can be accurately estimated by those who have been around long enough.
Flame or flame war	1. To post an article with the intent to insult and provoke. 2. To speak incessantly and/or rabidly on a relatively uninteresting subject or with a patently ridiculous attitude. 3. Either #1 or #2, directed with hostility at a particular person or people. Flames are often found in large numbers (known as a flame war) during holy wars (discussed later in this table). The newsgroup `alt.flame` is dedicated to perfecting the art of flaming.
Flame bait	A posting that is intended to trigger a flame war, or one that invites flames in reply. For example, posting an article on how to run dogs over in `rec.pets.dogs` is sure to draw scathing flames from the readers of that group.
Kibo	Also known as "He who greps" (grep is a UNIX text-searching tool). Kibo was the first person to grep (search) the entire news stream for his name, generating a reply if the string `kibo` was found. Eventually (we think), he modified his search pattern to find various modifications of `kibo`, such as `Kibo` and `KIBO`. Kibo is the closest thing to a god on Usenet. We worship you, almighty Kibo! See `alt.religion.kibology` for more information.
Kook	A term used for many things, but mostly for the weirdos who randomly appear in different groups and who cause no end of trouble. Often placed in kill files, they usually disappear only after everyone has finally stopped responding to their ridiculous or improperly posted articles.
Lurk	To read a newsgroup but not post articles. It is often hypothesized that upwards of 99 percent of the people reading a group do not post, or post very rarely. Of course, this hypothesis could be incorrect.

Term	Description
Religious issue	Questions that seemingly cannot be raised without touching off *holy wars* (a flame war about a religious issue), such as "What is the best operating system (or editor, language, architecture, shell, mail reader, newsreader, and so on)?" Almost every group has a religious issue of some kind. Anybody who was around the last time the issue exploded is careful not to provoke another war. Religious issues are universally guaranteed to start a long-running, tiresome, bandwidth-wasting flame war—with no truces.
September	The time when college students return to school and start to post silly questions, repost MAKE MONEY FAST, break rules of netiquette, and just generally make life on Usenet more difficult than at other times of the year. You can really tell when homework is due, because the "How do I…" articles begin to surface. Unfortunately, it has been September since 1993.
Signal-to-noise ratio (snr)	A subjective quantity (the snr has no units—it is usually just some obvious quantifier) describing someone's idea of just how much content a group has relative to its junk. The snr is *very* subjective. Generally, every person who reads news has a certain threshold for snr. If any group falls below that threshold, the reader will unsubscribe rather than wade through all the junk.
Sturgeon's Law	90 percent of everything is crud. What that 90 percent is depends on who you are, but this law is often the cause of strenuous debate about a thread's being either on or off topic. Note that this does not imply that the remaining 10 percent is not crud.
Troll	A posting designed specifically to generate follow-ups about something trivial, but not in the sense of a flame. Also a post designed to instruct readers to ignore obvious drivel by making the repliers feel utterly stupid.

There are many other terms. I suggest picking up a copy of *The New Hacker's Dictionary* by Eric S. Raymond (MIT Press, 1996). Keep this book by your side as you engage in Usenet.

NNTP Protocol

We now begin our journey to the server side of Usenet. Beginning with this section, we will explore the NNTP protocol and then move on to installing and configuring the nntp server.

The Network News Transfer Protocol (NNTP) utilizes the facilities of the Transmission Control Protocol (TCP) as the underlying connectivity medium (stream connection). An NNTP conversation between an NNTP client and server occurs at the well-known port number 119. Typically, an NNTP server runs as a daemon, accepting connections from other hosts and clients.

An NNTP conversation is similar to other TCP/IP protocols, such as HTTP, FTP, and so on. The client and server speak a language consisting of commands and their associated arguments or data (if applicable). The language is readable ASCII text. You can converse manually with an NNTP server as long as you know the commands and required data. The conversation consists of the NNTP client submitting commands to the server and the server responding with a numeric response code. The code may be followed by data.

The NNTP protocol is described in RFC 977, which identifies the requirements and the language or commands that are available. The Usenet system provides a central repository containing news articles. Also, there are programs allowing a subscriber to select and manipulate news articles.

The NNTP server is merely a gateway between the NNTP client and the NNTP databases that contain the articles. The NNTP server makes no assumptions about the client and provides no functionality for user interaction, including the presentation of articles.

NNTP Commands

As mentioned previously, an NNTP command is comprised of a textual command preceding some number of arguments. Commands and their associated argument(s) are delimited by a space or tab character. Each command line submitted can consist of only one command; multiple commands are not permitted. Each command line is terminated by a CR/LF character sequence.

A restriction is posed against the length of the command line. The complete line submitted to the server must not exceed 512 characters. If a command requires an argument (or data), the delimiter characters (spaces or tabs) are counted. Additionally, the terminating CR/LF pair is included in the count.

Table 17.2 summarizes the NNTP commands.

Table 17.2 **NNTP Commands**

Command	Description
ARTICLE	Used to request an article by its message identifier or numeric identifier. If available, the header and body of the article are returned.
BODY	Similar to the ARTICLE command, except that only the article's body is returned. The request is by the article's message ID or numerical identifier.
GROUP group	Used to join a newsgroup identified by the argument group.
HEAD messageID	Similar to the ARTICLE command, except that only the article's header is returned. The request is by the article's message ID or numerical identifier.
HELP	Used to obtain a list of applicable commands.
IHAVE	The client uses this command to inform the server it has the article identified by a message identifier. If the server wants the article, it tells the client to send the article. Otherwise, the server responds that it does not want the article.
LAST	The current article pointer is set to the previous article (not the last article available).
LIST	Used to obtain a list of newsgroups offered by the news server.
NEWGROUPS	Requests a list of new newsgroups created since a specified date and time. Some people think this command is NEWSGROUPS; however, it is not requesting a list of newsgroups, only groups that are new. See LIST for comparison.
NEWNEWS	Used to request a list of articles that have been posted since a specified date.
NEXT	Used to set the current article pointer to the next article.
POST	A request to submit (or post) an article (posting must be allowed). The article should be sent if the response code is 340.
QUIT	Tells the server to end the session and close the connection.
SLAVE	Tells the server that this client is a slave server.
STAT	Similar to the ARTICLE command, STAT is used to set the current article pointer. Data is not returned.

The following dialog shows a manual connection using the telnet program:

```
stimpy $ telnet news1.attglobal.net nntp
Trying 943.432.123.342...
Connected to news1.server.net.
Escape character is '^]'.
200 news1.server.net DNEWS Version 5.2c, S3, posting OK
HELPO
500 command not recognized
HELP
100 Legal commands
  authinfo user Name|pass Password
  article [MessageID|Number]
  body [MessageID|Number]
  check MessageID
  date
  group newsgroup
  head [MessageID|Number]
  help
  ihave
  last
  list [active|active.times|newsgroups|subscriptions]
  listgroup newsgroup
  mode stream
  mode reader
  newgroups yymmdd hhmmss [GMT] [<distributions>]
  newnews newsgroups yymmdd hhmmss [GMT] [<distributions>]
  next
  post
  slave
  stat [MessageID|Number]
  takethis MessageID
  xgtitle [group_pattern]
  xhdr header [range|MessageID]
  xover [range]
  xpat header range|MessageID pat [morepat...]
```

The HELP command is submitted, and a list of legal commands is returned. Notice that, initially and intentionally, the command submitted is HELPO. This command is invalid, and the server responded appropriately.

Commands are submitted from the client to the NNTP server. If the server does not respond, the command may be re-sent. The next section discusses server responses.

NNTP Server Responses

Responses can be one of two types—status or text. A *status* message from the server identifies the response associated with the last command received. The status code consists of a three-digit code. Table 17.3 describes the first-digit portion of the response code.

Table 17.3 **NNTP Status Responses, First-Digit Description**

First Status Code	Description
1xx	Identifies informative messages
2xx	Indicates success
3xx	Indicates that the command is okay so far, so continue with the next
4xx	Denotes that the command is correct but cannot be executed
5xx	Indicates that the command is not (yet) implemented, the command is incorrect, or some other error occurred

The second digit in the code identifies the functional response category. These functional codes are listed in Table 17.4.

Table 17.4 **NNTP Status Responses, Second-Digit Description**

Second Status Code	Description
x0x	Messages about the connection, setup, and other miscellaneous things
x1x	Used to designate a newsgroup selection
x2x	Used to designate an article selection
x3x	Identifies various distribution functions
x4x	Used to refer to posting
x8x	Indicates any nonstandard extensions
x9x	Provided for debugging output

Each command in the RFC 977 document identifies the codes that are expected responses from the server. Some status messages also contain data as an argument. The number and type of arguments are fixed. A single space character is used as a delimiter to separate the code from the argument(s) (if applicable).

Overall, the NNTP client can choose to ignore codes in the 1xx range. A code of 200 or 201 is a response code when a connection is initially established. The following dialog demonstrates this output:

```
stimpy $ telnet news1.attglobal.net nntp
Trying 32.97.166.128...
Connected to news1.prserv.net.
Escape character is '^]'.
```

continues ▶

continued

```
200 news1.prserv.net DNEWS Version 5.2c, S2, posting OK
QUIT
205 closing connection - goodbye!
Connection closed by foreign host.
stimpy $
```

A status code of 400 is sent by the NNTP server when it must discontinue the news service. The 5xx family of status codes indicates that the command could not be executed for some reason.

Table 17.5 describes the response codes that can be sent by the NNTP server. These are general responses.

Table 17.5 **NNTP Status Categories**

Status Code	Description
100	Help text is returned.
190 through 199	Identified for debug output.
200	The server is ready. Posting is allowed.
201	The server is ready. No posting is allowed.
400	Specifies that the nntp service is being terminated.
500	Specifies that the submitted command is not recognized.
501	Specifies that there is a syntax error in the supplied command.
502	Identifies an access restriction or specifies that permission is denied.
503	Identifies a program fault and specifies that the command is not executed.

The second type of response is the *text* response. It is sent after a numeric status response line has been sent, indicating that text follows. The format of the text is one or more lines, terminated with a CR/LF character pair. A single period (.), on a line by itself, is sent to indicate the end of text. The following dialog demonstrates this:

```
03# telnet news1.attglobal.net nntp
Trying 32.97.166.128...
Connected to news1.prserv.net.
Escape character is '^]'.
200 news1.prserv.net DNEWS Version 5.2c, S1, posting OK
HELP
100 Legal commands
  authinfo user Name|pass Password
  article [MessageID|Number]
  body [MessageID|Number]
```

```
    check MessageID
    date
    group newsgroup
    head [MessageID¦Number]
    help
    ihave
    last
    list [active¦active.times¦newsgroups¦subscriptions]
    listgroup newsgroup
    mode stream
    mode reader
    newgroups yymmdd hhmmss [GMT] [<distributions>]
    newnews newsgroups yymmdd hhmmss [GMT] [<distributions>]
    next
    post
    slave
    stat [MessageID¦Number]
    takethis MessageID
    xgtitle [group_pattern]
    xhdr header [range¦MessageID]
    xover [range]
    xpat header range¦MessageID pat [morepat...]
.
QUIT
205 closing connection - goodbye!
Connection closed by foreign host.
stimpy $
```

Notice that after the HELP command is submitted, the server responds with a list of commands. The list is terminated by a single period (.) on a line by itself. If the text contains a period as the first character, the line will contain two periods (..). The client program must validate each line, checking for a lone period or double period, and responding accordingly.

Text messages are normally used as display to the user. The status codes are normally interpreted and shielded from the user, because the code itself is not informative.

Command and Response Details

The NNTP commands and the responses associated with them are detailed in this section. Refer to RFC 977 for more details.

The ARTICLE Command

The syntax of the ARTICLE command is as follows:

```
ARTICLE message-id
```

Upon receipt of this command, the server displays the header, a blank line, and the body (text) of the identified article. The identifying *message-id* is the message ID of an article in its header. The internally maintained "current article pointer" is left unchanged.

Here is an optional usage of the ARTICLE command:

ARTICLE [*nnn*]

As in the previous usage of the ARTICLE command, the header, a blank line, and the body (text) of the current or specified article are displayed. The parameter *nnn*, which is optional, is the numeric ID of an article in the current newsgroup. If the parameter is not given, the current article is displayed.

If a valid article number is used, the current article pointer is set. The response indicates the current article number.

The *message-id* field can be used to purge duplicate articles, because this ID is unique for every article.

The following list shows the responses associated with the ARTICLE command. *n* represents the article number, and *a* represents the message ID for an article.

- **220** *n a*. The article is retrieved, and the head and body follow.
- **221** *n a*. The article is retrieved, and the head follows.
- **222** *n a*. The article is retrieved, and the body follows.
- **223** *n a*. The article is retrieved; the text must be requested separately.
- **412.** A newsgroup has not been selected.
- **420.** A current article has not been selected.
- **423.** The article number specified does not exist in this group.
- **430.** The identified article was not found.

The GROUP Command

The syntax of the GROUP command is as follows:

GROUP *ggg*

The name of the newsgroup is supplied as the parameter *ggg*. This is the newsgroup to join (or select). Use the LIST command to acquire a list of valid newsgroups offered.

If the command is successful, the first and last articles in the selected newsgroup are returned. Also, a total count of all articles available is given, but this count is only an estimate. The method by which the count is derived is implementation specific.

Once a newsgroup has been selected using this command, the current article pointer is set to the first article. If it's unsuccessful, the previous newsgroup and current article pointer are maintained.

The following list shows the responses that can be expected from submission of the GROUP command. *n* is the count of articles for the newsgroup. *f* designates the number of the first article. *l* designates the last article in the newsgroup. *s* indicates the name of the newsgroup.

- **211 *n* *f* *l* *s*.** Identifies the newsgroup selected.
- **411.** Specifies that the newsgroup does not exist.

The HELP Command

The syntax of the HELP command is as follows:

HELP

Upon receipt of this command, the server responds with a list of available commands supported by the server. A sole period on a line by itself identifies the end of the list.

The following response is applicable for the HELP command:

- **100.** The help text follows.

The IHAVE Command

The syntax of the IHAVE command is as follows:

IHAVE *messageid*

An NNTP client sends this command, with the argument, to the server, effectively telling the server, "I have this article named by the message identifier." The server can instruct the client to send the article. Otherwise, the server tells the client it does not want the article.

If the server requests the article, the client responds by sending the article's header and body. A response code is returned, indicating success or failure.

The IHAVE command is used to transfer an existing article. Use the POST command to submit a new article. Generally, the IHAVE command is not executed by a newsreader program; it is executed only by server processes.

A server may reject an article for a number of reasons, such as an invalid newsgroup (for the article), hardware issues, or a corrupted article. The decision is implementation specific and is not specified by the NNTP protocol.

The following are the responses for the IHAVE command:

- **235.** The article transfer was successful.
- **335.** The article is to be transferred. The termination sequence for the transmission is <CR-LF>.<CR-LF>.
- **435.** Do not send the identified article because it is not desired.
- **436.** The transfer failed. Attempt to retransmit at a later time.
- **437.** The article was rejected. Do not send it again.

The LAST Command

The syntax of the LAST command is as follows:

LAST

This command is used to set the current article pointer to the previous article in the newsgroup. If the pointer is at the first article in the list, an error is returned, and the pointer continues to point to the first article. The current article number and message identifier are returned.

The following are the responses for the LAST command. *n* designates the article number. *a* designates the unique article identifier.

- **223** *n* *a*. The article has been retrieved. The text must be requested separately.
- **412.** A newsgroup has not been selected.
- **420.** An article has been selected as current.
- **422.** There is no previous article in this group.

The LIST Command

The syntax of the LIST command is as follows:

LIST

The server returns a list of available newsgroups in reaction to this command. Each newsgroup entry exists on a separate line and is formatted as follows:

group last first posting

The name of the newsgroup is identified by *group*. The last article number for the newsgroup is identified by *last* and is numeric. The *first* field indicates the first article for the newsgroup and is a numeric value. Finally, the *posting* field indicates whether posting is allowed. The value of *posting* can be either y or n.

An empty list, identified by a lone period on a line, is considered a legitimate response. This response specifies that there are no newsgroups.

The following is the response for the LIST command:

- **215.** A list of newsgroups follows.

The NEWGROUPS Command

The syntax of the NEWGROUPS command is as follows:

```
NEWGROUPS date time [GMT] [distributions]
```

The server displays a list of newsgroups that have been created since the specified *date* and *time*. The date must be formatted as six digits, as in YYMMDD. Because the year is identified with two digits, the closest century is used. The *time* field is required and is also formatted to six digits, as in HHMMSS. If GMT is not present, the local time is assumed.

The parameter *distributions* is optional. It identifies a list of distribution groups.

As with the LIST command, an empty list is considered a legitimate response. This response specifies that there are no new newsgroups.

The following is the response for the NEWGROUPS command:

- **231.** A list of new newsgroups follows.

The NEWNEWS Command

The syntax of the NEWNEWS command is as follows:

```
NEWNEWS newsgroups date time [GMT] [distribution]
```

The server displays a list of article message identifiers that have been posted or received since the specified *date* and *time*. The *date* and *time* parameters follow the same format as the NEWGROUPS command. Each entry occupies a single line, and the list is terminated by a sole period on a line by itself.

An asterisk (*) can be used for the newsgroup field to act as a wildcard. For example, comp.lang.* will return entries such as comp.lang.c, comp.lang.c++, and so on.

The following is the response for the NEWNEWS command:

- **230.** A list of new articles by message ID follows.

The NEXT Command

The syntax of the NEXT command is as follows:

```
NEXT
```

This command is used to set the current article pointer to the next article in the newsgroup. If the pointer is at the last article, an error is returned, and the last article remains current.

The article number and message identifier are returned as a result of this command.

The following are valid responses for the NEXT command. *n* designates the article number, and *a* designates the unique article identifier.

- **223** *n* *a*. The article is retrieved. You must request the text separately.
- **412.** A newsgroup has not been selected.
- **420.** An article has not been selected as current.
- **421.** There is no next article in this newsgroup.

The POST Command

The syntax of the POST command is as follows:

POST

This command is used to submit a new article to the server. If posting is allowed, a **340** code is returned. Upon receipt of this code, the article should be transmitted. Otherwise, a code of **440** indicates that posting is not allowed.

After the article has been transmitted, the server returns a response code indicating success or failure. The format of the article should correspond to the specification established in RFC 850. A sole period on a line by itself indicates the end of the article's text.

The following are valid responses for the POST command:

- **240.** The article has been posted successfully.
- **340.** Transmit the article to be posted, and terminate with <CR-LF>.<CR-LF>.
- **440.** Article posting is not allowed.
- **441.** Posting has failed.
- **201.** The server is ready, and posting is not allowed.

The QUIT Command

The syntax of the QUIT command is as follows:

QUIT

The QUIT command is used to tell the server to terminate the session and close the connection. It is generally accepted practice for the client to submit this command to close the connection.

The following is the response for the QUIT command:

- **205.** Close the connection.

The SLAVE Command

The syntax of the SLAVE command is as follows:

SLAVE

This command effectively tells the server that the client is to be treated as a slave server. This helps ensure that priority should be given to a slave server versus an NNTP client, because a slave server normally serves many NNTP clients.

The following is the response for the SLAVE command:

- **202.** Slave status is acknowledged.

Configuring the NNTP Server

The name of the NNTP server follows the pattern of other server daemons—the server's name is nntpd. The server can be configured to execute in one of two methods, which applies to other Linux Internet servers as well. The nntpd server can be started at bootup from an rc startup script, or it can be executed on demand by the `inetd` daemon.

If you're using `inetd`, an entry should exist in the `/etc/inetd.conf` file. The following shows a sample entry for the `nntpd` daemon:

```
# inetd.conf file
...
# service_name sock_type proto flags user server_path args
nntp     stream  tcp nowait     news    /usr/etc/in.nntpd    nntpd
...
# To re-read this file after changes, just do a 'killall -HUP inetd'
# end of file
```

If you choose the first option, running nntpd as stand-alone, you should make sure you comment out any line referencing nntpd in the `/etc/inetd.conf` file.

Regardless of the mode of execution, you should be sure that an nntp entry exists in the `/etc/services` file, as shown in the following snippet:

```
# /etc/services ...
...
auth         113/tcp     authentication    tap     ident
sftp         115/tcp
uucp-path    117/tcp
```

continues ▶

continued

```
nntp            119/tcp     readnews        untp    # USENET News Transfer Protocol
ntp             123/tcp
ntp             123/udp     # Network Time Protocol
netbios-ns      137/tcp     # NETBIOS Name Service
netbios-ns      137/udp     netbios-dgm     138/tcp # NETBIOS Datagram Service
...
#
```

To store news articles, the nntpd daemon requires a temporary directory. The following dialog demonstrates the creation of this directory:

```
stimpy $ mkdir /var/spool/news/.tmp
stimpy $ chown news.news /var/spool/news/.tmp
stimpy $
```

Restricting NNTP Access

The /usr/lib/news/nntp_access file determines the accesses to NNTP resources. The format for an entry is as follows:

```
site    read¦xfer¦both¦no    post¦no    [!exceptgroups]
```

When a client establishes a connection, the server queries for the fully qualified domain name of the host client using a reverse lookup.

Table 17.6 describes the procedure, based on the match made by the server. A match can be either partial or exact.

Table 17.6 **nntpd Hostname Matching**

Matched By	Description
Hostname	The fully qualified domain name of the host. If the match is literal, the entry applies.
IP address	The IP address (dotted quad notation). The entry applies. All other entries are ignored.
Domain name	A match if the client's hostname matches the domain name, as in *.domain.
Network name	The name of a network identified in the /etc/networks file.
Default	Matches any client.

The access rights for a client are governed by an entry's second and third fields. A value of read specifies news article retrieval. xfer specifies the transmission of news articles. The both value permits read and xfer. no denies all access. The third field is used to govern the client's rights to post articles without header information. This information is completed by the news server. The third field is ignored if the value of the second field is no.

The fourth field is optional. If it's specified, it contains a list of groups that the client is not allowed to access.

Summary

This chapter covered most of the functionality of Usenet. We began with an overview of Usenet and its community.

Next, the overall mechanics, or concepts, of Usenet were covered. This included descriptions of terminology such as *articles, newsgroups,* and *newsreaders*. An overview of article processing was also given.

The next section described the client side of Usenet, covering the use of two newsreaders. You use a newsreader to access newsgroups and manipulate articles contained within a newsgroup. An overview of the krn newsreader, provided as part of the KDE package, was given. Netscape's newsreader, Messenger, was also covered.

Next, we covered some common Usenet terms, such as *flame* and *flame bait*. Any Usenet participant worth his salt will have *The New Hacker's Dictionary* by his side.

The next section dealt with the NNTP commands that are sent to a server. Also, the response codes were described in detail. Some of the commands discussed were ARTICLE, BODY, and GROUP, to name just a few.

Finally, we closed the chapter with a section concerning the configuration of the nntpd server daemon.

18

Print Services

WE CAN DO A LOT WITH OUR COMPUTERS. We can crunch numbers using spreadsheets and produce documents using word processors. It would be great if all documents we produced could be sent directly to the parties concerned, enabling them to view the documents on their computer. Unfortunately, the reality is that we often have to produce paper copies of our documents.

In this chapter, we see what it takes to get paper output from the documents we produce.

Print Overview

Linux, like other UNIX systems, performs the process of printing using the concept of spooling. Printers are slow mechanical devices, and even the printing of the smallest document can hold up a process. However, we do not want other processes (such as a word processor) to wait for a print job to finish.

Linux includes various software applications to implement and manage a print queue. When we send a file to the printer under Linux, that file does not immediately go to the printer. Instead, the file is sent to a temporary area, logically known as the print queue, to wait its turn to be printed. If the file to be printed is the only file in the queue, it is processed immediately. If one or more files are in the queue, those files are printed first. Later in the chapter you will see how you can send a file directly to the printer. However, this is not an optimal method.

Because Linux is a multiuser operating system, the concept of the print queue is very effective for multiple users printing to a single printer. Users simply send their print jobs off and the print queue manages the task of printing each user's documents in the correct sequence. The printer services under Linux remove the burden of printer management and control from users on the network.

The overall process to print a document from software (or command line) to the printer is straightforward and simple. Let us use the example of a word processor. You tell the program that you want to print the current document. The program gathers the text, along with any special formatting characters, and sends a data stream to the print queue software. The print queue software stores the print data to a temporary file on the disk. This relieves the word processor from waiting for the file to be printed; the print queue software is now the owner of the file to be printed. Of course, the word processor program thinks that the file has been printed because the streaming of data has completed. If you have ever printed a document under a single-user operating system such as DOS, you may remember that the program (printing the document) remains unavailable until the print job is complete.

Now that the print queue software has spooled the print job to disk, it is simply a matter of the print queue manager determining the next file to print. If no other files are in the queue, the newly spooled file is opened and sent to the printer. If other files are in the queue, they are opened one at a time and sent to the printer. This process continues until all files have been sent to the printer.

This all seems simplistic, but there is more detail to printing under Linux than can be captured in a few paragraphs. Let us continue our journey into the world of printing under Linux.

Printer Preliminaries

Most all distributions of Linux ask if you want to configure a printer during the installation process. The more robust distributions even have a list of printers to choose from; these distributions take away much of the anguish of setting up a printer under Linux. Still, it is a good idea to know what is happening, especially if problems arise.

Table 18.1 lists the most popular printers supported by Linux. The printer capabilities are fully supported under Linux.

Table 18.1 **Printers Fully Supported by Linux**

Manufacturer	Model(s)
Apple	LaserWriter 16/600, LaserWriter IINTX, LaserWriter Select 360
Brother	HL-1070, HL-10V, HL-10h, HL-1260, HL-2060, HL-4Ve, HL-630, HL-660, HL-720, HL-730, HL-760, HL-8
Canon	BJC-210, BJC-250, BJC-4000, BJC-4100, BJC-4200, BJC-4300, BJC-4400, BJC-600, BJC-6000, BJC-610, BJC-620, BJC-70, BJC-800, BJ-10e, BJ-20, BJ-200, BJ-330, BJ-5, LBP-1260, LBP-1760, LBP-4+, LBP-4U, LBP-8A1, LBP-8II, LIPS-III
Citizen	ProJet II, ProJet IIc
Digital	DECwriter 520ic, DECwriter 500i, DECwriter 110I, LN03
Epson	SQ 1170, Stylus Color, Stylus Color 400, Stylus Color 440, Stylus Color 640, Stylus Color 660, Stylus Color 800, Stylus Color 850, Stylus Color II, Stylus Color IIs, Stylus Pro XL, ActionLaser 1100, LP 8000
Fujitsu	PrintPartner 10V, PrintPartner 16DV, PrintPartner 20W, PrintPartner 8000
Hewlett Packard	DeskJet 500, DeskJet 510, DeskJet 520, 2000C, 2500C, DeskJet 1200C, DeskJet 1200C/PS, DeskJet 1600C, DeskJet 1600Cm, DeskJet 310, DeskJet 400, DeskJet 420C, DeskJet 500C, DeskJet 540, DeskJet 550C, DeskJet 600, DeskJet610C, DeskJet 610CL, DeskJet 612C, DeskJet 660C, DeskJet 670C, DeskJet 672C, DeskJet 682C, DeskJet 690C, DeskJet 694C, DeskJet 697C, DeskJet 810C, DeskJet 812C, DeskJet 850C, DeskJet 855C, DeskJet 882C, DeskJet 890C, PaintJet XL300, Color LaserJet 4500, LaserJet 1100, LaserJet 1100A, LaserJet 2 w/PS, LaserJet 2100M, LaserJet 2P, LaserJet 3, LaserJet 3P w/PS, LaserJet 4, LaserJet 4 Plus, LaserJet 4050N, LaserJet 4L, LaserJet 4M, LaserJet 4P, LaserJet 5, LaserJet 5000, LaserJet 5L, LaserJet 5M, LaserJet 5MP, LaserJet 5P, LaserJet 6L, LaserJet 6MP, LaserJet 8000, LaserJet 8100, Mopier 320
Kyocera	F-3300, FS-1700+, FS-3750, FS-600, FS-800, P-2000
Lexmark(/IBM)	Optra Color 40, Optra Color 45, 4303 Network Color Printer, Optra Color 1200, Optra Color 1275, 4019, 4029 10P, Page Printer 3112, 4039 10plus, Optra E, Optra E+, Optra E310, Optra Ep, Optra K 1220, Optra R+, Optra S 1250, Optra S 1855, Valuewriter 300

continues ▶

Table 18.1 **Continued**

Manufacturer	Model(s)
Minolta	PagePro 6, PagePro 6e, PagePro 6ex, PagePro 8
NEC	SilentWriter LC 890, Silentwriter2 S60P, Silentwriter2 model 290, SuperScript 660i
Oce	3165
Okidata	Okipage 8c, 8p, OL 410e, OL 600e, OL 610e/PS, OL 800, OL 810e/PS, OL400ex, OL810ex, OL830Plus, Okipage 10e, Okipage 12i, Okipage 20DXn, Okipage 4w, Okipage 6e, Okipage 6ex
Olivetti	JP350S, JP450, PG 306
Panasonic	KX-P8420, KX-P8475, KX-P4410, KX-P4450, KX-P5400
QMS	2425 Turbo EX
Ricoh	4801, 6000
Samsung	ML-5000a
Sharp	AR-161
Tally	MT908
Seiko	SpeedJET 200
Tektronix	4696, 4697, Phaser 780
Xerox	DocuPrint C55, DocuPrint 4508, DocuPrint N17, DocuPrint N32

Printer Type

You need to consider several things when you set up your Linux system for printer support. One item is the printer itself. Is the printer a dot matrix, an inkjet, or a laser printer? Although most software can send files to any printer, it is always a good idea to take advantage of a printer's feature set. What am I talking about here? Well, you can send documents as flat ASCII text files to a laser printer, but why not take advantage of the formatting features that the laser printer offers?

Each type of printer does particular things well. A mechanical dot matrix printer is good for printing multipart forms.

Laser printers are good at scaling fonts to various sizes and are quite adept at applying font styles, such as bold and italics; and effects, such as outline and shadow.

Inkjet printers are really geared for individual use. Inkjet printers are quite flexible, providing the option to print in black and white or in color.

Printer Language

You can choose from two printer languages: PostScript and Printer Control Language (PCL). PostScript was popularized by Apple, specifically by the introduction of its LaserWriter printer. As can be expected, each language has its advantages and disadvantages.

The best choice, if you can opt for it, is to go with a PostScript printer. I say "if you can opt for it" because PostScript is specifically supported by laser printers. Another reason is that the PostScript option is, as a rule, more expensive than PCL. The benefits of PostScript, in the long run, should outweigh the extra cost. Most UNIX software speaks PostScript because, historically, PostScript is the native printer language of the UNIX community. PostScript is also the native tongue used within the publishing industry.

PostScript is also independent of device. In other words, PostScript is not specific to printers; some programs display PostScript to computer screens and can send PostScript files to fax machines.

PCL is a page-description language developed by Hewlett Packard. The PCL language is implemented in many HP (and other vendor) laser and inkjet printers. PCL version 5 and later versions support Intellifont, which is a scalable font.

A PCL command is identified using Escape character (ASCII value 27) as the first command character. The remaining characters, which identify the command, are usually printable characters. The printer ignores PCL syntax errors without warning.

You should always ensure that your printer is using the latest PCL language version. The most current version (at the time of this writing) is PCL 5e. Most (current) inkjet and laser printers are PCL compatible. PCL version 5e supports 600dpi, whereas previous versions support only 300dpi.

Printer Interface

The next obvious thing to consider is the interface to the printer. Is the interface serial or parallel? Some printers offer both options, providing flexibility of service. The most common, of course, is the parallel interface.

Do not discount the use of a serial printer, because this interface provides some flexibility. A serial interface printer can be set up at a remote location; you can dial it up and then transmit data to it. A case in point: Not too long ago, I developed a system for a client that is in the business of preparing loan packages for home mortgages. A package is a set of documents for a single mortgage; it can consist of 100 pages or more. The client would print the packages and then courier those packages to the various mortgage companies. I suggested that the client put a single printer with a modem at the (remote) client site and then transmit the packages on demand. Initially, the packages were transmitted manually by an operator at the server site. Eventually, this manual process was automated by software that automatically dialed a remote site, established a connection, and then transmitted the package. Figure 18.1 graphically depicts the process.

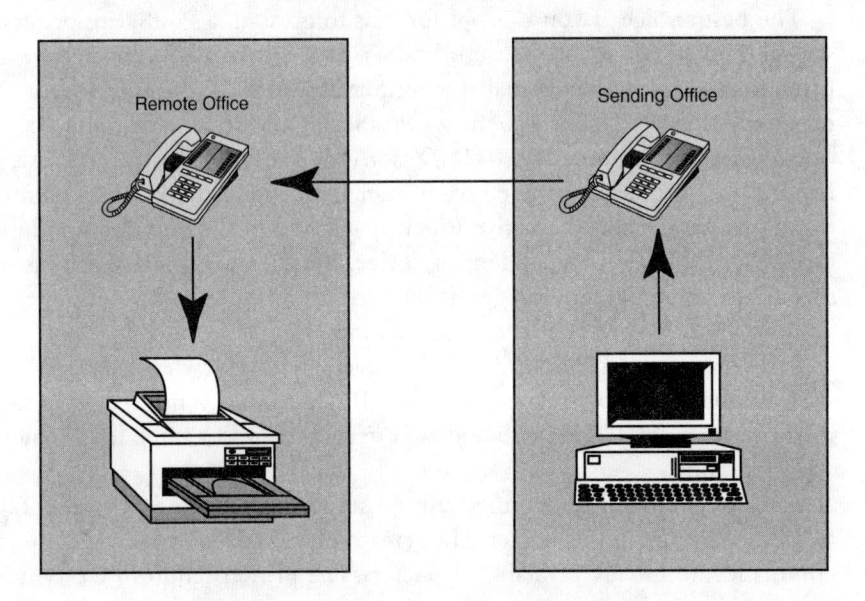

Figure 18.1 Transmitting to a remote serial printer.

Another advantage of using serial is the length of cable. You can easily run a 50-foot length of serial cable between the computer and a serial printer (for RS 232). You can jump a greater distance if you opt for the RS 422 interface. Using eight-pin wire, I have placed printers more than 100 feet from the computer, with no degradation in delivery of data.

There are advantages to the parallel interface. For one, the parallel interface is faster than the serial interface, although I have seen some serial printers coaxed into accepting data at 115,200 baud. Some interesting hacking took place on the part of the hardware and software engineers to achieve this baud rate. Regardless, parallel ports can achieve speeds of 150Kbps with ease. The downside to the parallel interface is the length of the delivery cable. Delivery of data through a parallel cable is good up to about 20 feet. Degradation of data delivery increases as the length of the parallel cable increases (beyond 20 feet). Signal fade occurs on the wire and data is lost.

A third interface for data delivery is Ethernet. As a rule, only high-end printers have the capability to use an Ethernet interface. In general, it makes sense to use Ethernet in conjunction with a high-speed laser printer—print data is delivered faster and the data is printed faster. Keep in mind, however, that depending on the amount of print traffic, the Ethernet bandwidth is reduced. This is because the print data must first travel from the (source) workstation to the print server and finally to the printer; the data travels from source to final destination via Ethernet wire. Another downside to a network printer becomes apparent when the network goes down. Dependency on network printing decreases flexibility with respect to printer usage.

Configuring Print Services

Linux has adopted the BSD-style printer services, and the services are sometimes referred to as lpr. Be warned, however, that some distributions of Linux use the lpsched system. Some distributions offer (or will offer) LPRng, which reduces the administration load for systems that have more than one printer on the network. In addition, LPRng is a good fit if you are using serial printers or other unique printers. Another advantage is that LPRng is freely available.

In a pinch, you can send data directly to the printer from the command line, as in the following dialog:

```
stimpy $ ls -al > /dev/lp0
```

Be sure to check the exact device for your system using the dmesg command. Running dmesg should reveal the device that Linux has detected.

Print Commands

Several commands are used to support printer services under Linux. Table 18.2 briefly describes these commands. You should note that the commands begin with a lowercase L—*not* the numeral 1.

Table 18.2 Linux Printer Commands

Command	Description
lpc	This command is used to control the printing system. You use lpc to start, stop, and otherwise manipulate the print queue.
lpd	This is the spool daemon. There is an lpd daemon running for every (running) printer known to the system. There is also one "master" lpd for the system as a whole. The lpd daemon will fork a child to handle any incoming request.
lpq	This command lists the current jobs found in a print queue.
lpr	This is the user-centric spool command. The lpr command, when executed, communicates to the lpd command submitting print jobs into the spool.
lprm	This command is used to remove a print job from the print spool.

In a nutshell, when your Linux system boots up, the lpd daemon is executed. The lpd daemon reads the /etc/printcap to obtain configuration information. The /etc/printcap file contains entries for each printer and identifies options for each of the printer entries.

Whenever a user submits a file to print using the lpr command, lpr submits the file, the print options, and user information to the lpd daemon. The lpd daemon then uses this information to print the file.

Let us examine each of the commands in a little more detail. Then, we take a look at the /etc/printcap file.

lpc

The lpc command is the line printer control program and is used by a system administrator to control the line printer system. You can use the lpc command to disable/enable a printer, disable/enable a printer's spooling queue, or rearrange print jobs that are in a spooling queue. You can also use lpc to check the status of printers and their associated queues and daemons.

The usage for lpc follows:

lpc [command]

Table 18.3 describes the available command options for lpc.

Table 18.3 The lpc Options

Option	Description
? [command ...]	Print a description of each command specified in the argument list or a list of the commands if no argument is given.

Option	Description
help [command ...]	Print a description of each command specified in the argument list or a list of the commands if no argument is given.
abort No all ¦ printer	Terminate an active daemon on the host and disable printing for the identified printers.
clean No all ¦ printer	Remove control, data, and temporary files that cannot be printed for the specified queue.
disable No all ¦ printer	Turn the identified queues off. This is used to prevent any new print jobs from being submitted into the queue using lpr.
down No all ¦ printer message	Turn the specified queue off, disable printing, and submit a message into the (identified) printer status file.
enable No all ¦ printer	Enable spooling on the queue for identified printers.
exit	Exit from the lpc command.
quit	Exit from the lpc command.
restart all ¦ printer	Start a new printer daemon. If a daemon is running, kill and restart the daemon.
start all ¦ printer	Enable printing and start the daemon for the printers listed.
status No all ¦ printer	Display a status for the daemons and queues.
stop all ¦ printer	Stop a daemon after the current print job completes, then disable printing.
topq printer [jobnum...][user ...]	Reorganize the jobs listed to the top of the queue.
up all ¦ printer	Enable printing and start a printer daemon.

The commands may be abbreviated, provided no ambiguity occurs.

lpd

The lpd command is the line printer spooler daemon. The lpd command is usually executed when the Linux system is booted. The lpd command reads the /etc/printcap file to discover available printers and their options. The daemon prints any files lingering in the queue.

At the lowest level, lpd uses the listen-and-accept system calls to process requests. As mentioned previously, one master lpd is running—this master lpd will fork a child process to perform any type of queue request. The lpd command can be invoked with a number of options. The following is the usage for lpd:

lpd [option] [port]

One option is -l (lowercase L). This option tells lpd to log any requests received. This can be quite helpful when debugging printing problems.

Another option is specified by port#, which identifies the Internet port number to use whenever the system call getservbyname is invoked.

The lpd command attempts to open a file to be printed. If lpd cannot open the file, a message to that effect is submitted to syslog. If the lpd command cannot open the file after 20 tries, it skips that file and moves on.

lpq

The lpq command is used to list the current jobs found in the print queue. Information reported includes the username that submitted the print job, the job's position in the queue, the job number, and the total file size. The usage for lpq is as follows:

lpq [options] [name]

If *name* is supplied, only information pertaining to the specified username is reported.

The -P option identifies the printer to obtain status for. The default is to report on the system printer or the printer identified by the environment variable PRINTER.

The -l option to lpq is used to report information about each file owned by a job.

The third option available is #jobnum, allowing you to obtain information about a specific job number.

lpr

The lpr command is used to submit print jobs. The lpr command uses the spooling daemon to print the indicated files. The following shows the usage for lpr:

lpr [-Pprinter] [-#num] [-C class] [-J job] [-T title][-U user] [-i [numcols]]
    [-1234 font] [-wnum] [-cdfghlnmprstv] [name ...]

The lpr command will complain about printing binary files. Also, any files that are too large will be truncated. If lpr cannot connect to the lpd daemon, lpr prints a message stating that the spooler cannot be started.

If the spooler is disabled and a nonroot user attempts to print a file, a message is displayed and no files are queued.

A number of options can be provided to the lpr command.

You will see references to the *burst* page—sometimes called the cover or banner page. The burst page is similar to a fax cover sheet. It contains information such as the user, the job number, and the file that is being printed. The burst page always precedes the file that is printed. In a small network with five or fewer people, you probably do not need to print a burst page. If you have more than five users and a fair amount of printing is being done, a burst page should be required.

Table 18.4 lists some of the more common options.

Table 18.4 **Some Common lpr Options**

Option	Description
-P	Directs the output to the specified printer. The default printer is usually used or the environment variable PRINTER is queried for the printer.
-h	Does not print the burst page.
-m	Sends mail on completion of the print job.
-r	Deletes the file after spooling or printing (if -s is used) is complete.
-s	Forces the use of symbolic links. Normally, files are copied to the spool directory. This option forces the use of the symlink call to link to the actual file; thus, the files are not copied. This allows large files to be printed. This also implies that the files to be printed should not be deleted or modified in any way until after they are printed.
-#*num*	Uses the value identified by *num* as the number of copies of the file to print.
-T *title*	The title to be used. Normally, the filename is used for the title.
-U *user*	Prints the specified username on the burst page.
-i [*numcols*]	Indents the output. The *numcols* argument specifies the number of spaces (or blanks) to be output before the text of the line. Otherwise, eight characters are printed. If *numcols* is not specified, eight spaces are printed.
-w*num*	Uses the value identified by *num* as the page width.

Several other options can be specified. These options are used to signal that the files are not standard text files. The spool daemon uses the appropriate filter before printing the files, based on the option.

lprm

The `lprm` command is used to remove print jobs from the queue. The usage for `lprm` is as follows:

```
lprm [-Pprinter] [-] [job # ...] [user ...]
```

Table 18.5 lists the available options and their descriptions.

Table 18.5 **The lprm Options**

Option	Description
-P*printer*	This option is used to designate the queue for a specific printer; otherwise, the default printer is used.
-	This option tells the `lprm` command to remove all jobs owned by the user. If the user submitting this option is the superuser, the queue will be completely cleared.
user	This option tells the `lprm` command to delete jobs (that are queued) that belong to the identified *user*. Only the superuser can use this option.
job #	This option allows a user to remove a job number from the queue.

If files are removed from the queue, the `lprm` command displays the files removed. If no print jobs exist, `lrpm` does not display a message.

If a user invokes the `lprm` command without any options, all files owned by the user are purged from the queue.

If a spool daemon is running, `lrpm` kills the daemon before purging any files; `lrpm` then launches a new daemon after the files are purged.

The /etc/printcap File

The `/etc/printcap` file is referred to as the printer capability database. Although identified as a database file, it is not one in the strictest sense. The `/etc/printcap` file is a text file that contains configuration information for printers on the network. The following is a snippet from a fairly comprehensive `/etc/printcap` file:

```
#
# the definition that follows is
# for a DecWriter printer
```

```
#lp¦ap¦arpa¦LA-180 DecWriter III:\
#         :br#1200:fs#06320:tr=\f: \
# of=/usr/lib/lpf:lf=/usr/adm/lpd-errs:
#lp:lp=/dev/lp0:sd=/usr/spool/lpd/lp0: \
# of=/usr/lib/lpf: lf=/usr/adm/lpd-errs
#
# Generic
lp:lp=/dev/lp1:sd=/var/spool/lpd/lp1:sh
#
```

The /etc/printcap file is similar in structure to the /etc/termcap file. Whereas the /etc/termcap file is used to describe terminals, the /etc/printcap file is used to describe printers.

Any time that the printing system is activated to print a file (or files), the /etc/printcap is accessed and read to retrieve printer information. This allows you to modify the /etc/printcap file to add a printer, to delete a printer, or to change the settings for a printer. This makes the /etc/printcap file's information dynamic in nature.

Each line (entry) in the /etc/printcap file, like other Linux configuration files, describes only one printer. You can break a printcap entry across several lines by using the \ character, the line-continuation character. This can help with readability for any lines that span beyond the rightmost column of the display or text editor. Each entry is broken into distinct fields. The first field is the name of the printer. Beyond this requirement, all other fields can be placed in any order on the line. The following snippet is the Generic entry shown in the previous example:

```
# Generic
lp:lp=/dev/lp1:sd=/var/spool/lpd/lp1:sh
#
```

Each field is delimited by a colon character. A comment line begins with the # character. I highly recommend that you sprinkle comments generously within your /etc/printcap file; the file is cryptic enough. Be sure you are consistent with the layout and content for each entry in the file. In other words, place the option fields at the same point for each entry. For example, the sd option field should always be the third field for an entry. You can also make a rule that says, "There should be no more than four fields on a physical line (for each entry)." Be sure to break each entry that spans multiple lines with a \ character. Consistency provides for more readability and ease of editing. Again, the snippet for the Generic entry follows:

```
# Generic
lp:lp=/dev/lp1:sd=/usr/spool/lp1:sh
#
```

The first field is lp and identifies the printer name. A colon ends that field and the next field is lp, not to be confused with the printer name. This field is the device name for output. The value for the lp field is /dev/lp1. A value is defined for a field using the = character. The third field is sd and identifies the spool directory. This field identifies where files are sent and stored to be spooled. In this snippet, files are stored in the /var/spool/lpd/lp1 directory. The last field, sh, is used to suppress the printing of burst pages. Recall that a burst page is a cover page that precedes a print job and provides information about that print job.

Each field option is a two-letter designation. Each field can be one of three types: Boolean, numeric, and string. Table 18.6 lists the available field names, their type, the default value, and a brief description.

Table 18.6 **Field Options for /etc/printcap**

Option	Type	Default	Description
af	str	NULL	Name of the accounting file.
br	num	none	If lp is a tty device, set the baud rate for it.
cf	str	NULL	The cifplot data filter.
df	str	NULL	Identifies the tex data filter.
fc	num	0	If lp is a tty device, clear flag bits.
ff	str	`\f'	The string to send for a form feed.
fo	bool	false	Used to send a form feed when the device is first opened.
fs	num	0	Similar to fc field, but sets the bits.
gf	str	NULL	Identifies the graph data filter format.
hl	bool	false	Identifies that the burst header page is to be printed last.
ic	bool	false	Identifies that the driver supports ioctl to indent the printout; using ioctl is a non-standard method.
if	str	NULL	Identifies the name of the text filter that does accounting.

Option	Type	Default	Description
lf	str	/dev/console for some distributions; NULL for others	Identifies the filename for errorlogging.
lo	str	Lock	Identifies the filename for the lock file.
lp	str	/dev/lp	Identifies the device name to open for output.
mx	num	1000	Identifies the maximum file size, using BUFSIZ blocks. If the value is zero (0), it is an unlimited size.
nd	str	NULL	Identifies the next directory for the list of queues. (May not yet be implemented.)
nf	str	NULL	Identifies the ditroff data filter, for device-independent troff.
of	str	NULL	Identifies the name of the program for output filtering.
pc	num	200	Identifies the price per foot (or page) in hundredths of cents.
pl	num	66	Identifies the page length in lines.
pw	num	132	This field identifies the page width in characters.
px	num	0	Identifies the page width in pixels.
py	num	0	Identifies the page length in pixels.
rf	str	NULL	Identifies the filter used for printing FORTRAN text files.
rg	str	NULL	Identifies the restricted group; only members of the group are allowed access.

continues ▶

Table 18.6 **Continued**

Option	Type	Default	Description
rm	str	NULL	Identifies the machine name for the remote printer.
rp	str	lp	The name of the remote printer.
rs	bool	false	Identifies that remote users are restricted to those with local accounts.
rw	bool	false	Identifies that the printer device should be open for reading and writing.
sb	bool	false	Identifies that short banner, one line only, should be used.
sc	bool	false	Identifies that multiple copies are to be suppressed.
sd	str	/var/spool/lpd	Identifies the spool directory.
sf	bool	false	Identifies that form feeds are to be suppressed.
sh	bool	false	Identifies that the burst page header is to be suppressed.
st	str	status	Identifies the name of the status file.
tf	str	NULL	Identifies the troff data filter.
tr	str	NULL	Identifies the trailer string to print when the queue empties.
vf	str	NULL	Identifies the raster image filter.

Although the previous table is comprehensive, you should check the printcap man page on your Linux distribution. It is not uncommon for a Linux distribution to not include the man page for printcap. If so, you can find the Linux man pages at http://metalab.unc.edu/mdw/index.html, which is the home page for the Linux Documentation Project.

The `PRINTER` Environment Variable

As mentioned previously in this chapter, the `PRINTER` environment variable identifies the default printer. If you use a specific printer a majority of the time, you can set the `PRINTER` environment variable in your login shell script. The following shows a sample entry for the bash shell:

```
export PRINTER=laserjet5
```

You can do this to avoid having to specify the `-P` option to the various printer commands.

Printer Configuration Under SuSE

Under SuSE Linux, configuration of a printer can be handled using the YaST utility. In this section, we show the steps involved in getting a printer up and running quickly.

You can run the YaST utility from the (text) command line or from within the graphical environment. Figure 18.2 shows the YaST main menu running in the KDE terminal emulation console named Konsole.

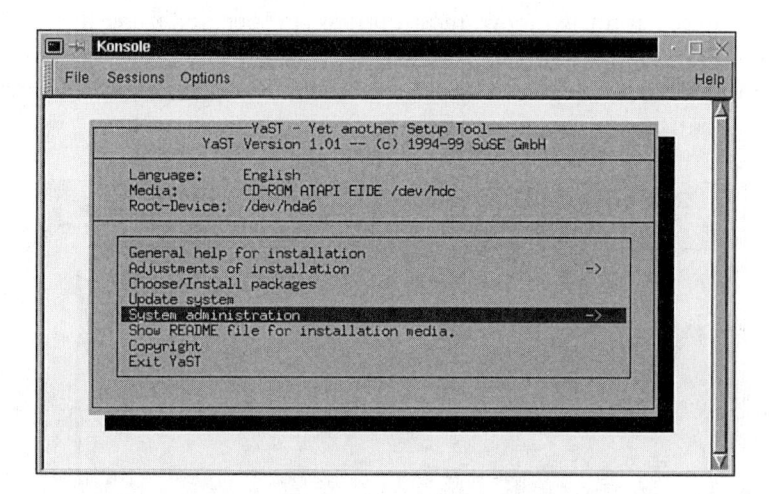

Figure 18.2 YaST running in Konsole.

From the main menu, select the System Administration option. At the next menu window, select the Integrate Hardware into System menu option. Finally, at the third menu window, select the Configure Printers option. Figure 18.3 shows YaST at the Configure Printers option.

516 Chapter 18 Print Services

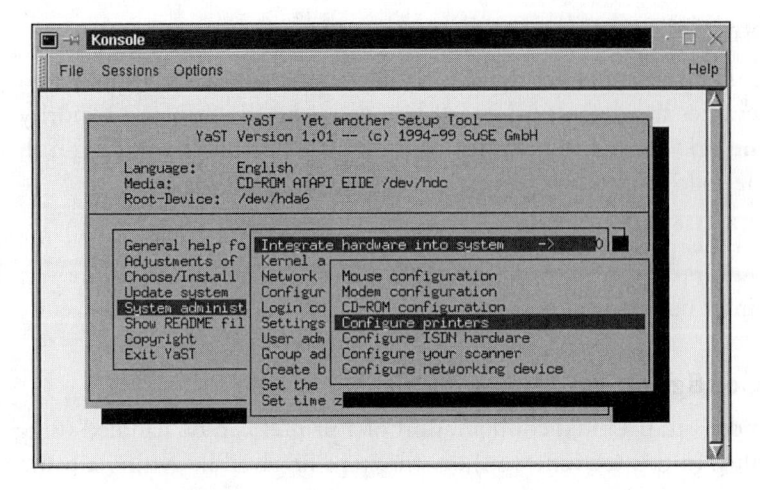

Figure 18.3 YaST at Configure printers menu option.

Next, you see the Installation of Apsfilter window. This provides an easy way to configure `apsfilter`, which is a universal printer filter. A number of fields are required at this window; most options are specified using menu-based lists. After you have identified all the fields required for this window, select the Install button. Figure 18.4 shows the window prior to selecting the Install button.

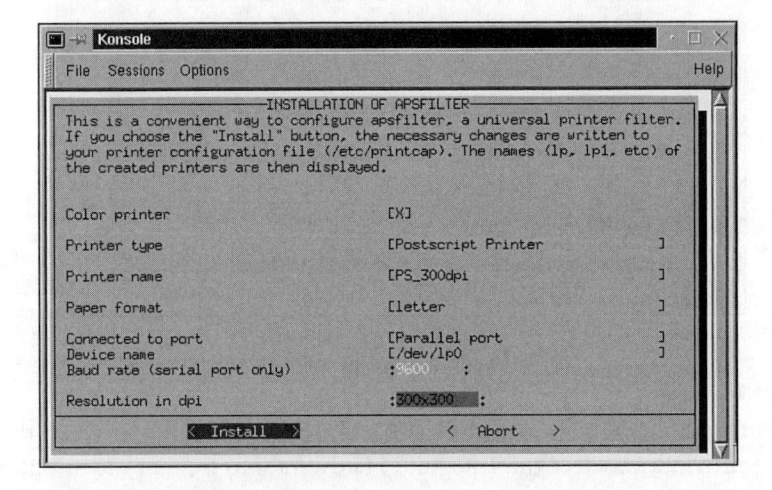

Figure 18.4 YaST at Installation of Apsfilter window.

The YaST utility runs a script file to assist in creating the printer. When it is complete, a message box is displayed. Figure 18.5 shows a sample of the message window.

Configuring Print Services

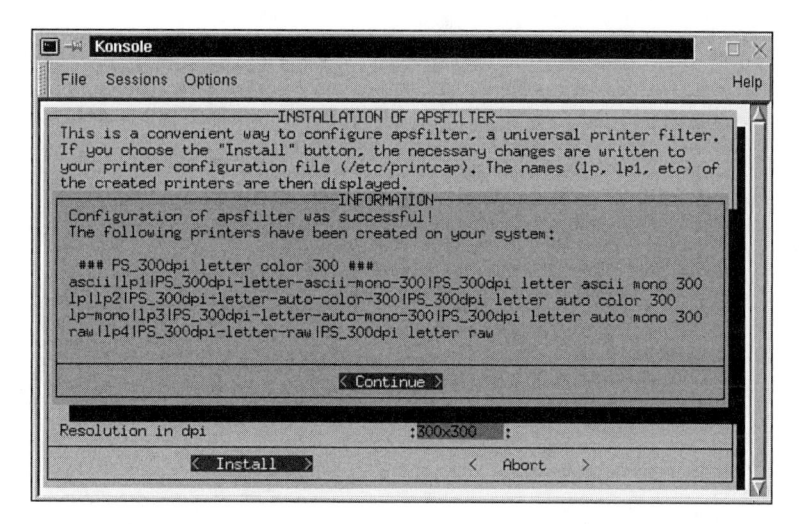

Figure 18.5 Message Confirmation dialog window.

At this point, simply select the Continue button on the Confirmation window and you will be returned to the last YaST menu window selected. You can now exit YaST.

Changes are made to the `/etc/printcap` file. The following is a snippet from the file, showing only the `apsfilter` entries:

```
### BEGIN apsfilter: ### PS_300dpi letter color 300 ###
#   Warning: Configured for apsfilter, do not edit the labels!
#           apsfilter setup Tue Dec 14 05:40:01 CST 1999
#
ascii|lp1|PS_300dpi-letter-ascii-mono-300|PS_300dpi letter ascii mono 300:\
        :lp=/dev/lp0:\
        :sd=/var/spool/lpd/PS_300dpi-letter-ascii-mono-300:\
        :lf=/var/spool/lpd/PS_300dpi-letter-ascii-mono-300/log:\
        :af=/var/spool/lpd/PS_300dpi-letter-ascii-mono-300/acct:\
        :if=/var/lib/apsfilter/bin/PS_300dpi-letter-ascii-mono-300:\
        :la@:mx#0:\
        :tr=:cl:sh:sf:
#
lp|lp2|PS_300dpi-letter-auto-color-300|PS_300dpi letter auto color 300:\
        :lp=/dev/lp0:\
        :sd=/var/spool/lpd/PS_300dpi-letter-auto-color-300:\
        :lf=/var/spool/lpd/PS_300dpi-letter-auto-color-300/log:\
        :af=/var/spool/lpd/PS_300dpi-letter-auto-color-300/acct:\
        :if=/var/lib/apsfilter/bin/PS_300dpi-letter-auto-color-300:\
        :la@:mx#0:\
        :tr=:cl:sh:sf:
#
```

continues ▶

Chapter 18 Print Services

continued

```
lp-mono¦lp3¦PS_300dpi-letter-auto-mono-300¦PS_300dpi letter auto mono 300:\
        :lp=/dev/lp0:\
        :sd=/var/spool/lpd/PS_300dpi-letter-auto-mono-300:\
        :lf=/var/spool/lpd/PS_300dpi-letter-auto-mono-300/log:\
        :af=/var/spool/lpd/PS_300dpi-letter-auto-mono-300/acct:\
        :if=/var/lib/apsfilter/bin/PS_300dpi-letter-auto-mono-300:\
        :la@:mx#0:\
        :tr=:cl:sh:sf:
#
raw¦lp4¦PS_300dpi-letter-raw¦PS_300dpi letter raw:\
        :lp=/dev/lp0:\
        :sd=/var/spool/lpd/PS_300dpi-letter-raw:\
        :lf=/var/spool/lpd/PS_300dpi-letter-raw/log:\
        :af=/var/spool/lpd/PS_300dpi-letter-raw/acct:\
        :if=/var/lib/apsfilter/bin/PS_300dpi-letter-raw:\
        :la@:mx#0:\
        :tr=:cl:sh:sf:
### END    apsfilter: ### PS_300dpi letter color 300 ###
```

Your /etc/printcap entries will most likely look different from what is shown here.

You can also use YaST to configure remote printers. If you need to configure a remote printer, start YaST. When the main menu is displayed, select the System Administration option. At the next menu window, select the Network Configuration menu option. Finally, at the third menu window, select the Administer Remote Printers option. Figure 18.6 shows YaST at this stage.

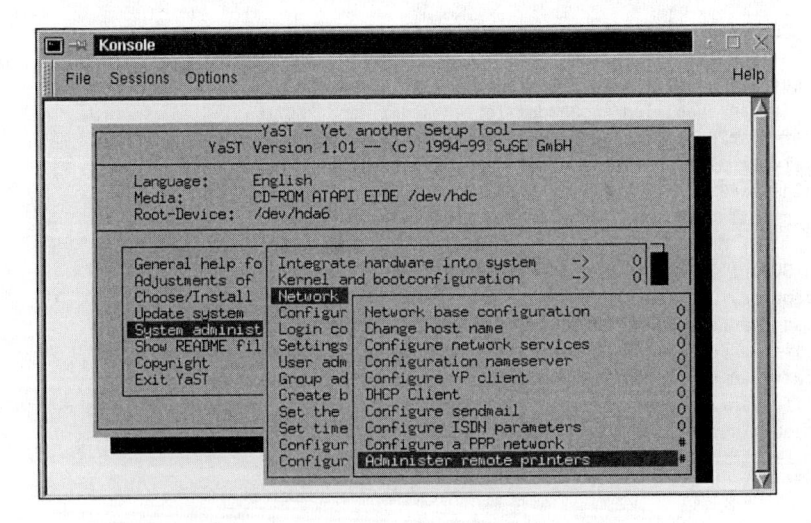

Figure 18.6 Administer remote printers menu option.

A new window is displayed, showing a number of fields. The first field, Name of Remote Printer, is highlighted. At the bottom of the window, you will see various command buttons. Some of the fields on this screen can present options by selection. You do this using the F3=Selection command button. Figure 18.7 shows the Printer Selection window displayed, after the F3 keyboard key is selected.

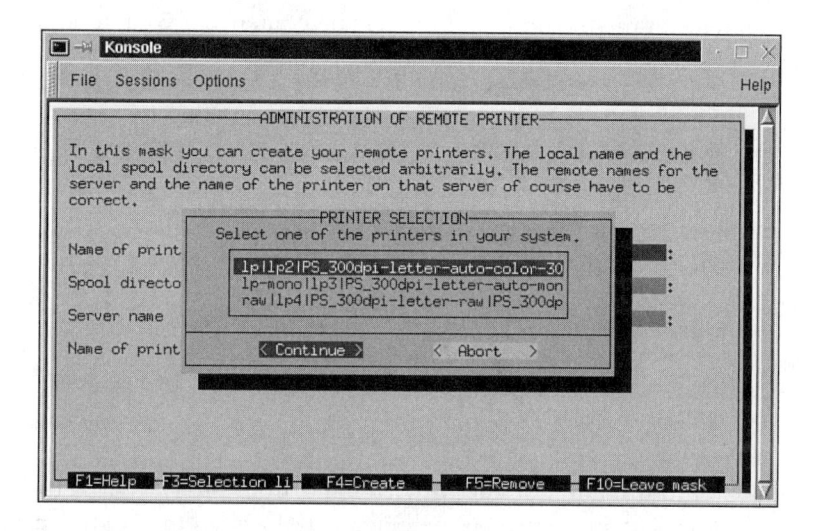

Figure 18.7 Printer Selection window.

After you have supplied values for the fields, press the F4 keyboard key. This writes the changes and applies them to the /etc/printcap file. The following shows (only) the changes that are applied.

```
### BEGIN apsfilter: ### PS_300dpi letter color 300 ###
#   Warning: Configured for apsfilter, do not edit the labels!
#           apsfilter setup Tue Dec 14 05:40:01 CST 1999
#
\
        :rm=remote.server.com:\
        :rp=lp:\
        :sd=/var/spool/lpd/PS_300dpi-letter-ascii-mono-300:
#
lp-mono|lp3 ...
```

You need to be cautious about using this option under YaST. If you define the same remote printer, it will be added to the /etc/printcap file and you will have duplicate entries for that remote printer. After running YaST, you should check the /etc/printcap file in your editor and make any appropriate modifications. After YaST has applied the required changes, you are returned to the main menu.

Printer Configuration Under Red Hat

Under Red Hat Linux, configuration of a printer can be handled using the Printer Configuration utility in the Control Panel. This utility provides a user-friendly graphical front end to configure all types of printers. It is assumed that you are running the GNOME environment. Before we add a new printer, let us take a look at the /etc/printcap file. The following shows the contents of the file on my machine. The contents of your /etc/printcap file will be different.

```
#
# Please don't edit this file directly unless you know what you are doing!
# Be warned that the control-panel printtool requires a very strict format!
# Look at the printcap(5) man page for more info.
#
# This file can be edited with the printtool in the control-panel.
##PRINTTOOL3## LOCAL cdj550 300x300 letter {} DeskJet550 3 1
lp:\
        :sd=/var/spool/lpd/lp:\
        :mx#0:\
        :sh:\
        :lp=/dev/lp0:\
        :if=/var/spool/lpd/lp/filter:
#end
```

If the Control Panel is not currently running, from the GNOME main menu, select System, Control-Panel. Figure 18.8 shows the control-panel with the Printer Configuration utility icon highlighted.

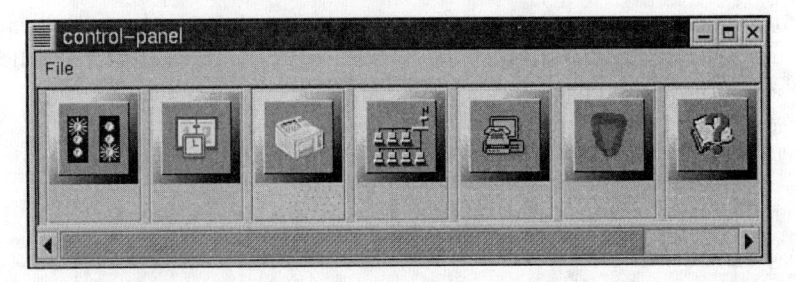

Figure 18.8 Printer Configuration in Red Hat's control-panel.

Click the Printer Configuration icon in the control-panel to execute the utility. Figure 18.9 shows the Red Hat Linux Print System Manager window. Notice that the configuration shows a printer installed. Existing entries can be modified or a new entry defined. Three command buttons are located at the bottom of the window. The Edit button enables you to modify an existing printer entry, the Add button enables you to define a new printer entry, and the Delete button removes an existing printer entry.

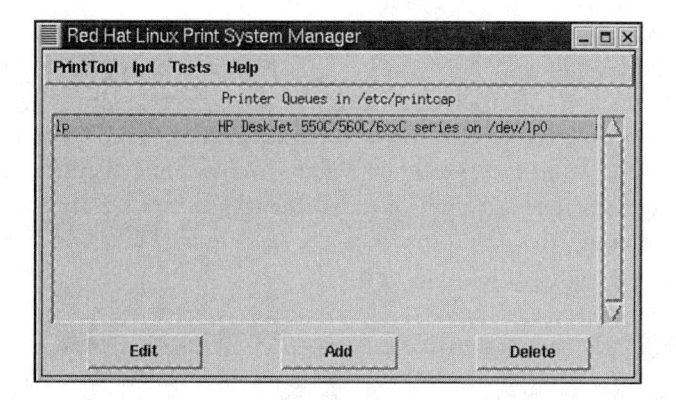

Figure 18.9 Red Hat Linux Print System Manager.

Because we want to add a new printer definition, click the Add button. Figure 18.10 shows the Add a Printer Entry window. On this window, we can define the new printer to be a Local Printer, Remote UNIX Queue, SMB/Windows printer, or a NetWare Printer. For now, click the Local Printer option button and then click OK.

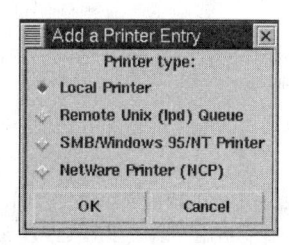

Figure 18.10 Add a Printer Entry dialog window.

Next, the Edit Local Printer Entry window is displayed, as shown in Figure 18.11. Several fields need to be filled. For the Input Filter field, you can click the Select button to bring up a list of printers.

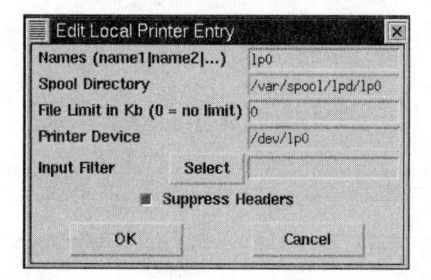

Figure 18.11 Edit Local Printer Entry dialog window.

522 Chapter 18 Print Services

Go ahead and click the Select button located to the right of the Input Filter field. The Configure Filter window is displayed, as shown in Figure 8.12. From this list, you can select various popular printers. Simply scroll down the list of available printers and select your printer. As you select a printer, the other fields on the Configure Filter window change automatically. You can accept the default values or make changes as you see appropriate. After you have completed the settings on the Configure Filter window, click OK. This dismisses the dialog window.

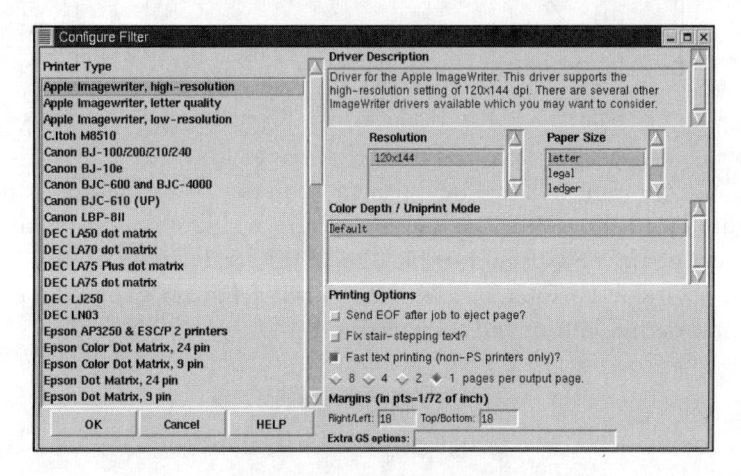

Figure 18.12 Configure Filter dialog window.

Finally, you should see the Red Hat Linux Print System Manager displayed with the new printer entry you have chosen (Figure 8.13).

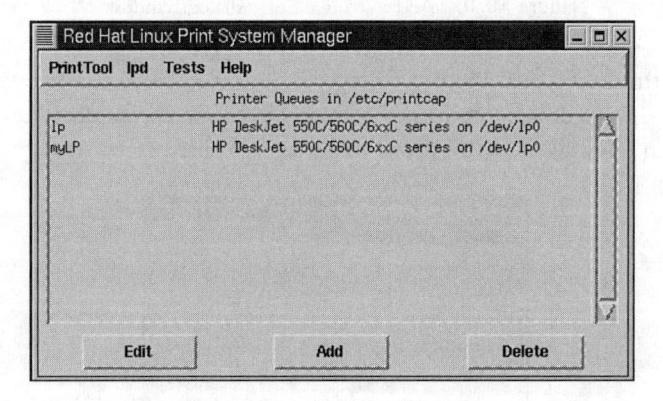

Figure 18.13 Red Hat Linux Print System Manager.

To exit this dialog window, click the Close button on the title bar, or from the menu, select PrintTool and then Quit. Before exiting, you may need to restart the `lpd` daemon. If so, select the `lpd` menu option and then select the Restart option.

Changes are automatically made to the `/etc/printcap` file. The following is the contents of the file. Compare this with the output shown earlier.

```
#
# Please don't edit this file directly unless you know what you are doing!
# Be warned that the control-panel printtool requires a very strict format!
# Look at the printcap(5) man page for more info.
#
# This file can be edited with the printtool in the control-panel.
##PRINTTOOL3## LOCAL cdj550 300x300 letter {} DeskJet550 3 1
lp:\
        :sd=/var/spool/lpd/lp:\
        :mx#0:\
        :sh:\
        :lp=/dev/lp0:\
        :if=/var/spool/lpd/lp/filter:
##PRINTTOOL3## LOCAL cdj550 300x300 letter {} DeskJet550 3 {}
myLP:\
        :sd=/var/spool/lpd/lp0:\
        :mx#0:\
        :sh:\
        :lp=/dev/lp0:\
        :if=/var/spool/lpd/lp0/filter:
#end
```

Notice that the printer entry named `myLP` has been added to the file. The entry is also preceded with a comment stating that the PrintTool utility created the new printer entry.

Summary

We started this chapter with an overview of the Linux print services. We learned that when we send a file to the printer, the file does not immediately go to the printer. Rather, the file is sent to a temporary area known as the print queue to await its turn to be printed.

Various popular printers supported by Linux are shown in Table 18.1. If your printer is not supported, it might be time for an upgrade. Even if your printer is not directly supported, you might be able to choose a different printer that your printer will mimic.

We discussed some items that need to be considered when selecting and configuring a printer. Printer type should be considered. Do you need a dot-matrix, laser, or inkjet printer? Printer language also needs to be considered.

Linux supports both PostScript and PCL-style printers. The PostScript is a more flexible printer, but with this flexibility comes higher costs.

The printer interface is another consideration when configuring a printer. Printers are offered with either a parallel or a serial interface. Some high-end printers provide both interfaces. Parallel cables have a length limit of about 20 feet; beyond this distance, data can be lost on the way to the printer. A serial interface is preferred if the distance from print server to printer is beyond 20 feet.

Next, the print commands and daemons were covered. The `lpc` command is used to start, stop, and otherwise manipulate the print queue. The `lpd` daemon is the spool daemon and controls the printing of files. The `lpq` command is used to list jobs in the print queue. The `lpr` command communicates to the `lpd` command, submitting print jobs. Finally, the `lprm` command is used to remove print jobs from the queue.

The `/etc/printcap` file was covered next. Each line in the file is a printer entry. There should be an entry in the `/etc/printcap` file for each printer on the system. Each entry in the `/etc/printcap` file consists of individual fields describing attributes about the printer and how to operate it. Each field is separated by a colon character.

We closed the chapter with two sections specific to two Linux distributions. First, printer configuration under SuSE Linux was covered using the YaST configuration utility. Finally, we covered printer configuration under Red Hat, using the PrintTool utility.

IV

System Administration

19 The Tools

20 Booting and Shutdown

21 Security

22 Managing Accounts

23 Other Administrative Tasks

19

The Tools

Now there is a chapter title that sounds all-encompassing! What does "The Tools" refer to? Good question. This chapter is about some of the more interesting tools that are used with various Linux distributions. Many of the "generic" tools have been covered in other chapters of this book. Some of the generic tools covered are Samba, Apache, and system administration tools including user management (such as adduser), file management (such as mkdir), process management (such as ps and kill), and printing. Most of those tools are quite commonplace and are fairly well documented in this book and in the public domain.

What we will do here is examine some of the more popular distributions of Linux and the tools they offer. Some of the tools are *distribution-agnostic*—in other words, if we are discussing the StarOffice suite, we do not need to address a specific Linux distribution. But if we want to discuss YaST (SuSE) or Linuxconf (Red Hat) or TurboWMCfg (TurboLinux), the discussion will be vendor-specific.

Overview

It seems like quite an endeavor to try to address the many tools available for different distributions of Linux. Although I would like to talk about *all* the possible tools, I cannot. A whole book would have to be dedicated to that chore. In this chapter, we will discuss only the tools that would be used most often by the average Linux user.

Some books are distribution specific (or vendor specific) and are good if you are staying with one distribution. The truth of the matter is that many Linux users like to experiment with different Linux distributions. This could be because of pure curiosity and interest in researching them, or it could be that you need to evaluate several distributions to find the best fit.

Some people argue that a single-distribution operating system is the best answer to an organization's needs. Some companies would like you to think *their* operating system is the all-encompassing and all-enduring solution. The problem with that belief is that you must (strictly) adhere to *their* standards. You must be satisfied with *their* user interface. You must be satisfied with *their* filesystem. You must be happy with *their*—well, you better be happy with *them* as a company. Many of these companies are just happy to pocket *your* money and continue to do what *they* want.

It doesn't have to be that way—that is a pledge from the world of Linux. You are free to choose the distribution of Linux you want, based on your needs and the features and benefits offered by a particular Linux distribution. Are you unhappy with your Linux vendor and can't get resolution? Fine; switch to another vendor. You say you are dissatisfied with the window manager? Switch to one of several that are available for Linux. I think you get the idea.

We will begin our journey through the tools landscape by investigating some of the more general tools and then moving on to the distribution-specific tools. Then we will address so-called productivity tools—programs that are used for everyday office tasks such as word processing. Follow along as we unravel some of the more popular tools in use today.

Configuration, Maintenance, and Management Tools

This section covers various tools that you can use to configure, maintain, or manage Linux and Linux programs.

Red Hat Package Manager (RPM)

RPM, although considered vendor-specific, has found its way onto the CD-ROMs of many Linux (and UNIX) distributions. RPM is a powerful package manager that is used to build, install, query, uninstall, update, and verify individual software packages. Many Linux vendors have recognized the power of RPM and use it for their distribution. Some vendors furnish a front end to RPM, relieving the user of having to decide which RPM option(s) to use. RPM is open software, distributable under the GNU Public License (GPL).

Here is the command-line usage for RPM:

```
rpm [options]
```

An RPM package consists of an archive of files, plus package information including name, version, and description. The features provided by RPM are many, making software maintenance easier than what is possible with tar/zip packages.

RPM has five basic modes of operation: install, query, uninstall, update, and verify. The next five sections address each of these. Let's see how to become productive with RPM.

Installing an RPM Package

This has to be the most popular mode of operation for RPM. The main reason we use RPM is to install software.

You have probably seen an RPM package filename. Here is a real-world example of an RPM filename:

```
xfree86-doc-3.3.5-3.i386.rpm
```

The filename can be broken down into its individual identifiers. `xfree86` is the software identifier. `-doc-` further identifies the software as containing documentation for XFree86. `3.3.5` designates the version of the software, and `-3` is the software release. The last identifier is `i386`, which identifies the architecture. Other architectures might be `sparc` or `alpha`.

The key to installing an RPM package lies with the letters `ivh`. These letters, as you might guess, are options to the `rpm` command. The following dialog demonstrates how to install the XFree86 package just mentioned:

```
stimpy $ rpm -ivh xfree86-doc-3.3.5-3.i386.rpm
XFree86                     ###############################
stimpy $
```

Upon execution of the `rpm` command, the package name is displayed, and then a series of hash marks (#). The hash marks provide a visual clue, like a progress meter.

A number of errors can appear. If the package already exists, or there are conflicting files or unresolved dependencies, you will see an error message reflecting the problem.

If the package already exists or there are conflicting files, you can force the installation using the `−replacefiles` option to the `rpm` command.

For an unresolved dependency, it is recommended that you install the package that is required. Obviously, the package you want to install requires some other software to run and cannot be found. If you absolutely insist on installing the package, you can force the installation using the `−nodeps` option to the `rpm` command.

Querying with RPM

When you query a package or RPM database, nothing really happens to your system. In other words, nothing is installed, removed, or updated. The intent is to just check out the contents of the package or installed packages. The following usage shows the easiest way to query a package:

```
stimpy $ rpm -q [option / packageName]
```

You can specify an option to the query switch. You can also specify the package name to query. The following dialog demonstrates the query option:

```
stimpy $ rpm -qa
aaa_base-99.11.9-0
aaa_dir-99.11.1-0
aaa_skel-99.10.31-0
at-3.1.8-95
base-99.9.13-11
...
ypserv-1.3.9-4
bind8-8.2.2-41
samba-2.0.6-16
stimpy $
```

This dialog lists the installed packages on the system. Of course, this list does not represent all packages installed. The following dialog demonstrates the results of two different queries (each in bold text) to the bind8 package:

```
stimpy $ rpm -qi bind8
Name        : bind8                   Relocations: (not relocateable)
Version     : 8.2.2                      Vendor: SuSE GmbH, Nuernberg, Germany
Release     : 41                      Build Date: Thu Feb  3 02:51:09 2000
Install date: Fri Feb  4 02:05:39 2000 Build Host: waerden.suse.de
Group       : unsorted                Source RPM: bind8-8.2.2-41.src.rpm
Size        : 2353522                    License: 1989 The Regents of the
                                                  University of California.
Packager    : feedback@suse.de
Summary     : BIND v8 - Name Server (new version)
Description :
The new named daemon with examples.
The support utilities nslookup, dig, dnsquery and host
are found in the package bindutil.
Documentation on setting up a name server can be
found in /usr/doc/packages/bind .
Authors:
----
    ISC Software <bind@isc.org>
    Paul Vixie <vixie@vix.com>
SuSE series: n
stimpy $ rpm -qc bind8
/etc/named.conf
/sbin/init.d/named
```

```
/var/named/127.0.0.zone
/var/named/localhost.zone
/var/named/root.hint
stimpy $
```

The first option displays general package information and the second query displays the files marked as configuration files.

Uninstalling an RPM Package

Uninstalling an RPM package is as simple as installing a package. There is a slight difference, though, because you identify the package name and not the (original) package filename. The following dialog demonstrates the execution of RPM with the uninstall option:

```
stimpy $ rpm -e bind8
...
stimpy $
```

This dialog uninstalls the package from the system. The following dialog demonstrates the use of the —test option. Nothing is removed, but RPM goes through the functional procedure as if to remove the named package. Be sure to use the -vv option to see the output.

```
stimpy $ rpm -e —test -vv bind8
D: opening database mode 0x0 in //var/lib/rpm/
D: will remove files test = 1
D:     file: /var/named/slave action: remove
D:     file: /var/named/root.hint action: remove
D:     file: /var/named/localhost.zone action: remove
D:     file: /var/named/127.0.0.zone action: remove
D:     file: /var/named action: skip
D:     file: /var/adm/fillup-templates/rc.config.bind action: remove
...
D:     file: /sbin/init.d/rc2.d/S11named action: remove
D:     file: /sbin/init.d/rc2.d/K34named action: remove
D:     file: /sbin/init.d/named action: remove
D:     file: /etc/named.conf action: remove
D: removing database entry
stimpy $
```

You might receive a dependency error. This will occur if some other package on the system depends on the package you want to remove. If you want to remove the package anyway, simply supply the —nodeps option.

Updating an RPM Package

There are two ways to update a package on your system: an *upgrade* and a *freshen*. An upgrade installs a package; a freshen doesn't install a package if the package doesn't currently exist.

The following dialog demonstrates an upgrade and a freshen. The commands are in bold:

```
stimpy $ rpm -Uvh xfree86-doc-3.3.5-3.i386.rpm
XFree86                ###############################
stimpy $ rpm -Fvh xfree86-doc-3.3.5-3.i386.rpm
XFree86                ###############################
stimpy $
```

The difference between the invocations, as you can see, is in the options used. To upgrade, -Uvh is used. The option -Fvh is used to freshen a package. If you want to freshen a group of packages in one shot, simply issue the rpm command like this:

```
stimpy $ rpm -Fvh *.rpm
```

This allows you go about your business while RPM takes care of freshening multiple packages.

Verifying an RPM Package

If you need to compare the contents of a package with what is installed, use the verify feature of RPM. You can verify one or more individual files within a package, check the complete package, or check all installed packages. The following dialog demonstrates the use of each invocation:

```
stimpy $ rpm -Vf /usr/bin/addr
...
stimpy $rpm -Va
...
stimpy $rpm -Vp xfree86-doc-3.3.5-3.i386.rpm
...
stimpy $
```

The first invocation of RPM verifies the file named /usr/bin/addr. To further the example, the following dialog is presented. The switch -vv is added to show more verbose output from the rpm command.

```
stimpy $ rpm -vv -Vf /usr/bin/addr
D: opening database mode 0x0 in //var/lib/rpm/
D: record number 6660248
D: dependencies: looking for bindutil
D: dependencies: looking for /bin/sh
D: dependencies: looking for /bin/sh
D: dependencies: looking for ld-linux.so.2
D: dependencies: looking for libc.so.6
D: dependencies: looking for libc.so.6(GLIBC_2.0)
D: dependencies: looking for libc.so.6(GLIBC_2.1)
D: dependencies: looking for bind
stimpy $
```

The second execution verifies all installed packages on the system. The following dialog shows more detail for this execution (without showing every package installed):

```
stimpy $ rpm -Va
S.5....T c /etc/modules.conf
S.5....T c /etc/motd
.M...... c /etc/permissions
.M...... c /etc/permissions.easy
.M...... c /etc/permissions.paranoid
.M...... c /etc/permissions.secure
...
.......T   /usr/doc/packages/alsa/README.alsaconf
.......T   /usr/doc/packages/alsa/README.driver
.......T   /usr/doc/packages/alsa/SOUNDCARDS
.......T   /usr/doc/packages/alsa/TODO.driver
S.5....T c /etc/smb.conf
stimpy $
```

With the "verify all" option, expect the `rpm` command to run quite a while, especially if you have a legion of installed packages.

The third invocation verifies the installed package with the package file. The following dialog shows more detail:

```
stimpy $ rpm -vv -Vp ./root/DOWNLOADs/bind8.rpm
D: opening database mode 0x0 in //var/lib/rpm/
D: New Header signature
D: Signature size: 68
D: Signature pad : 4
D: sigsize        : 72
D: Header + Archive: 1046019
D: expected size   : 1046019
D: dependencies: looking for bindutil
D: dependencies: looking for /bin/sh
D: dependencies: looking for /bin/sh
D: dependencies: looking for ld-linux.so.2
D: dependencies: looking for libc.so.6
D: dependencies: looking for libc.so.6(GLIBC_2.0)
D: dependencies: looking for libc.so.6(GLIBC_2.1)
D: dependencies: looking for bind
stimpy $
```

The following shows the output from RPM when discrepancies are discovered:

```
stimpy $ rpm -Vp samba.rpm
S.5....T c /etc/smb.conf
stimpy $
```

RPM will be quiet (nothing will be output) if all is verified. If there are discrepancies, RPM will let you know, as it did in the previous dialog. What RPM has told us is that the `/etc/smb.conf` file is a configuration file (c) and that the size, MD5 checksum, and file modification time have failed verification. This stands to reason, because the file has been modified since the package was installed.

The following is a list of identifiers that signify a specific test:

- 5: MD5 checksum
- S: File size
- L: Symbolic link
- T: File modification time
- D: Device
- U: User
- G: Group
- M: Mode (includes permissions and file type)

The output is in the form of a string of eight characters. If the character c is present, it identifies the file as a configuration file. Finally, the filename is printed. A single . (period) means that the test passed. The following is the list of identifying characters for each test:

```
stimpy $ rpm -Va
S.5....T c /etc/modules.conf
S.5....T c /etc/motd
.M...... c /etc/permissions
.M...... c /etc/permissions.easy
.M...... c /etc/permissions.paranoid
.M...... c /etc/permissions.secure
.......T   /usr/doc/packages/aaa_base/fillup.txt
.......T   /usr/doc/support/suppengl.txt
.......T   /usr/doc/support/suppform.txt
.M......   /sbin/init.d
.M......   /sbin/init.d/boot.d
.M......   /sbin/init.d/rc0.d
.M......   /sbin/init.d/rc1.d
.M......   /sbin/init.d/rc2.d
.M......   /sbin/init.d/rc3.d
.M......   /sbin/init.d/rc6.d
.M......   /sbin/init.d/rcS.d
....L...   /usr/doc
missing    /var/catman
.....U..   /var/named
missing    /var/tmp/vi.recover
.......T   /usr/doc/packages/bash/COMPAT
.......T   /usr/doc/packages/bash/FAQ
.......T   /usr/doc/packages/bash/INTRO
.......T   /usr/doc/packages/bash/NEWS
.......T   /usr/doc/packages/bash/bashref.html
...
stimpy $
```

This dialog demonstrates the verification of all packages on the system. The output was truncated because the list grew to 4,482 lines.

Graphical RPM: Gnome-RPM

Gnome-RPM provides a graphical interface to the RPM system for those running the X Windows system. Basically, everything you can do with command-line RPM, you can do with Gnome-RPM. As the name suggests, Gnome-RPM integrates with the GNOME desktop environment.

The program is a full-featured graphical application, replete with pull-down menus, a toolbar, a tree view window, and a display window. Figure 19.1 shows Gnome-RPM after it is invoked from the desktop environment.

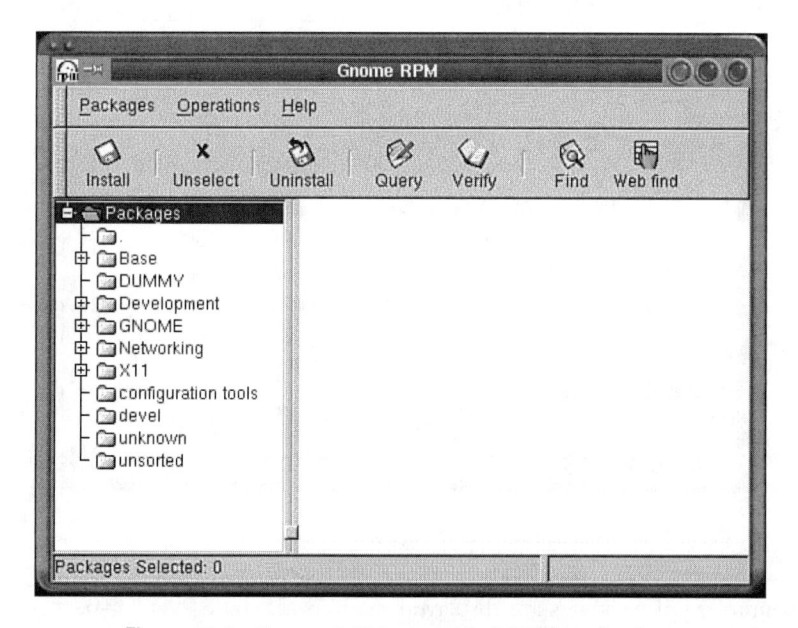

Figure 19.1 Gnome-RPM, a graphical RPM application.

If you are familiar with GNOME, you probably noticed that Figure 19.1 does not visually represent a GNOME application. To be fair, the application is running under the KDE desktop environment on SuSE 6.3 Linux. Additionally, the Photon theme is running.

Under the Packages menu, the options available are Query, Uninstall, Verify, and Create Desktop Entry. Under the Operations menu, the available options are Find, Web Find, Install, and Preferences. Toolbar icons match most of the menu options listed.

536 Chapter 19 The Tools

The basic operation of Gnome-RPM is straightforward. You browse around and select a package (or packages), and then you apply one of the commands using the menus or toolbar.

The Web find option is unique in that it offers you the chance to search the Internet for packages you want to install or update.

The interface for Gnome-RPM should be familiar to you. You select from categories of packages in the tree view pane, and then select packages that appear in the display pane (on the right side). Figure 19.2 shows the unsorted category selected and the corresponding packages in the right pane.

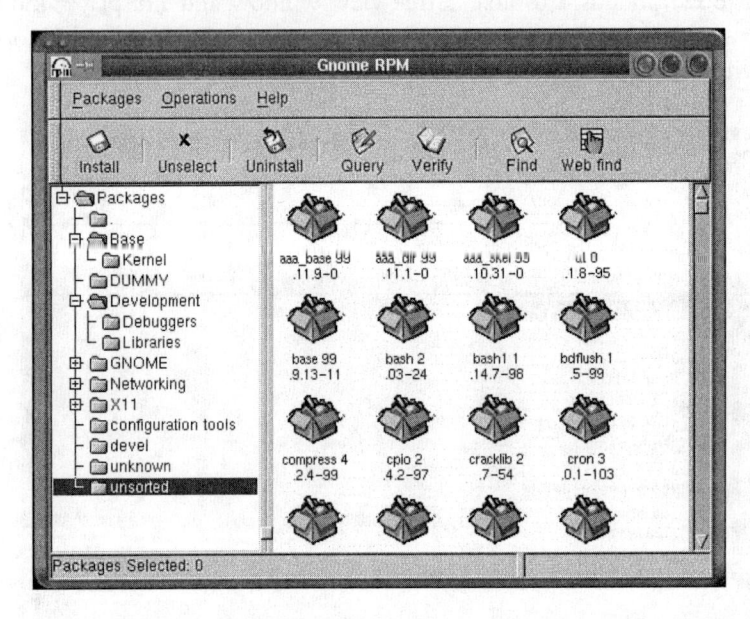

Figure 19.2 Gnome-RPM showing package icons in the display panel.

A number of packages are displayed, such as aaa_base.99.11.9-0, aaa_dir.99.11.1-0, aaa_skel.99.10.31-0, and so on.

As mentioned previously, you select a package and then apply the desired operation. Figure 19.3 shows the Query window after the modules-2.3.6-3 package was selected from the Kernel subcategory under the Base category (in the tree view).

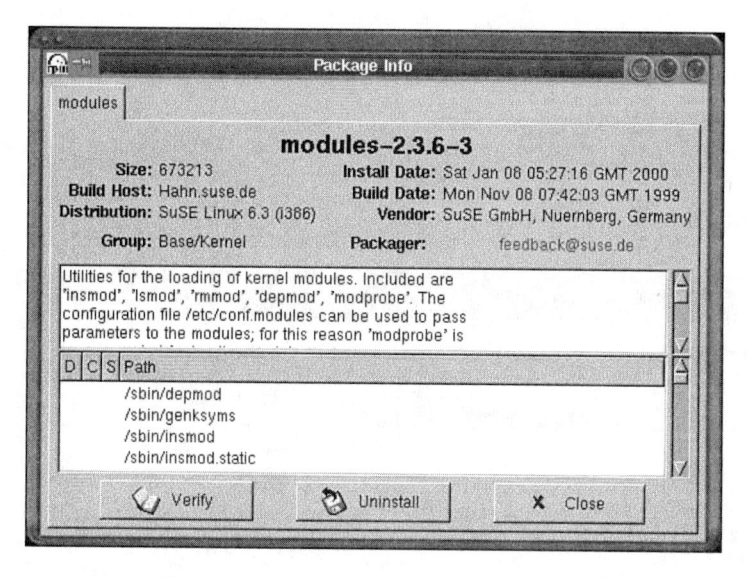

Configuration, Maintenance, and Management Tools 537

Figure 19.3 Gnome-RPM Query window.

The Query window shows vital information about the package, including a scrollable text area displaying the package description and a second scrollable text area showing the contents of the package. This window also has command buttons for Verify, Uninstall, and Close.

The Verify window, shown in Figure 19.4, shows the result of package verification. For every problem found, a message is displayed in the columnar list area.

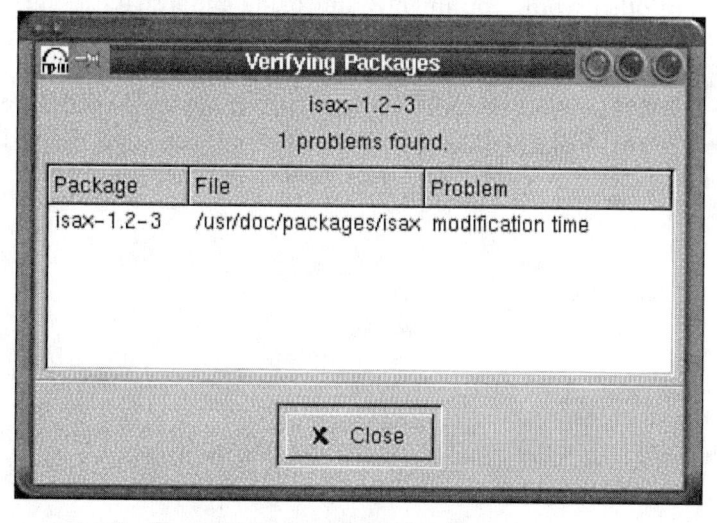

Figure 19.4 Gnome-RPM Verify window.

538 Chapter 19 The Tools

Notice that a verification failed concerning the modification time for the /usr/doc/packages/isax/rc.sax file in the isax-1.2-3 package, which is in the configuration category.

If you want to add a new package to Gnome-RPM, select the Install option from the Operations menu. You see the Install window, as shown in Figure 19.5.

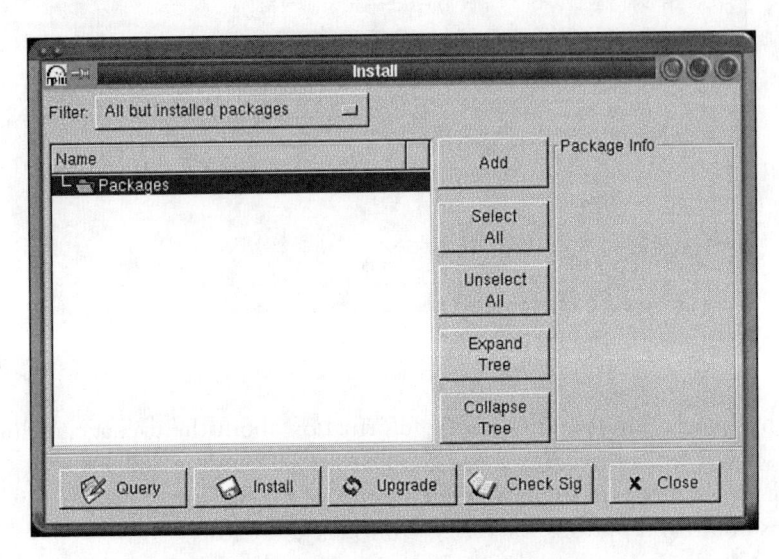

Figure 19.5 Gnome-RPM Install (Add/Install) window.

The intent here is to add new packages that are coming from the "outside" world. In other words, you might want to add and install packages from a CD-ROM, or maybe you downloaded some packages from the Internet. Using the Install window allows you to add packages to the database and then install them. Let's assume that we want to add and install the Samba package. First, click the Add button in the Install window. The Add Packages window appears, as shown in Figure 19.6.

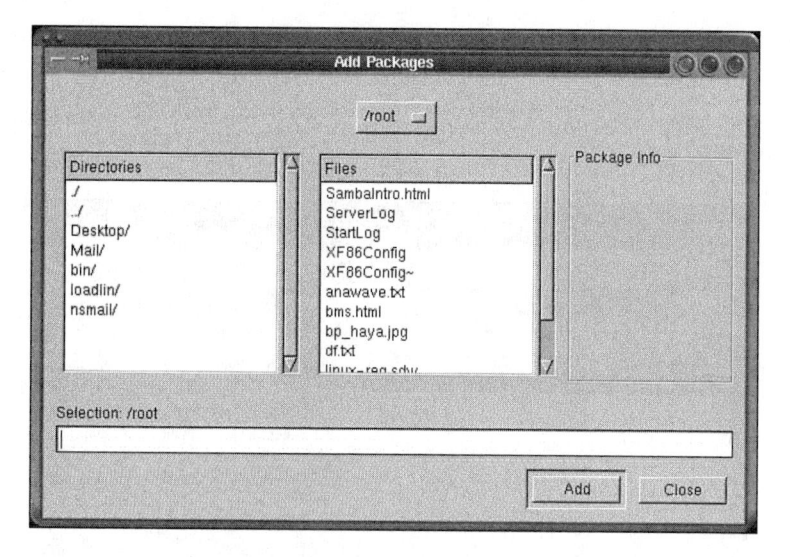

Configuration, Maintenance, and Management Tools 539

Figure 19.6 Gnome-RPM Add Packages window.

Notice that there are a number of ways to identify a package with this window. There is a tree view pane on the extreme left, showing the directory tree. You use this pane, along with the selection pane to the right of the tree view pane. There is a text box at the bottom of the window, allowing you to type the pathname manually. In Figure 19.7, the Samba package is selected, and the Add button has been clicked.

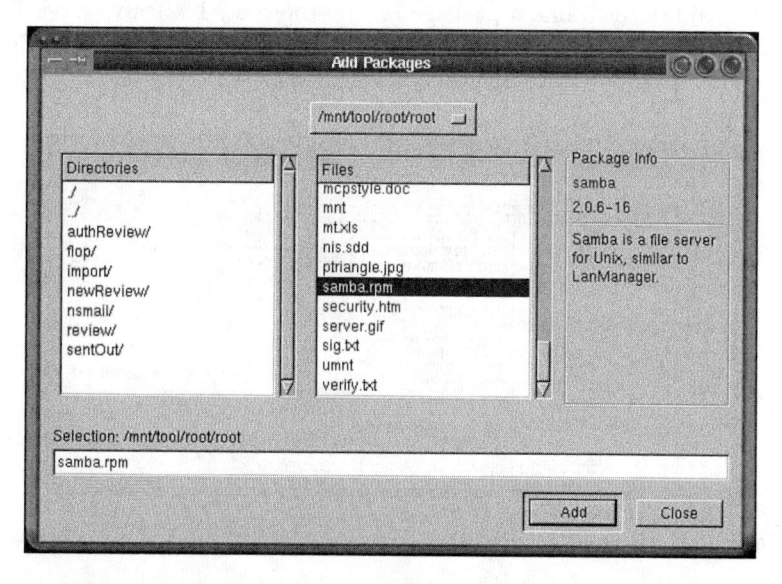

Figure 19.7 Gnome-RPM Add Packages window with Samba selected.

540 Chapter 19 The Tools

Next, click the Close button. Focus is returned to the Install window. At this point, you might not see the package, so select All Packages from the Filter combo box. Figure 19.8 shows the Samba package added to the unsorted category.

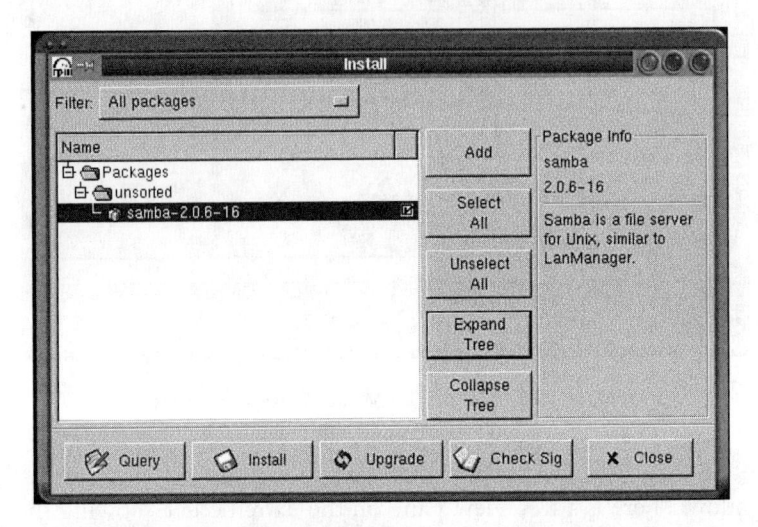

Figure 19.8 Gnome-RPM Install window with Samba selected.

From here, you can check the signature, perform a query, upgrade or install the package, or do nothing and close the window.

Do you need to find a package on the Internet? The easy way is to select the Web Find button or menu option. Figure 19.9 shows the Rpmfind window after the RPM list was downloaded.

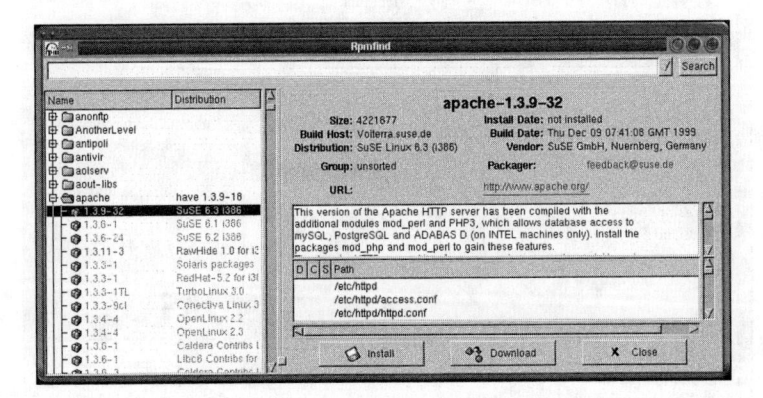

Figure 19.9 Gnome-RPM Rpmfind window with Apache for SuSE 6.3 selected.

At this point, you can decide to download and install the package (or packages) or close the window.

Armed with the well-respected RPM and Gnome-RPM package manager applications, you will discover that installing, updating, verifying, and removing packages is a breeze. Here's one last note about installing software packages under Linux: The best part is that you do not have to reboot the system in order to use the software.

Using YaST Under SuSE (6.3)

Yet another Setup Tool (YaST) is designed to be, well, another setup tool. YaST improves the installation process and helps relieve the user of some heartache. We will be looking at the YaST that is shipped in version 6.3 of SuSE Linux.

Before we get started, Table 19.1 describes the options to YaST.

Table 19.1 **Options for YaST**

Option	Description
-m	Does not use colors.
-v	Prints the compile time for YaST and exits.
-h	Prints this info.
—help	Prints this info.
-t`Terminal`	Uses the identified `Terminal` instead of stdout.
-d`Debug`	Writes debug output to the identified `Debug`.
—nomenu	Does not go into the main menu loop.
—plain	Removes the `/var/lib/YaST/install.inf` file before startup.
—version	Prints the YaST version number and exits.
—autoexit	Exits automatically after the end of the first screen.
—mask `name`	Executes the screen `name` automatically. Possible values for `name` are `help`, `install`, `update`, `readme`, `copyright`, `language`, `keymap`, `medium`, `fdisk`, `filesys`, `login`, `user`, `group`, `backup`, `consolefont`, `timezone`, `xfree`, `gpm`, `security`, `rcconfig`, `mouse`, `modem`, `cdrom`, `printer`, `isdn-hw`, `scanner`, `netcard`, `kernel`, `bootdisk`, `rescue`, `lilo`, `network`, `name`, `services`, `nameserver`, `ypclient`, `sendmail`, `netprinter`, `isdn-num`, `ppp`, `live-con`, and `live-discon`.

Chapter 19 The Tools

I would like to mention one other thing. This section deals with YaST-1, not Yast-2. For one thing, Yast-2 had some problems with the shipping product, so I chose to discuss YaST-1, because it is stable and the "least common denominator" of the two tools. Oddly enough, too, is the fact that I have more control over setup using YaST-1. Let's start with a screen shot of the top-level menu, shown in Figure 19.10.

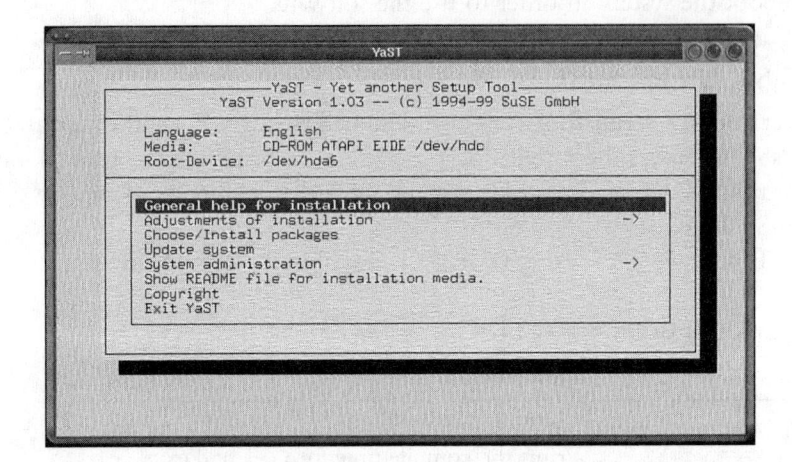

Figure 19.10 YaST-1 at the top-level menu.

Some of the menu options are just one-time items, such as General Help for Installation, Copyright, and Show README File for Installation Media. Let's jump right into the first (real) menu option, Adjustments of Installation. Figure 19.11 shows the resulting menu.

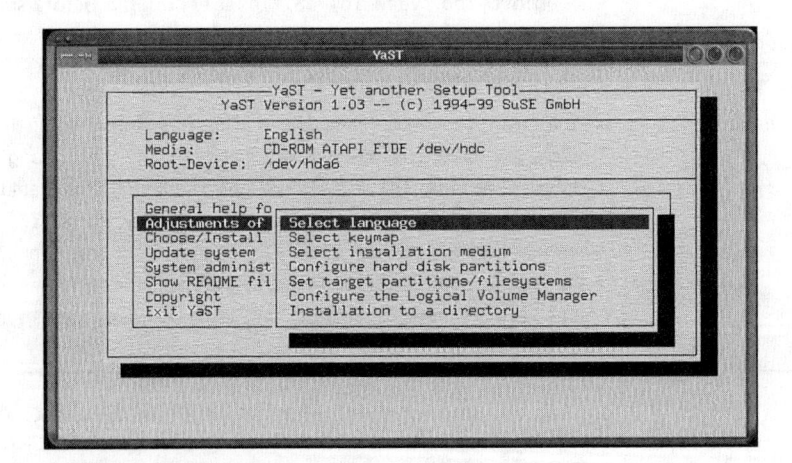

Figure 19.11 YaST-1 at the Adjustments of Installation pop-up menu.

Configuration, Maintenance, and Management Tools 543

You can perform a number of operations here. You can set your language, such as English or Russian, using the Select Language option.

The Select Keymap option allows you to choose from among different keyboard types, such as QWERTY, DVORAK, AMIGA, and others. You can also select the keyboard's language.

The Select Installation Medium menu option allows you to select the origin of the installation medium. The options available are installation via NFS or from a CD-ROM, directory, hard drive partition, or FTP site.

The Configure Hard Disk Partitions option lets you partition one or more hard drives. You can do a lot with this tool. It is easy to use and gets the job done. Figure 19.12 shows this tool in action. The second hard drive is currently selected, waiting to be massaged.

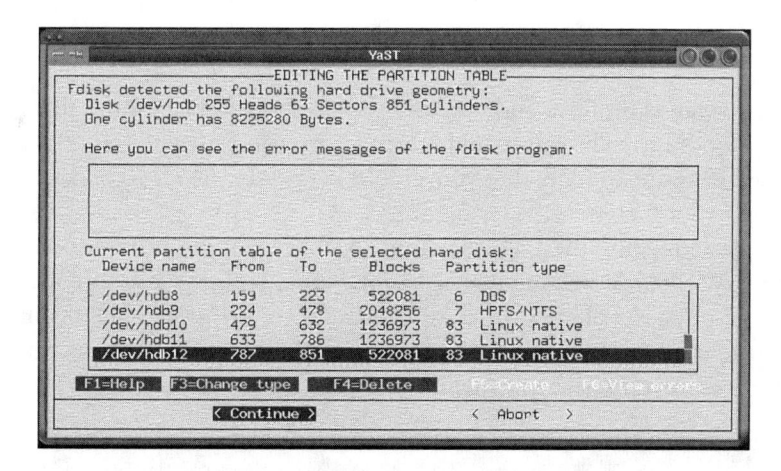

Figure 19.12 Editing the Partition Table screen.

Personally, I prefer a tool that is focused on the partitioning challenge. PartitionMagic (currently 5.0) from PowerQuest is a top choice and has been around longer than most other tools in its class. Other honorable mentions are Partition Commander from V Communications and Quarterdeck's Partition-It. You can go to http://www.pcmag.com to read the reviews and decide which tool you prefer.

The next menu option is Set Target Partitions/Filesystems. It allows you to set mount points, select an inode density, format a partition, and so on. Figure 19.13 shows the Creating Filesystems screen.

544 Chapter 19 The Tools

Figure 19.13 Creating Filesystems.

This screen is intuitive and easy to use. You should create more than one partition. Normally, you would create a partition for root, /usr, /tmp, and /var. Be aware, though, that you should keep /bin, /dev, /etc, /lib, and /sbin on the root filesystem.

The Configure the Logical Volume Manager option is used to set up the LVM (logical volume manager) for Linux. It allows you to concatenate several physical volumes (such as hard disks) to a *volume group,* forming a storage pool (such as a virtual disk). Figure 19.14 shows the screen that is displayed if you select this menu option.

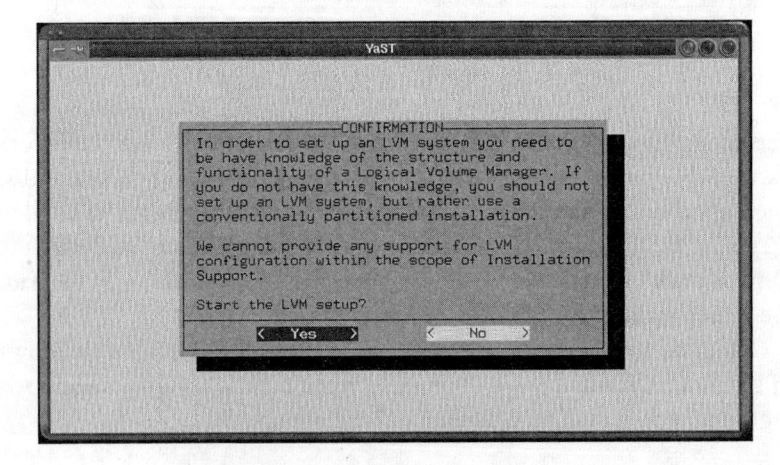

Figure 19.14 LVM Confirmation screen.

You should read the warning *very* carefully. This option is not detailed, for obvious reasons.

The last option on the current submenu is Installation to a Directory. It is used to install the whole Linux system into a directory. Why would you want to do this? You might need to update another machine using NFS. This method provides an easy and painless way to update other machines.

You can press the Esc key to return to the top-level menu. The next option of interest is System administration. This menu has 15 choices, as shown in Figure 19.15.

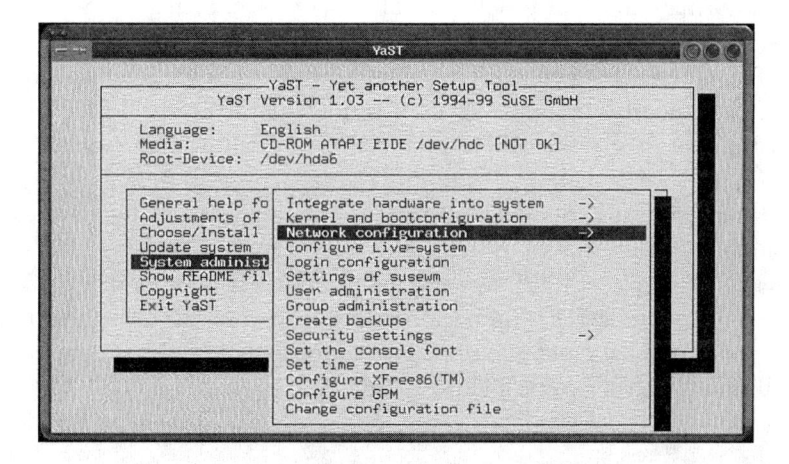

Figure 19.15 System Administration submenu.

Selecting the Integrate Hardware into System option takes you to another menu. Here, you can modify settings for the mouse, modem, CD-ROM, printers, ISDN hardware, scanner, and networking device.

The next menu option, Kernel and Bootconfiguration, provides you with three options. You can select a boot kernel, create a rescue disk, or configure LILO. These options are fairly straightforward—most of them were set during installation. Use these if you have an update kernel or your system has changed and you want to update your rescue disk. You *do* have a rescue disk, right?

Next on the menu list is Network Configuration. Be cautious with the Configure Network Services option. Even if you choose to use the Esc key to back out, you will be carried through all the choices, and the SuSE configuration scripts will be executed. Some of the options prompted for here are Start inetd?, Start portmapper?, and Start NFS server?, among others. You should also be cautious about wandering off into the Configuration Nameserver menu option. You could end up overwriting your DNS configuration files with empty data. If you are connected to the Internet at the time, you will begin getting errors about unresolved addresses. I know, because it happened to me!

The next menu option is Configure YP Client. The SuSE people really should change this to NIS (Network Information System). The whole reason behind the name change is because "Yellow Pages" is a registered trademark. This option lets you set up an NIS client, allowing you to access NIS map file information. Refer to Chapter 11, "Network Information Service (NIS)," for more information.

The Configure Sendmail Option is used to configure sendmail, which is an electronic mail transport agent. It is not supposed to be a user interface for Internet mail. sendmail's responsibility is to deliver preformatted email messages.

If you are using ISDN, Configure ISDN Parameters is the place to go if you need to alter the ISDN settings.

The Configure a PPP Network menu option is worth a trip too because many people utilize dial-up networking. When you select this menu option, the SuSE WvDial Configuration tool is executed, and you are presented with the screen shown in Figure 19.16.

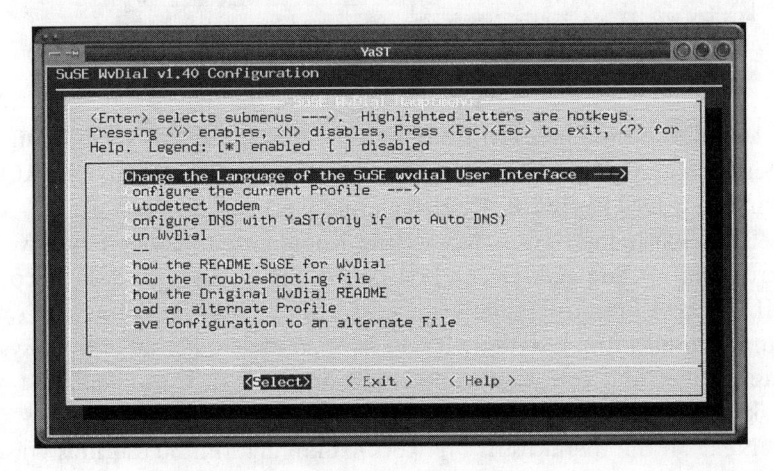

Figure 19.16 SuSE WvDial Configuration screen.

A number of options are available on this screen. Be sure that you are not currently online before continuing with this tool. The most important option here is the Configure the Current Profile menu option. Selecting this choice offers up the Profile screen, as shown in Figure 19.17.

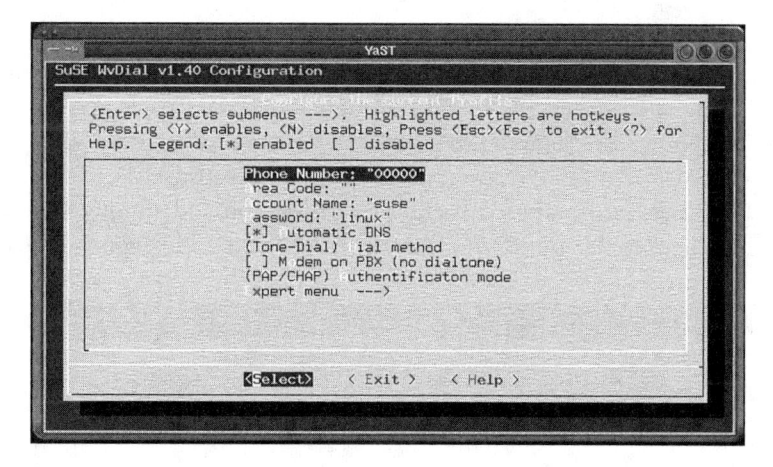

Figure 19.17 SuSE WvDial Profile screen.

At this screen, you simply supply the ISP's phone number, your account name, and password. You can also specify whether automatic DNS is enabled, the dial method, and the authentication mode. Automatic DNS must be supported by your ISP. If it isn't, you should obtain the DNS server configuration and set it with YaST. When you have completed the required entries, select the Exit option. You see a "Do you wish to save ..." screen. If you want to commit your changes, select Yes; otherwise, select No.

If you want to add a remote printer, select the Administer Remote Printers menu option. These are printers that exist remotely from your machine. You will have to supply a server and printer name.

If you want to add a remote printer using Samba, select the Administer Remote Printers menu option. On the APSFilter For Samba screen, you must supply the printer type, name, paper format, and DPI settings. Additionally, you must provide the Samba server name, the printer service, a username, and finally a password. Refer to Chapter 15, "Samba: Merging Linux and Windows," for more information on Samba. Press Esc to return to the previous menu.

Next on the menu list is Configure Live-System, allowing you to integrate a live filesystem from a CD-ROM or disconnect from one. Doing this allows you to use the programs directly from a CD-ROM. You do not have to install the packages to your hard disk partition(s). If you mount the live filesystem, you must keep the CD-ROM in the drive at all times. Note that although disk space is conserved, performance will be slower.

The next menu option is Settings of susewm. This option allows you to set up the default window manager and the configuration files required by the window managers. If you add or remove software packages, you come here to update the menus. Once you have set everything the way you want, select the <Continue> option; otherwise, select <Abort>.

The User Administration menu option lets you add, modify, and remove users. Selecting this option displays the screen shown in Figure 19.18.

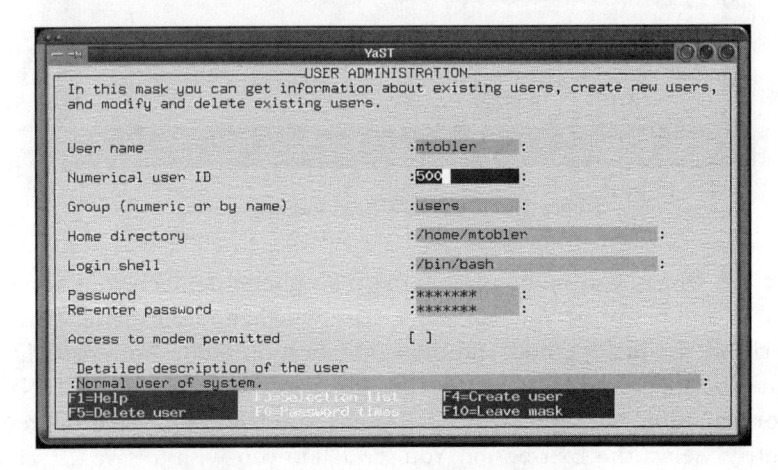

Figure 19.18 User Administration screen.

As you can see, a new user is being added to the system. All the pertinent information is on the screen; the next step is to press the F4 key to create the user. A processing window pops up momentarily as the user information is added to the system. The user information remains on the screen; you need to press the F10 key to leave the screen and return to the menu.

The Group Administration menu option permits you to add, modify, or delete group information. This is very similar to adding users.

Next on the list is the Create Backups menu option, which allows you to back up all or a portion of your system. Figure 19.19 shows the screen that is displayed.

This greatly reduces the fatigue experienced from doing backups at the command line. To add a directory, press the + key. To remove a directory, press the - key. When you are satisfied with the selections, press the F10 key to continue with the process.

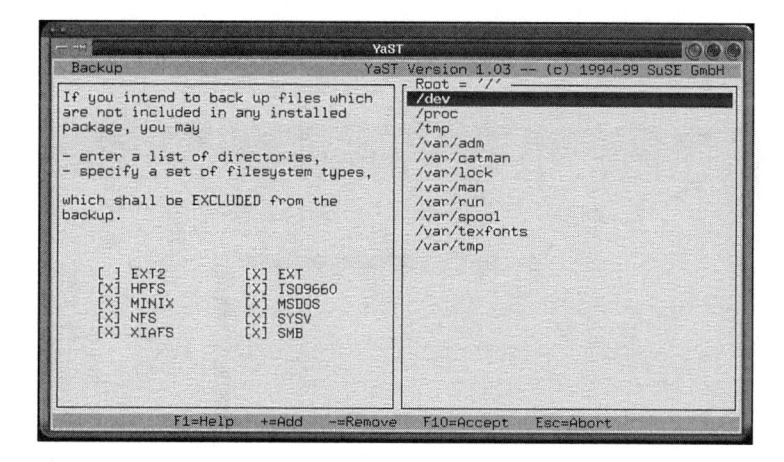

Figure 19.19 Backup screen.

As we progress down the menu options, we come to the Security Settings option. Two options are available: General Information on Security and Configuration of the /etc/login.defs File. In the general security screen, you can control the level of system security. For the /etc/login.defs configuration screen, you set the login failed attempts, password expiration, and group ID information, among others.

You can set the default console font using the Set the Console Font menu option. To set the time zone information, select the Set Time Zone menu option.

The Configure XFree86 menu option permits you to configure your XFree86 Windows system. All this menu option does is start the xf86config command-line script. Running YaST just to execute this is redundant and time consuming.

The Configure GPM menu option allows you to determine whether gpm is executed at boot time or not. gpm permits you to use the mouse to cut and paste text among virtual consoles.

Change Configuration File is the last menu option on this submenu. This option allows you to set the environment variables that are used to configure a SuSE Linux system. These environment variables are found in the /etc/rc.config file. When the SuSE system configuration scripts are executed, this file is parsed, and the settings there determine which configuration options to employ.

Chapter 19 The Tools

Let's return to the top-level menu. The Choose/Install Packages menu option is our last endeavor within YaST (see Figure 19.20).

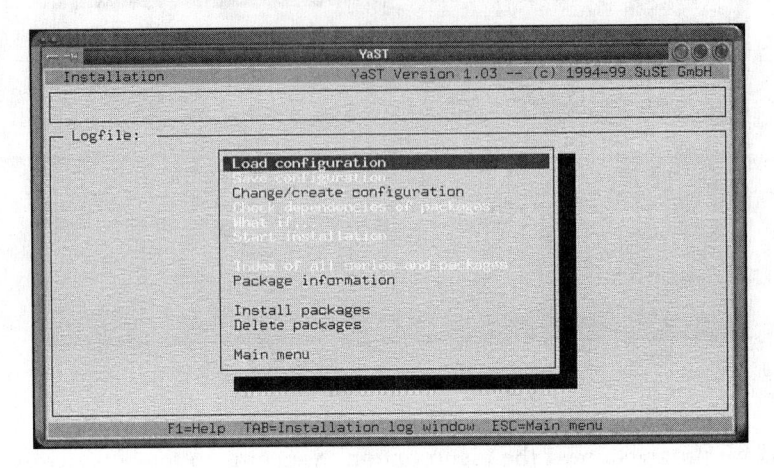

Figure 19.20 YaST Choose/Install packages screen.

A number of menu options are available on this screen; some might be disabled. The Install Packages menu option provides you with a visual interface for installing packages on the system. Selecting this option displays the screen shown in Figure 19.21.

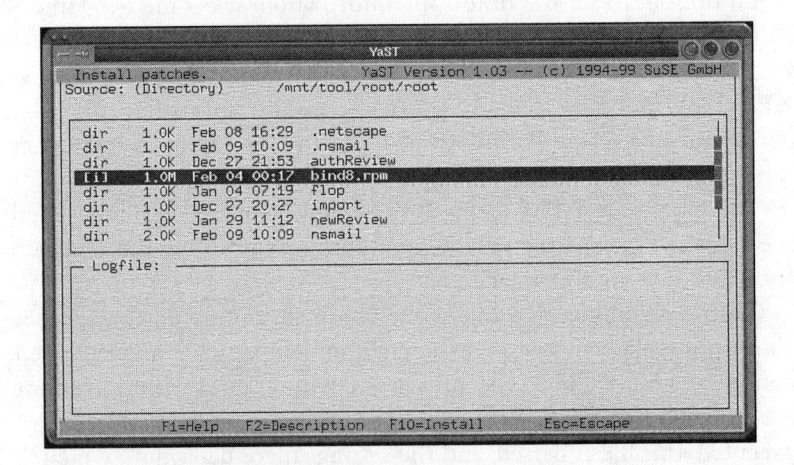

Figure 19.21 Install Patches screen.

The browse method selected was directory; notice that a directory path is selected. In the display pane, you see a number of entries, mostly directories. The currently selected item, bind8.rpm, shows its status as installed. Pressing the Spacebar toggles this entry from installed to upgrade. To continue with the installation, press the F10 key.

To delete a package that is currently installed, select the Delete Packages menu option. Scroll through the list, using the Spacebar to select packages to be deleted. When you have completed the selections, press the F10 key to remove the software packages.

The Change/Create Configuration option allows you to select packages to be added, updated, or removed from the system. The packages are grouped into functional categories such as networking and games, among many others. Be sure you have identified the source medium for the installation. For example, if you're installing from a CD-ROM, be sure you have identified it and that the CD-ROM medium is in the drive before continuing.

Running Linuxconf Under Red Hat 6.1

Linuxconf is a graphical, interactive tool used to perform various maintenance activities, plus it dynamically activates any changes so that those changes are immediately realized. So, Linuxconf provides two benefits to its user: It helps you properly configure the item at hand, and it writes and activates the changes immediately.

Let's start with a screen shot of Linuxconf after startup (see Figure 19.22).

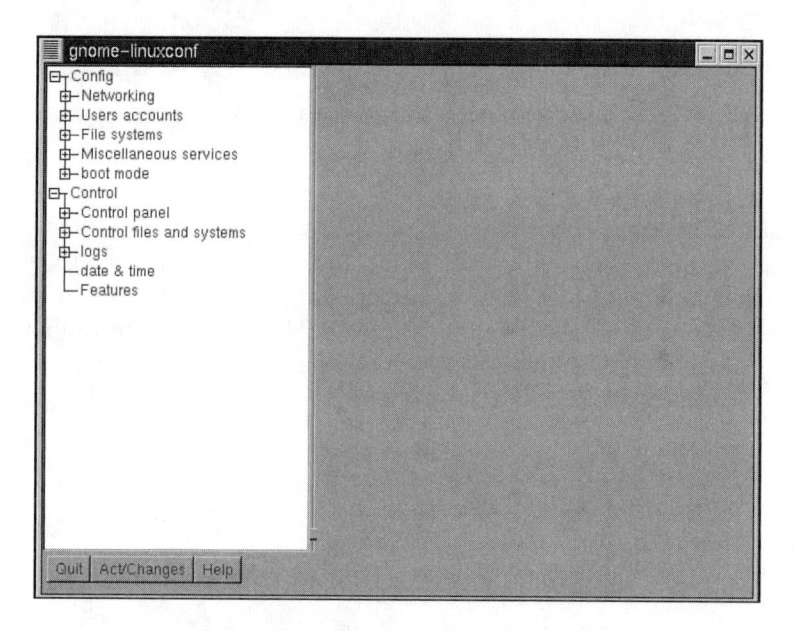

Figure 19.22 Linuxconf upon execution.

Notice that Linuxconf has two top-level categories, and within those categories are various topics. You see categories named Config and Control. Within the Config tree, the topics are Networking, Users Accounts, File Systems, Miscellaneous Services, and Boot Mode. Within the Control tree, the topics are Control Panel, Control Files and Systems, Logs, Date & Time, and Features. Each of these topics, with the exception of Date & Time and Features, can be expanded to reveal subtopics. As an example, we will open the File systems topic and then select the Access Local Drive subtopic. Figure 19.23 shows the Local Volume tab page.

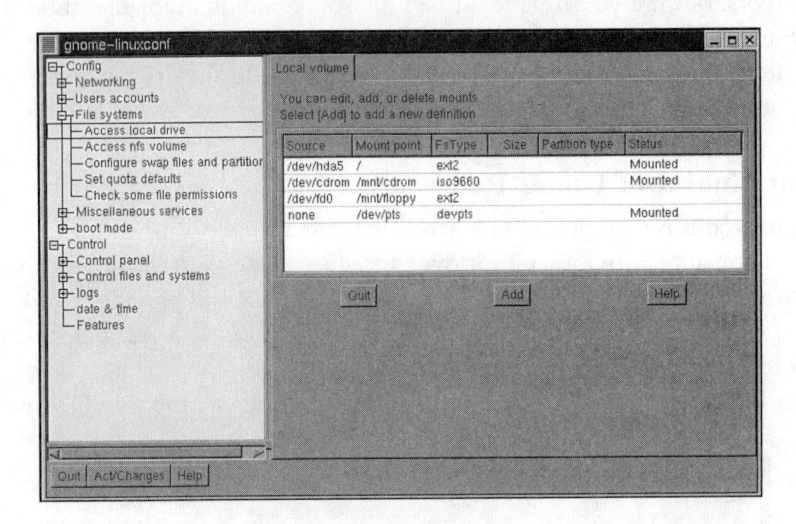

Figure 19.23 Local Volume tab.

On the Local Volume tab, you can add, delete, and edit mount points. As you can see, the status of the mount point is given, in addition to the partition type, size, mount point, filesystem type, and source. If you need to create a new mount, you click the Add button. This takes you to the Volume Specification tab page, shown in Figure 19.24, which consists of four tab pages named Base, Options, Dos options, and Misc.

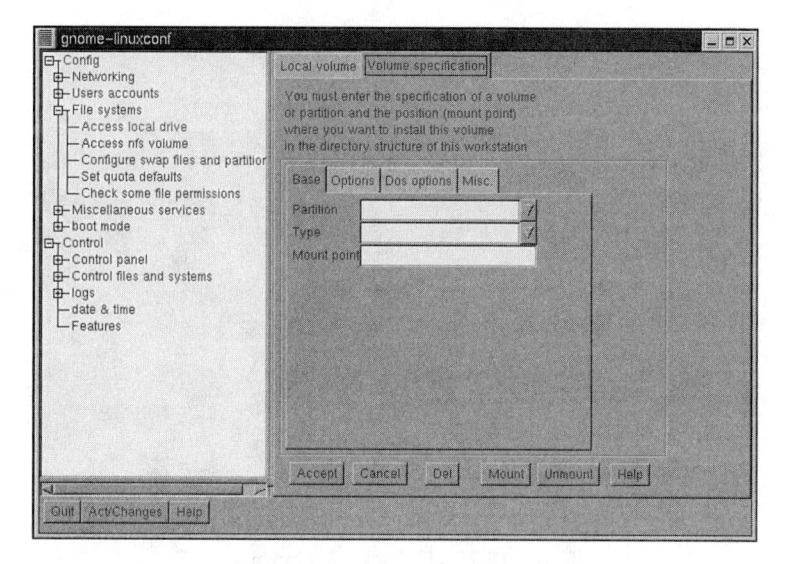

Figure 19.24 Volume Specification tab.

Notice the Partition combo box on the Base tab. It would be nice if Linuxconf could fill that combo box with valid partitions. Linux, when booting up, detects all partitions that exist on the computer; Linuxconf could derive this information and make the partitions available for the choosing. It might even be able to make a best guess as to the filesystem type.

The next option we will examine is the Networking topic. There are three subtopics to choose from: Client Tasks, Server Tasks, and Misc. Each of these subtopics has a tree that can be expanded further. Figure 19.25 shows the Networking subtopic tree expanded.

554 Chapter 19 The Tools

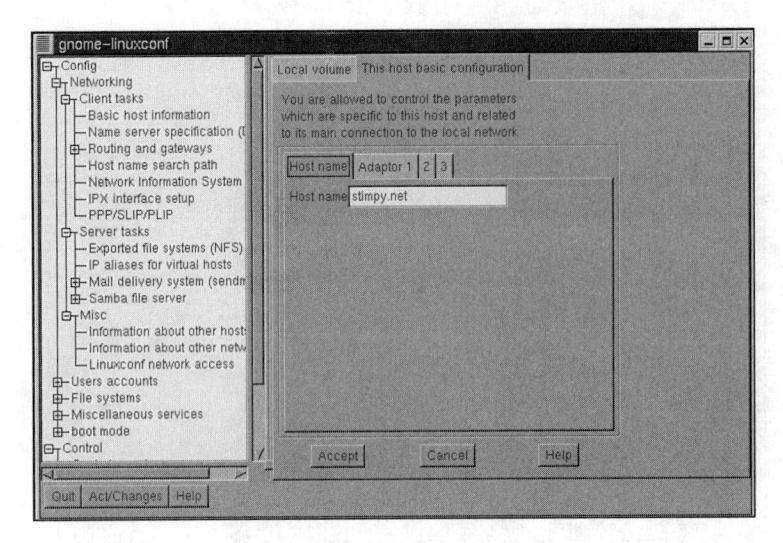

Figure 19.25 Networking branch.

Here, the Client tasks topic tree is expanded and the Basic Host Information subtopic is selected. Notice that this page consists of four tabs: Host Name, Adapter 1, 2, and 3. Each tab page maintains information specific to the topic tab. On each tab, you can view and change (if applicable) the data on the tab page. After you have made the appropriate changes, be sure to click the Accept button.

In the previous section on SuSE's YaST tool, we showed the procedure to set up PPP dial-up configuration. To provide some contrast, we will follow the same procedure using Linuxconf.

To get to the PPP dial-up configuration, open the Networking topic and then the Client Tasks subtopic. Finally, click the PPP/SLIP/PLIP subtopic. Figure 19.26 shows the result of these selections.

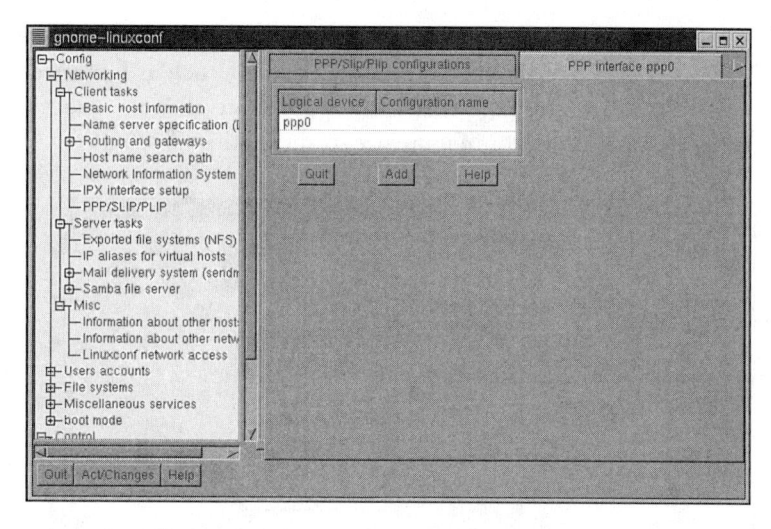

Configuration, Maintenance, and Management Tools   555

Figure 19.26   PPP/Slip/Plip Configurations tab.

This tab page shows the available devices for use with PPP/SLIP/PLIP—specifically, the ppp0 device is shown. To continue the configuration, click the device you want. If there is no device, click the Add button. Figure 19.27 shows the result of selecting the ppp0 entry.

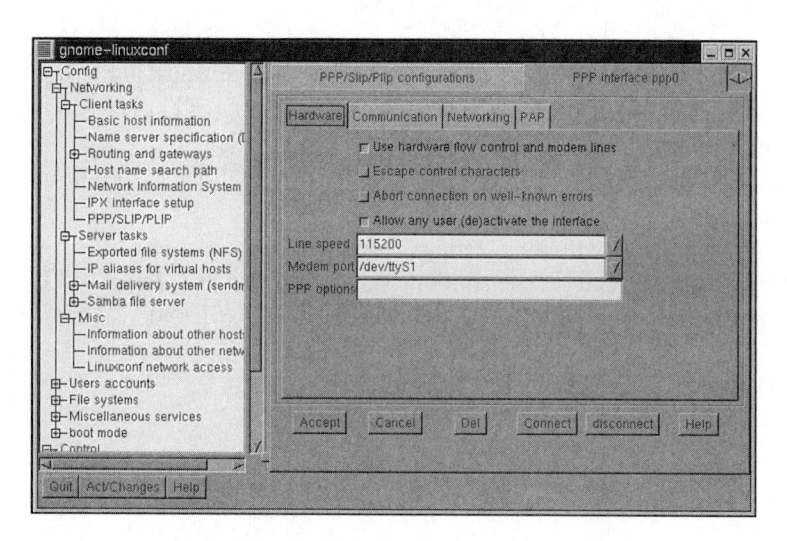

Figure 19.27   PPP Interface ppp0 Hardware tab.

This is the Hardware tab page, the first of four tab pages for the ppp0 interface. A number of properties can be modified, such as line speed and modem port. When you have made the appropriate changes, select the next tab, named Communication. Figure 19.28 shows this tab page.

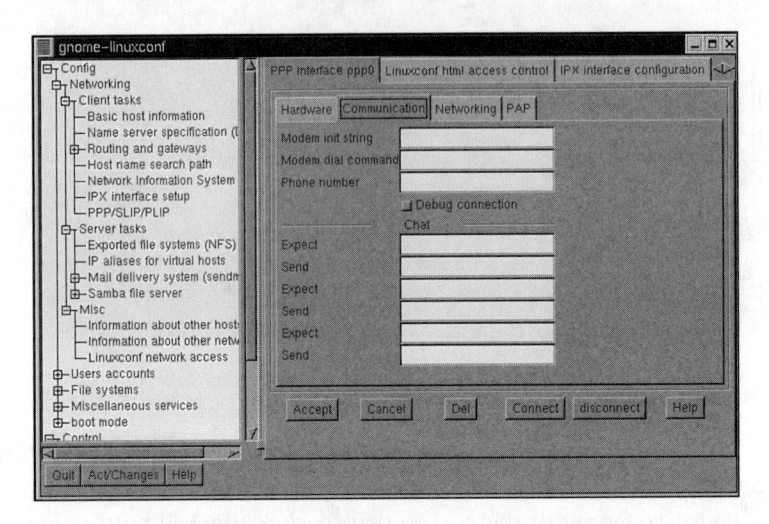

Figure 19.28 PPP Interface ppp0 Communication tab.

This page maintains information relating to the modem device. You can change properties such as the modem initialization string and phone number. You can also create a chat script, consisting of expect-send string pairs.

Clicking the next tab reveals the Networking tab page, shown in Figure 19.29.

This tab page maintains settings for an established connection. Some of the settings you can set are timeout values and the MRU and MTU values.

Finally, select the PAP tab page, shown in Figure 19.30.

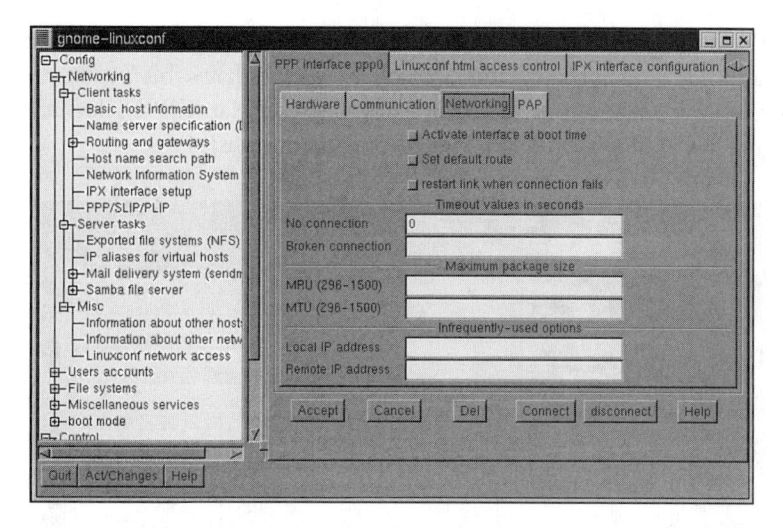

Figure 19.29 PPP Interface ppp0 Networking tab.

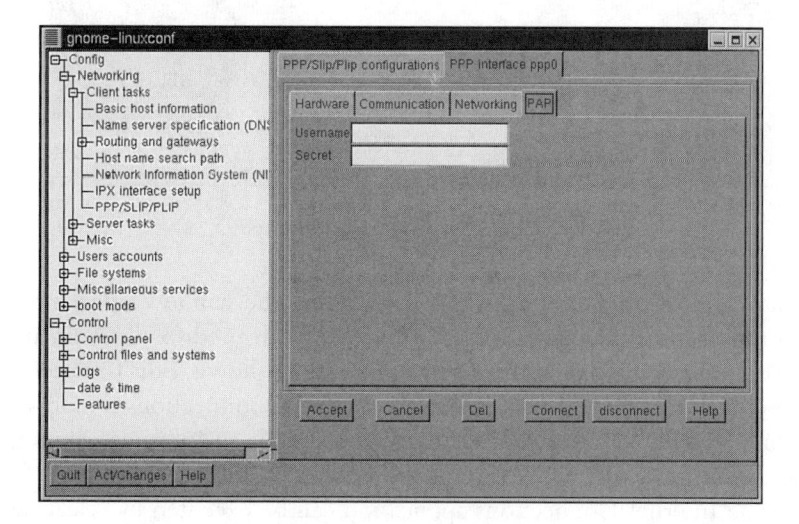

Figure 19.30 PPP Interface ppp0 PAP tab.

This page allows you to change the Username and Secret (password) fields. Oddly enough (and I have never understood this), the Secret field is not so secret—your password is revealed as plain text. If you walk away from your workstation, anyone can walk up and check out your login sequence, so be cautious! To test your settings, you click the Connect button at the bottom of the tab page.

558 Chapter 19 The Tools

Personally, I have found using Linuxconf to connect to the Internet to be a rather quirky affair. Other people obviously have this same opinion, because Red Hat has introduced RP3, the Red Hat PPP Dialer utility. Figure 19.31 shows two of the tools involved with RP3.

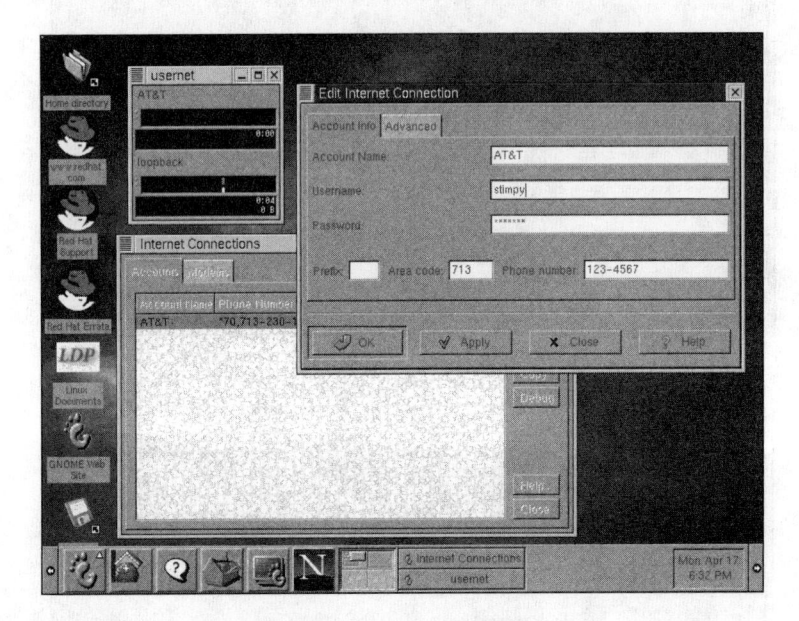

Figure 19.31 Red Hat's RP3 PPP tools.

The window titled usernet is the RP3 dialer. The window titled Internet Connections is the configuration program that is used to add, edit, and delete Internet connections. The third window shown, Edit Internet Connection, is a child window of the Internet Connections window. This is where you apply the changes required for an Internet account. In this instance, the AT&T account is being modified.

The Internet Connections application can be executed by selecting Internet, Dialup Configuration Tool. The second application, RP3, can be found under Internet, RH PPP Dialer.

As soon as you have a valid Internet account set up, you use the RP3 application to dial up and connect to the service provider. These tools are found under Internet, GNOME (if they are installed).

This section provided an overview of the use of the Red Hat Linuxconf tool. Feel free to explore its other configuration possibilities.

Running Configuration Tools Under TurboLinux 4.0

TurboLinux comes with a number of tools to configure the system. Not all of them offer a graphical interface. TurboLinux does not offer a one-stop shopping configuration tool, such as SuSE's YaST or Red Hat's Linuxconf. Instead, TurboLinux offers individual tools to tackle configuration categories. The following list describes the TurboLinux configuration tools. If the tool is offered in an X Windows interface (its name begins with an X), it is also listed.

- **TurboFSCfg/XturboFSCfg.** Used to configure and manage filesystems (create, mount, unmount).
- **TurboHW.** Used to determine hardware devices.
- **Turbonetcfg/Xturbonetcfg.** Used to configure the network.
- **TurboPkg/XturboPkg.** Used to manage RPM (Red Hat Package Manager) packages.
- **TurboPNPCfg.** Used to configure PNP (Plug and Play) devices.
- **TurboPrintCfg.** Used to configure local and remote printers.
- **Turboservice/Xturboservice.** Used as a real-time service manager.
- **TurboSoundCfg.** Used to configure sound card information.
- **TurboTimeCfg.** Used to configure time zone information.
- **TurboUserCfg/XturboUserCfg.** Used to configure users and groups.
- **TurboWMCfg.** Used for selecting which window manager to use.
- **XturboFind.** Used to find and locate commands and files.

For the sake of consistency, we will examine the tool for PPP dial-up connectivity. This will give us a comparison to the tools offered by SuSE (YaST) and Red Hat (Linuxconf). First, however, you might need to set up your network configuration. In this section, we will check the network settings and then move on to the PPP configuration tool.

From the Wharf toolbar, open the Managers tray. The Wharf is the strip of icon buttons that run down the right side of the screen. Next, click the Net Mngr icon button. This invokes the Xturbonetcfg configuration application, shown in Figure 19.32.

560 Chapter 19 The Tools

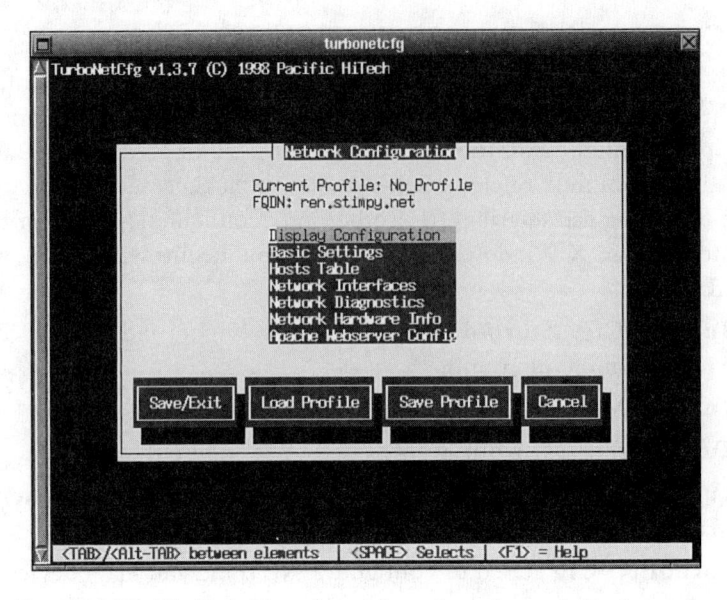

Figure 19.32 The TurboLinux network configuration tool, Xturbonetcfg.

Xturbonetcfg consists of a menu of seven options and four command buttons. You use the up and down arrow keys to select a menu option, and then you press the Enter key. For example, to modify the host table entries, select the Hosts Table menu option and press Enter. Figure 19.33 shows the Hosts Table configuration screen.

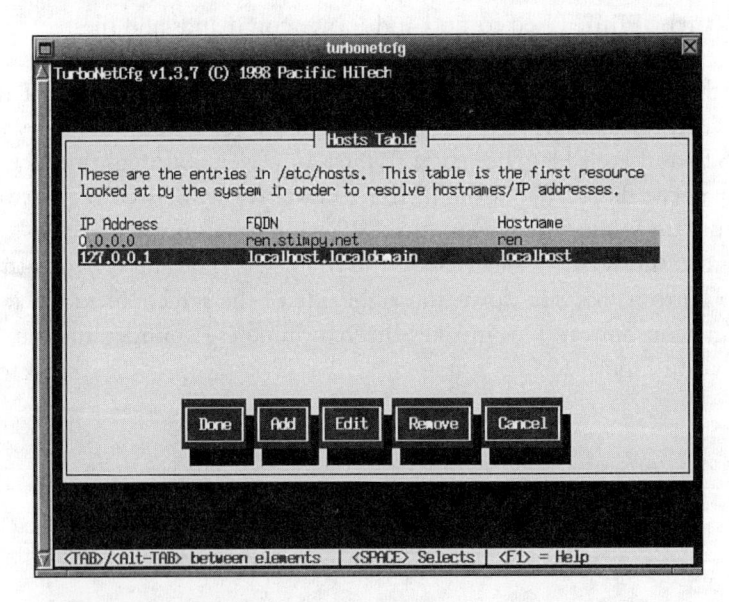

Figure 19.33 The Xturbonetcfg Hosts Table configuration screen.

This screen displays the entries found in the /etc/hosts file. You see that you can add, edit, and remove entries using this screen. The Cancel button discards any changes you have made, and the Done button saves the changes and returns you to the main menu.

The Basic Settings menu option (refer to Figure 19.32) allows you to change global network settings. These options include the hostname, domain name, search domains, DNS name servers, gateway IP, and gateway device.

The menu options offering you the opportunity to apply changes are Basic Settings, Hosts Table, Network Interfaces, and Apache Webserver Configuration. Visit each of these, excluding the Apache option for now, and apply the settings that are appropriate for your network. When you are done, click the Save/Exit command button.

Next, it is time to launch the TurboPPPCfg application. From the Wharf toolbar, open the Tools tray and click the PPP/Dialup icon button. This launches the TurboPPPCfg configuration tool, shown in Figure 19.34.

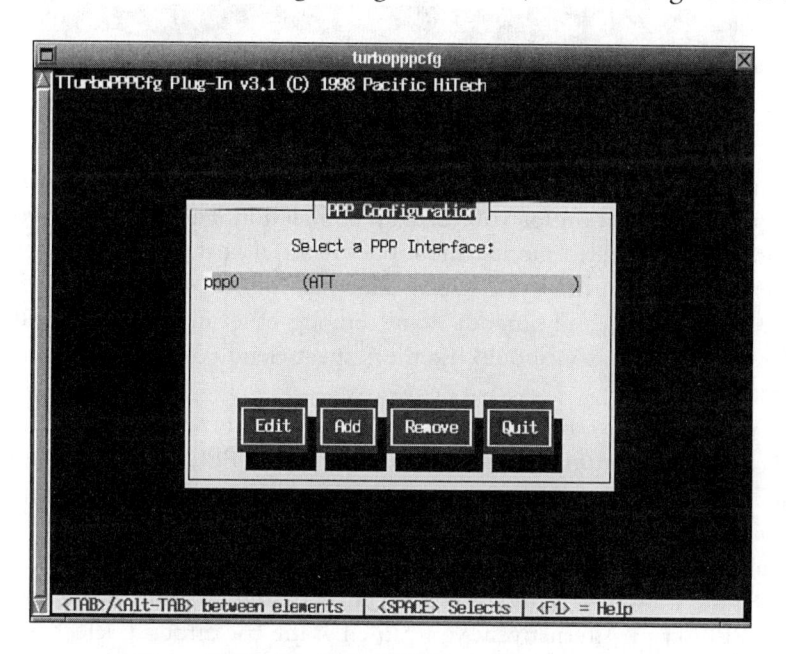

Figure 19.34 The TurboPPPCfg application window.

Click the Add button to create a new entry. Highlight the entry you need to modify, and click the Edit command button. You see the Configuring ppp*X* (*X* is the PPP number) screen, shown in Figure 19.35.

562 Chapter 19 The Tools

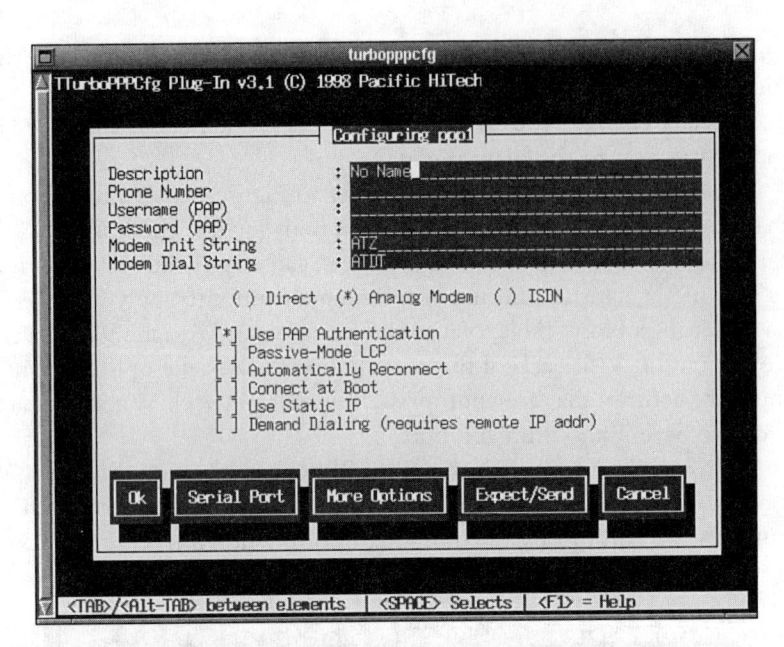

Figure 19.35 The TurboPPPCfg Configuring pppX screen.

A number of items can be modified on this screen. You should provide the required information for your dial-up connection. The Serial Port command button allows you to modify the modem's serial port. The More Options command button displays a screen, allowing you to configure such things as the MRU, MTU, and timeout values, among other items. If your ISP does not support PAP, you should use the Expect/Send command button to provide a log script.

When you have finished with all the appropriate settings for your ISP, click the OK command button. This tells TurboPPPCfg to write the changes and returns you to the main menu. Click the Quit command button in the main menu to quit the application. You are now ready to test your connection to your ISP.

At the bottom-left side of the screen, click the modem icon. This initiates the PPP script. Alternatively, you can click the background, select Network, PPP Menu, PPP Start. Once the connection is established, you can execute the Netscape application and go surfing.

Before we finish with TurboLinux, let's look at the TurboFSCfg tool. From the Wharf toolbar, open the Manager tray and select the File Systems icon button. This launches the TurboFSCfg configuration tool, shown in Figure 19.36.

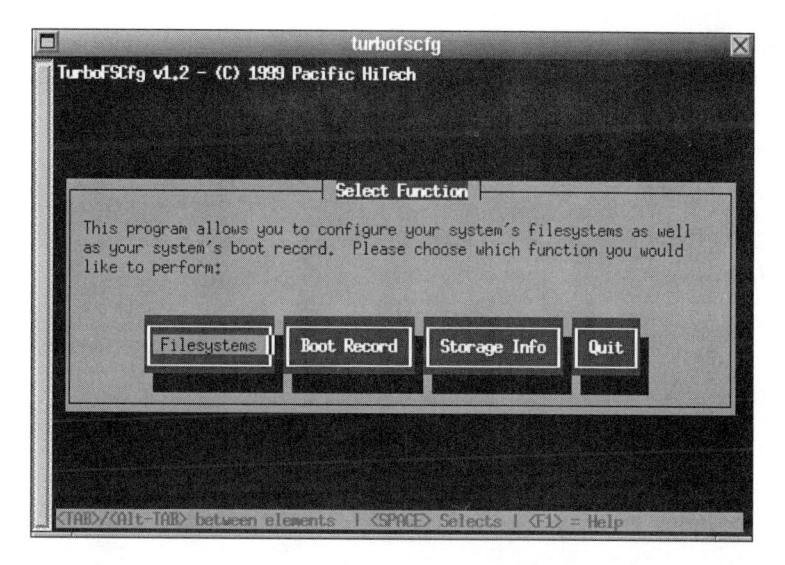

Configuration, Maintenance, and Management Tools   563

Figure 19.36 The TurboFSCfg application.

The opening screen offers four choices. For this exercise, click the Filesystems command button. The Configure Filesystems screen is displayed (see Figure 19.37), allowing you to perform actions on the filesystems. For example, you can mount, unmount, and check filesystems.

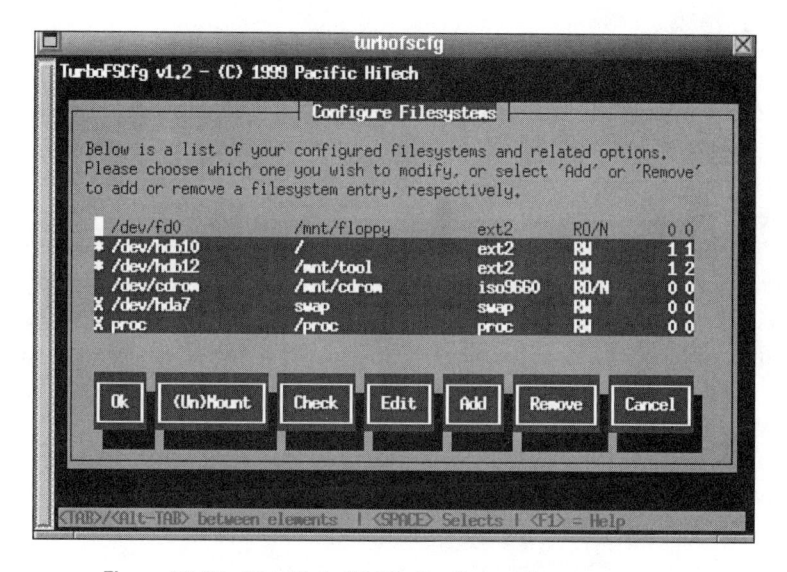

Figure 19.37 The TurboFSCfg Configure Filesystems screen.

Chapter 19 The Tools

For this exercise, we will add and mount a new filesystem. Click the Add command button. The Filesystem Type pop-up window appears. Select the Local Filesystem option. The Edit Filesystem screen is displayed, as shown in Figure 19.38.

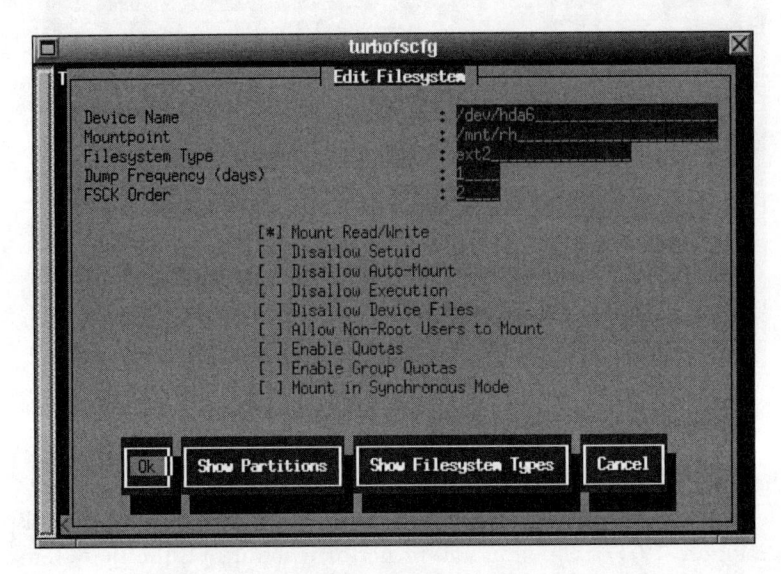

Figure 19.38 The TurboFSCfg Edit Filesystem screen.

In this figure, the settings are already filled in. For this system, the /dev/hda6 partition holds the Red Hat distribution, so the mount point is at /mnt/rh (you can choose another name). You will, of course, provide different settings for the partition and mount point. When you are finished with the settings, click the OK command button. You are returned to the Configure Filesystems screen, as shown in Figure 19.39.

The new filesystem should show up as a new entry on this screen. Indeed, the second entry in Figure 19.39 shows that the /dev/hda6 partition is mounted at the /mnt/rh directory. When you are finished with filesystem maintenance, return to the main menu and click the Quit command button.

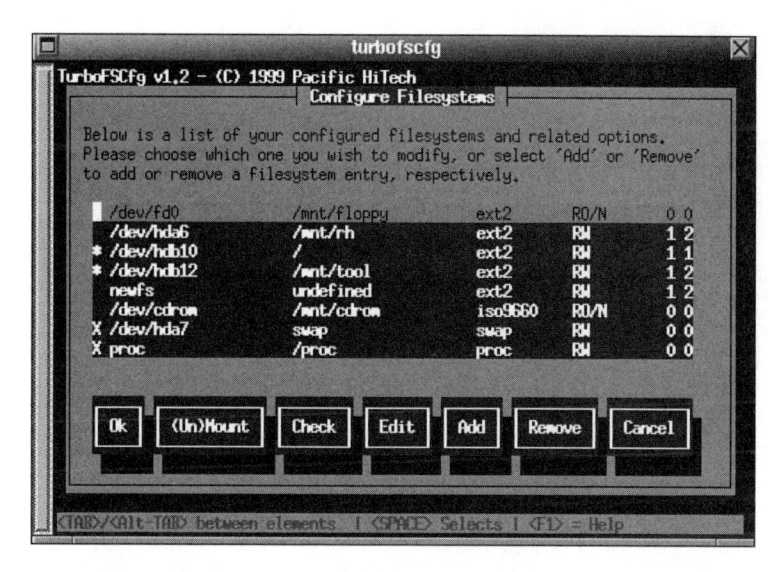

Figure 19.39 The TurboFSCfg Configure Filesystems screen.

Productivity Tools

There are increasing numbers of applications for Linux. We will focus here on the most well-known general office-type application, StarOffice.

Running StarOffice

This section takes a brief look at version 5.1 of StarOffice. StarOffice is an integrated office suite that runs on a variety of platforms, providing seamless access to files and applications. It provides a consistent interface that is quite easy to use. StarOffice provides one window to all the suite products: files, email, spreadsheets, graphics, and presentations, just to name a few. Plus, other applications can be invoked from within the StarOffice workplace. Figure 19.40 shows StarOffice after it is invoked.

566   Chapter 19   The Tools

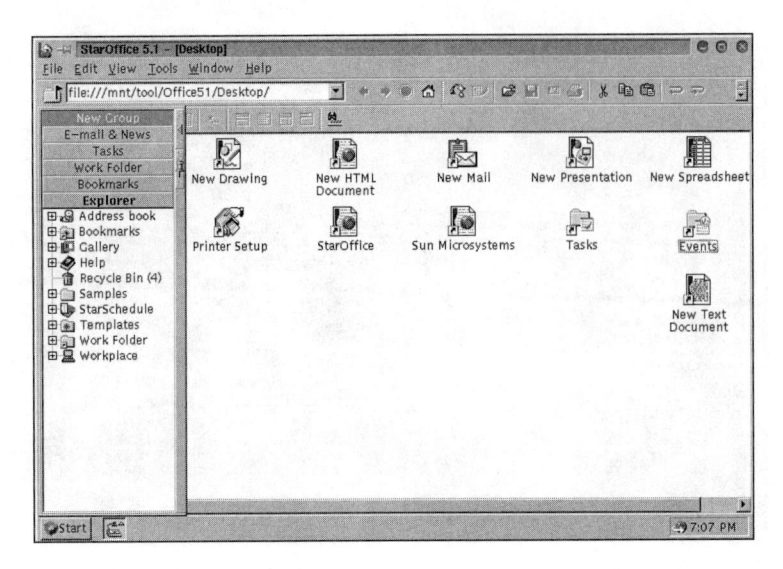

Figure 19.40   StarOffice 5.1 desktop.

The opening screen of StarOffice offers a window with a number of icons. Each of these represents a different file type in StarOffice.

As mentioned, you can use StarOffice to create word processing documents, surf the Web, create HTML documents, process your email, create graphics images, run spreadsheets, and create presentations. You do not have to execute a separate application for each product type. Figure 19.41 shows the StarOffice Browser in action at the `http://www.sun.com` Web site.

It's nice to be able to jump between windows within a tool, rather than having to search for an individual application window on the desktop. StarOffice is a truly integrated office suite. You can create a word processing document and instantly turn it into an HTML document, and vice versa.

Look at the bottom toolbar in Figure 19.41. You see two icons, each representing a file type. One is titled Chapter 19 (what you are reading), and the other is titled Sun Micro.... Each icon represents an individual window with its specified type. These buttons allow you to quickly switch to the desired window. You might have noticed that the Chapter 19 icon looks like a Microsoft Word document icon. That is because StarOffice knows how to read and write Word 95 and 97 file types. (I used StarOffice to write the manuscript for this book.)

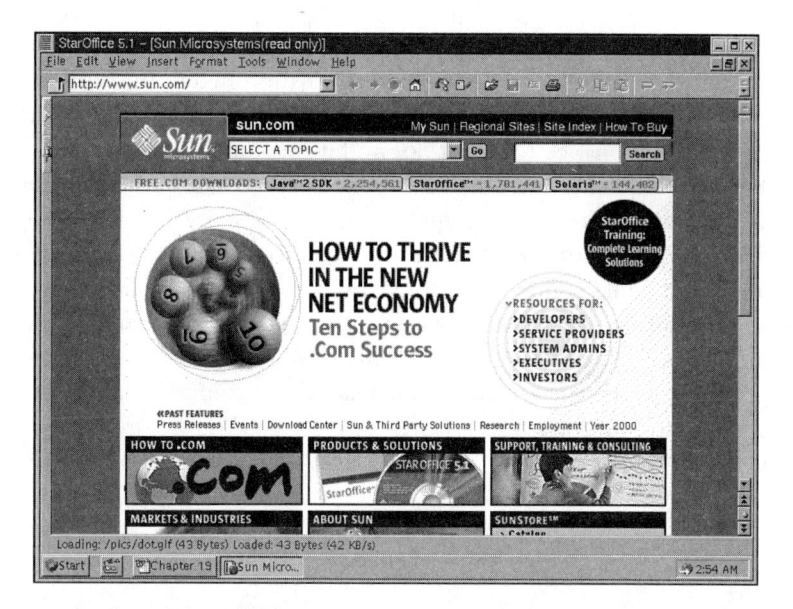

Figure 19.41 StarOffice 5.1 at the Sun Microsystems Web site.

I leave you to try out the StarOffice suite. Most popular distributions of Linux include it (among other software products). If StarOffice is not included, you can download it from http://www.sun.com.

Summary

This chapter covered a few of the important tools that are used to install Linux software, configure an installed Linux system, and provide office productivity.

We first looked at the Red Hat Package Manager (RPM) tool. Although Red Hat is in the name, RPM is an open source application designed to build, install, query, uninstall, update, and verify individual software packages. Most Linux distributions are now using RPM to install and maintain software packages. We also looked at Gnome-RPM, which provides a graphical interface to the RPM system.

Next, we went through an overview of the Yet another Setup Tool (YaST), which is included in the SuSE Linux distribution. It improves the installation process and provides maintenance of the system after installation. The Linuxconf tool, distributed with Red Hat, is a graphical tool used to perform various maintenance activities. It also activates any changes so that they are immediately realized.

We also took a look at some of the tools offered under the TurboLinux distribution. Specifically, we examined the Xturbonetcfg, TurboPPPCfg, and TurboFSCfg configuration tools. TurboLinux does not provide an integrated setup and maintenance tool, but does offer individual tools.

Finally, we quickly examined StarOffice and its capabilities. It provides a truly integrated suite of office applications.

This chapter is not meant to be an exhaustive resource for all the tools you will use while running Linux. Many other quality applications and tools are available for Linux. Covering them all would become a book in itself. Check Appendix A, "Other Sources of Information," and Appendix B, "Common Questions," for more information regarding Linux applications and where to find them.

Cheers!

20

Booting and Shutdown

IN THIS CHAPTER, WE EXPLORE the Linux boot process. If you want to use Linux, booting is unavoidable, so it is important to understand the boot process.

The average person running an operating system views the boot process as a black box. As a rule, he does not think much about what is happening—he just sits and waits until the logon prompt is available. But most Linux users are a little more adventurous and curious than the average user. It is not uncommon to want to know more about Linux and its inner workings. In this chapter, we see what is happening before we can use Linux.

Many Linux users have more than one operating system on their machines. This provides many challenges for booting. For example, my machine contains four distributions of Linux, IBM's OS/2, IBM DOS 6.2 with the Microsoft Windows 3.11 shell, and Microsoft Windows NT. Linux is my operating system of choice; the others exist because I am forced to use them.

Overview

The complete boot process, called *bootstrapping*, is a natural progression that starts when you turn the power switch on. The bootstrap process is straightforward. After you have turned on the power, the computer's BIOS (Basic Input Output System) goes to a well-known address on the hard disk (or floppy disk) and loads a small executable known as the bootstrap loader. The bootstrap loader is then responsible for loading and starting the operating system.

This process is common to personal computers; other computer architectures may use a different sequence for bootstrapping. For the PC, the bootstrap loader can be found in the first sector of the hard drive or floppy disk.

The two-step process is required to maintain flexibility. The bootstrap loader is small in size and very focused with respect to functionality. The only role that the bootstrap loader plays is starting the operating system—no other functionality is included. This results in a very small executable, only hundreds of bytes. An added bonus is that the bootstrap loader does not care which operating system it is starting; this allows you to install any operating system or boot manager you want.

After Linux is loaded, various hardware items are initialized and device drivers are loaded. Next, the init process is started by the kernel; init is given the process ID of 1. Init is the parent of all future processes within the Linux system. You can find the init executable in the /sbin directory.

Opposite Linux startup is shut down. You cannot simply turn the power off to the computer. You must first bring Linux down from its running status. Linux is not alone in this requirement—other operating systems require proper shutdown before a system reset or power down. Linux uses memory buffers to store information about the file system and its state. This information is cached for performance reasons. Occasionally, Linux will flush the cached information out to disk. If you power the system down before Linux has flushed the data, the file system will be suspect and, in most instances, will be corrupted. This is why it is imperative that Linux is properly shut down.

When your Linux system is starting up, you will see numerous messages displayed to the console—so many messages, in fact, that the screen is inevitably scrolled. There are times when you need to examine these messages. Constantly rebooting the system to try to catch any message(s) is not an option. So, how can you examine these messages after the system has started and you are logged on? Easy—you use the dmesg command. The dmesg command is used to examine the kernel ring buffer or, more specifically, for you to show the boot messages. In a pinch, you can invoke dmesg as in the following dialog:

```
stimpy $ dmesg > booting.txt
```

This will invoke `dmesg` and write its output to the file named `booting.txt`. The following is a sample dialog to examine boot messages.

```
stimpy $ cat booting.txt
Linux version 2.2.10 (root@Mandelbrot.suse.de) (gcc version 2.7.2.3)
Detected 166196481 Hz processor.
Console: colour VGA+ 80x25
Calibrating delay loop... 66.36 BogoMIPS
Memory: 95456k/98304k available (1172k kernel code, 416k reserved (endbase 0x9e000),
VFS: Diskquotas version dquot_6.4.0 initialized
CPU: Intel Pentium 75 - 200 stepping 0c
Checking 386/387 coupling... OK, FPU using exception 16 error reporting.
Checking 'hlt' instruction... OK.
Checking for popad bug... OK.
Intel Pentium with F0 0F bug - workaround enabled.
POSIX conformance testing by UNIFIX
PCI: PCI BIOS revision 2.10 entry at 0xfc7c1
PCI: Using configuration type 1
PCI: Probing PCI hardware
Linux NET4.0 for Linux 2.2
Based upon Swansea University Computer Society NET3.039
NET4: Unix domain sockets 1.0 for Linux NET4.0.
NET4: Linux TCP/IP 1.0 for NET4.0
IP Protocols: ICMP, UDP, TCP, IGMP
Initializing RT netlink socket
Starting kswapd v 1.5
Detected PS/2 Mouse Port.
pty: 256 Unix98 ptys configured
Real Time Clock Driver v1.09
RAM disk driver initialized:  16 RAM disks of 20480K size
PIIX: IDE controller on PCI bus 00 dev 38
PIIX: not 100% native mode: will probe irqs later
PIIX: neither IDE port enabled (BIOS)
PIIX: IDE controller on PCI bus 00 dev 39
PIIX: not 100% native mode: will probe irqs later
    ide1: BM-DMA at 0xffa8-0xffaf, BIOS settings: hdc:pio, hdd:pio
hda: ST32140A, ATA DISK drive
hdb: Maxtor 87000A8, ATA DISK drive
hdc: DC5-E6, ATAPI CDROM drive
ide0 at 0x1f0-0x1f7,0x3f6 on irq 14
ide1 at 0x170-0x177,0x376 on irq 15
hda: ST32140A, 2015MB w/128kB Cache, CHS=1023/64/63
hdb: Maxtor 87000A8, 6679MB w/256kB Cache, CHS=14475/15/63
hdc: ATAPI 6X CD-ROM drive, 256kB Cache
Uniform CDROM driver Revision: 2.55
Floppy drive(s): fd0 is 1.44M
...
```

The contents of this file continue, as can be expected. Using the `dmesg` command can be quite useful for debugging a booting system.

Usage for the `dmesg` command is as follows:

```
dmesg [-c] [-n level]
```

The init Process

The `-c` switch is used to clear the contents of the ring buffer after printing the messages. The `-n level` switch is used to set the level of messages that are printed to the console. For example, `-n 1` shows only panic messages.

The init Process

As mentioned previously, the init process is the parent of all processes within a running Linux system. The init process refers to its configuration file named /etc/inittab. The /etc/inittab file contains information that init uses to bring the system up into a specific run level. The following is a sample /etc/inittab file:

```
# /etc/inittab
# This is the main configuration file of /sbin/init
# All scripts for runlevel changes are in /sbin/init.d/ and the main
# file for changes is /etc/rc.config.
# default runlevel
id:2:initdefault:
# check system on startup
si:I:bootwait:/sbin/init.d/boot
# /sbin/init.d/rc takes care of runlevel handling
#
# runlevel 0 is halt
# runlevel S is single user
# runlevel 1 is multiuser without network
# runlevel 2 is multiuser with network
# runlevel 3 is multiuser with network and xdm
# runlevel 6 is reboot
l0:0:wait:/sbin/init.d/rc 0
l1:1:wait:/sbin/init.d/rc 1
l2:2:wait:/sbin/init.d/rc 2
l3:3:wait:/sbin/init.d/rc 3
#l4:4:wait:/sbin/init.d/rc 4
#l5:5:wait:/sbin/init.d/rc 5
l6:6:wait:/sbin/init.d/rc 6

# what to do in single-user mode
ls:S:wait:/sbin/init.d/rc S
~~:S:respawn:/sbin/sulogin
# what to do when CTRL-ALT-DEL is pressed
ca::ctrlaltdel:/sbin/shutdown -r -t 4 now
# special keyboard request (Alt-UpArrow)
# look into the kbd-0.90 docs for this
kb::kbrequest:/bin/echo "Keyboard Request -- edit /etc/inittab to let this work."
# what to do when power fails/returns
pf::powerwait:/sbin/init.d/powerfail     start
pn::powerfailnow:/sbin/init.d/powerfail now
#pn::powerfail:/sbin/init.d/powerfail now
po::powerokwait:/sbin/init.d/powerfail   stop
# for ARGO UPS
```

```
sh:12345:powerfail:/sbin/shutdown -h now THE POWER IS FAILING
# getty-programs for the normal runlevels
# <id>:<runlevels>:<action>:<process>
# The "id" field  MUST be the same as the last
# characters of the device (after "tty").
1:123:respawn:/sbin/mingetty --noclear tty1
2:123:respawn:/sbin/mingetty tty2
3:123:respawn:/sbin/mingetty tty3
4:123:respawn:/sbin/mingetty tty4
5:123:respawn:/sbin/mingetty tty5
6:123:respawn:/sbin/mingetty tty6
#  Note: Do not use tty7 in runlevel 3, this virtual line
#  is occupied by the program xdm.
#
#  This is for the package xdmsc, after installing and
#  and configuration you should remove the comment character
#  from the following line:
#7:2:respawn:+/sbin/init.d/rx tty7
# modem getty.
# mo:23:respawn:/usr/sbin/mgetty -s 38400 modem
# fax getty (hylafax)
# mo:23:respawn:/usr/lib/fax/faxgetty /dev/modem
# vbox (voice box) getty
# I6:23:respawn:/usr/sbin/vboxgetty -d /dev/ttyI6
# I7:23:respawn:/usr/sbin/vboxgetty -d /dev/ttyI7
# end of /etc/inittab
```

The scripts that are used to bring Linux into a specific run level are found in the /sbin/init.d directory. Note that some distributions of Linux locate the startup directories in the /etc/rc.d directory. For example, under SuSE Linux (6.2), the /etc/rc.d directory is a link to the /sbin/init.d directory. The following dialog confirms this:

```
stimpy $ ls -al ¦ grep rc.d
lrwxrwxrwx   1 root     root     14 Oct 13 13:09 rc.d -> ../sbin/init.d
stimpy $
```

The following is a partial listing of the /sbin/init.d directory.
```
drwxr-xr-x  2 root      root      1024 Oct 13 13:09 rc0.d
drwxr-xr-x  2 root      root      1024 Oct 13 13:14 rc1.d
drwxr-xr-x  2 root      root      2048 Oct 13 13:17 rc2.d
drwxr-xr-x  2 root      root      2048 Oct 13 13:17 rc3.d
drwxr-xr-x  2 root      root      1024 Oct 13 13:09 rc4.d
drwxr-xr-x  2 root      root      1024 Oct 13 13:09 rc5.d
drwxr-xr-x  2 root      root      1024 Oct 13 13:09 rc6.d
drwxr-xr-x  2 root      root      1024 Oct 13 13:09 rcS.d
```

Eight run levels are identified; the range of run levels is 0–6 inclusive. The eighth run level is known as "S" or "s." Table 20.1 details the various run levels.

Table 20.1 **Summary of Run Levels**

Run Level	Description
0	Halt. This level halts the system. The `halt` script, found in `/sbin/init.d/rc0.d`, is used to satisfy the `halt` functionality. The `halt` script may invoke the script `halt.local` found in the `/sbin/init.d` directory. This file is user editable so that you can include any special shutdown operations.
1	Single-user mode. This level is for single-user mode without a network. You can have more than one virtual console under this run level.
2	Multiuser, no NFS or X. This level sets multiuser mode with a network. This is primarily used for servers not running X.
3	Multiuser. This level sets multiuser mode with a network and runs xdm, the X Display Manager. Be sure you have set up X for this level.
4	Reserved, not used yet.
5	X11.
6	Reboot. This level reboots the system. The `reboot` script, found in `/sbin/init.d/rc6.d`, is used to satisfy reboot functionality. As in run level 0, the reboot script invokes the script `halt.local` found in the `/sbin/init.d` directory. This file is user editable so that you can include any special reboot operations.
S, s	Single-user mode. This level brings the system into single-user mode. The script `single`, found in the `/sbin/init.d/rcS.d` directory, is executed. Only one console is available in this run level.

If you recall, the `/sbin/init.d` directory contains a directory that is associated with each run level. The format for the directory is `/sbin/init.d/rc#.d`, where the # is replaced with a run level. Thus, the directory named `/sbin/init.d/rc3.d` is dedicated to run level 3 script files. The following is a snippet of a directory listing for the `/sbin/init.d/rc3.d` directory.

```
drwxr-xr-x    2 root     root        2048 Oct 13 13:17 .
drwxr-xr-x   11 root     root        1024 Oct 13 13:17 ..
lrwxrwxrwx    1 root     root           6 Oct 13 13:09 K10xdm -> ../xdm
lrwxrwxrwx    1 root     root           7 Oct 13 13:09 K19cron -> ../cron
lrwxrwxrwx    1 root     root           7 Oct 13 13:09 K19nscd -> ../nscd
lrwxrwxrwx    1 root     root           8 Oct 13 13:17 K19smbfs -> ../smbfs
lrwxrwxrwx    1 root     root           9 Oct 13 13:16 K20apache -> ../apache
lrwxrwxrwx    1 root     root          11 Oct 13 13:17 S20sendmail -> ../sendmail
lrwxrwxrwx    1 root     root           6 Oct 13 13:17 S20smb -> ../smb
lrwxrwxrwx    1 root     root           8 Oct 13 13:17 S20squid -> ../squid
```

```
lrwxrwxrwx   1 root      root             7 Oct 13 13:09 S21cron -> ../cron
lrwxrwxrwx   1 root      root             7 Oct 13 13:09 S21nscd -> ../nscd
lrwxrwxrwx   1 root      root             8 Oct 13 13:17 S21smbfs -> ../smbfs
lrwxrwxrwx   1 root      root             6 Oct 13 13:09 S30xdm -> ../xdm
lrwxrwxrwx   1 root      root             5 Oct 13 13:09 K20at -> ../at
lrwxrwxrwx   1 root      root             8 Oct 13 13:09 K20inetd -> ../inetd
lrwxrwxrwx   1 root      root             6 Oct 13 13:16 K20lpd -> ../lpd
lrwxrwxrwx   1 root      root             8 Oct 13 13:09 K20rwhod -> ../rwhod
lrwxrwxrwx   1 root      root            11 Oct 13 13:17 K20sendmail -> ../sendmail
lrwxrwxrwx   1 root      root             6 Oct 13 13:17 K20smb -> ../smb
```

Notice that the file names are coded in a special format. A script file begins with either the letter K or S. A script that begins with an S is used to start a service. A script that begins with a K is used to kill (or stop) a service. The number that is between the S or K and the filename is used for sequencing of the scripts. For example, for a service such as lpd running under a network, the sequence number should be greater than the sequence number for the network service. Conversely, the sequence number for shutting down a service, lpd for example, should be less than the sequence number for the network service. This ensures that the daemon service, lpd for example, is stopped before the network is brought down.

You will also note from the previous directory listing that each file is actually a link to a file in the /sbin/init.d directory. You can manually restart a service, if required, by invoking the associated script to stop the service and then start the service. For example, to manually restart the apache service, you would do so as shown in the following dialog:

```
stimpy $ /sbin/init.d/apache stop
stimpy $ /sbin/init.d/apache start
```

Some administrators invoke the "stop" a second time, before invoking the "start" line. Doing this provides some assurance that the service is indeed stopped.

You will recall that the init process examines the /etc/inittab file upon invocation. The init process first looks for an entry matching initdefault—this entry specifies the default (or initial) run level of the system. The following is an extract from an /etc/inittab file, showing the initdefault entry:

```
id:3:initdefault:
```

It is quite possible that the initdefault entry does not exist, or worse yet, the /etc/inittab file is nonexistent. If either is the case, you must manually enter the run level at the console.

The files rc.sysinit, rc, and rc.local are found in the /etc/rc.d directory. Each of these scripts is used for a specific purpose, such as during boot or for changing run levels.

The `rc.sysinit` script is the first script that the init process executes. This script provides functionality such as checking the file systems and setting system variables.

The `rc` script is used to bring the system into a run level or when changing run levels. The `rc` script accepts a single argument representing the run level desired.

The `rc.local` script is run after all other startup scripts have been executed. This script is user editable, allowing you to add your own customizations for startup. The following shows a sample `rc.local` script file.

```
stimpy $ cat rc.local
#!/bin/sh
# This script will execute after other init scripts.
if [ -f /etc/redhat-release ]; then
    R=$(cat /etc/redhat-release)
    arch=$(uname -m)
    a="a"
    case "_$arch" in
        _a*)  a="an";;
        _i*)  a="an";;
    esac
    echo "" > /etc/issue
    echo "$R" >> /etc/issue
    echo "Kernel $(uname -r) on $a $(uname -m)" >> /etc/issue
    cp -f /etc/issue /etc/issue.net
    echo >> /etc/issue
fi
```

For some distributions, such as SuSE Linux, the startup files are located in the /sbin/init.d directory. Additionally, the files (for this distribution) are named differently.

The boot-level master script is named /sbin/init.d/boot and is comparable to the /etc/rc.d/rc.sysinit file. The /sbin/init.d/boot file also executes various hardware initialization scripts found in the /sbin/init.d/boot.d directory. Next, the /sbin/init.d/boot script file calls on the /sbin/init.d/boot.local file to execute local commands, similar to the /etc/rc.d/rc.local file. After system startup is complete, /sbin/init will switch to the default run level identified in /etc/inittab. Finally, it calls /sbin/init.d/rc to start or stop services (using scripts) under the /sbin/init.d directory.

As mentioned previously, the `initdefault` entry in the /etc/inittab file identifies the default run level. In Table 20.1, the various run levels were detailed. Recall that run level 0 sets the system to halt and run level 6 sets the system to reboot. Do not change the `initdefault` entry to one of these two run levels. Obviously, you will never be able to use your system if `initdefault` is set to 0 or 6.

Using LILO, the Linux Loader

LILO, which is short for LInux LOader, is a boot manager that allows you to choose an operating system to start whenever you power up your computer. LILO is installed to and runs from your hard disk and is used to automatically boot your Linux system from a kernel image stored on the hard disk.

LILO can be installed to the master boot record on the hard disk or to a floppy disk. Even if you install LILO to your hard disk, you should also install one to a floppy to act as an emergency disk in the event of hard-disk failure.

LILO boots the default operating system defined in the /etc/lilo.conf file. After LILO is invoked, a timeout sequence is started; if this timer expires, the default operating system will be booted.

You can manually override this feature by pressing the Shift key during the boot sequence. Alternatively, you can provide the prompt option in the /etc/lilo.conf file. If either method is employed, LILO will sit patiently until you select an operating system to boot. You select an operating system by typing its name, which could be **msdos** or, of course, **linux**. At the LILO prompt, you can touch the Tab key to bring up a list of available operating system that LILO can boot.

Configuring LILO

LILO is configured through its configuration file named lilo.conf, which is found in the /etc directory. As with other Linux configuration files, /etc/lilo.conf is a text file that can be modified in your favorite editor.

Some of the information found in /etc/lilo.conf provides guidance to LILO for its operation. Other data in the file contains information specific to each operating system that LILO will boot. The following dialog shows a real-world sample of an /etc/lilo.conf file on a SuSE 6.2 system.

```
stimpy $ more /etc/lilo.conf
# LILO configuration file
# begin LILO global Section
boot=/dev/hda6
#compact        # faster, but won't work on all systems.
vga = normal    # force sane state
read-only
prompt
timeout=20
# End LILO global Section
# begin operating system specific section(s)
image = /boot/vmlinuz
  root = /dev/hda6
  label = SuSE
stimpy $
```

As a point of contrast, the following is an /etc/lilo.conf for RedHat 6.0 on the same computer.

```
stimpy $ more /mnt/redhat/etc/lilo.conf
boot=/dev/hda5
map=/boot/map
install=/boot/boot.b
prompt
timeout=50
# os specific
image=/boot/vmlinuz-2.2.5-15
        label=linux
        root=/dev/hda5
        read-only
other=/dev/hda1
        label=dos
        table=/dev/hda
stimpy $
```

The label line refers to the text that is displayed in the LILO boot menu list. This is the text identifier that you type to boot the associated operating system. As mentioned previously, the first few lines pertain to LILO's general operation and the operating system specific entries follow.

Notice in the previous /etc/lilo.conf examples that the boot entry identifies a logical partition where the Linux system is installed. If LILO were configured as the primary boot loader, the boot entry would be boot=/dev/hda. This particular machine uses System Commander as the primary boot manager. Based on the Linux operating system chosen, System Commander loads the appropriate LILO boot loader, which is installed on the (associated) Linux logical partition.

A number of options to LILO are available. Table 20.2 shows the options.

Table 20.2 **Summary of Options to LILO**

Option	Description
backup=*backup-file*	Copies the original boot sector to the named *backup-file*.
boot=*boot-device*	Sets the name of the device (or partition) containing the boot sector. If boot is omitted, the boot sector is read from the device mounted as root.
change-rules	Defines boot-time changes to partition-type numbers.
compact	Tries to merge read requests for adjacent sectors into a single read request. You should use this option when booting from a floppy disk.

Option	Description
`default=`*name*	Uses the named image as the default boot image.
`delay=`*tsecs*	Identifies the number of tenths of a second the boot loader waits before booting the default image.
`disk=`*device-name*	Defines nonstandard parameters for the specified disk. See the man page for more details.
`disktab=`*disktab-file*	Identifies the name for the disk parameter table. This option is not recommended.
`fix-table`	Allows LILO to adjust 3D addresses in partition tables. See the man page for more details.
`force-backup=`*backup-file*	Similar to the `backup` option, but will overwrite the backup copy.
`ignore-table`	Informs LILO to ignore any corrupt partition tables.
`install=`*boot-sector*	Installs the named file as the new boot sector. The `/boot/boot.b` file is the default if install is not used.
`linear`	Generates linear sector addresses instead of sector/head/cylinder addresses. See the man page for more information.
`lock`	Enables the automatic recording of boot command lines as default for the boot that follows.
`map=`*map-file*	Specifies the location of the map file. The file `/boot/map` is the default.
`message=`*message-file*	Identifies a file containing a message to be displayed before the boot prompt.
`nowarn`	Disables any warnings about eventual future problems.
`prompt`	Forces a boot prompt without requiring a keypress.
`restricted`	The per-image option `restricted` applies to all images.
`serial=`*parameters*	Enables control from a serial line. See the man page for more information.

continues ▶

Table 20.2 **Continued**

Option	Description
`timeout=`*tsecs*	Sets a timeout, in tenths of a second, for keyboard input; if timeout occurs, the first image is automatically booted.
`verbose=`*level*	Enables progress messages. Higher numbers provide more verbose output.

When your system boots with LILO as the boot manager, you will see a LILO 0 prompt. If you accepted the defaults during installation, you have a couple of options at the LILO prompt. You can let LILO time out and allow it to boot the default operating system, or you can type the name of the desired operating system at the LILO prompt to boot it. If you cannot remember the available choices, you can press the Tab key to obtain a list of available operating systems that LILO can boot.

Using LOADLIN, another Linux Loader

If you are running DOS in addition to Linux, you should consider using the LOADLIN boot loader. LOADLIN is a viable alternative to LILO because LOADLIN is easier to use.

The nice thing about LOADLIN is that it does not require specialized installation. In addition, the Linux kernel images can exist on any DOS medium. You can even boot Linux from a CD-ROM without using a (floppy) boot disk.

So, how does LOADLIN perform its magic? What LOADLIN does is execute the Linux kernel, completely replacing the DOS operating system that is currently executing. Be forewarned, however, you cannot exit Linux when you are done and return to DOS. You will have to reboot the system to get back to DOS.

LOADLIN Requirements

The requirements for LOADLIN are quite minimal. Obviously, you will need the DOS operating system. Optionally, you can be running Windows 95.

At a minimum, your machine must be sporting an 80386 processor. You will also need a Linux kernel image, such `zImage`, `bzImage`, or `/vmlinuz`.

Finally, you must have the LOADLIN package named LODLIN16.TGZ. This package contains various DOS-specific files, such as LOADLIN.EXE, MANUAL.TXT, TEST.PAR, PARAMS.DOC, and other files. The last two files, TEST.PAR and PARAMS.DOC, are sample parameter files.

You can find a copy of LODLIN16.TGZ at the following URLs: ftp://ftp.cdrom.com/pub/linux/sunsite/system/boot/dualboot or http://metalab.unc.edu/pub/Linux/system/boot/dualboot.

Easy LOADLIN Setup

You should create a directory named LOADLIN on the C: drive (let us assume C: drive for the sample). Copy the LODLIN16.TGZ file into the directory and use a decompression (unzipper) utility to extract the contents. The following dialog shows the files that were extracted onto my system:

```
C:\LOADLIN> dir /S /X
Directory of C:\LOADLIN
12/29/99  10:22a        <DIR>                    .
12/29/99  10:22a        <DIR>                    ..
12/29/99  10:22a                  87,210         lodlin16.tgz
04/30/96  06:30p                   2,830         readme.1st
04/30/96  05:44p                  32,208         loadlin.exe
03/22/94  03:29a                  18,324         copying
04/30/96  03:51p                   2,420         test.par
05/16/94  08:31a                     220         linux.bat
03/18/96  02:16a                   1,376         initrd.tgz
05/04/96  08:14a                     327         files
12/29/99  10:24a        <DIR>                    doc
12/29/99  10:24a        <DIR>                    src
  Directory of C:\LOADLIN\doc
12/29/99  10:24a        <DIR>                    .
12/29/99  10:24a        <DIR>                    ..
03/31/96  06:34p                   7,241         announce.txt
04/30/96  04:01p                   8,508         changes
04/30/96  07:15p                  32,719         manual.txt
05/04/96  08:31a                   1,303         lodlin16.lsm
04/30/96  06:28p                   1,808         quicksta.rt
04/30/96  06:53p                  12,511         params.doc
04/30/96  08:23a                  12,004         initrd.txt
  Directory of C:\LOADLIN\src
12/29/99  10:24a        <DIR>                    .
12/29/99  10:24a        <DIR>                    ..
04/28/96  03:13p                  59,643         loadlin.asm
04/28/96  10:23a                     140         loadlina.asm
04/28/96  03:17p                  28,025         loadlini.asm
04/28/96  05:25p                  35,983         loadlinj.asm
03/30/96  05:41p                  23,528         loadlinm.asm
04/30/96  09:16a                     860         makefile
03/16/96  06:28p                   3,721         pgadjust.asm
04/30/96  07:49a                   4,020         srclinux.tgz
C:\LOADLIN>
```

I suggest that you read the various text and documentation files so that you get the latest and greatest information.

After unzipping the LODLIN16.TGZ file, you are almost ready to fly. Next, copy the image file (zImage, bzImage, or /vmlinuz) to the root DOS partition, such as C:\. That is really all there is to it.

Booting Linux Using LOADLIN

This is the easy part. The following dialog demonstrates the use of LOADLIN to boot Linux (for most installations):

```
C:\> cd \LOADLIN
C:\LOADLIN> loadlin c:\vmlinuz root=/dev/hdb2 ro
```

If you have many parameters that span beyond the DOS limit of a 128-byte DOS command line, you can use a parameter file, as demonstrated in the following dialog. The Linux partition specified in the previous dialog is /dev/hdb2—this is only for demonstration purposes. Be sure to specify the Linux partition that exists on your system.

```
C:\> cd \LOADLIN
C:\LOADLIN> loadlin @param.fil
```

Check out the TEST.PAR file found in the C:\LOADLIN directory; it is a sample parameter file. Also, check out the PARAMS.DOC file in the C:\LOADLIN\DOC directory. It contains a list of Linux parameters. You might also check out the parameters list found at the following URL: http://sunsite.unc.edu/mdw/HOWTO/BootPrompt-HOWTO.html.

In a pinch, you can get help from the LOADLIN executable by typing its name alone on the DOS command line, as shown in the following dialog:

```
C:\LOADLIN> loadlin <enter>
LOADLIN v1.6 (C) 1994..1996 Hans Lermen <lermen@elserv.ffm.fgan.de>
USAGE:
  LOADLIN @params
  LOADLIN [zimage_file] [options] [boot_params]
    without any params, LOADLIN displays this help message.
  @params:
      params is a DOS file containing all other options
    zimage_file:
      DOS file name of compressed Linux kernel image
    options:
      -v        verbose, show information on params and configuration
      -t        test mode, do all but starting Linux, also sets -v
      -d file   debug mode, same as -t, but duplicates output to "file"
      -clone    ( Please read MANUAL.TXT before using this switch! )
      -n        no translation for root=/dev/...
      -txmode   switch to textmode 80x25 on startup
      -noheap   disable use of setup heap
```

```
       -wait=nn  after loading wait nn (DOS)ticks before booting Linux
       -dskreset after loading reset all disks before booting Linux
   boot_params:
      root=xxx  filesystem to be mounted by Linux as "/"
                (string passed unchanged to the kernel)
           xxx = hex number (e.g. root=201 for /dev/fd1)
               = /dev/mmmn (e.g. root=/dev/hda2)
                      mmm = fd,hda,hdb,sda,sdb...
                      n   = 1..10.. decimal
      ro         mount "/" readonly
      rw         mount "/" read/write
      initrd=x   (for kernels > 1.3.72) load file x into /dev/ram. If FS in x
                 contains /linuxrc, execute it, and then remount to root=xxx.
                 If root=/dev/ram, just load, bypass execution of /linuxrc

   for more boot params see PARAMS.TXT or Paul Gortmakers HOWTO:
     http://sunsite.unc.edu/mdw/HOWTO/BootPrompt-HOWTO.html
     http://rsphy1.anu.edu/~gpg109/BootPrompt-HOWTO.html
...etc...
```

To simplify the booting process, you should create a DOS batch file to execute any processes required. You can find a sample batch file named `LINUX.BAT` in the `C:\LOADLIN` directory.

You can also use the `CONFIG.SYS` file to boot multiple configurations if you are using DOS 6.0 or later. Be sure to check the LOADLIN documentation for more details on how to do this.

Emergency Boot Floppy Disks

Almost all Linux distributions, during installation, will prompt you to create an emergency boot floppy. I highly recommend that you do this because there are times when Linux may not boot. Be forewarned, though: These boot floppies only contain the Linux kernel—just enough to get the system booted up. After the system is up, you will have to use the distribution's disks, such as CD-ROMs, to repair any damage.

If you are using LILO as the boot manager and it becomes unusable because of a failed configuration, booting from the hard disk may not be an option. To handle this type of situation, you will also need a root floppy disk.

Be sure to update these emergency floppy disks whenever your Linux system changes—specifically, changes to the kernel.

Summary

In this chapter, we covered Linux bootstrapping. You discovered that the `dmesg` command can be used to examine the boot messages.

The init process, the parent of all processes, was covered in detail. The `/etc/inittab` file was discussed and an example provided. The scripts used to bring Linux to a specific run level were also discussed. Next, a discussion of the available run levels was covered. In addition, the run-level scripts were discussed.

The Linux Loader (LILO) was covered, including coverage of `/etc/lilo.conf`, the LILO configuration file. You learned that LILO can, in addition to booting a Linux system, boot other operating systems living on the same machine. Additionally, the available options to LILO were presented.

The Load Linux (LOADLIN) DOS boot utility was discussed. LOADLIN is a great option for booting Linux from the DOS command line. Setting up LOADLIN for use is a very simple process: Download `LODLIN16.TGZ` into a DOS directory, unzip it, and you are ready to go.

Finally, we closed the chapter with a discussion about building Linux emergency boot disks. This is important because there may be a time when you will be unable to boot your Linux system from the hard drive.

21

Security

OBVIOUSLY, IN THIS DAY AND AGE, security is a major concern among system administrators. We can take this a step further and say that security is a concern among all users. You need to consider many things when approaching security.

This chapter explains tactics and measures you can use to reduce security risks and concerns.

Overview

Surprisingly enough, some system administrators are rather lazy when it comes to security. A general "no problems here" attitude exists among some system administrators. I believe the problem boils down to one of two thoughts: Some system administrators think their system is secure enough, and some just do not know what the potential threats are. Many security features are disabled or not initially installed, by default, when users install a Linux distribution. Some distributions of Linux attempt to address this by offering a "server install" option during the installation process. The vendor may also offer other versions of its base product, such as a secure server edition.

I want to be rather bold and tell you that your system cannot be crack-free. The crack I am talking about here is synonymous with system break-in. All systems are susceptible to break-in by crackers. As a matter of fact, it is my opinion that every system has been cracked at one time or another. Believe it or not, some systems are cracked on a weekly basis! Probably the only system that has not been cracked is the standalone home PC that has never made an outside (network) connection and that is used by only one person.

Intruders

There is a difference between a cracker and a hacker. The intent of a *cracker* is to break in to a system. Secondary to that is whether the cracking is malicious in nature. It is true that after the cracker gets in to a system, the course of events usually leads to destruction of data or the collection of corporate data. But not all crackers intend to be malicious; a lot of crackers are interested only in the challenge of a break in.

A *hacker*, on the other hand, is someone who has an extreme interest in computers. The interest may be broad or focused. For example, for a programming hacker, the focus might be in deep technical knowledge about the Java or C++ programming language. In this extreme case, the programmer may dig deep into the mechanics of the language and may even become intimate with the compilers, linkers, and other tools. A hacker has no interest in breaking in to systems, and malicious actions are not a part of the hacker's regimen. The hacker with broad computer interest just wants to know everything about computers—from details about hardware to operating systems to software.

You should establish sound security policies within your organization. When they are in place, you should enforce those policies. You can find a Request For Comment (RFC) at http://www.rfc-editor.org that defines a fairly comprehensive security policy Search for RFC2196. RFC1244 is a good example of a network security policy. You should also check out RFC1281, which is a sample security policy with descriptions for each step.

Most crackers fall into one of several categories. Although the following list is not comprehensive, it does provide some of the major categories.

- **The Celebrity.** This intruder wants "celebrity" fame among his or her peers and will break into your system as an advertising technique. The more visible your site, the more likely this person is to try to break in.
- **Espionage.** This is a rather broad category, consisting of corporate espionage, competitive espionage, or what is known as data marketing. For the corporate type, the intent is to discover what the "other guy" is up to with respect to products and/or services. The same holds true for the competitive espionage type, but on a much smaller scale. This one

usually involves gaming companies. For the data marketer, the intent is to extract useful data that can be sold on the open (or closed) market. The intent here is for financial gain.

- **Investigative.** This group is more curious than anything else. This could be someone who just wants to see what "breaking in" is all about. This person might also be curious about what is on your system.
- **Leeches.** These people actually have the nerve to use your machines' resources. It is amazing how much this happens. One or more groups might be using your system(s) as a chat site, as an FTP site, for mass storage, as a pornography site, and so on.
- **Malicious.** This person has only one thing in mind, and that is to cause some type of damage. This cracker might bring your system(s) down, damage data, or modify files on your Internet site.
- **Piggyback.** If your system is connected to other hosts on the network, this category of cracker will use your system to gain access to the other hosts.

Let's move forward and see what it takes to secure your Linux system. Always remember—prevention is your best friend.

Physical Security

No, I am not talking about some big, hefty security guard here, although a security guard is a form of physical security. When we think of security, we usually think of viruses, worms, crackers breaking into a system, and other such computer system torment.

However, I am talking about the physical surroundings and physical influences that impact our system(s). A computer system is susceptible to its environment.

Another aspect of physical security is ensuring that your systems are habitually backed up. Surprisingly enough, I visit many client sites only to discover that system backup is viewed as a nuisance rather than as a positive effort.

Natural Elements

Dust plays a big part in the destruction of our computer equipment. Have you ever opened up the case on a computer that has been sealed up for months? Remember how those dust rodents scurried about when you took the case off? I am not talking about a real rodent, of course, but I am referring to the amount of dust that can accumulate in a computer (and peripherals). Other computer equipment is vulnerable to attack by dust, not just the computer. Printers need occasional attention to remove dust from their internals. External modems and keyboards require "dust maintenance," too. Personally, I clean my keyboard and computer once every two months. I remove the keys (keyboard) and clean all the garbage out and then blow all the dust out of the computer.

Electricity is another physical threat to computer equipment. The real problem here is electrical surges. Most computer equipment is delicate when it comes to electrical surges; modems are notorious for electrical surge damage. You should ensure that all your computer equipment is receiving power through a surge protector. Although an inexpensive surge protector will provide some relief, you should invest in a high-end surge protector with battery backup. You should also ensure that your telephone and answering machine are attached to a surge protector because these items can receive damage.

Smoke and fire are both threats to computer systems. Be sure you have fire-fighting equipment that is easily accessed. Your safety and that of the people around you is the primary concern here; the computer equipment is secondary. Be sure to install smoke and fire detectors, alarms, and automatic extinguishers, if available.

Physical Elements

Let's get back to the security guard subject. We really need to touch on this subject because it relates to theft and malicious damage (disgruntled employees). Small computer equipment is easily concealed, such as modems (external and internal), hardware cards, laptops, and some keyboards. Digital cameras are becoming commonplace in the computer-savvy office. Keep these sometimes-used items under lock and key. Theft is an issue that must be dealt with.

Physical access to your equipment should be a concern, too. You do not want unauthorized people accessing your computer room or browsing through office space. Crackers are known for watching people log in to a system, or they pick up sticky notes that have login instructions on them.

BIOS Locks

Many of today's personal computers provide password facilities in the BIOS. Most allow you to set a boot password and a BIOS setup password.

The boot password is used when you turn the computer's power on. After the power on self test (POST), the computer prompts you for the boot password; this happens before booting any operating system or boot manager software. You are usually given three chances to enter the correct password, and then the computer locks up or reboots. You set the boot password in the BIOS setup.

The BIOS setup password is required when you enter into the BIOS setup after powering up the computer. You cannot modify any BIOS settings until you supply the setup password. This password is separate from the boot password. A BIOS setup password is a good administrative tool; it keeps your users from altering the BIOS settings. You should engage the BIOS password for all machines in your organization.

These BIOS locks are not foolproof. Anyone with knowledge of computers can disable (or reset) the boot and BIOS setup passwords. To reset or disable these passwords requires physical access to the motherboard, so you should provide some sort of physical computer lock. Computer locks are discussed in the next section.

Computer Locks

Many of today's computers come with a physical locking mechanism. Some machines have an integrated lock, requiring a key to lock and unlock the case. These case locks are good for keeping a thief from opening up the case and stealing network cards, video cards, and other internal hardware.

The case locks also keep people from opening the case to disable or reset the BIOS and boot passwords. Most machines allow you to disable or reset the passwords by moving a jumper to the "disable" position. With some machines, you can reset the password by removing wall power and momentarily removing the internal battery. The battery is designed to maintain BIOS settings while a machine is unplugged from the power source.

Some machines provide loop-lock mechanisms. You simply purchase a key or a combination lock and attach the lock through the loops. For more expensive machines, you can run a cable through the case loops and anchor the cable to the wall or floor. This helps prevent the unauthorized removal of the machine.

System Backup

As mentioned previously, some organizations view system backup as an annoyance. It seems that a backup occurs only when someone with authority asks, "When was the last backup performed?" Delaying backups should never happen. Backups are even more crucial if you are running a business.

If you are the system administrator of your single PC home system, a backup is not as critical. Do not misunderstand me—I am not saying that you should not back up your home machine on a regular basis. If you are the system administrator for a 24/7 organization of 1,000 employees who rely on their computers, then you had better be backing up the systems daily. If you are responsible only for your home box, a weekly or monthly backup is sufficient.

Believe it or not, some system administrators have been relieved of their employment because of failure to perform periodic backups. I have witnessed companies go into total panic because of invalid or missed backups. A case in point—a telecommunications company was having problems with its database system. So severe was the problem that the database vendor sent its top technicians to find and fix the problem. In the meantime, the vendor recommended that the client re-create the databases and restore the data from their most recent backups. The telecommunications company had already lost two days worth of critical data. Guess what? The system administrator discovered that the most current and valid backup was more than 20 days old! The lesson here is that not only do you have to perform backups, but you should ensure that those backups are valid. The telecommunications company lost critical accounting and call-routing data.

Backups are not useful only for recovering from the effects of malicious conduct. As mentioned previously, the database failed, which prompted a restore of data. This shows that poorly written software can wreak havoc on a disk's data, too.

Hardware can also be at fault. Hard drives are electromechanical devices that are susceptible to failure at some point in time. You should not rely on the failure statistics presented by disk manufacturers. You must be prepared for failure at any time. If you are diligent with hard-drive maintenance and backups, you reduce the risk of failure and increase your chances of recovery. Surprisingly, I had a hard drive that lasted eight long years on a machine being used as a file and application server!

A complete discussion of backup routines is beyond the scope of this section. A universally accepted schedule is the six-tape cycle. This is both easy to implement and practical. Four of the tapes are used for days Monday through Thursday. One tape is earmarked for "even" Fridays and the sixth tape is dedicated for "odd" Fridays. For the Monday-to-Thursday routine, you perform an incremental backup; this implies that only changed data (files) are backed up. Each Friday, you perform a complete backup of all hard-disk data.

The ultimate backup routine is to modify the six-tape routine to include the whole month. If you are responsible for a 24/7 operation, this expense is minimal. If you have a four-week month, you will require 20 tapes. The daily incremental backups are performed as usual, in addition to the Friday full backup. The difference is that you stow those tapes (Monday–Friday) away—preferably in a safe—and start with fresh tapes beginning on Monday. This method enables you to go back a full month if you need to.

You should refer to the section "System Backup and Restoration" in Chapter 23, "Other Administrative Tasks," for more information concerning system backup.

Decreasing the Risk

Some tips to decrease the chance of physical security violations are as follows:

- **Revealing paperwork.** A policy should be in place that disallows the display (or storage) of sticky notes or other note paper with login information. Instructions concerning login procedures should also be stowed away in a desk. Some people are notorious for pasting sticky notes to their monitors with their usernames and passwords!

- **Unattended hardware.** Do not leave computer equipment unattended. This is particularly true of smaller items, such as disk drives, modems, digital cameras, backup tapes and drives, and so on. You might as well include software, too.

- **Unattended terminals.** Do not log in to a system and then run off to lunch, especially if that session is the root user. This allows any user to wreak havoc on your system. You should set up your system so that the terminal automatically logs off after a specified period of idle time (or use a screen lock or screen saver).

- **User education.** This one is very important because it helps to ensure that the previous three items are understood and, hopefully, enforced.

What is important is to establish sound security policies, to publish those policies, and to enforce those policies.

Threats to Security Caused by Social Engineering

Now there is a fancy phrase! What is social engineering? In a nutshell, it is the ability of a person to negotiate something from another person. People use many tactics to do this, from misrepresentation to persuasion.

Social engineering involves the use and abuse of people and their waste—waste being paper garbage and the like. A typical example is a cracker that befriends the system administrator of a large system. The cracker spends time discovering personal things about the administrator. Why? Because people usually create passwords that are personal in nature, such as their dog's name or the type of car they own. So the cracker learns these things to help gain access to the system. Crackers are also known to rummage through office trash, either in the office or in the outside dumpster. I knew someone who once obtained a 200-page list of usernames and passwords! Apparently, the system administrator printed the list to weed out dead accounts and she simply threw the list away in the public receptacle.

Crackers also exercise their social engineering skills by "visitation methods." A prime example is a cracker that visits a company to apply for a position. The cracker, of course, has no intention of accepting the job. Rather, she is there to take a tour of the facility to discover any system access hints that might be lying around. Anything will do—sticky notes, printouts, and even watching people log in to the system. This method is quite popular because the candidate is expected to be interested in the office surroundings, so the interviewer never thinks twice about the inquisitiveness of the candidate. Other visitation methods are taking a tour, engaging the company as a potential client, or visiting friends or relatives.

A cracker might pretend to be the system administrator and call upon some poor unsuspecting user. During the conversation, he asks the person for his or her username and password so that he can "fix" the damaged password file (`/etc/passwd`).

What can you do to prevent such social engineering occurrences from happening? As mentioned previously, educate your users. Explain what social engineering is all about and how they can prevent it from happening. You might even run some practice sessions to see if you can get past your users.

Authentication

This section covers the most typical approaches taken to secure Linux systems. I discuss weak passwords and what you can do to alleviate the problem. Also, account types are addressed, such as command and dead accounts. Last, I address encryption as a security measure and describe some of the products available.

Passwords

Weak passwords, weak passwords, weak passwords, weak passwords... It cannot be said enough: An easy way to breach a computer system is through weak passwords. Some crackers can just sit down at a terminal and guess at passwords, especially if they have employed their social-engineering skills. Some crackers also employ the use of password-cracking software, which automates the task of breaking into a system.

There exists a list of the top 100 passwords used by people. You might be surprised to learn that system administrators consistently use the password "GOD." Why? Because these system administrators might believe that they are the "GOD" of the system.

The best defense for weak passwords is to employ a number of policies concerning passwords. First, you should enforce the concept of password reset at regular intervals. Common practice states that you should enforce a change of password every eight weeks. This requires each user to change his or her password at regular intervals. Another policy is to enforce the use of multiple-word passwords. Some examples are hungryBear, goHome, flatTire, and so on. Have your users create their passwords in mixed-case text. Remember, passwords are case sensitive. And better yet, have your users inject a number or two in the password.

Some good password samples are coffee8Tea, half9Half, book4Shelf, phone3Book, fast4Track, and so on. The best passwords are not words at all. As mentioned previously, most crackers use software to automate system cracking. These programs use the dictionary to draw out passwords. The program also concatenates words to use as passwords. Therefore, the stronger passwords consists of random words, numbers, and symbols. The man page for the `passwd` command states that you can use lowercase alphabetic, uppercase alphabetic, the digits 0 through 9, and punctuation marks.

The acronym approach to creating a password should be employed, rather than using common words out of the dictionary. It is really easy; just think of some easy-to-remember phrase or song lyric and create an acronym for it. For example, "it is raining cats and dogs" becomes iirc&d. You could throw in a number to toughen up the password, such as i9irc&d. Just be sure you choose a phrase that you will remember.

The CERN Security Handbook provides a wealth of security information at the following URL: `http://consult.cern.ch/writeup/security/main.html` and more specifically (for passwords) at `http://consult.cern.ch/writeup/security/security_3.html`.

Shadow Passwords

The /etc/passwd file serves several purposes. The file is used to store users of the system. Specifically, it stores a username and an encrypted password for each user on the system. A problem with this method is that the encrypted password is available to prying eyes. This is because the /etc/passwd file contains other user information, such as user and group IDs. This means that the /etc/passwd file must be readable by the world. All a user needs to do is utilize a password-cracking program to determine the real password.

Shadow passwords provide a means to reduce the risk of password cracking. Shadow passwords are stored in the /etc/shadow file. Only privileged users can read the /etc/shadow file; usually only the root user is allowed to examine and modify the /etc/shadow file. You must ensure that your system supports shadow passwords because some utilities expect the encrypted passwords to be in the /etc/passwd file.

The following shows four entries in the /etc/passwd file.

```
root:x:0:0:root:/root:/bin/bash
lp:x:4:7:lp daemon:/var/spool/lpd:/bin/bash
news:x:9:13:News system:/etc/news:/bin/bash
uucp:x:10:14::/var/lib/uucp/taylor_config:/bin/bash
```

Notice that the second field, the password field, contains only the letter x. The password is actually stored in the /etc/shadow file. The following snippet shows the associated entries for the /etc/passwd file.

```
root:j9fd.Np9bUTk:10968:0:10000::::
lp:*:9473:0:10000::::
news:*:8902:0:10000::::
uucp:*:0:0:10000::::
```

The last three entries do not have encrypted passwords associated with the usernames lp, news, and uucp.

Several commands are used to add, delete, modify, and verify users and shadow passwords. The useradd command is used to add a new user to the system. The userdel command is used to delete an existing user from the system. The command usermod is used to modify an existing user account. The passwd command is used to change the password for a user. Finally, the pwck command is used to validate the consistency of the /etc/passwd and /etc/shadow files. Be sure to check Chapter 22, "Managing Accounts," for more information on these commands.

Accounts

Numerous types of accounts can figure in your security plan. They are reviewed in the following sections.

Command Accounts

Some administrators utilize the facilities of *command* accounts. Quite simply, if you log in using one of these accounts, an associated command is executed and the account is then logged out automatically.

A well-known account is the finger account. If you log in using finger, the associated command, `finger`, is executed and then the log in session is closed.

Most distributions of Linux no longer implement this account—or other command accounts, for that matter. Their popularity has dwindled because of the security risks they pose. Command accounts provide crackers with signatures, or identifying information, about a system site. Also, these commands have well-exposed flaws that can be exploited by crackers.

Yet, it is good to know about this risk. Check your system to be sure these accounts are disabled or password enabled.

Dead Accounts

A *dead* account is one that is no longer valid. This could be for many reasons, such as an employee that is no longer employed or on an extended leave of absence.

The optimal solution, of course, is to completely remove the account. The other solution is to disable the account, as discussed in the previous section. To disable the account, place a * character in the password (second) field of the `/etc/passwd` file. If your system uses shadow passwords, place the * character in the second field of the `/etc/shadow` file.

If you decide to remove an account, you should use the `userdel` command. This command is used to delete a user account and its related files. If you do not use this command, you will have to manually remove all the files and directories associated with the account. Simply execute the command as shown in the following example:

userdel [*-r*] *accountName*

The command modifies the system account files, removing the entries that refer to `accountName`. The named account must exist. If the `-r` option is specified, files in the account's home directory will be removed along with the home directory itself. You will have to seek out files located in other file system(s) and delete them manually.

Default Accounts

During the install process, Linux creates a number of *default* accounts that are required for Linux to operate properly. In most distributions, many of these accounts are disabled. This is done by placing a * character in the password field of the /etc/passwd file or the /etc/shadow file if shadow passwords are employed. You should be aware that some software packages create special accounts.

If any of these accounts are not disabled, you should ensure that each account has a valid and strong password attached to it.

Guest Accounts

A *guest* account is used in cases where guests are required to use the system. This relieves the system administrator from having to create an account and then remove it when the guest departs. The problem is—what if a cracker discovers that your system uses guest accounts? Half the battle of cracking a system is knowing a valid account (user) name.

Typically, the password associated with the guest account is going to be something such as guest or password or temp. Do not fall prey to this absurdity. If you are utilizing the guest account on your system, be sure that a strong password is associated with it, and change it periodically. You can also disable the account when there are no visitors.

You can also employ password aging to alleviate security risks that guest accounts present. Password aging is discussed in the earlier section "Passwords."

Password-Free Accounts

I will tell you straight up—do not allow *password-free* accounts. This is just too easy for crackers and their software. You should not allow a password-free account.

You can disable an account by placing a * in the password field of the /etc/passwd file (or the /etc/shadow file if shadow passwords are used). This will disallow anyone from logging in to the system. The following is a snippet from an /etc/passwd file:

```
root:x:0:0:root:/root:/bin/bash
lp:x:4:7:lp daemon:/var/spool/lpd:/bin/bash
news:x:9:13:News system:/etc/news:/bin/bash
uucp:x:10:14::/var/lib/uucp/taylor_config:/bin/bash
```

The password field is the second field of an entry. Each line constitutes a user on the system.

If your system implements shadow passwords, the entry will be found in the /etc/shadow file. The following is a snippet that is associated with the previous /etc/passwd file snippet:

```
root:j9fd.Np9bUTk:10968:0:10000::::
lp:*:9473:0:10000::::
news:*:8902:0:10000::::
uucp:*:0:0:10000::::
```

Notice that the root account has an associated password, whereas the other three accounts (lp, news, and uucp) are disabled.

Encryption

Encryption provides another level of security. Kerberos authentication, the first form of encryption discussed next, provides a strong form of security.

Kerberos Authentication

Developed at MIT in the mid 1980s, Kerberos is used as a distributed authentication service. Kerberos authenticates a user when the user logs in to the system. If a host or server on the network requires authentication, Kerberos provides a method to prove the user's identity. With Kerberos, a client process runs on behalf of a user. This process is used to prove the user's identity. Kerberos does this without sending data on the network, thus precluding an attacker from obtaining a password or authentication packet.

Kerberos implements authentication by assigning a unique key to the network user. This unique key is called a *ticket*. The ticket is subsequently embedded in network messages to authenticate the sender.

Spoofing has always been a network security concern. *Spoofing* is the act of a client fooling a server into thinking the client is someone else. Kerberos helps in this regard by preventing users from spoofing the system.

You can find more information on Kerberos at http://web.mit.edu/kerberos/www.

Pluggable Authentication Modules (PAM)

The most basic method of authentication and authorization to use in a system is a username and password scheme. At a log in prompt, you enter your username; then you are challenged to verify who you are by providing a password. If a match is made, the system authorizes your access into the system. At that point, your environment is adjusted to reflect your level of authorization at the point of authentication.

Pluggable Authentication Modules (PAM) is a system implemented as a suite of shared libraries enabling the system administrator to elect how applications perform user authentication. PAM allows you to alter the methods of authentication at will and it offers this functionality as loadable modules. Thus, you can switch the authentication mechanism without rewriting and recompiling a PAM application. This implies that you can completely modify your authentication system without modifying your PAM applications.

The following lists some highlights of PAM:

- You can identify particular users as able to log in to the system during a range of hours.
- You can set resource limits (amount of memory, maximum processes, and so on) for users, thereby disallowing denial-of-service attacks. A denial-of-service attack is when the attacker tries to make a resource too busy so that it cannot answer legitimate network requests or tries to deny legitimate users access to your machine.
- You can use password encryption methods other than DES.
- You can enable shadow passwords at will.

The PAM library is locally configured with a combination of files in the /etc/pam.d directory. The dynamically loadable modules are usually located in the /usr/lib/security directory. Older versions of Linux configure PAM using the /etc/pam.conf file. The following is a listing of the /etc/pam.d directory under SuSE 6.3; other distributions of Linux may locate the files in another directory tree.

```
bash-2.03# ls -al
total 21
drwxr-xr-x    2 root     root         1024 Jan  8 18:33 .
drwxr-xr-x   28 root     root         3072 Jan 18 23:57 ..
-rw-r--r--    1 root     root          230 Nov  8 15:40 chfn
-rw-r--r--    1 root     root          230 Nov  8 15:40 chsh
-rw-r--r--    1 root     root          580 Nov  8 14:30 ftpd
-rw-r--r--    1 root     root          437 Nov  8 23:54 gdm
-rw-r--r--    1 root     root          500 Nov  8 15:40 login
-rw-r--r--    1 root     root          443 Nov  6 09:49 other
-rw-r--r--    1 root     root          230 Nov  8 15:40 passwd
-rw-r--r--    1 root     root          311 Nov  8 16:52 ppp
-rw-r--r--    1 root     root          263 Nov  8 14:30 rexec
-rw-r--r--    1 root     root          454 Nov  8 14:30 rlogin
-rw-r--r--    1 root     root          292 Nov  8 14:30 rsh
-rw-r--r--    1 root     root          317 Nov  8 14:35 su
-rw-r--r--    1 root     root          108 Nov  8 17:05 su1
-rw-r--r--    1 root     root           60 Nov  8 17:06 sudo
-rw-r--r--    1 root     root          265 Nov  6 08:57 xdm
-rw-r--r--    1 root     root           67 Nov  8 17:53 xlock
-rw-r--r--    1 root     root           67 Nov  8 17:59 xscreensaver
bash-2.03#
```

The following list shows the contents of the /etc/pam.d/passwd file, taken from the list shown previously.

```
#%PAM-1.0
auth       required     /lib/security/pam_unix.so    nullok
account    required     /lib/security/pam_unix.so
password   required     /lib/security/pam_unix.so    strict=false
session    required     /lib/security/pam_unix.so
```

The syntax of each file in the /etc/pam.d directory is made up of individual lines taking the following form:

```
module-type    control-flag    module-path    arguments
```

The module-type can be one of four types: auth, account, session, and password. The control-flag tells the PAM library how to react to the success or failure of the associated module. The module-path is the path of the dynamically loadable object file or the pluggable module itself. The args is a token list that is passed to the module.

A good site for PAM can be found at http://www.kernel.org/pub/linux/libs/pam/Linux-PAM-html/pam.html.

File Security

The filesystem employed by Linux is a hierarchical one, consisting of a tree of directories and files that are contained within those directories. Linux maintains information about each directory and file within the system. The following list shows some of the attributes of a file.

- Filename
- Protection (access permissions)
- Number of hard links
- User ID of owner
- Group ID of owner
- Total size, in bytes
- Time of last access
- Time of last modification
- Time of last change

This can open up a host of problems within a Linux system. One of the most important aspects of file security relates to access permissions. You should pay close attention to how your system implements file security and be certain to employ it properly.

Chapter 21 Security

The file permission settings control who has access to a file, but they go beyond that. The permissions also state what those users can do to the file. The following dialog demonstrates the use of the `ls` command.

```
bash-2.03# ls -l
total 9094
-rwxr--r--   1 root     root       33869 Oct 22 17:09 SuSEconfig
-rwxr-xr-x   1 root     root     3670780 Nov  9 08:56 YaST
-rwxr-x---   1 root     root       17159 Nov  9 03:31 actctrl
-rwxr-xr-x   1 root     root        4756 Nov  8 18:28 activate
-rwxr-xr-x   1 root     root       14004 Nov  8 17:23 agetty
-rwxr-xr-x   1 root     root       31704 Nov  8 14:17 arp
-rwxr-x---   1 root     root       21951 Nov  9 03:31 avmcapictrl
-rwxr-xr-x   1 root     root        9708 Nov  8 18:28 badblocks
-rwxr--r--   1 root     root        3185 Apr 30  1999 bootp
-rwxr-xr-x   1 root     root       14520 Nov  8 14:33 bootpc
-rwsr-xr-x   1 root     root       22377 Nov  9 09:07 cardctl
-rwxr-xr-x   1 root     root       51848 Nov  9 09:07 cardmgr
-rwxr-xr-x   1 root     root       50456 Nov  8 17:23 cfdisk
-rwxr-xr-x   1 root     root       17668 Nov  9 10:46 checkproc
-rwxr-xr-x   1 root     root       67304 Nov  8 13:52 ckraid
lrwxrwxrwx   1 root     root           7 Jan  8 11:29 clock -> hwclock
drwxr-xr-x   2 root     root        1024 Jan  8 11:51 conf.d
-rwxr-xr-x   1 root     root        4308 Nov  8 17:23 ctrlaltdel
-rwxr-xr-x   1 root     root       86192 Nov  8 18:28 debugfs
-rwxr-xr-x   1 root     root       39608 Nov  8 13:41 depmod
bash-2.03#
```

The leftmost column shows us the file's type and its permissions. The first character, -, designates a normal file. If this character is the letter d, the file type is a directory. The letter l designates the file type to a link.

The remaining nine characters in the first column designate the access permissions for the file's owner, group, and "world." Each of the three classifications has three settings: r for read permission, w for write permission, and x for execute permission. If the letter is present, the permission is considered on; otherwise, it is off and is visually represented by the - character.

Consider the entry debugfs from the previous list. The entire permission setting for debugfs is rwxr-xr-x, which yields rwx for the owner, r-x for the group, and r-x for the world.

The rwx for the owner states that the owner root can read and write the file and execute it. The r-x for the root group states that the group can read the file and execute it. The permissions for the group are also applicable to the world (everyone else); that is, the rest of the world can read the file and execute it.

Network Access

Local area networks (LANs) provide for an easy portal into a system. Most system administrators feel secure about their LANs with respect to system security, but do not be fooled. The LAN provides an easy entry point into an otherwise secure system. All that is required is a machine with weak security to provide a penetration point for a cracker. If the security for just one machine on a LAN is weak, all systems on that LAN can be compromised.

You should require that all machines on a LAN be challenged for authentication. The machine name and username should both be authenticated. A trusted host allows a machine to connect to a host with a minimum of hassle. Usually, the names of the machines that are trusted can be found in the /etc/hosts, /etc/hosts.equiv, and any .rhosts files. Traditionally, passwords are not required for a trusted host connection.

Network File System

The *Network File System* (NFS) is a popular and widely used protocol for file sharing. It is discussed in detail in Chapter 12, "Network File Service (NFS)." NFS allows servers running the nfsd daemon and mountd to export entire filesystems to client machines utilizing the NFS filesystem support built in to their kernels or to machines that provide for NFS support in the kernel. The mountd daemon keeps track of mounted filesystems in the /etc/mtab file and can display them with the showmount command.

Many organizations use NFS to serve up users' home directories. This allows users to roam about and use more than one machine; thus, each user has access to her home directory.

If you are using NFS, be sure that you export only to the machines that actually require those services. You should never export your entire root directory. Take your time and set up NFS so that only the required directories are exported.

Network Information Service

The *Network Information Service* (NIS) is a method by which information can be distributed to a group of machines. It is discussed in detail in Chapter 11, "Network Information Service (NIS)." Fundamentally, the NIS master maintains the information tables, and it converts these tables to NIS map files. These map files are then distributed about the network to other machines.

The NIS clients can then obtain login, password, home directory, and shell information from these NIS map files. Incidentally, this information is the same as that found in the /etc/passwd file. Users can then manipulate their account information, such as changing passwords just one time and having that change take effect for all other NIS machines in the domain.

As you would expect, this type of functionality reduces the security that NIS can control. This is just a side effect of NIS being a flexible and easy information system. If a cracker could discover just the NIS domain name, accessing the /etc/passwd file is a piece of cake. NIS is also easily spoofed, so be sure you know the risks of running NIS before doing so.

The update to NIS is NIS+. NIS+ is more secure than NIS. If you are running NIS, you should check out NIS+ at http://metalab.unc.edu/mdw/HOWTO/NIS-HOWTO.html.

Firewalls

Firewalls have been around for quite a while. The concept is simple—the *firewall* is used to control the information that is allowed to flow into and out of your network.

To use an analogy, townhouses and office buildings use firewalls as a form of protection from fire. Although they are used to reduce the movement of fire, the concept is the same. Walls are strategically placed within the structure to retard the movement of fire to other parts of the structure. Even automobiles employ firewalls—a metal wall that separates the engine and passenger compartments. A computer firewall is the same, but it utilizes software as the "wall."

The very first firewall utilized a UNIX machine that had a connection to two distinct networks. One network card was connected to the Internet and the other card was connected to the internal network. If you wanted to get to the Internet, you had to log on to the UNIX firewall server. From that point, you would use the resources on the UNIX firewall server.

To this day, the firewall host is connected to both the Internet and your internal LAN. Any access to the Internet from your client machine (or vice versa) must travel through the firewall. This allows the firewall to have power over the data that is moving in and out of your private network.

As you would expect, Linux machines are a natural choice for firewall systems. You have flexibility in the number of options you can employ to set up a firewall. For Linux versions 2.0 and later, firewall support can be provided directly by the kernel.

If you have a Linux system utilizing an older Linux kernel, previous to 2.1.102, you can obtain a copy of the `ipfwadm` package from http://www.xos.nl/linux/ipfwadm.

If you are using Linux with a kernel version of 2.1.102 or later, you can obtain the `ipchaining` package from http://www.rustcorp.com/linux/ipchains. Regardless of the package, you can control the type of network traffic you will allow, and you can change the rules dynamically.

Good resources for firewall support are available. An excellent, yet dated, document can be found at the National Institute of Standards and Technology (NIST). The URL to the document is http://csrc.nist.gov/nistpubs/800-10/main.html.

Another good site is The Freefire Project, which can be found at http://sites.inka.de/sites/lina/freefire-l/index_en.html. You can get information on firewall tools, resources, and join their mailing list. Unfortunately, I find the site not very browser friendly.

Accounting Data

A lot of important information can be found in the `/var/log` directory. The following dialog shows the contents of a typical Linux `/var/log/` directory.

```
bash-2.03# ls -al
total 296
drwxr-xr-x    3 root     root         1024 Jan 21 01:33 .
drwxr-xr-x   17 root     root         1024 Jan  8 11:38 ..
-rw-r--r--    1 root     root         6419 Jan  8 18:07 Config.bootup
-rw-r--r--    1 root     root         3127 Jan 21 01:33 boot.msg
-rw-------    1 root     root           24 Jan 21 01:34 faillog
-rw-r--r--    1 root     root            0 Jan  8 11:34 httpd.access_log
-rw-r--r--    1 root     root         3682 Jan 21 01:34 httpd.error_log
-rw-rw-r--    1 root     tty           292 Jan 21 01:34 lastlog
-rw-r-----    1 root     root         1065 Jan  9 00:03 mail
-rw-r-----    1 root     root        45238 Jan 21 04:53 messages
drwxr-xr-x    2 news     news         1024 Jan  8 11:29 news
-rw-r-----    1 root     root          616 Jan  9 00:03 sendmail.st
-rw-------    1 wwwrun   root            0 Jan  8 11:34 ssl_scache.dir
-rw-------    1 wwwrun   root            0 Jan  8 11:34 ssl_scache.pag
-rw-r-----    1 root     root         9191 Jan 21 03:15 warn
-rw-rw-r--    1 root     tty        221568 Jan 21 04:53 wtmp
-rw-r-----    1 root     root            0 Nov  6 08:57 xdm.errors
bash-2.03#
```

You should ensure that the files in the `/var/log` directory can be viewed (read/write) only by appropriate personnel—only people in system administrator roles.

You should be familiar with your logging facility because different Linux distributions will perform their logging differently. You can discover where your Linux distribution is logging by viewing the /etc/syslog.conf file. The syslogd daemon uses this file to know where it is to log system messages. The following shows the contents of the /etc/syslog.conf on a freshly installed SuSE 6.3 Linux distribution:

```
# /etc/syslog.conf - Configuration file for syslogd(8)
# print most on tty10 and on the xconsole pipe
#
kern.warn;*.err;authpriv.none       /dev/tty10
kern.warn;*.err;authpriv.none       |/dev/xconsole
*.emerg                             *
#
# enable this, if you want that root is informed immediately
#*.alert      root
#
# all email-messages in one file
#
mail.*            -/var/log/mail
#
# all news-messages
# these files are rotated and examined by "news.daily"
news.crit         -/var/log/news/news.crit
news.err          -/var/log/news/news.err
news.notice       -/var/log/news/news.notice
# enable this, if you want to keep all
# news messages in one file
#news.*           -/var/log/news.all
#
# Warnings in one file
#
*.=warn;*.=err            -/var/log/warn
*.crit                    /var/log/warn
#
# save the rest in one file
#
*.*;mail.none;news.none    -/var/log/messages

# enable this, if you want to keep all
# messages in one file
#*.*              -/var/log/allmessages
```

As you can see, SuSE's syslogd daemon performs its logging to various files in the /var/log directory. The following shows the contents of a newly installed Red Hat 6.1 (Deluxe) distribution:

```
# Log all kernel messages to the console.
# Logging much else clutters up the screen.
#kern.*           /dev/console
# Log anything (except mail) of level info or higher.
```

```
# Don't log private authentication messages!
*.info;mail.none;authpriv.none        /var/log/messages
# The authpriv file has restricted access.
Authpriv.*              /var/log/secure
# Log all the mail messages in one place.
Mail.*                  /var/log/maillog
# Everybody gets emergency messages, plus log them on another
# machine.
*.emerg                         *
# Save mail and news errors of level err and higher in a
# special file.
uucp,news.crit          /var/log/spooler
# Save boot messages also to boot.log
local7.*           /var/log/boot.log
```

With this distribution of Red Hat, the logging is also performed to files in the /var/log directory. For contrast, the following is the contents of a version 4.0 distribution of Slackware.

```
# /etc/syslog.conf
# For info about the format of this file,
# see "man syslog.conf" (the BSD man page),
# and /usr/doc/sysklogd/README.linux.
*.=info;*.=notice      /usr/adm/messages
*.=debug               /usr/adm/debug
# We don't log messages of level 'warn'. Why?  Because if you're running
# a news site (with INN), each and every article processed generates a
# warning and a disk access.  This slows news processing to a crawl.
# If you want to log warnings, you'll need to uncomment this line:
#*.warn            /usr/adm/syslog
*.err              /usr/adm/syslog
#
# This might work instead to log on a remote host:
# *         @hostname
```

You should always be in the habit of analyzing your log files. Scripts can be created to automate repetitive tasks, such as validating idle time in log files. Idle time, you ask? If your system is heavily used, your log files might show a maximum of 60 seconds between log entries. This is considered the log idle time. Crackers are notorious for removing entries of their activities from log files before leaving the system. They do this for a couple of reasons. One is that they want to remove any traces of their existence on the system, especially those that would leave a trail to them. This also allows them to return again, especially if they find things on your system that they want. They also remove their trail of existence because it is part of the routine (challenge). The first part of the challenge is breaking in; the second part is getting out undetected.

Check for idle time in the log files. This is indicative of someone tampering with the log file—specifically, removing entries.

Look for short-lived entries, too. Scan for a log in session that is very short. Many crackers just want to get the right username and password. Some crackers will peruse your system for structure and content, and then log off. They capture the structure and content and review the data offline. They examine the data and then form a plan of attack.

Watch for usernames being used when they should not be. For example, suppose you discover a log in entry for the username `guest` and you have not had any visitors using your system. This should raise some suspicion. You then want to disable the guest account and change its password.

Make it a point to keep the `auth` facility from any other log information. This should include information such as log in, using `su` to switch user, and any other special accounting facts. Other facility keywords besides `auth` are `authpriv`, `cron`, `daemon`, `kern`, `lpr`, `mail`, `mark`, `news`, `security` (same as `auth`), `syslog`, `user`, `uucp`, and `local0` through `local7`. The facility specifies the subsystem that produced the message.

You should also force syslog to forward logging data to a secure machine. To enable this, use the at (@) sign (REMOTE MACHINE option) to relay the messages. This allows syslogd to send messages to a remote host also running `syslogd` and to receive messages from remote hosts. The remote host will not forward the message; rather, it will log them locally. If you want to forward messages to a remote host, you have to prepend the hostname using the @ sign. By doing this, you can control the syslog messages on one host if other machines will log (remotely) to it.

Refer to the man page for `syslog.conf` for more detailed information about other information pertaining to syslog rules.

Several more advanced syslogd programs are out there. Take a look at http://www.core-sdi.com/english/slogging/ssyslog.html for Secure Syslog. Secure Syslog allows you to encrypt your syslog entries and make sure no one has tampered with them.

Another syslogd providing more features is syslog-ng. It allows you a lot more flexibility in your logging facilities and uses remote syslog streams to prevent tampering.

The swatch (Simple Watchdog) tool is used for monitoring events. Swatch will modify specified programs, enhancing their logging capabilities. Software is also provided to monitor the system logs for important messages.

Finally, log files are much less useful when no one is reading them. Take some time out every once in a while to look over your log files and get a feeling for what they look like on a normal day. Knowing this can help make unusual things stand out.

Summary

We covered a lot of information concerning security in this chapter. We began with an overview of security, specifically discussing intruders. You learned the difference between a hacker and a cracker: a hacker is someone who has an extreme interest in computers, whereas a cracker is more interested in breaking into a system and potentially causing malicious damage. Crackers can fall into one of several categories: leeches, espionage, celebrity, investigative, piggyback, and malicious. Others exist, but these are the major categories.

Physical security was covered next, including natural and physical elements. Some of the natural elements are dust, electricity, smoke, and fire. You can guard against electrical problems by installing surge protectors and battery backup units. For fire, there are many methods of (reactive) prevention, such as smoke and fire detectors, alarms, and automatic extinguishing systems.

Some of the physical elements concern subjects such as security guards and access cards, BIOS locks, computer (case) locks, and system backup. I also discussed how to reduce the risk, including "revealing" paperwork, unattended hardware, unattended terminals, and user education.

Next, social engineering was covered, which is the ability for someone to negotiate something from another person utilizing tactics such as misrepresentation and persuasion.

Other security issues were discussed, such as passwords, account types, and encryption. Some of the account types discussed were command accounts, dead accounts, default accounts, guest accounts, and password-free accounts. Each of these account types has its weaknesses, and you should ensure that preventative measures are put into place.

Next, we jumped into the world of authentication, specifically discussing Kerberos Authentication and Pluggable Authentication Modules (PAM). Kerberos provides a method to prove the user's identity without sending user data on the network. PAM is a suite of shared libraries that enables the administrator to decide how applications perform user authentication.

Shadow passwords are a popular staple in the fight against intrusion. Traditionally, the /etc/passwd file contains the username and associated password for each user on the system. Shadow passwords are stored in the /etc/shadow file, allowing only privileged users access to it.

Then, we moved into file security, covering file permission settings, which control who has access to the file. These settings also state what those users can do to the files. Also covered are Network File System (NFS), Network Information Service (NIS), and firewalls. NFS is a widely used protocol for file sharing. NIS is a method to distribute information to a group of machines on the network. A firewall controls information that is allowed to flow into and out of a network. Each has its own special security limitations that should be addressed.

Finally, we covered accounting information and the need to safeguard it. You should ensure that files in the /var/log directory are viewed only by appropriate personnel. The /etc/syslog.conf file will reveal the directory your Linux distribution is logging to.

22

Managing Accounts

IN THIS CHAPTER, WE FOCUS primarily on the management of user and group accounts. It is important to understand what it takes to add, modify, and remove users and groups.

Beginning with the section that follows, an overview of user management is provided, followed by sections dealing with user account management and group account management.

Overview

Linux is a multitasking and multiuser operating system. When we talk about *multitasking*, we are referring to the fact that the operating system can execute more than one process at a time. Actually, only one process has the attention of the processor, but you can have multiple applications running and Linux will switch between these processes, allowing each application a slice of processor time.

Linux is also a multiuser operating system. This feature allows more than one user to be logged in to a single computer. Because Linux allows multiple users to be on the system at one time, each user on the system must be uniquely identified. There are a number of reasons for this.

First, each user on the system must be acknowledged and be held accountable for usage on the system. Many organizations require accounting information for each user on the system. In other words, each user's time is accounted for so that the user's time on the system can be billed to the appropriate department. Logging a user's time on a system provides a measure of accountability concerning activities while the user is utilizing the system.

Another reason that each user needs to be uniquely identified is for file storage requirements. When users log on to a Linux system, they are assigned a home directory where they can store files and other electronic artifacts. Many applications that are used with a Linux system store configuration information specific to the user currently using the application. For example, you might be using a word processing application and might have changed various options in the configuration window. When you save these options, the application stores your options to a special data file in your home directory (or other similar scheme).

A third reason is security. Some people might classify this subject as "classification of work." In other words, it's not so much that security is a concern, but it's the capabilities that are enabled for specific users. So, if Mary (an accountant) logs in to the system, she will be able to use the accounting system and examine all accounts and records. She will also be able to examine payroll records and perform other financially sensitive functions within the system. John, on the other hand, who is a data entry clerk, can access the accounting system only to add new shipping orders and inventory records. In addition, John can run spreadsheet and word processing applications pertaining only to his area of responsibility. This example shows both a concern for security and a focus for roles played within the system. We do not want John to access the accounting system and view everyone's payroll information. From a role perspective, we want to allow John to run only the spreadsheet and word processing applications. This helps to provide a focus of activities for John while he is in the system.

To help with these situations (and others), Linux provides support for multiple users to be logged in. Each user is given a unique name, known as a *username*, for identification. You cannot view a username just as something that is specific to one user—the picture is much greater than that. It is the artifacts that result from a user's use of the system. These artifacts include items such as files, system resources, and other system-oriented pieces of information that are specific to one user.

Managing Users

This section delves into the world of user management. Although this is an easy chore, it can be a consuming responsibility. This is especially true in a large organization employing hundreds or thousands of employees. Someone has to keep up with all the users on the system, and that someone is the system administrator.

It is not just the adding and removing of users from the system that can be so overwhelming. It is the change in status or directory paths. It might be the addition of an application to the system that applies only to 2 of the 500 people using the system. Yet, as an administrator, you must start somewhere when dealing with users. This involves adding a new user, removing a user, and associating a user with a group. Associating a user with a group adds another level of complication. We discuss groups in a section that follows.

In this section, we address the layout and functionality of the /etc/passwd file. We also examine what it takes to add a new user to the system and to remove a user from the system. Starting with the next section, we discuss the purpose and the use of the /etc/passwd file.

The /etc/passwd File

The /etc/passwd file can be viewed as the central repository for all users on a Linux system. The /etc/passwd file is not specific to Linux; indeed, the /etc/passwd file was born from UNIX systems. Most people refer to the file simply as the *password file*.

A word of caution: Before modifying the /etc/passwd file, you should always make a copy of the file. Although some text editors automatically create a backup file, you cannot rely on this happening with all editors.

The password file contains more than just a username. Many other pieces of information about a specific user are maintained in the password file. Also, various applications use the password file for various reasons, such as user verification and group information.

The structure of the /etc/passwd file is similar to that of other configuration-oriented files in Linux. Each line is dedicated to one user. Each line contains a number of fields that are separated by a colon. Seven fields compose a user's entry in the password file. Table 22.1 identifies these seven fields.

Table 22.1 **Entries in the `/etc/passwd` File**

Field	Description
`Username`	This is the username that uniquely identifies one user of the system. Each organization (usually) has a policy concerning the naming convention to be used for username creation.
`Password`	This is an encrypted form of a password that is specific to the username.
`Numeric user ID`	Each user is identified within the system with a unique ID that is numeric.
`Numeric group ID`	Each user is identified within the system to be a member of some group. Each group within the system can have zero or more usernames associated with it.
`Full name`	This is usually reserved for the user's full name (first and last names). You can also use it to store other information about a user.
`Home directory`	This field is a directory path indicating the user's home directory.
`Login shell`	This identifies the shell program to run after the user logs in to the system.

As mentioned previously, each of these fields (the file data) is separated by a colon, and each line is specific to one user. The following could represent a typical entry for the `/etc/passwd` file:

`sjcat:gTfs4Ggvfes4ws:122:100:Stimpson J. Cat:/home/sjcat:/bin/bash`

In this sample entry, the username is `sjcat`. The second field is the (unreadable) password entry. The third entry is the unique numeric ID that is associated with the username. The next field is the numeric group ID, 100, that is associated with `sjcat`. The entry `Stimpson J. Cat` is the full name entry, and the sixth entry is sjcat's home directory. The last field is the shell command to be launched, which is `/etc/bash`. The following is a sample `/etc/passwd` file.

```
stimpy $ cat /etc/passwd
root:x:0:0:root:/root:/bin/bash
bin:x:1:1:bin:/bin:/bin/bash
daemon:x:2:2:daemon:/sbin:/bin/bash
lp:x:4:7:lp daemon:/var/spool/lpd:/bin/bash
news:x:9:13:News system:/etc/news:/bin/bash
uucp:x:10:14::/var/lib/uucp/taylor_config:/bin/bash
games:x:12:100::/tmp:/bin/bash
man:x:13:2:::/var/catman:/bin/bash
```

```
at:x:25:25::/var/spool/atjobs:/bin/bash
postgres:x:26:2:Postgres Database Admin:/var/lib/pgsql:/bin/bash
lnx:x:27:27:LNX Database Admin:/usr/lib/lnx:/bin/bash
mdom:x:28:28:Mailing list agent:/usr/lib/majordomo:/bin/bash
wwwrun:x:30:65534:Daemon user for apache:/tmp:/bin/bash
squid:x:31:65534:WWW proxy squid:/var/squid:/bin/bash
fax:x:33:14:Facsimile Agent:/var/spool/fax:/bin/bash
gnats:x:34:65534:Gnats Gnu Backtracking System:/usr/lib/gnats:/bin/bash
adabas:x:36:100:Adabas-D Database Admin:/usr/lib/adabas:/bin/bash
irc:x:39:65534:IRC Daemon:/usr/lib/ircd:/bin/bash
ftp:x:40:2:ftp account:/usr/ftp:/bin/bash
anonymous:*:222:2:ftp account:/usr/ftp:/bin/false
firewall:x:41:31:firewall account:/tmp:/bin/false
informix:x:43:34:Informix Database Admin:/usr/lib/informix:/bin/bash
named:x:44:44:Name Server Daemon:/var/named:/bin/bash
db2fenc1:x:46:46:DB2 Instance UDF user:/usr/lib/db2/db2fenc1:/bin/bash
db2inst1:x:47:47:DB2 Instance main user:/usr/lib/db2/db2inst1:/bin/bash
db2as:x:48:48:DB2 Administration:/usr/lib/db2/db2as:/bin/bash
fnet:x:49:14:FidoNet:/var/spool/fnet:/bin/bash
gdm:x:50:15:Gnome Display Manager:/var/lib/gdm:/bin/bash
postfix:x:51:51:Postfix:/var/spool/postfix:/bin/false
cyrus:x:52:12:User for Imapd:/usr/cyrus:/bin/bash
nps:x:53:100:NPS admin:/opt/nps:/bin/bash
nobody:x:65534:65534:nobody:/tmp:/bin/bash
stimpy $
```

Notice that the root account has a userID of zero (0). The root account is also known as the superuser account. The username for the superuser account does not have to be root, although this is standard practice. You can, for example, use the name king or master if you like. Whatever name you choose, the userID is the determining factor by the system.

The first field for a user is the user's assigned username. Most organizations maintain a policy for username naming conventions. The most popular naming conventions are the concatenation of the user's first (name) initial and the user's last name. In the previous example, Stimpson J. Cat becomes scat because the first letter of the first name is prefixed to the last name. This is the most popular convention used, although other schemes can be employed. Another popular scheme is the user's first name spelled out fully, followed by an underscore (_) character, and then followed by the user's last name. Using our example then, the username would be stimpson_cat. This alleviates the duplication that can arise from the first name letter plus last name scheme. For example, Valarie Findlay and Vince Findlay will both resolve to the same username (using the first scheme). Another consideration for usernames is that some systems restrict the length of a username to eight characters. Letters, digits, the underscore (_), and period (.) can be used in the creation of a username.

The second field is the password and is unreadable because it is in an encrypted form. The password is not in human-readable form—and for good reason. Most every user on a Linux system can print (or view) the contents of the /etc/passwd file; this is why the password is encrypted. The encryption algorithm provides a high level of security. This is not, however, an excuse to choose simple and easy-to-crack passwords. Most Linux distributions use *shadow passwords*. The encrypted password is stored in a separate file named /etc/shadow. Only the root user can read this file. In the /etc/passwd file, a special marker is used in the second field. Refer to the previous /etc/passwd sample; the "x" character denotes this special marker. To change a user's password, you invoke the passwd command.

The third field is a unique number that is associated with the username, often called the UID. The system refers to a username using its associated UID, rather than the username. The system can process that number much faster than it can a string of text (username). Let's face it, computers are number-crunching machines.

UIDs and Shared Accounts

If more than one account has the same UID, they are considered to be equivalent. There are times when several users must share an account (in contrast to being members of the same group), when doing this is preferable to having those users share one account/password combination.

The fourth field is the group ID (GID) and is used to associate a user with some group. Group information is found in the file /etc/group and is discussed in a section that follows. Users should be associated with a group such as users or staff; they should not be associated with groups such as bin or mail.

The fifth field is the user's full name. Some organizations use this field for other identification purposes. This field is not used by Linux for any purpose; it is simply a free-form text field.

The sixth field is the user's home directory and should be unique. When users log in to the system, their current working directory will be the home directory specified in this field. A user's home directory is typically a subdirectory under the /home directory. The directory name is usually the same as the username, but it is not restricted to using it.

The last field designates the shell command that is launched for the user. For most Linux distributions, the login shell used is /bin/bash.

Next, we will see what we can do to add a user to the system.

Adding a User

We can edit the /etc/passwd file directly to add a user to the system. This can be somewhat cumbersome and can lead to trouble. Before demonstrating this method, we first examine two commands that can be used to add a user. Then, if you are feeling brave, we detail the manual method of adding a user by editing the /etc/passwd file.

You should note that not all Linux systems offer both the adduser and useradd commands. The most popular is (probably) the adduser command. In the next section, we detail the adduser command. If your Linux distribution offers both commands, be sure that the command files are unique (no link from one command to the other). For example, under RedHat, adduser is a symbolic link to the useradd command; erroneous results can be expected if you pass adduser options.

Using the adduser Command

The first command we examine is the adduser command. This command is used to add a nonexistent user to the system. The various forms of usage for adduser are as follows:

```
adduser [--system [--home directory] [--group]] [--quiet] [--force-badname] [--help]
        [--version] [--debug] username
adduser [--quiet] [--force-badname] [--help] [--version] [--debug] username group
adduser [--group] [--quiet] [--force-badname] [--help] [--version] [--debug] group
```

Table 22.2 lists the options to the adduser command.

Table 22.2 **Options to the adduser Command**

Option	Description
--system	Creates a new system user and is assigned the /bin/false shell; an asterisk is identified in the password field.
--home directory	Identifies the directory as the user's home directory. If the directory does not currently exist, it is created.
--group	Creates a group with the given name.
--quiet	Suppresses any progress messages.
--force-badname	Forces the commands (addgroup or adduser) to be less stringent. Usually, the username and group names must consist of a lowercase letter followed by lowercase letters or numbers.
--help	Shows any help text for the command.
--version	Displays the version information.
--debug	Provides debugging information.

The `adduser` command adds a user to the system. The command utilizes information found in the configuration file named /etc/adduser.conf. The `adduser` command automatically assigns an appropriate (and unique) UID and places the value into the /etc/passwd file.

If required, the `adduser` command creates a home directory for the username. Next, it copies the skeletal files (from /etc/skel) to the home directory. Finally, the command allows the system administrator to set a default password, plus finger information for the new user. The `adduser` command must be run as root.

If the `adduser` command is invoked with a single name, `adduser` creates a new user with the supplied name. If adduser is passed two names, `adduser` uses the first name as an existing user and the second name signifies an existing group; then adduser adds the existing user to the group.

Using the `useradd` Command

The next command we examine is the `useradd` command, which is a variation of the `adduser` command. This command is also used to add a nonexistent user to the system. The various forms of usage for `useradd` are as follows:

```
useradd [-c comment ] [-d dir ] [-e expire ] [-f inactive ] [-g group ]
[-G group [, group...]] [-m [ -k skel_dir ]] [-u uid [-o]] [ -s shell ] login
useradd -D [ -b base_dir ] [ -e expire ] [ -f inactive ] [ -g group ]
```

You should note that not all Linux systems offer both commands. The most popular is (probably) the `adduser` command. Table 22.3 identifies the options to the `useradd` command.

Table 22.3 **Options to the `useradd` Command**

Option	Description
-c comment	Comment is any text string. It is used as the field of the user's full name and is stored in the user's /etc/passwd entry.
-d dir	Home directory for the new user. The default is base_dir/username; base_dir is the base directory for login home directories (usually /home) and username is the new username.
-e expire	The expiration date for a login. Beyond this date, the user will not be able to access this login; usually used for temporary logins.
-f inactive	Specifies the maximum number of days between uses for a login ID.

Option	Description
-g *group*	Specifies an existing group's ID or string name.
-G *group*	Defines the new user's supplementary group membership for an existing username account.
-k *skel_dir*	The directory containing the skeleton information that can be copied to a user's home directory.
-m	Creates the new user's home directory if it does not already exist.
-s *shell*	Specifies the full pathname of the user's login shell.
-u *uid*	The UID of the new user; it must be a non-negative decimal number.
-o	Allows a UID to be duplicated.
-b *base_dir*	Identifies the default base directory if the -d option is not specified.

The useradd command performs two steps. First it adds the new user entry into the /etc/passwd file, and then it applies the password to the /etc/shadow file. The command also creates any group memberships for the user if the -G option is specified. It also creates the user's home directory if the -m option is specified. The new username entry is locked until you apply the passwd command for the account. You should note that the limit for a line using this command is set to 512 characters. Take this into consideration when supplying a new username account.

The username (or login) field is a string of no more than eight characters, although some distributions of Linux allow more characters. The legal characters can consist of alphabetic characters, numeric characters, the period (.), the underscore (_), and the hyphen (-). The first character specified must be alphabetic. The generally accepted practice is to use all lowercase alphabetic characters for a username. Most versions of useradd produce a warning message if you have not adhered to the rules.

Manually Create a New User

You can create a username account manually, without the use of the adduser or useradd commands. The following steps detail the sequence that is required. A quick note before starting: the vipw (or vi) command may not be available on your system; use whatever editor is appropriate.

1. Using the vipw command, edit the /etc/passwd file. Insert a new line and the required fields. You should not use another editor to edit this file; the vipw command applies appropriate locks to the /etc/passwd file while editing. Verify that you have supplied a username, UID,

GID, the user's full name, the home directory, and the user's login shell. For the password entry, use the star (*) character. You will use another command to set a default password. For the time being, a * for the password will disallow the use of the username.

2. Next, create the user's home directory that you identified in the /etc/passwd file. For example, if the username is newuser, execute the command **mkdir /home/newuser**.

3. After creating the user's home directory, you need to copy all the files from /etc/skel to the user's home directory. Using our example, issue the command **cp /etc/skel/* /home/newuser**.

4. Next, you need to set the ownership and permission using the chown and chmod commands. The recommended sequence of commands is as follows: **cd /home/newuser, chown -R username.group.**, and **chmod -R go=u,go-w**.

5. Finally, you need to set an initial password using the passwd command. This command is used to change the password and its attributes for a specified username. If your distribution uses an /etc/shadow file, you must be sure to add the user to that file.

If you require a new group for this new user, you will have to edit the /etc/group file. To edit this file, you need to use the vigw command, which is similar in operation to the vipr command. Supply the appropriate additions for the new group account and save the file.

After you have completed the final step (setting the password), the account should be accessible. The password step should be the last step in the manual process. If you change the password as an early step, the user will have the ability to log in before you have completed the remaining steps.

This exercise is beneficial because you may be required to create special accounts, such as the FTP account. This account is not used by any one person in particular. This account is normally called the *anonymous ftp* account. You may already be familiar with this if you have downloaded files from an FTP site. Most Linux systems create this account automatically during the installation process.

Removing a User

The commands in this section are fairly straightforward. Not many options can be applied because the focus of the commands is to simply remove a specified username from the system.

When removing a user from the system, you have to remember that besides the entry in the /etc/passwd file, you must remove all files, mailboxes, print jobs, cron jobs, and all references for the user. The `userdel` command is used to help facilitate all this housekeeping. The use of the `userdel` command is addressed in the next section.

Using the `userdel` Command

The `userdel` command is used to delete a user's login from the system. The syntax is as follows:

```
userdel [ -r ] login
```

The `userdel` command first deletes the specified username from the system and causes other changes in the system for that username. The only option to the `userdel` command is the `-r` option. This option removes the user's home directory from the system. After the command has completed, the associated files and directories will not be accessible.

Manually Removing a User

You can also manually remove a user from the system, the same as you can manually add a user to the system. This section addresses the removal of a user from the system; the user `dummy` is assumed here.

First, you must remove the `dummy` entry found in the /etc/passwd file. This is quite easy; just fire up your editor and bring the /etc/passwd into the editor. Locate the line for `dummy` and delete the line. Save the file and return to the command prompt. Also, if your distribution uses an /etc/shadow file, be sure to remove the user's entry in that file, too.

Next, you should check for a `dummy` entry in the /etc/group file. This is also easy; just bring /etc/group into your favorite editor. Locate any line(s) containing `dummy` and remove the `dummy` user entry (or entries). Save the file and return to the command prompt.

Next, you need to remove the user's home directory. Assuming the standard /home/... directory path, issue the `rm` command as follows:

```
stimpy $ rm -r /home/dummy
```

Be absolutely sure you are removing the appropriate home directory before submitting the recursive delete.

Finally, you need to purge the mail spool file and crontab entries for the user. In a pinch, you can run the `rm` command against the user's spool file, such as in the following dialog. This dialog also demonstrates the use of the `crontab` command to remove entries for user `dummy`.

```
stimpy $ rm -r /var/spool/mail/dummy
stimpy $ crontab -u dummy -r
```

You can also follow up these steps by performing a systemwide search for the username `dummy`.

Managing Groups

Each user is a member of one or more groups within a Linux system. The magic of groups pertains to file permissions and accessibility. Each file maintains group ownership attributes and permissions that define how the users in that group can access the file.

Some of the more common system-defined groups are `bin`, `mail`, and `sys`. No user should be a member of any of the system-defined groups. A group such as `users` is a more appropriate group for user.

In the next section, we discuss adding a new group to the system, followed by a section concerning the removal of a group.

Adding a Group

The `groupadd` command is used to create a new group and its definition. The command applies the attributes by adding the new entry to the /etc/group file. The syntax for the command is as follows:

```
groupadd [ -g gid [ -o ] ] group
```

Table 22.4 details the options for the `groupadd` command.

Table 22.4 **Options to the `groupadd` Command**

Option	Description
-g gid	Assigns the group ID gid for the new group. This group ID must be a non-negative decimal integer below MAXUID as defined in /usr/include/sys/param.h.
-o	Allows the gid to be duplicated.

The following dialog shows the contents of a sample /etc/group file:

```
stimpy $ cat /etc/group
root:x:0:root
bin:x:1:root,bin,daemon
daemon:x:2:
tty:x:5:
disk:x:6:
lp:x:7:
wwwadmin:x:8:
kmem:x:9:
wheel:x:10:
mail:x:12:cyrus
```

```
news:x:13:news
uucp:x:14:uucp,fax,root,fnet
shadow:x:15:root,gdm
dialout:x:16:root
at:x:25:at
lnx:x:27:
mdom:x:28:
yard:x:29:
dosemu:x:30:
firewall:x:31:
public:x:32:
video:x:33:
informix:x:34:
game:x:40:
xok:x:41:
trusted:x:42:
modem:x:43:
named:x:44:named
postfix:x:51:postfix
dbmaker:x:52:
users:x:100:
nogroup:x:65534:root
stimpy $
```

The information contained in the /etc/group file is similar in structure to the /etc/passwd file detailed previously. Each group entry exists on a single line. Each line is separated into four distinct fields, using the colon (:) as the separator.

The first field is the group name and should consist of alphanumeric characters. The second field is the password and is usually left blank (or an asterisk is used). This field usually exists for backward compatibility because most versions of Linux do not support this field. The third field is the group ID number—each group should have a unique value. The fourth field is a list of all user IDs that are members of the group.

Modify a Group

You can modify a group using the groupmod command. The syntax for this command is as follows:

```
groupmod [ -g gid [ -o ] ] [ -n name ] group
```

The groupmod command allows you to modify the definition of a group. The command will modify the associated entry found in the /etc/group file. Table 22.5 details the options that are supported by the groupmod command.

Table 22.5 **Options to the `groupmod` Command**

Option	Description
`-g gid`	Identifies the new group ID for the group. The group ID must be a non-negative decimal integer less than `MAXUID`.
`-o`	Allows the GID to be duplicated.
`-n name`	Specifies the new name for the group.

The `groupmod` command is used to modify a group definition in the `/etc/group` file. If NIS or NIS+ is used to supplement the local `/etc/group` file, the `groupmod` command will not change information supplied by NIS. The `groupmod` command validates the group name and group ID to the external name service. Refer back to Chapter 11, "Network Information Service (NIS)," for more information concerning NIS.

Removing a Group

The `groupdel` command is used to delete a group definition from the `/etc/group` file. The syntax is as follows:

`groupdel group`

The command deletes the appropriate entry from the `/etc/group` file.

You should note that the `groupdel` command will delete only a group definition that is found in the `/etc/group` file. If a NIS or NIS+ is used to complement the (local) `/etc/group` file, the `groupdel` command will not be able to change the information supplied by NIS.

Summary

In this chapter, we covered the management of user accounts. Because Linux is a multiuser operating system, we need a way to maintain the users who access the system. This is done by creating a user account for each user on the system. Unique usernames are used so that each user's work can be uniquely identified and stored on the system, providing a way to isolate a user's work (from other users). There are security reasons for maintaining unique username accounts for all users on the system.

We examined the structure of the `/etc/passwd` file. We discovered that the `/etc/passwd` file consists of seven fields, including username, password, user ID, group ID, full name, home directory, and login shell command.

We examined how to add a new user to the system. Two commands are available to add a user: adduser and useradd. Some Linux systems have both commands, and some Linux systems have one or the other. Refer to your system documentation for details. We also examined how to manually add a user to the system.

Also covered in this chapter is the removal of users from the system. The userdel command is covered; this command automates the process of removing the username entries from the /etc/passwd and /etc/group files and also any crontab and mail entries. We also covered the process of manually removing a user.

We covered the use of the /etc/group file and the commands associated with adding and removing groups. The groudadd, groupmod, and groupdel commands were covered. These commands allow you to manipulate groups on your system and the users that are related to those groups.

23
Other Administrative Tasks

THIS CHAPTER DEALS WITH THE administrative tasks that are of great importance on a Linux system. Other chapters have discussed Linux installation and maintenance, user administration, and some of the tools that would be used on a weekly basis by a system administrator.

This chapter covers some of the deep technical administrative chores such as backup and recovery, security, and file maintenance.

Overview

System administration, in my opinion, is really a state of mind. Yes, there are daily chores that must be accomplished to maintain a Linux (or UNIX) system. These daily chores *must* be adhered to in order to keep the users happy and their daily routines trouble-free. Yet there is more to administration than checking off a list of tasks day after day.

Good system administrators have a curiosity about what makes the system tick and a need to troubleshoot. It must seem strange that someone would want to troubleshoot a system, but it is true. Troubleshooting presents a challenge to the administrator. Yet at the same time, it presents some heartaches and sleepless nights.

Performing some preventative maintenance can alleviate some of the heartaches and sleepless nights. In order to cut down on future maintenance costs, organizations implement preventative measures. What is the old saying—an ounce of prevention is worth a pound of cure? This also applies to system administration.

For example, if you perform weekly preventative maintenance on the system's hard disk(s), the life of the hard disk(s) will be prolonged—assuming that there are no manufacturer defects.

Performing weekly maintenance on user account configuration reduces the likelihood of crackers gaining access to the system. Of course, you must ensure that other security holes are corked up. You should pay attention to security notices posted on the Internet describing new methods of attack performed by crackers. Some people will disagree with me, but as a system administrator, you should subscribe to *2600 Magazine*. Why subscribe to a magazine that is advertised as the "hacker's quarterly"? This magazine (and others like it) can make you aware of methods employed by crackers. One good site is `http://www.rootshell.com`, which provides security news, exploits, and more. For a fairly comprehensive moderated mailing list for the discussion and announcement of computer security vulnerabilities, join the BugTraq mailing list. To join, simply send an email to `listserv@securityfocus.com` with the text `SUBSCRIBE BUGTRAQ Lastname, Firstname` in the body of the email.

Staying informed is the key to successful system administration. Administrators who maintain a true interest in their work will be far ahead of the game compared to administrators who wait for the end of the day.

Root Account

This was discussed in another chapter, but it is worth repeating here. You must remember that the root account is the most privileged account on a Linux system. You can do absolutely anything you want if you have root privileges: add, edit, and remove users; modify user passwords; install and remove software; and delete unwanted files (and *wanted* files, if you aren't careful).

Bad things can happen while you're logged in as the root account. I have seen system administrators do what is shown here:

```
bash-2.03#
bash-2.03# cd / tmp
bash-2.03# rm * -r
bash-2.03#
```

This looks fairly harmless at first glance. There are no errors or warnings. But look closer. The first command executed is `cd / tmp`, not `cd /tmp`, which produces a different outcome. The `cd` command used in the dialog changes to the `root` directory, not `/tmp` as the administrator anticipated. Try it on your system—execute `cd / tmp` and then execute the `pwd` command. You will discover that you are indeed in the root directory. So the administrator executed the two commands without thinking about or verifying the results of her actions. Some administrators execute the ls command before committing to the rm command. But back to the administrator. She stared in disbelief at the commands she had executed. By the time she pressed Ctrl+C, the damage had been done. If you are unfamiliar with the potential results of the rm* -r command, it obliterates all files in the current (or specified) directory and continues this operation recursively in subdirectories.

You should always log in using a normal user account, unless you have to perform root-level maintenance. Many administrators feel less than adequate if they log in as anything but the root account. Do not let your ego get in the way, or you might have the same experience as the administrator just described.

If you are logged in as root under Red Hat Linux and you execute the GNOME file manager, an error message is displayed informing you that you are running as root. If you are logged in as the root account, the # is displayed as the last character in the prompt. This is a reminder that you are running as the root account. I know an administrator who modifies the shell prompt to read !RooT!-> to remind him of his power.

Beware the strength of the root account. Execute every command with caution. Always think twice about what you are about to execute, and then think again. It pays to be prepared and cautious.

Rotating User Passwords

You should always set up each user account so that its password expires on a rotating basis. Most users do not like to change their passwords all the time, but it is a good security measure to combat crackers.

On really large corporate systems, you should rotate passwords at least every 45 days. Many administrators rotate passwords every 30 days. If you are running a small office system of about 30 users, rotating passwords can be relaxed to about 60 days, especially if the system has Internet access. If the system is a fully enclosed LAN, you might relax rotation beyond 60 days. I do not recommend this, however, because certain employees can become disgruntled and wreak havoc on the system.

If you are using SuSE Linux, you can use the YaST tool to set the expiration of a password for an account. From the YaST menu, select the System Administration, User Administration menu option. The User Administration window appears. Once you have a user profile loaded, press the F6 function key to reveal the Duration of Password screen.

Generically (regardless of distribution), you can set password expiration for user accounts utilizing the `passwd` command. The -x, -n, -w, and -i options are used to execute password aging on an account.

Use the -x *max* option to set the maximum number of days that a password remains valid. After *max* days have passed, the user is required to change the password.

Use the -n *min* option to set the minimum number of days before a password can be changed. The user cannot change his or her password until *min* days have elapsed.

The -w *warn* option sets the number of days the user is warned before his or her password expires. The warning begins to occur *warn* days before the password expiration. The warning tells the user how many days remain.

Use the -i *inact* option to disable an account after *inact* days have passed after the password has expired. The user will no longer be able to sign on to the account.

You can also edit the /etc/shadow file directly to change the password aging information. This makes it easier to change multiple users at one time.

Some distributions of Linux, such as Red Hat, utilize the `chage` command to support the options just listed. The usage of `chage` is as follows:

```
chage [-m mindays] [-M maxdays] [-d lastday] [-I nactive]
   [-E xpiredate] [-W warndays] user
```

System Backup and Restoration

You must perform system backups at regular intervals. This cannot be stressed enough. Failures can occur, so it is always prudent to be prepared for a system restoration.

Many problems can occur. There are various hardware failures, such as a hard disk crash or power outage. Human error accounts for many system outages, from accidental to deliberate acts. Earlier you read about an administrator who accidentally executed the `rm -r *` command at the root directory.

A typical backup procedure consists of copying partition data onto an external medium. This external medium can take many forms, such as CD-ROM, tape, or removable drives. This affords you the ability to keep the medium off site and in a safe place. You can also reuse the medium to help save money.

You can also perform a backup to another machine. On a large corporate system, this makes sense, because the backup to moveable media can be executed on one machine. For example, say you have servers scattered about the country. Each of these servers can execute a `cron` job to archive data files to a central server. Then, only this server will require a backup to external media.

Backup Considerations

Just as there are many distributions of Linux, there are many ways to execute a backup. Some command-line tools have been with us for quite a while, such as cpio, dd, dump, and tar. There are tools supplied by the distribution's vendor, both text-based and graphics-based. For example, the YaST tool that is included with SuSE Linux provides an interactive front end for performing a backup. Archiving utilities are provided with some of the graphical desktops such as KDE's Kdat, a tar-based tape archive utility. We cannot forget about the commercial tools, such as BRU (Enhanced Software Technologies), UNiBACK (Orbit Software), and PerfectBackup+ (Merlin Software).

When reviewing these tools, you should consider a few things. One, of course, is ease of use. Do you need a user interface to ease the selection of files and directories and unattended scheduling? Along these lines, technical support can be thought of as providing ease of use (and piece of mind). Unattended backup is another consideration. If you require fairly sophisticated scheduling, look for this feature in a product. There are other things to consider, such as portability and network backups.

You should make a checklist of the features that are important for your organization and use it when comparison shopping.

Backup Tools

We will look at a couple of tools that can be used to perform routine backup. We will take a quick look at a number of tools, both graphical and command-line.

Using KDE's KDat

Most distributions of Linux now include the K Desktop Environment (KDE). KDE offers a graphical tool called KDat. KDat provides a nice graphical interface and uses the tar utility for creating archives. This offers you the choice of moving the archive to another Linux (or UNIX) system. Figure 23.1 shows the KDat utility after invocation.

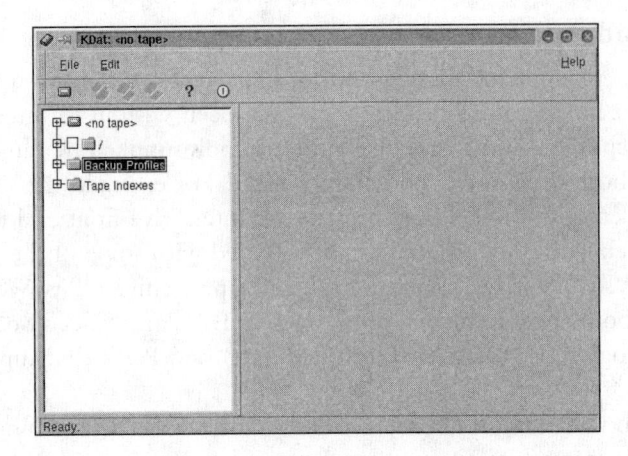

Figure 23.1 KDE's KDat archive utility.

If you have installed the K Desktop Environment, you can find the KDat tool on the Utilities menu, labeled as Tape Backup Tool. You can also execute it using the command window. Press Alt+F2, type **kdat**, and press Enter. The interface consists of a tree view in the left panel and a data panel on the right side.

If you have never used this tool, you should first select the File, Create Backup Profile menu option. The data panel on the right displays a number of fields and two tab pages, Backup and Tar Options. You need to provide a profile name and archive name. The profile names are helpful in describing the type of backup. For example, you might have a backup profile named Incremental or Full Backup.

Next, you need to specify the directories and files you want to include in the backup. First, click the Working directory pull-down (in the right panel). Next, click the + associated with the root directory (in the left panel). Figure 23.2 shows the result of clicking the tree and shows the right panel opened.

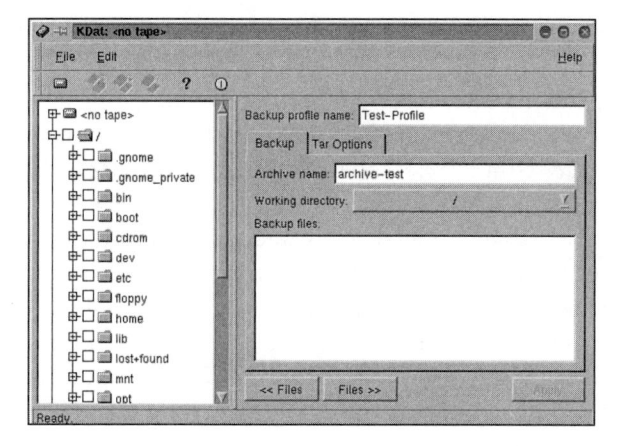

Figure 23.2 KDE's KDat with the root tree open.

Notice that there is an empty box between the + and the folder icon for each folder. If you click in this box, an x appears. A file or directory that is marked (that has an x) will be included in the backup. To perform a full backup, mark the root directory. This will select all the subdirectories and the files within them. Next, remove the x from the box next to the /proc and /mnt subdirectories. You do not want to back up the contents of /proc and probably do not want to back up whatever filesystems are mounted. When you have all the directories and files selected, click the Files >> button in the right panel. Figure 23.3 shows the results.

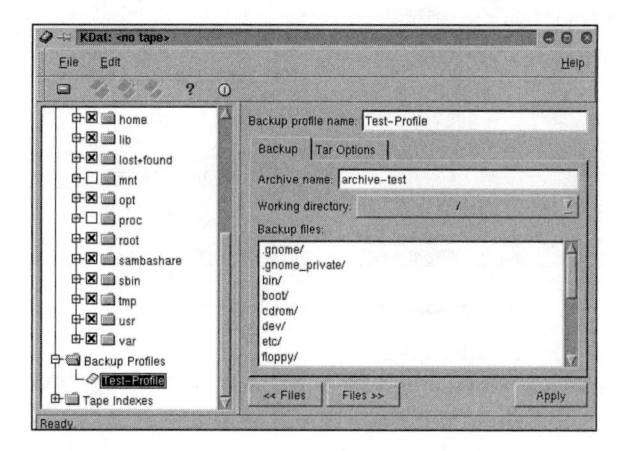

Figure 23.3 KDE's KDat with directories selected.

Be sure to click the Apply button. The final step is to actually back up to tape. Be sure that you have a tape inserted in the drive. Next, select the Mount Tape menu selection from the File menu.

If you receive an error message that says the tape is not available, check the preference settings. Select the Edit, Preferences menu option and be sure that the correct tape drive device is selected. Ensure that the profile you want to use is selected, right-click it, and choose the Backup option. A dialog box appears. Simply click the OK button after you have confirmed the details. The backup will begin. KDat shows the progress of the backup in a dialog box. When the backup is complete, be sure to unmount and eject the tape. To unmount, select File, Unmount Tape. Optionally, you can click the tape drive toolbar icon, or right-click the tape drive tree node and select Unmount Tape.

For more information about KDat, select Help, Contents.

Using YaST Under SuSE

SuSE's YaST configuration utility offers a simple way to back up files. Start YaST, and then select the System Administration, Create Backups menu option. The screen shown in Figure 23.4 is displayed.

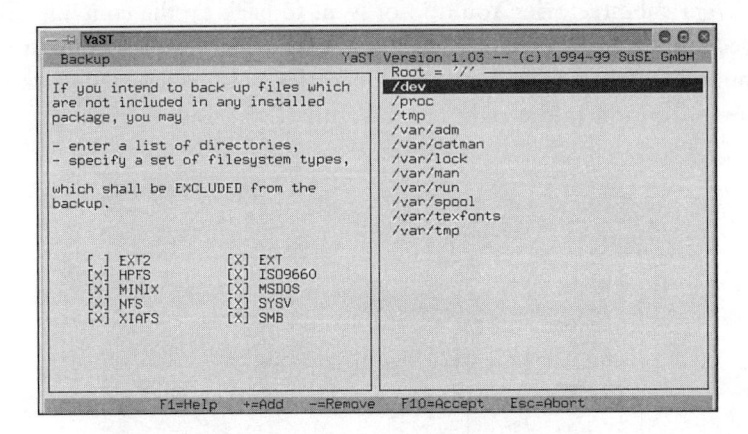

Figure 23.4 SuSE's YaST backup utility.

The right pane is where everything happens. Select the directories to *exclude* from the backup, and press the F10 key to continue. The utility scans the disk for files that have changed. When the tool is finished with its scan, it displays the file selection screen, shown in Figure 23.5.

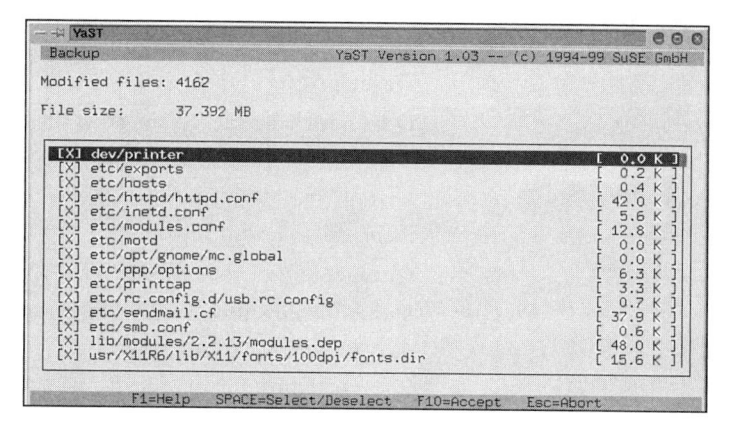

Figure 23.5 SuSE's YaST backup file selection screen.

At this screen, you can further refine the files to be included in the backup. Once you are satisfied with the choices, press the F10 key to continue.

Next, you have the option of specifying the archive name and specific options. If you decide to save to a partition, be sure sufficient space is available.

Using the tar Utility

If you want to use the tar utility, you should become familiar with the appropriate options to satisfy your type of backup. Table 23.1 shows the functional options for tar (you must select one option from this table). Table 23.2 shows the miscellaneous options available for tar.

Table 23.1 **Functional Options for tar**

Option	Description
-A, —catenate, —concatenate	Appends tar files to an archive.
-c, —create	Creates a new archive.
—delete	Deletes files from the archive (do not use magnetic tapes).
-r, —append	Appends files to the end of an archive.
-t, —list	Lists the contents of an archive.
-u, —update	Appends only files that are newer than the copies in the archive.
-x, —extract, —get	Extracts files from an archive.

Table 23.2 Miscellaneous Options for tar

Option	Description
`--atime-preserve`	Does not change access times on the dumped files.
`-b, --block-size N`	Uses a block size of $N{\times}512$ bytes.
`-B, --read-full-blocks`	Reblocks as reads happen.
`-C, --directory DIR`	Changes to directory named *DIR*.
`--checkpoint`	Shows the directory names while reading the archive.
`-f, -file [HOSTNAME:]file`	Uses an archive file or a device named *file*.
`--force-local`	Archive file is local.
`-F, --info-script F` `--new-volume-script file`	Runs a script at the endof each tape.
`-G, --incremental`	Creates, lists, or extracts an old GNU-format incremental backup.
`-g, --listed-incremental F`	Creates, lists, or extracts a new GNU-format incremental backup.
`-h, --dereference`	Does not dump the symbolic links. Rather, it dumps the files the symbolic links point to.
`-i, --ignore-zeros`	Specifies to ignore blocks of zeros in the archive, which usually signifies EOF.
`--ignore-failed-read`	Does not exit with nonzero status if files are unreadable.
`-k, --keep-old-files`	Keeps existing files and does not overwrite them in the archive.
`-K, --starting-file file`	Begins at the file named *file* in the archive.
`-l, --one-file-system`	Stays in the local filesystem when creating an archive.
`-L, --tape-length N`	Changes tapes after writing $N{\times}1024$ bytes.
`-m, --modification-time`	Does not extract the file-modified time.
`-M, --multi-volume`	Creates, lists, or extracts a multivolume archive.
`-N, --after-date DATE,` `--newer DATE`	Stores only files newer than named *DATE*.
`-o, --old-archive, --portability`	Writes a V7 format archive rather than ANSI format.
`-O, --to-stdout`	Extracts files to the standard output.
`-p, --same-permissions,` `--preserve-permissions`	Extracts all protection information.

Option	Description
-P, --absolute-paths	Does not strip leading /s (slashes) from filenames.
--preserve	The same as -p -s; all protection information is extracted and a list of names to extract is sorted to match the archive.
-R, --record-number	Shows a record number within the archive with each message.
--remove-files	Removes files after adding them to the archive.
-s, --same-order, --preserve-order	A list of names to extract is sorted to match the archive.
-S, --sparse	Handles sparse files in an efficient manner.
-T, --files-from F	Gets names to extract or create from file F.
--null -T	Reads null-terminated names.
--totals	Prints the total bytes written with —create.
-v, --verbose	Verbosely lists files processed.
-V, --label NAME	Creates an archive with a volume named NAME.
--version	Prints the tar program's version number.
-w, --interactive, --confirmation	Asks for confirmation for every action.
-W, --verify	Attempts to verify the archive after writing it.
--exclude FILE	Excludes the file named FILE.
-X, --exclude-from FILE	Excludes files listed in FILE.
-Z, --compress, --uncompress	Filters the archive through compress.
-z, --gzip, --ungzip	Filters the archive through gzip.
--use-compress-program PROG	Filters the archive through a program named PROG.
--block-compress	Blocks the output of the compression program for tapes.
-[0-7][lmh]	Specifies the drive and density.

As an extreme example, the following performs a complete backup of your system and writes it to the /backup filesystem. As usual, you want to exclude the /proc, /mnt, and /backup filesystems.

```
tar -zcvpf /backup/full-backup.tar.gz \
    —directory / —exclude=mnt —exclude=proc —exclude=backup .
```

If you refer to the previous tables, you can quickly decipher the options being used. The z specifies compression of the archive. c specifies that the archive is to be created. v produces verbose output. p specifies to preserve permissions. `f` names the file for the archive. The `—directory` option tells tar to move to the named directory. The `—exclude` options identify the directories to exclude from the backup. The final . is intentional. It tells tar to back up everything in the current directory. Remember, the `—directory` option told tar to move to the / (root) directory.

Once the archive is written, you can move it to any medium you choose. If you want to write to magnetic tape, be sure to check out the `mt` command.

Finally, to restore the previous archive, you would execute the following command:

```
tar -zxvpf /backup/full-backup.tar.gz
```

That's all there is to it.

Using cron and crontab Files

If you're like me, you execute certain commands on a regular basis. You might want to execute a command every hour on the hour or once a day at midnight.

The `cron` command and `crontab` files are used to schedule commands and processes that repeat at specified intervals. Dates and times are specified in the crontab files. The `cron` daemon is started at system startup and can be seen running using the `ps x` command. The `cron` command should not be executed from the command line, even by a system administrator.

Here is the format of a `crontab` file:

```
minute    hour    day    month    day    command
```

Each of the date and time components can be expressed as an integer. The following list shows the values for each of the fields.

- Minute: 0 to 59
- Hour: 0 to 23
- Day of month: 0 to 31
- Month: 0 to 12 (or names; see the following discussion)
- Day of week: 0 to 7 (or use names)

You can use the * (asterisk) to logically designate "all" for the component. For example, a * for the *year* component means "every year."

A range of numbers can be specified. A range consists of two numbers separated by a hyphen (-), the range being inclusive. For example, `7-10` for the *hours* entry specifies execution at hours 7, 8, 9, and 10.

Lists are also allowed. They are a set of numbers (or ranges) separated by commas. For example, `1,2,5,9` and `0-4,8-12` are valid range specifications.

Names can be used for the *month* and *day* of week fields. This is the preferred method, because the month and day are obvious. Use the first three letters of the day or month. Unfortunately, ranges and lists of names are disallowed.

A couple of examples are in order:

```
15 09 * * 03 date
```

This `crontab` entry is used to execute the `date` command at 9:15 a.m. every Wednesday.

```
00 10 * * * cat /var/log/messages | mail root
```

This `crontab` entry mails the contents of the `/var/log/messages` file to the root account at 10 a.m. every morning.

Most Linux distributions offer the following crontab directories:

- `/etc/cron.hourly`: Runs the command every hour.
- `/etc/cron.daily`: Runs the command once a day.
- `/etc/cron.weekly`: Runs the command once a week.

Scripts or any other executables can be placed into any of these directories. This relieves you of having to develop a `crontab` entry. If you have a command that fits into one of these categories, place it in the appropriate directory. The file can be a symbolic link to the actual command.

System Monitoring

System monitoring must be an aggressive effort. This doesn't mean you should sit at your computer every minute of every day and watch the system running. It means you should take a proactive role in monitoring the system. Be aware of the potential for break-ins. Keep up with current events in the security arena. Read the hacker magazines and Web sites to gain insight into the habits and methods of attack.

A principle of software development is that of change management (versioning). The intent is to create an initial baseline of the software and then continue creating versions throughout the software's life cycle. Version-control software, complete with a repository, is used to check software components into and out of the repository. This allows you to go back to a previous version of a component if necessary.

The same concept should be applied to an operating system such as Linux. Some of the smarter system administrators create a snapshot of a system after initial installation. This might seem extreme, but if the system is being used as a Web or application server, it's a small price to pay to be secure. Running `ls -AlR / > sys.list`, `netstat -a -n > net.list`, `vmstat > virtmem.list`, `free > free.list`, and `df -k > disk.list` can help with respect to intrusion detection. Most of these tools can help in the area of allocating system resources—an area that can reveal processes that might be stealing resources.

Be sure to back up your system regularly. If your business relies on computer operations, you should maintain at least a month's worth of backup media.

Any time a system configuration file is modified, its statistics should be recorded. This helps in pinpointing the date that an intrusion might have occurred. Also, save those important log files for future reference.

Some very good tools are available to detect and prevent intrusion. We will examine some of the tools available.

Monitoring the Network

This one is very important because it is the network that is compromised when a break-in occurs. There are times when the intrusion happens from within the corporate walls, but most are from the outside. The intent here is to place the proper safeguards on network intrusion. The use of firewalls plays an important role in the prevention of a network breach. Other tools can aid in the prevention and detection of a network breach; we will discuss them in this section.

To keep in sync with the tradition of Linux, many of the tools are freely available. Many corporations see free software (actually, open-source software) as inadequate. For software, this rationale is incorrect. If you are going to be using software to safeguard your system, it makes sense to use software that has source code included. This allows you to alter the software to your needs and also to gain an understanding of the software's internal workings.

Some of the following tools are well known and are used in the Linux community.

Deception ToolKit (DTK)

This toolkit provides the functionality of deception to oppose an attack. To the attacker, the system appears to have a number of vulnerable entry points (which hopefully are not there). The attacker tries a security hole, and DTK provides the proper response, leading the attacker to believe he has compromised the system.

The DTK package listens for inputs on the system and supplies expected responses (of security flaws). DTK also logs the activity, providing a blueprint of the attacker.

You can find DTK at `http://www.all.net/dtk`.

Klaxon

Klaxon is useful for detecting port scanner attacks, such as those committed by ISS and SATAN, among others. It also has optional support for IDENT to reveal the remote user.

Klaxon is available at `ftp://ftp.eng.auburn.edu/pub/doug/`.

Psionic HostSentry

HostSentry is used as a host-based login detection and response tool. This tool works by monitoring the interactive login sessions and identifying unusual behavior that might point to an intrusion. HostSentry uses a dynamic database and signatures to detect any misuse. It also reports and reacts to the events in real time.

The HostSentry product can be found at `http://www.psionic.com/abacus`.

Psionic PortSentry

PortSentry is a component of the Abacus Project suite of security tools. PortSentry is designed to detect, log, and respond specifically to port scans performed against a host.

The product runs on TCP and UDP sockets and detects port scans against a system. You can configure PortSentry to run on multiple sockets simultaneously, so only one copy of PortSentry is required to handle multiple services. PortSentry can react to port scans by blocking the host in real time. PortSentry can report violations to either the local or remote syslog daemons. Information logged includes the system name, the time of the attack, the attacking host IP, and the TCP or UDP port the connection was made to.

The PortSentry product can be found at `http://www.psionic.com/abacus`.

TCP-WRAPPERS

Wietse Venema's TCP-WRAPPERS allows you to restrict connections to various services based on IP address and other criteria.

Using TCP-WRAPPERS, you can monitor and filter incoming requests for the EXEC, FINGER, FTP, RLOGIN, RSH, SYSTAT, TALK, TELNET, TFTP, and other network services. The package supports both 4.3BSD-style sockets and System V.4-style TLI.

The package provides daemon wrapper programs that can be installed without changes to existing software or configuration files. The wrappers identify the client host and the requested service. The wrappers do not exchange information with the client or server applications.

TCP-WRAPPERS comes standard with source code, so it can be adapted to most distributions. It is available via FTP at `ftp://ftp.porcupine.org/pub/security`.

Monitoring the Filesystem

You should never overlook filesystem monitoring. The majority of attacks are aimed at modifying the filesystem in some way. Malicious destruction of files and directories is typical. In other instances, files are stored on the host system in hidden directories.

Audits should be conducted on your systems' filesystems. Determining the frequency of audits depends on many variables, such as the number of users and whether your systems are exposed to the outside world. If your systems have high visibility to the outside world, you should think about bringing in ethical crackers. These are people who try to break in to your systems and provide feedback as to the security flaws they uncover.

To help provide a more proactive stance with respect to invasion of your filesystems, you should investigate and choose one of the packages described in the following sections. These packages offer a way to "take inventory" of your files and to make comparisons (verify them) in the future.

AIDE

The Advanced Intrusion Detection Environment (AIDE) is an alternative to Tripwire (described later) and is free for the downloading. The author claims that AIDE provides the same functionality (and more) as the semi-free Tripwire.

AIDE creates a database based on the regular expression rules defined in the configuration file. Once the database is baselined, it is used to verify the integrity of files. Some of the algorithms used to check the integrity of the files are haval, md5, rmd160, sha1, and tiger, in addition to others. You can add other algorithms as required. The tool can check file attributes for inconsistencies. AIDE can be found at `http://www.cs.tut.fi/~rammer/aide.html`.

Big Brother

The Big Brother product includes local clients to test system conditions and availability of network services. The results are sent to DISPLAY servers or PAGER servers, notifying administrators.

Big Brother runs on Linux (and UNIX), Windows NT, and Novell. You can find more information on the Web at `http://www.maclawran.ca/bb-dnld`.

confcollect

confcollect gathers all the system-specific configuration information and sends it by mail to a centralized administrator.

You can download confcollect from `http://www.skagelund.com/confcollect`.

Gog&Magog

The Gog&Magog system-monitoring tool is broken down into two separate tasks—collecting information and analyzing information. The collection phase is handled by the `gog` command. The analysis portion is handled by the `magog` command.

For each host that is monitored, a cron job invokes the `/usr/local/bin/magog` script command. The script creates a file named `/tmp/hostname.chk`. All relevant information about the host is stored in this file.

Data collected at each host is transferred to a central host. A profile containing a valid image for each system is defined for each machine. The Magog tool is then used to analyze the data.

A third tool, GogView, offers graphical control panels that are written in HTML.

You can obtain Gog&Magog and GogView from `http://www.multimania.com/cparisel/gog`.

Nannie

Nannie is a tool that monitors identified files that should (conceptually) not change or be touched. When Nannie executes, it builds a linked list of filenames itemized in its `/etc/nannie.cfg` configuration file and obtains information about each file using the `stat` command.

Armed with this persistent data, it can check the files to verify that the values have not been altered. Nannie is released under the GNU GPL and is available via FTP at `ftp://tools.tradeservices.com/pub/nannie`.

PIKT

The Problem Informant Killer Tool (PIKT) is an innovative tool for the administration of heterogeneous networked workstations. PIKT monitors systems, reports and fixes problems, and supervises system configurations.

PIKT provides an embedded scripting language that exhibits a straightforward syntax. The PIKT scripting language shares many elements with other languages and is advertised to break new ground by providing features that make programming easier.

PIKT offers a script preprocessor and control mechanism for managing administrative scripts. You can also use it for version control, installation, error logging, and the scheduling of programs written in other languages. It can also be used to invoke macros, metacomments, and C-like `#if`, `#ifdef`, and `#include` directives in Perl, AWK, and so on.

PIKT is distributed under the GNU GPL and is available at http://pikt.uchicago.edu/pikt.

Sentinel

Sentinel is a file- and drive-scanning utility providing functionality similar to both the Tripwire and Viper.pl utilities. It employs a database similar to Tripwire, but it implements a RIPEMD 160-bit MAC checksumming algorithm, which is said to be more secure than MD5 128-bit checksum.

Also available is gSentinel, which is a graphical front-end to the Sentinel product. The gSentinel system is packaged as an RPM package. The gSentinel product is currently under development and might not be as polished as other GUI packages. You can get each of these packages on the Web at http://zurk.netpedia.net/zfile.html.

SuSEauditdisk

SuSEauditdisk consists of a bootable disk and provides tools for integrity checks, offering a means to inspect for potential damage.

It comes with the SuSE Linux distribution, but it can be adapted for use with any Linux distribution. SuSEauditdisk can be found at http://www.suse.de/~marc.

Sxid

Sxid is used to track changes in SUID or GUID files. Sxid reports any changes that have occurred to these files. The author recommends that Sxid run as a cronjob. You can also execute Sxid manually to perform spot checking.

Sxid also tracks SUID or GUID files using MD5 checksums, providing detection of installed root kits that are normally not detected using typical name and permissions checking. You can download Sxid at `ftp://marcus.seva.net/pub/sxid` using FTP.

Tripwire

Tripwire gives a system administrator the ability to create fingerprints of filesystems, objects, or registry keys. Just like a fingerprint, the signature produced by Tripwire uniquely identifies each file (or other object) so that the system administrator can see whether any changes have occurred. This lets the administrator know with certainty whether a file has been breached according to the policy he set. You can find Tripwire at `http://www.tripwiresecurity.com`.

ViperDB

ViperDB is alternative to Tripwire. It is advertised that ViperDB is faster than Tripwire. ViperDB does not utilize a single database for recording, but implements a plain-text database that is stored in each directory that is watched. This suggests that there is not a single attack point for an attacker to focus on.

If the owner and group settings have changed, ViperDB can change those settings back to their original values. It can also revert the permission settings to the original permissions. ViperDB has the ability to take away permissions if a change is detected on an SUID or GUID file. Email notification provides the ability to send summaries when changes are detected. You can find ViperDB at `http://www.resentment.org/projects/viperdb`.

Packet Sniffers

A packet sniffer is a program that can capture and record network packets traveling across a given network interface, computer, or network. They are used by network engineers to troubleshoot network problems. Crackers use them to extract confidential and sensitive network traffic, such as unencrypted logins. A packet sniffer is, effectively, a wiretap for network traffic.

Since network traffic can be viewed as fairly random, a protocol analyzer is used to decipher the type of network traffic and put the information into context.

tcpdump

The oldest and most common packet sniffer is the tcpdump command. This command prints the headers of packets on a specified network interface. Executing tcpdump on the command line puts it into receptive mode, waiting for network traffic to cross the interface. The default mode dumps a single-line decode of the packets to the standard output. Each output packet is presented on a separate line.

The tcpdump command is available on virtually every distribution of Linux (and UNIX). Check the tcpdump man page for more information.

Ethereal

Ethereal is a network protocol analyzer for Linux and UNIX. It is used to examine data from a network or from a file on disk. You can use Ethereal to browse data, viewing summary or detailed information for each packet. Ethereal includes a display filter language, and you can view the ASCII contents of a TCP connection.

Ethereal can be obtained from http://ethereal.zing.org.

Karpski

Karpski is an Ethernet protocol analyzer and sniffer. Although its sniffer and scanner are limited, the sniffer is easier to use than other sniffers such as tcpdump. You can add other protocols using the protocol definition file.

Karpski can be used to launch programs against addresses on your local network and as a local network intrusion tool. This tool is free and comes with source code. You can find karpski on the Web at http://niteowl.userfriendly.net/linux/RPM/karpski.html.

sniffit

The sniffit tool is a packet sniffer and monitoring tool designed for TCP, UDP, and ICMP packets. It gives you detailed technical information on these packets, such as SEQ, ACK, TTL, Window, and so on. The packet contents can be viewed in different formats, such as hex or plain text.

By default, sniffit can handle both Ethernet and PPP network devices. With proper effort, however, it can be easily forced to use other devices. The sniffer can be configured to filter incoming packets, capturing only identified packets. The configuration file allows you to identify the packets that should be processed.

The sniffit tool has an interactive mode for active monitoring. It can be used for continuous monitoring. sniffit can be obtained from http://sniffit.rug.ac.be/~coder/sniffit/sniffit.html.

Snort

Snort is a packet sniffer and logger that is based on libpcap. It features protocol analysis, rules-based logging, and content searching.

You can use Snort to detect buffer overflows, stealth port scans, CGI attacks, SMB probes, and OS fingerprinting attempts. It has other capabilities as well. This tool includes real-time alerting capability. These alerts can go to syslog or an alert file, or appear as a popup message using Samba's smbclient.

You can find Snort at http://www.clark.net/~roesch/security.html.

SPY

SPY is a protocol analyzer available on UNIX and Linux platforms. It can capture data for any attached network interface, supporting Ethernet, FDDI, PPP and PLIP, and SLIP/CSLIP. You can also feed data packets to SPY using your own software. SPY can store captured data to disk, allowing you to analyze the data later.

SPY uses prefilters, allowing you to capture relevant network traffic based on addresses or encapsulated protocols. SPY has a built-in protocol description language, making it possible to define protocols and the method required for decoding them. You can get SPY from http://pweb.uunet.de/trillian.of/Spy.

Packet Sniffer Detection

As mentioned previously, a packet sniffer is a "bugging device" used to listen in on network traffic. If a computer is running in promiscuous mode, it is likely that someone is performing packet sniffing. In other words, he is viewing network traffic, such as clear-text passwords, email, file transfers, and so on. This information allows a potential attacker to easily penetrate your network.

So how do you detect whether a packet sniffer is running on your network? You use a tool that detects conditions favorable for packet sniffing. One of the best tools for this is AntiSniff, from L0pht Heavy Industries, described in the next section.

AntiSniff

AntiSniff is a proactive security monitoring tool. It is used to detect packet sniffing. You can use it to scan the network, detecting whether any computers are set in promiscuous mode, which (normally) indicates that a computer has been compromised.

AntiSniff is not designed to detect hardware-based network probes. In addition, it is not designed to detect special-purpose network analyzers, which require an attacker to physically install them. You can find AntiSniff at http://www.l0pht.com/antisniff.

Summary

This chapter discussed some preventative tasks that are important in maintaining a Linux system.

We first covered the root account, discussing some of the drawbacks of using it. The root account is a powerful account, and you can make mistakes while using it without realizing it. You should use the root account only when required.

Next, we discussed the practice of rotating passwords. As an aid to combating crackers, you should always set user accounts to change their password on a rotating basis.

System backup and restoration is a necessary evil. Many problems can occur, such as a hard disk crash or power outage, and even human error (accidental or malicious), requiring the execution of a data restoration. Be sure you have a backup plan in place, and execute it. KDE's kdat (graphical) application was covered, showing you how to archive files and write them to tape. SuSE's YaST tool was demonstrated, and the command-line tar command was described.

Next, we covered the cron command and the crontab files. The cron command and crontab files are used for scheduling recurring commands and processes.

System monitoring should become a part of your daily routine. You should take a proactive role in order to head off potential break-ins. Staying current with security subjects is a part of playing a proactive role. There are a number of major playing fields you should be aware of, such as network monitoring, filesystem monitoring, and packet sniffing.

Monitoring the network involves tools that watch for, detect, and report on potential network breaches.

Filesystem monitoring includes inventory and verification of the filesystem. Filesystem monitoring is as important on a corporate system as it is on a stand-alone machine. Be sure to practice it daily.

Packet sniffing is the act of capturing and recording network packets that travel across a network. Network engineers use packet sniffers to troubleshoot network problems. Crackers use them to extract confidential and sensitive network traffic, allowing them to breach a system. You should consider using them occasionally as a means of system monitoring. You should also run a packet sniff detector, allowing you to check on crackers who might be sniffing your network.

V

Quick Reference

24 Utility Programs

25 Regular Expressions

24

Utility Programs

As you have seen in other chapters, Linux is a very powerful operating system, and it comes with an endless supply of software. I use the word software to refer collectively to user commands and programs. Most Linux distributions include two to four CD-ROMs (beyond the required) packed full of software and source code. If you do not find the software you are looking for, chances are it exists somewhere on the Internet.

Most of what is covered in this chapter pertains to the Linux user commands, with a couple of side trips to some specialized programs.

Overview

Linux, a UNIX look-alike, provides for small, very focused commands. The concept is simple and straightforward—the idea is to be able to tie programs together. Most Linux commands are flexible. This flexibility comes from two functional concepts: command options and redirection.

Command options, as you have seen elsewhere in this book, provide flexibility by allowing the user to tailor a command to suit the situation. Command options can either broaden or fine-tune a command.

Redirection, which includes both input and output, is used to send the output of one command to the input pipe of a second command.

The commands presented in this chapter are geared for use at the command line. I will not address any graphically oriented programs that might exist within a graphical environment such as KDE or GNOME.

The power of Linux comes from the many command-line programs and commands. You can, however, execute command-line programs and commands from within a graphical shell window.

Online Help

One of the fastest ways to learn Linux is to make use of the Help system. Traditionally, however, we do not refer to it as the Help system, but as the *man pages*. The term *man* is short for manual, as in a user manual. As a rule, a man page exists for every Linux command. Be forewarned, though, a man page might not be available for some commands. There are a number of reasons why this is true. Also, the shell itself will offer help. Let us see what commands we have to use and access the Linux Help system.

The Man Pages

The command used most often for obtaining help is man. A man page is available even for the man command. The syntax for man is as follows:

```
man [options] [section] title
```

The *title* refers to the command you want to obtain help with. If you execute man without a section or title, you will get a message similar to the following dialog:

```
bash-2.03# man
What manual page do you want?
bash-2.03#
```

Here, man is asking you to specify a command on which to obtain help. The man pages are functionally categorized by the user audience. This categorization refers to the man page *section*. For example, library calls are found in section 3 of the man pages, and section 8 contains the system administration commands.

No restrictions are placed on the length of a man page. A man page for one command may occupy only a few lines, whereas the man page for another command might consist of 30 or more printed pages. For example, the following is the complete man page for the rev command.

```
bash-2.03# man rev
...
REV(1)           UNIX Reference Manual                    NAME
     rev - reverse lines of a file
SYNOPSIS
     rev [file]
DESCRIPTION
```

```
     The rev utility copies the specified files to the standard output, reversing the order
of characters in every line.   If no files are specified, the standard input is read.
BSD Experimental                March 21, 1992
```

For contrast, the `ls` command consumes 396 lines on the SuSE distribution. The man page for the `less` command surpasses the `ls` man page—the `less` man page consumes 1,848 lines!

Back to the `man` command. In its simplest form of execution, you provide the command name (title) to man as an option. The following sample dialog shows how to get the man page for the `ls` command.

```
bash-2.03# man ls
...
```

It is as simple as that—no magic involved.

What if you do not know the name of a command, but you want to know what command(s) support some functionality? Appropriately enough, the command is `apropos`. The following is the usage for `apropos`.

```
apropos string ...
```

Notice the ellipses after the option named *string*. This means that you can supply more than one string and apropos will return entries that match all the strings that you supply.

Let us watch this command in action; the following dialog demonstrates the use of the apropos command.

```
bash-2.03# apropos printer
QPrinter (3qt)         - Paint device that prints graphics on a printer
a2ps (1)               - format files for printing on a PostScript printer
curs_print (3x)        - ship binary data to printer
gs-hpdj (1)            - Ghostscript device driver for printers understanding PCL-3
lp (4)                 - line printer devices
lpc (8)                - line printer control program
lpd (8)                - line printer spooler daemon
lprm (1)               - remove jobs from the line printer spooling queue
lptest (1)             - generate lineprinter ripple pattern
pac (8)                - printer/plotter accounting information
printcap (5)           - printer capability data base
psmandup (1)           - print duplex on non duplex printers
qprinter (3qt)         - Paint device that prints graphics on a printer
testprns (1)           - check printer name for validity with smbd
pbmto10x (1)           - convert a portable bitmap into Gemini 10X printer graphics
pbmtoepson (1)         - convert a portable bitmap into Epson printer graphics
pbmtoptx (1)           - convert a portable bitmap into Printronix printer graphics
bash-2.03#
```

654   Chapter 24   Utility Programs

To demonstrate the use of apropos with multiple strings, the following dialogs are presented. Three distinct invocations to apropos can be used, which are bolded to enhance identification.

```
bash-2.03# apropos architecture
__setfpucw (3)       - set fpu control word on i386 architecture
arch (1)             - print machine architecture
bash-2.03# apropos machine
arch (1)             - print machine architecture
kaffe (1)            - a virtual machine to execute Java(tm) bytecode
load (n)             - Load machine code and initialize new commands.
ripquery (8)         - querying remote machine running routed for routing informations
routed-trace (8)     - utility to switch trace logging on/off on routed running on remote
                       machine
rquota (3)           - implement quotas on remote machines
ruptime (1)          - show host status of local machines
rusers (1)           - who is logged in to machines on local network
rwho (1)             - who is logged in on local machines
XGetWMClientMachine (3x) - set or read a window's WM_CLIENT_MACHINE property
XSetWMClientMachine (3x) - set or read a window's WM_CLIENT_MACHINE property
lispmtopgm (1)       - convert a Lisp Machine bitmap file into pgm format
pgmtolispm (1)       - convert a portable graymap into Lisp Machine format
ppmdist (1)          - simplistic grayscale assignment for machine generated, color images
xon (1x)             - start an X program on a remote machine
bash-2.03# apropos architecture machine
__setfpucw (3)       - set fpu control word on i386 architecture
arch (1)             - print machine architecture
arch (1)             - print machine architecture
kaffe (1)            - a virtual machine to execute Java(tm) bytecode
load (n)             - Load machine code and initialize new commands.
ripquery (8)         - querying remote machine running routed for routing informations
routed-trace (8)     - utility to switch trace logging on/off on routed running on remote
                       machine
rquota (3)           - implement quotas on remote machines
ruptime (1)          - show host status of local machines
rusers (1)           - who is logged in to machines on local network
rwho (1)             - who is logged in on local machines
XGetWMClientMachine (3x) - set or read a window's WM_CLIENT_MACHINE property
XSetWMClientMachine (3x) - set or read a window's WM_CLIENT_MACHINE property
lispmtopgm (1)       - convert a Lisp Machine bitmap file into pgm format
pgmtolispm (1)       - convert a portable graymap into Lisp Machine format
ppmdist (1)          - simplistic grayscale assignment for machine generated, color images
xon (1x)             - start an X program on a remote machine
bash-2.03#
```

Notice how the call to `apropos architecture machine` combines the output of both individual calls `apropos architecture` and `apropos machine`. Submitting multiple strings to apropos can be useful in certain situations. Interestingly enough, apropos is synonymous with the `man -k` command, as shown in the following dialog:

```
bash-2.03# man -k architecture
__setfpucw (3)          - set fpu control word on i386 architecture
arch (1)                - print machine architecture
bash-2.03#
```

Notice that the output is the same as the previous example that used the `apropos` command.

If this is your first exposure to the man pages, you might feel a little shortchanged with the detail of the text. The objective for a man page is to be revealing, yet terse. There should be just enough to explain the command, but not too much explanation. As previously mentioned, the man page for `less` consumes 1,848 lines—think how long the man page would be if the authors were not succinct.

The man pages are categorized into sections, as shown in the following list:

- **man1.** This section describes the user commands.
- **man2.** This section describes Linux system calls.
- **man3.** This section describes the library functions, excluding the library functions described in the man2 section.
- **man4.** This section describes the special files.
- **man5.** This section describes the file formats and protocols, and C structures.
- **man6.** This section describes games and other programs available.
- **man7.** This section describes miscellaneous commands, such as the `nroff` macro package, some tables, C header files, the file hierarchy, and other things that don't fit into the other sections.
- **man8.** This section describes administrative and privileged commands to be used by the superuser, such as daemons and machine- or hardware-related commands.
- **man9.** This section describes the kernel-related commands.

To find out more information about a section, you can issue the `"man section # intro"` command. This will output a man page for the section desired.

Help Under the bash Shell

The default shell under Linux is bash. The bash shell is quite powerful, offering features derived from other command shells. The bash shell is a command interpreter, watching your every keystroke and acting on those submissions. Any time that you type a command and press Enter, bash first attempts to resolve the command internally. If the command is not a built-in command, it looks externally and executes it (if found). How do you find out the built-in commands for bash? An appropriate question because this section deals with online help. The bash shell offers its own online help, appropriately enough, using the help command. The following dialog shows the output from bash's online help.

```
bash-2.03# help
GNU bash, version 2.03.0(1)-release (i686-pc-linux-gnu)
These shell commands are defined internally.  Type `help' to see this list.
Type `help name' to find out more about the function `name'.
Use `info bash' to find out more about the shell in general.
A star (*) next to a name means that the command is disabled.

 %[DIGITS ¦ WORD] [&]                    . filename
 :                                       [ arg... ]
 alias [-p] [name[=value] ... ]          bg [job_spec]
 bind [-lpvsPVS] [-m keymap] [-f fi      break [n]
 builtin [shell-builtin [arg ...]]       case WORD in [PATTERN [¦ PATTERN].
 cd [-PL] [dir]                          command [-pVv] command [arg ...]
 continue [n]                            declare [-afFrxi] [-p] name[=value
 dirs [-clpv] [+N] [-N]                  disown [-h] [-ar] [jobspec ...]
 echo [-neE] [arg ...]                   enable [-pnds] [-a] [-f filename]
 eval [arg ...]                          exec [-cl] [-a name] file [redirec
 exit [n]                                export [-nf] [name ...] or export
 false                                   fc [-e ename] [-nlr] [first] [last
 fg [job_spec]                           for NAME [in WORDS ... ;] do COMMA
 function NAME { COMMANDS ; } or NA      getopts optstring name [arg]
 hash [-r] [-p pathname] [name ...]      help [pattern ...]
 history [-c] [n] or history -awrn       if COMMANDS; then COMMANDS; [ elif
 jobs [-lnprs] [jobspec ...] or job      kill [-s sigspec ¦ -n signum ¦ -si
 let arg [arg ...]                       local name[=value] ...
 logout                                  popd [+N ¦ -N] [-n]
 printf format [arguments]               pushd [dir ¦ +N ¦ -N] [-n]
 pwd [-PL]                               read [-r] [-p prompt] [-a array] [
 readonly [-anf] [name ...] or read      return [n]
 select NAME [in WORDS ... ;] do CO      set [—abefhkmnptuvxBCHP] [-o opti
 shift [n]                               shopt [-pqsu] [-o long-option] opt
 source filename                         suspend [-f]
 test [expr]                             time [-p] PIPELINE
 times                                   trap [arg] [signal_spec ...] or tr
 true                                    type [-apt] name [name ...]
 typeset [-afFrxi] [-p] name[=value      ulimit [-SHacdflmnpstuv] [limit]
 umask [-p] [-S] [mode]                  unalias [-a] [name ...]
 unset [-f] [-v] [name ...]              until COMMANDS; do COMMANDS; done
```

```
variables - Some variable names an wait [n]
while COMMANDS; do COMMANDS; done  { COMMANDS ; }
bash-2.03#
```

The built-in commands (functions) provide for a performance boost because the shell does not have to search and execute an external command. If you need additional help on a shell built-in command, type **help** *command*, as shown in the following sample dialog.

```
bash-2.03# help pwd
pwd: pwd [-PL]
    Print the current working directory.  With the -P option, pwd prints
    the physical directory, without any symbolic links; the -L option
    makes pwd follow symbolic links.
bash-2.03#
```

These shell commands can also be used in shell scripts.

Process Commands

Linux is a busy beast, keeping track of active users and processes. Whenever a new process is launched (command or program), Linux keeps a record of the process and its attributes. Various commands support the manipulation and verification of processes. In this section, we take a look at these commands.

Process Status with the ps Command

Probably the most important command is ps. Quite simply, ps stands for *process status* and is used to report on the status of one or more processes. The usage for the ps command is as follows:

```
ps [-][lujsvmaxScewhrnu][txx][O[+|-]k1[[+|-]k2...]] [pids]
```

The ps command provides a snapshot of currently running processes. This snapshot provides information only at the time of the execution of the ps command. Executing ps without any arguments will list processes owned by you. The following demonstrates this:

```
bash-2.03# ps a
  PID TTY      STAT   TIME COMMAND
  166 tty1     S      0:00 login -- root
  167 tty2     S      0:00 /sbin/mingetty tty2
  168 tty3     S      0:00 /sbin/mingetty tty3
  169 tty4     S      0:00 /sbin/mingetty tty4
  170 tty5     S      0:00 /sbin/mingetty tty5
  171 tty6     S      0:00 /sbin/mingetty tty6
  179 tty1     S      0:00 -bash
  294 tty1     S      0:00 sh /usr/X11R6/bin/startx
  295 tty1     S      0:00 tee /root/.X.err
  323 tty1     S      0:00 xinit /root/.xinitrc --
```

continues ▶

continued

```
337 tty1      S       0:03 kwm
350 tty1      S       0:10 kfm -d
356 tty1      S       0:01 kbgndwm
359 tty1      S       0:00 krootwm
362 tty1      S       0:03 kpanel
376 tty1      S       0:32 /opt/Office51/bin/soffice.bin
384 tty1      S       0:00 /opt/Office51/bin/soffice.bin
385 tty1      S       0:00 /opt/Office51/bin/soffice.bin
386 tty1      S       0:00 /opt/Office51/bin/soffice.bin
387 tty1      S       0:00 /opt/Office51/bin/soffice.bin
388 tty1      S       0:00 /opt/Office51/bin/soffice.bin
389 tty1      S       0:00 /opt/Office51/bin/soffice.bin
420 tty1      S       0:01 kvt -T ption Terminal -icon kvt.xpm -miniicon kvt.xpm
421 pts/0    S       0:00 bash
481 tty1      S       0:01 kscd -caption CD Player -icon kscd.xpm
484 tty1      S       0:02 ark -caption Archiver -icon /opt/kde/share/icons/ark.
509 tty1      S       0:00 konsole -icon konsole.xpm -miniicon konsole.xpmi -cap
510 pts/1    S       0:00 /bin/bash
512 pts/1    R       0:00 ps a
bash-2.03#
```

The PID column shows the process ID for a process. Each process that is launched is assigned a unique process identification number. Other Linux commands, such as `kill`, require the PID as an argument.

The TTY column indicates the terminal from which the process was executed. Take a look at the previous dialog; it shows that the `ps` command executed was from terminal `p0`. The ? character designates that the process does not have a controlling terminal.

The STAT column provides the current status of the process. The STAT column contain one of several character entries; the most common are R and S. An R designates a *runnable* state and an S signifies a *sleeping* state. Other values are D for *uninterruptible sleep*, T for stopped or *traced*, and Z for a *zombie* process. This value is not static because processes alternate from one state to another.

The TIME column displays the amount of system time that is used by the process.

Finally, the COMMAND column is the process name that is executing. There are other column fields, depending on the options to the `ps` command.

Table 24.1 shows the options that are available to the `ps` command. The list is not all-inclusive; be sure to check the `ps` man page for more information.

Table 24.1 **Common Options to the ps Command**

Option	Description
a	Shows processes for other users
l	Long format
H	Does not display a header
u	Displays username and start time for the process
m	Displays memory information
F	Displays in "forest" (family) tree format—graphically shows the parent/child relationship between processes
x	Displays processes that do not have a controlling terminal.
S	Adds child CPU time and page faults
r	Displays only running processes
e	Displays the environment after command line
w	Displays as wide output; does not truncate command lines to fit on one line

The following dialogs demonstrate the use and output of ps, using different options. Each ps execution is bolded to highlight it.

```
bash-2.03# ps u
USER       PID %CPU %MEM  SIZE   RSS TTY STAT START   TIME COMMAND
root       162  0.0  1.0  1704  1024   1 S    12:40   0:00 login -- root
root       163  0.0  0.4  1112   444   2 S    12:40   0:00 /sbin/mingetty tty2
root       164  0.0  0.4  1112   444   3 S    12:40   0:00 /sbin/mingetty tty3
root       168  0.0  1.3  2256  1292   1 S    12:40   0:00 -bash
root       189  0.1  4.4  6616  4288   1 S    12:40   0:06 kwm
root       206  0.1  4.9  8468  4744   1 S    12:40   0:04 kfm -d
root       212  0.0  3.8  6456  3672   1 S    12:40   0:01 kbgndwm
bash-2.03# ps l
 FLAGS  UID  PID PPID PRI NI  SIZE   RSS WCHAN      STA TTY TIME COMMAND
   100    0  162    1   0  0  1704  1024 wait4      S     1 0:00 login -- root
   100    0  163    1   0  0  1112   444 read_chan  S     2 0:00 /sbin/mingetty...
   100    0  164    1   0  0  1112   444 read_chan  S     3 0:00 /sbin/mingetty...
     0    0  206    1   0  0  8468  4744 do_select  S     1 0:04 kfm -d
     0    0  212    1   0  0  6456  3672 do_select  S     1 0:01 kbgndwm
     0    0  215    1   0  0  6108  3584 do_select  S     1 0:00 krootwm
     0    0  218    1   0  0  6620  4336 do_select  S     1 0:03 kpanel
   100    0  168  162   0  0  2256  1292 wait4      S     1 0:00 \bash
```

Using the `top` Command for Process Status

The `ps` command is very useful, but the list is static in nature. If you want to see a continual update of processes, the `top` command is the ticket. Figure 24.1 shows a snapshot of the `top` display.

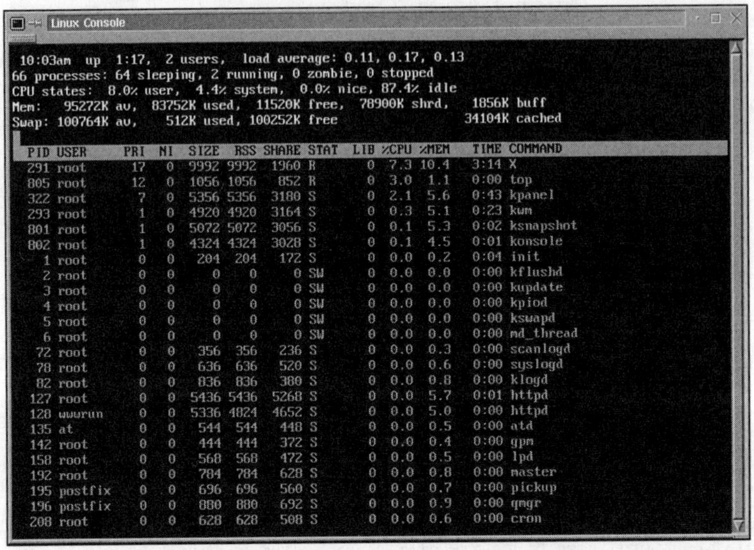

Figure 24.1 The top command display.

The `top` command accepts a number of command keys while it is running. For example, you can change the sort order of the display, or you can use the s command key to change the amount of time between screen updates. To display the help screen for top commands, press the ? key. Figure 24.2 shows the keystroke commands available to this version of top.

The `top` command can utilize a significant amount of CPU time, so use it sparingly.

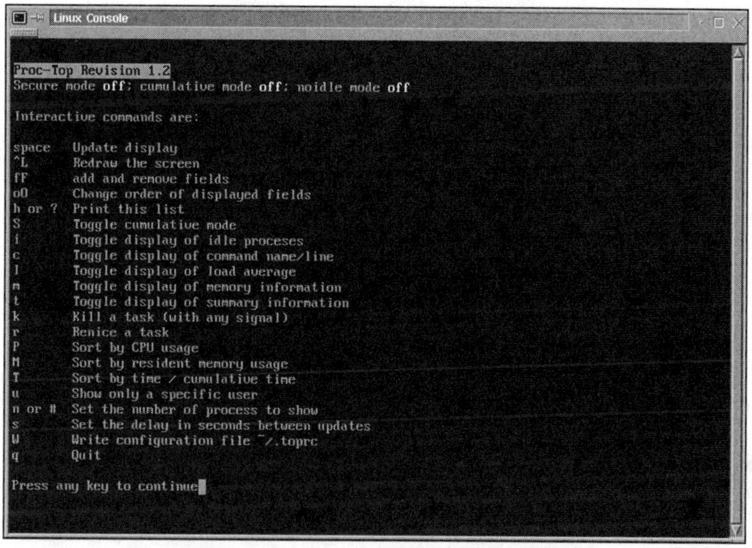

Figure 24.2 The top command help display.

Using at to Schedule a Process

The at command is used to execute a command (or commands) at a specified time. The usage for at is as follows:

```
at [-V] [-q queue] [-f file] [-mldbv] TIME
at -c job [job...]
```

At a minimum, you should execute at specifying a time and the command to execute. Optionally, you can specify a date. Commands can be read (by at) from standard input or from a file. Input to at is terminated with EOF.

Table 24.2 lists the available options for the at command.

Table 24.2 **Options to the at Command**

Option	Description
-V	Displays the version number.
-q queue	Tells at to use the named queue. A queue is identified by a letter: a to z and A to Z. The a queue is the default for at and the b queue is for batch. The default queue is c. Queues that have a higher letter have a higher nice value.
-m	When the job (executed by at) has completed, sends email to the user.

continues ▶

Table 24.2 **Continued**

Option	Description
-f file	Tells at to read the job from the named file, instead of standard input.
-l	Alias for atq.
-d	Alias for atrm.
-b	Alias for batch.
-c	Concatenates the jobs listed on the command line to standard output. Does not take a time specification.

The following sample dialog demonstrates a simple use of the at command:

```
bash-2.03# at 21:55
at> date > date.txt
at> echo "Done"
at> mail -s"Completed" root
at> <EOT>
warning: commands will be executed using /bin/sh
job 5 at 1999-10-15 21:55
bash-2.03#
```

When you type the at command, you enter into its interactive shell. Notice that this version of at displays a prompt, at>, awaiting your input. At the end of each line, simply press Enter. When you have completed all required commands, execute EOF (Ctrl+D). In the dialog shown, EOF is executed at the line that reads at> *EOT*—the at command outputs the *EOT* upon receipt of EOF. Upon receipt of EOF, the at command outputs information about the job submission. In this sample, at displays a warning message about using /bin/sh, displays a job number, and confirms the time for the job.

The at command allows for flexible and complex time specifications. Time can be formatted as HHMM or HH:MM; the default time is the 24-hour clock.

You can also specify midnight, noon, or tea time (4 p.m.) and you can have a time of day suffixed with a.m. or p.m. for running in the morning or in the evening. You can specify what day the job will be run, by giving a date in the form month day with an optional year, or by giving a date of the form MMDDYY or MM/DD/YY or DD.MM.YY. You can give times such as now + count time-units, where the time-units can be minutes, hours, days, or weeks. You can tell at to run the job today by suffixing the time with today, or to run the job tomorrow by suffixing the time with tomorrow.

For example, to run a job at 4 p.m. three days from now, you would type **at 4 p.m. + 3 days**; to run a job at 10:00 a.m. on July 31, you would type **at 10 a.m. Jul 31**; and to run a job at 1:00 a.m. tomorrow, you would type **at 1 a.m. tomorrow**.

Process Termination with the `kill` Command

The `kill` command is used to terminate an executing process. Why would you want to kill a command? There are times when a process is locked up or running rampant.

Before you can execute the `kill` command for some process, you need to obtain its process ID (PID). You read about the `ps` command in a previous section of this chapter; use it to obtain the PID. The usage for the `kill` process follows.

```
kill [-s signal ¦ -p] [-a] pid ...
kill -l [signal]
```

The simplest execution of the `kill` command is shown in the following dialog. Notice the ellipses after *pid* in the preceding usage—you can submit more than one PID to the kill command.

```
bash-2.03# kill 485
bash-2.03#
```

If you do not designate the signal to use, the SIGTERM signal is sent to the process. Use the `ps` command to verify that the process is terminated. If it isn't, you can issue the `kill` command, using the signal 9 (SIGKILL) option. Many processes will ignore the SIGTERM signal but cannot ignore the SIGKILL signal. The following dialog demonstrates the use of `kill`, sending signal 9 to the process.

```
bash-2.03# kill -9 485
bash-2.03#
```

Another reason a process may not appear to terminate is that another process may be creating it. This is obvious if you execute `kill -9` for a process and that process surfaces again with a new PID. What has happened is that the parent process has detected that the child process is terminated, and the parent re-creates the child process. In this situation, you will have to kill the parent process, too. You can use the `ps l` (lowercase L) command to see parent processes.

If you are logged in as anything other than the superuser account (root), you cannot kill other users' processes. This functionality is deliberate to keep a user from inadvertently (or maliciously) killing another user's process. The superuser can, of course, kill any process—except the init process, which is the parent of all processes and has the PID of 1. You can also kill processes while the `top` command is executing on your terminal, using the **k** keystroke.

Using su to Become Another User

To some Linux users, the `su` command means "super user" and for others it means "switch user." Regardless of what it means, executing the `su` command creates a shell with the effective user ID of the named user. The usage for the `su` command is as follows:

su [options] [user] [shell arguments]

The `su` command can be executed without any arguments. If a user is not specified, a shell is created and executes as the superuser account. If you are running as a user other than root, you will be prompted for the root password. If you log on successfully, you will have all the privileges of the root account.

If a username is provided to `su` and you are logged on as root, you will become the named user. If you are logged on as a user other than root and you execute `su` with another username, you will be prompted for that password.

When `su` is executed, the environment variables HOME, SHELL, USER, and LOGNAME are set to USER, unless root executed the `su` command. The shell that is run is not an actual login shell. Table 24.3 lists the options available to the `su` command.

Table 24.3 **Options to the su Command**

Option	Description
-c COMMAND, --command=COMMAND	Passes COMMAND to the shell with a -c option instead of executing an interactive shell.
-f, --fast	Passes the -f option to the shell; you should supply this option only if csh or tcsh is the executing shell. This option prevents the reading of the startup file .cshrc.
--help	Displays a message on standard output about su's usage.
-, -l, --login	Makes the shell a login shell.
-m, -p, --preserve-environment	Prevents the environment variables HOME, USER, LOGNAME, or SHELL from being changed. Also, executes the shell specified in the SHELL environment variable versus the USER's shell identified in /etc/passwd.

Option	Description
-s, --shell shell	Executes SHELL instead of the USER's shell identified in /etc/passwd. The exception is if the user running su is not superuser and the USER's shell is restricted.
--version	Displays version information on standard output.

When you are finished executing under su, enter EOF (normally Ctrl+D) to exit the su shell. Optionally, you can execute the exit command to exit the su shell.

Summary

We began this chapter with an overview of Linux utility commands, starting with the available Linux Help system.

The Linux online Help system is accessed by using the man command. You simply execute the man *title* command, where the *title* is the command page you require help with. The man pages are categorized into various sections. The apropos command is discussed, which allows you to search for commands based on one or more supplied keywords.

Next, the Help system built in to the bash shell was discussed. Many functions are built in to the bash shell—the available commands can be shown by executing the help command. More detailed help for a particular built-in command can be displayed with the help [*command*] command. For example, to get help on the bash pwd command, you would execute the command help pwd on the bash command line.

The process commands were covered next. The commands covered in this section are ps, top, at, and kill. The ps command is used to list running processes. The list produced by ps is static in nature and is a snapshot of processes at the time of the execution of ps. The top command also shows running processes, but it runs as a (full) screen process, with continual updates of the running processes. The at command is used to execute commands at a specified time and optional date. The kill command is used to terminate one or more processes.

Finally, the su command was discussed, which allows you to become another user. Executing the su command creates a shell with the effective user ID of the named user. When the su command is executed, the HOME, SHELL, USER, and LOGNAME environment variables are set to USER, unless root has executed the su command.

25
Regular Expressions

A REGULAR EXPRESSION IS A SERIES OF CHARACTERS and operators used for string matching. It is used most often for string searching in one or more files. Regular expressions are used in more places than most people think.

In this chapter, we will examine the use of regular expressions and show you how to make them work to your advantage.

Overview

If you use Linux (or UNIX), you will undoubtedly use regular expressions. Although you might not use them on a daily basis, you will use them occasionally. A regular expression is not a tool itself, but is an integrated component of many Linux tools (commands).

Many of the commands you use in Linux expect regular expressions, the most famous of them being the egrep command. Scripting languages such as Perl, Python, and Tcl rely on regular expressions. Regular expressions are used by programming-language tools for C, C++, Pascal, and so on. Even editors are in on the act: Emacs and vi are known for their use of regular expressions.

The successful use of regular expressions depends partly on having the correct frame of mind. To fully exploit their power, you should have a good understanding of regular expressions. If you think like a regular expression, you will reduce the time and effort needed to exploit them.

A regular expression can be detailed, convoluted, complicated, and downright nasty. If you want to understand system scripts and how they operate, you need to understand regular expressions. Different tools interpret (and expect) regular expressions to be formatted in different ways, but having a common ground from which to work is advantageous.

Keep in mind that regular expressions are used for text processing, so their use might not be obvious. Popular word processors use regular expressions to parse and validate text. Knowing when a regular expression is used can aid in the use of a tool, even if it is as simple as a word processor.

The real world has real problems to solve. Many of the tools we use, especially with Linux, require our knowledge of regular expressions. Very few people are armed with this knowledge. You will be at an advantage knowing the power of regular expressions.

Pattern Matching

If you have used a text editor or word processor, you have no doubt performed pattern matching. This concept is central to regular expressions.

For example, you have probably performed a text search or possibly a search and replace. The simplest of pattern matching involves an exact match. For example, to find the word *find*, you simply supply that word to the search utility. The search engine uses the regular expression "find" to match text from the input source. There are case-insensitive searches, but let's not cloud the issue right now. In this case, the word processor searches for every occurrence of the word "find" exactly. Not "Find" or "finD" or "FIND" or "find40," but "find." "find40" will not be found if you specify a *whole-word* search only.

Another form of pattern matching is wildcard matching. If you come from the DOS world, you will recognize such pattern-matching characters as ? and *. These are also used in the Linux world, so anything you knew before Linux will be usable. These special characters are used in DOS for filename matching. The following dialog demonstrates sample usage for these special characters. The two sample uses are in bold:

```
C:\> dir *.txt
chap-1.txt
chap-2.txt
chap-22.txt
chap-3.txt
chap-5.txt
hello.txt
source.txt
C:\> dir chap-?2.txt
chap-22.txt
C:\>
```

The first example, `dir *.txt`, exploits the special character `*`, which means "match anything." In DOS, a filename consists of two parts: the file's *name* and its *extension*, separated by a period.

So, we interpret `*.txt` to mean "all files that have an extension matching txt exactly." By the way, in DOS, filenames are converted to uppercase, meaning that DOS is not case-sensitive.

In the second example, `dir chap-?2.txt`, the special character `?` means "match any (legal) single character in place of the `?`". The output shows that the file `chap-22.txt` matches the pattern. If there were files named `chap-32.txt` and `chap-42.txt`, those would have been listed too. However, `chap-2.txt` would not be listed, because a character is required just before the 2. The use of `?` and `*` is not restricted to a single instance of those special characters. The following dialog demonstrates some other variations:

```
C:\> dir he*.*
hello.txt
herk.dat
heel.doc
C:\> dir h??l*.*
hello.txt
heel.doc
C:\>
```

The first example includes all files beginning with he. The second example includes all files that begin with h and have the fourth letter in the name equal to l. Okay, enough of the DOS world; let's get back to Linux.

Pattern matching includes what I have been referring to as *special characters*. The fancy name used for these special characters is *metacharacters*. Besides metacharacters, the other classification of characters in a regular expression is that of *literals*. The following is a group of metacharacters that you might have seen in expressions:

. ^ $ * + ? [\ | ( )

Each metacharacter has a special meaning within the context of a regular expression. Literal is just what it means—*exact* or *verbatim*.

The wildcards used for filename expansion are rather limiting when you consider the power that is available using metacharacters. The wildcard characters used for filename expansion are just good enough for their intended use. But we need something more powerful for text searching, parsing, and processing. You will see the power behind metacharacters as we move through this chapter.

Metacharacters

Before we move on to examples of the use of regular expressions, a listing of the metacharacters and their meanings is in order.

As mentioned, a metacharacter is a special character that has meaning in the context of a regular expression. Table 25.1 details the metacharacters.

Table 25.1 **Metacharacter Definitions**

Metacharacter	Name	Description
.	Dot	Matches any character
^	Caret	Start of the line
$	Dollar sign	End of the line
*	Asterisk, star	Repeats zero or more times
+	Plus sign	Repeats one or more times
?	Question mark	Optional character
[...]	Character group, brackets	Any character in the list (represented by ellipses)
[^...]	Character group, negated	Any character not listed
\	Backslash	Escape
|	Or (vertical bar)	Matches an expression on either side
(...)	Parentheses	Provides focus for the | (or) metacharacter

The rules for metacharacters can be frustrating at times, especially when you're trying to understand their usage. For example, the dot (.) has one meaning within brackets (character class) but another meaning outside a character set. Let's examine some of these metacharacters in more detail.

The Dot (.)

The . metacharacter matches any single character. It is a sort of shorthand for the [...] (character class) containing all characters. You are effectively saying, "Replace the dot with any character possible."

It is worth repeating that the dot (.) represents *any* character, not just some legal character within the context of dot's usage. You must consider the context of the expression for which it is used. Not all characters are legal in a filename, so the dot is overbearing, expanding into possibilities unforeseen. This could have disastrous results if you are creating (random) filenames.

This goes back to what I mentioned previously—you have to think from the perspective of the regular expression. You have to execute the expression in your mind. You should also have some understanding of the data source. Knowing whether the data is highly random or very structured will help you develop effective regular expression statements. Granted, you might have to experiment with sample data in the beginning, but it will eventually become intuitive.

Let's look at an example. You have been asked to extract names from a file that meets specific criteria. The structure of the text file consists of an employee number, hire date, and social security number. Each line in the file represents a single employee record. The content is demonstrated in the following snippet:

```
10332    01/01/1970    001-23-4567
10333    12.14.1987    001.34.5678
10354    06-23-1977    001-45-6789
10387    11 08 1992    001 56 7890
10363    02 13 1992    001 67 8901
10309    12/02/1988    001-78-9012
...
```

As you can see, the data is structurally consistent. There is a five-digit employee number, followed by a date, and finally an 11-character social security number. I said that the data is structurally consistent, but I did not say that the format of the data is consistent. There is a difference. As a point of contrast, the following shows a file that is not structurally consistent (or format-consistent):

```
10332        01/01/1970    001-23-4567
10333        John Jones    1515 Carpet Ln.    001.34.5678
10354        Mary Smith    5463 Whim Rd.      001-45-6789
(713)999-1212    10387     11 08 1992     001 56 7890
10363        02 13 1992    001 67 8901
(281)878-1111    10309     12/02/1988
...
```

This file's structure is not consistent from line to line. You will have to give some thought to structure in order to effectively scan, parse, and process the second sample file.

Getting back to the first sample file, you have been asked to clean up the file. All dates and social security numbers must be in a consistent format. Both the dates and the social security numbers must use the dash (-) character as a separator.

Initially, your manager just wants a list of employee numbers who started on 06/23/1977. A first crack at the regular expression might look like this:

```
stimpy $ egrep '06.23.1977' test.txt
10354    06-23-1977    001-45-6789
21354    06-23-1977    991-45-6789
31354    06-23-1977    881-45-6789
41354    06-23-1977    771-45-6789
51354    06-23-1977    661-45-6789
61354    06-23-1977    551-45-6789
71354    06-23-1977    441-45-6789
stimpy $ egrep '06.23.1977' test.txt
10354    06-23-1977    001-45-6789
21354    06.23.1977    991-45-6789
31354    06.23.1977    881-45-6789
41354    06/23-1977    771-45-6789
51354    06-23/1977    661-45-6789
61354    06.23.1977    551-45-6789
71354    06-23.1977    441-45-6789
stimpy $
```

Notice that there are two executions of the egrep command, using the same regular expression. The records extracted are the same. The difference is that the date separators were changed for the second execution. This is a rather simple example, yet quite effective and useful.

An alternative to this would be the following regular expression:

```
stimpy $ egrep '06[/-.]23[/-.]1977' test.txt
stimpy $ egrep '06[-./]23[-./]1977' test.txt
10354    06-23-1977    001-45-6789
21354    06.23.1977    991-45-6789
31354    06.23.1977    881-45-6789
41354    06/23-1977    771-45-6789
51354    06-23/1977    661-45-6789
61354    06.23.1977    551-45-6789
71354    06-23.1977    441-45-6789
stimpy $
```

Notice that the first execution does not result in any output, but the second execution does. As in the first regular expression, the dash (-) character has special meaning within a character set if it is not the first character. In this case, the dash specifies a range of characters. So, for the first execution, the expression specifies that the characters in the range from / to . are included in the expansion. In the second execution, the dash is not classified as a metacharacter and is included as part of the character set (and is examined literally).

The Caret (^)

The ^ metacharacter represents the beginning of a line that is being scanned. The caret must be at the beginning of the expression. So, using the previous file as an example, we can extract all the records that have the characters 1033 at the beginning. The following dialog demonstrates the use of the caret:

```
stimpy $ egrep '^1033' test.txt
10332   01/01/1970      001-23-4567
10333   12.14.1987      001.34.5678
stimpy $
```

So what if you execute the egrep command using a lone caret as the expression? You will get all lines, including any blank lines. This regular expression:

```
stimpy $ egrep '^' test.txt
```

is not the same as this:

```
stimpy $ egrep '^.' test.txt
```

Remember, the . means any character, which seems similar to the lone caret. Or is it? Actually, the processing is not the same. The following is a complete file that we will use to test the theory:

```
10333   12.14.1987      001.34.5678
41354   06/23-1977      771-45-6789

10387   11 08 1992      001 56 7890
10363   02 13 1992      001 67 8901
```

The blank line is intentional—there is actually a blank line in the file. The following dialog demonstrates the two variations just mentioned. Each execution is highlighted in bold.

```
stimpy $ egrep '^' test2.txt
10333   12.14.1987      001.34.5678
41354   06/23-1977      771-45-6789

10387   11 08 1992      001 56 7890
10363   02 13 1992      001 67 8901
stimpy $ egrep '^.' test2.txt
10333   12.14.1987      001.34.5678
41354   06/23-1977      771-45-6789
10387   11 08 1992      001 56 7890
10363   02 13 1992      001 67 8901
stimpy $
```

With the first `egrep` command, all lines from the file are extracted and printed to the console. With the second `egrep` command, only lines that have at least one character at the start of the string are displayed. The reason is that the newline characters are removed first, before processing for a character matching the . metacharacter.

The caret metacharacter can be quite useful if you need to search for lines beginning with a sequence of characters. An example might be a file in which each line begins with a ZIP code. To extract all records in which the ZIP code begins with the character sequence 77, you would execute this:

```
stimpy $ egrep '^77' filename
```

The inverse of the caret is the dollar sign ($), discussed in the following section.

The Dollar Sign ($)

The $ metacharacter represents the end of a line that is being scanned. The dollar sign must be at the end of the expression. So, using the file in the previous section as an example, we can extract all the records that have the characters 567 at the end of the line. The following dialog demonstrates the use of the $ metacharacter:

```
stimpy $ egrep '567$' test.txt
10332    01/01/1970      001-23-4567
stimpy $
```

So, what if you execute the `egrep` command using only a dollar sign as the expression? You will get all lines, including blank lines. Would this regular expression:

```
stimpy $ egrep '$' test.txt
```

be synonymous with this one?

```
stimpy $ egrep '.$' test.txt
```

If you recall, the . signifies any character, which could be the same as the $ metacharacter. Or is it? Realistically, the processing is not the same. The following shows the same five-line file used in the preceding section. We will use it to test the theory.

```
10333    12.14.1987      001.34.5678
41354    06/23-1977      771-45-6789

10387    11 08 1992      001 56 7890
10363    02 13 1992      001 67 8901
```

Again, the blank line is intentional, because there is a blank line in the file. The following dialog shows two executions of the egrep command using the same regular expression:

```
stimpy $ egrep '$' test2.txt
10333   12.14.1987      001.34.5678
41354   06/23-1977      771-45-6789

10387   11 08 1992      001 56 7890
10363   02 13 1992      001 67 8901
stimpy $ egrep '$' test2.txt
10333   12.14.1987      001.34.5678
41354   06/23-1977      771-45-6789

10387   11 08 1992      001 56 7890
10363   02 13 1992      001 67 8901

stimpy $
```

Notice that the output from the second execution includes a blank line before the last stimpy $ prompt. To prove a point, I added a new line just after the last textual line in the file.

```
stimpy $ egrep '$' test2.txt
10333   12.14.1987      001.34.5678
41354   06/23-1977      771-45-6789

10387   11 08 1992      001 56 7890
10363   02 13 1992      001 67 8901
stimpy $
```

Now let's execute the test. The following dialog shows the results of the two expressions. Each individual execution is highlighted in bold:

```
bash-2.03# egrep '$' test2.txt
10333   12.14.1987      001.34.5678
41354   06/23-1977      771-45-6789

10387   11 08 1992      001 56 7890
10363   02 13 1992      001 67 8901
bash-2.03# egrep '.$' test2.txt
10333   12.14.1987      001.34.5678
41354   06/23-1977      771-45-6789
10387   11 08 1992      001 56 7890
10363   02 13 1992      001 67 8901
stimpy $
```

The first egrep command prints all lines, even blank lines, to the console. With the second egrep command, only the lines that have at least one character at the end of the string are displayed. We do not see the blank lines because the newline characters are removed before processing for the . metacharacter.

Using the $ metacharacter can be quite useful if you want to search for lines that end with a sequence of characters. An example might be a file in which each line ends with a certain subset of text. For example, to extract and print all records in which a line ends with the character sequence Linux., you would execute this command:

stimpy $ egrep 'Linux.$' *filename*

Before we leave this section, let's see what would happen if we mixed the caret and dollar sign metacharacters in an expression:

stimpy $ egrep '^$' test2.txt

stimpy $ egrep '^.$' test2.txt
stimpy $

The first egrep execution prints only the blank lines, discarding all other lines. This expression states that the line will be printed if there is a beginning of a line, followed by an end of a line. There are no characters within the blank lines, so they are shown.

The second execution of egrep does not print any lines. The end-of-line characters are removed, and then the line is interpreted for the . metacharacter. Because no character is present, the line is not printed.

The Character Class ([. . .])

A character class is identified using the open and close brackets ([ ]). The character class is used to match any character enclosed within the brackets, at the insertion point. The following sample helps you understand the use of the character class:

st[oe]p

This is interpreted as "Find an s, followed by a t, followed by an o or e, followed by a p, and end the match." Therefore, the two possible matches are stop and step. This seems easy enough, but things can get a little messy.

In a previous section, I mentioned that the dash can take on a couple of different meanings, depending on its location within the character class. If the dash is the first character in a character class, it is not a metacharacter, but a literal. If the dash is between characters, it indicates a range. The following example demonstrates this:

'Room 1[012345]'
'Room 1[0-5]'

These two regular expressions are identical. In the first example, the characters are identified literally. In the second example, the dash metacharacter is used to specify the range of allowable values.

Within a character class, you can intermingle ranges and literal characters. Also, ranges can be intermixed with other ranges and literal characters. The following examples demonstrate this magic:

```
'Room 1[0-36-9]'
```

Consider the following input file:

```
Room 12
Room 14
Room 15
Room 18
```

If we execute `egrep` with the preceding regular expressions, we will see the following output:

```
stimpy $ egrep 'Room 1[0-36-9]' test3.txt
Room 12
Room 18
stimpy $
```

The 3 and the 6 within the character class are not treated as literals, but are integral to the ranges they are associated with. The records shown in the preceding dialog prove this. The following lines from the file are not printed, because the 4 and the 5 do not fall within the ranges specified:

```
Room 14
Room 15
```

The ranges shown so far have been numeric, but you are not restricted to numbers. Letters are often used within character class ranges. For example, the following demonstrates a way to parse for hexadecimal values:

```
'[0-9A-Fa-f]'
```

For programmers, this might be useful information. Nonprogrammers might find this information uninteresting.

Remember, some characters maintain one trait inside a character class and another when outside. And some characters, such as the dash, have different meanings depending on their location within the character class.

The Negated Character Class ([^...])

The preceding section introduced the character class and provided examples to clarify its use. This section looks at the character class in reverse.

Earlier, you discovered that the caret represents the beginning of a line that is being scanned. As you have learned, however, the meaning of a character can change based on the context in which it is being used. And yes, it has happened again.

The caret, when used within a character class expression, negates the interpretation of the character class. (You should note that the caret, now a metacharacter, must be the first character after the opening bracket.) So what does it mean to negate the character class? Quite simply, characters are matched that do not occur in the list. An example is in order. The following example is taken from the preceding section, with the addition of a caret in the character class:

`st[^oe]p`

This expression means "Match an s, followed by a t, followed by any character that is not an o or an e, followed by a p, and end the match." This expression will reveal some strange words, such as `stip`, `stap`, `stup`, and so on. At the same time, we might find some interesting words. If we run egrep with this expression against the words file, the result is interesting. The following dialog shows the output (on my system):

```
stimpy $ egrep 'st[^oe]p' /usr/share/dict/words
Gestapo
mistype
mistyped
mistypes
mistyping
staphylococcus
staple
stapler
staples
stapling
stipend
stipends
stipulate
stipulated
stipulates
stipulating
stipulation
stipulations
stupefy
stupefying
stupendous
stupendously
stupid
stupidest
stupidities
stupidity
stupidly
stupor
stimpy $
```

The words (dictionary) file can provide debugging functionality for your regular expressions. If you are not quite sure what the result of an expression will be, use the words file for sample results. Note that some Linux distributions locate the words file in the /usr/dict directory.

Repeat Zero or More Times (*)

The star (*) metacharacter is actually an enhancing quantifier. In other words, the * enhances (or modifies) the item that precedes it.

I say "enhances" because the * is used to repeat the item in front of it. The interpretation is flexible in that the repetition can happen zero or more times. This implies that the * expression will always succeed.

A simple example is in order. Suppose you are developing an operating system that will eventually take over the computing world. Let's further assume that the current code name for this system is "LNX." You have just discovered that "LNX" is copyrighted, and you need to find a new name. You have written a lot of documentation, and you want to make the new name change as effortless as possible. At the same time, you want to retain recognition of "LNX." The dictionary seems like a good place to start. The regular expression might look something like this:

```
'L.N.X'
```

Simple enough. With this expression, you can scan the dictionary for words that could have any letter (or none) between each of the letters "LNX." Give it a try. The following is a sample result:

```
stimpy $ egrep 'L.N.X' /usr/share/dict/words
stimpy $
```

That execution was not very fruitful. There could be a couple of problems with this expression. One problem might be that more than one letter exists between the letters we are supplying. To fix this problem, we use the * to specify that the . should repeat zero or more times. The following dialog demonstrates this:

```
stimpy $ egrep 'L.*N.*X' /usr/share/dict/words
stimpy $
```

Still no luck. Obviously, there is a problem with the letters' capitalization. We can use character classes to help with this problem. Let's provide the option to search for uppercase and lowercase occurrences of the letters:

```
stimpy $ egrep '[Ll].*[Nn].*[Xx]' /usr/share/dict/words
larynx
Lennox
Linux
lynx
```

continues ▶

continued

```
lynxes
plaintext
plaintexts
planoconvex
stimpy $
```

This list certainly provides some variations on our original three letters. A quick scan of the list yields the name we are looking for: Linux. Sounds like a great name for the ultimate operating system.

Repeat One or More Times (+)

The + metacharacter is also an enhancing quantifier. This means that the + enhances the item preceding it.

The + metacharacter enhances the item in front of it one or more times. This implies that the + expression might or might not succeed.

To provide an example and some contrast to the * metacharacter, let's use the example from the preceding section. Another glance into the dictionary using + versus * should provide similar results:

```
stimpy $ egrep '[Ll].*[Nn].*[Xx]' /usr/share/dict/words
larynx
Lennox
Linux
lynx
lynxes
plaintext
plaintexts
planoconvex
stimpy $ egrep '[Ll].+[Nn].+[Xx]' /usr/share/dict/words
Lennox
Linux
plaintext
plaintexts
planoconvex
stimpy $
```

Two different executions of `egrep` are shown, each supplying a different expression. In the first execution, the regular expression from the preceding section is re-executed. In the second `egrep` execution, all occurrences of * are replaced with the + metacharacter.

As you can see from the output, the number of matches returned is less when using the + metacharacter in the expression. Remember, when using the +, the preceding item must be repeated one or more times. One word that is in the * list, but not in the + list, is `lynx`. The * metacharacter says

"Match the preceding item zero or more times." The + metacharacter says "Match the preceding item one or more times." Because there is a . between the n and the x characters, there must be at least one character between these two characters. This is why the word lynx is not listed in the + list.

Optional (?)

The ? metacharacter is used to specify whether the preceding item can exist or not. You name the item that could exist and follow it with the ? metacharacter. An expression using ? might look like this:

```
'pen(cil)?'
```

In this example, the ? is associated with the expression in parentheses. As with other metacharacters, you need to give some forethought as to the expression's results.

```
stimpy $ egrep 'pen(cil)?' /usr/share/dict/words | wc -l
    215
stimpy $
```

The reason, of course, is that the results return words that have pen as a subexpression. The words pen, pencil, penciled, and pencils show up—this was the expression's intent. So how can we get just pen and pencil out of the dictionary? The following dialog should bring home the answer:

```
stimpy $ egrep '^pen(cil)?$' /usr/share/dict/words
pen
pencil
stimpy $
```

You should try to predict the outcome of your regular expressions. If you cannot be certain, try the expression on the dictionary or a test file.

Alternatives (|)

There are times when you want to choose between subexpressions. For example, *Angie* is an acceptable alternative for *Angela,* as is *Mike* for *Michael*.

To accomplish this task, two metacharacters are used. The first is |, known as the vertical bar (or bar for short). The other metacharacters are the ( ) (parentheses).

You use the | to delimit the alternatives (or choices). The ( ) provide scope for the alternatives. Using the examples just mentioned gives you the following alternative expressions:

```
(Angie|Angela)
(Mike|Michael)
```

For that matter, you could even do this:

```
(Angie¦Michael)
(Mike¦Angela)
```

The `egrep` command couldn't care less, because it doesn't provide for any logical reasoning. It would be interesting to see just how popular these names might be. We will check the dictionary using the names in an alternative regular expression. The following dialog is taken directly from a KDE konsole session:

```
stimpy $ egrep '(Angie¦Angela¦Mike¦Michael)' /usr/share/dict/words
Angela
Angie
Michael
Michaels
stimpy $
```

This might be fun if you want to see whether your children's names are in the dictionary:

```
stimpy $ egrep '(Madison¦Ashton¦Drew)' /usr/share/dict/words
Madison
stimpy $
```

You can use other metacharacters to modify the alternatives. For example, you might want to match only subexpressions that are at the beginning (or end) of a line. The following dialog demonstrates this use:

```
stimpy $ egrep '^(Angie¦Angela¦Mike¦Michael)' /usr/share/dict/words
Angela
Angie
Michael
Michaels
stimpy $ egrep '(Angie¦Angela¦Mike¦Michael)$' /usr/share/dict/words
Angela
Angie
Michael
stimpy $
```

Notice that the second invocation of `egrep` does not include `Michaels` in the list. If you recall, the `$` metacharacter says to "Match the expression at the end of a line."

You should be cautious with alternative expressions, because they follow some of the same rules as standard expressions. The following dialog shows the potential results of such an expression:

```
stimpy # egrep '(and¦wand)' /usr/share/dict/words ¦ wc -l
    508
stimpy #
```

It appears that our alternative subexpressions can be subexpressions in the search for a match. The preceding expression brings up an interesting point. If you look again, you will see that the first alternative is a subexpression of the second alternative. As it turns out, the order doesn't matter, because the tool scans for all listed alternatives until a match is found (or not found).

Be careful when using alternatives, because you can get skewed results. The following dialog shows the potential output from an expression that should have had a space character as an alternative:

```
stimpy $ egrep '(|Angie)' /usr/share/dict/words | wc -l
  45407
stimpy $
```

The `egrep` command matched every entry in the dictionary with this regular expression.

Escaping

We have examined a number of metacharacters and their usage. The question that is raised by most people is "How can I match a character that is used as a metacharacter?" This is a very good question, and there is an answer.

The backslash (\) character is used to *escape* a metacharacter, which forces the metacharacter to lose its meaning. In other words, the metacharacter becomes a literal character.

Let's assume that you are writing a book on the C++ programming language. Before submitting each chapter, you want to ensure that every occurrence of "C" in the string "C++" is in uppercase. The following dialog might be your first attempt:

```
stimpy $ egrep 'c++' /usr/share/dict/words | wc -l
  12682
stimpy $
```

You piped the output of `egrep` to the `wc` command because you wanted to test your expression first. It is quite possible that you have 12,682 occurrences of "c++," but this is unlikely. Just to be sure, you re-execute the `egrep` command without piping the output to the `wc` command. The following dialog demonstrates this:

```
stimpy $ egrep 'c++' /usr/share/dict/words
aback
abduct
abducted
abduction
abductions
abductor
abductors
```

continues ▶

continued

```
...
zinc
zodiac
zoological
zoologically
Zurich
stimpy $
```

Obviously, my hunch was correct. I am using the local dictionary in this example, but it is (probably) representative of the real world. So what is the problem with our expression?

First of all, the + is a metacharacter. The expression used says "Match the preceding item one or more times." The item in question is the character c. If you look at the snippet's output, you will see that every word matched contains the letter c. Because we are talking about escaping metacharacters in this section, let's try the expression again, this time escaping the + metacharacter.

Becuse we need some sample output here, I created a 13-line text file. Each line contains the string c++ within a phrase, with the exception of two lines. The c++ string occurs at the beginning, middle, and end of a line. I also threw in a single blank line. Here are the file's contents:

```
The c++ programming language
You should program in c++
I am writing in the c++ language.
This C++ is in upper.
I like to use c++.

c++ is my language.
c++ thrives on the Linux environment.
Consider using c++
This line has some characters.
Trust in c++.
c++ will light your way.
Try c++ and you will never go back.
```

The following dialog shows the results of executing the expression we hope will work:

```
stimpy $ egrep 'c++' testc.txt
The c++ programming language
You should program in c++
I am writing in the c++ language.
I like to use c++.
c++ is my language.
c++ thrives on the Linux environment.
Consider using c++
This line has some characters.
```

```
Trust in c++.
c++ will light your way.
Try c++ and you will never go back.
stimpy $
```

As you can see, the line `This line has some characters.` is also selected as matching the expression. The following dialog is our next attempt at finding only lines containing the c++ text string:

```
stimpy $ egrep 'c\+\+' testc.txt
The c++ programming language
You should program in c++
I am writing in the c++ language.
I like to use c++.
c++ is my language.
c++ thrives on the Linux environment.
Consider using c++
Trust in c++.
c++ will light your way.
Try c++ and you will never go back.
stimpy $
```

It appears that the expression works correctly. To verify the expression's accuracy, we can use it to test for the single line that contains the C++ text string. The following dialog shows the results:

```
stimpy $ egrep 'C\+\+' testc.txt
This C++ is in upper.
stimpy $
```

Obviously, the expression now works as intended.

Whole Words

Many times we want to find a (whole) word in a file, only to discover that our word is actually a subword. For example, let's say that we want to search the words file for the word (or character string) pitch. This seems simple enough—we should be able to pass that expression to egrep and get the word back. The following dialog shows the results:

```
stimpy $ egrep 'pitch' /usr/share/dict/words
pitch
pitched
pitcher
pitchers
pitches
pitchfork
pitching
stimpy $
```

This list contains a few more words than expected. Although this list is short, some expressions will yield lengthy lists, such as out or able. So how can we reduce the list to the exact word we specified? There are a couple of ways to do this.

If your egrep command supports the \< and \> metacharacter sequence, you can use those to delineate the word. One drawback is that not all egrep commands support this metacharacter sequence. Another drawback is that this sequence requires some extra typing. Yet another drawback is that of aesthetics. The following dialog shows the results of using these metacharacter sequences:

```
stimpy $ egrep '\<pitch\>' /usr/share/dict/words
pitch
stimpy $
```

Obviously, this version of egrep supports the sequence. Besides being a little cumbersome to type, the expression looks a little confusing. I have seen some people try to "correct" the expression like this:

```
stimpy $ egrep '\<pitch>\' /usr/share/dict/words
egrep: Trailing backslash
stimpy $
```

There is another option to get the exact word. Recall the "start of line" and "end of line" metacharacters from earlier in this chapter. We can combine these to give focus to the single word we are interested in. Let's see if this works, using the preceding example:

```
stimpy $ egrep '^pitch$' /usr/share/dict/words
pitch
stimpy $
```

It worked! Personally, I prefer this method of exact-word searching to the previous use of metacharacter sequences. We can test it on an expression that should yield a fair number of word hits:

```
stimpy $ egrep 'or' /usr/share/dict/words | wc -l
   2975
stimpy $ egrep '^or$' /usr/share/dict/words | wc -l
      1
stimpy $ egrep '^or$' /usr/share/dict/words
or
stimpy $
```

Wow! The count of words matching the expression or is 2,975 on this system (SuSE 6.3). Encasing the word or in the caret and dollar sign metacharacters reveals a single match, according to the output from the wc command. Indeed, the result of the third egrep execution reveals the exact word or, as specified by the expression.

There is one caveat to this method of exact-word matching: It works only if each line in the file is a single word.

Summary

This chapter tackled the use of regular expressions. We began with an overview of regular expressions and some concepts of pattern matching. A regular expression is a series of characters and operators that are used for pattern matching.

An overview of metacharacters was discussed next. A metacharacter is a special character that has meaning in the context of a regular expression. In subsequent sections, each of the important metacharacters was discussed in more detail.

The . (dot) metacharacter is used to match any single character. This metacharacter effectively says, "Replace the . with any character."

Next, the ^ (caret) metacharacter was discussed. This metacharacter represents the beginning of the line being scanned. The caret must be at the beginning of the expression, as in the expression ^1033.

At the other end of the spectrum is the $ (dollar sign) metacharacter. This metacharacter is used to represent the end of the line being scanned. The dollar sign must be at the end of the expression, as in the expression 567$.

Next, the character class was described. It is used to match any of the enclosed characters (within the brackets) at the point of insertion. The character class is delimited by brackets ([ ]). The expression st[oe]p demonstrates a character class.

The negated character class, represented as [^...], is used to exclude any characters in the character class. The sample expression st[^oe]p means "Match an s, then a t, then any character that is not an o or an e, followed by a p."

The * (star) metacharacter is used to enhance an expression. It is used to repeat the item immediately before the *. This metacharacter is useful if you need to repeat zero or more occurrences of an item.

The + (plus sign) metacharacter enhances the item in front of it. This metacharacter says, "Repeat the previous item one or more times." This implies that the + metacharacter can fail (no match found).

Next, the ? (question mark) metacharacter was discussed. This metacharacter specifies whether the preceding item can exist or not. In the expression June?, the e can be present or not to satisfy the expression.

The | (vertical pipe) metacharacter, plus parentheses, is used to delimit alternatives. The expression `(Jan|Feb|Mar|1st)` might be used to find lines containing text pertaining to the first quarter of the year.

Next, we discussed the backslash (\) character, which is used to escape a metacharacter. This forces the metacharacter to lose its meaning and be treated as a literal character.

Finally, the chapter closed with a discussion of exact-word matches. For example, you might want to match all lines that contain the text string `pitch`. It is possible that words such as `pitch`, `pitched`, `pitcher`, and `pitchers` will match the expression. If the tool supports the `\<` and `\>` metacharacter sequence, you can implement exact-word matches.

VI

Appendixes

A Other Sources of Information

B Common Questions

A

Other Sources of Information

A WEALTH OF INFORMATION ON LINUX can be found rather easily. One of the most obvious places is on the Internet. Of course, you can be overwhelmed by the vast amounts of information returned from an Internet search. Also, you will find many dead-end Internet addresses.

With this appendix I hope to provide you with the most current sources of information about Linux at the time of this writing.

Books

An advantage of Linux is that it is POSIX compatible. POSIX is an acronym for Portable Operating System Interface for UNIX. POSIX is a set of standards defined by IEEE and ISO that define an interface between software and operating systems. When software conforms to POSIX, there is some assurance that the software can be easily ported to other POSIX-compliant operating systems. Most varieties of UNIX and Windows NT fall into this category. The POSIX standards are currently maintained by the Portable Applications Standards Committee (PASC), which is an arm of the IEEE. This means that you can obtain books on UNIX and find the content very useful for Linux.

General UNIX Books

The *Hip Pocket Guide to UNIX* (by Michele Petrovsky and Tom Parkinson, IDG Books Worldwide, 1998) summarizes UNIX commands at a glance.

More than 90 commands are listed alphabetically, including a description, a summary of the syntax, some examples, and characteristics for each command. The guide also provides an overview of UNIX basics, a glossary, and print and online resources.

Learning the UNIX Operating System, Fourth Edition (by Jerry Peek, Grace Todino, and John Strang, O'Reilly, 1997) provides a thorough introduction to UNIX, giving you a good jump-start. It is a good primer for those coming from other operating systems.

A book providing an exploration into the UNIX kernel is *Unix Internals: A Practical Approach* (by Steve Pate, Addison Wesley, 1996). The book provides a description of the UNIX kernel internal and how it interacts with the Intel x86 processor family.

Windows NT and UNIX (by G. Robert Williams and Ellen Beck Gardner, Addison Wesley, 1998) provides information concerning the coexistence of the Windows NT and UNIX operating systems. Various topics on networking are covered, including CORBA and DCOM, TCP/IP, electronic mail, and so on.

The *UNIX System Administration Handbook, Second Edition* (by Evi Nemeth, Garth Snyder, and Scott Seebass, Prentice Hall, 1995) is a popular book among system administrators. This book covers all aspects of system administration from basic administrative topics to UNIX. It also provides guidelines for dealing with six popular versions of UNIX. The third edition of this book is due around April, 2000 and is rumored to include Linux information.

Although somewhat dated, *Essential System Administration, Second Edition* (by Aeleen Frisch, O'Reilly, 1995) is a good system-administration book that cuts right to the core.

UNIX Programming Books

When most programmers think of UNIX programming, they think of *Advanced Programming in the UNIX Environment* (by W. Richard Stevens, Addison Wesley, 1993), which has descriptions for more than 200 UNIX system calls and functions. The book goes beyond descriptions by providing examples of working, usable code. If you are programming for UNIX or Linux, this book should be on your bookshelf.

POSIX Programmer's Guide: Writing Portable UNIX Programs (by Donald Lewine, O'Reilly, 1991) provides an explanation of the POSIX standard. This book is also a good reference for the POSIX.1 library, providing you with the tools to create portable software.

Programming with GNU Software (by Mike Loukides and Andy Oram, O'Reilly, 1996) comes with a CD-ROM and is aimed at the programmer that is new to UNIX. The CD-ROM includes software such as the GNU Emacs text editor; gcc, C and C++ compiler; the GNU libraries; the gdb debugger; RCS, version control software for source code maintenance; GNU make, a build utility; and the gprof profiler utility package.

Magazines

Here again, in addition to the Linux magazines that are available, UNIX-oriented magazines can provide a wealth of information for the Linux enthusiast. Also, do not limit yourself only to Linux- and UNIX-oriented magazines. Many other magazines provide content for Linux. The following is a brief list of magazines and e-zines that are recommended reading.

32 Bits Online Magazine	Designed for Mac, Linux, OS/2, and Windows enthusiasts. The URL is http://www.32bitsonline.com.
Bleeding Edge Magazine	An online Linux-specific magazine. The URL is http://www.gcs.bc.ca/bem.
EXT2	A monthly Web magazine for Linux users. The URL is http://news.tucows.com/ext2/index.shtml.
Linux Answers Magazine	A British Linux magazine, both hard copy and online. The site contains many online tutorials, tips, and helpful information. The URL is http://www.linuxanswers.co.uk/mainpage.htm.
Linux Focus	An online magazine devoted to the Linux community, providing tips, information, and recent news. The URL is http://www.linuxfocus.org.
Linux Gazette	Monthly online magazine for Linux users, including columns for new users, Q&As, graphics, and articles from software developers. The URL is http://www.linuxgazette.com.
Linux Journal	Monthly publication serving the Linux community. The URL is http://www.linuxjournal.com.

Linux Magazine	Monthly publication serving the Linux community. The URL is `http://www.linux-mag.com`.
LinuxSpirit.Com	Their mission is to show today's average computer user why they might be interested in Linux, how they might use it, and to help them along the way. The URL is `http://www.linuxspirit.com`.
LinuxWorld	A Web-only magazine that provides news and technical information about Linux and Open Source software. The URL is `http://www.linuxworld.com`.
Maximum Linux Magazine	Magazine from the publishers of Maximum PC. Lots of online material and downloads. The URL is `http://www.maximumlinux.com`.
Sys Admin	Targets UNIX systems administrators who seek to improve the performance or extend the capabilities of their system. The URL is `http://www.samag.com`.
UNIX and Linux Computing Journal	A free periodic resource for UNIX and GNU/Linux users, administrators, programmers, and hobbyists featuring subscriptions and feedback forums. The URL is `http://www.diverge.org/ulcj`.
UNIX Review	Dedicated to helping UNIX professionals around the world develop and administer superior systems and solutions. The URL is `http://www.performancecomputing.com/unixreview`.
UnixWorld	The URL is `http://www.networkcomputing.com/unixworld`.

Other printed and online magazines will appear in the future; be sure to check the sites listed in this appendix's section "Linux Web Sites."

Usenet Newsgroups

A number of newsgroups exist for discussion of various Linux-related topics—from installing and configuring a Linux system, to writing applications for Linux, to discussing how Linux can be improved, to major announcements.

Be sure to check with your Internet service provider for details concerning availability, connectivity, and usage of its Usenet server.

`comp.os.linux.advocacy`	For the discussion of the benefits of Linux compared to other operating systems.
`comp.os.linux.announce`	For the posting of announcements of general interest to the Linux community.
`comp.os.linux.answers`	For posting Linux FAQs, How-Tos, READMEs, and other documents that answer questions about Linux. This will help keep the traffic down in other c.o.l.* groups.
`comp.os.linux.development.apps`	For questions and discussion regarding writing of applications for Linux and porting of applications to Linux.
`comp.os.linux.development.system`	For questions and discussion regarding the development of the Linux operating system proper: kernel, device drivers, loadable modules.
`comp.os.linux.hardware`	For questions and discussion specific to a particular piece of hardware; for example, "Can this system run Linux?", "How do I use this disk drive with Linux?", and so on.
`comp.os.linux.misc`	For questions and discussion relating to Linux but not covered by a more specific Linux newsgroup.
`comp.os.linux.networking`	For questions and discussion relating to networking or communications, including Ethernet boards, serial communications, SLIP, and so on.
`comp.os.linux.setup`	For questions and discussion relating to Linux installation and system administration.
`comp.os.linux.x`	For questions and discussion relating to X Window System, version 11, compatible software including servers, clients, libraries, and fonts running under Linux. XFree86 issues not unique to Linux will be directed to `comp.windows.x.i386unix`.

`linux.*news hierarchy` — The `linux.* news hierarchy` is a set of gated mailing lists relevant to the Linux user community. They are typically very narrow in topic, and some, especially in the `linux.dev.*` and `linux.act.*` subhierarchies, are intended primarily for developers and alpha/beta testers. Please read the introduction on this newsgroup before posting to it.

Miscellaneous Linux Newsgroups

Many of the following newsgroups may also be available on your server (or Deja.com). These newsgroups begin with `linux.*`; some samples follow. Be sure to access your Usenet server for a complete list.

`linux.appletalk`

`linux.apps.bbsdev`

`linux.apps.flexfax`

`linux.apps.linux.bbs`

`linux.apps.seyon`

`linux.apps.seyon.development`

`linux.apps.xword`

`linux.bbs.rocat`

`linux.debian.alpha`

`linux.dev.680x0`

`linux.dev.admin`

`linux.dev.apps`

`linux.dev.atm`

`linux.fido.ifmail`

`linux.free-widgets.announce`

`linux.free-widgets.development`

`linux.i18n`

`linux.jobs`

`linux.largesites`

`linux.local.chicago`

`linux.local.novat-scotia`

`linux.local.silicon-valley`

`linux.motif.clone.lesstif`

linux.net.atm

linux.net.masqarade

linux.new-tty

linux.news.groups

linux.ports.alpha

linux.ports.hp-pa

linux.ports.powerpc

linux.postgres

linux.redhat.applixware

linux.redhat.axp

linux.redhat.devel

linux.samba

linux.samba.announce

This list is not all inclusive—be sure to download a complete list of newsgroups from your ISP's Usenet server. You can also check for available newsgroups at the http://www.deja.com site. You can also use Deja.com to post new messages and read and respond to posted messages.

UNIX-Related Newsgroups

The following list is geared to UNIX (in general), but provides a community of participation for Linux users, as well.

comp.unix.admin

comp.unix.advocacy

comp.unix.bsd

comp.unix.misc

comp.unix.pc-clone.32bit

comp.unix.programmer

comp.unix.questions

comp.unix.security

The X Windows Newsgroups

The following list of newsgroups is geared to UNIX X Windows, but it can also provide a community for Linux X Windows users, as well.

comp.windows.x.i386unix

comp.windows.open-look

Appendix A Other Sources of Information

```
comp.windows.x
comp.windows.x.announce
comp.windows.x.apps
comp.windows.x.intrinsics
comp.windows.x.motif
```

Networking Newsgroups

The following list is geared to UNIX networking, but it can provide a community for Linux networking, as well.

```
comp.protocols.ppp
comp.protocols.tcp-ip
comp.dcom.modems
comp.dcom.lans.ethernet
alt.internet.services
```

Regional Newsgroups

The following newsgroups are specific to regions around the world.

alt.os.linux	
alt.uu.comp.os.linux.questions	
at.fido.linux	
aus.computers.linux	Australia
cn.bbs.comp.linux	China
cribx1.linux	
dc.linux	Washington, DC (USA)
dc.org.linux-users	Washington, DC (USA)
de.alt.sources.linux.patches	Germany
de.comp.os.linux	Germany
de.comp.os.linux.hardware	Germany
de.comp.os.linux.misc	Germany
de.comp.os.linux.networking	Germany
de.comp.os.linux.x	Germany
ed.linux	
es.comp.os.linux	Spain
essi.linux	Spain
fido.belg.fra.linux	

```
fido.ger.linux
fido.linux-ger
fido7.linux
fido7.unix.linux
fj.os.linux
fr.comp.os.linux          France
gwdg.linux
han.comp.os.linux         Korea
han.sys.linux             Korea
hannet.ml.linux.680x0
hr.comp.linux.m
it.comp.linux             Italy
```

Newsgroup Archives

You can also find archived articles at the following sites:

- Archived articles from `comp.os.linux.announce` can be found at `ftp://sunsite.unc.edu/pub/Linux/docs/linux-announce.archive`.

- Most Usenet newsgroup archives can be found at `http://www.deja.com`. If your Internet service provider (ISP) does not offer newsgroup service, you can use Deja.com to post, search, and read Usenet messages.

Mailing Lists

Many mailing lists are available, each one covering specific subject matter about Linux. The focal point for most of these mailing lists is for the benefit of developers and alpha and beta testers, so that they can coordinate and discuss their work on Linux.

One of the top mailing lists is served up by the Majordomo mailserver located at `majordomo@vger.rutgers.edu`.

The following is a fairly comprehensive list of mailing lists found at vger.

linux-680x0—Linux on the 680×0 arch

linux-admin—Linux administration discussions

linux-all

linux-alpha—Linux on the ALPHA arch

linux-announce—Linux announce

linux-apps—Linux application discussions

linux-atm—Using ATM with Linux

linux-bbs—Linux bulletin board discussions

linux-c-programming—C language programming on Linux

linux-config—Linux configuration discussions

linux-diald—Using diald on Linux

linux-doc—Linux documentation discussions

linux-fido—Using FIDO with Linux

linux-fsf

linux-ftp—Using FTP with Linux

linux-gcc—Using gcc on Linux

linux-gcc-digest

linux-hams

linux-hppa

linux-ibcs2

linux-interviews—Interviews with people on Linux

linux-ipx—Linux and IPX networking

linux-japanese—For Japanese ports of Linux

linux-kernel—Discussion about the Linux kernel

linux-kernel-digest

linux-kernel-patch

linux-laptop—The use of Linux on laptops

linux-linuxbsd—Linux and BSD UNIX discussions

linux-linuxss

linux-localbus—Linux and local bus architecture

linux-lugnuts

linux-mca

linux-mgr

linux-mips—Linux on the MIPS architecture

linux-msdos—Linux and DOS interoperability

linux-msdos-digest

linux-net—Networking list

linux-new-lists

linux-newbie—List for the new (or occasional) Linux user

linux-normal

linux-nys

linux-oasg

linux-oi—Using the Object Interface toolkit

linux-pkg—Making package installation easier

linux-ppc—The Power-PC port of Linux

linux-ppp—Using PPP networking under Linux

linux-pro—Discussion about the Linux PRO distribution

linux-qag—Linux Quality Assurance Group

linux-scsi—SCSI drive development and usage

linux-serial—Using serial devices under Linux

linux-seyon—Talk about Seyon, the terminal program

linux-sound—Using sound cards and utilities under Linux

linux-standards—Standardizing various aspects of Linux

linux-svgalib—SVGA library discussion

linux-tape—Using tape storage devices under Linux

linux-term—Talk about using the Term suite of programs

linux-uucp—Using UUCP under Linux

linux-wabi—Linux Windows App Binary Interface emulation

linux-word—Discussion about the Linux-Word project

Linux-x11—Using the X-Window system under Linux

To obtain information on how to subscribe to any of the mailing lists, send an email message to `majordomo@vger.rutgers.edu` using the word **help** in the body of the email message. The mailing list server will respond with an email containing instructions on how to subscribe to the mailing lists and the command supported.

Linux Web Sites

The following is provided, hopefully, as a fairly comprehensive list of Web sites that support Linux in some way. Keep in mind that Internet addresses may change; these sites are valid as of the time of this writing.

Applications

Support for applications can be found at the following:

AcuCOBOL: `http://www.acucobol.com/acucobol.html`

BSCSoft: Load balancing and high availability: `http://www.bscsoft.com/`

Catalog of Free Compilers and Interpreters: `http://www.idiom.com/free-compilers`

Comware International: Provides ISP software products: http://www.comnets.com

CRiSP editor: http://www.vital.com

Cyberscheduler: http://www.envicon.de

High Performance Cluster Computing Resources: http://www.dgs.monash.edu.au/~rajkumar/cluster/index.html

High-Availability Linux Project: http://www.henge.com/~alanr/ha

Java Linux: http://www.blackdown.org/java-linux.html

Linux Applications and Utilities Page: http://www.chariott.com/linapps.html

Linux Databases and Tools: http://linas.org/linux/db.html

Linux Software Encyclopedia: http://stommel.tamu.edu/~baum/linuxlist/linuxlist/linuxlist.html

MySQL: http://www.tcx.se

OMNIS Studio Evaluation: http://www.blyth.com/download/download.html

Open Sound System: http://www.4front-tech.com/ossfree

Print, Scan, Fax and OCR: http://www.vividata.com

RPM repository: http://www.rpmfind.net/linux/RPM

SAMBA: http://samba.anu.edu.au

Scanner Access Now Easy: http://www.mostang.com/sane

Scientific Applications on Linux: http://ftp.llp.fu-berlin.de/lsoft

StarOffice: http://www.stardivision.de

The Linux Software Map: http://www.execpc.com/lsm

The Project Mnemonic Development Site: http://www.mnemonic.browser.org

Uninet Perl Co.: http://www.uninetsolutions.com/free.html

Web Browsers for Linux: http://www.linux.trix.net/browsers.en.htm

Wolfram Research (Mathematica): http://www.wolfram.com

XMCD - Motif CD Audio Player: http://sunsite.unc.edu/~cddb/xmcd/

Applix Office for Linux: http://www.applix.com/applixware/main.cfm

Applixware: http://www.applix.com/appware/appware.htm

Cary's Applixware Page: http://www.radix.net/~cobrien/applix

SuSE Mailing List Archive: http://lists.suse.com/archives

Architectures

Support for Linux under various architectures can be found at the following sites:

ARM Linux: http://www.arm.uk.linux.org/~rmk

Current ports of Linux OS:
http://perso.wanadoo.es/xose/linux/linux_ports.html

ELKS The Embeddable Linux Kernel Subset:
http://www.elks.ecs.soton.ac.uk/cgi-bin/ELKS

Linux on L4: http://os.inf.tu-dresden.de/L4/LinuxOnL4

Linux on SGI: http://www.linux.sgi.com

Linux on the Alpha: http://www.alphalinux.org

Linux on VAX: http://www.mssl.ucl.ac.uk/~atp/linux-vax

Linux/AP: http://cap.anu.edu.au/cap/projects/linux

Linux/MIPS: http://www.fnet.fr/linux-mips

Linux/Sun3: http://www.netppl.fi/~pp/sun3

Linux7k: http://www.calcaria.net

LinuxPPC: http://www.linuxppc.org

MkLinux: http://www.mklinux.apple.com

SPARC Linux: http://www.geog.ubc.ca/sparclinux.html

VMELinux: http://www.vmelinux.org

Benchmarks

Benchmark information is available at these sites:

Spectable: ftp://ftp.cdf.toronto.edu/pub/spectable

The Performance Database Server:
http://netlib2.cs.utk.edu/performance/html/PDSbrowse.html

Transaction Processing Performance Council: http://www.tpc.org/

BLINUX: http://leb.net/blinux

Commercial Software

Information on commercial software is available at these sites:

FlagShip: http://www.fship.com

MetroLink: http://www.metrolink.com

VMWare: http://www.vmware.com

Linux Forum: http://datania.com/linux

Games

Games are out there too! Support is available at the following sites:

Linux DOOM FAQ: http://jcomm.uoregon.edu/~stevev/Linux-DOOM-FAQ.html

Linux Penguin: http://home.knuut.de/Bernhard.Hailer/penguin

The Linux Game Tome: http://www.happypenguin.org/news

GNU, the Free Software Foundation—Cygnus Solutions: http://www.cygnus.com

GNU's Not Unix!: http://www.gnu.ai.mit.edu

The GNU Project: http://www.delorie.com/gnu

Hardware Vendors

Some hardware vendors include the following:

MikroTik Systems: http://www.mt.lv

PSSC Labs: http://www.pssclabs.com

VA Linux Systems: http://www.varesearch.com

HOW-TOs and Information

Some other sources of information include the following:

Advice and guidance on performance tuning Linux systems: http://www.tunelinux.com

comp.protocols.tcp-ip.domains FAQs: http://www.intac.com/~cdp/cptd-faq

External Parallel Port devices and Linux: http://www.torque.net/linux-pp.html

FAQs about wu-ftpd: http://www.cetis.hvu.nl/~koos/wu-ftpd-faq.html

Freshmeat: http://freshmeat.net

Linux and Linux-Related Development Projects

These sites describe ongoing developments in Linux:

http://sunsite.unc.edu/LDP/devel.html

Linux HowTos: http://metalab.unc.edu/linux/HOWTO/HOWTO-INDEX.html

Linux on Laptops: http://www.cs.utexas.edu/users/kharker/linux-laptop

Linux PCMCIA Information: http://pcmcia.sourceforge.org

Micro Channel Linux: http://www.dgmicro.com/mca

Network Management & Monitoring with Linux: http://www.develnet.es/~david/papers/snmp

Porting Applications to Linux: http://www.cs.berkeley.edu/~mdw/linux/porting-linux/html/paper.html

Slashdot News for Nerds: http://slashdot.org

The 86open Project: http://www.telly.org/86open

The programmer's file formats collection: http://www.wotsit.org

Wim's BIOS Page: http://ping4.ping.be/bios

Free Patents: http://www.freepatents.org

Linux Home Pages

Some important Linux home pages include the following:

Linus Torvalds: http://www.cs.helsinki.fi/~torvalds

Linux BBS: http://www.linuxbbs.org

Linux Books and Resources: http://www.dragonfire.net/~garym/linux/

Linux Journal: http://207.178.22.52/index.html

Linux Mama: http://www.linuxmama.com

Linux Savvy: http://www.linuxsavvy.com

Macmillan Linux Resources: http://www.informit.com

SuSE Inc.: http://www.suse.com

The Internet Operating System Counter: http://leb.net/hzo/ioscount

The Linux Counter: http://counter.li.org

Linux Portals

Linux Portals include the following:

Freshmeat: http://freshmeat.net

Linux Berg: http://www.linuxberg.com

Linux International: http://www.li.org

Linux Start: http://www.LinuxStart.Com

Linux Ticker: http://LinuxTicker.com

Linux Today: http://linuxtoday.com/index.html

LINUX.DE (Germany): http://www.linux.de

Linux.org.uk (United Kingdom): http://www.linux.org.uk

LinuxInfo.de (Germany): http://www.linuxinfo.de/de

LinuxLinks.com: http://www.linuxlinks.com

LinuxPowered: http://www.linuxpowered.com

Slashdot: http://slashdot.org

Projects

Linux-related projects include the following:

Beowulf Project: http://www.beowulf.org

Linux SMP: http://www.uk.linux.org/SMP/title.html

Real Time Linux: http://luz.cs.nmt.edu/~rtlinux

The 86open Project: http://www.telly.org/86open

Security

Security issues are covered on these sites:

CERT Coordination Center: http://www.cert.org

COAST Hotlist: http://www.cerias.purdue.edu/coast/hotlist

SecurityFocus: http://www.securityfocus.com

The Linux Security Home Page: http://www.ecst.csuchico.edu/~jtmurphy

UNIX System Security Checklist:
http://staff.washington.edu/dittrich/R870/security-checklist.html

User Groups

User groups include the following:

Linux User Groups: http://lugww.nllgg.nl

Linux Users' Group Orléans (France): http://perso.magic.fr/obenassy/lugo

LUG list overview (Germany): http://lugww.counter.li.org

Ottawa Carleton Linux Users Group: http://www.oclug.on.ca

runix: http://runix.aful.org/

SuSE Linux Users: http://clubs.yahoo.com/clubs/suselinuxusers

Wabi 2.2 for Linux FAQ: http://www.caldera.com/tech-ref/wabi/faq/faq.html

X Windows System

X Windows sites include the following:

comp.windows.x.apps FAQ:
http://www.ee.ryerson.ca:8080/~elf/xapps/faq.html

GNOME: http://www.gnome.org

LessTif is the Hungry Programmers' version of OSF/Motif:
http://www.lesstif.org

Metro Link, Inc.: http://www.metrolink.com

The K desktop environment (KDE): http://www.kde.org

The Open Group: http://www.opengroup.org

The XFce project: http://tsikora.tiac.net/xfce

The XFree86 Project: http://www.xfree86.org

Xi Graphics, Inc.: http://www.xig.com

Linux FTP Sites

The following lists the well-known FTP sites for Linux. FTP sites come and go, so be sure to check out the following document:

http://sunsite.unc.edu/LDP/HOWTO/INFO-SHEET.html

The following three sites are considered to be the main Linux FTP sites:

ftp://tsx.mit.edu/pub/linux

ftp://sunsite.unc.edu/pub/Linux

ftp://ftp.kernel.org/pub/linux

You can also obtain Linux from the following FTP sites:

tsx-11.mit.edu

sunsite.unc.edu

ftp.funet.fi

net.tamu.edu

ftp.mcc.ac.uk

src.doc.ic.ac.uk

ftp.informatik.tu-muenchen.de

ftp.dfv.rwth-aachen.de

ftp.informatik.rwth-aachen.de

ftp.lip6.fr

ftp.uu.net

wuarchive.wustl.edu

ftp.win.tue.nl

ftp.stack.urc.tue.nl

srawgw.sra.co.jp

cair.kaist.ac.kr

NCTUCCCA.edu.tw

Appendix A Other Sources of Information

```
nic.switch.ch
sunsite.cnlab-switch.ch
cnuce_arch.cnr.it
ftp.monash.edu.au
ftp.dstc.edu.au
ftp.sydutech.usyd.edu.au
```

More information can be obtained from the `http://www.linux.org` and `http://www.li.org` sites.

B

Common Questions

LINUX HAS BEEN A GREAT INSPIRATION for many people, both programmers and users. All Linux users, no matter what their level of expertise, come upon a barrier of one type or another. These barriers always generate questions. And as anyone who is new to Linux can attest, there are many questions.

In this appendix, we unveil some of the most common questions that almost every Linux user asks. And, hopefully, we will expose some questions that are not always raised. As an added bonus, we will answer all these questions.

Overview

This appendix will undoubtedly be accessed many times by the new Linux user—and even more so if that user is new to UNIX, in general.

For the experienced UNIX user, Linux is a breath of fresh air. But in that same breath are questions: "Where is the *blah* command?" "Why does Linux do operation *so-and-so* this way?"—and so on and so forth. Remember, Linux was built from the ground up and was born from its own shell. Linux is also considered a hybrid, supporting many commands found on SystemV UNIX and BSD UNIX, as well as some commands specific to Linux.

So What Is Linux?

Linux is an operating system that is a clone of UNIX. It offers true multitasking and provides support for multiple users. Linux also provides for virtual memory support, shared libraries, demand loading, TCP/IP networking, and sophisticated memory management.

Linux began its life as a school project, written by Linus Torvalds. People across the globe contributed to the Linux effort by writing software for Linux. Linux distribution falls under the GNU Public License.

The main platform of choice for Linux is the 80386 processor (and later). Other processor platforms are supported and others are on the way.

Linux interoperates well with other operating systems, including Windows, NetWare, and MacOS. It supports a wide range of software, including X Windows, Emacs, and TCP/IP networking.

Benchmarks of Linux have shown results comparable with midrange workstations from Sun and Digital.

What Distributions of Linux Are Available?

Linux comes in all shapes and sizes. Many organizations have taken the basic Linux package and enhanced it to reflect their culture. Some distributions can be purchased on CD-ROM, downloaded from an FTP site, or found in the back of a book (on CD-ROM).

Some organizations allow you to download their distribution free of charge and, optionally, purchase their distribution on CD-ROM with documentation.

The following list of Linux distributions is not all-inclusive. Check Appendix A, "Other Sources of Information," for more information.

armedLinux

The armedLinux distribution is considered the "Linux for Windows users." The armedLinux system is an optimized Linux system that installs and runs under Microsoft Windows 95 or 98.

You can reach armedLinux at http://www.armed.net.

Caldera OpenLinux

OpenLinux is designed as a business workstation. It comes with Applixware and StarOffice so that you you can create and manipulate office documents, such as word processing, presentations, and spreadsheets. It comes with

Netscape Communicator, and you can host your own Web site with the Apache Web server. Files and printers can be shared among Linux, Macintosh, OS/2, UNIX, and Windows clients.

Caldera created and offers the LIZARD (Linux Wizard) graphical installation utility. LIZARD can detect many devices, such as the mouse, the keyboard, CD-ROM and hard drives, sound, video, and network cards (and other devices).

Caldera OpenLinux bundles PartitionMagic and BootMagic to enable other operating systems to share the PC. You can create separate partitions for each operating system that will reside on the PC and then boot each of those systems with a minimal amount of fuss.

You can find Caldera OpenLinux at http://www.calderasystems.com.

Corel LinuxOS

Corel's distribution of Linux was launched at the Comdex Fall/99 show. Corel has taken and enhanced Debian GNU/Linux and packages the K Desktop Environment (KDE), providing a graphical desktop environment.

Corel Linux OS features Corel Install Express, a simple four-step installation utility. Also included are a file manager, centralized configuration and system updates, an email client, and a Web browser.

You can find Corel Linux OS at http://linux.corel.com.

Debian GNU/Linux

The Debian GNU/Linux package is a free distribution of Linux. The Debian distribution is maintained through the efforts of people who volunteer their time.

The Debian distribution contains many prepackaged software titles and contains advanced package-management tools to allow ease of installation and maintenance.

You can reach Debian at http://www.debian.org.

DLX Linux

The DLX Linux distribution is considered a full-featured Linux system for Intel PCs that comes on one 3 1/2-inch floppy disk. Also, DLX has a 130KB writeable ext2 filesystem on the disk to store configuration files. Support is provided for the parallel port Zip drive so that you can mount the 100MB disks. DLX Linux is distributed only in source form.

You can find DLX at http://www.wu-wien.ac.at/usr/h93/h9301726/dlx.html.

DragonLinux

DragonLinux can coexist with and live on the same partition as your Windows system, and it takes up less space than a word processor. The DragonLinux distribution is an Internet-ready distribution of Linux and is very small—consuming only 150MB. It uses the UMSDOS file system, eliminating the need to repartition the system's hard drive(s). DragonLinux also comes complete with networking tools and documentation.

You can find DragonLinux at `http://www.dragonlinux.nu`.

easy Information Technology's (eIT) easyLinux

easyLinux offers an easy-to-use GUI-based (using a VGA X Server) installation utility. It offers three installation modes: Beginner Mode, Advanced Mode, and Professional Mode. Beginner Mode hides many of the details of installing Linux; Advanced Mode offers more information and installation options to the user; and Professional Mode provides full details for installation and dialog boxes to offer alterations.

The easyLinux distribution does not target UNIX gurus who want to experiment with different window managers, work at the text-mode console, or drive Linux hard. The eIT people want to recommend easyLinux to users who want to use Linux as a desktop workstation with a minimal amount of fuss.

You can reach eIT easyLinux at `http://www.eit.de`.

hal91

The hal91 distribution is described as a minimalist Linux that fits on one 1.44MB floppy disk. It is intended to be used as a rescue disk and as a portable Linux system.

You can find hal91 at `http://home.sol.no/~okolaas/hal91.html`.

Linux by LibraNet

The LibraNet Linux distribution is based on the Debian/GNU Linux distribution and provides an enhanced desktop setup and configuration utility.

LibraNet has provided for ease of installation for those packages that are usually hard to install. Doing this eliminates many hours of finding, comprehending, installing, and configuring these packages. For example, included are packages such as Netscape Communicator, RealPlayer G2 (now RealPlayer 7), WordPerfect, and StarOffice. Also included are KDE, GNOME, and window managers such as IceWM, Enlightenment, and Windowmaker.

You can find Libranet at http://www.libranet.com.

Linux Mandrake

According to Mandrake, the Linux Mandrake distribution is 99 percent compatible with Red Hat Linux. It is available for most Pentium and compatible processors. It includes the KDE graphical interface, GNOME, AfterStep, WindowMaker, IceWM, and many others.

Software included with Linux Mandrake are the Apache Web Server, GIMP (image manipulation program), Netscape Communicator, and many other excellent software packages.

You can find Mandrake at http://www.linux-mandrake.com.

LinuxPPC for the PowerPC

LinuxPPC is a native port of Linux to the PowerPC platform. It runs natively on the PCI-based Apple PowerMacs, Amiga Power-UP systems, and many IBM/Motorola PreP/CHRP workstations. It will also run on several embedded platforms, including the Motorola MBX and RPX. LinuxPPC provides support for multiple processors (SMP) found on some Power Macs and IBM RS/6000 (4-CPU) computers.

You can reach LinuxPPC at http://www.linuxppc.org.

LinuxPro by Workgroup Solutions Group (WGS)

The Linux Pro distribution consists of a six-CD set. Also, it includes the *Linux Encyclopedia*, a 1600+ page reference manual of information with tutorials on setup, configuration, and much more. A CD-ROM containing a large amount of online text (too much to print), such as newsgroup postings and the HOWTOs, is included.

You can find LinuxPro at http://www.wgs.com.

LinuxWare by TransAmeritech Systems

The LinuxWare distribution provides an installation utility that runs under Windows/Windows95. Virtually anyone can install the base LinuxWare in less than 30 minutes.

The package can be installed from any DOS-supported CD-ROM drive. You are not required to repartition your hard drive(s) to install LinuxWare—only an uncompressed DOS drive with enough space is required. Also, LinuxWare can be installed to a drive other than the c: drive.

You can find LinuxWare at `http://www.trans-am.com/index1.htm`.

LoopLinux (DOS Linux)

LoopLinux is a Linux distribution that can be installed on and run from a DOS system; therefore, you do not need to repartition your hard disk(s).

You can find LoopLinux at `http://www.tux.org/pub/people/kent-robotti/index.html`.

MkLinux

MkLinux is a Linux distribution designed for the Power Macintosh platform. The MkLinux distribution operates on the Open Group Mach PMK1.1 microkernel that runs natively on the PowerPC microprocessor.

You can reach MkLinux at `http://www.mklinux.apple.com`.

Red Hat Linux

The Red Hat distribution is available for Intel, Alpha, and SPARC platforms. The distribution includes the Red Hat Linux operating system, StarOffice, Installation and Reference Guides, and installation support.

Red Hat offers several packages, including Standard, Deluxe, and Professional. Red Hat employs a graphical installation utility to ease the installation process. Other features include software RAID, hardware probing, easy-to-use PPP Dialer, high-availability clustering, LDAP integration, and many other features.

You can find Red Hat at `http://www.redhat.com`.

Slackware Linux

The Slackware distribution of Linux was developed by Patrick Volkerding. It is designed with two goals: ease of use and stability. It includes most of the latest popular software packages.

The distribution provides an easy-to-use installation utility, online documentation, and a menu-driven package system. A full installation provides the X Windows System, C/C++ development environments, FTP server, mail server, networking utilities, news server, Web server, Netscape Communicator, and many more.

You can reach Slackware at `http://www.slackware.com`.

Stampede GNU/Linux

The Stampede GNU/Linux distribution is designed to be fast and easy to use for the new user, yet versatile for the power user.

The goals for Stampede are high performance and quality, stability and compatibility, expandability, easy updating, and strong security.

You can find Stampede at http://www.stampede.org.

Storm Linux

The Storm Linux distribution is based on the Debian GNU/Linux distribution. Enhancements include easier installation, configuration, administration, and updating.

The distribution includes the KDE and GNOME graphical environments. Some other software packages are provided, including StarOffice, Partition MagicSE, Applixware Office demo version, BRU Backup demo, VMWare demo, and many others.

You can reach Storm Linux at http://www.stormix.com.

SuSE Linux

The SuSE distribution contains 1,500 applications and utilities and claims to offer the most Linux applications in one package. The package includes a menu-driven graphical installation utility with automatic hardware detection. A complete Linux system and desktop can be installed in less than 30 minutes.

Many software packages are included for the office, image manipulation, programming, sound, multimedia, typesetting, Web hosting, networking, demo software, games, Internet, mail, databases, video, and much more.

You can find SuSE Linux at http://www.suse.com.

TurboLinux

The TurboLinux distribution provides powerful desktop applications, such as WordPerfect and Netscape Communicator. Also included are System Commander Deluxe TL, the GNOME, and KDE and TurboDesk graphical environments.

TurboLinux is available in three great flavors:

- Workstation 4.0—The high-performance choice for Linux on the desktop.
- TurboLinux Server 4.0—Claims to be the most secure Linux server out of the box.

- TurboLinux TurboCluster Server 4.0—Builds scalable, available, and affordable server clusters.

You can reach TurboLinux at http://www.turbolinux.com.

Yggdrasil Plug and Play Linux

The Yggdrasil distribution consists of two CD-ROMs. The first CD-ROM includes all the system programs, and the second CD-ROM contains the source code. On supported hardware configurations, Plug and Play Linux can be run by inserting the boot floppy, inserting the first CD-ROM, and starting the computer. DOS and network installation is also supported.

A 170-page installation guide is included, along with enhancements to the system-administration graphical-control panels.

You can reach Yggdrasil at http://www.yggdrasil.com.

WinLinux

The WinLinux distribution installation and configuration tasks are run directly under Windows. Some of the features of WinLinux are Windows integration, Smart configuration (hardware devices are detected and automatically configured), Easy start (start WinLinux by double clicking it), Safe installation (no hard disk repartitioning), Optimal Disk Usage (WinLinux shares free disk space with Windows), K Desktop Environment, and many other features.

You can find WinLinux at http://www.winlinux.net.

What Processors Does Linux Run On?

As most of us know, the 80386 family of processors (and later) is supported. Linux runs okay on a 386, but a Pentium should be the minimum configuration.

Machines utilizing the Motorola 68000 series of processors, such as Amiga, Apple, and Atari, are supported. You can find the m68k URL at http://www.linux-m68k.org.

There is a Linux port to the PowerPC processor. Linux/PPC will run on PCI-based Apple PowerMacs, IBM and Motorola PReP and CHRP workstations, and the Amiga Power-UP systems. Some embedded platforms also are supported, including the Motorola MBX and RPX. The Linux/PPC URL is at http://www.linuxppc.org.

The Alpha, SPARC, PowerPC, and ARM platforms are supported by the Debian GNU/Linux distribution. You can get more information at http://www.debian.org/ports. Red Hat also supports the SPARC and Alpha platforms; you can find Red Hat at http://www.redhat.com.

SGI is working to bring Linux to various MIPS-based machines. The URL for more information is at http://www.linux.sgi.com.

Apple computer supports a port of Linux to various Power Macintosh platforms. MkLinux runs natively on the PowerPC microprocessor. You can get more information at http://www.mklinux.apple.com.

UltraLinux is the Linux port for the SPARC family of processors (such as Sun workstations). The current port is considered very stable and supports most workstations, including the 32-bit SPARC processors and 64-bit UltraSPARC workstations. You can find information on UltraLinux at http://www.ultralinux.org.

Many other ports of Linux are available, including Compaq (Digital), (IBM) MicroChannel, Intel SMP, NEC architectures, various RISC architectures, handhelds, microcontrollers, and embedded system—just to name a few. An excellent URL for Linux ports can be found at http://perso.wanadoo.es/xose/linux/linux_ports.html.

What Are Some of the Requirements of Linux?

The most popular platform is the Intel platform; the minimum processor is the 80386. Linux supports most PC motherboard bus architectures, including ISA, EISA, VESA, and PCI. Linux also supports the IBM MicroChannel Architecture (MCA).

For disk requirements, you might be able to squeeze a Linux system in under 20MB, but for any serious system you will need more space. For an installation with X Windows GUI support, you should expect to use about 120MB.

Installing almost any of the commercial-grade distributions will set your hard disk back from 250MB to 500MB. If you install everything, including source code, disk requirements can soar upwards of 4GB.

For memory requirements, Linux requires a minimum of 4MB of RAM, but for Linux to be truly usable, you will want more RAM. If you want to run X Windows, a minimum of 16MB of RAM is required. Of course, the more the better. If you are running applications such as Netscape Communicator under a GUI, you will require about 64MB (physical memory). The swap partition size should be twice the amount of physical RAM.

Linux supports a broad range of PC video cards, including Hercules, IBM monochrome, CGA, EGA, VGA, and SVGA video cards. Many accelerated video cards are also supported by Linux.

A wide range of network interface cards are supported by Linux. Most ARCnet, Ethernet, FDDI, Frame Relay, and Token Ring cards are supported; the most popular are Ethernet cards.

Linux supports a vast array of internal and external serial modems. The exception is WinTel (internal Windows) modems.

Most all CD-ROM drives are supported by Linux, and the most common interfaces are IDE, EIDE, ATAPI, and SCSI. Linux can read only the ISO 9660 and High Sierra extensions for CD-ROM file formats.

Linux supports all MFM, IDE, and EIDE controllers, and most RLL and ESDI controllers. Linux also supports a wide range of SCSI controllers from manufacturers such as Adaptec, Future Domain, and Buslogic.

Mouse support under Linux includes serial, bus, and PS/2 mouse interfaces. Other pointing devices, such as trackballs and touchpads, should work under Linux.

Most SCSI tape drives are supported by Linux, as long as the SCSI controller is supported. Some QIC drives that interface with the floppy controller (or parallel port) are also supported. The QIC-02 interface is also supported by Linux.

Linux supports practically every popular parallel-port printer. Serial printers are also supported by Linux. Table 18.1 in Chapter 18, "Print Services," lists many printers supported by Linux.

In addition to this book, you can find information regarding Linux requirements at the Linux Documentation Project at http://metalab.unc.edu/mdw/index.html. The Hardware Compatibility HOW-TO at http://metalab.unc.edu/mdw/HOWTO/Hardware-HOWTO.html lists the most popular hardware. You can also check the Installation and Getting Started Guide at http://metalab.unc.edu/mdw/docs.html from Matt Welsh.

Where Can I Get Linux?

Many distributions can be acquired by purchase or by download. Some of the more popular distributions are covered in the previous section "What Distributions of Linux Are Available?" Obviously, your best bet is to purchase a distribution on CD-ROM. A good, high-end Linux system can be purchased for less than $100.

A good URL for categories of Linux distributions is http://www.linuxhq.com.

Where Can I Find Software for Linux?

Many software titles that run natively under Linux are available, including database, groupware, math, office applications and suites, games, graphics-oriented, multimedia, networking, programming and development packages, servers, science, Web-oriented, and X Windows applications.

For office applications, there is Applixware from Applix, WordPerfect for Linux from Corel Corporation, and StarOffice from Sun Microsystems. This list is not all inclusive.

MagicPoint is an X11-based presentation tool and is designed to construct presentations. Its presentation file is text-only so that you can create presentation files quickly with your favorite editor. The current release is an alpha release. You can find MagicPoint at http://www.mew.org/mgp.

Most major database vendors support Linux, including Informix Dynamic Server and Informix-SE from Informix Software, InterBase 5 from InterBase Software, Oracle from Oracle, and UniVerse from Ardent Software.

You can choose from many software development packages. Some of them are CodeWarrior from Metrowerks, CodeWizard for C++ from ParaSoft, GNUPro for Linux from Cygnus, IBM ViaVoice Run Time and the SDK for Linux from IBM, ISE Eiffel SDK from Interactive Software Engineering, Install Toolkit for Java from IBM, JdesignerPro from BulletProof, KAI C++ Compiler from Kuck & Associates, MKS Source Integrity from MKS, Magic from Magic Software, and many others.

A good URL to start with is Linux Online at http://www.linux.org; select Applications.

Can I Access Data on Drive Types Other Than Linux?

Yes, Linux has the capability to read and write DOS and OS/2 FAT partitions and floppy disks. Linux can use the DOS filesystem type that is built into the kernel or mtools package. The VFAT filesystem used by Windows 9x and Windows NT is also supported by the kernel.

The dmsdos package offers support for reading and writing compressed file systems, such as DoubleSpace and DriveSpace in DOS 6.xx and Window95. Stacker versions 3 and 4 also are supported by this package.

Linux can access HPFS partitions in read-only mode. You can provide for HPFS support as a module or when compiling the kernel.

Linux supports the Amiga Fast File System (AFFS) hard-drive partitions (but not floppies). Support is provided for AFFS version 1.3 and later.

The UFS filesystem that is used by BSD, Coherent, FreeBSD, NetBSD, NeXTStep, SunOS, System V, and XENIX is supported only for read-only access. Support is provided by module or as a kernel compile-time option.

Linux supports Windows for Workgroups and Windows NT SMB drives for read-and-write access. The Samba package also supports Windows for Workgroups filesystems. Windows NTFS is also supported, but in read-only mode.

Can I Run Software Written for Other Operating Systems?

Yes and no. The MS Windows (3.xx) Emulator (WINE), is still under construction; in other words, it is not ready for prime time. You can run some applications, but it is still quirky at best. You can get the WINE FAQ at `ftp://sunsite.unc.edu/pub/Linux/ALPHA/wine/Wine.FAQ`.

Here is something rather unique: VMware from vmware. This product will run multiple virtual computers on a single PC at the same time. Partitioning or rebooting is not required with VMware. The VMware product features full networking, multimedia support, sound, and undoable virtual disks. If you run multiple operating systems on your PC, and you do not want the hard-drive-partitioning hassles or to have to reboot every time you want to run another operating system, you should check out this product. You can find Vmware for Linux at `http://www.vmware.com`.

Where Can I Get Linux Information on the Internet?

Linux information can be found from many sources. New sites are launched every month.

You should also check out any Linux user groups that might exist within your community. User groups provide a wealth of information; in addition, most user groups offer Linux CD-ROM (or floppy disk) distributions. User groups also provide a mechanism for the exchange of ideas.

Other sources of Linux information follow.

Web Sites

One obvious source is to start at any Internet search engine, such as `http://www.yahoo.com`, `http://www.excite.com`, `http://www.hotbot.com`, `http://www.altavista.com`, `http://www.directhit.com`, `http://www.google.com`, http://www.dogpile.com, to name a few. Each search engine has its strengths and weaknesses; you should decide which search engine works best for a given type of search.

The Linux Documentation Project URL is http://www.linuxdoc.org. You can find the man pages, HOWTOs and mini-HOWTOs, Guides Series, and FAQs.

The Linux International Web site is found at http://www.li.org. Linux International is a not-for-profit association, consisting of groups, corporations, and others working to promote and help grow Linux and the Linux community.

The Linux Online site is a central clearing house for information and the promotion of Linux. This is a good jumping-off point to other places on the Internet. The URL is http://www.linux.org.

Usenet Newsgroups

Many Linux Usenet newsgroups can be found, mostly within the comp.os.linux.* hierarchy. You can also check in the comp.unix.* hierarchy of newsgroups because Linux is a POSIX-compatible system.

Some of the more popular newsgroups are comp.os.linux.misc, comp.os.linux.setup, comp.os.linux.advocacy, comp.os.linux.networking, comp.os.linux.hardware, and the comp.os.linux.development.apps.

If you do not have access to a news server, you can always read and participate at http://www.deja.com (formerly http://www.dejanews.com).

FTP Sites

The best way to get Linux distributions, applications, and documentation is to use File Transfer Protocol (FTP). Many FTP sites are available. The main FTP sites are ftp.funet.fi/pub/OS/Linux in Finland, ftp.sunsite.unc.edu/pub/Linux in the U.S., and ftp.tsx-11.mit.edu/pub/linux, also in the U.S.

The popular distributions of Linux are Debian GNU/Linux, available at ftp.debian.org/pub/debian; Red Hat, available at ftp.redhat.com; Slackware, available at ftp.slackware.com; Caldera OpenLinux, available at ftp.caldera.com/pub/OpenLinux; and SuSE, which is available at ftp.suse.com/pub/SuSE-Linux. You can also find information about other distributions in this appendix in "What Distributions of Linux Are Available?"

If you are an operating-system tinkering type and want the latest kernel, go to ftp.cs.helsinki.fi/pub/Linux_Kernel. Linus Torvalds updates this site with the latest and greatest kernel versions.

Are Disk and File Utilities Available for Linux?

In general, no specialized disk and file utilities are available, like those that might be found with other operating systems (no dirty windows with Linux).

Some of the more common requests concern file defragmentation, file compression, and undelete utilities. We address these items in the next several subsections. Some great URLs for Linux software are the following:

http://www.linuxapps.com

http://www.freshmeat.net

http://happypenguin.org (games)

http://linux.tucows.com

Be sure to check these sites often because new software is continually updated and added.

File Defragmentation

If you are utilizing the ext2 filesystem (and its cousins), there is not much reason to use a file defragmentation utility. This filesystem contains code to keep file fragmentation at a minimum.

If you must have a defragmentor, look for defrag with a filename similar to defrag-0.70.tar.gz; you can find it at sunsite.unc.edu, in the /pub/Linux/system/filesystems directory or the Linux software URLs listed in the previous section.

Also, check out e2defrag, an enhanced version defrag that supports 2.2.x systems and defragments ext2 filesystems.

File Compression

File compression supported by the Linux kernel is provided for by the block device driver named *DouBle*. DouBle was developed by Jean-Marc Verbavatz and can be found at sunsite.unc.edu in the /pub/Linux/patches/diskdrives directory. Be forewarned, however, that directory information and inodes are compressed in addition to files. If you experience disk or file corruption of any type, you will probably not recover the data.

The tcx (Transparently Compressed Executables) allows you to compress infrequently used executables and to uncompress them when they are used. You can find tcx at sunsite.unc.edu in the /pub/Linux/utils/compress directory.

An application named zlibc provides applications with the capability to read compressed files (GNU gzip variety), eliminating the need to decompress (unzip) the file(s). You can find this utility at sunsite.unc.edu in the /pub/Linux/libs directory.

The e2compr utility provides transparent compression for the ext2 filesystem. Any new files added can be compressed automatically without explicitly identifying the new file. It is advertised as safer than DouBle when the filesystem becomes full or in the event of a system crash. Different parts of the filesystem can be compressed in different ways, such as leaving some disk areas uncompressed. Data files can be compressed, in addition to binary files.

File Undelete

Even as we speak (or read), utilities are being developed that provide undelete functionality. However, do not expect this functionality to be available any time soon.

A better option employs the use of commands that alias file manipulation commands. These alias commands mimic the real commands, except that they move files to an "undelete" directory, such as might be found on other operating systems. Think of this directory as a trash can that you might have at the office. You toss paper and other items that you no longer want. Some time later, though, you realize that you need the phone number written on a tossed piece of paper. You simply retrieve the paper from the trash can—sort of an "untrash" command. The Linux version of this works the same. For example, you execute the command as shown in the following dialog.

```
stimpy $ rm myPhoneFile.txt
stimpy $
```

The next thing out of your mouth is, "Holy bat chute, I need all those phone numbers!" Fortunately, the rm command you executed is an alias for the real rm command supplied with Linux. This alias command first moves the file to the "trash can" directory, and then executes the actual rm command. The functionality it performs might look like the following dialog.

```
stimpy $ cp myPhoneFile.txt /trashCan
stimpy $ rm myPhoneFile.txt
stimpy $
```

Of course, error-checking functionality would be used to make sure the move succeeded before deleting the file.

Other utility commands are available to view files in the trash can, to undelete files, and to purge the trash can.

The Undelete Utilities, which provide undelete functionality for the Linux ext2 filesystem in Linux, can be found at any of the utility sites listed previously.

Another undelete utility, named recover, automates the steps found in the Ext2fs-Undeletion-HOWTO to recover one or more deleted files.

The SafeDelete utility is another fine utility providing round-trip delete and undelete functionality. SafeDelete's undelete command can restore a file to its original directory, applying the original permission settings, timestamps, and so on. The software is provided as a command-line utility and also as an ncurses interface, providing a scrollable list of deleted files. Also provided in the SafeDelete package is a utility that permanently deletes files from the trashcan as they age.

The Deltree utility provides the user with a configurable application for file browsing and undelete functionality. It works in text mode and provides logging facilities. Deleted files and directories can be restored to their original location or an alternate path.

What Do I Do If I Forgot the root Password?

This is really an easy fix. Simply shut down the machine and boot init the shell, as in the following:

```
boot: Linux init=/bin/sh
bash# mount -o remount / -rw
bash# passwd root
```

The following steps demonstrate another method:

1. Reboot the system.
2. At the lilo prompt type **Linux 1**.
3. Next, at the prompt, type **passwd root**.
4. You will need to enter your (new) password twice.
5. Reboot as normal.

You should note that this is peculiar only to Linux, rather than a fix for a non-Linux UNIX system. For UNIXes, you will need to boot into single-user mode. If you get the message `Unable to lock passwd file`, check out the /etc directory; there might be a file named `passwd.lock` or some similar name.

How Can I Share Linux/Windows Printers and Filesystems?

Your best bet is to use Samba. Be sure to read Chapter 15, "Samba: Merging Linux and Windows" in this book. You can also find information about Samba at `http://samba.anu.edu.au`.

How Can I Mount a Windows95 Filesystem?

To get long filename support, mount the Windows drive vfat instead of msdos or umsdos. You will have to make some changes to the `/etc/fstab` file; specifically, change any msdos-type entries to the vfat type.

You will also have to ensure that vfat is loaded properly; the proc entry must come before the drives in the `/etc/fstab` file. Therefore, if your `/etc/fstab` file looks like the following:

```
/dev/hdc1                      ext2    defaults       1 1
/dev/hda1      /c              msdos   defaults       0 0
/dev/cdrom     /mnt/cdrom      iso9660 noauto,ro      0 0
none           /proc           proc    defaults       0 0
```

You will have to change it to the following:

```
none           /proc           proc    defaults       0 0
/dev/hdc1                      ext2    defaults       1 1
/dev/hda1      /c              vfat    defaults       0 0
/dev/cdrom     /mnt/cdrom      iso9660 noauto,ro      0 0
```

Do Viruses Exist on Linux?

In a nutshell—no. The most famous UNIX virus is the Morrison Worm, and it's probably the last. Why? Viruses have a hard time existing on a UNIX/Linux system because of the permission mechanism.

An automagic feature of Windows systems is to allow almost anything to run, such as ActiveX programs, Word macros, AutoRun CD-ROM, JavaScript, HTML energized email, and so on. UNIX and Linux do not like to run applications without your permission. This is another reason to run Linux over Windows.

How Are Linux Passwords Encrypted?

Actually, a hash is generated (from the given password) using the DES or MD5 algorithm, rather than using an encryption/decryption scheme.

The next time that you log in, the login program uses the algorithm to regenerate the hash and compares it to the hash entry in the /etc/passwd or /etc/shadow file.

How Large Can a File Be Under Linux?

This is largely dependent on the type of filesystem that is used. The ext2, minix, and ext filesystems running on a 32-bit platform can manage files up to 2GB. On a 64-bit platform, a patch is available to manage files greater than 2GB. Newer kernel versions will support this in the future.

Are There Comparisons of Linux to Other Operating Systems?

A popular site can be found at http://www.unix-vs-nt.org and is known as the "UNIX Versus NT Organization" (as if there is a comparison!). Be sure to read the Kirsch Paper; you will find this article to be very interesting. Some of the highlighted sections from the article are "Why Microsoft Uses Solaris Instead of NT" and "Microsoft Admits That NT Trails Solaris."

It is interesting to note that John Kirch is a Networking Consultant and a Microsoft Certified Professional (Windows NT).

What Is the Legal Status of Linux?

Linux is copyrighted software (not public domain), even though it is distributed with complete source code. Linux is available, free of charge under the GNU General Public License (GPL, known as *copyleft*). You can find GNU at http://www.gnu.org.

Many applications that run under Linux also fall under the GPL, although many are legally copyrighted. The X Windows system falls under the MIT X copyright, and other Linux utilities fall under the BSD copyright.

Do I Need to Repartition to Use Linux?

It is always wise to partition your hard disk(s) to accommodate more than one operating system. In some instances, it is recommended to partition your hard drive(s) even if you are using a single operating system, especially if you are using an OS that uses the DOS file system. With the DOS file system, the larger the (logical) drive, the more space that is wasted.

Can I Get Linux Preinstalled on a New Computer?

Absolutely!

A list of vendors can be found at: `http://www.linux.org/vendors/systems.html`.

You can get a machine as simple and as reasonably priced as an Intel-based PC to high-end machine such as an Alpha or Sparc system.

Some of the companies specialize in a single Linux distribution. Some vendors will install any distribution you prefer. When you are ready to shop around, be sure to refer to the provided URL.

Index

Symbols

= (assignment operator), defining environment variables, 74
* (asterisk) metacharacter, 679-680
  deleting files, 88
  wildcard matching, 668-669
@ (at sign), forwarding logging data, 606
\ (backslash character)
  command continuation, 86
  escaping metacharacters, 683-685
  line-continuation character, printcap file, 511
\\ escaped character
  chat program escape sequence, 377
  UUCP, 406
! (bang character)
  command
    FTP, 258
    smbclient program, 440
  command history list, 71
  UUCP pathnames, 404
^ (caret) metacharacter, 673-674
  in character classes, 678
[ ] (character class) metacharacter, 676-677
; (command separator character), 77
- (dash) metacharacter, 676
  UUCP subscripts, 407
- option
  lprm command, 510
  su command, 664
-- option (sendmail), 245

$ (dollar sign) metacharacter, 674-676
  FTP command, 258
  printing environment variable values, 76
. (dot) metacharacter, 670-672
  . (single dot) directory entry, 81, 85
  .. (double dot) directory entry, 81, 85
' ' (empty string), chat program escape sequence, 377
[^] (negated character class) metacharacter, 677-679
+ (plus sign) metacharacter, 680-681
? (question mark) metacharacter, 681
  command
    FTP, 261
    smbclient program, 440
  option (lpc command), 506-507
  wildcard matching, 668-669
-? option (httpd daemon), 464
> (redirection symbol), in commands, 69
/ (slash character), directories, 81, 86
~ (tilde character)
  home directory, 84
  UUCP pathnames, 404
| (vertical bar) metacharacter, 681-683
  in commands, 69
-[0-7][lmh] option (tar utility), 635
-#num option (lpr command), 509
/bin directory, 82
/dev directory, 82, 211
  sound device files, 219-220
/dev/audio file, 219

/dev/audio0 file, 219
/dev/audio1 file, 219
/dev/dsp file, 219
/dev/dsp0 file, 219
/dev/dsp1 file, 219
/dev/midi00 file, 220
/dev/midi01 file, 220
/dev/midi02, 220
/dev/midi03, 220
/dev/mixer file, 219
/dev/mixer0 file, 219
/dev/mixer1 file, 219
/dev/modem device, 211
/dev/mouse device, 211
/dev/music file, 219
/dev/null (special-device file), 79
  deleting directories/files, 89
/dev/sequencer file, 220
/dev/sequencer2 file, 220
/dev/sndstat, 220
/dev/ttyS0 serial port, 211
/etc directory, 82
  FTP, 277
/etc/aliases file (NIS), 311
/etc/bootparams file (NIS), 311
/etc/cron.daily directory, 637
/etc/cron.hourly directory, 637
/etc/cron.weekly directory, 637
/etc/diphosts file, defining entries for diplogin command, 371-372
/etc/ethers file (NIS), 311
/etc/exports file, 337-339
/etc/fstab file, 344, 346
/etc/group file, 620-621
  NIS, 311
/etc/host.conf file, 287-289
  environment variables, 289
  PPP hostname resolution, 374
  TCP/IP, 185

/etc/HOSTNAME file (TCP/IP), 182
/etc/hosts file, 282
  NIS, 311
  TCP/IP, 183-184
/etc/hosts.allow file, 335
/etc/hosts.deny file, 335
/etc/inetd.conf file, 421-422, 427, 495
/etc/inittab file, 572-573
/etc/lilo.conf file, 577-578
/etc/mtab file, 601
/etc/named.boot file, 291-295
/etc/named.pid file, 291
/etc/netgroup file (NIS), 311
/etc/netmasks file (NIS), 311
/etc/networks file
  NIS, 311
  TCP/IP, 184
/etc/pam.d directory, 598
/etc/pam.d/passwd file, 599
/etc/passwd file, 611-614
  defining entries for diplogin command, 370
  disabling accounts, 596
  NIS, 311
  shadow passwords, 594
/etc/ppp/options file (pppd daemon), 380-381
/etc/printcap file, 510-514
  Red Hat Linux printer configuration, 520, 523
  SuSE Linux printer configuration, 517-519
/etc/protocols file (NIS), 311
/etc/rc.d directory, 185-195
/etc/rc.d/serial file, 213
/etc/resolv.conf file, 290-291
  PPP hostname resolution, 374
  SLIP, 354
  TCP/IP, 185
/etc/rpc file (NIS), 311
/etc/services file, 421, 427, 495
  NIS, 311

accelerated video cards, Linux installation requirements 731

/etc/shadow file, 594
   disabling accounts, 596
   NIS, 311
   password expiration, 628
/etc/syslog.conf file, 604
/etc/termcap file, 511
/etc/uucp directory path, 388
/experimental/mod_auth_digest.o module, AddModule section (Apache Web server Configuration file), 456
/experimental/mod_mmap_static.o module, AddModule section (Apache Web server Configuration file), 454
/home directory, 82
/lib directory, 82
/proc directory, 83
/proc/interrupts contents, 213
/proxy/libproxy.a module, AddModule section (Apache Web server Configuration file), 456
/sbin/init.d directory, 573-575
/tmp directory, 83
/usr directory, 83
/usr/bin directory, 83
/usr/etc directory, 83
/usr/lib directory, 83
/usr/lib/uucp directory path, 388
/usr/lib/uucp/call file, 389, 394
/usr/lib/uucp/config file, 389-390
/usr/lib/uucp/Devices file, 399, 401-402
/usr/lib/uucp/dial file, 389, 394-395
/usr/lib/uucp/dialcodes file, 389, 395
/usr/lib/uucp/Dialers file, 399, 402-403
/usr/lib/uucp/password file, 389, 395
/usr/lib/uucp/Permissions file, 399, 403
/usr/lib/uucp/port file, 389, 393-394
/usr/lib/uucp/sys file, 389-393
/usr/lib/uucp/Systems file, 400-401
/usr/local directory, 83
/usr/local/apache directory, 448

/usr/local/samba/lib directory, 421
/usr/man directory, 83
/usr/src directory, 83
/usr/X11R6/lib/X11/doc directory, 207
/var directory, 83
/var/adm directory, 83
/var/lock/samba directory, 418
/var/log/ directory, 603
/var/log/messages file, 301
/var/named/root.cache file, 295
   retrieving, 293
/var/run/named.pid file, 291
/var/spool directory, 83
/var/tmp/named.run file, 291
/var/tmp/named.stats file, 291
/var/tmp/named_dump.db file, 291
32 Bits Online Magazine Web site, 693
86open Project Web site, 705-706
2600 Magazine, 626

A

-A option
   ftpd, 275
   tar utility, 633
-a option
   dip command, 358
   nmbd daemon, 437
   smbd daemon, 436
   uustat command, 409
%a variable substitution (smb.conf file), 425
A News, 470
a option (ps command), 659
Aahz's law (Usenet), 482
ABORT keyword (chat program), 378
abort option (lpc command), 507
--absolute-paths option (tar utility), 635
accelerated video cards, Linux installation requirements, 21

access permissions (file security), 599-600
access restrictions (NNTP servers), 496-497
access rules, ypserv.conf file (field descriptions), 316-317
access.conf file, 460
accessing non-Linux file systems, 719-720
access_log file, 465
account command (FTP), 258
accounts, 59. *See also* users
   anonymous ftp, 618
   command accounts (security), 595
   configuring (YaST utility), 548
   creating, 60-61
   dead accounts (security), 595
   default accounts (security), 595-596
   deleting, 595
   disabling, 595-596
   guest accounts (security), 596
   password-free accounts (security), 596-597
   passwords, 58, 61-63
      case sensitivity, 62
      changing, 63
      creating user accounts, 60-61
      encryption, 726
      expiration, 627-628
      root account, 62, 724
      shadow passwords, 594, 614
      weak passwords, 593
   root
      cautions about, 63-64, 626-627
      usernames for, 613
Action directive (Apache Web server), 466
active mode (NNTP), 473
active partitions, 28
AcuCOBOL Web site, 701
add command, 193
AddHandler directive (Apache Web server), 467

adding. *See also* creating
   groups to system, 620-621
   users to system, 615
      adduser command, 615-616
      manually, 617-618
      useradd command, 616-617
AddModule section (Apache Web server Configuration file), 453-456
address book (Kmail), 236-237
Address Book window (Netscape Messenger), 242
addresses
   gateway addresses, 180
   IP, 177-179
      lookup (DNS), 281
      mapping to hostnames. See DNS
      netmasks, 179
      SLIP, 352
      spoofing, 288
   name server addresses, 179
   serial ports, 213
adduser command, 615-616
administrative tasks, importance of, 625-626
Advanced Intrusion Detection Environment (AIDE), 640
Advanced Linux Sound Architecture (ALSA), 220-221
Advanced Programming in the UNIX Environment, 692
Advice and guidance on performance tuning Linux systems Web site, 704
af field (/etc/printcap file), 512
--after-date option (tar utility), 634
AfterStep (window manager), 136
AIDE (Advanced Intrusion Detection Environment), 640
alert option (/etc/host.conf file), 288
alias commands, 723
aliases, 67-68
AliasFile option (sendmail), 246

all_squash mapping option (/etc/exports file), 338
ALSA (Advanced Linux Sound Architecture), 220-221
alt Usenet category, 472
Alt+F2 procedure (virtual consoles), 65
alternatives metacharacter, 681-683
anongid mapping option (/etc/exports file), 338
anonuid mapping option (/etc/exports file), 338
anonymous FTP, 256-257
   accounts, 618
   server configuration, 278
AntiSniff utility, 645
Apache Software Foundation Web site, 445
Apache Web server, 8
   build process
      Configuration file, modifying, 451-457
      "easy way," 449-450
      executing, 457, 459
      manual method, 450-459
      requirements, 451
   checking for existence of, 446-447
   decompressing and unarchiving source packages, 447-449
   environment variables, 465-466
   handlers, 466-467
   httpd daemon command-line options, 463-464
   log files, 465
   obtaining, 445-446
   overview, 443-444
   restarting, 465
   runtime configuration, 459-461
   selecting platform for, 444-445
   starting, 461-462
   stopping, 462-464
append command (FTP), 258
--append option (tar utility), 633
applets, GNOME, 159
application layer (network model), 176

applications. *See also* **software; utilities**
   on desktop, 133
   in focus, 133
   launching
      GNOME, 168
      KDE, 149
   Main menu, 134-135
   office applications for Linux, 8
   taskbar, KDE, 139
   Web sites for, 701-702
Applications module (KDE desktop configuration), 144
Applix Office for Linux Web site, 702
Applixware Web site, 702
apropos command, 653-655
apsfilter (universal printer filter), 516
architecture
   NFS, 328
      clients, 329-332
      error recovery, 329
      protocol operational overview, 328
      servers, 332
      transport independence, 329
   Web sites for, 703
archives. *See also* **backups**
   Usenet newsgroups, 699
arguments, 68. *See also* **options**
   XF86Setup program, 112
ARM Linux Web site, 703
armedLinux distribution, 710
ARTICLE command (NNTP), 485, 489-490
articles (Usenet), 471
   headers, 471
   transferring among computers, 472-473
ascii command (FTP), 258, 265
ash shell, 66
assignment operator (=), defining environment variables, 74
asterisk (*) metacharacter, 679-680
   deleting files, 88
   wildcard matching, 668-669

asyncmap option (pppd daemon), 379
at command, 661-663
at sign (@), forwarding logging data, 606
atime option (mount command), 347
--atime-preserve option (tar utility), 634
attributes
    chatScript, 402
    COMMANDS, 403
    device, 400-401
    dialer, 402
    dialerLine, 402
    logScript, 401
    MACHINE, 403
    phoneNumber, 401
    READ, 403
    remoteSystem, 400
    REQUEST, 403
    schedule, 400
    SENDFILES, 403
    speed, 401-402
    ttyLine, 402
    WRITE, 403
audio, sound cards, 216-218
    Advanced Linux Sound Architecture (ALSA), 220-221
    Open Sound System (OSS) driver, 220
    SoundBlaster configuration, 218-220
auth option (pppd daemon), 379
authentication
    Kerberos, 597
    PAM (Pluggable Authentication Modules), 597-599
auto option (mount command), 347
--autoexit option (YaST utility), 541
autofs command, 331
automation (SLIP), dip command, 357-363
    dynamic IP connectivity, 368-370
    sample script, 363-366
    static IP connectivity, 367-368
automount command, 331

automountd daemon, 331
automounter, 328-332
Autostart folder, 132

B

\b (chat program escape sequence), 377
B News, 470
-B option
    sendmail, 244
    tar utility, 634
-b option
    at command, 662
    named daemon execution, 296
    smbclient program, 440
    useradd command, 617
    ypserv command, 315
-ba option (sendmail), 244
background, changing
    GNOME, 166-167
    KDE desktop, 144-146
backslash character (\)
    command continuation, 86
    escaping metacharacters, 683-685
    line-continuation character, printcap file, 511
backup option (LILO), 578
backups, 628
    importance of, 589-591
    KDat utility, 629-632
    planning considerations, 629
    tar utility, 633-636
    YaST utility, 548-549, 632-633
bang character (!)
    command
        FTP, 258
        smbclient program, 440
    command history list, 71
    UUCP pathnames, 404
banner pages, printing, 509

bar (|) metacharacter, 681-683
Barber, Brian (nntpd), 471
bash shell, 66
   command history list, 70-71
   help command, 656-657
Basic Networking Utilities (BNU). *See* HDB UUCP
batching articles (Usenet), 473
-bD option (sendmail), 244, 254
beep command (dip), 359
bell command (FTP), 258
benchmark information, Web sites for, 703
Beowulf Project Web site, 706
Berkeley Internet Domain System (BIND), 282
-bH option (sendmail), 244
-bi option (sendmail), 244
Big Brother utility, 641
bin directory (FTP), 276
binary command (FTP), 258, 265
binary distribution of Apache Web server, 445
BIND (Berkeley Internet Domain System), 282
binding clients to servers (NIS), 318-319
BIOS setup password, 589
Bleeding Edge Magazine Web site, 693
BLINUX Web site, 703
--block-compress option (tar utility), 635
--block-size option (tar utility), 634
block-special devices, 79
-bm option (sendmail), 244
BNU (Basic Networking Utilities). *See* HDB UUCP
BODY command (NNTP), 485
body
   email messages, 228-229
   SMTP protocol, 229
Boigy's Law (Usenet), 482

bookmarks (KDE), 154
books, Linux documentation sources, 691-693
boot floppies
   booting from, 55
   creating (Slackware Linux), 40-42
   emergency disks, 583
boot manager software, 56
boot option (LILO), 578
boot options, configuration (YaST utility), 545
boot password, 589
boot process, 29
   emergency boot floppy disks, 583
   init process, 572-576
   LILO, 577
      configuring, 577-580
   Linux, 55-56
      rc files, 185-195
   LOADLIN, 580
      booting Linux with, 582-583
      decompressing files from, 581-582
      requirements, 580-581
   message display, 570-572
   with multiple operating systems, 26-27
   overview, 569-570
   starting httpd daemon at, 462
bootp command (dip), 359
bootstrap loader, 570
-bp option (sendmail), 244
br field (/etc/printcap file), 512
brackets ([ ]). *See* character class ([ ]) metacharacter
Break command (dip), 359
-broadcast option (ypbind command), 318
-broken-server option (ypbind command), 319
browsers, connecting to local Web servers, 461-462
-bs option (sendmail), 244
BSCSoft Web site, 701

BSD Mail email program, 231
-bt option (sendmail), 244
BugTraq mailing list, 626
build package of Apache Web server, 445
build process
    Apache Web server
        Configuration file, modifying, 451-457
        "easy way," 449-450
        executing, 457, 459
        manual method, 450-459
        requirements, 451
    sendmail package, 249-250
Build script (.cf file creation), 250-253
built-in commands, 66
burst pages, printing, 509
bus architecture, 206
    requirements, installing Linux, 21
-bv option (sendmail), 245
bye command (FTP), 258

C

^C (chat program escape sequence), 378
\c escaped character
    chat program escape sequence, 377
    UUCP, 406
C News, 470
-C option
    httpd daemon, 463
    sendmail, 245
    uucp command, 405
-c option
    at command, 662
    pnpdump utility, 218
    slattach command, 355
    smbclient program, 440
    tar utility, 633-634
    useradd command, 616
    uustat command, 409
    ypbind command, 319
    ypxfr command, 322-323

cache option (/etc/named.boot file), 292-293
caching (DNS), 285, 287
Caldera OpenLinux distribution, 710-711
    installation, 30-33
    Samba installation, 419-420
call file (Taylor UUCP configuration), 394
capplets (GNOME), 164
Card window (Netscape Messenger), 242-243
caret (^) metacharacter, 673-674
    in character classes, 678
Cary's Applixware Page Web site, 702
case command (FTP), 258
case sensitivity
    of Linux, 64, 85
    passwords, 62
case_sensitive option (name mangling), 426
cat command, 90, 462
Catalog of Free Compilers and Interpreters Web site, 701
categories (Usenet), list of, 472
--catenate option (tar utility), 633
#CC option, Makefile section (Apache Web server Configuration file), 452
cd command, 84-86, 626
    FTP, 258, 268
    smbclient program, 440
CD-ROM drives, Linux requirements, 23-24, 718
CD-ROMs, Red Hat Linux installation, 34
CDE (Common Desktop Environment), 136
cdup command (FTP), 258
CERN Security Handbook Web site, 593
CERT Coordination Center Web site, 706
cf field (/etc/printcap file), 512
.cf file (sendmail), creating, 250-253

cgi-script handler (Apache Web server), 466
chage command, 628
change-rules option (LILO), 578
changing
  current working directory, 84
  passwords, 63
  shells, 66
character class ([ ]) metacharacter, 676-677
character-special devices, 79
characters, 669. *See also* metacharacters
chat keyword, 392
chat program (PPP), 375-379
chatkey command (dip), 359
chatScript attribute, 402
check-names option (/etc/named.boot file), 294
CheckAliases option (sendmail), 246
--checkpoint option (tar utility), 634
CheckpointInterval option (sendmail), 246
chip sets
  executing SuperProbe, 97-98
  Linux video card requirements, 21-22
  XFree86 hardware requirements, 96-97
chmod command, 278, 618
  FTP, 258
chown command, 396, 618
chroot command, 277
CIFS (Common Internet File System), 415
class A IP addresses, 178
class B IP addresses, 178
class C IP addresses, 178
class D IP addresses, 178
class E IP addresses, 178
class F IP addresses, 178
clean option (lpc command), 507

client/server model (NIS), 305-306
  server allocation, 308
clients
  FTP, startup, 266
  NFS, 329-332, 344-345
    formats, 339
    mount command, 345-348
  NIS, configuring, 318-319
  Samba. *See* smbclient program
  Usenet, 470
clock settings, XFree86 configuration, 109
Clockchip settings, XFree86 configuration, 109
close command (FTP), 258, 273
COAST Hotlist Web site, 706
Collyer, Geoff (origin of Usenet), 470
com organizational domain, 284
command accounts, security, 595
COMMAND column (ps command), 658
command interpreters, 65
command separator character (;), 77
command-line options. *See* options
command-line window
  GNOME, 169
  KDE, 149
commands. *See also* daemons
  add, 193
  adduser, 615-616
  alias commands, 723
  aliases, 67-68
  apropos, 653-655
  arguments, 68
  at, 661-663
  autofs, 331
  automount, 331
  bash shell, 656-657
  built-in, 66
  case sensitivity, 64
  cat, 90, 462
  cd, 84-86, 626
  chage, 628

738 commands

chmod, 278, 618
chown, 396, 618
chroot, 277
completion feature, 72
configure, 449
Configure (Apache build process), 458
cp, 68, 80, 91, 460
cron, 636-637
crontab, 619
del, 193
dip, 357-363
    beep, 359
    bootp, 359
    Break, 359
    chatkey, 359
    config, 359
    databits, 359
    dec, 359
    Default, 359
    dial, 359
    dynamic IP connectivity, 368-370
    echo, 359
    exit, 359
    flush, 359
    get, 360
    goto, 360
    Help, 360
    if ... goto, 360
    inc, 360
    init, 360
    label, 359
    mode, 360
    modem, 360
    netmask, 360
    onexit, 360
    parity, 361
    password, 361
    port tty, 361
    print, 361
    proxyarp, 361
    psend, 361
    quit, 361
    reset, 361
    sample script, 363-366
    securid, 361

    securidfixed, 361
    send, 361
    shell, 361
    skey, 362
    sleep, 362
    speed, 362
    static IP connectivity, 367-368
    stopbits, 362
    term, 362
    timeout, 362
    wait text, 362
diplogin, 370
    /etc/diphosts file entries, 371-372
    /etc/passwd file entries, 370
    executing, 372
dmesg, 212, 374, 505, 570-572
domainname, 309-310, 317
echo, 76
egrep
    caret (^) metacharacter, 673-674
    character class ([ ]), 677
    dollar sign ($) metacharacter, 674-676
    dot (.) metacharacter, 672
    escaping metacharacters, 683
    negated character class ([^]), 678
    plus sign (+) metacharacter, 680
    vertical bar (|) metacharacter, 682
    whole word pattern matching, 686-687
env, 73
exec, 66
executing, 68-69
exit, 59
export, 76
exportfs, 342
external, 67
file, 79
find, 248
finger, 67, 595
flags, 69
flexibility of, 651
FTP, 257-262
    ! (exclamation point), 258
    $ (dollar sign), 258
    ? (question mark), 261
    account, 258

append, 258
ascii, 258, 265
bell, 258
binary, 258, 265
bye, 258
case, 258
cd, 258, 268
cdup, 258
chmod, 258
close, 258, 273
cr, 259
debug, 259
delete, 259
dir, 259
disconnect, 259
form, 259
get, 259, 262, 272
glob, 259
hash, 259, 265
help, 259, 272
idle, 259
lcd, 259
ls, 259, 268
macdef, 259
mdelete, 259
mdir, 259
mget, 259, 263
mkdir, 260
mls, 260
mode, 260
modtime, 260
mput, 260, 263
newer, 260
nlist, 260
nmap, 260
ntrans, 260
open, 266
open host, 260
options for, 257
prompt, 260, 264
proxy, 260
put, 263
put local-file, 260
pwd, 260
quit, 260, 273

recv, 260, 263
reget, 260
remotehelp, 261
remotestatus, 261
rename, 261
reset, 261
restart, 261
rmdir, 261
runique, 261
send, 261, 264
sendport, 261
size, 261
status, 261, 264
struct, 261
sunique, 261
system, 261
tenex, 261
trace, 261
type, 261
umask, 261
user, 261
verbose, 261
GNOME, 158
grep, 335
groupadd, 620
groupdel, 622
groupmod, 621-622
gunzip, 447
gzip, 447
halt, 58
head, 82, 90
history, 71
history list, 70-71
hostname, 182, 400
ifconfig, 353-357
insmod, 220
KDE, 138
kill, 422, 462-463, 663-664
    sending signals, 298-299
less, 76, 90
    man page for, 653
logout, 59
lpc, 506-507
lpq, 506, 508
lpr, 506, 508-510

commands

lprm, 506, 510
ls, 67, 69, 84-87, 219, 418, 600, 627
   man page for, 653
make, 71, 449-450
man, 11, 76, 92, 652-655
mdir, 328
mkdir, 87
modprobe, 220
more, 76, 90
mount, 69, 344-348
mv, 91, 460
ndc, 296-298
netstat, 196-197
nfs, 343
NNTP, 484-486
   ARTICLE, 489-490
   GROUP, 490-491
   HELP, 491
   IHAVE, 491-492
   LAST, 492
   LIST, 492-493
   NEWGROUPS, 493
   NEWNEWS, 493
   NEXT, 493-494
   POST, 494
   QUIT, 494-495
   SLAVE, 495
nslookup, 300-301
passwd, 63, 594, 614, 618
   options, 628
ping, 197-198
pppd, 379-380
   options file, 380-381
   script files, 381-383
   testing script files, 383-385
for printing, list of, 505-506
ps, 334, 340, 378, 418, 422, 657-659
pwck, 594
pwd, 67, 83, 626
rcnfsserver, 343
reboot, 58
redirection, 651
rev, 652
rm, 88, 619, 627, 723

rmdir, 89
route, 184, 356-357
rpc, 335-337
rpcinfo, 335, 340
rpm, 419
   installing RPM packages, 529
   querying RPM packages, 530-531
   uninstalling RPM packages, 531
   updating RPM packages, 531-532
   verifying RPM packages, 532-535
scheduling, 636-637
set, 73
setserial, 211
shells, 65-68
showmount, 601
shutdown, 57-58
slattach, 355-356
smbclient program, 440-442
su, 664-665
tail, 301
tar, 249, 447-448
TCP/IP, 193
tcpdump, 644
top, 660-661
umount, 344
uncompress, 447
useradd, 60-61, 594, 616-617
userdel, 594-595, 619
usermod, 66, 594
uuchk, 388-390, 396-399
uucico, 405
uucp, 404-405
   sample dialogs, 408
uustat, 408-410
vigw, 618
vipw, 617
wc, 683
which, 248, 343
ypbind, 318-319
ypcat, 320
ypinit, 311-314, 317
ypmatch, 321
yppoll, 321
yppush, 323-324
ypserv, 315

ypwhich, 319-320
ypxfr, 321-323
COMMANDS attribute, 403
commercial software, Web sites for, 703
Common Desktop Environment (CDE), 136
Common Internet File System (CIFS), 415
comp Usenet category, 472
comp.protocols.tcp-ip.domains FAQs Web site, 704
comp.windows.x.apps FAQ Web site, 706
compact option (LILO), 578
compatibility, Linux with non-Linux software, 720
completion feature (commands), 72
Compose window (Netscape Messenger), 241
Composer window (Kmail), 235-236
--compress option (tar utility), 635
compression utilities, 722-723
computer locks, 589
Comware International Web site, 702
--concatenate option (tar utility), 633
conf directory, 460
confcollect utility, 641
config command (dip), 359
config file (Taylor UUCP configuration), 390
config.layout file, 461
configuration
    boot options (YaST utility), 545
    dial-up networking
        Linuxconf utility, 554-557
        RP3 utility, 558
        TurboLinux configuration tools, 559-562
        YaST utility, 546-547
    DNS, 287
        /etc/host.conf file, 287-289
        /etc/resolv.conf file, 290-291
        named daemon, 291-301

filesystems (TurboLinux configuration tools), 562-565
FTP servers, 274
    anonymous access, 278
    directory permissions, 277-278
    directory structure, 276-277
    ftpd daemon, 275-276
    site names, 274
    testing, 278
GNOME desktop, 164-165
    background changes, 166-167
    panel changes, 167-168
gpm (YaST utility), 549
hardware (YaST utility), 545
HDB UUCP, 399-400
    configuration files, 399-400
    Devices file, 401-402
    Dialers file, 402-403
    Permissions file, 403
    Systems file, 400-401
KDE desktop, 142-144
    background changes, 144-146
    panel changes, 146-147
LILO, 577-580
live filesystems (YaST utility), 547
master servers (NIS), 309-311
mount points (Linuxconf utility), 552-553
networks
    Linuxconf utility, 553-554
    YaST utility, 545
NIS
    clients, 318-319
    slave servers, 317-318
    YaST utility, 546
    ypinit command, 311-314
    ypserv command, 315
    ypserv.conf file, 316-317
NNTP servers, 495-496
    access restrictions, 496-497
printers
    Red Hat Linux, 520-523
    SuSE Linux, 515-519
remote printers (YaST utility), 547
runtime configuration (Apache Web server), 459-461

742   configuration

Samba, 420
   smb.conf file, 422-426
   SWAT (Samba Web Administration Tool),
      421-422, 426-435
sendmail
   .cf file creation, 250-253
   YaST utility, 546
serial ports, 211-216
SLIP, 354-355
   ifconfig and route commands, 356-357
   slattach command, 355-356
SoundBlaster sound cards, 218-220
SuSE Linux, environment variables, 549
Taylor UUCP, 388-389
   call file, 394
   checking initial configuration, 389-390
   config file, 390
   configuration files, 389
   dial file, 394-395
   dialcodes file, 395
   password file, 395
   port file, 393-394
   sys file, 390-393
   verifying configuration, 395-399
TCP/IP, 181
   /etc/host.conf configuration file, 185
   /etc/HOSTNAME configuration file, 182
   /etc/hosts configuration file, 183-184
   /etc/networks configuration file, 184
   /etc/resolv.conf configuration file, 185
   location of configuration files, 182
TurboLinux configuration tools, 559-565
user accounts (YaST utility), 548
UUCP, 388
window managers (YaST utility), 548
XFree86, 101-102, 209-210
   checklist, 209
   xf86config, 102-111
   XF86Config file, 118-130
   XF86Setup, 102, 111-118
   YaST utility, 549
Configuration file, modifying (Apache Web server build process), 451-457

configuration files
   distributing. *See* distributed database systems
   TCP/IP
      /etc/host.conf, 185
      /etc/HOSTNAME, 182
      /etc/hosts, 183-184
      /etc/networks, 184
      /etc/resolv.conf, 185
      location of, 182
Configure Account dialog box (Kmail), 233
configure command, 449
Configure command (Apache build process), 458
--confirmation option (tar utility), 635
connect script option (pppd daemon), 379
ConnectionCacheSize option (sendmail), 246
ConnectionCacheTimeout option (sendmail), 246
connectionless IP (Internet Protocol), 177
ConnectionRateThrottle option (sendmail), 247
connections to
   FTP hosts, 265
   FTP sites, 266
consoles (virtual), 64-65
Control Center
   configuring GNOME desktop, 164-165
      background changes, 166-167
      panel changes, 167-168
   configuring KDE desktop, 142-144
      background changes, 144-146
      panel changes, 146-147
controllers
   hard drives
      IDE and EIDE controllers, 203
      MFM and RLL controllers, 203
      SCSI controllers, 203-205
      Ultra-ATA controllers, 203
   Linux requirements, 718
cooperative multitasking, 5
copying directories/files, 91

GNOME, 170
KDE, 153
copyright issues, Linux, 726
Corel LinuxOS distribution, 711
cost of Linux, 7
cover pages, printing, 509
cp command, 68, 80, 91, 460
#CPP option, Makefile section (Apache Web server Configuration file), 452
CPU requirements, installing Linux, 19
cr command (FTP), 259
crackers
 compared to hackers, 586
 definition of, 3
 idle time in log files, 605-606
 social engineering threats to security, 591-592
 types of, 586-587
 Web site for security information, 626
--create option (tar utility), 633
creating. *See also* **adding**
 directories, 87
 files, 80
 user accounts, 60-61
CRiSP editor Web site, 702
cron command, 636-637
crontab command, 619
crontab files, 636-637
crtscts option (pppd daemon), 379
csh shell, 66
CSLIP (compressed SLIP), 354
Ctrl+Alt+Delete procedure (shutdown), 58
Current ports of Linux OS Web site, 703
current working directory, 83-84
CustomLog directive (Apache Web server), 465
Cyberscheduler Web site, 702
cyrus option (MAILER), 252

D

\d escaped character
 chat program escape sequence, 377
 UUCP, 406
-D option
 ftpd, 275
 smbd daemon, 436
-d option
 at command, 662
 FTP, 257
 httpd daemon, 463
 named daemon execution, 296
 nmbd daemon, 437
 sendmail, 245
 smbclient program, 439-440
 useradd command, 616
 uucp command, 405
 YaST utility, 541
 ypmatch command, 321
 yppoll command, 321
 yppush command, 323
 ypserv command, 315
 ypxfr command, 322
%d variable substitution (smb.conf file), 425
daemons
 automountd, 331
 ftpd, configuration, 275-276
 httpd, 446-447, 459
  command-line options, 463-464
  restarting Apache Web server, 465
  starting Apache Web server, 461-462
  stopping Apache Web server, 462-464
 inetd, 194, 275, 422, 427, 463
 lpd, 506-508
 mountd, 339-342, 601
 named, 291
  /etc/named.boot file, 292-295
  executing, 296-301
 nfsd, 339-342, 601
 nmbd, 415, 417, 437-438
 nntpd, 495-496
  access restrictions, 496-497

portmapper, 333-337
pppd, 373, 379-380
　options file, 380-381
　script files, 381-383
　testing script files, 383-385
rpc.ypxfrd, 316
smbd, 415, 417, 433-436
syslogd, 604
tcpd, 276
ypserv, 316
dash (-) metacharacter, 676
　UUCP subscripts, 407
databases, distributed. *See* **distributed database systems**
databits command (dip), 359
datagrams, IP (Internet Protocol), 177
\ddd (chat program escape sequence), 377
dead accounts, security, 595
Debian GNU/Linux distribution, 711
Debian GNU/Linux Web site, 717
debug command (FTP), 259
debug option (pppd daemon), 379
-debug option (ypbind command), 319
dec command (dip), 359
Deception ToolKit (DTK), 638
decompressing Apache Web server source package, 447-449
default accounts, security, 595-596
Default command (dip), 359
default option (LILO), 579
default-handler handler (Apache Web server), 466
DefaultCharSet option (sendmail), 247
defaultroute option (pppd daemon), 379
defaults option (mount command), 347
default_case option (name mangling), 426
defining environment variables, 74
defragmentation utilities, 722
Deja.com Web site, 12, 697, 699

del command, 193
　smbclient program, 440
delay option (LILO), 579
delete command (FTP), 259
--delete option (tar utility), 633
deleting. *See also* **uninstalling**
　accounts, 595
　directories, 89
　files, 88-89
　groups, 622
　print jobs from print queue, 510
　users, 618
　　manually, 619-620
　　userdel command, 619
DeliveryMode option (sendmail), 246
Deltree utility, 724
--dereference option (tar utility), 634
desktop, 133
　GNOME, 159
　　configuring, 164-168
　KDE, configuring, 142-147
　virtual. *See* virtual desktops
Desktop module (KDE desktop configuration), 144
dev directory (FTP), 277
dev option (mount command), 348
device attribute, 400-401
device keyword, 394
Device section (XF86Config file), 127
devices
　hard drives, 202
　　booting from, 55
　　IDE and EIDE controllers, 203
　　installation requirements, 24-25
　　MFM and RLL controllers, 203
　　partitioning, 27-29, 42-43, 543-544
　　Red Hat Linux installation, 34
　　SCSI controllers, 203-205
　　space requirements, 717
　　Ultra-ATA controllers, 203
　modems, 205, 210
　　Linux requirements, 718

mounting, 346
mouse, 205-206
    Linux requirements, 25, 718
    Pointer section (XF86Config file), 123-124
    Red Hat Linux installation, 34
    X Windows navigation, 134
    XFree86 configuration, 103-104, 113-114
serial ports, 210-211
    configuration, 211-216
    naming conventions, 211
sound cards, 216-218
    Advanced Linux Sound Architecture (ALSA), 220-221
    Open Sound System (OSS) driver, 220
    SoundBlaster configuration, 218-220
video cards, 207-209
    Device section (XF86Config file), 127
    Linux requirements, 21-22, 718
    Red Hat Linux installation, 34
    XFree86 configuration, 106-109, 115, 209-210

Devices file (HDB UUCP configuration), 401-402

DEV_RANDOM rule, Rules section (Apache Web server Configuration file), 457

df field (/etc/printcap file), 512

dial command (dip), 359

dial file (Taylor UUCP configuration), 394-395

Dial-Up IP Protocol. *See* **dip (Dial-Up IP Protocol) commands**

dial-up networking, configuration
Linuxconf utility, 554-557
RP3 utility, 558
TurboLinux configuration tools, 559-562
YaST utility, 546-547

dialcodes file (Taylor UUCP configuration), 395

DialDelay option (sendmail), 247

dialer attribute, 402

dialer keyword, 394

dialerLine attribute, 402

Dialers file (HDB UUCP configuration), 402-403

dialog boxes (Kmail)
Configure Account, 233
Please Set Password and Username, 235
Settings, 232-233

dip (Dial-Up IP Protocol) commands, 352, 357-363
beep, 359
bootp, 359
Break, 359
chatkey, 359
config, 359
databits, 359
dec, 359
Default, 359
dial, 359
dynamic IP connectivity, 368-370
echo, 359
exit, 359
flush, 359
get, 360
goto, 360
Help, 360
if ... goto, 360
inc, 360
init, 360
label, 359
mode, 360
modem, 360
netmask, 360
onexit, 360
parity, 361
password, 361
port tty, 361
print, 361
proxyarp, 361
psend, 361
quit, 361
reset, 361
sample script, 363-366
securid, 361
securidfixed, 361
send, 361
shell, 361

skey, 362
sleep, 362
speed, 362
static IP connectivity, 367-368
stopbits, 362
term, 362
timeout, 362
wait text, 362

diplogin command, 370
/etc/diphosts file entries, 371-372
/etc/passwd file entries, 370
executing, 372

dir command
FTP, 259
smbclient program, 440

directed broadcast addresses, 178

directives (Apache runtime configuration), 460

directories, 78-80. *See also* **file systems**
. and .. directory entries, 81
. and .. paths, 85
/bin, 82
/dev, 82, 211
sound device files, 219-220
/etc, 82
/etc/cron.daily, 637
/etc/cron.hourly, 637
/etc/cron.weekly, 637
/etc/pam.d, 598
/home, 82
/lib, 82
/proc, 83
/tmp, 83
/urs, 83
/usr/bin, 83
/usr/etc, 83
/usr/lib, 83
/usr/local, 83
/usr/local/apache, 448
/usr/local/samba/lib, 421
/usr/man, 83
/usr/src, 83
/usr/X11R6/lib/X11/doc, 207

/var, 83
/var/adm, 83
/var/lock/samba, 418
/var/log/, 603
/var/spool, 83
conf, 460
creating, 87
current working directory, 83-84
deleting, 89
directory tree, 80-83
FTP
  permissions, 277-278
  structure, 276-277
GNOME, 170
home directory, 84
  creating user accounts, 60
KDE
  bookmarking, 154
  copying/moving/linking, 153
  opening, 151-153
moving, 91
  within directory tree, 85-86
parent, 81
root, 81-82
viewing contents, 86-87

directory option (/etc/named.boot file), 292-293

--directory option (tar utility), 634

directory trees, 80-83
moving within, 85-86

disable option (lpc command), 507

disabling accounts, 595-596

disconnect command (FTP), 259

disconnect script option (pppd daemon), 379

disk drives. *See* **hard drives**

disk option (LILO), 579

disk space requirements
Linux, 717
Slackware Linux installation, 38-40
XFree86, 96

disktab option (LILO), 579

distributed database systems
   DNS, 281
   NIS
      client/server model, 305-306
      clients, configuring, 318-319
      domains, 307-308
      files handled by, 304, 311
      master server, configuring, 309-311
      purpose of, 303-305
      server allocation, 308
      slave servers, configuring, 317-318
      ypcat command, 320
      ypinit command, 311-314
      ypmatch command, 321
      yppoll command, 321
      yppush command, 323-324
      ypserv command, 315
      ypserv.conf file, 316-317
      ypwhich command, 319-320
      ypxfr command, 321-323

distribution-specific tools, compared to multi-distribution tools, 527-528

distributions of Linux, 9, 710
   armedLinux, 710
   availability of, 718
   Caldera OpenLinux, 710-711
      installation, 30-33
      Samba installation, 419-420
   Corel LinuxOS, 711
   Debian GNU/Linux, 711
   DLX Linux, 711
   DragonLinux, 712
   easyLinux, 712
   hal91, 712
   LibraNet Linux, 712
   Linux Mandrake, 713
   LinuxPPC, 713
   LinuxPro, 713
   LinuxWare, 713
   LoopLinux, 714
   MkLinux, 714
   Red Hat Linux, 714
      /etc/syslog.conf file, 604-605
      installation, 33-38
      Linuxconf utility, 215, 551-558
      printer configuration, 520-523
      Samba installation, 419
   Slackware, 714
      /etc/syslog.conf file, 605
      installation, 38-49
      Samba installation, 420
   Stampede GNU/Linux, 715
   Storm Linux, 715
   SuSE Linux, 715
      /etc/syslog.conf file, 604
      configuration (environment variables), 549
      installation, 49-53
      password expiration, 627
      printer configuration, 515-519
      Samba installation, 419
      YaST utility, 213-214, 541-551, 632-633
   TurboLinux, 715
      configuration tools, 559-565
      Samba installation, 419
      TurboHW utility, 215-216
   WinLinux, 716
   Yggdrasil, 716

dlopen( ) function, 451

dlsym( ) function, 451

DLX Linux distribution, 711

dmesg command, 212, 374, 505, 570-572

DNS (Domain Name Service), 281
   configuration, 287
      /etc/host.conf file, 287-289
      /etc/resolv.conf file, 290-291
      named daemon, 291-301
   hostname resolution (PPP), 374
   name servers, 286-287
   operational overview, 282-287
   organizational domains, 283-284
   result caching, 285, 287
   zones, 286

dns option (ypserv.conf file), 316

documentation sources for Linux, 10-13
   books, 691-693
   FTP sites, 707-708, 721
   magazines, 693-694

mailing lists, 699-701
Usenet newsgroups, 694-699, 721
user groups, 720
Web sites, 701-706, 720-721
dollar sign ($) metacharacter, 674-676
   printing environment variable values, 76
Domain Name Service. *See* **DNS**
domain name spaces, 286
domain option (/etc/resolv.conf file), 290
domainname command, 309-310, 317
domains
   naming conventions, 284
   NIS, 307
      naming, 307-308
   organizational domains, 283-284
DOS
   LOADLIN boot loader, 580
      booting Linux with, 582-583
      decompressing files from, 581-582
      requirements, 580-581
   LoopLinux distribution, 714
dot (.) metacharacter, 670-672
dot matrix printers, 502
DouBle utility, 722
down option (lpc command), 507
downgrade-1.0 Apache environment variable, 466
downloading
   files (FTP), 262-263
   Samba, 416
DragonLinux distribution, 712
drives. *See* **hard drives**
DSO (Dynamic Shared Object) support feature, Apache Web server, 451
DTK (Deception ToolKit), 638
dummy interface, 353-354
dumpdb option (ndc command), 297
duplicating. *See* **copying directories/files**
dust, danger to computer equipment, 587
dynamic IP connectivity (dip command), 368-370
Dynamic Shared Object (DSO) support feature, Apache Web server, 451
dynamically shared libraries, 5

E

-E option (smbclient program), 439
e option (ps command), 659
-e option
   chat program, 375
   useradd command, 616
   uustat command, 409
e-zines (Linux documentation sources), 10, 693-694
e2compr utility, 723
easyLinux distribution, 712
echo command, 76
   dip program, 359
edu organizational domain, 284
egrep command
   caret (^) metacharacter, 673-674
   character class ([ ]), 677
   dollar sign ($) metacharacter, 674-676
   dot (.) metacharacter, 672
   escaping metacharacters, 683
   negated character class ([^]), 678
   plus sign (+) metacharacter, 680
   vertical bar (|) metacharacter, 682
   whole word pattern matching, 686-687
EIDE controllers (hard drives), 203
EightBitMode option (sendmail), 247
EISA bus architecture, 206
eIT (easy Information Technology) easyLinux distribution, 712
electricity, danger to computer equipment, 588
ELKS the Embeddable Linux Kernel Subset Web site, 703
Ellis, Jim (origin of Usenet), 470
elm email program, 230
Emac, as email program, 230-231
email services

mailboxes, 226
MDA (mail delivery agent), 228
messages, header and body, 228-229
MTA (mail transfer agent), 227-228
MUA (mail user agent), 227
   Kmail, 231-237
   Netscape Messenger, 237-243
   programs, list of, 230-231
overview, 225-226
processing model, 226-227
sendmail, 243-245
   building the package, 249-250
   .cf file creation, 250-253
   executing, 254
   obtaining, 247-248
   options, 244-247
SMTP, 229
UUCP. *See* UUCP

emergency boot floppy disks, 583
enable option (lpc command), 507
encryption
Kerberos authentication, 597
PAM (Pluggable Authentication Modules), 597-599
passwords, 726

Enlightenment (window manager), 136
env command, 73
envelope (SMTP), 229
environment variables, 72-77
/etc/host.conf file, 289
Apache Web server, 465-466
defining, 74
exported, 73
exporting local, 76
FTP, 262
HISTSIZE, 70
MAILCHECK, 75
PAGER, 76
PATH, 77
PRINTER, 515
printing values, 76
su command, 664

SuSE Linux configuration, 549
equal sign (=), defining environment variables, 74
$errlvl variable (dip script files), 363
error recovery (NFS), 329
ErrorLog directive (Apache Web server), 465
ErrorMode option (sendmail), 246
errors, httpd daemon, 447
error_log file, 465
escape option (pppd daemon), 379
escape sequences (chat program), 377-378
escaped characters (UUCP), 406
escaping metacharacters, 683-685
ESDI controllers (hard drives), 203
Essential System Administration, Second Edition, **692**
Ethereal protocol analyzer, 644
Ethernet, printer interface, 505
Ethernet cards
Linux installation requirements, 22
networking hardware requirements, 180

exclamation point (!), command history list, 71
--exclude option (tar utility), 635
--exclude-from option (tar utility), 635
exec command, 66
exec option (mount command), 348
execute bits (files), 79
executing. *See also* **starting**
commands, 68-69
named daemon, 296-301
Samba
   nmbd daemon, 437-438
   smbd daemon, 435-436
sendmail, 254
SuperProbe, 97-98
SWAT, 427

exit command, 59

dip program, 359
smbclient program, 441
exit option (lpc command), 507
exiting Linux, 56-58, 570
exmh email program, 230
EXPAT rule, Rules section (Apache Web server Configuration file), 457
expect-send scripts (UUCP), 406-407
expiration of passwords, 627-628
export command, 76
exported environment variables, 73
exportfs command, 342
exporting
filesystems, 332, 342-343
local environment variables, 76
expressions. *See* **regular expressions**
EXT2 Web site, 693
extended partitions, 28
external commands, 67
external modems, 205
External Parallel Port devices and Linux Web site, 704
--extract option (tar utility), 633
EXTRA_CFLAGS option, Makefile section (Apache Web server Configuration file), 452
EXTRA_DEPS option, Makefile section (Apache Web server Configuration file), 452
EXTRA_INCLUDES option, Makefile section (Apache Web server Configuration file), 452
EXTRA_LDFLAGS option, Makefile section (Apache Web server Configuration file), 452
EXTRA_LIBS option, Makefile section (Apache Web server Configuration file), 452

F

F option (ps command), 659
-F option (sendmail), 245
-f option
at command, 662
chat program, 375
httpd daemon, 463
mount command, 347
su command, 664
tar utility, 634
useradd command, 616
uucp command, 405
ypbind command, 319
ypxfr command, 322
FAQs (Frequently Asked Questions), Linux documentation sources, 11
FAQs about wu-ftpd Web site, 704
--fast option (su command), 664
fax modems, 205
fax option (MAILER), 251
fc field (/etc/printcap file), 512
ff field (/etc/printcap file), 512
fields
/etc/passwd file, 612
/etc/printcap file, 512-514
access rules (ypserv.conf file), 316-317
file command, 79
file management
GNOME, 169-170
copying directories/files, 170
linking directories/files, 170
moving directories/files, 170
opening directories/files, 170
properties, 170
KDE, 149-150
bookmarking directories/files, 154
copying directories/files, 170
linking directories/files, 170
moving directories/files, 170
file properties, 154
history list, 154
opening directories/files, 151-153

file option (pppd daemon), 379
--file option (tar utility), 634
file sizes (Linux), 726
file systems, 77. *See also* **directories**
    configuration (TurboLinux configuration tools), 562-565
    exporting, 332, 342-343
    importing, 344
    live filesystems, configuration with YaST utility, 547
    mounting, 328-332, 344-345
        /etc/exports file, 337-339
        mount command, 345-348
    non-Linux, accesing, 719-720
    operational overview, 78-80
File Transfer Protocol. *See* **FTP**
files, 78-80
    /etc/exports, 337-339
    /etc/fstab, 344, 346
    /etc/group, 620-621
    /etc/host.conf, 287-289
        environment variables, 289
    /etc/hosts, 282
    /etc/hosts.allow, 335
    /etc/hosts.deny, 335
    /etc/inetd.conf, 421-422, 427, 495
    /etc/mtab, 601
    /etc/named.boot, 291-295
    /etc/named.pid, 291
    /etc/pam.d/passwd, 599
    /etc/passwd, 611-614
        disabling accounts, 596
        shadow passwords, 594
    /etc/printcap, 510-514
        Red Hat Linux printer configuration, 520, 523
        SuSE Linux printer configuration, 517-519
    /etc/rc.d/serial, 213
    /etc/resolv.conf, 290-291
    /etc/services, 421, 427, 495
    /etc/shadow, 594
        disabling accounts, 596
        password expiration, 628
    /etc/syslog.conf, 604
    /etc/termcap, 511

/var/log/messages, 301
/var/named/root.cache, 295
    retrieving, 293
/var/run/named.pid, 291
/var/tmp/named.run, 291
/var/tmp/named.stats, 291
/var/tmp/named_dump.db, 291
compression utilities, 722-723
config.layout, 461
Configuration file, modifying (Apache Web server build process), 451-457
copying, 91
creating, 80
crontab, 636-637
defragmentation utilities, 722
deleting, 88-89
downloading (FTP), 262-263
execute bits, 79
fully qualified filenames, 78
GNOME
    copying, 170
    linking, 170
    moving, 170
    opening, 170
    properties, 170
handled by NIS, 304, 311
handlers (Apache Web server), 466-467
HDB UUCP configuration, 399-400
.htaccess, 461
KDE
    bookmarking, 154
    copying, 153
    linking, 153
    moving, 153
    opening, 151-153
    properties, 154
log files
    Apache Web server, 465
    LAN security, 603-606
moving, 91
named pipes, 80
ordinary, 78
permission bits, 79
runtime configuration files (Apache Web server), 460-461
security, 599-600

sharing. *See* NFS (Network File Service)
smb.conf, 420, 422-424
    name mangling, 426
    variable substitutions, 425-426
sound devices files in /dev directory, 219-220
special, 79
storing in home directory, 84
Taylor UUCP configuration, 389
transferring. *See* FTP
truncating, 80
types of, 78
undelete utilities, 723-724
uploading (FTP), 263-264
viewing, 90
words, 679
ypserv.conf, 316-317
--files-from option (tar utility), 635
Files section (XF86Config file), 119-120
filesystem monitoring tools, 640
    AIDE, 640
    Big Brother, 641
    confcollect, 641
    Gog&Magog, 641
    Nannie, 641
    PIKT, 642
    Sentinel, 642
    SuSEauditdisk, 642
    Sxid, 642
    Tripwire, 643
    ViperDB, 643
find command, 248
finger command, 67, 595
FIPS, partitioning hard drives, 42-43
fire, danger to computer equipment, 588
firewalls, 602-603
flags, 69. *See also* **options**
FlagShip Web site, 703
flame bait (Usenet), 482
flaming (Usenet), 482
flexibility of commands, 651
flooding (Usenet), 472

floppy disks
    boot and root floppies (Slackware Linux), creating, 40-42
    booting from, 55
    emergency boot floppy disks, 583
flush command (dip), 359
fo field (/etc/printcap file), 512
focus (applications), 133
folders. *See* **directories**
fonts, Files section (XF86Config file), 119-120
force-backup option (LILO), 579
--force-badname option (adduser command), 615
--force-local option (tar utility), 634
force-no-vary Apache environment variable, 466
force-response-1.0 Apache environment variable, 466
forgotten root password, troubleshooting, 724
ForkEachJob option (sendmail), 247
form format command (FTP), 259
forwarders option (/etc/named.boot file), 293
forwarding logging data, 606
FQDN (fully qualified domain name), 284
Free Patents Web site, 705
Freefire Project Web site, 603
Frequently Asked Questions (FAQs), Linux documentation sources, 11
freshening RPM packages, 531-532
Freshmeat Web site, 704-705
fs field (/etc/printcap file), 512
FTP (File Transfer Protocol), 176, 255
    anonymous ftp accounts, 618
    clients, startup, 266
    commands, 257-262
        ! (exclamation point), 258
        $ (dollar sign), 258
        ? (question mark), 261
        account, 258

append, 258
ascii, 258, 265
bell, 258
binary, 258, 265
bye, 258
case, 258
cd, 258, 268
cdup, 258
chmod, 258
close, 258, 273
cr, 259
debug, 259
delete, 259
dir, 259
disconnect, 259
form, 259
get, 259, 262, 272
glob, 259
hash, 259, 265
help, 259, 272
idle, 259
lcd, 259
ls, 259, 268
macdef, 259
mdelete, 259
mdir, 259
mget, 259, 263
mkdir, 260
mls, 260
mode, 260
modtime, 260
mput, 260, 263
newer, 260
nlist, 260
nmap, 260
ntrans, 260
open, 266
open host, 260
options for, 257
prompt, 260, 264
proxy, 260
put, 263
put local-file, 260
pwd, 260
quit, 260, 273
recv, 260, 263
reget, 260
remotehelp, 261
remotestatus, 261
rename, 261
reset, 261
restart, 261
rmdir, 261
runique, 261
send, 261, 264
sendport, 261
size, 261
status, 261, 264
struct, 261
sunique, 261
system, 261
tenex, 261
trace, 261
type, 261
umask, 261
user, 261
verbose, 261
downloading files, 262-263
environment variables, 262
hosts, connections to, 265
operational overview, 265-273
overview, 255-257
server configuration, 274
   anonymous access, 278
   directory permissions, 277-278
   directory structure, 276-277
   ftpd daemon, 275-276
   site names, 274
   testing, 278
sites
   connections to, 266
   Linux documentation sources, 12-13, 707-708, 721
   login, 267
uploading files, 263-264
ftpd daemon, configuration, 275-276
ftpmail utility program, 13
Full name field (/etc/passwd file), 612
fully qualified domain name (FQDN), 284

fully qualified filenames, 78
functions
    dlopen( ), 451
    dlsym( ), 451
    gethostbyaddress, 282
    gethostbyname, 282
future of Linux, 8-9
-Fvh option (rpm command), 532
fvwm (window manager), 136
fvwm95 (window manager), 137

G

-G option
    tar utility, 634
    useradd command, 617
-g option
    groupadd command, 620
    uucp command, 405
%g variable substitution (smb.conf file), 425
games, Web sites for, 704
gateway addresses, 180
get command
    dip program, 360
    FTP, 259, 262, 272
    smbclient program, 441
--get option (tar utility), 633
gethostbyaddress function, 282
gethostbyname function, 282
gf field (/etc/printcap file), 512
GID (Group ID), 614
    creating user accounts, 60
Glickman, Matt (origin of Usenet), 470
glob command (FTP), 259
global environment variables. *See* **exported environment variables**
[global] section (smb.conf file), 424
gmc (GNOME file management), 169-170
    copying directories/files, 170
    linking directories/files, 170
    moving directories/files, 170
    file properties, 170
    opening directories/files, 170
GNOME (window manager), 137, 159
    command-line window, 169
    configuration, 164-165
        background changes, 166-167
        panel changes, 167-168
    file management, 169-170
        copying directories/files, 170
        linking directories/files, 170
        moving directories/files, 170
        opening directories/files, 170
        properties, 170
    launching applications, 168
    Main menu, 160-162
    pager, 162-163
    panel, 159-160
    starting, 158
    sticky windows, 164
    virtual desktops, 162-163
GNOME Web site, 706
Gnome-RPM, 535-540
GNU General Public License (GPL), 726
GNU Network Object Model Environment. *See* **GNOME**
GNU Project Web site, 704
GNU's Not Unix! Web site, 704
GNU, the Free Software Foundation—Cygnus Solutions Web site, 704
Gog&Magog utility, 641
goto label command (dip), 360
gov organizational domain, 284
GPL (GNU General Public License), 726
gpm, configuration (YaST utility), 549
Graphical User Interface (GUI), 93. *See also* **X Windows; XFree86**
    desktop, 133
    KDE, 132
    overview, 132-133
    panel, 133
    taskbar, 133
grep command, 335
GROUP command (NNTP), 485, 490-491

Group ID (GID), 614
　creating user accounts, 60
--group option (adduser command), 615
groupadd command, 620
groupdel command, 622
groupmod command, 621-622
groups, 620
　adding to system, 620-621
　modifying, 621-622
　removing, 622
　system-defined, 620
guest accounts (security), 596
GUI (Graphical User Interface), 93.
　See also **X Windows; XFree86**
　desktop, 133
　KDE, 132
　overview, 132-133
　panel, 133
　taskbar, 133
gunzip command, 447
gzip command, 447
--gzip option (tar utility), 635

H

H option (ps command), 659
-h option
　ftpd, 275
　httpd daemon, 463
　lpr command, 509
　mount command, 347
　nmbd daemon, 437
　smbclient program, 439
　smbd daemon, 436
　tar utility, 634
　YaST utility, 541
　yppoll command, 321
　yppush command, 324
　ypxfr command, 322
%H variable substitution (smb.conf file), 425

hackers
　compared to crackers, 586
　definition of, 3
hal91 distribution, 712
halt command, 58
handlers (Apache Web server), 466-467
hard drives, 202
　booting from, 55
　IDE and EIDE controllers, 203
　Linux
　　installation requirements, 24-25
　　space requirements, 717
　MFM and RLL controllers, 203
　partitioning, 27-29, 543-544
　　with FIPS, 42-43
　Red Hat Linux installation, 34
　SCSI controllers, 203-205
　Ultra-ATA controllers, 203
hard links, 80
hardware
　bus architecture, 206
　configuration
　　YaST utility, 545
　hard drives, 202
　　booting from, 55
　　IDE and EIDE controllers, 203
　　installation requirements, 24-25
　　MFM and RLL controllers, 203
　　partitioning, 27-29, 42-43, 543-544
　　Red Hat Linux installation, 34
　　SCSI controllers, 203-205
　　space requirements, 717
　　Ultra-ATA controllers, 203
　modems, 205, 210
　　Linux requirements, 718
　mouse, 205-206
　　Linux requirements, 25, 718
　　Pointer section (XF86Config file), 123-124
　　Red Hat Linux installation, 34
　　X Windows navigation, 134
　　XFree86 configuration, 103-104, 113-114
　overview, 201-202

756 hardware

serial ports, 210-211
  configuration, 211-216
  naming conventions, 211
sound cards, 216-218
  Advanced Linux Sound Architecture (ALSA), 220-221
  Open Sound System (OSS) driver, 220
  SoundBlaster configuration, 218-220
video cards, 207-209
  Device section (XF86Config file), 127
  Linux requirements, 21-22, 718
  Red Hat Linux installation, 34
  XFree86 configuration, 106-109, 115, 209-210

Hardware Compatibility HOW-TO Web site, 718

hardware requirements
Linux, 8
networking, 180
Slackware Linux installation, 38-39
SLIP, 351
XFree86 installation, 95-98

hardware vendors, Web sites for, 704, 727

hash command (FTP), 259, 265

hashes (password encryption), 726

HDB (HoneyDanBer) UUCP, 387
configuration, 399-400
  configuration files, 399-400
  Devices file, 401-402
  Dialers file, 402-403
  Permissions file, 403
  Systems file, 400-401

HDLC (High-Level Data Link Control), 372

head command, 82, 90

HEAD command (NNTP), 485

headers
email messages, 228-229
Usenet articles, 471

HELP command (NNTP), 485, 491

Help command (dip), 360

help command
bash shell, 656-657
FTP, 259, 272
smbclient program, 441

--help option
adduser command, 615
su command, 664
uucp command, 405
YaST utility, 541

help system, 652
bash shell, 656-657
man pages, 92, 652-655

High Performance Cluster Computing Resources Web site, 702

High-Availability Linux Project Web site, 702

High-Level Data Link Control (HDLC), 372

Hip Pocket Guide to UNIX, **691**

history
of Linux, 6
of XFree86 development, 94

history command, 71

history list
commands, 70-71
KDE, 154

HISTSIZE environment variable, 70

hl field (/etc/printcap file), 512

HoldExpensive option (sendmail), 246

holy wars (Usenet), 483

HOME (FTP environment variable), 262

home directory, 84
creating user accounts, 60

Home directory field (/etc/passwd file), 612

--home directory option (adduser command), 615

[homes] section (smb.conf file), 424

HoneyDanBer (HDB). *See* **HDB UUCP**

Horton, Mark (origin of Usenet), 470

hostname command, 182, 400
hostname lookup (DNS), 281
hostname resolution
   /etc/resolv.conf file (SLIP), 354
   PPP, 374
hostnames, mapping to IP addresses. *See* DNS
hosts (FTP), connections to, 265
hosts argument (order option), /etc/host.conf file, 289
HostSentry utility, 639
Hotwired Web site, 444
HOWTOs
   Linux documentation sources, 11
   Web sites for, 704
.htaccess files, 461
httpd daemon, 446-447, 459
   command-line options, 463-464
   restarting Apache Web server, 465
   starting Apache Web server, 461-462
   stopping Apache Web server, 462-464
httpd.conf file, 460
httpd.pid file, 465
humanities Usenet category, 472
HUP signal, restarting Apache Web server, 464
hyphen. *See* dash (-) metacharacter

I

-I option
   smbclient program, 439
   uucp command, 405
   uustat command, 410
-i option
   dip command, 358
   FTP, 257
   lpr command, 509
   nmbd daemon, 438
   passwd command, 628

smbd daemon, 436
tar utility, 634
uustat command, 409
%I variable substitution (smb.conf file), 425
ic field (/etc/printcap file), 512
IDE controllers (hard drives), 203
idle command (FTP), 259
idle time in log files, checking, 605-606
if ... goto command (dip), 360
if field (/etc/printcap file), 512
ifconfig command, 193, 353-357
--ignore-failed-read option (tar utility), 634
ignore-table option (LILO), 579
--ignore-zeros option (tar utility), 634
IgnoreDots option (sendmail), 246
IHAVE command (NNTP), 485, 491-492
ihave/sendme protocol, 473
imap-file handler (Apache Web server), 466
importing filesystems, 344
inc command (dip), 360
include option (/etc/named.boot file), 294
--incremental option (tar utility), 634
inetd daemon, 194, 275, 422, 427, 463
--info-script option (tar utility), 634
Information module (KDE desktop configuration), 144
information sources for Linux, 10-13
   books, 691-693
   FTP sites, 707-708, 721
   magazines, 693-694
   mailing lists, 699-701
   Usenet newsgroups, 694-699, 721
   user groups, 720
   Web sites, 701-706, 720-721
init command (dip), 360
init process, 186, 570, 572-576

inkjet printers, 502
INN (Internet News), 471
inode numbers, 80
Input Devices module (KDE desktop configuration), 144
insmod command, 220
install option (LILO), 579
Installation and Getting Started Guide Web site, 718
installing
    Apache Web server
        build process, 449-459
        decompressing and unarchiving source package, 447-449
    Linux, 15, 29-30
        booting multiple operating systems, 26-27
        bus architecture requirements, 21
        Caldera Open Linux installation, 30-33
        CD-ROM requirements, 23-24
        CPU requirements, 19
        disk drive requirements, 24-25
        memory requirements, 20
        methods of, 26
        modem requirements, 23
        mouse requirements, 25
        network interface card requirements, 22
        partitioning hard drives, 27-29
        printer requirements, 26
        Red Hat Linux installation, 33-38
        requirements checklist, 16-18
        Slackware Linux installation, 38-49
        SuSE Linux installation, 49-53
        tape drive requirements, 25
        video card requirements, 21-22
    packages (YaST utility), 550-551
    RPM packages, 529
    Samba, 419-420
    XFree86, 95
        checking for previous installation, 99
        hardware requirements, 95-98
        manual installation, 100-101
        X servers, 98-99

int organizational domain, 284
integrated math coprocessors, Linux installation requirements, 19
integration of Windows with Linux. *See* Samba
interactive mode (NNTP), 473
--interactive option (tar utility), 635
interfaces. *See also* controllers
    printers, 503-505
internal modems, 205, 211
Internet
    email services. *See* email services
    FTP. *See* FTP
Internet News (INN), 471
Internet Operating System Counter Web site, 705
Internet Protocol. *See* IP
intrusions. *See* security; system monitoring
IP (Internet Protocol), 176-177
    addresses, 177-179
        lookup (DNS), 281
        mapping to hostnames. See DNS
        netmasks, 179
        SLIP, 352
        spoofing, 288
    networks, NFS client format, 339
ipchaining package, 603
IRIXN32 rule, Rules section (Apache Web server Configuration file), 457
IRIXNIS rule, Rules section (Apache Web server Configuration file), 457
IRQ settings (serial ports), 212-213
ISA bus architecture, 206
isapnp utility, 218-219
-ivh options (rpm command), 529

J-K

-j option (uucp command), 405
Java Linux Web site, 702
job # option (lprm command), 510
#jobnum option (lpq command), 508
\K (chat program escape sequence), 377
K Desktop Environment. *See* **KDE**
K desktop environment (KDE) Web site, 707
-K option
  tar utility, 634
  uustat command, 409
-k option
  dip command, 358
  useradd command, 617
  uustat command, 409
  ypcat command, 320
Karpski protocol analyzer, 644
KDat backup utility, 629-632
KDE (K desktop environment) Web site, 707
KDE (K desktop environment) window manager, 132, 137-138
  command-line window, 149
  configuration, 142-144
    background changes, 144-146
    panel changes, 146-147
  file management, 149-150
    bookmarking directories/files, 154
    copying directories/files, 153
    file properties, 154
    history list, 154
    linking directories/files, 153
    moving directories/files, 153
    opening directories/files, 151-153
  KDat backup utility, 629-632
  Kmail email program, 231-237
  krn newsreader, 474-477
  launching applications, 149
  Main menu, 140-141
  mounting CD-ROMs, 154-156
  panel, 140
  printer setup, 156-158
  starting, 138-139
  sticky windows, 142
  taskbar, 139
  themes, 147-149
  virtual desktops, 140, 142
kde command (KDE), 138
--keep-old-files option (tar utility), 634
Kerberos authentication, 597
key bindings (XFree86 configuration), 104
keyboard, XFree86 configuration
  xf86config program, 104-105
  XF86Setup program, 114-115
Keyboard section (XF86Config file), 122-123
Keys module (KDE desktop configuration), 144
keywords
  chat, 392
  chat program, ABORT, 378
  device, 394
  dialer, 394
  nodename, 390
  phone, 392
  port, 392, 394
  speed, 392, 394
  system, 391
  time, 392
  translate, 402
  type, 394
kfm (KDE File Manager), 149-150
  bookmarking directories/files, 154
  copying directories/files, 153
  file properties, 154
  history list, 154
  linking directories/files, 153
  moving directories/files, 153
  opening directories/files, 151-153
Kibo (Usenet), 482
kill command, 422, 462-463, 663-664
  sending signals, 298-299
killing services, 575

Klaxon utility, 639
Kmail email program, 231-237
kook (Usenet), 482
krn newsreader, 474-477
kvt (KDE command-line window), 149

L

-L option (mount command), 347
l option (ps command), 659
-l option
    at command, 662
    dip command, 358
    httpd daemon, 463
    lpd daemon, 508
    lpq command, 508
    nmbd daemon, 438
    smbclient program, 439-440
    smbd daemon, 436
    su command, 664
    tar utility, 634
%L variable substitution (smb.conf file), 425
label command (dip), 359
--label option (tar utility), 635
languages, printers, 503
LANs (Local Area Networks), security, 601
    firewalls, 602-603
    log files, 603-606
    NFS (Network File System), 601
    NIS (Network Information Service), 601-602
Lapsley, Phil (nntpd), 471
laser printers, 502
LAST command (NNTP), 485, 492
launching applications
    GNOME, 168
    KDE, 149

lcd command
    FTP, 259
    smbclient program, 441
LCP (Link Control Protocol), 372
LDP (Linux Documentation Project) Web site, 10, 266
Learning the UNIX Operating System, Fourth Edition, 692
legal issues (Linux copyright status), 726
less command, 76, 90
    man page for, 653
LessTif (window manager), 137
LessTif Web site, 706
lf field (/etc/printcap file), 513
lib directory (FTP), 277
LibraNet Linux distribution, 712
LILO (LInux LOader), 27, 577
    configuring, 577-580
limit option (/etc/named.boot file), 294
limited broadcast addresses, 178
line printer control (lpc command), 506-507
line printer spooler daemon (lpd), 507-508
line-continuation character (\), printcap file, 511
linear option (LILO), 579
Link Control Protocol (LCP), 372
link layer (network model), 176
linking directories/files
    GNOME, 170
    KDE, 153
links, 80
Linux
    accessing non-Linux file systems, 719-720
    advantages of, 6
    booting, 55-56
    case sensitivity, 64, 85
    compared to other operating systems, 726
    compatibility with non-Linux software, 720

copyright status, 726
cost of, 7
disk and file utilities, 722
    compression, 722-723
    defragmentation, 722
    file undelete, 723-724
distributions, 9, 710
    armedLinux, 710
    availability of, 718
    Caldera OpenLinux, 710-711
    Corel LinuxOS, 711
    Debian GNU/Linux, 711
    DLX Linux, 711
    DragonLinux, 712
    easyLinux, 712
    hal91, 712
    LibraNet Linux, 712
    Linux Mandrake, 713
    LinuxPPC, 713
    LinuxPro, 713
    LinuxWare, 713
    LoopLinux, 714
    MkLinux, 714
    Red Hat Linux, 714
    Slackware, 714
    Stampede GNU/Linux, 715
    Storm Linux, 715
    SuSE Linux, 715
    TurboLinux, 715
    WinLinux, 716
    Yddgrasil, 716
documentation sources, 10-13
    books, 691-693
    FTP sites, 707-708, 721
    magazines, 693-694
    mailing lists, 699-701
    Usenet newsgroups, 694-699, 721
    user groups, 720
    Web sites, 701-706, 720-721
file sizes, 726
free distribution, 4
future of, 8-9
hardware requirements, 8

history of, 6
installation, 15, 29-30
    booting multiple operating systems, 26-27
    bus architecture requirements, 21
    Caldera Open Linux installation, 30-33
    CD-ROM requirements, 23-24
    CPU requirements, 19
    disk drive requirements, 24-25
    memory requirements, 20
    methods of, 26
    modem requirements, 23
    mouse requirements, 25
    network interface card requirements, 22
    partitioning hard drives, 27-29
    printer requirements, 26
    Red Hat Linux installation, 33-38
    requirements checklist, 16-18
    Slackware Linux installation, 38-49
    SuSE Linux installation, 49-53
    tape drive requirements, 25
    video card requirements, 21-22
integration with Windows. See Samba
logging in, 59
logging out, 59
long filename support, 725
NFS support, 333
office applications for, 8
operating system support, 4
overview, 710
partition requirements, 727
performance, 7
preinstalled, 727
processor support, 3, 716-717
pronunciation of, 4
releases, 9
requirements, 717-718
security, 7
sharing printers with Windows, 725
shut down, 56-58, 570
software availability, 719
as UNIX clone, 3, 5
uses for, 7-8
viruses, 725

Linux Answers Magazine Web site, 693

Linux Applications and Utilities Page Web site, 702
Linux BBS Web site, 705
Linux Berg Web site, 705
Linux Books and Resources Web site, 705
Linux Counter Web site, 705
Linux Databases and Tools Web site, 702
Linux Documentation Project (LDP) Web site, 10, 266, 718, 721
Linux DOOM FAQ Web site, 704
Linux Focus Web site, 693
Linux Forum Web site, 703
Linux Game Tome Web site, 704
Linux Gazette Web site, 10, 693
Linux Guides (Linux documentation sources), 10-11
Linux HOWTOs
   Linux documentation sources, 11
   Web sites for, 704
Linux International Web site, 705, 721
Linux Journal, 10
Linux Journal Web site, 693, 705
LInux LOader. *See* LILO
Linux Magazine Web site, 694
Linux Mama Web site, 705
Linux Mandrake distribution, 713
Linux on L4 Web site, 703
Linux on Laptops Web site, 704
Linux on SGI Web site, 703
Linux on the Alpha Web site, 703
Linux on VAX Web site, 703
Linux Online Web site, 719, 721
Linux PCMCIA Information Web site, 704
Linux Penguin Web site, 704
Linux portals, Web sites for, 705
Linux Savvy Web site, 705
Linux Security Home Page Web site, 706
Linux SMP Web site, 706
Linux Software Encyclopedia Web site, 702
Linux Software Map Web site, 702
Linux Start Web site, 705
Linux Ticker Web site, 705
Linux Today Web site, 705
Linux User Groups Web site, 706
Linux Users' Group Orléans (France) Web site, 706
Linux Weekly News Web site, 10
Linux World Web site, 10
LINUX.DE (German) Web site, 705
Linux.org.uk (United Kingdom) Web site, 705
Linux/AP Web site, 703
Linux/MIPS Web site, 703
Linux/PPC Web site, 716
Linux/Sun3 Web site, 703
Linux7k Web site, 703
Linuxconf utility, 215, 551-558
LinuxInfo.de (German) Web site, 705
LinuxLinks.com Web site, 705
LinuxOS distribution, 711
LinuxPowered Web site, 705
LinuxPPC distribution, 713
LinuxPPC Web site, 703
LinuxPro distribution, 713
LinuxSpirit.Com Web site, 694
LinuxWare distribution, 713
LinuxWorld Web site, 694
LIST command (NNTP), 485, 492-493
--list option (tar utility), 633
--listed-incremental option (tar utility), 634
listings, sample smb.conf file, 423-424
literals, 669
live filesystems, configuration (YaST utility), 547
lo field (/etc/printcap file), 513

LOADLIN boot loader, 580
　booting Linux with, 56, 582-583
　decompressing files from, 581-582
　requirements, 580-581
Local Area Networks. *See* **LANs**
local environment variables, exporting, 76
local option
　MAILER, 251
　pppd daemon, 379
$local variable (dip script files), 363
local Web servers, connecting browsers to, 461-462
$locip IP variable (dip script files), 363
lock option
　LILO, 579
　pppd daemon, 379
locks, computer, 589
log files
　Apache Web server, 465
　LAN security, 603-606
logical partitions, 28
logical volume manager (LVM), 544
login, 59
　FTP sites, 256-257, 267
login option (pppd daemon), 380
--login option (su command), 664
login prompts, 56, 58
login scripts (UUCP), 406-407
Login shell field (/etc/passwd file), 612
LogLevel option (sendmail), 246
logout command, 59
logScript attribute, 401
long filename support (Linux), 725
loopback addresses, 178
loopback interface (SLIP), 353-354
LoopLinux distribution, 714
low-bandwidth connections (NFS performance optimization), 348-349

lowercase command (smbclient program), 441
lp field (/etc/printcap file), 513
lpc command, 506-507
lpd daemon, 506-508
lpq command, 506, 508
lpr command, 506, 508-510
lpr print services, 505
lprm command, 506, 510
LPRng print services, 505
lpsched print services, 505
ls command, 67, 69, 84-87, 219, 418, 600, 627
　FTP, 259, 268
　man page for, 653
　smbclient program, 441
LUG list overview (GERMANY) Web site, 706
lurking (Usenet), 482
LVM (logical volume manager), 544

M

-M option
　ftpd, 275
　smbclient program, 439
　tar utility, 634
m option (ps command), 659
-m option
　at command, 661
　dip command, 358
　lpr command, 509
　su command, 664
　useradd command, 617
　uucp command, 405
　uustat command, 409
　YaST utility, 541
　ypinit command, 312
　ypwhich command, 320
%M variable substitution (smb.conf file), 425
m68k Web site, 716

macdef command (FTP), 259
MACHINE attribute, 403
Macmillan Linux Resources Web site, 705
magazines (Linux documentation sources), 10, 693-694
MagicPoint Web site, 719
mail. *See* email services
mail delivery agent (MDA), 228
Mail Reader window (Kmail), 234
mail transfer agent (MTA), 227-228
   sendmail, 243-245
      building the package, 249-250
      .cf file creation, 250-253
      executing, 254
      obtaining, 247-248
      options, 244-247
mail user agent (MUA), 227
   Kmail, 231-237
   Netscape Messenger, 237-243
   programs, list of, 230-231
mail11 option (MAILER), 252
mailboxes, 226
MAILCHECK environment variable, 75
MAILER options, 251-252
mailing lists
   BugTraq, 626
   compared to Usenet, 469
   Linux documentation sources, 699-701
mailx email program, 230
Main menu, 134-135
   GNOME, 160-162
   KDE, 140-141
make command, 71, 449-450
Makefile section (Apache Web server Configuration file), 452
man command, 11, 76, 92, 652-655
man pages, 92, 652-655
Mandrake distribution, 713
mangle_case option (name mangling), 426
manual installation, XFree86, 100-101

manually creating new users, 617-618
manually removing users, 619-620
map option (LILO), 579
mapname option (ypxfr command), 323
mapping hostnames to IP addresses. *See* DNS
mapping options (/etc/exports file), 338
maps
   automounter, 330
   NIS, 305-306
      building, 311-314
      ypcat command, 320
      ypmatch command, 321
      yppoll command, 321
      yppush command, 323-324
      ypxfr command, 321-323
map_daemon mapping option (/etc/exports file), 338
map_nis mapping option (/etc/exports file), 338
map_static mapping option (/etc/exports file), 338
mask command (smbclient program), 441
--mask option (YaST utility), 541
masks. *See* netmasks, IP addresses
master servers (NIS), 305-306
   configuring, 309-311
   starting, 315
math coprocessors (Linux installation requirements), 19
MaxDaemonChildren option (sendmail), 247
MaxHopCount option (sendmail), 246
Maximum Linux Magazine Web site, 694
MCA (Micro Channel Architecture), 206
md command (smbclient program), 441
MDA (mail delivery agent), 228
mdelete command (FTP), 259
mdir command, 328
   FTP, 259

memory
  Linux requirements, 20, 717
  Red Hat Linux installation, 34
  Slackware Linux installation, 38
  virtual, 5
  XFree86 hardware requirements, 95
menus, Main menu, 134-135
  GNOME, 160-162
  KDE, 140-141
message display during boot process, 570-572
message option (LILO), 579
messages
  email. *See also* email services
    header and body, 228-229
  Usenet. *See* articles (Usenet)
Messenger email program (Netscape), 230, 237-243
Messenger newsreader (Netscape), 477-481
metacharacters, 669
  asterisk (*), 679-680
  caret (^), 673-674
  character class ([ ]), 676-677
  dollar sign ($), 674-676
  dot (.), 670-672
  escaping, 683-685
  list of, 670
  negated character class ([^]), 677-679
  plus sign (+), 680-681
  question mark (?), 681
  vertical bar (|), 681-683
METALAB Web site, 266
MeToo option (sendmail), 246
Metro Link, Inc. Web site, 703, 707
MFM controllers (hard drives), 203
mget command
  FTP, 259, 263
  smbclient program, 441
mice. *See* **mouse**
Micro Channel Architecture (MCA), 206
Micro Channel Linux Web site, 704

MikroTik Systems Web site, 704
mil organizational domain, 284
MinQueueAge option (sendmail), 247
misc Usenet category, 472
MIT AI Laboratory Web site, 444
mkdir command, 87
  FTP, 260
  smbclient program, 441
MkLinux distribution, 714
MkLinux Web site, 703, 717
mls command (FTP), 260
mode command
  dip program, 360
  FTP, 260
modem command (dip), 360
modem option (pppd daemon), 380
$modem variable (dip script files), 363
modems, 205, 210
  Linux requirements, 23, 718
--modification-time option (tar utility), 634
modifying groups, 621-622
modprobe command, 220
modtime command (FTP), 260
modules
  AddModule section (Apache Web server Configuration file), 453-456
  KDE desktop configuration, 144
Modules section (XF86Config file), 120
modules/example/mod_example.o module, AddModule section (Apache Web server Configuration file), 456
mod_access module, AddModule section (Apache Web server Configuration file), 453
mod_actions.o module, AddModule section (Apache Web server Configuration file), 455
mod_alias.o module, AddModule section (Apache Web server Configuration file), 455

mod_asis.o module, AddModule section (Apache Web server Configuration file), 455

mod_auth module, AddModule section (Apache Web server Configuration file), 453

mod_auth_anon.o module, AddModule section (Apache Web server Configuration file), 456

mod_auth_db.o module, AddModule section (Apache Web server Configuration file), 456

mod_auth_dbm.o module, AddModule section (Apache Web server Configuration file), 456

mod_auth_digest module, AddModule section (Apache Web server Configuration file), 453

mod_autoindex.o module, AddModule section (Apache Web server Configuration file), 455

mod_browser module, AddModule section (Apache Web server Configuration file), 453

mod_cern_meta.o module, AddModule section (Apache Web server Configuration file), 456

mod_cgi module, AddModule section (Apache Web server Configuration file), 453

mod_cgi.o module, AddModule section (Apache Web server Configuration file), 455

mod_cookies module, AddModule section (Apache Web server Configuration file), 453

mod_digest module, AddModule section (Apache Web server Configuration file), 453

mod_digest.o module, AddModule section (Apache Web server Configuration file), 456

mod_dir module, AddModule section (Apache Web server Configuration file), 453

mod_dir.o module, AddModule section (Apache Web server Configuration file), 455

mod_dld module, AddModule section (Apache Web server Configuration file), 453

mod_dll module, AddModule section (Apache Web server Configuration file), 453

mod_env module, AddModule section (Apache Web server Configuration file), 453

mod_env.o module, AddModule section (Apache Web server Configuration file), 454

mod_example module, AddModule section (Apache Web server Configuration file), 453

mod_expires module, AddModule section (Apache Web server Configuration file), 453

mod_expires.o module, AddModule section (Apache Web server Configuration file), 456

mod_headers module, AddModule section (Apache Web server Configuration file), 453

mod_headers.o module, AddModule section (Apache Web server Configuration file), 456

mod_imap module, AddModule section (Apache Web server Configuration file), 453

mod_imap.o module, AddModule section (Apache Web server Configuration file), 455

mod_include module, AddModule section (Apache Web server Configuration file), 453 mod_include.o module, AddModule section (Apache Web server Configuration file), 455

mod_info module, AddModule section (Apache Web server Configuration file), 453

mod_info.o module, AddModule section (Apache Web server Configuration file), 455

mod_isapi module, AddModule section (Apache Web server Configuration file), 453

mod_log_agent module, AddModule section (Apache Web server Configuration file), 453

mod_log_agent.o module, AddModule section (Apache Web server Configuration file), 455

mod_log_common module, AddModule section (Apache Web server Configuration file), 453

mod_log_config module, AddModule section (Apache Web server Configuration file), 454

mod_log_config.o module, AddModule section (Apache Web server Configuration file), 454

mod_log_referer module, AddModule section (Apache Web server Configuration file), 454

mod_log_referer.o module, AddModule section (Apache Web server Configuration file), 455

mod_mime module, AddModule section (Apache Web server Configuration file), 454

mod_mime.o module, AddModule section (Apache Web server Configuration file), 455

mod_mime_magic module, AddModule section (Apache Web server Configuration file), 454

mod_mime_magic.o module, AddModule section (Apache Web server Configuration file), 455

mod_mmap_static module, AddModule section (Apache Web server Configuration file), 454

mod_negotiation module, AddModule section (Apache Web server Configuration file), 454

mod_negotiation.o module, AddModule section (Apache Web server Configuration file), 455

mod_proxy module, AddModule section (Apache Web server Configuration file), 454

mod_rewrite module, AddModule section (Apache Web server Configuration file), 454

mod_rewrite.o module, AddModule section (Apache Web server Configuration file), 456

mod_setenvif module, AddModule section (Apache Web server Configuration file), 454

mod_setenvif.o module, AddModule section (Apache Web server Configuration file), 456

mod_so module, AddModule section (Apache Web server Configuration file), 454

mod_so.o module, AddModule section (Apache Web server Configuration file), 456

mod_speling module, AddModule section (Apache Web server Configuration file), 454

mod_speling.o module, AddModule section (Apache Web server Configuration file), 455

mod_status module, AddModule section (Apache Web server Configuration file), 454

mod_status.o module, AddModule section (Apache Web server Configuration file), 455
mod_unique_id module, AddModule section (Apache Web server Configuration file), 454
mod_unique_id.o module, AddModule section (Apache Web server Configuration file), 456
mod_userdir module, AddModule section (Apache Web server Configuration file), 454
mod_userdir.o module, AddModule section (Apache Web server Configuration file), 455
mod_usertrack module, AddModule section (Apache Web server Configuration file), 454
mod_usertrack.o module, AddModule section (Apache Web server Configuration file), 456
mod_vhost_alias module, AddModule section (Apache Web server Configuration file), 454
mod_vhost_alias.o module, AddModule section (Apache Web server Configuration file), 454
Monitor section (XF86Config file), 125-127
monitoring. *See* system monitoring
monitors
   Red Hat Linux installation, 34
   video cards, 207-209
      XFree86 configuration, 209-210
   XFree86 configuration
      xf86 config program, 105-106, 110-111
      XF86Setup program, 115-117
more command, 76, 90
Morrison Worm (UNIX virus), 725
mount command, 69, 344-348
mount points, 330
   configuration (Linuxconf utility), 552-553

mountd daemon, 339-342, 601
mounting
   CD-ROMs in KDE, 154-156
   filesystems, 328-332, 344-345
      /etc/exports file, 337-339
      mount command, 345-348
      Windows 95, 725
mouse, 205-206
   Linux requirements, 25, 718
   Pointer section (XF86Config file), 123-124
   Red Hat Linux installation, 34
   X Windows navigation, 134
   XFree86 configuration
      xf86config program, 103-104
      XF86Setup program, 113-114
moving
   directories/files, 91
      GNOME, 170
      KDE, 153
   within directory tree, 85-86
mput command
   FTP, 260, 263
   smbclient program, 441
mru option (pppd daemon), 379
MS Windows (3.xx) Emulator (WINE), 720
MTA (mail transfer agent), 227-228
   sendmail, 243-245
      building the package, 249-250
      .cf file creation, 250-253
      executing, 254
      obtaining, 247-248
      options, 244-247
mtu option (pppd daemon), 379
$mtu variable (dip script files), 363
MUA (mail user agent), 227
   Kmail, 231-237
   Netscape Messenger, 237-243
   programs, list of, 230-231
multi option (/etc/host.conf file), 288
--multi-volume option (tar utility), 634

multiple operating systems, booting, 26-27
multitasking, 609
   cooperative, 5
   preemptive, 5
multiuser operating systems, 5
   Linux as, 609-610
mutt email program, 230
mv command, 91, 460
mx field (/etc/printcap file), 513
mySQL Web site, 702

N

\N (chat program escape sequence), 377
-N option
   tar utility, 634
   uustat command, 409
-n option
   mount command, 347
   nmbd daemon, 438
   passwd command, 628
   smbclient program, 439
   uucp command, 405
%N variable substitution (smb.conf file), 425
\n (UUCP escape character), 406
name mangling (smb.conf file), 426
name resolution
   /etc/resolv.conf file (SLIP), 354
   PPP, 374
name servers
   addresses, 179
   DNS, 286-287
   named daemon, 291
      /etc/named.boot file, 292-295
      executing, 296-301
named daemon, 291
   /etc/named.boot file, 292-295
   executing, 296-301
named pipes, 80

nameserver option (/etc/resolv.conf file), 290
naming conventions
   domains, 284
   FTP sites, 274
   NIS domains, 307-308
   partitions, 28
   serial ports, 211
   usernames, 613
Nannie utility, 641
National Institute of Standards and Technology (NIST) Web site, 603
navigation in X Windows, 134
nd field (/etc/printcap file), 513
ndc command, 296-298
negated character class ([^]) metacharacter, 677-679
net organizational domain, 284
Netcraft Web site, 443
netgroups (NFS client format), 339
netmask command (dip), 360
netmask option (pppd daemon), 380
netmasks, IP addresses, 179
Netscape Messenger email program, 230, 237-243
Netscape Messenger newsreader, 474, 477-481
netstat command, 196-197
network addresses. *See* **IP addresses**
Network File Service. *See* **NFS**
network information, Red Hat Linux installation, 34
Network Information Center (NIC), hostname/IP address mapping, 282
Network Information Service. *See* **NIS**
network interface cards (NICs)
   Linux requirements, 22, 718
   Red Hat Linux installation, 34
network layer (network model), 176
Network Management & Monitoring with Linux Web site, 704

Network module (KDE desktop configuration), 144
network monitoring tools, 638
    DTK (Deception ToolKit), 638
    HostSentry, 639
    Klaxon, 639
    PortSentry, 639
    TCP-WRAPPERS, 639
Network News Transfer Protocol. *See* **NNTP**
Network Solutions, Inc. (NSI) Web site, 178
Network World, **10**
networking, 175
    configuration
        Linuxconf utility, 553-554
        YaST utility, 545
    dial-up networking configuration
        Linuxconf utility, 554-557
        RP3 utility, 558
        TurboLinux configuration tools, 559-562
        YaST utility, 546-547
    FTP. *See* FTP
    hardware requirements, 180
    LANs (Local Area Networks), 601
        security, 601-606
    packet sniffers, 643
        detecting, 645-646
        Ethereal, 644
        Karpski, 644
        sniffit, 644
        Snort, 645
        SPY, 645
        tcpdump command, 644
    PPP (Point-to-Point Protocol), 372
        chat program, 375-379
        hostname resolution, 374
        overview, 372-373
        pppd daemon, 379-385
        requirements, 373-374
    rc files, 185-195
    serial connections, 211
    SLIP (Serial Line Internet Protocol), 351
        /etc/resolv.conf file, 354
        automation with dip command, 357-370
        configuration, 354-357
        loopback interface, 353-354
        overview, 351-352
        running server with diplogin command, 370-372
    TCP/IP, 175-176
        configuring, 181-185
        gateway addresses, 180
        IP (Internet Protocol), 177
        IP addresses, 177-179
        name server addresses, 179
        TCP (Transmission Control Protocol), 177
    testing the network, 195-198
    trusted hosts, 601
    Usenet newsgroups, 698
--new-volume-script option (tar utility), 634
newer command (FTP), 260
--newer option (tar utility), 634
NEWGROUPS command (NNTP), 485, 493
NEWNEWS command (NNTP), 485, 493
news servers, 472
news Usenet category, 472
newsgroups, 471. *See also* **NNTP; Usenet**
    Linux documentation sources, 12, 694-699, 721
newsreaders, 12, 473-474
    krn, 474-477
    Netscape Messenger, 477-481
NEXT command (NNTP), 485, 493-494
nf field (/etc/printcap file), 513
NFS (Network File Service), 325
    architecture, 328
    clients, 329-332, 344-345
        formats, 339
        mount command, 345-348
    error recovery, 329

Linux support for, 333
overview, 325-327
performance optimization, 348-349
protocol operational overview, 328
security concerns, 601
servers, 332
/etc/exports file, 337-339
benefits, 333
exporting filesystems, 342-343
mountd and nfsd daemons, 339-342
portmapper, 333-337
transport independence, 329

nfs command, 343

nfs script, 341-342

nfsd daemon, 339-342, 601

NIC (Network Information Center), hostname/IP address mapping, 282

NICs (network interface cards), Linux requirements, 718

NIS (Network Information Service), 282, 303
client/server model, 305-306
server allocation, 308
clients, configuring, 318-319
configuration (YaST utility), 546
domains, 307
naming, 307-308
files handled by, 304, 311
master server, configuring, 309-311
purpose of, 303-305
security concerns, 601-602
slave servers, configuring, 317-318
ypcat command, 320
ypinit command, 311-314
ypmatch command, 321
yppoll command, 321
yppush command, 323-324
ypserv command, 315
ypserv.conf file, 316-317
ypwhich command, 319-320
ypxfr command, 321-323

NIS+, 602

NIST (National Institute of Standards and Technology) Web site, 603

nlist command (FTP), 260

nmap command (FTP), 260

nmbd daemon, 415, 417, 437-438

nmblookup utility, 415

NNTP (Network News Transfer Protocol), 469-471. *See also* **Usenet**
commands, 484-486
ARTICLE, 489-490
GROUP, 490-491
HELP, 491
IHAVE, 491-492
LAST, 492
LIST, 492-493
NEWGROUPS, 493
NEWNEWS, 493
NEXT, 493-494
POST, 494
QUIT, 494-495
SLAVE, 495
modes, 473
operational overview, 484
server configuration, 495-496
access restrictions, 496-497
server responses, 486-489

nntpd daemon, 471, 495-496
access restrictions, 496-497

-no-ping option (ypbind command), 319

noatime option (mount command), 348

noauto option (mount command), 348

nodename keyword, 390

--nodeps option (rpm command), 529

nodetach option (pppd daemon), 380

nodev option (mount command), 348

noexec option (mount command), 348

nokeepalive Apache environment variable, 466

--nomenu option (YaST utility), 541

non-Linux file systems
accessing, 719-720
compared to Linux, 726

non-Linux software, Linux compatibility with, 720
NoRecipientAction option (sendmail), 247
nospoof option (/etc/host.conf file), 288
nosuid option (mount command), 348
notrace option (ndc command), 297
nouser option (mount command), 348
nowarn option (LILO), 579
no_root_squash mapping option (/etc/exports file), 338
NSI (Network Solutions, Inc.) Web site, 178
nslookup command, 300-301
ntrans command (FTP), 260
--null -T option (tar utility), 635
Numeric group ID field (/etc/passwd file), 612
Numeric user ID field (/etc/passwd file), 612

O

-O option (smbclient program), 439
-o option
  groupadd command, 620
  groupmod command, 622
  mount command, 347-348
  nmbd daemon, 437
  smbd daemon, 436
  tar utility, 634
  uustat command, 409
of field (/etc/printcap file), 513
office applications for Linux, 8
--old-archive option (tar utility), 634
OldStyleHeaders option (sendmail), 246
olvwm (window manager), 138
olwm (window manager), 137
OMNIS Studio Evaluation Web site, 702
--one-file-system option (tar utility), 634
onexit command (dip), 360

online help. *See* help system
open command (FTP), 266
Open Group Web site, 707
open host command (FTP), 260
Open Sound System (OSS) driver, 220
Open Sound System Web site, 702
opening directories/files
  GNOME, 170
  KDE, 151-153
OpenLinux distribution, 710-711
  installation, 30-33
  Samba installation, 419-420
operating systems
  booting with multiple, 26-27
  compared to Linux, 726
  Linux support for, 4
  multitasking, 5
  multiuser, 5
  partitions, 727
#OPTIM option, Makefile section (Apache Web server Configuration file), 452
optimization (NFS), 348-349
options, 69. *See also* commands
  /etc/host.conf file, 288
  /etc/named.boot file, 292-295
  /etc/printcap fields, 512-514
  /etc/resolv.conf file, 290-291
  AddModule section (Apache Web server Configuration file), 453-456
  adduser command, 615
  at command, 661-662
  chat program, 375-376
  dip command, 358
  FTP commands, 257
  ftpd daemon, 275-276
  groupadd command, 620
  groupmod command, 622
  httpd daemon, 463-464
  LILO, 578, 580
  lpc command, 506-507
  lpr command, 509-510

lprm command, 510
MAILER, 251-252
Makefile section (Apache Web server Configuration file), 452
mapping options (/etc/exports file), 338
mount command, 346-348
name mangling (smb.conf file), 426
named daemon execution, 296
ndc command, 296-297
nmbd daemon, 437-438
passwd command, 628
pppd daemon, 379-380
ps command, 659
Rules section (Apache Web server Configuration file), 457
sendmail, 244-247
slattach command, 355
smbclient program, 438-440
smbd daemon, 436
su command, 664-665
tar utility, 633-635
useradd command, 616-617
uucp command, 405
uustat command, 409-410
YaST utility, 541
ypbind command, 318-319
ypcat command, 320
ypinit command, 312
ypmatch command, 321
yppoll command, 321
yppush command, 323-324
ypserv command, 315
ypserv.conf file, 316
ypwhich command, 320
ypxfr command, 322-323

options file (pppd daemon), 380-381

order option (/etc/host.conf file), 288-289

ordinary files, 78

org organizational domain, 284

organizational domains, 283-284

OSS (Open Sound System) driver, 220

Ottawa Carleton Linux Users Group Web site, 706

P

\p escaped character
  chat program escape sequence, 377
  UUCP, 406
-P option
  lpq command, 508
  lpr command, 509
  lprm command, 510
-p option
  dip command, 358
  named daemon execution, 296
  nmbd daemon, 438
  slattach command, 355
  smbclient program, 439
  smbd daemon, 436
  su command, 664
  tar utility, 634-635
  uustat command, 409
  ypbind command, 319
  yppush command, 324
  ypserv command, 315
  ypxfr command, 323

%p variable substitution (smb.conf file), 425

packages
  defined, 33
  installing with YaST utility, 550-551
  ipchaining, 603
  RPM (Red Hat Package Manager), 528-529
    Gnome-RPM, 535-540
    installing, 529
    querying, 530-531
    uninstalling, 531
    updating, 531-532
    verifying, 532-535
  sendmail, building, 249-250
  uninstalling with YaST utility, 551

packet sniffers, 643
  detecting, 645-646
  Ethereal, 644
  Karpski, 644
  sniffit, 644

Snort, 645
SPY, 645
tcpdump command, 644
pager (GNOME), 162-163
PAGER environment variable, 76
PAM (Pluggable Authentication Modules), 597-599
panel, 133
GNOME, 159-160
changing, 167-168
KDE, 140
changing, 146-147
parallel printers, 504
parameters. *See also* **options**
smb.conf file, 422
PARANOID rule, Rules section (Apache Web server Configuration file), 457
parent directory, 81
parity command (dip), 361
Partition Commander utility, 543
partition table, 28
Partition-It utility, 543
partitioning hard drives, 27-29, 543-544
with FIPS, 42-43
PartitionMagic utility, 543
partitions
Linux requirements for, 727
Linuxconf utility, 553
PASC (Portable Applications Standards Committee), 691
passive mode (NNTP), 473
passive option (pppd daemon), 379
passwd command, 63, 594, 618
options, 628
password command, 614
dip program, 361
Password field (/etc/passwd file), 612
password file. *See also* **/etc/passwd file**
Taylor UUCP configuration, 395

password option (smbclient program), 439
password-free accounts (security), 596-597
passwords, 58, 61-63
BIOS setup password, 589
boot password, 589
case sensitivity, 62
changing, 63
creating user accounts, 60-61
encryption, 726
expiration, 627-628
root account, 62
troubleshooting forgotten passwords, 724
shadow passwords, 594, 614
weak passwords, 593
PATH environment variable, 77
paths
. and .. directories, 85
. and .. directory entries, 81
pattern matching, 668-669. *See also* **metacharacters**
whole words, 685-687
pc field (/etc/printcap file), 513
PCI Local Bus, 206
PCL (Printer Control Language), 503
pdksh shell, 66
performance
Linux, 7
NFS, 348-349
Performance Database Server Web site, 703
permissions
file security, 79, 599-600
FTP directories, 277-278
Permissions file (HDB UUCP configuration), 403
personal files, storing in home directory, 84
phone keyword, 392
phoneNumber attribute, 401

phquery option (MAILER), 252
physical security, 587
   BIOS locks, 588-589
   computer locks, 589
   dust, danger to computer equipment, 587
   electricity, danger to computer equipment, 588
   importance of, 588
   smoke and fire, danger to computer equipment, 588
   system backups, 589-591
   tips for, 591
PID (httpd.pid file), 465
PID column (ps command), 658
PIKT (Problem Informant Killer Tool), 642
pine newsreader, 473
ping command, 197-198
pipe symbol (|), in commands, 69
pl field (/etc/printcap file), 513
--plain option (YaST utility), 541
planning Linux installation, 15
   booting multiple operating systems, 26-27
   bus architecture requirements, 21
   CD-ROM requirements, 23-24
   CPU requirements, 19
   disk drive requirements, 24-25
   memory requirements, 20
   methods of installation, 26
   modem requirements, 23
   mouse requirements, 25
   network interface card requirements, 22
   partitioning hard drives, 27-29
   printer requirements, 26
   requirements checklist, 16-18
   tape drive requirements, 25
   video card requirements, 21-22
platform, selecting for Apache Web server, 444-445
Please Set Password and Username dialog box (Kmail), 235
Plug-and-Play. *See* **PNP**

Pluggable Authentication Modules (PAM), 597-599
plus sign (+) metacharacter, 680-681
PNP (Plug-and-Play), 218
   SoundBlaster sound card configuration, 218-219
pnpdump utility, 218
Point-to-Point Protocol. *See* **PPP**
Pointer section (XF86Config file), 123-124
pointing devices (X Windows navigation), 134
policies, security, 586
pop option (MAILER), 251
popularity of Linux, reasons for, 6
port file (Taylor UUCP configuration), 393-394
port keyword, 392, 394
port# option (lpd daemon), 508
port tty name command (dip), 361
$port variable (dip script files), 363
--portability option (tar utility), 634
Portable Applications Standards Committee (PASC), 691
Portable Operating System Interface for UNIX (POSIX), 691
portals (Linux), Web sites for, 705
Porting Applications to Linux Web site, 704
portmapper (NFS server), 333-337
ports
   Apache Web server, 462
   serial. *See* serial ports
   Web site for information, 717
PortSentry utility, 639
POSIX (Portable Operating System Interface for UNIX), 691
POSIX Programmer's Guide: Writing Portable UNIX Programs, **692**
POST command (NNTP), 485, 494

PostScript, 503
PPP (Point-to-Point Protocol), 372.
See also **dial-up networking**
    chat program, 375-379
    hostname resolution, 374
    overview, 372-373
    pppd daemon, 373, 379-380
        options file, 380-381
        script files, 381-383
        testing script files, 383-385
    requirements, 373-374
pppd daemon, 373, 379-380
    options file, 380-381
    script files, 381-383
    testing script files, 383-385
preemptive multitasking, 5
preinstalled Linux, 727
--preserve option (tar utility), 635
preserve_case option (name mangling), 426
--preserve-environment option (su command), 664
--preserve-order option (tar utility), 635
--preserve-permissions option (tar utility), 634
primary name servers (DNS), 286
primary option (/etc/named.boot file), 293-294
primary partitions, 28
primary servers (DNS), 294
print command
    dip program, 361
    smbclient program, 441
print queues
    lpq command, 508
    overview of print process, 499-500
    removing print jobs from, 510
Print, Scan, Fax and OCR Web site, 702
Printer Control Language (PCL), 503
PRINTER environment variable, 515

printers. *See also* **printing**
    configuration
        Red Hat Linux, 520-523
        SuSE Linux, 515-519
    interfaces, 503-505
    KDE, setup, 156-158
    languages, 503
    Linux requirements, 26, 718
    remote printers, configuration with YaST utility, 547
    sharing between Linux and Windows, 725
    supported by Linux, 500-502
    types of, 502
[printers] section (smb.conf file), 424
printing. *See also* **printers**
    /etc/printcap file, 510-514
    burst pages, 509
    commands, list of, 505-506
    environment variable values, 76
    line printer control (lpc command), 506-507
    line printer spooler daemon (lpd), 507-508
    overview of process, 499-500
    print queue, removing print jobs from, 510
    print services, 505
    PRINTER environment variable, 515
    submitting print jobs (lpr command), 508-510
printmode command (smbclient program), 441
privilege levels, 58
Problem Informant Killer Tool (PIKT), 642
process ID (httpd.pid file), 465
processes
    scheduling (at command), 661-663
    status
        ps command, 657-659
        top command, 660-661
    terminating (kill command), 663-664
processors
    Linux support, 3, 716-717
    requirements, installing Linux, 19

procmail option (MAILER), 251
products, defined, 33
programmer's file formats collection Web site, 705
Programming with GNU Software, 693
programs, MUA (mail user agent)
  Kmail, 231-237
  list of, 230-231
  Netscape Messenger, 237-243
Project Mnemonic Development Site Web site, 702
projects (Linux), Web sites for, 706
prompt command
  FTP, 260, 264
  smbclient program, 441
prompt option (LILO), 579
prompts, login, 56, 58
pronunciation of Linux, 4
properties
  GNOME files, 170
  KDE files, 154
protocol analyzers. *See* **packet sniffers**
protocols
  FTP (File Transfer Protocol), 255
    commands, 257-262
    downloading files, 262-263
    environment variables, 262
    operational overview, 265-273
    overview, 255-257
    server configuration, 274-278
    uploading files, 263-264
  ihave/sendme, 473
  LCP (Link Control Protocol), 372
  NFS (Network File Service), 325
    /etc/exports file, 337-339
    architecture, 328
    clients, 329-332, 344-345
    error recovery, 329
    exporting filesystems, 342-343
    mount command, 345-348
    mountd and nfsd daemons, 339-342
    overview, 325-327
    performance optimization, 348-349
    portmapper, 333-337
    protocol operational overview, 328
    server benefits, 333
    servers, 332
    transport independence, 329
  NNTP (Network News Transfer Protocol), 469-471
    commands, 484-486
    modes, 473
    operational overview, 484
    server configuration, 495-497
    server responses, 486-489
  PPP (Point-to-Point Protocol), 372
    chat program, 375-379
    hostname resolution, 374
    overview, 372-373
    pppd daemon, 379-385
    requirements, 373-374
  SLIP (Serial Line Internet Protocol), 351
    /etc/resolv.conf file, 354
    automation with dip command, 357-370
    configuration, 354-357
    loopback interface, 353-354
    overview, 351-352
    running server with diplogin command, 370-372
  SMTP (Simple Mail Transfer Protocol), 229
  TCP/IP, 175-176
    gateway addresses, 180
    IP (Internet Protocol), 177
    IP addresses, 177-179
    name server addresses, 179
    TCP (Transmission Control Protocol), 177
  UUCP (UNIX-to-UNIX Copy Protocol), 387, 470
    configuration, 388
    HDB configuration, 399-403
    login scripts, 406-407
    overview, 387-388
    sample dialogs, 408
    Taylor configuration, 388-399
    uucp command, 404-405
    uustat command, 408-410
  XNP (X Network Protocol), 94
proxy command (FTP), 260

proxyarp command (dip), 361
ps command, 334, 340, 378, 418, 422, 657-659
psend command (dip), 361
Psionic HostSentry utility, 639
Psionic PortSentry utility, 639
PSSC Labs Web site, 704
pub directory (FTP), 277
pull mode (NNTP), 473
push mode (NNTP), 473
put command
    FTP, 263
    smbclient program, 441
put local-file command (FTP), 260
pw field (/etc/printcap file), 513
pwck command, 594
pwd command, 67, 83, 626
    FTP, 260
px field (/etc/printcap file), 513
py field (/etc/printcap file), 513

Q

\q (chat program escape sequence), 377
-q option
    at command, 661
    named daemon execution, 296
    uustat command, 409
-q1h option (sendmail), 254
-qI option (sendmail), 245
-qR option (sendmail), 245
-qS option (sendmail), 245
querying RPM packages, 530-531
querylog option (ndc command), 297
question mark (?) metacharacter, 681
    wildcard matching, 668-669
queue command (smbclient program), 441
QueueDirectory option (sendmail), 247
queues. *See* print queues

QUIT command (NNTP), 485, 494-495
quit command
    dip program, 361
    FTP, 260, 273
    smbclient program, 441
quitting. *See* shutting down

R

\r escaped character
    chat program escape sequence, 377
    UUCP, 406
-R option
    mount command, 347
    sendmail, 245
    smbclient program, 439
    uustat command, 409
r option (ps command), 659
-r option
    chat program, 375
    lpr command, 509
    named daemon execution, 296
    tar utility, 633, 635
    uucp command, 405
    uustat command, 409
%R variable substitution (smb.conf file), 425
RAM
    Linux requirements, 20, 717
    Red Hat Linux installation, 34
    Slackware Linux installation, 38
    XFree86 hardware requirements, 95
RAMDAC settings (XFree86 configuration), 109
ranges in character classes, 676
#RANLIB option, Makefile section (Apache Web server Configuration file), 452
RAWRITE program, creating boot and root floppies (Slackware Linux), 41-42
rc files, 185-195
rc script, 576

rc.local script, 576
rc.sysinit script, 576
rcnfsserver command, 343
rd command (smbclient program), 441
READ attribute, 403
--read-full-blocks option (tar utility), 634
Real Time Linux Web site, 706
reboot command, 58
rec Usenet category, 472
--record-number option (tar utility), 635
recover utility, 724
recurse command (smbclient program), 441
recv command (FTP), 260, 263
Red Hat Linux distribution, 714
   /etc/syslog.conf file, 604-605
   installation, 33-38
   Linuxconf utility, 215, 551-558
   printer configuration, 520-523
   Samba installation, 419
Red Hat Package Manager. *See* RPM
Red Hat Web site, 33, 717
redirection, 651
redirection symbol (>), in commands, 69
reference sources for Linux, 10-13
   books, 691-693
   FTP sites, 707-708, 721
   magazines, 693-694
   mailing lists, 699-701
   Usenet newsgroups, 694-699, 721
   user groups, 720
   Web sites, 701-706, 720-721
reget command (FTP), 260
regional newsgroups (Linux documentation sources), 698-699
regular expressions
   metacharacters, 669
      asterisk (*), 679-680
      caret (^), 673-674
      character class ([ ]), 676-677
      dollar sign ($), 674-676
      dot (.), 670-672
      escaping, 683-685
      list of, 670
      negated character class ([^]), 677-679
      plus sign (+), 680-681
      question mark (?), 681
      vertical bar (|), 681-683
   overview, 667-668
   pattern matching, 668-669
      whole words, 685-687
release versions
   Linux, 9
   XFree86, 93-94
religious issues (Usenet), 483
reload option (ndc command), 297
remote execution (SWAT), 428
remote printers, configuring with YaST utility, 518-519, 547
$remote variable (dip script files), 363
remotehelp command (FTP), 261
remotestatus command (FTP), 261
remoteSystem attribute, 400
remount option (mount command), 348
--remove-files option (tar utility), 635
removing. *See* deleting
rename command (FTP), 261
renaming virtual desktops, 141
reorder option (/etc/host.conf file), 288
repartitioning. *See* partitioning hard drives
--replacefiles option (rpm command), 529
REQUEST attribute, 403
requirements
   Apache Web server build process, 451
   disk space (Slackware Linux installation), 39-40
   hardware (Slackware Linux installation), 38-39
   installing Linux, 717-718
      bus architecture requirements, 21
      CD-ROM requirements, 23-24
      checklist, 16-18

    CPU requirements, 19
    disk drive requirements, 24-25
    hardware requirements, 8
    memory requirements, 20
    modem requirements, 23
    mouse requirements, 25
    network interface card requirements, 22
    partitions, 727
    printer requirements, 26
    tape drive requirements, 25
    video card requirements, 21-22
  LOADLIN, 580-581
  networking, hardware requirements, 180
  PPP, 373-374
  SLIP, 351
  XFree86 installation, 95-98

reset command
  dip program, 361
  FTP, 261

resolvers (DNS), 282

RESOLV_ADD_TRIM_DOMAINS environment variable (/etc/host.conf file), 289

RESOLV_HOST_CONF environment variable (/etc/host.conf file), 289

RESOLV_MULTI environment variable (/etc/host.conf file), 289

RESOLV_OVERRIDE_TRIM_DOMAINS environment variable (/etc/host.conf file), 289

RESOLV_REORDER environment variable (/etc/host.conf file), 289

RESOLV_SERV_ORDER environment variable (/etc/host.conf file), 289

RESOLV_SPOOF_CHECK environment variable (/etc/host.conf file), 289

restart command (FTP), 261

restart option
  lpc command, 507
  ndc command, 297

restarting Apache Web server, 465

restricted option (LILO), 579

result caching (DNS), 285, 287

retrans option (NFS), 349

Retrieving messages window (Kmail), 235

rev command, man page for, 652

reverse lookup (DNS), 281

rf field (/etc/printcap file), 513

RFCs, security policies, 586

rg field (/etc/printcap file), 513

RIP (Routing Information Protocol), 176

RLL controllers (hard drives), 203

rm command, 88, 619, 627, 723
  smbclient program, 441

rm field (/etc/printcap file), 514

rmail mode (Emacs), 231

rmdir command, 89
  FTP, 261
  smbclient program, 442

$rmtip IP variable (dip script files), 363

ro option (mount command), 348

root account
  passwords, 62
  precautions, 63-64, 626-627
  usernames for, 613

root directory, 81-82

root floppies (Slackware Linux), creating, 40-42

root password, troubleshooting forgotten, 724

root.cache file. *See* /var/named/root.cache file

root_squash mapping option (/etc/exports file), 338

route command, 184, 356-357
  TCP/IP, 193

Routing Information Protocol (RIP), 176

rp field (/etc/printcap file), 514

RP3 utility, 558

RPC, portmapper, 333-337

RPC broadcasts, 334

rpc command, 335-337

rpc script, 340

rpc.ypxfrd daemon, 316
rpcinfo command, 335, 340
RPM (Red Hat Package Manager), 33, 528-529
   Gnome-RPM, 535-540
   packages
      installing, 529
      querying, 530-531
      uninstalling, 531
      updating, 531-532
      verifying, 532-535
rpm command, 419
   installing RPM packages, 529
   querying RPM packages, 530-531
   uninstalling RPM packages, 531
   updating RPM packages, 531-532
   verifying RPM packages, 532-535
RPM repository Web site, 702
rs field (/etc/printcap file), 514
RS-232 ports. *See* **serial ports**
rtin newsreader, 473
Rules section (Apache Web server Configuration file), 457
run command files, 185-195
run levels
   /sbin/init.d directory, 573-575
   list of, 574
runique command (FTP), 261
runix Web site, 706
running processes (Apache Web server), examining, 462
runtime configuration (Apache Web server), 459-461
rw field (/etc/printcap file), 514

S

\s escaped character
   chat program escape sequence, 377
   UUCP, 406
S option (ps command), 659

-S option
   ftpd, 275
   httpd daemon, 463
-s option
   chat program, 375
   lpr command, 509
   mount command, 347
   nmbd daemon, 438
   slattach command, 355
   smbclient program, 439
   smbd daemon, 436
   su command, 665
   tar utility, 635
   uustat command, 409
   ypinit command, 312, 317
   ypxfr command, 323
%S variable substitution (smb.conf file), 425
SafeDelete utility, 724
Salz, Rich (Internet News), 471
Samba, 413
   checking for existence of, 416-419
   configuration, 420
      smb.conf file, 422-426
      SWAT (Samba Web Administration Tool), 421-422, 426-435
   installing, 419-420
   nmbd daemon, 415, 417, 437-438
   nmblookup utility, 415
   obtaining, 416
   overview, 413-415
   security, 414
   share mode, 414
   sharing printers between Linux and Windows, 725
   smbclient program, 415, 417, 438-442
   smbd daemon, 415, 417, 435-436
   smbpasswd utility, 415
   smbstatus utility, 415
   testparm utility, 415, 417
   testprns utility, 415
   user mode, 414
Samba Web Administration Tool, 421-422, 426-435

SAMBA Web site, 702
--same-order option (tar utility), 635
--same-permissions option (tar utility), 634
SaveFromLine option (sendmail), 246
sb field (/etc/printcap file), 514
sc field (/etc/printcap file), 514
Scanner Access Now Easy Web site, 702
schedule attribute, 400
scheduling
    commands, 636-637
    processes, 661-663
sci Usenet category, 472
Scientific Applications on Linux Web site, 702
Screen section (XF86Config file), 127-130
script (chat program option), 376
scripts. *See also* shells
    Build (.cf file creation), 250-253
    dip variables, 363
    nfs, 341-342
    pppd daemon, 381-383
        testing, 383-385
    rc, 576
    rc.local, 576
    rc.sysinit, 576
    rpc, 340
    sample dip script, 363-366
    UUCP login, 406-407
SCSI adapters (Red Hat Linux installation), 34
SCSI controllers (hard drives), 203-205
sd field (/etc/printcap file), 514
search and replace (pattern matching), 668
search option (/etc/resolv.conf file), 290-291
secondary name servers (DNS), 286
secondary option (/etc/named.boot file), 293
secondary servers (DNS), 294

sections (smb.conf file), 422, 424
Secure Syslog Web site, 606
securid command (dip), 361
securidfixed command (dip), 361
security, 585-586
    accounts
        command accounts, 595
        dead accounts, 595
        default accounts, 595-596
        guest accounts, 596
        password-free accounts, 596-597
    BugTraq mailing list, 626
    chat program, 378
    crackers
        compared to hackers, 586
        definition of, 3
        idle time in log files, 605-606
        social engineering threats to security, 591-592
        types of, 586-587
        Web site for security information, 626
    encryption
        Kerberos authentication, 597
        PAM (Pluggable Authentication Modules), 597-599
    file security, 599-600
    LANs, 601
        firewalls, 602-603
        log files, 603-606
        NFS (Network File System), 601
        NIS (Network Information Service), 601-602
    Linux, 7
    passwords, 58, 61-63
        BIOS setup password, 589
        boot password, 589
        case sensitivity, 62
        changing, 63
        creating user accounts, 60-61
        encryption, 726
        expiration, 627-628
        root account, 62
        shadow passwords, 594, 614
        troubleshooting forgotten root account passwords, 724
        weak passwords, 593

permissions
  files, 79, 599-600
  FTP directories, 277-278
physical security, 587
  BIOS locks, 588-589
  computer locks, 589
  dust, danger to computer equipment, 587
  electricity, danger to computer equipment, 588
  importance of, 588
  smoke and fire, danger to computer equipment, 588
  system backups, 589-591
  tips for, 591
policies, 586
Samba, 414
social engineering threats, 591-592
system administration, importance of, 626
system monitoring
  filesystem monitoring tools, 640-643
  importance of, 637-638
  network monitoring tools, 638-639
  packet sniffers, 643-646
Web sites for information, 626, 706
YaST utility settings, 549

Securityfocus Web site, 706

semicolon (;), command separator character, 77

send command
dip program, 361
FTP, 261, 264

send-as-is handler (Apache Web server), 466

SENDFILES attribute, 403

sendmail, 243-245
building the package, 249-250
.cf file creation, 250-253
configuration (YaST utility), 546
executing, 254
obtaining, 247-248
options, 244-247

SendMimeErrors option (sendmail), 246

sendport command (FTP), 261

Sentinel utility, 642

September (Usenet), 483
serial option (LILO), 579
Serial Line Internet Protocol. *See* **SLIP**
serial ports, 210-211
configuration, 211-216
naming conventions, 211
serial printers, 503-504
serial-line connectivity. *See* **PPP; SLIP**
Server Message Block (SMB), 413
server-info handler (Apache Web server), 466
server-parsed handler (Apache Web server), 466
server-status handler (Apache Web server), 466
ServerFlags section (XF86Config file), 120, 122
ServerRoot directive (Apache runtime configuration), 460
servers
Apache. *See* Apache Web server
binding NIS clients to, 318-319
client/server model (NIS), 305-306
FTP, configuration, 274-278
master servers (NIS), starting, 315
name servers
  DNS, 286-287
  named daemon, 291-301
news servers, 472
NFS, 332
  /etc/exports file, 337-339
  benefits, 333
  exporting filesystems, 342-343
  mountd and nfsd daemons, 339-342
  portmapper, 333-337
NIS
  master server configuration, 309-311
  server allocation, 308
NNTP
  configuration, 495-497
  responses, 486-489

slave servers (NIS), configuring, 317-318
SLIP, running with diplogin command, 370-372
Usenet, 470
Web. *See* Apache Web server
X servers. *See* X servers (XFree86)
servicename option (smbclient program), 439
services, starting/stopping, 575
set command, 73
SetHandler directive (Apache Web server), 467
setmode command (smbclient program), 442
setserial command, 211
Settings dialog box (Kmail), 232-233
SevenBitInput option (sendmail), 247
sf field (/etc/printcap file), 514
SGI Web site, 717
sh field (/etc/printcap file), 514
shadow passwords, 594, 614
share mode (Samba), 414
shared libraries, 5
shared resources (smb.conf file), 424
sharing
 files. *See* NFS (Network File Service)
 printers between Linux and Windows, 725
SHELL (FTP environment variable), 262
shell command (dip), 361
--shell option (su command), 665
shell scripts, 67
shells, 65-68. *See also* **names of specific shells**
 changing, 66
 types of, 66
Shlashdot News for Nerds Web site, 705
short_preserve_case option (name mangling), 426
showmount command, 601
shutdown command, 57-58
shutting down Linux, 56-58, 570

SIGHUP signal (named daemon), 299
SIGINT signal (named daemon), 299
SIGIOT signal (named daemon), 299
signal-to-noise ratio (snr), Usenet, 483
signals sent via kill command, 298-299
signature files (Kmail email program), 235
SIGSYS signal (named daemon), 299
SIGTERM signal (named daemon), 299
SIGUSR1 signal (named daemon), 299
SIGUSR2 signal (named daemon), 299
SIGWINCH signal (named daemon), 299
Simple Mail Transport Protocol (SMTP), 176, 229
Simple Network Management Protocol (SNMP), 176
Simple WATCHdog (swatch) tool, 606
single host (NFS client format), 339
single-distribution operating systems, compared to multiple distributions, 527-528
sites
 FTP
  connections to, 266
  login, 267
  naming, 274
 Web. *See* Web sites
size command (FTP), 261
skey command (dip), 362
Slackware Linux distribution, 714
 /etc/syslog.conf file, 605
 installation, 38-49
 Samba installation, 420
slash character (/), directories, 81, 86
Slashdot Web site, 705
slattach command, 355-356
SLAVE command (NNTP), 485, 495
slave option (/etc/named.boot file), 293-294
slave servers (NIS), 305-306
 configuring, 317-318

sleep command (dip), 362
SLIP (Serial Line Internet Protocol), 351
  /etc/resolv.conf file, 354
  automation with dip command, 357-363
    dynamic IP connectivity, 368-370
    sample script, 363-366
    static IP connectivity, 367-368
  configuration, 354-355
    ifconfig and route commands, 356-357
    slattach command, 355-356
  loopback interface, 353-354
  overview, 351-352
  running server with diplogin command, 370
    /etc/diphosts file entries, 371-372
    /etc/passwd file entries, 370
    executing diplogin, 372
smail mode (Emacs), 231
SMB (Server Message Block), 413
smb.conf file, 420, 422-424
  name mangling, 426
  variable substitutions, 425-426
smbclient program, 415, 417, 438-442
smbd daemon, 415, 417, 433, 435-436
smbpasswd utility, 415
smbstatus utility, 415
smoke, danger to computer equipment, 588
SMTP (Simple Mail Transport Protocol), 176, 229
smtp option (MAILER), 251
sndconfig utility, 218
sniffit packet sniffer, 644
SNMP (Simple Network Management Protocol), 176
Snort packet sniffer, 645
snr (signal-to-noise ratio), Usenet, 483
soc Usenet category, 472
social engineering, threats to security, 591-592
SOCKS4 rule, Rules section (Apache Web server Configuration file), 457

SOCKS5 rule, Rules section (Apache Web server Configuration file), 457
software. *See also* applications; utilities
  availability for Linux, 719
  non-Linux, Linux compatibility with, 720
  Web sites for information, 703
software packages. *See* packages
sortlist option (/etc/named.boot file), 294
sound cards, 216-218
  Advanced Linux Sound Architecture (ALSA), 220-221
  Open Sound System (OSS) driver, 220
  SoundBlaster configuration, 218-220
Sound module (KDE desktop configuration), 144
SoundBlaster (sound card configuration), 218-220
SPARC Linux Web site, 703
--sparse option (tar utility), 635
special characters. *See* metacharacters
special files, 79
Spectable Web site, 703
speed attribute, 401-402
speed command (dip), 362
speed keyword, 392, 394
$speed variable (dip script files), 363
Spencer, Henry (origin of Usenet), 470
spoofing, 288
  prevention of, 597
spooling. *See* print queues
SPY protocol analyzer, 645
square brackets ([ ]). *See* character class ([ ]) metacharacter
squash_gids mapping option (/etc/exports file), 338
squash_uids mapping option (/etc/exports file), 338
srm.conf file, 460
St field (/etc/printcap file), 514
Stampede GNU/Linux distribution, 715

star. *See* **asterisk (*) metacharacter**
StarOffice office suite, 565-567
StarOffice Web site, 702
start option
    lpc command, 507
    ndc command, 297
starting. *See also* **boot process; executing**
    Apache Web server, 461-462
    FTP clients, 266
    GNOME, 158
    KDE, 138-139
    NIS master servers, 315
    services, 575
--starting-file option (tar utility), 634
startx command
    GNOME, 158
    KDE, 138
STAT column (ps command), 658
STAT command (NNTP), 485
static IP connectivity (dip command), 367-368
stats option (ndc command), 297
status codes (NNTP), 486-488
status command (FTP), 261, 264
status option
    lpc command, 507
    ndc command, 297
status of processes
    ps command, 657-659
    top command, 660-661
StatusFile option (sendmail), 247
sticky windows, 136
    GNOME, 164
    KDE, 142
stop option
    lpc command, 507
    ndc command, 297
stopbits command (dip), 362
stopping
    Apache Web server, 462-464
    services, 575

Storm Linux distribution, 715
strings. *See* **regular expressions**
struct command (FTP), 261
Sturgeon's Law (Usenet), 483
su command, 664-665
substitutions (smb.conf file), 425-426
sunique command (FTP), 261
SuperProbe, executing, 97-98
superuser account. *See also* **root account**
    su command, 664-665
support
    hardware
        bus architecture, 206
        hard drives, 202-205
        modems, 205
        mouse, 205-206
        overview, 201-202
        serial ports, 210-216
        sound cards, 216-221
        video cards, 207-210
    long filenames, 725
    NFS, 333
        list of vendors, 326-327
    operating systems, 4
    printers, 500-502
    processors, 3, 716-717
survey results (Apache Web server), 443-444
SuSE Inc. Web site, 705
SuSE Linux distribution, 715
    /etc/syslog.conf file, 604
    configuration (environment variables), 549
    installation, 49-53
    password expiration, 627
    printer configuration, 515-519
    Samba installation, 419
    YaST utility, 213-214, 541-551
        backups, 632-633
SuSE Linux Users Web site, 706
SuSE Mailing List Archive Web site, 702
SuSEauditdisk utility, 642

swap partitions, 5
    Linux installation requirements, 20, 24-25
SWAT (Samba Web Administration Tool), 421-422, 426-435
swatch (Simple WATCHdog) tool, 606
switches. *See* options
switching users (su command), 664-665
Sxid utility, 642
symbolic links, 80
    XFree86 configuration, 108
sync option (mount command), 348
syntax errors (httpd daemon), 447
Sys Admin, 10, 694
Sys Admin Web site, 694
sys file (Taylor UUCP configuration), 390-393
syslog-ng tool, 606
syslogd daemon, 604
system administration
    importance of, 625-626
    root account, precautions, 63-64
system administrators, 59
system backups, importance of, 589-591
system command (FTP), 261
system keyword, 391
system monitoring
    filesystem monitoring tools, 640
        AIDE, 640
        Big Brother, 641
        confcollect, 641
        Gog&Magog, 641
        Nannie, 641
        PIKT, 642
        Sentinel, 642
        SuSEauditdisk, 642
        Sxid, 642
        Tripwire, 643
        ViperDB, 643
    importance of, 637-638
    network monitoring tools, 638
        DTK (Deception ToolKit), 638
        HostSentry, 639
        Klaxon, 639
        PortSentry, 639
        TCP-WRAPPERS, 639
    packet sniffers, 643
        detecting, 645-646
        Ethereal, 644
        Karpski, 644
        sniffit, 644
        Snort, 645
        SPY, 645
        tcpdump command, 644
system requirements. *See* requirements
system-defined groups, 620
Systems file (HDB UUCP configuration), 400-401

T

\t escaped character
    chat program escape sequence, 377
    UUCP, 406
-T option
    httpd daemon, 464
    lpr command, 509
    smbclient program, 440
-t option
    chat program, 375-376
    dip command, 358
    ftpd, 276
    mount command, 347
    sendmail, 245
    tar utility, 633, 635
    YaST utility, 541
    yppush command, 323
%T variable substitution (smb.conf file), 425
tail command, 301
talk Usenet category, 472
tape drives, Linux requirements, 25, 718
--tape-length option (tar utility), 634
tar utility, 249, 447-448, 633-636
    smbclient program, 442

taskbar, 133
   KDE, 139
Taylor UUCP, 387
   configuration, 388-389
      call file, 394
      checking initial configuration, 389-390
      config file, 390
      configuration files, 389
      dial file, 394-395
      dialcodes file, 395
      password file, 395
      port file, 393-394
      sys file, 390-393
      verifying configuration, 395-399
TCP (Transmission Control Protocol), 176-177
TCP-WRAPPERS utility, 639
TCP/IP, 175-176
   configuring, 181
      /etc/host.conf *configuration file, 185*
      /etc/HOSTNAME *configuration file, 182*
      /etc/hosts *configuration file, 183-184*
      /etc/networks *configuration file, 184*
      /etc/resolv.conf *configuration file, 185*
      location of configuration files, 182
   gateway addresses, 180
   IP (Internet Protocol), 177
   IP addresses, 177-179
      lookup (DNS), 281
      mapping to hostnames. See DNS
      netmasks, 179
      SLIP, 352
      spoofing, 288
   name server addresses, 179
   TCP (Transmission Control Protocol), 177
tcpd daemon, 276
tcpdump command, 644
tcsh shell, 66
tcx (Transparently Compressed Executables), 722
Templates folder, 132
tenex command (FTP), 261
term command (dip), 362

TERM signal, stopping Apache Web server, 462, 464
terminating processes (kill command), 663-664
--test option (rpm command), 531
testing
   FTP server configuration, 278
   network configuration, 195-198
   script files (pppd daemon), 383-385
testparm utility, 415, 417
testprns utility, 415
text processing. *See* **regular expressions**
text responses (NNTP), 488-489
Tf field (/etc/printcap file), 514
themes (KDE), 147-149
tickets (Kerberos authentication), 597
tilde (~)
   home directory, 84
   UUCP pathnames, 404
TIME column (ps command), 658
time keyword, 392
timeo option (NFS), 349
timeout command (dip), 362
timeout option (LILO), 580
Timeout.queuereturn option (sendmail), 247
timeouts (NFS performance optimization), 349
tin newsreader, 473
--to-stdout option (tar utility), 634
tools. *See also* **applications; software**
   AIDE, 640
   AntiSniff, 645
   Big Brother, 641
   confcollect, 641
   disk and file utilities, 722
      compression, 722-723
      defragmentation, 722
      file undelete, 723-724
   DTK (Deception ToolKit), 638
   Ethereal, 644

ftpmail, 13
Gog&Magog, 641
HostSentry, 639
isapnp, 218-219
Karpski, 644
KDat, 629-632
Klaxon, 639
Linuxconf, 215, 551-558
Nannie, 641
nmblookup, 415
Partition Commander, 543
Partition-It, 543
PartitionMagic, 543
PIKT, 642
pnpdump, 218
PortSentry, 639
RP3, 558
RPM (Red Hat Package Manager), 528-529
   Gnome-RPM, 535-540
   installing packages, 529
   querying packages, 530-531
   uninstalling packages, 531
   updating packages, 531-532
   verifying packages, 532-535
Sentinel, 642
single-distribution operating systems, compared to multiple distributions, 527-528
smbpasswd, 415
smbstatus, 415
sndconfig, 218
sniffit, 644
Snort, 645
SPY, 645
StarOffice office suite, 565-567
SuSEauditdisk, 642
Sxid, 642
tar, 633-636
TCP-WRAPPERS, 639
testparm, 417
testpart, 415
testprns, 415
Tripwire, 643
TurboHW, 215-216
TurboLinux configuration tools, 559-565
ViperDB, 643
xf86config, 209
XF86Setup, 210
xvidtune, 210
YaST, 213-214, 541-551
   backups, 632-633
   password expiration, 627
   printer configuration, 515-519
   Samba installation, 419

top command, 660-661

top-level domains, 283-284

topq option (lpc command), 507

Torvalds, Linus (creator of Linux), 4, 6
   home page, 705

--totals option (tar utility), 635

Tr field (/etc/printcap file), 514

trace command (FTP), 261

trace option (ndc command), 297

Transaction Processing Performance Council Web site, 703

TransAmeritech Systems LinuxWare distribution, 713

transfer queue (UUCP), checking status of, 408-410

TransferLog directive (Apache Web server), 465

transferring files. *See* **FTP (File Transfer Protocol)**

translate keyword, 402

Transmission Control Protocol (TCP), 176-177

Transparently Compressed Executables (tcx), 722

transport independence (NFS), 329

transport layer (network model), 176

Trash icon, 132

tree. *See* **directory tree**

trim option (/etc/host.conf file), 288

Tripwire utility, 643

troll (Usenet), 483

troubleshooting forgotten root
  password, 724
truncating files, 80
Truscott, Tom (origin of Usenet), 470
trusted hosts, 601
TTY column (ps command), 658
ttyLine attribute, 402
TurboFSCfg utility, 559, 562-565
TurboHW utility, 215-216, 559
TurboLinux distribution, 715
  configuration tools, 559-565
  Samba installation, 419
  TurboHW utility, 215-216
Turbonetcfg utility, 559
TurboPkg utility, 559
TurboPNPCfg utility, 559
TurboPPPCfg utility, 561-562
TurboPrintCfg utility, 559
Turboservice utility, 559
TurboSoundCfg utility, 559
TurboTimeCfg utility, 559
TurboUserCfg utility, 559
TurboWMCfg utility, 559
twm (window manager), 138
type command (FTP), 261
type keyword, 394
type-map handler (Apache Web
  server), 466
TypesConfig directive (Apache runtime
  configuration), 460

U

-U option
  chat program, 376
  ftpd, 275
  lpr command, 509
  sendmail, 245
  smbclient program, 439

u option (ps command), 659
-u option
  ftpd, 276
  tar utility, 633
  useradd command, 617
  uustat command, 409
%U variable substitution (smb.conf
  file), 425
UART (Universal Asynchronous
  Receiver-Transmitter) chip, 210
UDP (User Datagram Protocol), 176
UID (User ID), 614
  creating user accounts, 60
Ultra-ATA controllers (hard drives), 203
UltraLinux Web site, 717
umask command (FTP), 261
umount command, 344
unarchiving Apache Web server source
  package, 447-449
uncompress command, 447
--uncompress option (tar utility), 635
undelete utilities, 723-724
--ungzip option (tar utility), 635
Uninet Perl Co. Web site, 702
uninstalling
  packages (YaST utility), 551
  RPM packages, 531
Universal Asynchronous Receiver-
  Transmitter (UART) chip, 210
UNIX
  books about, 691-693
  Linux as clone for, 3, 5
  Morrison Worm virus, 725
  Usenet newsgroups, 697
UNIX and Linux Computing Journal
  Web site, 694
Unix Internals: A Practical Approach, 692
UNIX Review Web site, 694
*UNIX System Administration Handbook,
  Second Edition*, 692

utilities 791

UNIX System Security Checklist Web site, 706
UNIX Versus NT Organization Web site, 726
UNIX-to-UNIX Copy Protocol. *See* UUCP
UnixWorld, 10
UnixWorld Web site, 694
unreliable IP (Internet Protocol), 177
up option (lpc command), 507
--update option (tar utility), 633
updating RPM packages, 531-532
upgrading RPM packages, 531-532
uploading files (FTP), 263-264
URLs. *See* Web sites
--use-compress-program option (tar utility), 635
Usenet, 469. *See also* NNTP
   articles, 471
      headers, 471
      transferring among computers, 472-473
   compared to mailing lists, 469
   historical overview, 469-471
   news servers, 472
   newsgroups, 471
      Linux documentation sources, 12, 694-699, 721
   newsreaders, 473-474
      krn, 474-477
      Netscape Messenger, 477-481
   operational overview, 471-473
   terminology, list of, 481-483
   top-level categories, list of, 472
usenet option (MAILER), 251
user accounts. *See* accounts; users
User Datagram Protocol (UDP), 176
user command (FTP), 261
user groups
   Linux documentation sources, 720
   Web sites for, 706

User ID (UID), 614
   creating user accounts, 60
user mode (Samba), 414
user option
   lprm command, 510
   mount command, 348
useradd command, 60-61, 594, 616-617
UserDatabaseSpec option (sendmail), 247
userdel command, 594-595, 619
usermod command, 66, 594
Username field (/etc/passwd file), 612
usernames, 58, 610. *See also* accounts
   naming conventions, 613
   root accounts, 613
users. *See also* accounts
   /etc/passwd file, 611-614
   adding to system, 615
      adduser command, 615-616
      manually, 617-618
      useradd command, 616-617
   groups, 620
      adding to system, 620-621
      modifying, 621-622
      removing, 622
      system-defined, 620
   Linux as multiuser operating system, 609-610
   overview of user management, 611
   removing, 618
      manually, 619-620
      userdel command, 619
   switching (su command), 664-665
USR1 signal, restarting Apache Web server, 465
utilities. *See also* applications; software
   AIDE, 640
   AntiSniff, 645
   Big Brother, 641
   confcollect, 641
   disk and file utilities, 722
      compression, 722-723
      defragmentation, 722
      file undelete, 723-724

DTK (Deception ToolKit), 638
Ethereal, 644
ftpmail, 13
Gog&Magog, 641
HostSentry, 639
isapnp, 218-219
Karpski, 644
KDat, 629-632
Klaxon, 639
Linuxconf, 215, 551-558
Nannie, 641
nmblookup, 415
Partition Commander, 543
Partition-It, 543
PartitionMagic, 543
PIKT, 642
pnpdump, 218
PortSentry, 639
RP3, 558
RPM (Red Hat Package Manager), 528-529
   Gnome-RPM, 535-540
   installing packages, 529
   querying packages, 530-531
   uninstalling packages, 531
   updating packages, 531-532
   verifying packages, 532-535
Sentinel, 642
single-distribution operating systems, compared to multiple distributions, 527-528
smbpasswd, 415
smbstatus, 415
sndconfig, 218
sniffit, 644
Snort, 645
SPY, 645
StarOffice office suite, 565-567
SuSEauditdisk, 642
Sxid, 642
tar, 633-636
TCP-WRAPPERS, 639
testparm, 417
testpart, 415
testprns, 415
Tripwire, 643
TurboHW, 215-216
TurboLinux configuration tools, 559-565
ViperDB, 643
xf86config, 209
XF86Setup, 210
xvidtune, 210
YaST, 213-214, 541-551
   backups, 632-633
   password expiration, 627
   printer configuration, 515-519
   Samba installation, 419

uuchk command, 388-390, 396-399

uucico command, 405

UUCP (UNIX-to-UNIX Copy Protocol), 387, 470
   configuration, 388
   HDB configuration, 399-400
      configuration files, 399-400
      Devices file, 401-402
      Dialers file, 402-403
      Permissions file, 403
      Systems file, 400-401
   login scripts, 406-407
   overview, 387-388
   sample dialogs, 408
   Taylor configuration, 388-389
      call file, 394
      checking initial configuration, 389-390
      config file, 390
      configuration files, 389
      dial file, 394-395
      dialcodes file, 395
      password file, 395
      port file, 393-394
      sys file, 390-393
      verifying configuration, 395-399
   uucp command, 404-405
   uustat command, 408-410

uucp command, 404-405
   sample dialogs, 408

uucp option (MAILER), 251

uustat command, 408-410

-Uvh option (rpm command), 532

V

-V option
   at command, 661
   chat program, 375
   nmbd daemon, 437
   sendmail, 245
   smbd daemon, 417, 436

-v option
   dip command, 358
   FTP, 257
   httpd daemon, 464
   mount command, 347
   tar utility, 635
   uucp command, 405
   uustat command, 410
   YaST utility, 541
   yppush command, 324
   ypserv command, 315

%v variable substitution (smb.conf file), 425

VA Linux Systems Web site, 704

variable substitutions (smb.conf file), 425-426

variables
   in dip files, 363
   environment. *See* environment variables

vendors, NFS support, 326-327

verbose command (FTP), 261

verbose option (LILO), 580

--verbose option (tar utility), 635

--verify option (tar utility), 635

verifying RPM packages, 532-535

--version option
   su command, 665
   tar utility, 635
   YaST utility, 541
   ypbind command, 319

vertical bar (|) metacharacter, 681-683

VESA Local Bus (VLB), 206

Vf field (/etc/printcap file), 514

video adapter requirements, Slackware Linux installation, 38

video cards, 207-209
   Device section (XF86Config file), 127
   Linux requirements, 21-22, 718
   Red Hat Linux installation, 34
   XFree86 configuration, 209-210
      xf86 config program, 106-109
      XF86Setup program, 115

VIEW program, creating boot and root floppies (Slackware Linux), 41

viewing
   directory contents, 86-87
   files, 90

vigr command, 618

ViperDB utility, 643

vipw command, 617

virtual consoles, 64-65

virtual desktops, 133
   GNOME, 162-163
   KDE, 140, 142

virtual memory, 5
   requirements, 20

virtual terminals, 5

viruses on Linux, 725

VLB (VESA Local Bus), 206

VMELinux Web site, 703

VMWare for Linux Web site, 720

VMWare Web site, 703

-Vn option (ypwhich command), 320

-vv option (rpm command), 531-532

W

-W option
   smbclient program, 440
   uucp command, 405
   uustat command, 409

w option (ps command), 659

-w option
   mount command, 347
   passwd command, 628
   tar utility, 635

Wabi 2.2 for Linux FAQ Web site, 706

wait command (dip), 362
wallpaper (KDE desktop), changing, 145
WANTHSREGEX rule, Rules section (Apache Web server Configuration file), 457
wc command, 683
weak passwords, 593
Web Browsers for Linux Web site, 702
Web Server Survey, 443
Web servers. *See* Apache Web server
Web sites
    32 Bits Online Magazine, 693
    ALSA (Advanced Linux Sound Architecture), 221
    AntiSniff, 646
    Apache sites, list of, 444
    Apache Software Foundation, 445
    armedLinux, 710
    Big Brother, 641
    binary distribution of Apache Web server, 445
    Bleeding Edge Magazine, 693
    build package of Apache Web server, 445
    Caldera OpenLinux, 711
    CERN Security Handbook, 593
    confcollect, 641
    Corel LinuxOS, 711
    Debian, 711
    Debian GNU/Linux, 717
    Deja.com, 12, 697, 699
    DLX Linux, 711
    DragonLinux, 712
    DTK (Deception ToolKit), 639
    eIT easyLinux, 712
    Ethereal, 644
    EXT2, 693
    firewall information, 603
    GNU, 726
    GNU C compiler location, 451
    Gog&Magog, 641
    hal91, 712
    Hardware Compatibility HOW-TO, 718
    hardware vendors, 727
    HostSentry, 639

Hotwired, 444
Installation and Getting Started Guide, 718
ipchaining package, 603
Karpski, 644
KDE themes, 147
Kerberos information, 597
Klaxon, 639
LibraNet, 713
Linux Answers Magazine, 693
Linux distribution availability, 718
Linux Documentation Project, 10, 718, 721
Linux documentation sources, 701-706, 720-721
    applications, 701-702
    architectures, 703
    benchmarks, 703
    commercial software, 703
    games, 704
    hardware vendors, 704
    HOWTOs, 704
    Linux home pages, 705
    portals, 705
    projects, 706
    security, 706
    user groups, 706
    X Windows, 706-707
Linux Focus, 693
Linux Gazette, 10, 693
Linux International, 721
Linux Journal, 693
Linux Magazine, 694
Linux Online, 719, 721
Linux ports, 717
Linux software, 722
Linux Weekly News, 10
Linux World, 10, 694
LinuxPPC, 713, 716
LinuxPro, 713
LinuxSpirit.Com, 694
LinuxWare, 714
LoopLinux, 714
m68k, 716
MagicPoint, 719
Mandrake, 713
Maximum Linux Magazine, 694

METALAB (Linux Documentation Project), 266
MIT AI Laboratory, 444
MkLinux, 714, 717
mutt email program information, 230
Nannie, 641
Netcraft, 443
newsgroups, list of, 472
NIS+ information, 602
NSI (Network Solutions, Inc.), 178
Open Sound System (OSS) driver, 220
PAM (Pluggable Authentication Modules) information, 599
partitioning utilities reviews, 543
PortSentry, 639
Red Hat, 33, 714, 717
Samba, 416, 725
Secure Syslog, 606
security information, 626
security policy RFCs, 586
Sentinel, 642
SGI, 717
Slackware, 714
sniffit, 644
Snort, 645
SPY, 645
Stampede, 715
Storm Linux, 715
SuSE Linux, 715
Sxid, 643
Sys Admin, 694
Tripwire, 643
TurboLinux, 716
UltraLinux, 717
UNIX and Linux Computing Journal, 694
UNIX Review, 694
UNIX Versus NT Organization, 726
UnixWorld, 694
ViperDB, 643
VMWare for Linux, 720
Web Server Survey, 443
WinLinux, 716
XFree86, 22
XFree86 Project, 95
Yggdrasil, 716

WGS (Workgroup Solutions Group) LinuxPro distribution, 713
whack character (/), directories, 81
which command, 248, 343
whole words, pattern matching, 685-687
widgets (XFree86), 94
wildcard character. *See* asterisk (*) metacharacter
wildcard matching, 668-669
wildcards (NFS client format), 339
Wim's BIOS Page Web site, 705
Win32 platform, running Apache Web server on, 445
window managers, 6, 135
   AfterStep, 136
   CDE (Common Desktop Environment), 136
   configuration (YaST utility), 548
   Enlightenment, 136
   fvwm, 136
   fvwm95, 137
   GNOME, 137, 159
      command-line window, 169
      configuration, 164-168
      file management, 169-170
      launching applications, 168
      Main menu, 160-162
      pager, 162-163
      panel, 159-160
      starting, 158
      sticky windows, 164
      virtual desktops, 162-163
   KDE, 137-138
      command-line window, 149
      configuration, 142-147
      file management, 149-154
      launching applications, 149
      Main menu, 140-141
      mounting CD-ROMs, 154-156
      panel, 140
      printer setup, 156-158
      starting, 138-139
      sticky windows, 142
      taskbar, 139

themes, 147-149
virtual desktops, 140, 142
LessTif, 137
olvwm, 138
olwm, 137
twm, 138
XFree86, 94
window noise, 140
Windows
integration with Linux. *See* Samba
sharing printers with Linux, 725
Windows 95 filesystems, mounting, 725
Windows module (KDE desktop configuration), 144
Windows NT and UNIX, **692**
WINE (MS Windows (3.xx) Emulator), 720
WinLinux distribution, 716
-wnum option (lpr command), 509
Wolfram Research (Mathematica) Web site, 702
words file, 679
Workgroup Solutions Group (WGS) LinuxPro distribution, 713
WRITE attribute, 403

X

X Consortium, 94
X Network Protocol (XNP), 94
-X option
httpd daemon, 464
sendmail, 245
x option (ps command), 659
-x option
passwd command, 628
tar utility, 633, 635
uucp command, 405
uustat command, 410
ypcat command, 320
ypmatch command, 321

X servers (XFree86)
configuration, 107-108
installation, 98-99
X Windows, 5, 93, 131. *See also* **GUI**
Main menu, 134-135
navigation, 134
Usenet newsgroups, 697-698
Web sites for information, 706-707
window managers, 135
AfterStep, 136
CDE (Common Desktop Environment), 136
Enlightenment, 136
fvwm, 136
fvwm95, 137
GNOME, 137, 158-170
KDE, 137-158
LessTif, 137
olvwm, 138
olwm, 137
twm, 138
XF86Config file, 118-119
Device section, 127
Files section, 119-120
Keyboard section, 122-123
Modules section, 120
Monitor section, 125-127
Pointer section, 123-124
Screen section, 127-130
ServerFlags section, 120, 122
xf86config program, 102-111, 209
XF86Setup program, 102, 111-118, 210
XFce project Web site, 707
XFree86, 6, 93
configuration, 101-102, 209-210
checklist, 209
xf86config, 102-111
XF86Config file, 118-120, 122-130
XF86Setup program, 102, 111-118
YaST utility, 549
development of, 94
installation, 95
checking for previous installation, 99
hardware requirements, 95-98

manual installation, 100-101
X servers, 98-99
memory requirements, 20
release versions, 93-94
widgets, 94
window manager, 94
XFree86 Project, 94
XFree86 Project Web site, 95, 707
XFree86 Web site, 22
xfr_check_port option (ypserv.conf file), 316
Xi Graphics, Inc. Web site, 707
Xlib function library, 94
XMCD - Motif(©) CD Audio Player Web site, 702
XNP (X Network Protocol), 94
xonxoff option (pppd daemon), 380
XturboFind utility, 559
XturboFSCfg utility, 559
Xturbonetcfg utility, 559-561
XturboPkg utility, 559
Xturboservice utility, 559
XturboUserCfg utility, 559
xvidtune utility, 210

Y

-y option (uustat command), 409
YaST utility, 213-214, 541-551
backups, 632-633
password expiration, 627
printer configuration, 515-519
Samba installation, 419
Yellow Pages (YP), 282, 304
Yggdrasil Linux distribution, 716
ypbind command, 318-319
ypcat command, 320
ypinit command, 311-314, 317
ypmatch command, 321
yppoll command, 321

yppush command, 323-324
ypserv command, 315-316
ypserv.conf file, 316-317
-ypset option (ypbind command), 318
-ypsetme option (ypbind command), 319
ypwhich command, 319-320
ypxfr command, 321-323

Z

-Z option (tar utility), 635
zlibc utility, 723
zones (DNS), 286
zsh shell, 66

Linux & Open Source Solutions

Selected Titles from New Riders Publishing

MySQL teaches readers how to use the tools provided by the MySQL distribution, covering installation, setup, daily use, security, optimization, maintenance, and troubleshooting. It also discusses important third-party tools, such as the PerlDBI and Apache/PHP interfaces that provide access to MySQL.

ISBN: 0-7357-0921-1

Avoiding the dry and academic approach, the goal of *Python Essential Reference* is to concisely describe the Python programming language and its large library of standard modules, collectively known as the Python programming environment. This is an informal reference that covers Python's lexical conventions, datatypes, control flow, functions, statements, classes and execution model. A truly essential reference for any Python programmer.

ISBN: 0-7357-0901-7

Web Application Development with PHP explains PHP's advanced syntax including classes, recursive functions and variables. The authors present software development methodologies and coding conventions which are a must-know for industry quality products and make developing faster and more productive. Included is coverage on Web applications and insight into user and session management, e-commerce systems, XML applications and WDDX.

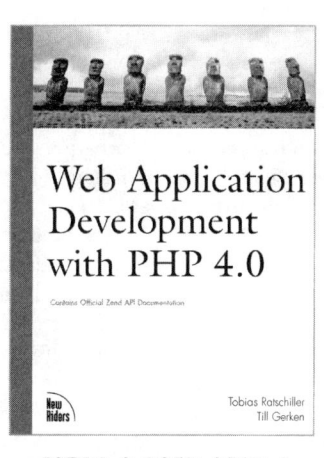

ISBN: 0-7357-0997-1

New Riders: Books for Networking Professionals

Windows NT/2000 Titles

Windows 2000 Professional
By Jerry Honeycutt
1st Edition
350 pages, $34.99 US
ISBN: 0-7357-0950-5

Windows 2000 Professional explores the power available to the Windows workstation user on the corporate network and Internet. The book is aimed directly at the power user who values the security, stability and networking capabilities of NT alongside the ease and familiarity of the Windows 9X user interface. This book covers both user and administration topics, with a dose of networking content added for connectivity.

Windows 2000 Registry
By Sandra Osborne
2nd Edition
550 pages, $34.99
ISBN: 0-7357-0944-0
December 2000

Windows 2000 Registry is a powerful tool for accomplishing many important administration tasks, but little information is available on registry settings and how they can be edited to accomplish these tasks. This title offers unique insight into using registry settings to configure client systems in a Windows 2000 environment. The approach of the book is that of revealing the GUI through the registry, allowing system administrators to to edit the registry settings to efficiently accomplish critical tasks such as configuration, installation, and management.

Windows 2000 DNS
By Herman Knief, Jeffrey Graham, Andrew Daniels, and Roger Abell
2nd Edition
450 pages, $39.99
ISBN: 0-7357-0973-4

The Domain Name System is a directory of registered computer names and IP addresses that can be instantly located. Without proper design and administration of DNS, computers wouldn't be able to locate each other on the network, and applications like email and Web browsing wouldn't be feasible. Administrators need this information to make their networks work. *Windows 2000 DNS* provides a technical overview of DNS and WINS, and how to design and administer them for optimal performance in a Windows 2000 environment.

Windows 2000 Deployment & Desktop Management
By Jeffrey A. Ferris
1st Ediition
400 pages, $34.99
ISBN: 0-7357-0975-0

More than a simple overview of new features and tools, this solutions-driven book is a thorough reference to deploying Windows 2000 Professional to corporate workstations. The expert real-world advice and detailed exercises make this a one-stop, easy-to-use resource for any system administrator, integrator, engineer, or other IT professional planning rollout of Windows 2000 clients.

Planning for Windows 2000
By Eric K. Cone, Jon Boggs, and Sergio Perez
1st Edition
400 pages, $29.99
ISBN: 0-7357-0048-6

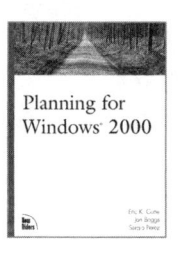

Windows 2000 is poised to be one of the largest and most important software releases of the next decade, and you are charged with planning, testing, and deploying it in your enterprise. Are you ready? With this book, you will be. *Planning for Windows 2000* lets you know what the upgrade hurdles will be, informs you how to clear them, guides you through effective Active Directory design, and presents you with detailed rollout procedures. Eric K. Cone, Jon Boggs, and Sergio Perez give you the benefit of their extensive experiences as Windows 2000 Rapid Deployment Program members by sharing problems and solutions they've encountered on the job.

Inside Windows 2000 Server
By William Boswell
1st Edition
1550 pages, $49.99
ISBN: 1-56205-929-7

Taking the author-driven, no-nonsense approach we pioneered with our Landmark books, New Riders proudly offers something unique for Windows 2000 administrators—an interesting, discriminating book on Windows 2000 Server written by someone who can anticipate your situation and give you workarounds that won't leave a system unstable or sluggish.

Windows 2000 Security
By Roberta Bragg
1st Edition
500 pages, $39.99
ISBN: 0-7357-0991-2
October 2000

No single authoritative reference on security exists for serious network system administrators. The primary directive of this title is to assist the Windows networking professional in understanding and implementing Windows 2000 security in their organization. Included are best practices sections which make recommendations for settings and security practices.

Windows 2000 Server Professional Reference
By Karanjit S. Siyan, Ph.D.
3rd Edition
1800 pages, $75.00
ISBN: 0-7357-0952-1

Windows 2000 Server Professional Reference is the benchmark of references available for Windows 2000. Although other titles take you through the setup and implementation phase of the product, no other book provides the user with detailed answers to day-to-day administration problems and tasks. Real-world implementations are key to help administrators discover the most viable solutions for their particular environments. Solid content shows administrators how to manage, troubleshoot, and fix problems that are specific to heterogeneous Windows networks, as well as Internet features and functionality

Windows 2000 User Management
By Lori Sanders
1st Edition
300 pages, $34.99
ISBN: 1-56205-886-X

With the dawn of Windows 2000, it has become even more difficult to draw a clear line between managing the user and managing the user's environment and desktop. This book, written by a noted trainer and consultant, provides a comprehensive, practical guide to managing users and their desktop environments with Windows 2000.

Windows 2000 Active Directory Design & Deployment
By Gary Olsen
1st Edition
450 pages, $45.00
ISBN: 1-57870-242-9
September 2000

This book focuses on the design of a Windows 2000 Active Directory environment, and how to develop an effective design and migration plan. The reader is led through the process of developing a design plan by reviewing each pertinent issue, and then provided expert advice on how to evaluate each issue as it applies to the reader's particular environment. Practical examples illustrate all these issues.

Windows 2000 Quality of Service
By David Iseminger
1st Edition
300 pages, $45.00
ISBN: 1-57870-115-5

As the traffic on networks continues to increase, the strain on network infrastructure and available resources has also grown. *Windows 2000 Quality of Service* teaches network engineers and administrators to how to define traffic control patterns and utilize bandwidth in their networks.

Windows 2000 Server: Planning and Migration
By Sean Deuby
1st Edition
450 pages $40.00
ISBN: 1-57870-023-X

Windows 2000 Server: Planning and Migration can quickly save the NT professional thousands of dollars and hundreds of hours. This title includes authoritative information on key features of Windows 2000 and offers recommendations on how to best position your NT network for Windows 2000.

Windows 2000 and Mainframe Integration
By William Zack
1st Edition
400 pages, $40.00
ISBN: 1-57870-200-3

Windows 2000 and Mainframe Integration provides mainframe computing professionals with the practical know-how to build and integrate Windows 2000 technologies into their current environment.

Windows NT/2000 Thin Client Solutions
By Todd Mathers
2nd Edition
750 pages $45.00
ISBN: 1-57870-239-9

A practical and comprehensive reference to MetaFrame 1.8 and Terminal Services, this book should be the first source for answers to the tough questions on the Terminal Server VCx2/MetaFrame platform. Building on the quality of the previous edition, additional coverage of installation of Terminal Services and MetaFrame on a Windows 2000 Server is included, as well as chapters on Terminal Server management, remote access, and application integration.

Windows NT/2000 Native API Reference
By Gary Nebbett
1st Edition
500 pages, $50.00
ISBN: 1-57870-199-6

This book is the first complete reference to the API functions native to Windows NT and covers the set of services that are offered by the Windows NT to both kernel- and user-mode programs. Coverage consists of documentation of the 210 routines included in the NT Native API, and the functions that have been be added in Windows 2000. Routines that are either not directly accessible via the Win32 API or offer substantial additional functionality are described in especially great detail. Services offered by the NT kernel, mainly the support for debugging user mode applications, are also included.

Windows NT/2000 ADSI Scripting for System Administration
By Thomas Eck
1st Edition
700 pages, $45.00
ISBN: 1-57870-219-4

Active Directory Scripting Interfaces (ADSI) allow administrators to automate administrative tasks across their Windows networks. This title fills a gap in the current ADSI documentation by including coverage of its interaction with LDAP and provides administrators with proven code samples that they can adopt to effectively configure and manage user accounts and other usually time-consuming tasks.

Windows 2000 Virtual Private Networking
By Thaddeus Fortenberry
1st Edition
400 pages, $45.00
ISBN 1-57870-246-1
October 2000

Because of the ongoing push for a distributed workforce, administrators must support laptop users, home LAN environments, complex branch offices, and more—all within a secure and effective network design. The way an administrator implements VPNs in Windows 2000 is different than that of any other operating system. In addition to discussions about Windows 2000 tunneling, new VPN features that can affect Active Directory replication and network address translation are also covered.

Windows NT Terminal Server and Citrix MetaFrame
By Ted Harwood
1st Edition
400 pages, $29.99
ISBN: 1-56205-944-0

It's no surprise that most administration headaches revolve around integration with other networks and clients. This book addresses these types of real-world issues on a case-by-case basis, giving tools and advice for solving each problem. The author also offers the real nuts and bolts of thin client administration on multiple systems, covering relevant issues such as installation, configuration, network connection, management, and application distribution.

Windows NT Power Toolkit
By Stu Sjouwerman and Ed Tittel
1st Edition
800 pages, $49.99
ISBN: 0-7357-0922-X

This book covers the analysis, tuning, optimization, automation, enhancement, maintenance, and troubleshooting of Windows NT Server 4.0 and Windows NT Workstation 4.0. In most cases, the two operating systems overlap completely. Where the two systems diverge, each platform is covered separately. This advanced title comprises a task-oriented treatment of the Windows NT 4 environment. By concentrating on the use of operating system tools and utilities, Resource Kit elements, and selected third-party tuning, analysis, optimization, and productivity tools, this book will show its readers how to carry out everyday and advanced tasks.

Windows NT Performance: Monitoring, Benchmarking, and Tuning
By Mark T. Edmead and Paul Hinsberg
1st Edition
288 pages, $29.99
ISBN: 1-56205-942-4

Performance monitoring is a little like preventive medicine for the administrator: No one enjoys a checkup, but it's a good thing to do on a regular basis. This book helps you focus on the critical aspects of improving the performance of your NT system by showing you how to monitor the system, implement benchmarking, and tune your network. The book is organized by resource components, which makes it easy to use as a reference tool.

Windows NT Device Driver Development
By Peter Viscarola and W. Anthony Mason
1st Edition
700 pages, $50.00
ISBN: 1-57870-058-2

This title begins with an introduction to the general Windows NT operating system concepts relevant to drivers, then progresses to more detailed information about the operating system, such as interrupt management, synchronization issues, the I/O Subsystem, standard kernel mode drivers, and more.

Windows NT Shell Scripting
By Tim Hill
1st Edition
350 pages, $32.00
ISBN: 1-57870-047-7

A complete reference for Windows NT scripting, this book guides you through a high-level introduction to the shell language itself and the shell commands that are useful for controlling or managing different components of a network.

Windows Script Host
By Tim Hill
1st Edition
400 pages, $35.00
ISBN: 1-57870-139-2

Windows Script Host is one of the first books published about this powerful tool. The text focuses on system scripting and the VBScript language, using objects, server scriptlets, and ready-to-use script solutions.

Internet Information Services Administration
By Kelli Adam
1st Edition
200 pages, $29.99
ISBN: 0-7357-0022-2

Are the new Internet technologies in Internet Information Services giving you headaches? Does providing security on the Web take up all of your time? Then this is the book for you. With hands-on configuration training, advanced study of the new protocols, coverage of the most recent version of IIS, and detailed instructions on authenticating users with the new Certificate Server and implementing and managing the new e-commerce features, *Internet Information Services Administration* gives you the real-life solutions you need. This definitive resource gives you detailed advice on working with Microsoft Management Console, which was first used by IIS.

Windows NT/2000 Network Security
By E. Eugene Schultz
1st Edition
437 pages, $45.00
ISBN: 1-57870-253-4

Windows NT/2000 Network Security provides a framework that will promote genuine understanding, a "big picture," of the Windows security model and associated capabilities. The goal is to acquaint readers with the major types of Windows security exposures when used in both peer-to-peer and client-server settings and to teach readers the specific security controls ansd settings that address each exposure, and how to evaluate tradeoffs to determine which control (if any) to apply.

SMS 2 Administration
By Michael Lubanski
and Darshan Doshi
1st Edition
350 pages, $39.99
ISBN: 0-7357-0082-6

Microsoft's new version of its Systems Management Server (SMS) is starting to turn heads. Although complex, it allows administrators to lower their total cost of ownership and more efficiently manage clients, applications, and support operations. So if your organization is using or implementing SMS, you'll need some expert advice. Michael Lubanski and Darshan Doshi can help you get the most bang for your buck with insight, expert tips, and real-world examples. Michael and Darshan are consultants specializing in SMS and have worked with Microsoft on one of the most complex SMS rollouts in the world, involving 32 countries, 15 languages, and thousands of clients.

SQL Server System Administration
By Sean Baird,
Chris Miller, et al.
1st Edition
352 pages, $29.99
ISBN: 1-56205-955-6

How often does your SQL Server go down during the day when everyone wants to access the data? Do you spend most of your time being a "report monkey" for your coworkers and bosses? *SQL Server System Administration* helps you keep data consistently available to your users. This book omits introductory information. The authors don't spend time explaining queries and how they work. Instead, they focus on the information you can't get anywhere else, like how to choose the correct replication topology and achieve high availability of information.

SQL Server 7 Essential Reference
By Sharon Dooley
1st Edition
400 pages, $35.00
ISBN: 0-7357-0864-9

SQL Server 7 Essential Reference is a comprehensive reference of advanced how-tos and techniques for developing with SQL Server. In particular, the book addresses advanced development techniques used in large application efforts with multiple users, such as developing Web applications for intranets, extranets, or the Internet. Each section includes detail on how each component is developed and then integrated into a real-life application.

Networking Titles

Understanding the Network: A Practical Guide to Internetworking
By Michael Martin
1st Edition
650 pages, $39.99
ISBN: 0-7357-0977-7

Understanding the Network addresses the audience in practical terminology, and describes the most essential information and tools required to build high-availability networks in a step-by-step implementation format. Each chapter could be read as a standalone, but the book builds progressively toward a summary of the essential concepts needed to put together a wide-area network.

Understanding Data Communications
By Gilbert Held
Sixth Edition
600 pages, $39.99
ISBN: 0-7357-0036-2

Updated from the highly successful fifth edition, this book explains how data communications systems and their various hardware and software components work. More than an entry-level book, it approaches the material in textbook format, addressing the complex issues involved in internetworking today. A great reference book for the experienced networking professional that is written by the noted networking authority, Gilbert Held.

Cisco Router Configuration & Troubleshooting
By Mark Tripod
2nd Edition
400 pages, $34.99
ISBN: 0-7357-0999-8

Want the real story on making your Cisco routers run like a dream? Pick up a copy of *Cisco Router Configuration & Troubleshooting* and see what Mark Tripod of Exodus Communications has to say. Exodus is responsible for making some of the largest sites on the Net scream, like Amazon.com, Hotmail, USAToday, Geocities, and Sony. In this book, the author provides advanced configuration issues, sprinkled with advice and preferred practices. By providing real-world insight and examples instead of rehashing Cisco's documentation, Mark gives network administrators information they can start using today.

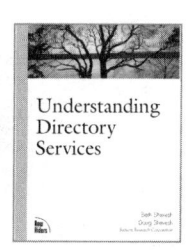

Understanding Directory Services
By Beth Sheresh and Doug Sheresh
1st Edition
400 pages, $39.99
ISBN: 0-7357-0910-6

Understanding Directory Services provides the reader with a thorough knowledge of the fundamentals of directory services: what DSs are, how they are designed, and what functionality they can provide to an IT infrastructure. This book provides a framework to the exploding market of directory services by placing the technology in context and helping people understand what directories can, and can't, do for their networks.

Local Area High Speed Networks
By Dr. Sidnie Feit
1st Edition
650 pages, $50.00
ISBN: 1-57870-113-9

A great deal of change is happening in the technology being used for local area networks. As Web intranets have driven bandwidth needs through the ceiling, inexpensive Ethernet NICs and switches have come into the market. As a result, many network professionals are interested in evaluating these new technologies for implementation. This book provides real-world implementation expertise for these technologies, including traces, so that users can realistically compare and decide how to use them.

Network Performance Baselining
By Daniel Nassar
1st Edition
700 pages, $50.00
ISBN: 1-57870-240-2

Network Performance Baselining focuses on the real-world implementation of network baselining principles and shows not only how to measure and rate a network's performance, but also how to improve the network's performance. This book includes chapters that give a real "how to" approach for standard baseline methodologies along with actual steps and processes to perform network baseline measurements. In addition, the proper way to document and build a baseline report is provided.

Directory Enabled Networks
By John Strassner
1st Edition
700 pages, $50.00
ISBN: 1-57870-140-6

Directory Enabled Networks is a comprehensive resource on the design and use of DEN. This book provides practical examples side-by-side with a detailed introduction to the theory of building a new class of network-enabled applications that will solve networking problems. It is a critical tool for network architects, administrators, and application developers.

Wide Area High Speed Networks
By Dr. Sidnie Feit
1st Edition
600 pages, $50.00
ISBN:1-57870-114-7

Networking is in a transitional phase between long-standing conventional wide area services and new technologies and services. This book presents current and emerging wide area technologies and services, makes them understandable, and puts them into perspective so that their merits and disadvantages are clear.

Quality of Service in IP Networks
By Grenville Armitage
1st Edition
300 pages, $50.00
ISBN: 1-57870-189-9

Quality of Service in IP Networks presents a clear understanding of the architectural issues surrounding delivering QoS in an IP network, and positions the emerging technologies within a framework of solutions. The motivation for QoS is explained with reference to emerging real-time applications such as Voice/Video over IP, VPN services, and supporting service level agreements.

Intrusion Detection
By Rebecca Bace
1st Edition
300 pages, $50.00
ISBN: 1-57870-185-6

Intrusion detection is a critical new area of technology within network security. This comprehensive guide to the field of intrusion detection covers the foundations of intrusion detection and system audit. *Intrusion Detection* provides a wealth of information, ranging from design considerations to how to evaluate and choose the optimal commercial intrusion detection products for a particular networking environment.

Open Source Titles

MySQL
By Paul DuBois
1st Edition
750 pages, $49.99
ISBN: 0-7357-0921-1

MySQL teaches readers how to use the tools provided by the MySQL distribution, covering installation, setup, daily use, security, optimization, maintenance, and troubleshooting. It also discusses important third-party tools, such as the Perl DBI and Apache/PHP interfaces that provide access to MySQL.

Python Essential Reference
By David Beazley
1st Edition
350 pages, $34.95
ISBN: 0-7357-0901-7

Avoiding the dry and academic approach, the goal of Python Essential Reference is to concisely describe the Python programming language and its large library of standard modules, collectively known as the Python programming environment. This is an informal reference that covers Python's lexical conventions, datatypes, control flow, functions, statements, classes and execution model. A truly essential reference for any Python programmer.

Linux Firewalls
By Robert Ziegler
1st Edition
500 pages, $39.99
ISBN: 0-7357-0900-9

A Linux machine connected to the Internet is in a high-risk situation. This book details security steps that a small, non-enterprise business user might take to protect himself. These steps include packet-level firewall filtering, IP masquerading, proxies, tcp wrappers, system integrity checking, and system security monitoring with an overall emphasis on filtering and protection. The goal is to help people get their Internet security measures in place quickly, without the need to become experts in security or firewalls.

GIMP Essential Reference
By Alex Harford
1st Edition
400 pages, $24.95
ISBN: 0-7357-0911-4

As the use of the Linux OS gains steam, so does the use of the GIMP. Many Photoshop users are starting to use the GIMP, recognized for its power and versatility. Taking this into consideration, GIMP Essential Reference has shortcuts exclusively for Photoshop users and puts the power of this program into the palm of the reader's hand.

DCE/RPC over SMB: Samba and Windows NT Domain Internals
By Luke Leighton
1st Edition
300 pages, $45.00
ISBN: 1-57870-150-3

Security people, system and network administrators, and the folks writing tools for them all need to be familiar with the packets flowing across their networks. Authored by a key member of the SAMBA team, this book describes how Microsoft has taken DCE/RPC and implemented it over SMB and TCP/IP.

Grokking the GIMP
By Carey Bunks
1st Edition
350 pages, $39.99
ISBN: 0-7357-0924-6

Grokking the GIMP is a technical reference that covers the intricacies of the GIMP's functionality. The material gives the reader the ability to get up to speed quickly and start creating great graphics using the GIMP. Included as a bonus are step-by-step cookbook features used entirely for advanced effects.

KDE Application Development
By Uwe Thiem
1st Edition
200 pages, $39.99
ISBN: 1-57870-201-1

KDE Application Development offers a head start on KDE and Qt. The book covers the essential widgets available in KDE and Qt, and offers a strong start without the "first try" annoyances which sometimes make strong developers and programmers give up.

Other Books By New Riders

Microsoft Technologies

ADMINISTRATION

Inside Windows 2000 Server
1-56205-929-7 • $49.99 US
Windows 2000 Essential Reference
0-7357-0869-X • $35.00 US
Windows 2000 Active Directory
0-7357-0870-3 • $29.99 US
Windows 2000 Routing and Remote Access Service
0-7357-0951-3 • $34.99 US
Windows 2000 Deployment & Desktop Management
0-7357-0975-0 • $34.99 US
Windows 2000 DNS
0-7357-0973-4 • $39.99 US
Windows 2000 User Management
1-56205-886-X • $34.99 US
Windows 2000 Professional
0-7357-0950-5 • $34.99 US
Planning for Windows 2000
0-7357-0048-6 • $29.99 US
Windows 2000 Server Professional Reference
0-7357-0952-1 • $75.00 US
Windows 2000 Security
0-7357-0991-2 • $39.99 US
Windows 2000 Registry
0-7357-0944-0 • $34.99 US
Available 2001
Windows 2000 Terminal Services and Citrix MetaFrame
0-7357-1005-8 • $39.99 US
Available 2001
Windows NT/2000 Network Security
1-57870-253-4 • $45.00 US
Windows NT/2000 Thin Client Solutions
1-57870-239-9 • $45.00 US
Windows 2000 Virtual Private Networking
1-57870-246-1 • $45.00 US
Available January 2001
Windows 2000 Active Directory Design & Migration
1-57870-242-9 • $45.00 US
Available September 2000
Windows 2000 and Mainframe Integration
1-57870-200-3 • $40.00 US
Windows 2000 Server: Planning and Migration
1-57870-023-X • $40.00 US
Windows 2000 Quality of Service
1-57870-115-5 • $45.00 US
Windows NT Power Toolkit
0-7357-0922-X • $49.99 US
Windows NT Terminal Server and Citrix MetaFrame
1-56205-944-0 • $29.99 US
Windows NT Performance: Monitoring, Benchmarking, and Tuning
1-56205-942-4 • $29.99 US
Windows NT Registry: A Settings Reference
1-56205-941-6 • $29.99 US

Windows NT Domain Architecture
1-57870-112-0 • $38.00 US

SYSTEMS PROGRAMMING

Windows NT/2000 Native API Reference
1-57870-199-6 • $50.00 US
Windows NT Device Driver Development
1-57870-058-2 • $50.00 US
DCE/RPC over SMB: Samba and Windows NT Domain Internals
1-57870-150-3 • $45.00 US

APPLICATION PROGRAMMING

Delphi COM Programming
1-57870-221-6 • $45.00 US
Windows NT Applications: Measuring and Optimizing Performance
1-57870-176-7 • $40.00 US
Applying COM+
ISBN 0-7357-0978-5 • $49.99 US

WEB PROGRAMMING

Exchange & Outlook: Constructing Collaborative Solutions
ISBN 1-57870-252-6 • $40.00 US

SCRIPTING

Windows Script Host
1-57870-139-2 • $35.00 US
Windows NT Shell Scripting
1-57870-047-7 • $32.00 US
Windows NT Win32 Perl Programming: The Standard Extensions
1-57870-067-1 • $40.00 US
Windows NT/2000 ADSI Scripting for System Administration
1-57870-219-4 • $45.00 US
Windows NT Automated Deployment and Customization
1-57870-045-0 • $32.00 US

BACK OFFICE

SMS 2 Administration
0-7357-0082-6 • $39.99 US
Internet Information Services Administration
0-7357-0022-2 • $29.99 US
SQL Server System Administration
1-56205-955-6 • $29.99 US
SQL Server 7 Essential Reference
0-7357-0864-9 • $35.00 US

Open Source

MySQL
0-7357-0921-1 • $49.99 US
Web Application Development with PHP
0-7357-0997-1 • $39.99 US
PHP Functions Essential Reference
0-7357-0970-X • $35.00 US
Available February 2001

Python Essential Reference
0-7357-0901-7 • $34.95 US
Autoconf, Automake, and Libtool
1-57870-190-2 • $35.00 US

Linux/Unix

ADMINISTRATION

Linux System Administration
1-56205-934-3 • $29.99 US
Linux Firewalls
0-7357-0900-9 • $39.99 US
Linux Essential Reference
0-7357-0852-5 • $24.95 US
UnixWare 7 System Administration
1-57870-080-9 • $40.00 US

DEVELOPMENT

Developing Linux Applications with GTK+ and GDK
0-7357-0021-4 • $34.99 US
GTK+/Gnome Application Development
0-7357-0078-8 • $39.99 US
KDE Application Development
1-57870-201-1 • $39.99 US

GIMP

Grokking the GIMP
0-7357-0924-6 • $39.99 US
GIMP Essential Reference
0-7357-0911-4 • $24.95 US

SOLARIS

Solaris Advanced System Administrator's Guide, Second Edition
1-57870-039-6 • $39.99 US
Solaris System Administrator's Guide, Second Edition
1-57870-040-X • $34.99 US
Solaris Essential Reference
0-7357-0023-0 • $24.95 US

Networking

STANDARDS & PROTOCOLS

Cisco Router Configuration & Troubleshooting, Second Edition
0-7357-0999-8 • $39.99 US
Understanding Directory Services
0-7357-0910-6 • $39.99 US
Understanding the Network: A Practical Guide to Internetworking
0-7357-0977-7 • $39.99 US
Understanding Data Communications, Sixth Edition
0-7357-0036-2 • $39.99 US
LDAP: Programming Directory Enabled Applications
1-57870-000-0 • $44.99 US
Gigabit Ethernet Networking
1-57870-062-0 • $50.00 US
Supporting Service Level Agreements on IP Networks
1-57870-146-5 • $50.00 US

Directory Enabled Networks
1-57870-140-6 • $50.00 US
Differentiated Services for the Internet
1-57870-132-5 • $50.00 US
Quality of Service on IP Networks
1-57870-189-9 • $50.00 US
Designing Addressing Architectures for Routing and Switching
1-57870-059-0 • $45.00 US
Understanding & Deploying LDAP Directory Services
1-57870-070-1 • $50.00 US
Switched, Fast and Gigabit Ethernet, Third Edition
1-57870-073-6 • $50.00 US
Wireless LANs: Implementing Interoperable Networks
1-57870-081-7 • $40.00 US
Wide Area High Speed Networks
1-57870-114-7 • $50.00 US
The DHCP Handbook
1-57870-137-6 • $55.00 US
Designing Routing and Switching Architectures for Enterprise Networks
1-57870-060-4 • $55.00 US
Local Area High Speed Networks
1-57870-113-9 • $50.00 US
Available June 2000
Network Performance Baselining
1-57870-240-2 • $50.00 US
Economics of Electronic Commerce
1-57870-014-0 • $49.99 US

SECURITY

Intrusion Detection
1-57870-185-6 • $50.00 US
Understanding Public-Key Infrastructure
1-57870-166-X • $50.00 US
Windows NT/2000 Network Security
1-57870-253-4 • $45.00 US
Linux Firewalls
0-7357-0900-9 • $39.99 US

LOTUS NOTES/DOMINO

Domino System Administration
1-56205-948-3 • $49.99 US
Lotus Notes & Domino Essential Reference
0-7357-0007-9 • $45.00 US

Software Architecture & Engineering

Designing for the User with OVID
1-57870-101-5 • $40.00 US
Designing Flexible Object-Oriented Systems with UML
1-57870-098-1 • $40.00 US
Constructing Superior Software
1-57870-147-3 • $40.00 US
A UML Pattern Language
1-57870-118-X • $45.00 US

Professional Certification

TRAINING GUIDES

MCSE Training Guide: Networking Essentials, 2nd Ed.
156205919X • $49.99 US
MCSE Training Guide: Windows NT Server 4, 2nd Ed.
1562059165 • $49.99 US
MCSE Training Guide: Windows NT Workstation 4, 2nd Ed.
1562059181 • $49.99 US
MCSE Training Guide: Windows NT Server 4 Enterprise, 2nd Ed.
1562059173 • $49.99 US
MCSE Training Guide: Core Exams Bundle, 2nd Ed.
1562059262 • $149.99 US
MCSE Training Guide: TCP/IP, 2nd Ed.
1562059203 • $49.99 US
MCSE Training Guide: IIS 4, 2nd Ed.
0735708657 • $49.99 US
MCSE Training Guide: SQL Server 7 Administration
0735700036 • $49.99 US
MCSE Training Guide: SQL Server 7 Database Design
0735700044 • $49.99 US
CLP Training Guide: Lotus Notes 4
0789715058 • $59.99 US
MCSD Training Guide: Visual Basic 6 Exams
0735700028 • $69.99 US
MCSD Training Guide: Solution Architectures
0735700265 • $49.99 US
MCSD Training Guide: 4-in-1 Bundle
0735709122 • $149.99 US
CCNA Training Guide
0735700516 • $49.99 US
A+ Certification Training Guide, 2nd Ed.
0735709076 • $49.99 US
Network+ Certification Guide
073570077X • $49.99 US
Solaris 2.6 Administrator Certification Training Guide, Part I
157870085X • $40.00 US
Solaris 2.6 Administrator Certification Training Guide, Part II
1578700868 • $40.00 US
MCSE Training Guide: Windows 2000 Professional
0735709653 • $49.99 US
MCSE Training Guide: Windows 2000 Server
0735709688 • $49.99 US
MCSE Training Guide: Windows 2000 Network Infrastructure
0735709661 • $49.99 US
MCSE Training Guide: Windows 2000 Network Security Design
073570984X • $49.99 US
MCSE Training Guide: Windows 2000 Network Infrastructure Design
0735709823 • $49.99 US
MCSE Training Guide: Windows 2000 Directory Svcs. Infrastructure
0735709769 • $49.99 US
MCSE Training Guide: Windows 2000 Directory Services Design
0735709831 • $49.99 US
MCSE Training Guide: Windows 2000 Accelerated Exam
0735709793 • $59.99 US
MCSE Training Guide: Windows 2000 Core Exams Bundle
0735709882 • $149.99 US

How to Contact Us

Visit Our Web Site

www.newriders.com

On our Web site you'll find information about our other books, authors, tables of contents, indexes, and book errata.

Email Us

Contact us at this address:

nrfeedback@newriders.com

- If you have comments or questions about this book
- To report errors that you have found in this book
- If you have a book proposal to submit or are interested in writing for New Riders
- If you would like to have an author kit sent to you
- If you are an expert in a computer topic or technology and are interested in being a technical editor who reviews manuscripts for technical accuracy

nrfeedback@newriders.com

- To find a distributor in your area, please contact our international department at this address.

nrmedia@newriders.com

- For instructors from educational institutions who want to preview New Riders books for classroom use. Email should include your name, title, school, department, address, phone number, office days/hours, text in use, and enrollment, along with your request for desk/examination copies and/or additional information.
- For members of the media who are interested in reviewing copies of New Riders books. Send your name, mailing address, and email address, along with the name of the publication or Web site you work for.

Write to Us

New Riders Publishing
201 W. 103rd St.
Indianapolis, IN 46290-1097

Call Us

Toll-free (800) 571-5840 + 9 + 7477

If outside U.S. (317) 581-3500. Ask for New Riders.

Fax Us

(317) 581-4663

We Want to Know What You Think

To better serve you, we would like your opinion on the content and quality of this book. Please complete this card and mail it to us or fax it to 317-581-4663.

Name _____

Address _____

City _____ State _____ Zip _____

Phone _____

Email Address _____

Occupation _____

Operating System(s) that you use _____

What influenced your purchase of this book?
- ❏ Recommendation
- ❏ Cover Design
- ❏ Table of Contents
- ❏ Index
- ❏ Magazine Review
- ❏ Advertisement
- ❏ New Rider's Reputation
- ❏ Author Name

How would you rate the contents of this book?
- ❏ Excellent
- ❏ Very Good
- ❏ Good
- ❏ Fair
- ❏ Below Average
- ❏ Poor

How do you plan to use this book?
- ❏ Quick reference
- ❏ Self-training
- ❏ Classroom
- ❏ Other

What do you like most about this book? Check all that apply.
- ❏ Content
- ❏ Writing Style
- ❏ Accuracy
- ❏ Examples
- ❏ Listings
- ❏ Design
- ❏ Index
- ❏ Page Count
- ❏ Price
- ❏ Illustrations

What do you like least about this book? Check all that apply.
- ❏ Content
- ❏ Writing Style
- ❏ Accuracy
- ❏ Examples
- ❏ Listings
- ❏ Design
- ❏ Index
- ❏ Page Count
- ❏ Price
- ❏ Illustrations

What would be a useful follow-up book to this one for you? _____

Where did you purchase this book? _____

Can you name a similar book that you like better than this one, or one that is as good? Why?
_____

How many New Riders books do you own? _____

What are your favorite computer books? _____

What other titles would you like to see us develop? _____

Any comments for us? _____
_____
_____

Inside Linux 0-7357-0940-8

www.newriders.com • Fax 317-581-4663

Fold here and tape to mail

Place
Stamp
Here

New Riders Publishing
201 W. 103rd St.
Indianapolis, IN 46290